BILLS OF EXCHANGE
AND BANKER'S DOCUMENTARY CREDITS

This book is to be returned on
or before the date stamped below

8/7/02
Business.

BILLS OF EXCHANGE AND BANKERS' DOCUMENTARY CREDITS

By

WILLIAM HEDLEY, MA, LLB

of Swepstone Walsh
Solicitors
Member of the Association de Droit Internationale, Paris

THIRD EDITION

|L|L|P|

LONDON   HONG KONG
1997

LLP Limited
Legal & Business Publishing Division
69–77 Paul Street
London EC2A 4LQ
Great Britain

SOUTH-EAST ASIA
LLP Asia Limited
Room 1101, Hollywood Centre
233 Hollywood Road
Hong Kong

© William Hedley, 1986, 1994, 1997

British Library Cataloguing in Publication Data

A catalogue record
for this book is available
from the British Library

ISBN 1–85978–122–5

Typeset by
Interactive Sciences Ltd, Gloucester
Printed in Great Britain by
WBC Print Ltd,
Bridgend, Mid Glamorgan

PREFACE TO THE THIRD EDITION

There have been considerable changes introduced into the subjects covering the scope of this book since the last edition in January 1994. During those three years the ICC have produced new Uniform Rules for Collections (ICC URC No. 522), replacing the former URC 322. The new rules came into force on the 1st of January 1996. In addition the ICC introduced Uniform Rules for Bank-to-Bank Reimbursements under Documentary Credits (ICC No. 525) which came into force on 1st July 1996. All these rules have been suitably incorporated in the text.

During the period since the last edition, there has also been a growing practice of UK banks to guarantee cheques by the use of the Continental European system of *aval*; strictly speaking this has no recognition in English Law, though it has been recognised by our Courts where some foreign law applies; and at all events, the practice has now spread to such a degree I thought it proper to include a reference to *avals*, and a more extended reference to the only case which has been considered by our courts, that is, *G & H Montage GmbH v. Irvani* (1990). The same must be said of the developing pattern in non recourse dealings, particularly with promissory notes, under, again, the Continental influence of forfaiting, and reference is now made in the text to this development also.

However, by far the greatest change to the banking world is the increased amendments brought about by the expanding use of electronic technology in the bank clearing system, whereby cheques can be cleared without the need physically to present each cheque to the drawee bank. To accommodate this, the Bills of Exchange Act 1882 has been amended, and this was achieved by the Bills of Exchange (Deregulation) Order 1996, which came into effect on 28th November 1996; interestingly enough, this amendment to the 1882 Act was achieved not by another Act of Parliament, but by a Statutory Instrument by powers conferred upon Parliament by the Deregulation and Contracting Out Act 1994. These changes in the clearing system are still evolving, and it will be some time yet before the changes are fully implemented. I have been indeed fortunate again to have had the assistance of friends at the Association for Payment Clearing Services (APACS), in particular Frederick Galbraith, without whose assistance I could not adequately have described the new arrangements. Moreover, because of the continuing changes, my publishers and I came to the conclusion that it was not feasible to include in this edition a copy of the Clearing House Rules, since they are in a state of change and updating, and would, almost certainly, be out of date in many respects by the time this edition is published.

The Courts continue to be asked to adjudicate upon difficulties which arise on various aspects of these subjects, and well over fifty new cases have been added to the text. *Deutsche Rückversicherung AG* v. *Walbrook Insurance Co Ltd* (1994) continued to show, on rather complicated facts, that payment under documentary credits remains inviolate; though by contrast, under a bank guarantee the Court of Appeal in *Themehelp Ltd* v. *West* (1995) held that the guarantor could be excused if he could show a *prima facie* case of fraud. Cases continue to appear on the theme of *O'Brien* v. *Barclays Bank plc* where wives (and it is usually wives or female partners) attempt to save their homes from guarantees given to banks in respect of their husbands' debts. Indeed, *Bank of Scotland* v. *Bennett* (1997) went further than previously, by the charge being set aside where a wife had been "morally blackmailed coerced and victimised" by her husband into giving the bank a charge over the matrimonial home.

The entitlement to have money returned by way of restitution has also been an active topic between various banks and equally various Borough Councils; *Westdeutsche Landesbank Girozentrale* v. *Islington London Borough* (1994), *Kleinwort Benson Ltd* v. *South Tyneside Metropolitan Borough Council* (1994) *South Tyneside Metropolitan Borough Council* v. *Svenska International plc* (1995) to mention but a few. In spite of all this judicial activity, the legal basis for the return of money is none too clear, being based either on the fact that one party or the other has been "unjustly enriched" or under the old common law remedy of money had and received.

As in the case of previous editions, I have been fortunate in having the support of friends, colleagues and family. Readers of previous editions will not be surprised to know that our barrister son Richard Hedley, once more, made time to read the updated drafts, and made a number of suggestions which have undoubtedly improved the book. The efforts which go into the task inevitably disrupt domestic arrangements, and once more my wife has not only been forced to tolerate the inevitable disruptions to family life, particularly so when weekends have ceased to be part of the domestic scene and have been given over regularly to further checking and research, but also has never ceased to provide encouragement when my efforts appeared to be losing momentum. I must also mention our younger son, Stuart, who has assisted with the chore of verifying various references which has helped greatly. As ever, my colleagues have been indulgent in the amount of time I have spent in preparing the new edition, because inevitably, this work impinges not only on one's professional life, but on the amount of time devoted to the task by those who helped me in the office. In particular, I must mention Linda Evans, who made time in the busiest of lives to type, and re-type, many of the amendments and additions, and much of this she accomplished by utilising her own time, when the pressures of office work prevented her from carrying out the task during normal hours; and also, Pauline Harte who has assisted me in the final run-in to completion of the new edition. Both these ladies have given unstinting help, and I am grateful indeed to have had their support. Finally, as always, my publishers have been most patient in the preparation of this edition, particularly so, since a number of the amendments which have been necessary (particularly with the new banking clearing system) had to be made when delivery of the manuscript was already well delayed.

Whilst writing and preparing a new edition can be a lonely task, the work could not have been completed without the help of all those whom I mention, and I am ever grateful to them all for the assistance which has been given to me.

I have tried to state the law as I thought it to be as at 31st March 1997, and if I have erred in any way, of course, the fault is wholly mine.

Lincoln's Inn Fields   WILLIAM HEDLEY
London
21 April 1997

CONTENTS

TABLE OF CASES

*(Page numbers in **bold type** indicate where an extract from the case is set out)*

TABLE OF STATUTES

*(Page numbers in **bold** type indicate where the text of the Act is set out)*

TABLE OF STATUTORY INSTRUMENTS

*(Page numbers in **bold type** indicate where the text of the Statutory Instrument is set out)*

TABLE OF INTERNATIONAL
CONVENTIONS

*(Page numbers in **bold type** indicate where the text of the item in question is set out)*

SECTION ONE

BILLS OF EXCHANGE

CHAPTER 1

INTRODUCTION

A bill of exchange is a piece of paper which is used to transfer money from one person to another instead of using the actual money itself.

It is a personal humbug and is inconvenient to carry large quantities of coins in our pockets and we gladly change these for banknotes whenever possible. Even this, however, is less convenient than leaving the money with a bank and merely carrying a cheque-book. Bearing this in mind it is not difficult to appreciate how in dealing with large quantities of money it is a practical impossibility to pay in cash, and it is obviously very desirable to use the alternative of paying by the giving of a slip of paper.

The best known type of bill of exchange is a "cheque" by which we transfer money at our bank to people to whom we are indebted. A cheque is payable "on demand", that is, at any time, whereas an "ordinary" bill (sometimes called a "time" bill) is often not payable until, say, three months after it is drawn up and signed. Thus, bills of exchange (apart from cheques) are more commonly employed in commercial transactions where the person who is paying for the goods does not wish, for one reason or another, to make immediate settlement of his account. Thus, if on 1 April Y buys 10,000 tons of coal from Z in Poland to be shipped to Liverpool to arrive on 1 July, Y can pay for the goods with a three months' bill. By this method, Y gets a fixed period of credit, and in the meanwhile Z has a document which he can use immediately.

What usually happens is that Y (the buyer of the coal) makes arrangements with a finance house that they will provide the money for the purchase. Y then draws the bill on the finance house, and they accept it to show that *they* have agreed to pay it in three months' time. Y then sends the bill to Z in exchange for the documents of title to the coal. Z now has a bill which he knows will be paid by the finance house on 1 July. Z is then in a position, if he wishes, to take the bill to another finance house, perhaps in Poland or Switzerland or London for that matter, and get them to discount the bill: that is, pay him immediately (less whatever commission or interest they may charge) and then *they* will take the bill from Z by negotiation, and, as the new owners of it, will present it for payment to the original finance house in London on 1 July. This way, Y gets his coal and three months' credit. Z gets paid immediately, and the two finance houses assist by carrying out their specialist function. Everything does, of course, depend on the standing of the finance house in London who "accept" the bill. Unless the acceptor is unimpeachable the transaction never really can get under way.

The use of bills of exchange is, therefore, an important and essential part of financing international trade, and, of course, they are used widely within the British Isles,[1] even where no foreign element is present.

The system of accepting bills and their discounting and presentment for payment is today a highly sophisticated part of the financial and banking scene, but, of course, it was not always so. In the beginning it was the merchant traders who, for a suitable rate of interest, were prepared to accept bills of exchange to give efficacy to transactions of smaller concerns. This was the beginning of the merchant banks, and on the outbreak of the First World War in 1914, a group of these merchant banks in London formed an informal committee to deal with the obligations of German customers. This laid the foundations for the Accepting Houses Committee, which is now one of the most powerful institutions in the City of London, and co-ordinates the business interests of the member banks. Obviously, a bill accepted by a member of the Committee is deemed to be a first-class security, and is, therefore, able to command the best possible terms and rates of interest.

The law relating to bills of exchange had developed through the usage of traders from about the 14th century into a body of law called the "Law Merchant".[2] This body of law was only lightly touched on by Parliament, until it was codified by the Bills of Exchange Act 1882.[3]

The 1882 Act was drafted by that great commercial lawyer, Sir Mackenzie Chalmers, after reading some 2,500 cases, which made up the law prior to the Act. The Act was simply intended to state the law as it was, but obviously, here and there a change had to be introduced if common sense dictated, or, if a particular point was not clear, a decision one way or another had to be taken. It is for this reason that cases decided prior to 1882 are still available, where appropriate, as authority for, or examples of, the points with which they deal. The 1882 Act has lasted over the years without substantial amendment; the only statutory modification of any consequence being the Cheques Acts 1957

---

1. The law of Scotland differs in one or two important aspects. See, for example, ss. 98 and 100 of the Bills of Exchange Act 1882.

2. For a history of this subject, see Holdsworth, H E L VIII, pp. 113 et seq. See also a short account per Cockburn LCJ in *Goodwin v. Robarts* (1875) 33 LT 272, at pp. 275 et seq; affirmed on appeal (1876) 35 LT 179. By far the best history of the subject is Dr Holden's book *History of Negotiable Instruments in English Law* (1955), University of London.

3. S. 1 of the 1882 Act. One great commercial judge considered it " . . . the best drafted Act of Parliament ever passed": per MacKinnon LJ, in *Bank Polski v. Mulder* [1942] 1 KB 497, at p. 500. The 1882 Act repealed and mostly re-enacted the few statutory provisions as did at that time exist: s. 96. Where any other Act or any document makes reference to any of the statutory provisions replaced by the 1882 Act, those Acts or documents are to be construed as if reference was to the corresponding provisions of the 1882 Act: s. 99.

and 1992, which gave bankers some additional protection when dealing with unindorsed or irregularly indorsed cheques.

One of the most important functions of the Act was to assist the concept of negotiability[4] by creating a special type of holder who would get a good title to a bill of exchange even if there had been all manner of irregularities in the prior dealings with it, provided he acted in good faith and without any knowledge of the irregularities. He is called by the Act a "holder in due course" and is referred to many times. He is given substantial protection, and a variety of presumptions are made in his favour, not available to lesser legal mortals. To reach the status of a "holder in due course" the Act lays down stringent rules which must be complied with, but, assuming the heights of Parnassus are reached, a "holder in due course" has little to fear of claims which may be made against him.

At one time, bills of exchange carried an *ad valorem* stamp duty, but this was abolished from 1 February 1971, and need not now be considered.[5]

All countries use bills of exchange, and many have adopted a code similar in terms to the 1882 Act.[6]

4. See *infra* Chap. 4.
5. Finance Act 1970, s. 32.
6. Almost all the Commonwealth countries and the USA. Different systems have been adopted by most Continental European jurisdictions. This is considered *infra* in more detail in Chap. 10.

CHAPTER 2

CONTRACT ON A BILL

It follows from all that has been said that a bill of exchange is part of a contract, and, like any other contract, can be legally enforced. The ordinary law of contract applies to bills of exchange, and the elements needed for a valid contract will be considered in a moment, but before doing so something must be said of the liability of the parties generally.

Often the giving of a bill of exchange is only part—sometimes the *final* part—of a larger transaction. For example, if someone in London buys machinery from a company in Germany, the payment for it (if by giving a bill of exchange) will be the final step of the agreement, which will have covered everything from the suitability of the machinery itself, to its carriage, installation, maintenance and so on. The payment for the machinery, while being important, is only one aspect of the transaction, and the seller will be entitled to payment whether a bill of exchange is given or not; it may well be in many instances some other method of payment will be employed, but in any event, the liability to pay is on the *original contract*.

If the buyer uses a bill of exchange to pay for the goods *a new contract on the bill* is created, which will exist *in addition* to the original contract to pay for the machinery. So that if the bill of exchange is not paid (that is, if it is dishonoured) the seller of the machinery can sue the buyer *either* under the original contract *or* on the dishonoured bill.

It is not always fully appreciated or understood that a bill of exchange (including a cheque) is *as cash*, and once having given it, it is to be treated *as cash*. The giving of a piece of paper in lieu of the money is simply a matter of convenience. This means—and this is the point which is frequently overlooked—that the giver of the bill cannot disclaim his liability on the bill just because something has gone wrong with the original contract.

Consequently, it matters not that he has a substantial counter-claim under the original contract, even exceeding the amount of the bill. The bill must first be paid, and any such claim then pursued as a separate action. One cannot simply refuse to honour a bill or "stop" a cheque just because something has gone amiss with the original contract; and the courts will not, other than in the most exceptional circumstances, grant a stay of judgment of a claim on the bill while a counter-claim is pursued and settled.[1]

The two immediate parties are always liable to one another, but time and again, the 1882 Act provides for liability *on the bill* in addition to any other liability which may exist under the original contract.

We must now consider each of the elements needed to support a valid contract.

It will be remembered these elements are (i) agreement between the parties; (ii) an intent to have the agreement legally enforceable; (iii) the parties must have capacity at law; (iv) there must be consideration.

Contracts involving bills of exchange have additional requirements, in that the bill must be: (v) in the proper form; and (vi) delivered.

I. AGREEMENT

In every contract the parties must be in agreement upon the terms, and if there is no agreement there can be no contract.

As we have seen, once a bill is given there is created a separate contract *on the bill*, and it will be rare indeed that the drawer or any of the other parties to the bill will be in a position, in a claim on the bill, to say there was no agreement to draw the bill or to become a party to it. There might be no agreement on the bill if, for example, there was some mistake or misunderstanding in the giving of the bill of exchange; but one must not confuse a lack of agreement under the original contract with the necessary agreement to give and receive a bill.

As when a claim is made *on the bill* it will be for dishonour (that is, that it has not been paid) and the defences open on such a claim are limited.

If the drawer (that is, the buyer of the machinery in the example above), finds the goods not up to standard he may wish to countermand his instructions to the drawee (that is, tell him not to pay the bill) but this cannot be done without running the risk that the payee (that is, the seller of the goods) will treat the bill as dishonoured, and set in motion the proceedings which follow the dishonour of a bill.[2]

II. INTENT TO CREATE LEGAL RELATIONS

In some agreements the parties may not intend that their arrangements should be legally enforceable. For example, a wager on a football pools coupon is expressed specifically to be "binding in honour only"[3]; or some arrangements

1. See the cases cited in Chap. 5 where the subject is considered in some detail.
2. This subject is discussed more fully *infra* Chap. 8.
3. *Jones v. Vernons Pools* [1938] 2 All ER 626.

between members of the same family are usually not intended to be sued on if one side or the other does not perform.[4]

In all these cases no action can lie *on the bill* if it was not intended that the giving of it was to have legal effect.

Once more, care must be taken not to confuse a lack of intent to create legal relations under the original contract, with that intended under the agreement *on the bill*.[5]

III. CAPACITY AND AUTHORITY

"Capacity" is a different thing from "authority". Capacity deals with the ability in law of the party concerned to make *himself* liable for his acts; whereas authority is the power to bind *someone else* to an agreement.

Capacity or the lack of it may be, and often is, temporary. It is at the time the act was done that capacity is important: if one did not have capacity then, no subsequent act or ratification is possible. Whereas a lack of authority can always be cured by ratification.

Capacity

The capacity to incur liability as a party to a bill of exchange is co-extensive with the capacity to contract.[6]

The theory of capacity is based on the notion that there must be agreement before there can be a contract; and if someone is under a disability they are (or are deemed to be) incapable of giving the necessary consent to an agreement. In the case of a bill of exchange where it is drawn or indorsed by someone who has no capacity or power to incur any liability on it, a holder can, nevertheless, enforce it against any *other* party to the bill.[7]

The various "incapacities", as they are sometimes called, can be classified as follows[8]:

(a) Infants

The common law

An infant (or minor as he is sometimes known) is a person, male or female, who has not attained the age of 18 years.[9] The common law rule is that an

---

4. *Jones v. Padavatton* [1969] 2 All ER 616.
5. This is discussed more fully *infra* in the section headed "The Two-Contract Liability" in Chap. 5.
6. Bills of Exchange Act 1882, s. 22(1).
7. *Ibid.*
8. Before 1 November 1935 the law denied to married women the right to contract. This need not now be considered further here: Law Reform (Married Women and Tortfeasors) Act 1935.
9. Family Law Reform Act 1969, s. 1. Before this, coming of age used to be the attaining of one's 21st birthday.

infant has no liability in contract; with the exception that contracts to acquire "necessities" can be binding.[10] However, under the terms of the Infants Relief Act 1874, some contracts were declared "absolutely void", and the minor could not be sued, even if the contract was one for the supply of "necessities". One of the types of contract made "absolutely void" by the 1874 Act related to bills of exchange by providing that all bills drawn, accepted or indorsed would be unenforceable against the infant (although they can be enforced against any other party[11]): "He is not liable upon a bill of exchange or a promissory note under any circumstances",[12] even for necessities.[13] For example, in *Hutley v. Peacock*,[14] an infant made out a cheque and post-dated it to a date a few days after he became of age, and when he was ultimately sued on the cheque, it was held that he was not liable.

All this was done to protect infants of course, but in fact there are several cases illustrating that it was the adult population which needed protecting! The rule was inviolate, however, and an infant could not be sued on a bill even if he has fraudulently represented himself to be of full age.[15]

It followed that since an infant could have no liability, any separate agreement of guarantee was also unenforceable.[16] In *Coutts & Co v. Browne-Lecky*,[17] an infant had an account with the bank, the debit balance on which was guaranteed by his father; when the bank tried to recover on the guarantee, it was held that as the loan to the infant was unenforceable under the terms of the Infants Relief Act, so therefore, was the father's guarantee, and the bank could not recover.

The Minors Contract Act 1987

If an infant enters into a contract after 9 June 1987[18] the transaction is affected by the Minors Contract Act 1987, which repeals the Infants Relief Act,[19] and

---

10. *Nash v. Inman* [1908] 2 KB 1, see now s. 3(2) Sale of Goods Act 1979.

11. Bills of Exchange Act 1882, s. 22(2).

12. *Per* Lord Esher MR in *Re Soltykoff* [1891] 1 QB 413, at p. 415.

13. It is not appropriate here to discuss what are, or what are not, "necessities". Note also, the mere fact that liability on a bill was totally unenforceable, did not mean that no action could be brought against an infant *on the original contract: per* Lord Esher, *ibid.*, p. 415.

14. (1913) 30 TLR 239.

15. *Leslie Ltd v. Sheill* [1914] 3 KB 607. Neither can be sued for deceit, as this would be an indirect way of recovering the money. However, if the subject-matter of the agreement was *property*, equity would compel the infant to return the property to the rightful owner: *Lempriere v. Lange* (1879) 12 Ch D 675.

16. A guarantee is where one person agrees to be answerable for the debt or default of another. There are *three* parties, and the primary liability is on the debtor. An indemnity (sometimes called "suretyship") is where the person agreeing, assumes direct liability with the creditor. The creditor is then able to sue the surety without first pursuing the debtor. In the *Browne-Lecky* case, if the agreement had been one of indemnity, with the father directly liable for the debt, perhaps, the bank could have recovered: *Wauthier v. Wilson* (1910) 28 TLR 239.

17. [1946] 2 All ER 207.

18. S. 5(2). The Act does not apply to Scotland: s. 5(3).

19. S. 4(2). Also repealed is the Betting and Loans (Infants) Act 1892.

so the old common law rules now apply once more. The new law as affecting infants would seem to be this:

(1) Contracts which under the terms of the Infants Relief Act were "absolutely void", are now only voidable at common law. In other words, the old rules relating to "necessities" apply to all contracts, including those relating to bills of exchange, and the words of Lord Esher referred to above no longer apply, once the infant can now be sued on a cheque, for example, if given for the purchase of "necessities".

(2) The contract must, however, be "made by the minor after the commencement of this Act",[20] and therefore, no attempted ratification *after* the 9 July 1987 can affect a contract made *before* that date, which means the contract will remain unenforceable against the infant.

(3) A ratification, when the infant comes of age, of a contract made *after* 9 July 1987 will, of course, be effective and binding upon him.

(4) A contract made on or after 9 July 1987 by someone of full age to repay a loan which he obtained while an infant, will be enforceable against him; and if he gives a cheque in repayment of the loan, and that cheque is dishonoured, he can now be sued on it.

(5) A guarantor of an infant's contractual obligations may now be liable, even though the contract is unenforceable against the infant.[21] *Coutts & Co* v. *Browne-Lecky* would appear, therefore, no longer to be good law.

(6) If an infant has entered into a contract after 9 July 1987, and has acquired property under it, even though that contract is unenforceable against the infant, he can be ordered to return the property, provided the court considers it "just and equitable" that the infant does so.[22]

   The section goes on to state that the court has power to order not only that such property be returned, but "any property representing it". So that, for example, if the infant has sold the property, it seems he can be ordered to hand over the proceeds of sale; or, if he has exchanged the original property for some other property, he can be compelled to hand over *that* property.

   This is coming very close to enforcing the original "unenforceable" contract, and how far the plaintiff can trace the property in this way is far from clear.

---

20. *Ibid.*, s. 1.
21. *Ibid.*, s. 2.
22. S. 3(1). This has long been the case in equity: see *Lempriere* v. *Lange* (1879) 12 Ch D 675. This is without prejudice to any other remedies which may be available to the plaintiff: s. 3(2).

(7) An infant can operate a bank account, and even be granted overdraft facilities (often, these days, in the shape of student loans). He may be a payee or holder of a bill of exchange, and as such, has all the usual rights of an adult; notwithstanding this, if he is obliged to commence an action to enforce those rights, he must do so through his "next friend", who is usually his parent, guardian or other adult who is *in loco parentis*.

Since infants became of full age at eighteen instead of twenty-one, the significance of the rules protecting them has decreased. In regard to liability on cheques, it would seem that in practical terms, this will rarely now be considered except for students and their dealings with their bankers.

(b) Debilitated minds

The concept of a person's mind being "debilitated" is that it is a temporary enfeeblement, and not a condition brought about by disease which would render that person of "unsound" mind. If this distinction is accepted, it can be said that if a person is intoxicated by alcohol or drugs to such a degree that he does not know what he is doing, he will be able to avoid liability on a bill of exchange.

It is, of course, a question of degree, and the burden of proof is heavy upon the person attempting to negative his liability for this reason.

To avoid his liability he must prove: (a) that at the time he gave the bill he did not know what he was doing and (b) the other party knew it.

The liability is voidable[23] (not void altogether); consequently, his actions can be ratified when sobriety returns.[24]

(c) Unsoundness of mind

Actions taken by mentally disordered people can sometimes be avoided; however, once again it is a question of degree. If the person is a "patient" under the Mental Health Acts little problem will be experienced in showing the incapacity. In such a case, any contract is "absolutely void and of no effect"[25] even if, in fact, made during a lucid interval.[26] If, however, the incapacity is brought on by circumstances which would not justify their being detained under the Mental Health Acts all the circumstances must be looked at, and it is then a question of fact how far the person concerned was incapable. For example,

---

23. *Gore* v. *Gibson* (1845) 14 LJ Ex 151.
24. *Matthews* v. *Baxter* (1873) 42 LJ Ex 73. Even a drunkard must always pay a reasonable price for necessities: Sale of Goods Act 1979, s. 3(2).
25. *Per* Cozens-Hardy LJ, *Re Walker* [1905] 1 Ch 160, 178.
26. *Ibid.*

MANCHES v. TRIMBORN[27]

Mrs T was an old lady of 86 years of age. For the benefit of a neighbour she gave M a cheque as part of a highly involved transaction between the neighbour and M. The cheque was dishonoured and M sued Mrs T, who said she did not understand the transaction, although she did appreciate the act of signing the cheque. *Held*—that that was not enough. Mrs T was not capable of understanding the true nature and effect of the series of transactions of which the cheque formed only part; M knew this and Mrs T was not, therefore, liable.

In these circumstances the liability is voidable provided it can be proved: (a) that at the time the drawer gave the bill he was not capable of understanding the true nature and effect of the transaction; and (b) the other party knew this.[28]

Any act done during a lucid interval is, of course, binding.[29]

(d) Aliens

There is no disability on a foreign national as such, unless this country is at war with his country, in which case he becomes an *enemy* alien and all commercial relations with an enemy are illegal.[30]

(e) Insolvency[31]

The Insolvency Act 1986[32] and the Insolvency Rules[33] swept away the old law which had applied to individuals and corporations,[34] and while the Act contains the provisions applicable to both, they are still treated separately.

A "bankrupt" is an individual who has been adjudged bankrupt pursuant to a bankruptcy order made by the court.[35] In the case of corporations, the position is rather more complicated under the new law in that if there is a hope that an insolvent company may be saved it may go into "administration" or

27. [1946] WN 62.
28. *Imperial Loan Co v. Stone* [1892] 1 QB 599.
29. *Selby v. Jackson* (1844) LJ Ch 249. Moreover, a person under a mental disability must always pay a reasonable price for necessities: Sale of Goods Act 1979, s. 3(2).
30. Trading with the Enemy Act 1939, s. 1. However, there is no reason to prevent his enforcing an existing contract providing he is resident in Britain, and "enemy" character in a trading sense has never attached to him: *Schaffenius v. Goldberg* [1916] 1 KB 284; or to defend an action if he is sued here. Indeed, the test of *enemy* status has more to do with where the person is resident than his nationality: *Porter v. Freudenberg* [1915] 1 KB 857.
31. The insolvency laws relating to bills of exchange apply notwithstanding anything provided in the 1882 Act: Bills of Exchange Act 1882, s. 97(1). See also, *Re Keever* [1967] 1 Ch 182.
32. 1986 c. 45.
33. As amended by the Insolvency (Amendment) Rules 1987. As amended from time to time. The Rules as amended apply to proceedings whenever those proceedings were commenced.
34. Prior to the commencement of the Act the law relating to personal bankruptcy was contained in the Bankruptcy Act 1914, and that relating to corporations in the Companies Act 1985. The new legislation is based on the Report of the Review Committee under the Chairmanship of Sir Kenneth Cork, Cmnd 8558, in June 1982.
35. Insolvency Act 1986, s. 381(1).

"receivership," then if all attempts at rescue fail—the company may be subject to "winding up".

Once an individual is made bankrupt or a corporation is made subject to any of the orders referred to above, there are various restrictions and prohibitions to which they become subject. For example, in the case of an individual he cannot validly dispose of his property,[36] which would include attempting to draw a cheque on his bank account, or accept or indorse a time bill,[37] though in the case of individuals there is a saving for banks which have paid out funds in respect of a transaction (which is subsequently proved to be void), between the day the bankruptcy petition is presented and the day the trustee takes control of the bankrupt's assets, provided the bank had no notice of the bankruptcy.[38]

(f) Companies

Nothing in the Bills of Exchange Act 1882 enables a corporation to make itself liable as drawer, acceptor or indorser of a bill unless it is competent to do so under "the law for the time being in force relating to corporations".[39]

The basic concept was that a company, being a juristic person, had no capacity to do anything unless it was given the power by the terms of the "objects" clause in its memorandum of association. So, if it has been formed to operate oil wells, it could not manage a sweet shop, and all acts done in pursuance of the confectionary venture would be *ultra vires* (beyond the power of) the company, and completely void.

Even if the contract was within a company's objects, it may still not have capacity to sign bills of exchange as drawer, indorser or acceptor, unless this power is stated in the memorandum of association. It is usual to give the power specifically, for example:

To draw, accept, indorse, negotiate, discount, execute and issue promissory notes, bills of exchange, script warrants and other transferable or negotiable instruments.

If for any reason, this provision has been omitted, it may be implied in the case of a trading company.[40] All this was not very satisfactory, since, if there was a dispute, it could take expensive litigation to resolve the point.

Hence, the only way a party dealing with a company could be sure his contract would be valid, was to consult the terms of the memorandum of association of the company with the Registrar of Companies.

36. *Ibid.*, s. 284(1).
37. Unless his trustee in bankruptcy intervenes, it appears he can validly indorse a bill which was accepted prior to the adjudication: *Willis v. Freeman* (1810) 6 Dig (Repl) 307.
38. This is considered in greater detail *infra* in Chapter 11, "Capacity to Operate a Bank Account".
39. Proviso to the Bills of Exchange Act 1882, s. 22(1).
40. See generally, *Re Peruvian Railways Co* (1867) LR 2 Ch 617. In the event that the company had no power, the directors could well find themselves liable personally to a holder for value: *West London Commercial Bank v. Kitson* (1884) 13 QBD 360.

This, of course, was also highly inconvenient, and s. 35[41] of the Companies Act 1985,[42] attempted to give some protection to those dealing with companies to ameliorate the rigours of the *ultra vires* rule.

However, this section has been substantially amended by s. 108 of the Companies Act 1989, which substitutes a new s. 35 into the Companies Act 1985, sweeping away much of the old law on the *ultra vires* rule, and making almost obsolete the need of third parties dealing with a company to enquire as to its "objects clause" in its Memorandum of Association.[43]

The new rules in favour of third parties dealing with companies are these:

(1) The validity of any act done by a company shall not be called into question on the ground of lack of capacity by reason of anything in the company's memorandum.[44]

(2) A party to a transaction with a company is not bound to enquire as to whether the company is permitted by its memorandum to enter into that transaction.[45] However, the position is still not absolutely clear where a third party *does* inspect the memorandum, and finds the company is acting outside its objects; probably, such knowledge does not now matter, since new s. 35A 2(*b*) provides that such a party is not to be regarded as acting in bad faith by reason only that he knew the transaction was beyond the powers of the directors under the company's constitution.[46]

While this new legislation goes some way to protect people dealing with companies, it does not abolish the doctrine of *ultra vires*[47]: for example, the company may not be able to enforce an *ultra vires* contract.[48]

41. Replacing similar provisions contained in the European Communities Act 1972, s. 9.

42. This consolidating Act replaces the earlier companies legislation including the Companies Acts of 1948, 1967, 1976, 1980 and 1981, together with various parts of other statutes, but is now itself amended by the Companies Act 1989.

43. Section 110 Companies Act 1989 amends s. 3 of the 1985 Act by providing that where a company's memorandum states that the object of the company is to carry on business as "a general commercial company", the company can carry on "any trade or business whatsoever": new s. 3A(*a*) Companies Act 1985; further, the company is now given power " . . . to do all such things as are incidental or conducive to the carrying on of any trade or business . . . ": new s. 3A(*b*).

44. Companies Act 1985, new s. 35(1).

45. *Ibid.*, new s. 35B.

46. However, where a person receives money, *in breach of trust*, from a Company, in efffect "turning a blind eye in the obvious", he cannot then claim the protection of the Act, that the payment was within the powers of the directors and could not, therefore, be challenged: *International Sales and Agencies Ltd* v. *Marcus* [1982] 3 All ER 551 at page 558h. Though without the breach of trust, the position may well be different, and *Re David Payne & Co Ltd* [1904] 2 Ch. 608 may no longer be good law.

47. It remains the duty of the directors to observe any limitations on their powers flowing from the company's memorandum: new s. 35(3); and a shareholder can restrain an act which is, in fact, beyond the company's capacity: new s. 35(2). The new s. 35 still confuses two issues: (1) the corporate capacity; and (2) the authority of the directors. As we have seen above, "capacity" and "authority" are two different things.

48. See *per* Salmon J. (as he then was), in *Anglo Overseas Agencies Ltd* v. *Green* [1960] 3 All ER 244, 245F; also *Bell Houses Ltd* v. *City Wall Properties Ltd* [1966] 2 All ER 674.

The way the situation can arise in practice is, for example, where a company has given a series of promissory notes, and before some or all mature, the company goes into liquidation. The liquidator is duty-bound to raise all legal issues he can to protect the assets of the company for the benefit of creditors generally, and so, if he considers that the transaction was *ultra vires* the capacity of the company, he will, no doubt, still attempt to disclaim liability on the notes.[49]

It will then be open to the holder of the notes to claim the benefit of s. 35, as we have just discussed.

Authority

Authority to draw, accept or indorse a bill is to be considered where a signature is applied on behalf of some person, as for example where an employee signs for his employer, or one partner signs on behalf of a partnership. Of course, there is no problem where the person signing is duly authorized, but if this is not the case the ensuing difficulties must be examined.

Section 24 of the 1882 Act provides that:

Where a signature on a bill is . . . placed thereon without the authority of the person whose signature it purports to be, the . . . unauthorised signature is wholly inoperative, and no right to retain the bill or to give a discharge therefor or to enforce payment thereof against any party thereto can be acquired through or under that signature, unless the party against whom it is sought to retain or enforce payment of the bill is precluded from setting up the . . . want of authority.

Provided that nothing in this section shall affect the ratification of an unauthorized signature not amounting to a forgery.

Of course, if the person receiving payment *knows* the bill is given in excess of the necessary authority he is not entitled to the payment, and must refund any money he does obtain. An example of this is the case of *Reckett* v. *Barnett*,[50] where

T had a power of attorney on behalf of R which enabled him to draw cheques on behalf of R. T bought a motor car from B, and paid for it by cheque signed "R by T his attorney". B knew the car was bought by T for his own use. Eventually the fraud was discovered, and R claimed repayment from B. *Held*—that since B knew T was buying the car for himself, B must refund the amount of the cheque.

A man's money is property, and if it is taken from the rightful owner without his authority, he can recover it from anyone into whose hands it can be found, until it comes into the hands of someone who receives it in good faith and for value, and without notice of the want of authority.[51]

---

49. If a company has no capacity under its memorandum to accept bills of exchange, the directors may be personally liable on them: *West London Commercial Bank* v. *Kitson* (1883) 12 QBD 157.

50. [1929] AC 176.

51. *Per* Denning J (as he then was) in *Nelson* v. *Larholt* [1947] 2 All ER 751, 752, C.

"Notice" may be actual notice, or may be satisfied where the man ought to have known of the want of authority, as for instance, if the circumstances were such as to put a reasonable man on enquiry, or if he was put off by an answer that would not have satisfied a reasonable man, or if he was negligent in not perceiving the want of authority.[52]

On the other hand, if the person receiving payment does *not* know of the defect in authority, the situation is not entirely clear, and the position of both the principal and of the person signing must be considered.

Liability of the principal

(a) Signatures by procuration[53]

The usual way to sign *per pro*, is "p.—p. George Smith-Alan Brown".[54] A signature appearing this way operates as notice that the person signing has but limited authority to sign, and the principal is bound only if the agent was acting within the actual limits of his authority.[55]

(b) Partnerships

If a partner or an employee is specifically authorized to draw or indorse a bill of exchange, even if the transaction is not connected with the firm's ordinary course of business the firm will be bound.[56]

However, problems usually arise where the holder of a bill wishes to make the firm liable for some extraneous and unauthorized act of one of the partners.

If the holder knows of the lack of authority, or if he does not believe the bill was given on behalf of the firm but by the partner in his own right as a principal, then clearly there can be no liability on the other partners.[57] However, subject to this, the firm will be liable even if the partner had no authority, if a bill is given[58]: (a) "for the purpose of the business of the partnership"; and, (b) "for carrying on, in the usual way, business of the kind carried on by the firm".

A payee will, therefore, be put on enquiry if a bill is given for some purpose wholly unconnected with the type of business with which the partnership is involved, and if he does not satisfy himself he may find it impossible to sustain a claim against the partners.

52. *Ibid.*, 752, H. See also *International Sales and Agencies Ltd* v. *Marcus* [1982] 3 All ER 551, 558, a to d.

53. Commonly called "per (= by) pro".

54. See *per* Scrutton LJ in *Slingsby* v. *District Bank Ltd* [1932] 1 KB 544, at p. 557.

55. Bills of Exchange Act 1882, s. 25. The drawee paying on a "per pro" signature is always under risk that the authority of the signer has been exceeded. Banks paying under such signature should always pay strictly in accordance with the mandate lodged with them. In some cases, particularly where accounts of individuals are concerned, it is necessary that a power of attorney is used, under the terms of the Powers of Attorney Act 1971.

56. Partnership Act 1890, s. 7.

57. *Ibid.*, s. 5.

58. *Ibid.*, s. 5.

Moreover, even if the transaction is within the overall type of business carried on by the firm, the bill must still be given "in the usual way" of carrying on the business[59]; and what is usual in one firm may be unusual for another!

However, the rule is that in a *trading* partnership[60] the right to draw and indorse bills of exchange is presumed. In a non-trading firm there is no such presumption and the burden of proof is on the holder to show the partner signing was acting "in the usual way".

How then does one tell whether a partnership is *trading* or not? The position is rather unsatisfactory since no clear rules have been laid down, but professional partnerships (for example, accountants and solicitors), cinema organizations, mining partnerships and agricultural partnerships have all been held non-trading.[61] If a claim is made successfully against the partnership then all the partners are liable, for if a person signs the *name of the firm* it is equivalent to the signatures of all the persons liable as partners in that firm.[62]

(c) Companies

Corporations can, of course, act only through agents. It is usual that bills are signed by a director or manager or some such person in authority. A company can put its seal on a cheque or bill but there is no need for it to do so.[63]

Section 37 of the Companies Act 1985 provides that a bill of exchange is deemed to have been made, accepted or indorsed on behalf of a company if it is executed in the name of the company or on behalf or on account of the company by anyone *acting under its authority.*

If there is *express* authority there will, of course, be no problem; however, if there is no express authority (such as a decision of the board of directors to adopt the contract and authorize the signing and issuance of bills of exchange, evidenced by an entry in the company's minute book) then a holder of a bill may have a problem. The problem will usually arise in one of two ways: either the bills will have been signed by one or more directors (legitimately, perhaps, within the terms of, say, the bank mandate), but without the consent of the board as a whole, and the other directors who did not consent may attempt to set the transaction aside; or the company will have gone into liquidation, and it will be the liquidator who claims that the directors who signed had no authority, in order to attempt to disclaim the transaction, and the company's liability on the bills. It is, after all, quite common to find in the memorandum

59. See *Bank of Australasia* v. *Breillat* (1847) 13 ER 642.
60. As to which see *Higgins* v. *Beauchamp* [1914] 3 KB 1192: " . . . a trading business is one which depends on the buying and selling of goods", *per* Lush J at p. 1195.
61. The liability to a holder on a bill in no way affects the rights and duties of the partners *inter se.* If a firm is liable due to the actions of a partner who has exceeded his authority the other partners will almost always be able to recover from him.
62. Bills of Exchange Act 1882, s. 23(2) and Partnership Act 1890, ss. 6 and 9.
63. Bills of Exchange Act 1882, s. 91(2).

of association a limitation placed on the directors, particularly of private companies, that they cannot enter into transactions involving the borrowing of money beyond a stipulated limit without the consent of the shareholders.

In such circumstances, the holder will, doubtless, try to rely on the ostensible authority of those signing, in one of the following ways:

1. *Under the new s. 35 of the Companies Act 1985.*[64] We have already noted this section under the topic of *corporate capacity*, and the same provisions apply to the *authority of the directors* to bind the company, whether that company has capacity or not.

Therefore, the holder of a bill, faced with a disclaimer of liability because of lack of authority of those signing, can now rely on the new s. 35(1) which states:

In favour of a person dealing with a company in good faith, the power of the board of directors to bind the company, or authorise others to do so, shall be deemed to be free of any limitation under the company's constitution.

The following points should be noted:

(1) a person is "dealing" with a company if he is a party to any transaction (or other act) to which the company is a party.[65]

(2) "good faith" is presumed unless the contrary is proved,[66] and bad faith is not presumed by reason only that the other party knew the transaction was beyond the powers of the directors under the company's constitution.[67]

(3) "under the company's constitution" also includes any limitation placed on the powers of the directors by a resolution passed at a shareholders' meeting,[68] or incorporated in a shareholders' agreement.[69]

(4) A party to a transaction is not bound to enquire as to any limitation on the powers of the board of directors to bind the company.[70]

These are all-embracing provisions, and on the face of them would give the holder of a bill of exchange considerable protection in enforcing his claim against the company. However, four further points need to be mentioned:

---

64. As we saw above, this section has been substantially amended by s. 108 of the Companies Act 1989, which substitutes a new s. 35 into the Companies Act 1985, sweeping away much of the old law on the *ultra vires* rule, and making almost obsolete the need of third parties dealing with a company to enquire as to its "objects clause" in its memorandum of association. It is the practice now to form companies whose articles provide that "The object of the Company is to carry on business as a general commercial company", which covers virtually any activity at all!

65. New s. 35(2)(*a*).
66. New s. 35(2)(*c*).
67. New s. 35(2)(*b*).
68. New s. 35(3)(*a*).
69. New s. 35(3)(*b*).
70. New s. 35B.

(5) The notion of "good faith" under the terms of the Bills of Exchange Act 1882[71] is, that something is done "honestly"; it is, therefore, easy to envisage circumstances where the holder of a bill delivered to him, whether as payee or indorsee, if he knew the transaction was outside the powers of the directors, may not pass the test of "good faith" under the 1882 Act.

(6) The right of a shareholder to bring proceedings to restrain the directors from acting beyond their powers is not affected by the new legislation.[72] So that, again on the face of the words employed in the new legislation, a shareholder could obtain an injunction to restrain the directors from issuing bills of exchange as part of a transaction, if that transaction appeared to be outside the powers of the board of directors.

However, the subsection goes on to provide that no such proceedings (for injunction) can be brought if the act being carried out by the directors (for example, the delivery of bills of exchange) is " . . . in fulfilment of a legal obligation arising from a previous act of the company." It is not easy to envisage what type of "legal obligation" would be binding on the company, yet could be restrained by a shareholder because the directors had exceeded their powers; certainly, a holder of a bill of exchange could well be involved in expensive litigation before the exact interpretation of such provisions was made clear.

(7) If the board of directors exceeds its powers, a transaction may be voidable at the option of the company if one of the parties is one of its directors, or someone connected with him, or another company with whom the director is associated.[73]

This provision is meant to cover the possible abuse of the wide freedom given under s. 35A (1) by directors who could otherwise bind their company to a transaction without limitation or possible recourse.

(8) The position of persons who are *not* party to a transaction is covered by s. 322A (5)(*c*) of the Companies Act 1985, which states that the company cannot set the transaction aside if:

rights acquired *bona fide* for value and without actual notice of the directors' exceeding their powers by a person who is not a party to the transaction would be affected by the avoidance.

One assumes this provision could cover the case of a holder of a bill of exchange by indorsement, and, of course, the funds the bill represents. However, if a person *is party to a transaction*, it seems he must still satisfy himself

71. Section 90, Bills of Exchange Act 1882.
72. Companies Act 1985, new s. 35(4). Also, the directors remain liable for exceeding their powers: new s. 35(5).
73. Companies Act 1985, new s. 322A (1) and (2), by virtue of Companies Act 1989, s. 109.

that other parties are not directors of the company with whom he is dealing, or otherwise associated, within the terms of the new subsection,[74] otherwise he may find the transaction voidable at the option of the company, and any funds he has received will have to be returned.

The company could not avoid the transaction however, if the other party had parted with any money or property, for example, by negotiating any bills of exchange, and hence restitution was no longer possible.[75]

These are all new provisions, of course, and as with all new legislation we must await its application and interpretation, particularly on how, if at all, the other (following) rules relating to the authority of directors may be affected.

2. *Under the rule in* Royal British Bank *v.* Turquand.[76] This rule is to the effect that third parties can rely on the *ostensible* authority of the directors and other executives in their dealings with a company with whom they are dealing, provided: (a) Everything appears, externally at least, to be in order. (b) They have no notice of any irregularity, and are not put upon enquiry.[77] (c) The document is not a forgery.[78] (d) The transaction is not one absolutely prohibited by the memorandum and articles, nor exceeding the limitations on the powers of the directors contained in these documents.[79] (e) The person relying on the rule is an "outsider" third party not someone within the company, such as a director.[80]

The notion behind the *Turquand* rule is clear enough, in that third parties who are outside the company, and who cannot know whether meetings have been properly held, or other internal steps taken to validate a transaction, should not be prejudiced. Consequently, under the terms of the rule, a third party will be able to hold the company liable in respect of a transaction

74. That is Companies Act 1985, new s. 322A (1).

75. *Ibid.*, s. 322A (5)(a).

76. (1856) 6 E & B 327. The Turquand rule has no application to lack of capacity in corporations. See also *Freeman and Lockyer v. Buckhurst Park Properties (Mangal) Ltd* [1964] 2 QB 480.

77. Banks can be put upon enquiry by company cheques being indorsed by a director, and paid into his own account: *A L Underwood Ltd v. Bank of Liverpool & Martins Bank* [1924] 1 KB 775; or if one director tells the company's bank he considers another director is drawing cheques for private purposes: *B Liggett (Liverpool) Ltd v. Barclays Bank Ltd* [1928] 1 KB 48. Directors drawing on the company account in their own favour is not, of itself, suspicious, unless the amount is very large: *Corporation Agencies Ltd v. Home Bank of Canada* [1927] AC 318. A third party could be put on notice by the company's register of charges under ss. 396 and 401 of the 1985 Act, and also anything shown in the annual return filed under the terms of s. 363.

78. *Ruben v. Great Fingall Consolidated* [1906] AC 439; *Kreditbank Cassel GmbH v. Schenkers Ltd* [1927] 1 KB 826.

79. *Irvine v. Union Bank of Australia* (1877) 2 App Cas 366. The reason being that the third party has constructive notice of the memorandum and articles as filed with the Registrar of Companies. See, however, s. 35 of the 1985 Act which might protect the third party in such a case if he can bring himself within its terms.

80. *Morris v. Kanssen* [1946] AC 459.

notwithstanding the fact that the directors were not properly appointed[81]; or if a purported directors' meeting was irregularly called or held,[82] or even not held at all.[83] The company is also bound where a shareholders' meeting should have been held to approve the transaction, but it was not.[84]

3. *Estoppel.* In addition to the above rules, a company may also be bound under the rules of agency and estoppel, where a director, or employee for that matter, is held out as representing the company. If there are limitations on his authority unknown to the third party, provided the authority is one which such a representative might normally be expected to have, the company will be estopped from denying that ostensible authority.

In this context, the question is often posed as to whether it is obligatory for the third party to search the company's public documents (essentially, the memorandum and articles of association) to see if there are any limitations on the authority of the directors to act themselves or to delegate. The position is that, if the third party is attempting to rely on a term in a public document of the company, then he must have inspected it, otherwise he could not allege he was relying on it.[85] However, if the articles do give power to delegate (as they usually do), and one of the directors is, in fact, *de facto* acting on behalf of the company, the company will be estopped from denying the authority of that person, even though the third party has *not* inspected the articles.[86]

As we have already noted, in signing bills of exchange, s. 37 of the Companies Act 1985 states that they are deemed to have been made, accepted or indorsed on behalf of the company if the act is done in the name of, or by or on behalf of, or on account of, the company " . . . by a person acting under its authority". So that, if cheques are signed in the ordinary course of business by, say, the "Chief Accountant", then the rules outlined above will probably apply, and the holder will get a good title. However, the following points must be noted:

> (1) The chief accountant may have authority within the company's bank mandate to sign cheques, and so would be acting for the company

---

81. *Mahoney v. East Holyford Mining Co* (1875) LR 7 HL 869. "The acts of a director or manager are valid notwithstanding any defect that may afterwards be discovered in his appointment or qualifications: and this provision is not excluded by s. 292(2) (void resolution to appoint)": Companies Act 1985, s. 285. It seems this section is not limited to "outsider" third parties; see under earlier legislation *Dawson v. African Consolidated Land Co* [1898] 1 Ch 6, and *Channel Collieries v. Dover Light Rail Co* [1914] 2 Ch 506.

82. *Re Fireproof Doors Ltd* [1916] 2 Ch 142.

83. *Davies v. R Bolton & Co* [1894] 3 Ch 678; *Duck v. Tower Galvinising Co* [1901] 2 KB 314.

84. *Re Hampshire Land Co* [1896] 2 Ch 743. Except, perhaps, if the resolution is one which must be filed with the Registrar of Companies, and is not: see Companies Act 1985, s. 380(4).

85. *Rama Corporation Ltd v. Proved Tin & General Investments Ltd* [1952] 2 QB 147.

86. *Freeman & Lockyer v. Buckhurst Park Properties (Mangal) Ltd* [1964] 2 QB 480, in particular *see per* Diplock LJ (as he then was) at p. 505 *et seq.* Also, *Biggerstaff v. Rowatt's Wharf Ltd* [1896] 2 Ch 93; *British Thomson-Houston Co v. Federated European Bank Ltd* [1932] 2 KB 176; *Clay Hill Brick Co Ltd v. Rawlings* [1938] 4 All ER 100.

" . . . under its authority", even though he did not have authority to enter into the particular transaction of which the giving of the cheque was part. In other words, the bank would pay the cheque, even though the company tried, subsequently, to negative the contract which the chief accountant had made.

(2) If the chief accountant had no authority at all to enter into the transaction, the company may well still find itself bound to it within the rules stated above, yet the signing of the cheque could hardly then be said to have been done on behalf of the company " . . . under its authority"; this would mean the payee would get no title, and would have to refund the amount received.

(3) If the cheque were negotiated by the payee, a subsequent holder, being a holder in due course or a holder for value, could well get a good title to the cheque, even though the payee might have a problem over the question of the unauthorized signature.

From all this it will be seen that if a cheque or other bill is deemed to have been validly executed within these rules, it does not follow that the basic transaction, of which the cheque or bill is part, will, necessarily, be binding on the company.

Liability of persons signing

Where an agent signs a bill in his own name as drawer, indorser or acceptor he can be *personally* liable on the bill, if he does not add words indicating that he signs for or on behalf of a principal, or in a representative capacity. In doing so he must state for whom he is agent, mere words describing him as an agent or as filling a representative capacity, without more, does not exempt him from personal liability.[87]

The principles were well stated by Scrutton LJ in the case of *Elliott* v. *Bax-Ironside*[88]:

Where a person puts his name on a bill with an addition there are two classes of cases into which the addition may fall. It may be such as to show that he is contracting as agent for another, putting his name on the bill only as agent and excluding his personal liability. Where a man signs "for and on behalf of Jones as agent" he is clearly not undertaking any personal liability, but is purporting to make Jones liable. It is otherwise where the man puts after his signature a description for the purpose merely of showing who he is and how he came to sign. Thus, in a case where money had been lent to a parish and the churchwardens signed a note for the amount 'P and W, Churchwardens' they were held personally liable on the note as makers for the description of themselves as churchwardens did not mean that they were signing as agents for the parish and took no personal liability, but was merely an explanation of how they came to put their names on the note.

87. Bills of Exchange Act 1882, ss. 26(1) and 31(5). See also *The Elmville* [1904] P 319.
88. [1925] 2 KB 301, at p. 307.

One of the most common situations to be found is that of directors, officers and employees of companies, who daily sign on behalf of the corporate entities. The greatest care must be taken when these people sign, because, if the bill or cheque is not paid, it is quite usual for the person signing to be sued *personally*. The rule enunciated by Scrutton LJ, in so far as it applies to companies, is contained in s. 349 of the Companies Act 1985, subs. (1)(c) and (d) of which provides that every company must, *inter alia*, mention its name in "legible characters" in all " . . . bills of exchange, promissory notes, endorsements, cheques and orders for money or goods . . . and in all its bills of parcels, invoices, receipts and letters of credit", which are purported " . . . to be signed by or on behalf of the company . . . ".

If the name of the company is not in "legible characters", by virtue of subs. (4) of s. 349, " . . . an officer of a company or a person on its behalf . . . " who " . . . signs or authorizes to be signed . . . " any bills or cheques or other documents mentioned above, will be " . . . personally liable to the holder of the bill of exchange, promissory note, cheque or order for money or goods for the amount of it (unless it is duly paid by the company)".[89]

Everything, therefore, turns on the "legible characters", and in what manner the person signed. The name of the company which must appear is that which is stated in the memorandum of association,[90] as recorded with the Registrar of Companies, and nothing else will do. Moreover, the name of a public company must end with the words "public limited company", and, in the case of a private company, with the word "limited"[91]; or the specified abbreviations "plc" or "Ltd",[92] and if they were omitted the person signing could be personally liable,[93] as he would be if the company name was mis-stated,[94] or a trade name used instead.[95]

On these occasions, sizeable problems can arise with the use of rubber stamps, if the name is not legible within the rule[96]; and even the customary method of signing, "for and on behalf of", will not negative personal liability

---

89. Except if the plaintiff, who drew the bill, was estopped because he was responsible for the misdescription: *Durham Fancy Goods Ltd* v. *Michael Jackson (Fancy Goods) Ltd* [1968] 2 All ER 987. However, a subsequent holder, not affected by the estoppel, could recover from the director personally: *per* Donaldson J (as he then was) at p. 991E. Incidentally, the personal liability under s. 349 is in addition to the fine for the offence under the Companies Act.

90. Companies Act 1985, s. 2(1)(a).

91. *Ibid.*, s. 25, or the equivalent in Welsh, if the registered office is in the Principality.

92. Section 27(1) and (4). This provision gives statutory effect to what was the situation prior to the new Act: see *Banque de l'Indochine et de Suez SA* v. *Euroseas Group Finance Co Ltd* [1981] 3 All ER 198. These abbreviations would appear to be the only ones now to be used, and the position with "Ld" must be in doubt: see *Stacy & Co Ltd* v. *Wallis* (1912) 106 LT 544.

93. *Penrose* v. *Martyr* (1858) EB & E 499: *British Airways Board* v. *Parish* [1979] 2 Lloyd's Rep. 361.

94. *Atkins* v. *Wardle* (1889) 61 LT 23.

95. *Maxform SpA* v. *Mariani & Goodville Ltd* [1979] 2 Lloyd's Rep. 385.

96. *Dernatine & Co* v. *Ashworth* (1905) 21 TLR 510, where the word "Limited" was missing because of the way the rubber stamp was applied but this was excused on the facts.

if the name of the company is incorrect, or if there is evidence that those signing accepted personal responsibility for the signature.[97]

The signature should also be followed with some "addition" (to use Scrutton LJ's expression) excluding personal liability. In the case of companies, it is usual to indicate the position of the person signing as "director" or "secretary" or whatever, but this really is a description " . . . showing who he is and how he came to sign",[98] and will not, of itself, negative personal liability.[99] Nowadays, it is common to see under the signature the words "authorized signatory" which, while it has not been tested in the courts, should be adequate to indicate that the person is not accepting personal liability—provided, of course, the name of the company appears correctly and in "legible characters".

Another common situation is that of partnerships. A partner who signs without the authority of his partners is personally liable, whether he signs his own name or that of the firm, as a person who signs a bill in a trade or assumed name is liable as if he had signed it in his own name.[100]

Personal representatives are sometimes put in difficulties. In the ordinary way they can negative their personal liability by signing and clearly indicating their capacity:

J. Jones Exor. of A. Smith Dec'd.[101]

If bills are signed in this way there is no personal liability, provided the personal representatives are merely completing a transaction begun by the deceased. However, if once they embark on new transactions, even if on the deceased's express instructions, then they will be personally liable no matter how they sign.

For example:

LIVERPOOL BANK v. WALKER[102]

X, by his will, directed his executor B to carry on his (X's) business after his death. This the executor did and in the course of business accepted bills, signing them "B executor of X". B was sued personally. *Held*—that he was personally liable, even though he had signed to negative liability.

In determining whether a signature on a bill is that of principal or agent, the construction most favourable to the validity of the bill will be adopted.[103]

---

97. *Rolfe Lubell & Co v. Keith* [1979] 1 All ER 860.
98. *Per* Scrutton LJ in *Elliott v. Bax-Ironside* [1925] 2 KB 301, 307.
99. *Landes v. Marcus* (1909) 35 TLR 478; but see on similar facts *Chapman v. Smethurst* [1909] 1 KB 927, where the "managing director" escaped personal liability. In *Bondina Ltd* v. *Rollaway Shower Blinds Ltd* [1986] 1 All ER 564, the director was given leave to defend as " . . . when he signed the cheques he adopted all the printed wording on it, including the company's name and account number, thereby showing that the cheque was drawn on the company's account and not by him personally. That approach was in line with *Chapman* v. *Smethurst* . . . ": *per* Dillon LJ [1986] 1 WLR 517.
100. Bills of Exchange Act 1882, s. 23(1).
101. See *infra* under title "Negotiation and Transfer".
102. (1859) 4 De G & J 24.
103. Bills of Exchange Act 1882, s. 26(2).

Estoppel and ratification

Section 24 of the Bills of Exchange Act 1882 provides two exceptions to the status of unauthorized signatures being "wholly inoperative" (1) where the rule of estoppel operates; and (2) where the signature is ratified. Each must be considered.

1. Estoppel

Section 24 provides that an unauthorized signature is "wholly inoperative" —

... unless the party against whom it is sought to retain or enforce payment of the bill is precluded from setting up the ... want of authority.

As we saw with reference to companies, if a man is "precluded" from denying a state of affairs which he has led someone else to rely on, he is said to be "estopped". This rule of estoppel is found in several instances in connection with bills of exchange. For example, the drawer of a bill is precluded (that is, estopped) from denying to a holder in due course the existence or capacity of the payee[104]; likewise an indorser, the genuineness and regularity of the drawer's signature and all previous indorsements.[105]

Lord Cranworth has explained the doctrine of estoppel as follows:

Where a party has by words or by conduct made a representation to another leading him to believe in the existence of a particular fact or state of facts, and that other person has acted on the faith of such representation, then the party who made the representation shall not afterwards be heard to say that the facts were not as he represented them to be.[106]

Thus, before an estoppel will arise the following must be present: 1. An unambiguous representation made by one person, 2. As to an existing state of affairs, 3. Prejudicially affecting the rights of the other, if the estoppel were not to operate.

An example of the operation of the doctrine of estoppel is the case of

LLOYDS BANK v. COOKE[107]

Cooke banked with Lloyds. He asked for an overdraft, which he said would be secured by promissory notes signed by a more affluent relative by the name of Sanbrook. Sanbrook foolishly (as it turned out) signed two blank pieces of paper and gave them

104. *Ibid.*, s. 55(1)(*b*).
105. *Ibid.*, s. 55(2)(*b*).
106. *West v. Jones* (1851) 1 Sim (n.s.) 205, 207. There are various courses of conduct (as opposed to actual spoken words) which will operate as an estoppel, for example by acquiescence: *Proctor v. Bennis* (1887) 36 Ch D 740. Also, there sometimes operates a quasi or equitable estoppel which is a valid *defence* to some actions: *per* Lord Cairns in *Hughes v. Metropolitan Railway Co* (1877) 2 App Cas 439, 448. See also *infra* under heading "Lapse of time" in "Defences to liability on the bill" in Chap. 5.
107. [1907] 1 KB 794.

to Cooke to be filled up as promissory notes for £250 each. Cooke fraudulently made them up for £500 each, and obtained an overdraft of £1,000. In due course, Lloyds sued both Cooke and the unfortunate Sanbrook; claiming (so far as Sanbrook was concerned) that he could not, having issued the notes, say Cooke did not have authority to make them up for the larger figure as he had done. *Held*—that "the common law doctrine of estoppel applies, and the rights of the parties may be decided by reference to that doctrine";[108] consequently the bank were entitled to recover from Sanbrook.

2. Ratification

Section 24 also provides:

... that nothing in this Section shall affect the ratification of an authorized signature not amounting to a forgery.

Consequently, there is, of course, nothing to prevent a principal ratifying an unauthorized signature, provided the signature does not amount to a forgery,[109] that is, if the signature was not placed on the bill with criminal intent to deceive. However, even if this does happen, and the person whose signature it is supposed to be, takes no action to correct the fraud, he will be liable on the bill; in effect, as though ratification had taken place.[110]

To summarize, therefore, to constitute a valid ratification the following conditions must be satisfied[111]: (a) the agent must have purported to act for the principal; and (b) the principal must have had capacity to execute the bill at the time the act was done; and (c) the principal must legally be capable of signing the bill at the time of ratification.

IV. CONSIDERATION

It is not easy to define exactly what "consideration" is. It has been said[112] it is " ... some right, interest, profit or benefit accruing to the one party, or some forbearance detriment, loss or responsibility given, suffered or undertaken by the other."

The notion of consideration springs from the belief in English law[113] that no one should be able to claim under an agreement that is purely *voluntary*. For example, if A says to B, "I shall give you £10 at Christmas", that is a gratuitous promise, and if A does not make a gift of £10, there is nothing B can do about it. There must be a *quid pro quo*. So, if A had gone on to say, "I shall give you

108. [1907] 1 KB 794 *per* Collins MR, at p. 800.
109. Bills of Exchange Act 1882, s. 24.
110. That is by estoppel, see *infra* under heading "estoppel" in Chap. 6. See also *Greenwood* v. *Martins Bank Ltd* [1932] 1 KB 371.
111. *Per* Wright J in *Firth* v. *Staines* [1897] 2 QB 70, at p. 78.
112. *Per* Lush J in *Currie* v. *Misa* (1875) LR 10 Ex 153, at p. 162.
113. The law of Scotland and of many other European countries is different in not requiring consideration to support a promise.

£10 at Christmas if you will repair my car today", and if B then repaired the car, this would be good consideration for A's promise to pay the £10.

A. *The doctrine considered*

The rules relating to the doctrine of consideration as affecting contracts on bills of exchange differ in some important respects from the rules of ordinary contracts—that is, contracts not involving bills of exchange. Indeed, the doctrine of consideration is a complicated subject which cannot adequately be discussed here; but as it affects bills of exchange, and stripped of many of its complexities, there are three broad principles which require treatment: 1. Sufficiency of consideration. 2. Consideration must move from the promisee. 3. Consideration must not be "past".

1. Sufficiency of consideration

Consideration must have value, but it need not in any way be equal or appropriate to the value of the other promise. Indeed, to the ordinary man in the street it may seem strange that consideration can be found in circumstances which, at first sight, appear to have little or no *value* at all in the accepted sense of the word. For example, the payment of £1 per annum has been deemed sufficient to support an agreement to allow a widow to live in the matrimonial home.[114] Again, the forbearance to bring an action to rectify an agreement which was subsequently varied;[115] or an unsupported promise to give security to a bank in the furtherance of facilities made available;[116] or the drawing of cheques to third parties for the benefit of the other party;[117] or the taking of a cheque when cash could be demanded.[118] All these actions amount to "consideration" although not necessarily of very much intrinsic value in themselves.[119]

Take two examples involving bills of exchange.

POLLWAY LTD v. ABDULLAH[120]

Pollway owned some property in Surrey and instructed May & Philpot, a firm of estate agents, to sell it. An auction was held and the property was knocked down to Abdullah. He signed a form of memorandum of agreement and gave May & Philpot a cheque for

114. *Thomas v. Thomas* (1842) 2 QB 851.
115. *Horton v. Horton* [1961] 1 QB 215.
116. *Alliance Bank v. Broom* (1864) 11 LT 362.
117. *Cole v. Milsome* [1951] 1 All ER 311.
118. *Pollway Ltd v. Abdullah* [1974] 1 WLR 493.
119. Put technically, the courts will not enquire into the adequacy of the consideration, nor will they denounce an agreement merely because it appears to be unfair, as the parties are presumed to be capable of appreciating their own interests. See *Adib El Hinnaiui v. Yacoub Fahmi Abu El Huda El Faruqi* [1936] 1 All ER 638 (PC). Unless, perhaps, if the agreement falls within the terms of the Unfair Contract Terms Act 1977 and the Unfair Terms in Consumer Contracts Regulations 1994, which came into force on 1st July 1995.
120. [1974] 1 WLR 493.

the deposit. Immediately afterwards, Abdullah thought better of the matter, and stopped the cheque and refused to proceed. Pollway resold the property, treating the contract with Abdullah as repudiated. Both Pollway and May & Philpot sued Abdullah *on the cheque*. Abdullah claimed that there had been a total failure of consideration. *Held*—that Pollway (the original vendors) could not recover on the cheque made payable to their agents (May & Philpot) because they did not give consideration, and had never been holders.[121] "On the other hand, at the moment when the cheque was given and received by the auctioneers they warranted to the defendant their authority to sign the memorandum on the vendor's behalf and to receive the cheque payable to themselves as named payees in diminution of the defendant's obligation to pay the full amount of the purchase price to the vendors.[122] If this were the true consideration for the cheque, as I think it was, that consideration never failed . . . "[123] May & Philpot could, therefore, recover on the cheque.

COLE v. MILSOME[124]

A Mr Hignett was in financial difficulties. He was friendly with both Mrs Cole and Miss Milsome, and he hit on an idea how he could turn the relationship to his financial advantage. He pursuaded Miss Milsome to draw a cheque in favour of Mrs Cole; Hignett then took that cheque to Mrs Cole with a request that she pay it into her bank, and then draw cheques in favour of people to whom he was indebted. What story he told these two ladies is not known, but Miss Milsome became concerned and she "stopped" her cheque. Mrs Cole was, obviously, alarmed at this (as she had already drawn the cheques requested by Hignett), and she telephoned Miss Milsome, who—also for reasons not explained—assured Mrs Cole that she would get her money. Mrs Cole did not, and she sued Miss Milsome. The defence was that there was no relationship between the two ladies, and hence the giving of the cheque by Miss Milsome was gratuitous. *Held*—that by drawing the cheque, and by assuring Mrs Cole that she would get her money, Miss Milsome had acted in a manner " . . . wholly inconsistent with an attitude . . . that she had written out the cheque expressly payable to the plaintiff merely to indicate a voluntary promise on her part which could be withdrawn at any time before the bank had honoured the draft".[125]

The rules with regard to consideration as affecting bills of exchange are contained in s. 27(1) of the Bills of Exchange Act 1882, which states:

Valuable consideration for a bill may be constituted by
  (a) Any consideration sufficient to support a simple contract.
  (b) An antecedent debt or liability. Such a debt or liability is deemed valuable consideration whether the bill is payable on demand or at a future time.

121. [1974] 1 WLR 493 *per* Roskill LJ (as he then was), at p. 497B.
122. In taking a cheque instead of cash, the recipient is not always deemed to be giving consideration however. "No sensible distinction can be taken between payment . . . by cash and payment . . . by cheque. The cheque, when given, is conditional payment. When honoured, it is actual payment. It is then just the same as cash." *Per* Lord Denning in *D & C Builders* v. *Rees* [1966] 2 QB 617, at p. 623C. Payment by credit card is, however, *not* conditional payment, it is actual payment when the voucher is signed by the cardholder: *In re Charge Card Services Ltd* [1988] 3 WLR 764, 775F. See also *Marreco* v. *Richardson* [1908] 2 KB 584.
123. *Per* Roskill LJ (as he then was), at p. 497C.
124. [1951] 1 All ER 311. This case is also cited *infra* under the heading "Impersonal payees" in Chap. 12. There were two claims, this deals with the second.
125. *Per* Lloyd-Jacob J at p. 314E. There is just a suggestion of an estoppel in the judge's words.

Paragraph (*a*) is clear enough, if the consideration—whatever it may be—is adequate to support a contract not involving a bill, then it will be adequate to support the contract on the bill. Indeed, often the consideration which supports a bill of exchange is the same consideration which exists under the original contract of which the bill of exchange forms part. This aspect is dealt with more fully in Chapter 5, when considering liability on a bill of exchange.

The provisions of para. (*b*), however, make an important change in the common law rule. The reason being, as we shall see below in a little more detail, is that once a contract has been fully performed, there is no consideration left which can support the subsequent giving of, say, a cheque in payment. The recipient (the holder) of the cheque could sue under the original contract for his money, but—without para. (*b*)—he could not sue on the cheque. Speaking of the provisions of para. (*b*) Sir Raymond Evershed has explained that they " . . . are intended to get over what would otherwise have been *prima facie* the result at common law by which the giving of a cheque for an amount for which the drawer was already indebted imported no consideration since the obligation was past . . . "[126]

2. Consideration must move from the promisee

The consideration must come from the person who is trying to enforce the agreement: in the example given above concerning the repair of the motor car, the consideration (that is, the repair of the car) has to come from the person demanding payment. Put technically, the consideration must "move from the promisee". So that if some third party altogether tries to recover, he would be a stranger to the contract and, in the case of a bill of exchange, in the hands of a holder who had not given consideration, and who is, therefore, a volunteer, the bill would not be enforceable. For example, in

OLIVER v. DAVIS[127]

Oliver lent Davis £350 and in return Davis gave Oliver a post-dated cheque for £400. As the date of payment approached, it became clear to Davis that he could not meet the cheque, and so he asked a lady friend, a Miss Woodcock, to draw a cheque on her account to settle matters with Oliver. This Miss Woodcock did, but immediately afterwards changed her mind, and "stopped" her cheque. In due time Oliver presented Davis' cheque which was dishonoured, and Miss Woodcock's which was, of course, not paid either. Oliver sued both Davis and Miss Woodcock on their cheques. *Held*—(in the action against Miss Woodcock) that the giving of her cheque to Oliver was a purely

126. *Oliver* v. *Davis* [1949] 2 KB 727, at p. 735.

127. [1949] 2 KB 727. See also *Hasan* v. *Willson* [1977] 1 Lloyd's Rep. 431, where, on similar facts, the same decision was reached. Both cases clearly show that the "antecedent debt or liability" referred to in s. 72(1)(*b*) of the 1882 Act must be that of the promisor or drawer of the bill: see particularly the words of Sir Raymond Evershed MR in *Oliver* v. *Davis*, at p. 735.

gratuitous action on her part, and as no consideration came from Oliver for her cheque, he could not recover from her.

If there have been prior dealings with the bill (cheque) where value has "at any time" — prior to the bill coming into the hands of the holder — been given for it between the prior parties; then, if it subsequently comes into the hands of a holder by way of a gift, he is nevertheless, deemed to be "holder for value" under the terms of s. 27(2) of the Bills of Exchange Act 1882, and he can recover from his immediate transferor and prior parties, who became such after the giving of the consideration.

There must have been prior dealings when the consideration was given however; it is not possible, as between the immediate parties, to have consideration moving otherwise than from the promisee.[128]

In all these cases, where someone has signed a bill of exchange, the burden of proof is on them to show that no consideration was given, if that is to be their defence, because "every party whose signature appears on a bill is *prima facie* deemed to have become a party thereto for value."[129]

3. Consideration must not be past

Consideration is sometimes expressed to be *executory*. If X's promise to do something for Y is in exchange for Y's promise to do something for X. For example, if X orders goods from Y to be delivered at the end of the month and paid for at that time, there is an immediate binding contract between them, although neither has performed his promise. The contract is supported by the mutual executory consideration: Y to deliver the goods, and X to pay for them. This must not be confused with *executed* consideration, which is Y doing something *in return* for X's promise. For example, if X offers £1 if Y will cut the lawn: Y may accept, but there is still no consideration until he has cut the lawn and *executed* the task.

Difficulties frequently arise if the task is wholly executed *before* the promise to pay is made. In such a case, the doing of the work is not deemed valuable consideration, however, as the consideration is expressed to be "past". In fact, there exists no consideration at all. For example, if Y cuts X's lawn on Monday

128. *Diamond v. Graham* [1968] 1 WLR 1061 (on facts almost identical to those in *Oliver v. Davis*) must surely be wrongly decided. Certainly, it is to be regretted that *Oliver v. Davis* was not cited to the court. Consideration must move from the promisee, as we have seen, and the Court of Appeal (Danckwerts, Diplock and Sachs LJJ) must surely have been in error in believing that Diamond was a "holder for value", when he was the payee of Graham's cheque, which had been demanded by Diamond as a condition precedent to his making a loan to a third party, which loan was *not*, in any way, made at Graham's request. See the critical views of Robert Goff J in the case of *Hasan v. Willson* [1977] 1 Lloyd's Rep. 431, at p. 442. In *Pollway Ltd v. Abdullah* [1974] 1 WLR 493, Roskill LJ (as he then was) said of *Diamond v. Graham* that had he needed to consider the case, he would have required further argument upon "certain questions", which did not " . . . seem to have been argued in that case . . . ": at p. 497F.
129. Bills of Exchange Act 1882, s. 30(1).

and on Tuesday X says, "I shall give you £1 for cutting the lawn yesterday", Y could not recover, as the cutting of the lawn was completed, past and done with before X made his promise to pay for it.

Section 27(1) of the 1882 Act makes an important exception to this general common law principle, by providing that valuable consideration for a bill of exchange, in addition to any consideration sufficient to support a simple contract, can be "an antecedent debt or liability". So, if X gives Y a cheque for £1 for cutting the lawn, Y could sue on it if it were dishonoured, by virtue of s. 27(1); although at common law, he could not sue on X's original promise.[130]

B. Illegal consideration

It may well be, of course, that the parties have agreed to do something which is illegal, in which case the cheque or the bill of exchange will not be supported by consideration since "illegal" consideration is, in fact, no consideration. There is no definition of "illegality" for this purpose, and many acts have been held illegal. Obviously, a contract in contravention of an Act of Parliament is illegal and, hence, unenforceable; also, cheques given for an immoral purpose; or in settlement of a gaming debt.[131] In each case the transaction must be looked at, and if the consideration does transpire to be illegal then payment of the bill cannot be enforced at all *between the immediate parties to the illegality*. Usually, the parties will be *in pari delicto*, and there can be no hope of the payee of a cheque getting a good title; he knows of the illegality from the beginning. Moreover, even if the parties are not acting in concert, the payee is still not able to get a good title, because, as we have seen, illegal consideration is, in fact, no consideration at all; and it will not save the payee to show that he did not realize that what was being agreed to (the consideration) was illegal.

However, if a subsequent holder is not a party to the illegality, and can show he qualifies as a holder in due course, or claims through a holder in due course, he will be able to recover on the bill.[132] The burden of proof in such a case is, however, on the holder to show that after the alleged illegality, proper consideration was given for the bill.[133] Knowledge of the illegality by a subsequent holder would, of course, be fatal to any claim. Take for example the case of

---

130. See *per* Sir Raymond Evershed MR, in *Oliver* v. *Davis* [1949] 2 KB 727, at p. 735.

131. It would not be appropriate here to discuss the rather involved gaming laws. However, it should be noted that the Gaming Act 1968, while not legalizing loans for gaming, does allow the cashing of cheques by the licensee of a gaming establishment provided the cheque is given for an equivalent amount of cash or tokens. The cheque must not be post-dated and the payee must bank it within two "business" days as defined by s. 92 of the 1882 Act, as amended by s. 3 of the Banking and Financial Dealings Act 1971.

132. Bills of Exchange Act 1882, s. 29(3).

133. *Ibid.*, s. 30(2).

LADUP LTD v. SHAIKH[134]

Shaikh visited the Ritz Casino, and obtained chips by giving drafts drawn on a bank called "Euroseas". After playing for some time, and having lost heavily, he cashed the balance of his chips and was given a cheque by the Ritz Casino for £45,000, marked "A/C Payee Only, Not Negotiable". Shaikh then immediately went to a casino operated by Ladup, and was given chips there to a value of £37,000 in exchange for the Ritz cheque which Shaikh indorsed in favour of Ladup; the balance being kept as a reduction of debts Shaikh already had with Ladup. There was some discussion on the telephone between the staff of the two casinos, and the Ladup people were told that the Ritz cheque to Shaikh (and now in the hands of Ladup) would be paid if the "Euroseas" drafts were met. As it happened they were not, and Ritz stopped payment on their cheque to Shaikh. Ladup sued Shaikh as indorser of the cheque, and the Ritz Casino as the drawer. *Held*—that undoubtedly, the cheque given by the Ritz Casino to Shaikh was given for an illegal consideration within the terms of the Gaming Act 1968, so that he certainly could not have sued on it, and Ladup " . . . when they accepted the cheque, knew perfectly well of the illegality involved in the drawing of the cheque. They cannot show, within the meaning of s. 30(2) of the Bills of Exchange Act 1882, that they accepted without notice of the illegality".[135] Therefore, the claims against both Shaikh and Ritz Casino failed.

C. Lack of consideration

If it is proved, in an action on a bill, that consideration has not been given or does not exist, it will mean the party trying to claim may well be a volunteer, and as such, he will be unable to claim on the bill. It follows, therefore, that if a cheque is given in circumstances which show the drawer is not a party to the transaction, and is simply acting gratuitously in law, the drawer is a volunteer receiving no consideration, and cannot be liable on his cheque given in these circumstances.

AEG (UK) v. LEWIS[136]

Mr Cash owned a house in which was an AEG gas cooker requiring some maintenance work to be carried out upon it. The gas fitter of AEG (UK) Ltd called by arrangement and carried out some repair work. Mr Cash was not present, but his daughter, Mrs Lewis, let the engineer into the home, signed the "Field Service Repair Sheet" when the work was completed, and, at the request of the engineer, gave him her personal cheque for £80.05. When Mr Cash returned, he found the work unsatisfactory, and asked his daughter to "stop" her cheque which she did. AEG (UK) Ltd then sued Mrs Lewis on the cheque. *Held*—the fitter had no authority, express or implied, to accept Mrs. Lewis's cheque, or to release Mr Cash from his obligation to pay. Mrs Lewis was a volunteer

---

134. [1982] 3 WLR 172.
135. *Per* McCowan J at p. 180H. In any event, since the cheque was marked "not negotiable", by virtue of s. 81 of the 1882 Act, Ladup could not get a better title than Shaikh had. Indeed, it is remarkable that Ladup accepted a cheque, in all the circumstances, marked "A/C Payee Only, Not Negotiable", since they might have had difficulty collecting anyway, because of the "A/C Payee" marking, quite apart from the illegality problem.
136. *The Times*, 29 December 1992. This account is taken from the Official Transcript.

in the transaction and was entitled to stop her cheque at any time before it was paid.[137]

This is certainly the case between the immediate parties to the bill, but subsequent holders may be in a better position.

This will be considered in greater detail later under the heading of "Liability on Negotiation" below at p. 65.

V. FORM OF A BILL

A. The definition considered

A bill of exchange is defined by s. 3(1) of the 1882 Act as:

> ... an unconditional order in writing addressed by one person to another, signed by the person giving it, requiring the person to whom it is addressed to pay on demand or at a fixed or determinable future time a sum certain in money to or to the order of a specified person, or to bearer.

Any instrument which does not comply with these conditions is not a bill of exchange.[138]

Almost every word of the definition is important and must be considered in some detail.

(a) There must be "an unconditional order"

A mere *request* to pay is insufficient. For example: "Please let bearer have £7 — and place it to my account and you will oblige your humble servant" was held invalid.[139] Contrast: "Mr Nelson will much oblige Mr Webb by paying to J Ruff 20 guineas on his account" was held valid.[140]

---

137. McCowan and Nourse LJJ. Hirst LJ dissented, pointing out that on the receipt of the cheque by the fitter a new contract came into being between AEG (UK) Ltd (the payees of the cheque) and Mrs Lewis. He thought to hold otherwise "might imperil the legal basis of a large number of other everyday cheque transactions". The case of *Cole* v. *Milsome* [1951] 1 All ER 311 was not cited to the court, which is to be regretted. There, it will be remembered, Lloyd-Jacob J (at p. 314E) thought the giving of a cheque " ... wholly inconsistent ... to indicate a voluntary promise ... ". This must surely be so in day-to-day commercial transactions; if this were not the case, it would mean no one would accept a cheque unless the payee is satisfied that the drawer has received consideration. A point which may certainly baffle the layman, if he is even conscious of it. Mrs Lewis, the defendant, did not appear and took no part in the proceedings, so we do not know what her defence might have been. In these circumstances, the plaintiffs were entitled to judgment, since the 1882 Act, s. 30(1), provides that "every party whose signature appears on a bill is *prima facie* deemed to have become a party thereto for value". In other words, the burden of proof of lack of consideration is on the defendant, and as she did not appear, judgment for the plaintiff must surely have followed. This point was not raised before the court either, so far as one can tell from the transcript.

138. Bills of Exchange Act 1882, s. 3(2).

139. *Little* v. *Slackford* (1828) Moore & M 171.

140. *Ruff* v. *Webb* (1794) 1 Esp.130.

The order must be unconditional. For example, a sum to be paid "when John marries" is invalid, since John may never marry. However, to pay on John's death is valid, because it is ascertainable: John's death must happen some time.

An order to pay the bill out of a particular fund is not unconditional, and so prevents the document being a bill of exchange. However, if there is an unqualified order to pay, the document will be a valid bill notwithstanding the order is coupled with an indication of a particular fund out of which the drawee is to reimburse himself, or a particular account to be debited.[141]

For example: "We hereby *authorize* you to pay on our account to the order of X £6000" is invalid and not a bill. Contrast: "Pay £100 to John Smith and debit my private account" is valid.

Any instrument which orders any act to be done *in addition to the payment of money* is not a bill of exchange.[142]

(b) The bill must be "in writing"[143]

Any form of writing will suffice, and a bill drawn up in pencil is quite valid.[144] The writing can be on any kind of material: paper, parchment, wood or a paving stone.[145]

(c) The bill must be "signed by the person giving it"

The "person giving it" is, of course, the drawer. It is not necessary that the drawer should sign it with his own hand. It is adequate if *his signature* is written by some other person by his authority.[146]

(d) Requiring "the person to whom it is addressed"

The person "to whom it is addressed" is the drawee, and he must always be named or otherwise indicated with reasonable certainty,[147] and while a bill can be addressed to two or more drawees it must not be drawn in the alternative or in succession, if it is addressed in this way it is not a bill.[148] For example, if

141. Bills of Exchange Act 1882, s. 3(3).
142. *Ibid.*, s. 3 (2).
143. "Writing" includes print and "written" includes printed: s. 2.
144. *Geary v. Physic* (1826) LJKB Hil. T. 147, 149. See also *Importers Co v. Westminster Bank* [1927] 2 KB 297, 304.
145. See *The Sunday Times*: 16 February 1975. A Mr Toms in a rent dispute with Watford Council drew a £12 cheque on a 56lb paving stone. His bank agreed to honour it, but the payees refused to accept it.
146. Bills of Exchange Act 1882, s. 91(1). If there was no such authority the placing of another's name to a bill could amount to forgery and be wholly inoperative: s. 24.
147. *Ibid.*, s. 6(1).
148. *Ibid.*, s. 6(2).

a bill is drawn: "To John Jones or James Smith"—not valid. Contrast: "To John Jones and James Smith"—valid.

(e) Time of payment

The section says that the order must be to pay " . . . on demand or at a fixed or determinable future time . . . ". Therefore a bill may be payable: (1) on demand; or (2) at a future time.

1. Payable on demand

A bill is payable on demand which is expressed to be so payable, or payable on sight, or on presentation, or in which no time for payment is expressed, or is accepted for payment or indorsed when it is overdue.[149] A typical example of a bill payable on demand is, of course, a cheque.

2. Payable at a future time

A bill which is not payable on demand must be payable at some future time. A bill is payable at a future time when it is expressed to be payable at a fixed period after date or sight, or at a fixed period after the occurrence of a specified event which is certain to happen, even though the time of happening may be uncertain.[150]

However, an instrument expressed to be payable on a contingency is not a bill, and the happening of the event does not cure the defect.[151] For example, bills payable: "ten days after the death of X"—valid or "one year after my death"—valid. Contrast: "when I marry X"—invalid or "ninety days after the arrival of S.S. Sinbad in London"—invalid.

When a bill is drawn payable at or after "sight" it means sight by the drawee when presentment is made for acceptance.

Where a bill is expressed to be payable at a fixed period after date but is issued undated, or where the acceptance of a bill payable at a fixed period after sight is undated, any holder may insert the true date of issue or acceptance, and the bill is payable accordingly.[152] If the wrong date is inserted, if it is done in good faith or, even if done *male fidei*, if the bill comes into the hands of a holder in due course, the date will be treated as the correct date.[153] This is most

---

149. *Ibid.*, s. 10.
150. Bills of Exchange Act 1882, s. 11.
151. *Ibid.*, s. 11. A bill drawn for payment "at 90 days D/A" (arguably 90 days after acceptance) was held not to be at a fixed or determined future time, as the acceptance might never happen: *Korea Exchange Bank Ltd* v. *Debenhams (Central Buying) Ltd* [1979] 1 Lloyd's Rep. 548.
152. *Ibid.*, s. 12.
153. *Ibid.*, s. 12(2).

important as a bill must be presented for payment on the day it falls due, otherwise the drawer and indorsers are discharged from their liability.

Every date is deemed to be the true date until the contrary is proved;[154] and a bill can be *ante* or *post* dated and still be valid.[155]

Computation of the time of payment

Where a bill was payable on a date in the future, over the years it became customary to allow an additional three days called "days of grace" in the payment of bills. These days came to be claimable as of right and the practice was given statutory approval by the 1882 Act. They were, in modern times anyway, something of a nuisance and are now abolished,[156] so that where a bill is not payable on demand, the day on which it falls due is determined by the following rules[157]:

(1) A bill is payable on the last day fixed by the bill as the time of payment, or on the next business day if the date fixed by the bill is a non-business day.

(2) If the 1882 Act limits the time for doing anything to less than *three days*, "non-business" days must be excluded. These are Saturday, Sunday, Good Friday, Christmas Day, or a bank holiday under the Banking and Financial Dealings Act 1971 (or any Act amending it); or a day appointed by Royal Proclamation as a Public Fast or Thanksgiving Day; or any day declared to be a "non-business" day under the 1971 Act.[158]

154. *Ibid.*, s. 13(1).

155. *Ibid.*, s. 13(2). A post-dated "cheque" is not in fact a cheque at all. Section 73 defines a cheque as "a bill of exchange drawn on a banker *payable on demand*", and if an instrument is post-dated it is clearly *not* payable on demand. For further discussion see *infra* under the heading "Post dating" in Chapter 12.

156. The Banking and Financial Dealings Act 1971, s. 3(2), replacing s. 14(1) of the 1882 Act, except for bills drawn before the new Act came into force, which was on 16 January 1972.

157. Bills of Exchange Act 1882, s. 14(1) and (2), as amended by the Banking and Financial Dealings Act 1971. For banking purposes a "day" ends at the close of banking hours—a decision cannot be held in suspense until the following morning: *Momm v. Barclays Bank International Ltd* [1976] 3 All ER 588. Note also, the meaning of "due date" and "punctual" payment—if banks are closed it should be the last working day *BEFORE* due date: see *Mardof Peach v. Attica Sea Carriers Corp* [1976] 2 All ER 249.

158. Section 92 of the 1882 Act as amended by the Banking and Financial Dealings Act 1971 (which is substituted for the 1871 Act referred to in para. (*b*). By the schedule to the new Act the following are bank holidays:

     Easter Monday
     the last Monday in August
     26 December if not a Sunday
     27 December in a year in which the 25th or 26th is a Sunday.

New Year's Day is a bank holiday from 1974: proclamation under s. 3 of the 1971 Act, see *London Gazette* 26 October 1973. It will be noticed that Good Friday is not included—though it is in Scotland, which has slightly different bank holidays to England. Good Friday is, however, a "non-business" day under s. 92 (*a*) of the 1882 Act.

Where a bill is payable at a fixed period "after sight", time runs from the date of the acceptance for payment. If the bill is dishonoured for non-acceptance, time will run from the date of noting or protesting.[159] If anything is required to be done by reference to a "month" it is a calendar month.[160]

(f) "a sum certain in money"[161]

The sum payable is "certain in money" even if it is payable with interest or by *stated* instalments. The sum is also certain if it is to be payable by stated instalments with a proviso that upon default in the payment of any one instalment the whole shall become due.[162]

The instalment must, however, be stated. For example: a bill payable "by two equal instalments due January 1st and July 1st" is valid. Contrast: a bill payable "by instalments" and nothing more is invalid.[163] As is a bill drawn payable "by ten weekly instalments, payable on . . . All instalments to cease on the death of X".[164]

If interest is payable on a bill, unless it otherwise provides, interest runs from the date of the bill, and if the bill is undated from the date of issue.[165] A bill is perfectly valid provided the rate is indicated or is to be ascertained as directed by the bill.[166]

Although no section of the 1882 Act requires the sum payable to be *both* in words and in figures, and a bill in one or the other is perfectly valid, if both are used and the figures do not correspond, the drawee can, if he wishes, pay out on the sum denoted in the words.[167]

(g) " . . . to or to the order of . . . "

A bill is payable "to order" which is expressed to be so payable, and the words will be implied where a bill is expressed to be payable to a particular person, unless the bill contains words prohibiting transfer, or indicating that it should not be transferable.[168]

---

159. Bills of Exchange Act 1882, s. 14(3) where a bill payable *after* sight is accepted for honour, its maturity is calculated from the date of noting for non-acceptance, and *not* from the date of acceptance for honour; s. 65(5).

160. *Ibid.*, s. 14(4).

161. On or after 15 February 1971 a bill is invalid if the amount is stated wholly or partially in shillings and pence: Decimal Currency Act 1969, s. 2(1).

162. Bills of Exchange Act 1882, s. 9(1).

163. *Moffatt* v. *Edwards* (1841) 174 ER 388.

164. *Worley* v. *Harrison* (1835) 111 ER 568.

165. Bills of Exchange Act 1882, s. 9(3).

166. *Ibid.*, s. 9(1)(d).

167. Bills of Exchange Act 1882, s. 9(2). However, a banker is entitled to return the instrument marking it "words and figures differ" since he has a right to demand from his customers that their cheques be drawn in clear and unambiguous terms.

168. Bills of Exchange Act 1882, s. 8(4).

The effect of the words "or order" is to indicate that not only is the payee entitled to the money under the bill, but that he can order payment to be made to anyone he chooses. If there are specific words used giving a contrary intention they will override the words "or order" even if those words (i.e., "or order") appear on the bill. For example, bills would not be payable "to order" if made out "Pay John Smith only" or "Pay John Smith. Not transferable" or if the words "not transferable" appear anywhere on the bill.

A bill as originally drawn to be payable "to bearer" must have the word "bearer" on the bill. It is commonly thought that if a bill has the words "or order" crossed out and initialled, it therefore becomes payable to bearer—it does not. The words "or order" being implied they will be deemed present even if they are struck out, unless the words "the bearer" are substituted.

Where a bill is expressed to be payable to the order of a specified person, and not to him or his order, either originally or by indorsement, it is nevertheless payable to him or his order at his option.[169] For example: "Pay to the order of John Smith" means literally, do not pay John Smith but pay to his order. However, such drawings are payable to the person (that is, John Smith) or to his order in the normal way.

(h) "A specified person or to bearer"

The person to whom a bill is made out is called the "Payee". A bill can be made out: (i) to someone or his order; or (ii) to someone or bearer; or (iii) to bearer.

The effect of (ii) or (iii) is to require payment to be made to whomsoever is in *possession of the bill*[170]: such bills are called "bearer" bills and the person in whose possession they are is called "the bearer".

A bill can be drawn payable to or to the order of the drawer;[171] or to, or to the order of, the drawee, for example if a cheque is made out to the bank upon which it is drawn.[172]

A bill can be made payable to two or more payees jointly, or in the alternative, or to one or some of several payees. Also a bill can be made payable to the holder of an office for the time being, for example, "The Post Master" or "The Vicar of St. Michael's Church".[173]

---

169. *Ibid.*, s. 8(5).
170. *Ibid.*, s. 2.
171. It may not be immediately clear why a drawer should wish to draw a bill in favour of himself. The reason is the way a transaction is sometimes structured (see for example *infra* under the heading "Structuring the transaction—Part I" in Chap. 4). In the case of a cheque, the drawer may make it out to himself if he draws cash from his bank.
172. Bills of Exchange Act 1882, s. 5(1).
173. Bills of Exchange Act 1882, s. 7(2).

However, whoever is named he must be indicated with reasonable certainty, otherwise the bill will be deemed payable "to bearer".[174]

The fictitious or non-existing payee

It sometimes happens that a bill is, on the face of it, not payable to bearer but will be deemed so. Section 7(3) of the 1882 Act provides that where the payee is "fictitious" or "non-existing" the bill may be treated by the holder[175] as payable to bearer.[176]

If a bill is deemed payable "to bearer" even a thief will be able to pass a good title, and as no indorsement is necessary to transfer the bill, any forged indorsement will be superfluous, and a good title to the bill will still pass. It follows that the unfortunate drawer of the bill will, therefore, be liable to the ultimate holder.

It is not always easy to say when a payee is to be deemed "fictitious" or "non-existing". It is not, in fact, totally clear whether the two expressions are synonymous or not. One might well be forgiven for thinking that if a person were deemed to be "fictitious", he would perforce be "non-existing". The courts have, however, found for the view that the two expressions are capable of different meanings, although it is not entirely clear from the cases the precise meanings which can be ascribed to each. Much depends upon the facts in each case. With some hesitation, it can be said the following rules appear to emerge from the cases.

1. If the whole transaction is a sham, the payee is "fictitious" even if the named person is known to the drawer or acceptor

BANK OF ENGLAND v. VAGLIANO[177]

V carried on the business as a merchant. One of his employees drew bills on V in favour of "C Petridi & Co" (with whom V dealt in business) and signed the bills in the name of another business associate "Vucina". V accepted the bills and the employee obtained payment from the bank across the counter. The fraud was discovered and V sued the bank for return of the money. The bank claimed the bills were made out to a fictitious or non-existing payee within s. 7(3) of the 1882 Act, and this made the bills payable to bearer—which is what they had done. *Held*—that the whole transaction was a fiction from beginning to end, the named payee "C Petridi & Co" was, therefore, deemed

---

174. *Ibid.*, s. 7(1).
175. The subsection does not say who may treat the bill as payable to bearer, but from the authorities which have considered the wording over the years it is clear it is the holder of the bill who has the right.
176. See also Bills of Exchange Act 1882, s. 5(2) which deals with a "fictitious" drawee. In s. 5(2) no mention is made of a "non-existing" drawee. See also s. 46(2)(*b*) and *infra* under the heading "Presentment for payment excused" in Chap. 3.
177. [1891] AC 107.

fictitious and the bills were, therefore, payable to bearer. The bank, having paid the bearer, got a good discharge.[178]

2. If the drawer intends the payee to take under the bill (even though he is induced by fraud to form that intention) the payee is not fictitious

In such a case the bill is not, therefore, deemed payable "to bearer" and the ultimate holder gets no title. For example:

NORTH & SOUTH WALES BANK v. MACBETH[179]

M was induced by the fraud of Y to draw a bill in favour of K. M intended K should take under the bill. Y forged the indorsement and paid the bill into his own bank, which received payment. On discovery of the fraud M sued Y's bank. *Held*—that as M intended K to take he was not a fictitious payee and the bill was not, therefore, payable to "bearer" and as the bank had paid the wrong person M could recover.

3. If the drawer is unaware of the existence of the payee, the payee can be deemed "fictitious" or "non-existing"

CLUTTON v. ATTENBOROUGH[180]

X a clerk of Y induced Y to sign a bill made payable to a person called "Brett" by saying that money was owing to him. In fact there was no such money owing, and Y (the drawer) had never heard of anyone called "Brett" (although he no doubt knew that there was a possibility of persons of that name somewhere). Thus, although Y intended to make payment to "Brett" he did not know of his actual existence. *Held*—that the bill was payable "to bearer" as the payee was non-existent to the knowledge of the drawer.

It is not clear from the speeches delivered in the House of Lords in *Clutton's* case whether "non-existing" is to be given a different meaning from "fictitious". Lord Halsbury thought Brett "non-existing"[181] while Lord Shand thought him "fictitious".[182] Warrington J, in *Vinden v. Hughes*[183] thought the expressions capable of different meanings, when he said of *Clutton's* case, " . . . the House of Lords were dealing there, not with the word 'fictitious' with which I have to deal, but with a different word—'non-existent'." While Lord Halsbury in the *Vagliano* case[184] came to the conclusion, " . . . that, however expressed, the real meaning of the sub-section is to imply the unreality of any

---

178. Lords Bramwell and Field dissented. They took the view that the payees were *not* fictitious. Speaking of the employee's wrongful acts Lord Bramwell said (p. 168): " . . . I cannot see how that can render actual existing persons fictitious within the meaning of the statute."
179. [1908] AC 137; see also *Vinden v. Hughes* [1905] 1 KB 795.
180. [1897] AC 90.
181. *Ibid.*, at p. 93.
182. *Ibid.*, at p. 95.
183. [1905] 1 KB 795, 801.
184. [1891] AC 107, at p. 122.

person who is named upon the face of the instrument as the payee of the bill".[185]

Impersonal payee

The definition in s. 3(1) of the 1882 Act says that a bill is a document payable, *inter alia*, to " . . . a specified *person* . . . ".

It follows that documents drawn "Pay cash or order" or "Pay wages or order" or such similar terms, which often appear, particularly on cheques, make the documents not bills of exchange at all, as the payee is impersonal. These documents cannot be transferred from one person to another,[186] and can never be indorsed. They are, in fact, valueless, except in so far as the drawee bank can treat the document as a mandate from its customer to pay the cash to whomsoever is in possession of the documents.[187]

Examples of bills of exchange

A "short" form of a bill may appear as follows:

£10,000.   London 1st January 1997

One hundred and eighty days after sight pay Anglo-Transylvanian Trading Co. Ltd. or Order the sum of Ten thousand pounds Sterling for value received

                                                              Sidney Trading Syndicate

To Basil Industries Ltd.
    Bootle
    Lancs.

Rarely will a bill be this simple. More often bills are drawn with various clauses mentioned on the face of the bill itself. For example:

£10,000   London 1st January 1997

---

185. His Honour Judge Chalmers (the draftsman of the 1882 Act) preferred Lord Herschell's judgment: see (1891) 7 LQR 216. "During the controversy the draftsman of the sub-section must have felt much like the Professor of Divinity who was asked by a student to explain some passage he had written in a theological tractate. "My young friend," said the Professor, "when I wrote that passage only God and I knew what it meant, and now only God knows." (at p. 218). Lord Herschell said, " . . . that in order to establish the right to treat a bill as payable to bearer it is enough to prove that the payee is in fact a fictitious person . . . " [1891] AC 107, at p. 147. Mr John R Adams (1891) 7 LQR 295, thought the basis of the decision was that Vagliano had accepted a bill and could not, therefore, disclaim it.
186. *Cole* v. *Milsome* [1951] 1 All ER 311.
187. *N & S Insurance Corp* v. *National Provincial Bank* [1936] 1 KB 328 and *Orbit Mining and Trading Co Ltd* v. *Westminster Bank Ltd* [1963] 1 QB 794.

One hundred and eighty days after sight of this our First of Exchange (Second and Third of the same date and tenor unpaid) pay Anglo-Transylvanian Trading Co. Ltd. or Order the sum of Ten thousand pounds Sterling, payable at the collecting bank's selling rate for sight drafts on London, with interest at nine per cent. per annum added thereto from date hereof to due date of arrival of remittance in London, value received.

Sydney Trading Syndicate

To Basil Industries Ltd.
    Bootle
    Lancs.

B. Defects in form

An inchoate bill is a bill lacking in some material particular.

Everything depends upon what part of the bill is not complete as to whether its validity as a bill is affected. A bill is not invalid by reason only that it is not dated, or that it does not specify the value given for it, or that any value has been given, or that it does not specify the place where it was drawn or the place where it is payable.[188]

Where a signature on a blank piece of paper *is delivered* by the drawer *in order that it may be converted into a bill* it operates, *prima facie*, as an authority to complete it for any amount.[189]

Similarly, when a bill is wanting in a material particular, a holder has, *prima facie*, authority to fill up the omission in any way he thinks fit.[190]

If an inchoate instrument, after completion, is to be enforceable against any person who became a party *before* its completion, it must be filled up within a reasonable time of delivery[191] and strictly in accordance with the authority given.

However, even if this is not done, and the bill *after completion* comes into the hands of a holder in due course, it will be valid and effective for all purposes.[192]

---

188. Bills of Exchange Act 1882, s. 3(4).
189. Before the Finance Act 1970 all bills had to bear stamp duty, usually at *ad valorem* rates. If the blank piece of paper was stamped, the holder could—in the circumstances indicated in the text—complete the bill for any amount the stamp would cover. Schedule 8, Part V of the 1970 Act has removed from s. 20(1) of the 1882 Act the word "stamped" from the first line of the sub-section and the words "the stamp will cover" from lower in the subsection. The effect of this is that the delivery of a blank piece of paper under s. 20 is authority to complete it for *any* amount.
190. Bills of Exchange Act 1882, s. 20(1). See *Haseldine* v. *Winstanley* [1936] 1 All ER 137; *cf. Baxendale* v. *Bennett* (1878) 3 QBD 525.
191. *Griffith* v. *Dalton* [1940] 2 KB 264.
192. Bills of Exchange Act 1882, s. 20(2).

If there are defects of form created by a mistake in the way the bill is drawn, for example by virtue of it being drawn by someone not being accustomed to such business matters, the courts have power to rectify the instrument.[193]

The courts will not, of course, rewrite a bill because one of the parties has thought better of the transaction, and wishes to get out of his obligations.

C. *Inland and foreign bills*

A bill can be either an inland bill or a foreign bill. A bill is deemed always to be an inland bill: that is, that on the face of it, it purports to be drawn and payable within the British Isles[194] or drawn within the British Isles on someone resident here. Any other bill is a foreign bill.

VI. DELIVERY

Every contract on a bill, whether it is the drawer's, the acceptor's, or an indorser's is incomplete and revocable until delivery takes place in order to give effect to the transaction.[195]

"Delivery" means the transfer of possession, actual or constructive, from one person to another.[196]

"Actual" delivery needs no explanation, it is the handing over of the bill.

"Constructive" delivery is where there has been no physical dealing with the bill, but some overt action, in respect of it. For example, there would be constructive delivery in the sending of a bill through the post, in which case the delivery is complete as soon as the bill is posted.[197] Again, if X said to Y, "The bill is made out in your favour and I have it in my safe. You can collect it whenever you like," this would be constructive delivery of the bill.

Where a bill is no longer in the possession of a party who has signed it either as a drawer, acceptor or indorser, a valid and unconditional delivery by him is presumed until the contrary is proved.[198] Moreover, in the case of an acceptance by the drawee, once it is written on the bill, and the drawee gives notice that he has accepted it to the person entitled, the acceptance is then complete.[199]

---

193. *Druiff v. Parker* (1868) 18 LT 46.
194. Bills of Exchange Act 1882, s. 4. "The British Isles" means any part of the UK and Ireland, the Isles of Man, Guernsey, Jersey, Alderney and Sark and the islands adjacent to any of them.
195. Bills of Exchange Act 1882, s. 21(1).
196. *Ibid.*, s. 2. "Issue" means the first delivery of a bill or note, complete in form to a person who takes it as a holder. "Acceptance" means acceptance completed by delivery. "Indorsement" means indorsement completed by delivery.
197. *Kleinwort v. Comptoir D'Escompte* [1894] 2 QB 157.
198. Bills of Exchange Act 1882, s. 21(3).
199. *Ibid.*, s. 21(1).

In order for the delivery to be effectual, it must be made either by the party drawing, accepting or indorsing himself or by his authority.[200] For example,

BROMAGE v. LLOYD[201]

B owed C £100. He drew a promissory note, but died before he was able to meet with C, and the note was found among his papers. C attempted to sue. *Held*—that there had been no delivery, and C could not recover on the note.

ARNOLD v. CHEQUE BANK[202]

C was the holder of a bill which he specially indorsed to D, and put it in an envelope to be posted. One of C's clerks took the bill, forged D's indorsement, and attempted to negotiate. The bill finally came into the hands of X who sued on it. *Held*—that there had been no delivery, and the bill was still the property of C.

BAXENDALE v. BENNETT[203]

X put a blank acceptance of his own in his desk. Y stole it and filled up the paper into a complete bill. Eventually, it came into the hands of P. P sued X on the bill, *Held*—that there had been no delivery *for the purpose of converting the document into a bill*, and, therefore, P could not recover from X.

Problems of a valid delivery sometimes arise where the postal service is used as a means of effecting delivery. The general rule is that once a bill is posted, delivery is effected;[204] however, if it cannot be shown that there was agreement between the parties—express or implied—to use the postal services, then the bill will, even after posting, be at the sender's risk and no delivery will be presumed; and, in fact, the sender will be liable to issue another bill if it is lost in the post.[205]

Once, however, a bill comes into the hands of a holder in due course, valid delivery by all parties prior to him so as to make them liable to him is conclusively presumed.[206]

Conditional delivery

Delivery may be subject to a condition or for a special purpose only, and not for the purpose of transferring the bill at all. If this is the case, the property in the bill will not pass. However, if a bill delivered in this way subsequently

---

200. *Ibid.*, s. 21(2)(*a*).
201. (1847) 1 Ex 32.
202. (1876) 45 LJCL 562.
203. (1878) 3 QBD 525. Cf. *Ingham* v. *Primrose* (1859) 28 LJCP 294: " . . . sound in principle if wrong on the facts" *per* Collins MR, *Nash* v. *De Freville* [1900] 2 QB 72, 89.
204. *Kleinwort* v. *Comptoir D'Escompte* [1894] 2 QB 157.
205. See *Pennington* v. *Crossley* (1897) 13 TLR 513.
206. Bills of Exchange Act 1882, s. 21(2).

comes into the hands of a holder in due course, proper delivery will be conclusively presumed.[207]

Moreover, once a bill is delivered, oral evidence is inadmissible to defeat the delivery. So it is not possible, once having delivered the bill, subsequently to say it was conditional or that there were terms attached to it.[208]

207. *Ibid.*, s. 21(2)(*b*). It not infrequently happens that one firm of solicitors draws a cheque in favour of another firm, and sends it to that other, but asks that the cheque be held to the order of the drawer, until some term or condition of the transaction in which they are instructed is complied with. In such a case, this amounts to conditional delivery; however, once the condition is satisfied the firm holding the cheque are capable of being holders-in-due-course, and may sue for the cheque's dishonour: *Clifford Chance* v. *Silver* (CA), *Financial Times*, 31 July 1992.

208. *Hitchings* v. *North Leather Co* [1914] 3 KB 907. A bill of exchange, and the debt created by it, are perfectly valid even though (as used to be the case) Treasury permission for the payment had not been obtained. Moreover, the need for Treasury consent simply moved from the bill to the judgment debt, once judgment had been signed: *Contract and Trading Co (Southern) Ltd* v. *Barbey* [1960] AC 244.

CHAPTER 3

PRESENTMENT

As we have already seen, a bill which is not payable on demand must be presented to the drawee twice: once for acceptance and then for payment.

The following rules are laid down by the 1882 Act for presentment both for acceptance and payment. In fact, it has long been the practice for bills of exchange to be handled for presentation, both for acceptance and payment, by the banking system. Consequently, on the presentation for acceptance the acceptor (that is, the customer of the paying bank) will sign his name, and add words such as "Payable at the Blank Bank, Market Branch, Manchester" which shows his bank he desires them to make payment and debit his (the acceptor's) account. This method does *not*, of course, render *the bank* liable as an acceptor. When the due date for payment arrives the acceptor's bank will receive the bill from the holder's bank, and payment will be effected in the usual way.

In executing this function the banks are merely agents of their customers and must, of course, comply with the rules laid down by the 1882 Act. These rules are as follows.

I. ACCEPTANCE

Acceptance of a bill is the signification by the drawee of his assent to the order of the drawer,[1] and " . . . the only persons who can accept a bill are the drawees"[2] because "An acceptance is an engagement to pay the amount for which the bill is drawn in money, and can only be given by the person against whom the bill is drawn".[3] Without agreeing in this way to pay a bill, a drawee is under no obligation to pay it. Although this may, of course, leave the drawee open to a claim by the drawer if, say, he is holding funds belonging to the drawer.

A holder of a bill *must* present it for acceptance when a bill:

1. Bills of Exchange Act 1882, s. 17(1).
2. Except in the case of acceptance for *honour* under the Bills of Exchange Act 1882, s. 65(1).
3. *Per* Lopes LJ, *Re Barnard* (1886) 32 Ch D 447, at p. 453.

(i) *Is payable "after sight"* in order to fix its maturity. When a bill payable after sight is negotiated the holder must either present it for acceptance or negotiate it within a reasonable time. He cannot "hang on" to the bill indefinitely.[4] If the holder does not present, the drawer and all indorsers will be discharged,[5] as it is unreasonable that their liability should be retained indefinitely.

In determining what is a reasonable time in this context regard must had[6]: (a) to the nature of the bill; (b) any usage of trade applicable; (c) the facts of the particular case.

(ii) *Expressly so stipulates.*

(iii) *Is drawn payable elsewhere than at the residence or place of business of the drawee.*[7]

In no other case is presentment for acceptance necessary in order to render liable any party to a bill.[8]

However, although a holder is compelled to present for acceptance in the above cases only, he *should* present in all cases where a bill is payable otherwise than on demand, as the drawee will then become liable to pay the bill, which he is not necessarily bound to do.

When a bill has been accepted generally presentment for payment is not necessary to render the acceptor liable.[9]

Time for acceptance

A bill may be accepted: (a) before it has been signed by the drawer or is otherwise incomplete;[10] or (b) when it is overdue; or (c) after it has been dishonoured.[11]

Requisites of an acceptance

(1) Presentment must be made by or on behalf of the holder to the drawee or some person authorized to accept or refuse acceptance on his behalf.[12] Thus, presentment to a servant who happened to open the door would not suffice.

---

4. Bills of Exchange Act 1882, s. 40(1).
5. *Ibid.*, s. 40(2).
6. *Ibid.*, s. 40(3).
7. *Ibid.*, s. 39(1) and (2).
8. *Ibid.*, s. 39(3).
9. *Ibid.*, s. 52(1).
10. *Ibid.*, s. 18(1).
11. *Ibid.*, s. 18(2). Where a bill payable after sight is dishonoured by non-acceptance, and it is then subsequently accepted by the drawee the holder is entitled to have the bill accepted as at the date of first presentment to the drawee, unless some other date is agreed: s. 18(3).
12. Bills of Exchange Act 1882, s. 45(3).

(2) It must be made at a reasonable hour on a business day.[13]

(3) The acceptance must be written on the bill.

(4) The acceptance must be signed by the drawee. His signature alone, without any further words will suffice. However, it must not express that the drawee will perform his promise by any other means than the payment of money.[14]

Usually the drawee will add the word "accepted" and the date: the date is, of course, most important to a bill payable so many days "after sight".

Where a bill is addressed to two or more drawees who are not partners, presentment must be made to each, unless one has authority to accept on behalf of them all.[15] If the drawee dies before a bill is presented for acceptance the holder can still present for acceptance to the personal representatives of the deceased.[16] Likewise, where the drawee becomes bankrupt presentment can be made to the trustee in bankruptcy.[17]

Presentment through the post is quite valid when the parties have agreed to this or the practice is recognized by usage.[18]

Acceptance is not complete, however, until the bill has been returned to the person who presented it.[19] However, where an acceptance is written on a bill, and notice is given by the drawee to the person entitled that the bill is accepted, the acceptance becomes absolute and irrevocable, even though there is no actual delivery.[20]

After acceptance, the terminology changes. The drawee becomes "the acceptor" and the bill "an acceptance". If a bill is to be paid at the acceptor's bank the acceptance is called a "domicil".

Division of acceptances

An acceptance can be either (a) general or (b) qualified.[21]

A *general* acceptance assents unequivocally to the order of the drawer.

A *qualified* acceptance, in express terms, varies the effect of the bill as drawn.

Qualified acceptances can be:

13. As to "business day" see Bills of Exchange Act 1882, s. 92. "Reasonable hour" means business hours: s. 41(1)(a). See *Bains* v. *National Provincial Bank* (1927) 137 LT 631, where it was held quite proper for a bank to pay a cheque five minutes after the usual and advertised banking hours. As to payment of cheques see now Deregulation (Bills of Exchange) Order 1996.
14. Bills of Exchange Act 1882, s. 17(2).
15. Bills of Exchange Act 1882, s. 41(1)(b).
16. *Ibid.*, s. 41(1)(c).
17. *Ibid.*, s. 41(1)(d).
18. *Ibid.*, s. 41(1)(e).
19. See s. 21(1).
20. *Ibid.*
21. See s. 19(1).

(1) Conditional: a conditional acceptance makes payment by the acceptor dependent on the fulfilment of a condition. For example "Accepted—payable when in funds".

(2) Partial: a partial acceptance means that part only of the amount for which the bill is drawn will be paid.

(3) Local: that is on acceptance the acceptor undertakes to pay only at a specified place. For example: "Payable only at the Blank Bank".

However, an acceptance to pay at a particular place is *general* unless it expressly states it is to be paid there *only* and nowhere else. For example, an acceptance "Payable at the Blank Bank" is a general acceptance.

(4) Qualified as to time: for example, if a bill is drawn to be payable two months after date and is accepted "Payable four months after date".

(5) Acceptance by some of several drawees: this occurs where, for example, a bill is drawn on X, Y and Z and only X accepts.[22]

Of course, a holder of a bill may refuse to take a qualified acceptance, and he can treat the bill as dishonoured if he does not receive an acceptance which is unqualified.[23] Moreover, if a holder does take a qualified acceptance without the express or implied authority of the drawer or any indorsers, and they do not subsequently ratify the qualified taking, whoever has not assented will be discharged from his liability on the bill.[24] However, if they receive notice of the qualified acceptance, and do not within a reasonable time dissent, they will be deemed to have assented to the taking of the qualified acceptance.[25]

Presentment for acceptance excused

We have seen[26] that in some cases presentment for acceptance is obligatory. However, even in these cases, presentment for acceptance need not be made if[27]:

(1) The drawee is dead,[28] bankrupt, fictitious or has no capacity.

(2) Despite reasonable efforts presentment cannot be effected.

(3) Where presentment was made irregularly, for example, not in business hours, but the drawee refused acceptance on other grounds.

22. See Bills of Exchange Act 1882, s. 19(2)(a) to (e).
23. *Ibid.*, s. 44(1).
24. *Ibid.*, s. 44(2). This does not apply to a partial acceptance if due notice has been given.
25. *Ibid.*, s. 44(3).
26. *Ibid.*, s. 39.
27. *Ibid.*, s. 41(2).
28. If the drawee is dead, presentment can be made to his personal representatives: s. 41(1)(c). Usually this will be done; however, a holder can treat the bill as dishonoured if, for example, the drawee has no personal representatives.

In these cases the holder may treat the bill as dishonoured and act accordingly. The holder must, of course, still present for acceptance even though he believes that on presentment the bill will be dishonoured.[29]

II. PAYMENT

There are two reasons for presentment for payment. First, and the most obvious, is to obtain payment; and secondly, if this is refused, to retain the liability of prior parties.

All bills, whether payable on demand or otherwise, must be presented for payment at the proper time and in the proper manner, and if they are not, the drawer and indorsers are discharged.[30]

Time for presentment

(1) A bill payable at a future time must be presented on the day it falls due for payment.[31] Except:

   (a) If the bill as drawn is payable other than at the drawee's place of business or his residence and if the holder has not had time to present for acceptance before presenting for payment on the day it falls due, the delay caused by presenting the bill for acceptance before presenting for payment is excused, and does not discharge the drawer or the indorsers. Provided the holder exercised reasonable diligence in trying to present for acceptance.[32]

   (b) If the acceptance is qualified which requires presentment for payment, omission to present for payment on the day of maturity will not discharge the acceptor in the absence of a stipulation to that effect.[33]

(2) A bill payable on demand (which includes cheques) must be presented within a reasonable time of issue or indorsement to retain the liability of prior parties. In determining what is a reasonable time regard must be had[34] (a) to the nature of the bill; (b) any usage of trade applicable; (c) the facts of the particular case.

Manner of presentment

Presentment for payment must be made in accordance with the following rules:

29. Bills of Exchange Act 1882, s. 41(3).
30. *Ibid.*, s. 45.
31. *Ibid.*, s. 45(1).
32. *Ibid.*, s. 39(4).
33. *Ibid.*, s. 52(2).
34. *Ibid.*, s. 45(2).

(1) Presentment must be made by or on behalf of the holder, to the person designated by the bill as payer or to some person authorized to pay (or refuse payment) on his behalf.

(2) The holder presenting for payment must produce the bill to the acceptor (or whomsoever is to pay it) and when the bill is paid he must immediately deliver up the bill to the acceptor or whoever paid it.[35]

(3) Presentment must be made at a "reasonable hour" on a "business day" at the "proper place".[36] A "proper place" within the Act[37] is as follows:

  (a) *the place specified in the bill*. So, for example, if a bill is accepted payable at the acceptor's bank, presentment to him personally will not suffice;[38] if not

  (b) *the address of the drawee or acceptor as stated in the bill*, and it is good presentment even if the premises are shut up[39] or the acceptor has left[40] or has died;[41] if not

  (c) *the drawee or acceptor's place of business or ordinary residence if known*; if not

  (d) *Wherever the drawee or acceptor can be found*; if not

  (e) *the last known place of business or residence of the drawee or acceptor.*

Where a bill is presented at the "proper place" and no person can be found to pay the bill no further presentment is necessary, and the bill can be treated as dishonoured.[42]

As in the case of presentment for acceptance so in the case of presentment for payment, where a bill is drawn upon or accepted by two or more persons who are not partners, presentment must be made to each one, unless a place of payment is specified in the bill, in which case presentment must be made there.[43]

If the drawee or acceptor dies before the bill is paid, then if there is no place specified in the bill where it is to be payable presentment must be made to the deceased's personal representatives if he has any.[44] Presentment through the

---

35. *Ibid.*, s. 52(4), but this does not now apply to presenting *cheques* for payment: see Deregulation (Bills of Exchange) Order 1996, s. 4(1).

36. As to "reasonable hour" see s. 41(1)(a); "business day" see s. 92; "proper place" see s. 45(4). A bank cashing a cheque five minutes after the usual and advertised banking hours is quite proper: *Bains v. National Provincial Bank* (1927) 137 LT 631.

37. Bills of Exchange Act 1882, s. 45(4).

38. *Gibb v. Mather* (1832) 149 ER 110.

39. *Hine v. Alleby* (1833) 110 ER 591.

40. *Buckstone v. Jones* (1840) 9 LJCP East. 257.

41. *Philpott v. Bryant* (1827) 6 Digest 224, 1566.

42. Bills of Exchange Act 1882, ss. 45(5) and 47(1)(a).

43. *Ibid.*, s. 45(6).

44. *Ibid.*, s. 45(7).

post is quite valid if the parties have agreed to this method, or the practice is recognized by usage.[45] If presentment cannot be effected within these rules, all is not lost, as it may well be that presentment can be excused.

Presentment for payment excused [46]

Presentment for payment is dispensed with and the bill can be treated as dishonoured in the following circumstances[47]:

    (i) where presentment cannot be effected. For example:

CORNELIUS v. BANQUE FRANCO-SERBE[48]

X, a Jugoslav firm, owed money to Y, who carried on business in England. A cheque was sent to Y drawn on a bank in Amsterdam. By reason of the German occupation of Holland it was impossible to present the cheque for payment. Y informed X of this fact and asked that the London branch of X's bank should meet the payment. This X refused to do and Y sued X on the cheque claiming that presentment was unnecessary. *Held* that by virtue of s. 46(2)(*a*) of the 1882 Act presentment was excused and Y could recover.

However, it is not sufficient that the holder believes the bill will be dishonoured, he must still present it.[49]

    (ii) where the drawee is fictitious.[50]

   (iii) where the drawer of the bill has been accommodated by the drawee or acceptor, and he believes the bill will not be paid if presented.

   (iv) where a bill was accepted or made for a person who has become an indorser on the bill, and he believes the bill will not be paid if presented.

If the drawer of a bill has been accommodated the acceptor or drawee is under no obligation to the drawer to pay the bill. Thus, as presentment for payment is not necessary to retain the liability of the drawer, it follows that if the bill is not presented the drawer will still be liable on it. However, since previous indorsers would then be discharged, it also follows presentment should be made to retain their liability.

    (v) where there has been an express or implied waiver of the necessity for presentment. For example, if payment has been made before the due date of payment by some other means.

---

45. *Ibid.*, s. 45(8).
46. *Ibid.*, s. 46(1).
47. *Ibid.*, s. 46(2).
48. [1941] 2 All ER 728.
49. Bills of Exchange Act 1882, s. 46(2)(*a*).
50. See discussion *supra* under heading "The fictitious or non-existing payee" in Chap. 2.

III. LOST BILLS

When a bill is needed for presentment, whether for acceptance or payment, or for any other purpose for that matter, and it has been misplaced, the person who was the holder of it before it was lost, can ask the drawer to issue another bill of the same tenor, which the drawer *must* do, provided the bill was not overdue before it was lost and that he receives a suitable indemnity in case the original is found.[51]

A sufficient indemnity would be a letter saying in effect that the person who was the holder would pay to the drawer, or other party to whom the indemnity was given, the amount of the bill, if the original was subsequently presented for payment.

The one-time holder of the lost bill has no right to have the duplicate bill indorsed by the prior parties to the original. However, the loss of the bill does not affect the rights of the one-time holder to sue a prior party to the original, provided he gives an indemnity to any of the other parties to the bill.[52]

51. Bills of Exchange Act 1882, s. 69. If the drawer refuses to give another bill he can be compelled by the court to do so.
52. *Ibid.*, s. 70.

CHAPTER 4

NEGOTIATION AND TRANSFER

PART I—FORMALITIES

A bill of exchange must have at least three parties.

The Drawer: he is the person who makes out (draws) and signs the bill. By drawing a bill the drawer engages that when it is presented it will be accepted and paid according to its tenor. If it is not paid (that is, if it is dishonoured) the drawer must make good the loss.[1]

The Drawee: is the person who is required to pay the bill.[2] As a bill of itself does not operate as an assignment of funds in the hands of a drawee, a drawee who does not accept a bill is not liable *on the bill* itself[3] although he may well be liable to the drawer for breach of contract.

The Payee: is the person whose name appears on the face of the bill. He is the person who must present the bill for acceptance and payment.

If matters stopped there (as often they do, particularly with cheques), there would be few problems. The payee would get his money and that would be an end of the matter.

However, frequently the payee does not seek payment himself, but passes the bill on to someone to whom *he* is indebted; and in fact, the bill may be passed on several times before payment from the drawee is finally requested. We must now consider the rules governing the passing of a bill in this way.

Negotiability

Some hundreds of years ago bills of exchange could not be passed on from one person to another. To assist merchants with their trade, special rules came to be recognized allowing bills to be passed on providing *due notice was given* to all parties. For example:

If A bought goods from B and gave a three-month bill in payment; and B, not wanting to wait for his money, negotiated it to C for cash. In days of yore, one can imagine the surprise C's arrival on A's doorstep would create, A never having seen C before, nor

---

1. Bills of Exchange Act 1882, s. 55(1)(*a*).
2. In the case of a cheque the "paying" or "drawee" bank.
3. Bills of Exchange Act 1882, s. 53(1).

been given any prior explanation of how he (C) came to be in a position to demand payment! It seemed only reasonable that if B wanted to negotiate the bill of exchange he should tell A what was going on.

Communications were not what they are today, and the giving of notice was often a heavy burden to pay for being able to use a bill in this way. Complications also arose where a bill was passed on by someone who had no right to it, or if there was some prior claim between two parties through whose hands the bill had passed. These third party rights were called "equities" and a bill was passed on "subject to equities" which meant that the person in whose hands a bill came could never be absolutely sure whether someone else might suddenly appear making a claim to the bill. The general rule being that a man cannot transfer a better title than he possesses himself which is enshrined in the maxim: *nemo dat quod non habet.*

To avoid these difficulties, the merchants began to develop bills which could be passed on free from these "equities" which became part of the "Law merchant".[4]

These documents came to be called "negotiable instruments", and were deemed the equivalent of cash, and over the years the courts have been very quick to guard against any infringement which might detract from the doctrine of negotiability.[5] So much so, that all bills are negotiable (that is, passing free of all prior claims) unless they are expressly restricted.[6]

It will be apparent from this that the word "negotiate" has a specialized meaning in that it is used to indicate a passing on of a bill free of any "equities" which in fact exist in respect of it.[7] The word "transfer" means to pass a bill subject to any "equities" which may exist.

As we have seen all bills of exchange are freely negotiable unless they are restricted in some way, and where a bill is negotiable it continues to be negotiable until it has been either: (a) restrictively indorsed; or (b) discharged.[8]

A negotiable bill may, of course, be payable either "to order" or to "bearer"[9] and the method of passing on each type must be considered.

---

4. Which is expressly preserved by the 1882 Act, except in so far as it is inconsistent with any express provision of the Act: Bills of Exchange Act 1882, s. 97(2). See also *per* Willes J, *Whistler* v. *Forster* (1863) 32 LJCP 163.

5. "We have repeatedly said in this court that a bill of exchange or promissory note is to be treated as cash", *per* Lord Denning MR in *Fielding & Platt Ltd* v. *Najjar* [1969] 1 WLR 357, 361B.

6. For example, by being marked "not negotiable". See Bills of Exchange Act 1882, s. 36(1).

7. The words "transfer" and "negotiate" are frequently mixed up—even in Acts of Parliament. See Bills of Exchange Act 1882, 31(1): "A bill is *negotiated* when it is *transferred*" (author's italics). We also speak sometimes of "assigning" or "conveying" a bill.

8. Bills of Exchange Act 1882, s. 36(1).

9. *Ibid.*, s. 8(2).

Method of passing on a bill

The payee (or any subsequent person) who wishes to pass on his bill to another can do so in one of two ways.

If the bill is payable to him "or bearer" there is no problem, he simply hands it over; if, as is usual, the bill is made out to him "or order" he must add his name to the bill (as an indorsement) before passing it on. Both methods must now be considered.

1. Bearer bill

A bill is payable "to bearer" which is expressed to be so payable, or on which the only or last indorsement is an indorsement in blank.[10]

A bearer bill need not be indorsed[11] for the purpose of its negotiation[12] and the transferee will get a perfectly good title, even if it turned out the bill had been stolen. The person passing the bill (either payee or subsequent holder) becomes a *"transferor by delivery"*[13] and as he has not put his name to it he is not liable *on the bill*,[14] and will be liable only to the person to whom *he* passed the bill.[15] It not infrequently happens, of course, that the transferee will insist upon indorsement before he will take the bill so that the transferor will become *liable on the bill*.[16] If this does happen, the transferor is then *not* a "transferor by delivery" and all the liabilities of an "indorser" will attach to him.[17]

A bill may, of course, become a bearer bill even if it was originally drawn to the payee "or order" by his indorsing it in blank.

2. Order bill

A bill payable "to order" to be negotiated must be indorsed as well as delivered to the transferee.[18] The transferor (whether the payee or some other person) then becomes an "indorser"[19] and as such engages that the bill will be accepted and paid according to its tenor, and if it is not (that is, if it is dishonoured) he will pay the holder or any subsequent indorser who is out of pocket.[20]

10. *Ibid.*, s. 8(3).
11. The word is sometimes spelled "endorsed"; "indorsed" is used throughout the 1882 Act.
12. Bills of Exchange Act 1882, s. 31(2).
13. *Ibid.*, s. 58(1).
14. *Ibid.*, s. 58(2).
15. That is, his immediate transferee: *ibid.*, s. 58(3).
16. *Fairclough* v. *Pavia* (1854) 9 Ex 690.
17. Bills of Exchange Act 1882, s. 56. In which case the transferor is not liable under s. 58(3) but under s. 55(2) which means he is liable to subsequent indorsers! In *Grunzweig und Hartmann Montage GmbH* v. *Rohim Mottaghi Irvani* [1988] 2 Lloyd's Rep 14, a signature was written by a guarantor *"bon pour aval pour les tires"*, which created a liability *on the bill*. Affirmed on appeal *G & H Montage GmbH* v. *Irvani* [1990] 2 All E.R. 225.
18. Bills of Exchange Act 1882, s. 31(3).
19. If a payee indorses the bill by "special indorsement" (that is, by naming the person to whom it then becomes payable) that person is an "indorsee"—not a new payee.
20. Bills of Exchange Act 1882, s. 55(2).

If a bill is drawn: "Pay John Smith or Order" it is payable to John Smith alone until he indorses it, which he can do by signing his name on the bill.

He can indorse it "specially" by writing in the name of the person he wishes to benefit:

"Pay George Brown or Order John Smith"

The bill is then payable to George Brown only, until he indorses it. Alternatively, John Smith could indorse the bill "in blank", that is signing it without specifying the indorsee in which case the bill will then become payable to bearer. Any subsequent person into whose hands the bill comes can, of course, convert the bill back again to an order bill by indorsing it specially to someone else.

It is quite possible, therefore, for a payee to indorse an order bill (and hence assume the obligations of an indorser) but if it is indorsed in blank, the transferee can then pass on the bill by mere delivery, thus being a transferor by delivery only.

Types of indorsement

Indorsements can be either[21]: (i) special; or (ii) in blank.

(i) A special indorsement specifies the person to whom or to whose order the bill is to be payable.[22] For example: "Pay John Smith or Order".

The rules relating to a payee of a bill, with the necessary modifications, apply to an indorsee under a special indorsement.[23]

(ii) An indorsement in blank specifies no indorsee[24] and usually consists of only the signature of the indorser.[25]

If a bill has been indorsed in blank, any holder can convert the blank indorsement into a special indorsement by writing above *his*[26] indorser's signature, a direction to pay to or to the order of himself or some other person.[27]

---

21. *Ibid.*, s. 32(6).
22. *Ibid.*, s. 34(2).
23. *Ibid.*, s. 34(3).
24. *Ibid.*, s. 34(1).
25. *Ibid.*, s. 32(1).
26. Section 34(4) says " . . . *the* indorser's signature . . . " (author's italics). To convert an indorsement in this way can only be to the signature of the indorser immediately prior.
27. Bills of Exchange Act 1882, s. 34(4).

Requirements of indorsements

The requirements of an indorsement are as follows:

(i) An indorsement in the form of the signature of the indorser, without any additional words, is sufficient.[28]

(ii) The indorsement must be written on the bill itself. Usually it will be written on the back, but an indorsement on the front is perfectly valid.[29]

If the back becomes filled with indorsements, a slip of paper called an "*allonge*" can be fixed adhesively to the bill for further transactions. In such a case the first indorser to use the *allonge* should make his indorsement partly on the bill itself and partly on the *allonge*: otherwise it would be possible to take the *allonge* and fix it to another bill. In some countries, when a bill is filled with indorsements a "copy" bill is used and the original and the copy are transferred together. Whichever method is used, indorsements not actually made on the bill itself are deemed to be so made.[30]

(iii) An indorsement must be of the whole bill. An indorsement which purports to transfer part only of the amount of the bill, or which attempts to split up the bill between two or more indorsers, does not operate as a negotiation of the bill.[31]

(iv) If a bill is payable to the order of two or more persons who are not partners, both or all must indorse, unless one has authority to indorse on behalf of the others.[32]

(v) All indorsements are deemed to have been made in the order in which they appear on the bill, unless the contrary is proved.[33]

Irregular indorsements

It not infrequently happens that the payee's name or the indorsee's name on an order bill is misspelt or otherwise wrongly designated. For the purpose of transferring the bill, it does not matter whether the indorsement is made as wrongly designated or in the correct name.[34] For example, if a bill is drawn "Pay J. Smith or Order" but the man's real name is "T. Smyth" he can quite

---

28. *Ibid.*, s. 32(1).
29. *Ex parte Yates* (1858) 2 De G & J 191.
30. Bills of Exchange Act 1882, s. 32(1).
31. *Ibid.*, s. 32(2). While negotiation of part is of no effect, the courts do recognize a "set off" if the indorsee marks a bill that he has received the balance of it. If a bill for £10,000 is negotiated from X to Y "Pay Y £3,000", if Y then marks the bill that he has received £7,000 (perhaps in cash), this is perfectly valid and it means the bill is then worth only £3,000.
32. Bills of Exchange Act 1882, s. 32(3). Dividend warrants made payable to the order of two or more persons, are payable on the indorsement of any one signature: s. 97(3)(d).
33. *Ibid.*, s. 32(5).
34. *Ibid.*, s. 32(4).

properly transfer it by indorsing it "J. Smith" or "T. Smyth" or "J. Smith" following this with his proper signature if he wishes.[35]

There is, however, a major problem facing the holder of a bill where there is a misdescription such as this, for if he does not get the indorser to sign exactly as the name appears on the bill, the document cannot then be "regular on the face of it" for the purpose of making the holder a holder in due course.[36] It is essential, therefore, to get an indorser to indorse a bill exactly as it appears on the bill.[37]

Restrictive indorsements

An indorsement may contain terms making it restrictive.[38] A restrictive indorsement is one which:

> (a) prohibits further negotiation of the bill;[39] or
> (b) prohibits further transfer of the bill;[40] or
> (c) gives directions as to how the bill is thereafter to be dealt with.[41]

(a) As we have seen, the essence of negotiability of a bill is that it can be passed from one person to another *free from equities*. However, if a bill is marked "not negotiable" the rights of the true owner will still subsist. So that if someone steals the bill and passes it on to someone, the true owner (the person from whom it was stolen) can get back the value of the bill even from an innocent holder who took in good faith.

(b) Where a bill contains words prohibiting transfer (or indicating an intention that it should not be transferred) it is valid between the immediate parties only and is not negotiable.[42]

For example, a bill is drawn in favour of X and he indorses it to Y; then Y marks it "not transferable": the bill can go no further than the person to whom Y transfers it.

Take another example:

HIBERNIAN BANK v. GYSIN[43]

The Irish Casing Co drew a three-month bill in its own favour: "to the order of the Irish Casing Co Ltd Only". The bill was crossed and marked "not negotiable". G accepted

35. *Ibid.*, s. 32(4).
36. *Bird & Co v. Thomas Cook Ltd* [1937] 2 All ER 227.
37. There are at least two cases which cause trouble. Cheques drawn "pay Mrs John Brown or Order". The best way is for her to indorse "Elizabeth Brown, the wife of John Brown". Secondly, a cheque to "Smith & Co" when the proprietor's name is Thomas Robson, he should be asked to indorse "Smith & Co" as this keeps the bill "regular" and also Mr Robson will be liable personally under s. 23(1) of the Bills of Exchange Act 1882.
38. Bills of Exchange Act 1882, s. 32(6).
39. *Ibid.*, s. 35(1).
40. *Ibid.*, s 8(1).
41. *Ibid.*, s. 35(1).
42. *Ibid.*, s. 8(1).
43. [1939] 1 KB 483.

the bill. The Irish Casing Co then indorsed the bill to H for value. The bill was dishonoured for non-payment. H then sued G. *Held*—that at the time of acceptance the bill was marked "not negotiable" and because the word "only" appeared it was not transferable and was limited as to its effect to the drawer and drawee only. H could not, therefore, sue as a holder for value.

(c) An indorsement which expresses that it is a mere authority to deal with the bill as directed (and not as a transfer of the ownership of the bill)[44] can take a number of forms.

For example, if the bill is indorsed

"Pay D only".
"Pay D for the account of X".
"Pay D or Order for collection".

If a bill is marked with a restrictive indorsement but it does not prevent further transfer of the bill, all subsequent indorsers will take the bill with the same rights and subject to the same liabilities as the first indorsee after the restrictive indorsement.[45] That is, the right to receive payment of the bill and to claim against anyone *his* indorser could have sued, but it gives him no right to pass on the bill unless the restrictive indorsement allows it.[46]

While a bill may be indorsed restrictively, it cannot be indorsed *conditionally*, and any attempt to impose conditions can be disregarded by the payer, and any payment to an indorsee is valid whether the condition is fulfilled or not.[47]

Moreover, the title of a person who negotiates a bill is defective if he obtained it, or the acceptance of it, by fraud, duress, or force and fear, or other unlawful means or for an illegal consideration, or when he negotiates it in breach of faith or under such circumstances as amount to fraud.[48]

Negotiation to a party already liable

It does not happen very often that a bill finds its way back into the hands of a party already liable on it, but where a bill is negotiated back to the drawer or to anyone already liable on it, such as the acceptor or an indorser, he can re-issue it by negotiation, but he cannot then enforce payment against any intervening party to whom *he* was previously liable.[49] For example:

A issues a bill to B who negotiates it to C then C negotiates it to D and D negotiates it back to A.

---

44. Bills of Exchange Act 1882, s. 35(1).
45. *Ibid.*, s. 35(3).
46. *Ibid.*, s. 35(2).
47. *Ibid.*, s. 33. Note that an instrument expressed to be payable on a contingency is not a bill at all, and the happening of the event does not cure the defect: s. 11(2).
48. *Ibid.*, s. 29(2).
49. *Ibid.*, s. 37.

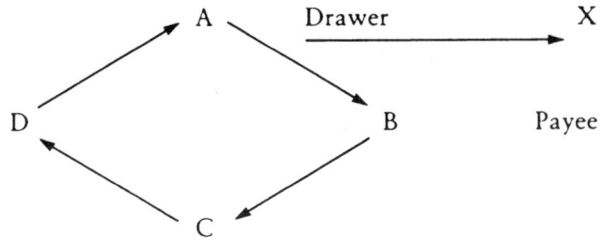

When A gets the bill negotiated back there is nothing to stop him re-issuing it to X; however, A cannot then claim payment from B, C or D.

Negotiation of overdue or dishonoured bills

Where a bill which is "overdue", or not overdue but dishonoured, is passed from one person to another, it can only be transferred[50] subject to any defect of title affecting it, and no one who takes it can acquire a better title than his transferor had.[51]

The onus of proof that a bill is overdue is on the person trying to avoid liability on it, and if an indorsement bears no date (and it often will not) it is *prima facie* deemed to have been made *before* the bill was overdue.[52]

A bill is deemed to be "overdue" after the last day of payment has passed, or if the bill is payable on demand, when it appears on the face of it to have been in circulation for an unreasonable time which is a question of fact in each case.[53]

Transmission by act of law

This occurs where, for some reason, the holder of a bill is dead or under some incapacity.

1. Death

If a man dies with a bill in his possession, the title passes to his personal representatives.[54] If the deceased left a will appointing executors they can act

---

50. Section 36(2) of the Bills of Exchange Act 1882 says: "Where an overdue bill is negotiated, it can only be *negotiated* subject to any defect of title . . . ": presumably the draftsman meant "*transferred*" (author's italics).

51. Bills of Exchange Act 1882, s. 36(2) and (5).

52. *Ibid.*, s. 36(4).

53. *Ibid.*, s. 36(3). Most banks will refuse to pay a cheque which is "stale" (usually six months old) even if not technically overdue.

54. *Re Robson* [1891] 2 Ch 559.

immediately; whereas, if he died intestate his administrators take their authority from the grant of Letters of Administration.[55]

If the personal representative indorses a bill in his own name, however, he should specify clearly the capacity in which he signs. For example, "J Jones Exor. of A Smith Decd."

When a personal representative indorses in this way he negatives his personal liability by indicating, not only that he is signing in a representative capacity, but also for *whom* he signs.[56]

If there are two or more personal representatives any one probably may sign for the estate. The point has never been decided finally, but is consistent with the rule that, so far as personalty is concerned, any *one* personal representative may sign on behalf of the estate. Of course, so far as the bank which handles the estate account is concerned, it will honour cheques and other instructions strictly in accordance with the mandate lodged with it. So that *vis-à-vis* the bank, the personal representatives can decide that all or any one or any two shall have power to sign on behalf of the estate. A testator can, if he wishes, (although rarely does) provide in the will as to whether or not some or all his executors shall have power to sign on behalf of the estate.

If the deceased had indorsed a bill but had not delivered it and it is found with his papers, it must be indorsed by the personal representatives before it can be delivered.[57]

It sometimes happens that a person with not long to live wishes to make a gift of money. Unfortunately, cheques uncashed at the time of death, drawn by the donor, do not constitute a transfer of funds at the bank, and cannot amount to a valid *donatio mortis causa* (a gift in contemplation of death).

RE BEAUMONT[58]

B was very ill, and in expectation of death she drew a cheque for £300 in favour of E. B had no funds at the bank but the bank would probably have loaned the money. E took the cheque to the bank. There was, in any event, some problem concerning the verification of B's signature, and B died before the cheque was paid. E sued B's personal representatives claiming the gift of the cheque was a valid gift. *Held*—that E was not entitled. " . . . there could not be an equitable assignment of funds at the bank, for the deceased had no funds there . . . and if the cheque had come back with the signature confirmed, and the manager had in the meantime changed his mind, he need not have paid. No right had been acquired by the payee[59] but an expectation only."[60]

55. *Chetty v. Chetty* [1916] 1 AC 603, at p. 609; for a more modern example see *Biles v. Caesar* [1957] 1 WLR 156.

56. Bills of Exchange Act 1882, s. 31(5). See also *supra* p.19 under the heading "Authority" in Chap. 2.

57. See *Bishop v. Curtis* (1852) 21 LJQB 391.

58. [1902] 1 Ch 889, and see *Re Leaper* [1916] 1 Ch 579, at p. 582.

59. The text says "drawee". This must be a slip for "payee". There is an *Errata* at the front of the volume but this is not included. There is no doubt Mrs Ewbank (E) was the payee.

60. *Per* Buckley J, p. 896.

Very similar circumstances arose in the case of *Re Swinburne*,[61] where it was held by the Court of Appeal that the payee could not recover. As we saw above, there is nothing to prevent the giving of bills of exchange (including cheques) *drawn by a third party in favour of the donor* (the deceased), even if he had not indorsed them.[62]

2. Insolvency

Upon adjudication all the bankrupt's property vests in his trustee in bankruptcy. Consequently, all bills of exchange in the possession of the bankrupt at the moment of adjudication which were his *beneficially*, will pass automatically without any form of transfer or indorsement.[63]

Subsequently, the trustee may indorse and negotiate these bills in the usual way, once more, taking care to negative his liability by making clear the capacity in which he signs.

In the case of companies, where an Administrator or Receiver is appointed he has power to take possession of the property of the company, and to deal with it in accordance with the powers contained in Schedule 1 to the Insolvency Act 1986. In particular[63a] to draw, accept, make and indorse any bill of exchange or promissory note in the name and on behalf of the company.

3. Order of the court

The court has no power to order the transmission of a bill of exchange.

However, under s. 12 of the Judgments Act 1838, the sheriff can seize any cheques, bills of exchange, promissory notes, bonds, specialities or other securities for money, and is empowered to hold them for the amount of the claim under the writ of *fieri facias*. If needs be, the sheriff can sue for the recovery of the money due under the cheques, bills of exchange, etc, which he has seized. Payment to the sheriff, by the person liable on these documents, is a good discharge, to the extent of such payment, from liability on these instruments.

If the seizure is by a County Court bailiff the position is slightly different. Under the provisions of s. 91 of the County Courts Act 1984, the Registrar of the County Court is empowered to hold any bills of exchange (or similar documents) as security for the amount directed to be levied by the execution. The person who is owed the money (that is the plaintiff in the County Court

---

61. [1926] Ch 38.
62. *Veal* v. *Veal* (1859) 27 Beav. 303; *Re Mead* (1880) 15 Ch D 651; *Clement* v. *Cheesman* (1884) 27 Ch D 631. A gift, in similar circumstances, of a bank deposit note is quite valid: *Re Dillon* (1890) 44 Ch D 76; as is a gift of banknotes even if retained for safe keeping by the deceased: *Re Hawkins* [1924] 2 Ch 47; as are savings certificates: *Darlow* v. *Sparks* [1938] 2 All ER 235; but not a bank deposit book: *Delgoffe* v. *Fader* [1939] 3 All ER 682.
63. Insolvency Act, s. 306(2).
63a. *Ibid.*, Schedule 1, para 10.

action) can then sue in the name of the holder (that is, the defendant in the action) for recovery of the money due under the cheques or bills. In neither case can the bills be negotiated.

PART II – LIABILITY ON NEGOTIATION

Holder in due course

A holder in due course is a creature of the 1882 Act[64] to whom all manner of protection is afforded in the cause of furthering negotiability. Providing the holder meets the terms of the definition he will get a good title to a bill, even if there have been irregularities in the prior transactions before he took. The Act[65] extends the protection by providing that every holder is deemed to be a "holder in due course" until the contrary is proved.[66]

None of this, of course, can make a party liable on a bill if he is not. For example, if the drawer's signature has been forged, the drawer will not be liable even to a person who might otherwise qualify as a holder in due course. However, as we shall see, if the bill has been accepted, the *acceptor* will be liable to a person qualifying as a "holder in due course" under the provisions of the Act.[67] Again, if it transpires that, say, one of the indorsements was made by an infant, if the bill comes into the hands of someone who satisfies the definition of "a holder in due course", that holder cannot claim from the infant, but he *can* claim from any *indorser* who signed before or after the infant.[68]

The requirements

Section 29(1) of the Bills of Exchange Act 1882 provides:

A holder in due course is a holder who has taken a bill complete and regular on the face of it, under the following conditions namely,
> (a) That he became a holder of it before it was overdue, and without notice that it had been dishonoured, if such was the fact;
> (b) That he took the bill in good faith and for value, and that at the time the bill was negotiated to him he had no notice of any defeat in the title of the person who negotiated it.

To be a holder in due course, therefore, the following requirements must be fulfilled. The person claiming must:

---

64. Under the previous law such a holder was expressed to be a "holder in good faith and without notice".
65. Bills of Exchange Act 1882, s. 30(2).
66. *Ibid.*, s. 30(2).
67. *Ibid.*, s. 54(2)(a).
68. *Ibid.*, ss. 55(2)(b) and 22(2).

(i) Be a "holder"

A holder is defined by s. 2 of the 1882 Act as "the payee or indorsee of a bill or note who is in possession of it or the bearer thereof". For reasons explained in para. (vii) below, a "payee" cannot be a holder in due course, so it follows that to be a holder in due course the holder must either be an "indorsee" or a "bearer".

There is no difficulty about being a "bearer". This is "the person in possession of a bill or note which is payable to bearer" (again s. 2). However, before there can be an "indorsee" there must be an indorsement; consequently, there cannot be a "holder" of a bill which requires indorsement, but which in fact is transferred by delivery only without indorsement.[69]

(ii) Take a bill "complete and regular on the face of it"

A person who takes an inchoate instrument, even if he has authority to complete it, cannot be a holder in due course. The "face" of a bill includes the back of it.[70] "Regularity" is a different thing from "validity". An indorsement can appear quite regular, but be invalid, for example, by being forged; yet an indorsement can be perfectly valid though most irregular, for example, a payee may be described by the wrong name, nevertheless an indorsement by that payee in his true name is valid to pass the bill,[71] but it would not be "regular" unless the payee added the misnomer by which he was described.[72]

"Regularity" is also different from "liability". For example, if the payee who is wrongly described indorses the bill in his own true name, the bill (as we have seen) is not "regular", but he is liable to any subsequent holder and cannot set up the irregularity as a defence.[73] When then is a bill not "regular"? The answer to this question is whenever it gives rise to doubt in the minds of bankers.[74] In other words, it depends upon the facts of each case.[75] In the following cases bills have been held not "regular":

---

69. See *Westminster Bank Ltd v. Zang* [1966] AC 182. "As the appellants had received the cheque from Mr Tilley without indorsement by him, they did not become holders of the cheque within the meaning of s. 2 of the Bills of Exchange Act 1882", *per* Lord Dilhorne, at p. 216F. *Midland Bank Ltd v. R V Harris Ltd* [1963] 2 All ER 685, would appear to be wrongly decided, though at no stage in the *Zang* case (at first instance, CA or HL) was this case disapproved. Indeed, it was only referred to at first instance ([1964] 3 All ER 683, 686B) where counsel for the defendant (Zang) thought it "entirely correct" but tried to distinguish it.

70. *Per* Denning LJ (as he then was) in *Arab Bank v. Ross* [1952] 2 QB 216, 226.

71. Bills of Exchange Act 1882, s. 32(4).

72. *Bird & Co v. Thomas Cook Ltd* [1937] 2 All ER 227. An indorsement in Arabic letters (or any other foreign lettering one assumes) would not be regular: *per* Denning LJ (as he then was) in the *Arab Bank* Case, *infra*, at p. 228.

73. *Per* Denning LJ, *ibid.*, p. 227.

74. *Ibid.*, p. 227: " . . . we shall not go far wrong if we follow the custom of bankers of the City of London on this point."

75. *Slingsby v. District Bank Ltd* [1932] 1 KB 544.

(a) if the indorsement is not made exactly to correspond with the name of the payee.

ARAB BANK LTD v. ROSS[76]

In pursuance of an agreement between R, and X and Y Co (a firm) for the purchase of shares, R drew a bill payable on demand to "X and Y and Co or Order": being the name of the firm of which X and Y were partners. X subsequently indorsed the bill to the plaintiff bank by signing "X and Y" the abbreviated word "Co" being omitted. "X" had the full authority of the firm to do this, and it was the recognized signature of the partnership. When the plaintiff bank presented the bill it was dishonoured as R said X and Y had got the bill by fraud. The bank claimed to be "holders in due course" and brought an action against R, the drawer. *Held*—that although the indorsement was valid to pass the title of the bill to the bank, the omission of the word "Co" gave rise to doubt whether the payees and indorsers were the same people, and therefore, the bill was not "regular" on the face. However, the bank was a "holder for value" and as the fraud was not proved the bill was payable to it.

Compare:

BIRD & CO v. THOMAS COOK LTD[77]

C & Son Ltd carried on a travel business and C & Son (Bankers) Ltd a separate banking business. A, a servant of B, had cheques payable to B and indorsed with B's signature. He then wrote on the cheques "Pay to the order of C & Son Ltd" and gave them to the banking branch in return for foreign currency. The cheques were then stamped by both branches of the firm. B then sued both branches for conversion. It was contended that C & Son (Bankers) Ltd were liable as they had given value for the cheques when C & Son Ltd, in whose favour they had been made, had not indorsed them. *Held*—that when B's employee wrote "Pay C & Son Ltd" he intended the "Bankers" to obtain payment, and although he misdescribed that company, the cheques were in law indorsed to that company.

(b) if it is marked "not negotiable" or "not transferable".

The whole purpose of the Act creating a holder in due course was to meet more easily the requirements of negotiability. If these rights are expressly negatived it is clearly the intention that the bill should pass, if at all, subject to whatever defects exist, and this is obviously contrary to there being a holder in due course.

It must now be remembered that under the Cheques Act 1992 a crossed cheque marked "account payee" means it is "not transferable".

(iii) Take the bill before it is "overdue"

For example, if a bill is payable on 1 June, on the 2nd the bill is overdue and if it is taken after this date the holder will obviously know that it is overdue

76. [1952] 2 QB 216.
77. [1937] 2 All ER 227.

and that rights against prior parties have been lost. If the bill is payable on demand (for example, a cheque) it is overdue if it has been in circulation for an unreasonable time. What is an "unreasonable" length of time is a question of fact.[78]

(iv) Take the bill "without notice that it had been dishonoured"

Notice means *actual* notice, not constructive notice. Obviously, if a holder has notice that at the time he takes a bill it has been dishonoured for non-acceptance (not non-payment of course) he will know that something is very wrong.

(v) Take the bill in "good faith"

A thing is deemed to be done "in good faith" within the meaning of the 1882 Act, where it is in fact done honestly whether it is done negligently or not.[79]

(vi) Take the bill "for value"

"Value" means valuable consideration[80] and the consideration must have been given by the holder. It is not enough that it was given by some prior party.

If anyone obtained a bill by fraud or some illegality and then passed it on, the burden of proof will be on the holder to show that he gave value for the bill. In other words, once fraud or illegality in the prior dealings with the bill is proved, the presumption that the holder is a "holder in due course" no longer applies.[81]

(vii) Have the bill "negotiated" to him

It follows that a payee cannot be a holder in due course, for a bill is "issued" to a payee[82] and the section requires the bill to be "negotiated" to a holder in due course. "It is true that under the definition clause in the Act (s. 2) the word "holder" includes the payee of a bill unless the context otherwise requires; but it appears from s. 29(1) that a holder in due course is a person to whom a bill has been negotiated and from s. 31 that a bill is negotiated by being transferred from one person to another and (if payable to order) by indorsement and delivery. In view of these definitions it is difficult to see how the original payee . . . can be a holder in due course within the meaning of the Act. Section 21(2), which distinguishes immediate from remote parties and includes a

78. Bills of Exchange Act 1882, s. 36(3).
79. *Ibid.*, s. 90.
80. *Ibid.*, s. 2.
81. *Ibid.*, s. 30(2).
82. *Ibid.*, s. 2. "'Issue' means the first delivery of a bill . . . "

holder in due course among the latter, points to the same conclusion".[83] This was decided in

R E JONES v. WARING & GILLOW[84]

B, posing as W's representative, induced J to pay to W a cheque for £5,000 stating fraudulently that J would receive valuable distribution rights in a new motor car, the cheque being the deposit for the supposed purchase of the car from W. B was already indebted to J for £5,000 but the true facts were not known either to J or to W. The fraud was finally discovered and J sued W for the return of the money. W claimed they were holders in due course of the cheque. *Held*—that as payees they could not be holders in due course, and they had to refund the money to J.

(viii) Show he had "no notice of any defect" in title

Once again the notice must be *actual* notice not constructive, and the defect is "in the title of the person who negotiated" the bill to the holder. In particular, the title of the transferor is "defective" in this context if *he* obtained the bill, or its acceptance, by fraud, duress, force or fear, or other unlawful means, or for an illegal consideration. Alternatively, if he negotiates the bill to the holder in breach of faith or under such circumstances as amount to fraud.[85] Obviously, if a holder knew that anything of this sort had been going on it would not be right that he should be able to benefit from the bill.[86]

If *all* these conditions are fulfilled the holder will be deemed a holder in due course and the following advantages will accrue:

(1) He holds the bill free from any defect of title of prior parties, as well as free from any personal defences the prior parties may have among themselves.[87]

(2) He can enforce payment against all parties liable on the bill. The parties must, however, be *liable*. The liability of the parties is considered below.

(3) If the title of the bill is in fact defective, he can nevertheless give the person who pays him a valid discharge; or if he negotiates the bill his transferee will get a good title.[88]

---

83. *Per* Lord Cave, *R E Jones* v. *Waring & Gillow* [1926] AC 670, 680.
84. [1926] AC 670.
85. Bills of Exchange Act 1882, s. 29(2).
86. Common illegal intention of the earlier parties to a bill will not, of course, affect a holder in due course: *Bank für Gemeinwirtschaft* v. *City of London* [1971] 1 All ER 541. See also definition of what can amount to constructive notice: *per* Denning J (as he then was) in *Nelson* v. *Larholt* [1947] 2 All ER 751, 752H. Also see *Agip (Africa) Ltd* v. *Jackson* [1991] 4 All ER 451, 467C for what can amount to "knowledge" of irregularities by a bank.
87. Bills of Exchange Act 1882, s. 38(2). *Any* holder of a bill has the right to sue in his own name: s. 38(1).
88. *Ibid.*, s. 38(3).

(4) If the bill has been dishonoured it will not affect him.[89] Moreover, if the dishonour is for non-acceptance, and proper notice is not given, it will not affect him if he takes after the omission.[90]

(5) It will not affect his rights, provided he takes without notice, if a previous holder has renounced the liabilities of any party.[91]

(6) In his hands it is presumed that an inchoate bill has been completed within a reasonable time and strictly in accordance with the authority given.[92]

(7) In his hands valid delivery of a bill by all parties is presumed.[93]

(8) In his hands, if a wrong date has been inserted in a bill it will nevertheless operate as the true date.[94]

(9) If a bill is materially altered, he can enforce payment for the amount as originally drawn, provided the alteration is not apparent.[95]

(10) Anyone who signs a bill otherwise than as a drawer or acceptor incurs the liabilities of an indorser to a holder in due course.[96]

(11) He is entitled to payment of each part which is accepted where a bill is drawn in a set.[97]

Holder for value

A "holder for value" is the holder of a bill on which value has at any time been given.[98] It does not matter that *he* did not give value so long as someone did.[99] It may be, for instance, that he can satisfy most, but not all, of the requirements to be a "holder in due course".

A holder for value takes a bill with whatever defects of title it may have, even though he himself has given valuable consideration and is innocent of any defect.

However, if the holder for value claims through a holder in due course, then even if there has been some fraud or illegality, so long as it was before the holder in due course took, the holder for value will have all the rights of a holder in due course.[100]

---

89. *Ibid.*, s. 36(5).
90. *Ibid.*, s. 48(1).
91. *Ibid.*, s. 62(2).
92. *Ibid.*, s. 20(2).
93. *Ibid.*, s. 21(2).
94. *Ibid.*, s. 12.
95. *Ibid.*, s. 64(1).
96. *Ibid.*, s. 56. See *Grunzweig und Hartmann Montage GmbH* v. *Rohim Mottaghi Irvani* [1988] 2 Lloyd's Rep 14. Affirmed on appeal *G & H Montage GmbH* v. *Irvani* [1990] 2 All ER 225.
97. Bills of Exchange Act 1882, s. 71(4) and (5).
98. *Ibid.*, s. 27(2). Reference should again be made to the topic of consideration for a bill, *supra* p. 21.
99. If the holder has a lien on a bill he is deemed to be a holder for value to the extent of the sum for which he has the lien: Bills of Exchange Act 1882, s. 27(3).
100. *Ibid.*, s. 29(3).

Holder without value

A holder "without value" (as we may call him) is one who takes a bill gratuitously as a gift without any consideration having been given for it; either by him or anyone prior to him. For example, if someone is given a cheque for £10 as a birthday present, he cannot sue on it. However, if he cashes it with a friend, the friend will have given value and *he* can recover from the drawer.

Liabilities of parties

If a bill of exchange is dishonoured a holder will presumably try to claim from one or more of the other parties to the bill. These are as follows:

(i) The drawer

The drawer is the person who draws the bill in the first place and starts off the whole series of transactions. By drawing the bill he undertakes that it will be paid, and if it is not, that he will compensate the holder or any indorser who has to pay it.[101]

In any claim made by a holder in due course, the drawer cannot set up as a defence the non-existence of the payee or that the payee had no capacity to indorse the bill.[102] This is only fair: surely the drawer must have known to whom he made out the bill, and if there was some irregularity about the payee it is not proper that the drawer should be able to use it to avoid his obligations on the bill.

In any event, if the drawer wishes, and his payee does not object, he can always negative his liability on the bill by writing on it "*sans recour*" or some such stipulation[103] or limit the bill's transferability by marking it "not transferable".

(ii) The acceptor

By accepting a bill the drawee undertakes to pay it according to the tenor of his acceptance.[104]

The obligations of an acceptor are onerous, and rightly so, as it is he who, by his conscious act, gives a bill its real value. Consequently, once an acceptance reaches the hands of a holder in due course, if it is then dishonoured, the acceptor will be liable and since he is presumed to know the drawer, his signature and all about him, he cannot be heard to say the drawer does not exist, or his (the drawer's) signature is forged, or that the drawer had no

---

101. *Ibid.*, s. 55(1)(*a*).
102. *Ibid.*, s. 55(1)(*b*).
103. *Ibid.*, s. 16.
104. *Ibid.*, s. 54(1).

capacity or authority to draw the bill in the first place, or to indorse the bill (if it is drawn to his own order). These are all matters which the acceptor could, if he wished, verify before accepting and, if he did not, it will be too late to try to set these matters up as a defence to a claim later.[105]

However, once the bill is accepted and is then returned either to the drawer (if it is drawn to his own order), or to the payee or other transferee, the acceptor will not see it again before it is due for payment and so the acceptor will not then know whether any subsequent indorsements (even the drawer's in the case of the bill to his own order) are genuine and valid, and so no obligation is implied. However, he cannot be heard to say the drawer had no capacity to indorse (if the bill was to the drawer's order) or that the payee (who would of course be named in the bill at the time of acceptance) does not exist or the payee had no capacity to indorse the bill;[106] both these facts could have been checked prior to the bill being accepted.

Heavy though the burden of the acceptor is, he owes no duty to anyone to accept the bill in such a way as to render impossible subsequent fraudulent "raising" of the bill, and if a bill has been tampered with in this way, the acceptor is liable to a subsequent holder in due course only for the amount of the bill as accepted, and not for the increased amount. For example, in

SCHOLFIELD v. LONDESBOROUGH[107]

X drew a three months' bill for £500 which was accepted by L. The bill was passed back to X who fraudulently raised the bill to £3,500. There was adequate space on the bill for this purpose. X then indorsed the bill to S. In due course, S presented the bill to L for payment. L refused to pay the higher figure and S sued, claiming that he took in good faith. *Held*—that L owed no duty of care in the manner of accepting a bill, and was not guilty of negligence by accepting the bill with spaces on it which facilitated fraud. Therefore L was not liable other than for the tenor of his original acceptance, namely £500.

(iii) The indorsers

By endorsing a bill an indorser undertakes that when it is presented it will be paid, and if it is not, that he will compensate the holder or any other indorser who signed the bill after the indorser who has to pay it.[108]

When one indorses a bill and passes it on, one will have received payment for the bill and have been paid out. Consequently, a heavy burden is exacted which should not be undertaken lightly!

105. *Ibid.*, s. 54(2)(*a*).
106. *Ibid.*, s. 54(2)(*b*) and (*c*).
107. [1896] AC 514. In reading the report one is faced in Lord Halsbury's speech, at p. 524 *et seq*, with the terrifying sight of over six pages of Latin (Seacciae, *Tract. de Commer*) and French (Pothier, *Du Contrat de Change*) which assisted the learned LC in his judgment! See also s. 54(1) of the Bills of Exchange Act 1882.
108. Bills of Exchange Act 1882, s. 55(2)(*a*).

An indorser is *always* liable to the person to whom he gave the bill, no matter what forgeries or irregularities have gone before.[109]

An even greater obligation is imposed if the person claiming is a holder in due course. In this case, the indorser is deemed to guarantee the genuineness, and regularity of the drawer's signature and *all* prior indorsements,[110] and is consequently liable even if there have been prior forgeries or whatever manner of irregularities.

Moreover, that the bill is valid and subsisting and he has a good title to it.[111]

All this is a very heavy burden, but, as in the case of a drawer, so with an indorser, if he wishes, and if his transferee will accept, he can negative his liability on the bill by writing "*sans recour*" or any other appropriate wording,[112] or by limiting the bill's further transferability.

There is, of course, no liability even to a holder in due course if the person being claimed against did not indorse it: for example, if he was a mere transferor by delivery, but even he is responsible to his immediate transferee.[113]

(iv) Accommodation party

Something must be said here of the liability of a party who, *quite gratuitously and for the purpose of lending his name to some other person*, signs a bill as drawer, acceptor or indorser. He is called "an accommodation party".[114]

There is, of course, no consideration for the accommodation party signing and he is, therefore, not liable to the person who asked for help (the relationship being one of principal and surety)[115] but he will be liable to a holder for value, whether that holder, at the time he took, knew or did not know of the accommodation.[116]

The purpose of accommodation is usually to give assistance to someone who is not himself totally credit worthy. For example: if A is being pressed for money and he arranges with B that he (A) will draw a bill on B which B will accept, A can then (on the strength of B's acceptance) raise money on the bill.

Note, however, that not every bill signed by an accommodation party is an accommodation *bill*, although often they are referred to as such. Strictly, an accommodation *bill* is one where the accommodation party is the *acceptor*.

---

109. *Ibid.*, s. 55(2)(*c*), and that person (i.e. the indorsee) need not be a holder in due course.
110. *Ibid.*, s. 55(2)(*b*).
111. *Ibid.*, s. 55(2)(*c*).
112. *Ibid.*, s. 16.
113. *Ibid.*, s. 58(2) and (3).
114. *Ibid.*, s. 28(1).
115. It is the duty of the party accommodated to provide funds to meet the bill at its maturity or otherwise to indemnify the accommodation party.
116. Bills of Exchange Act 1882, s. 28(2).

The reason is that an accommodation *bill* is only discharged when it is finally paid by the party accommodated;[117] if it is paid by any other party to the bill—usually the acceptor—they will have a claim against the person accommodated and hence the bill will still be alive.

The party accommodated is the one who is in need of the money, and it is ultimately his liability to provide the funds to pay the bill when it matures, by giving the money to the accommodation party if needs be. It follows that the party accommodated (who will usually be the drawer or an indorser) cannot normally defeat a claim because of default in notice of dishonour[118]—he would know there would be no funds: nor irregularities in presentment for payment[119]—as he would also know the bill would not have been paid even if it *had* been properly presented.[120]

An accommodation party must not be confused with a "referee in case of need"[121] who is another creature of the 1882 Act who may come to the aid of the impecunious.

A drawer of a bill or any indorser when they sign, can, if they wish, insert in the bill the name of a person to whom a holder may resort if the bill is dishonoured, either by non-acceptance or non-payment.

There is no obligation whatsoever on the referee in case of need. Unlike the accommodation party, he does not sign the bill and is liable to nobody. In fact it would be technically possible for him not even to know his name had been put forward as a referee! If reference is made to him, he may then accept the bill, and be of such assistance as he is prepared to be. Once he accepts the bill, he does, of course, become liable on it in the usual way.

A holder is not obliged to resort to a referee in case of need, and he has the option to do so or not as he thinks fit!

(v) Avaliste

The word *avaliste* is French and it means a "guarantor". An *aval* means a "guarantee".

As long ago as 1880 Lord Blackburn in *Steele* v. *McKinlay*[122] spoke of an indorsement on a bill of exchange by a person who was not a holder of the bill,

---

117. Bills of Exchange of Act 1882, s. 59(3).
118. *Ibid.*, s. 50(2)(*c*)(4) and (2)(*d*)(3).
119. *Ibid.* s. 46(2).
120. A guarantor of a bank account, and of bills of exchange discounted by the bank, guarantees that one of the parties to the bills, acceptor, drawer or indorser will pay, but the guarantor (not being a party to the bills) does not place himself on a level with the drawer so as to be answerable equally with the drawer if the acceptor defaults. In other words, all the parties to the bill must have defaulted, before the bank can call on the guarantor: *Scholefield Goodman & Sons Ltd* v. *Zyngier* [1985] 3 All ER 105, 112b (PC).
121. *Ibid.* s. 15. See also *infra* under the heading "Acceptance and Payment for Honour" in Chap. 8.
122. (1880) 5 App. Cas. 754 at p. 772.

but who put his name to it to facilitate the transfer of the bill to a holder. He explained how that might be achieved:

By the old foreign law, not in this respect entirely adopted by the English law, this might be done by what was called an *aval* (said to be an antiquated word signifying "underwriting"), either on the bill itself or on a separate paper; and if such an *aval* was given by anyone, his obligation to all subsequent holders of the bill was precisely the same as that of the person to facilitate whose transfer the *aval* was given. It appears from Pothier, *Du Contrat de Change*, Part 1., chap. 4, Article VII, *De l'obligation qui nait des avals*, that the *aval* might be made by one who gave his name, either by way of incurring responsibility for the drawer, placing the signature under the name of the drawer, or for the indorser, placing it under the indorsement, or for the acceptor, placing it under that of the acceptance. An *aval* for the honour of the acceptor, even if on the bill, is not effectual in English law, as appears by *Jackson* v. *Hudson* ((1810) 2 Camp 447, 170 ER 1213).

As Lord Blackburn states guaranteeing the payment of a bill of exchange in this way has no counterpart in English law[123] and is not mentioned in the Bills of Exchange Act 1882. However, it is widely used in continental Europe, taking its authority from the Geneva Convention 1930, Articles 30, 31 and 32.[124]

Article 30 states that payment of a bill of exchange may be guaranteed by an *aval* as to the whole or part of its amount, and this guarantee may be given by a third person (that is, who is not a party to the bill), or by someone who has signed as a party to the bill. Article 31 goes on to provide that the *aval* is expressed by the words "good as *aval*" ("*bon pour aval*") or by any other equivalent formula, and it may be written on the bill itself or on an *allonge*. The *aval* must specify for whose account the guarantee is given, and if it does not, it is deemed to be given for the account of the drawer of the bill.

Article 32 provides that the giver of the *aval* (*avaliste*[125]) is bound in the same way as the person for whom he has become guarantor, and his guarantee is valid ". . . even when the liability which he has guaranteed is inoperative for any reason . . ."—a heavy liability indeed—the only exception being in respect of any ". . . defect of form . . .".

As is noted elsewhere[126] the United Kingdom is not a subscriber to the Geneva Convention 1930 unifying the laws of bills of exchange, promissory notes and cheques.

The United Nations Convention on Bills of Exchange of 9 December 1988,[127] Article 46, provides for guarantees (in similar terms to the Geneva Convention), and states: "A guarantee is expressed by the words 'guaranteed', 'aval', 'good as aval' or words of similar import, accompanied by the signature

---

123. *G & H Montage GmbH* v. *Irvani* [1990] 2 All ER 225, *per* Purchas LJ, at p. 244c.
124. See *post* Appendix 7.
125. *G & H Montage GmbH* v. *Irvani* [1990] 2 All ER 225, p. 244d. Article 46 of the Geneva Convention 1930 uses the word *avaliseur*.
126. Chap. 10 *infra*.
127. See Appendix 6 *infra*.

of the guarantor."[128] Indeed, the guarantee can be effected by the signature of the guarantor alone, and any signature ". . . on the front of the instrument . . .", other than the maker, the drawer or the drawee, is a guarantee. One must assume, therefore, that a signature alone on the back of the bill, without more, will not be a guarantee.[129]

As ever, the liability of the guarantor is heavy, and he may not raise as a defence that he signed the instrument before it was signed by the person for whom he is guarantor, nor while the instrument was incomplete.

The United Kingdom is not a subscriber to this Convention either, indeed the only two countries who are, are the United States of America and the USSR, as was.

Notwithstanding the lack of provision in English law for the *aval*, over the past few years its use has gradually been adopted by businessmen, who have obtained a guarantee on bills of exchange (including promissory notes), and it is not uncommon today to see bills drawn and issued in Britain, marked:

> Good for aval
> for the account of [Blank Imports Limited]
>   (Signed)
> For and on behalf of [Blank Bank plc]

The English courts have not been called upon to pronounce on the validity of such arrangements, although they have recognised the *aval* when applying a foreign law which provides for such guarantees. In *G & H Montage GmbH* v. *Irvani*[130] bills of exchange drawn in Germany and payable in London were dishonoured. They had been marked *bon pour aval pour les tires*, and duly signed. It was held that German law applied, and as under German law the obligation of the guarantor was created, the *aval* was both recognisable and enforceable in the English courts.[131]

However, this is not the same as a bank in London giving an *aval* for its customer to purchase goods from, say, France, when almost certainly the law governing the *aval* would be English.

The following points must be noted:

> (1) While under English law it is always possible for one person to give a guarantee for another's debts, under the terms of the dust-encrusted Statute of Frauds, that guarantee must be in writing, or there must be a note or memorandum of it containing all the terms, and it must be signed by the guarantor.[132]

128. Art. 46(3).
129. *Cf.* under English law the "face" of a bill includes the "back"; *per* Denning LJ (as he then was) in *Arab Bank* v. *Ross* [1952] QB 216, 226.
130. [1990] 2 All ER 225.
131. *Per* Purchas LJ, at p. 244c.
132. For a more detailed consideration, see Cheshire, Fifoot & Furmston, *Law of Contract* (1996), 13th edition, pages 210 *et seq.*

A bank (or anyone else) could give such a guarantee on behalf of a buyer of goods to his supplier, but that would not make the bank (or anyone else) liable on the bill of exchange. The guarantee so given would be a wholly separate document and transaction.

Under English law the guaranteeing of payment of bills of exchange does not mean the guarantor is on a level with the other parties. "If a third party . . . guarantees a bill of exchange for the benefit of a bank which discounts it, the normal understanding will be that the surety guarantees that payment will be made by one or other of the parties to the bill who are liable on it . . ."[133]

(2) It has for many years been the case, and is provided by the Bills of Exchange Act 1882,[134] that the drawee (upon whom the bill is drawn), to be liable must accept the bill as his engagement to pay the amount for which the bill is drawn. If he does not accept the responsibility to pay, he is under no obligation. It follows that the "strength" of a bill depends almost exclusively on the "strength" of the acceptor.

Of course, the acceptor is liable on the bill, and he engages that he will pay it;[135] however, unless the bill comes into the hands of a holder in due course, the acceptor may not be liable if, for example, the drawer's signature has been forged, or he had no authority to draw the bill in the first place.

(3) Under the terms of section 56 of the Bills of Exchange Act 1882, if anyone signs a bill (a guarantor) ". . . otherwise than as a drawer or acceptor, he thereby incurs the liabilities of an indorser . . .", again to a holder in due course. It follows that a third party signing a bill to which the Bills of Exchange Act 1882 applies becomes an indorser, not a guarantor.

The only other "third party" to a bill is an "accommodation party"[136] who signs a bill as drawer, acceptor or indorser, quite gratuitously, for the purpose of lending his name to some other person who, very likely, is not credit worthy. Once he signs the bill, he will be liable on it to a holder for value.[137]

Because the *aval* is not recognised by English law (except as mentioned above where some foreign law is applied) it is difficult to see how a signature on a bill of exchange by way of an *aval* can have any validity in a transaction governed by English law. To give effect to an *aval* (as in the jurisdictions of continental Europe) would seem to

133. *Scholefield Goodman & Sons Ltd* v. *Zyngier* [1985] 3 All ER 105, 112b (PC).
134. S. 17(1).
135. Bills of Exchange Act 1882, s. 45(1).
136. Bills of Exchange Act 1882, s. 28.
137. *Ibid.*, s. 28(2). As to the definition of a holder for value, see *ibid.*, s. 27(2). It should be noted that a "referee in case of need" is not liable on a bill at all, unless, of course, he accepts the bill.

need an amendment to the Bills of Exchange Act 1882. Notwith-standing this situation, *avals* are in daily use in transactions governed by English law as is noted above.

Structuring the transaction—Part I [138]

It is not always clear why a transaction involving bills of exchange should be structured in the way it often is.

A bill is, in essence, a means of transferring money from X to Y. Unless the bill is a cheque (when X's money is held by his bank) it is never very clear, at first, why X has to order someone else to make payment to Y. Still less why Y sometimes draws the bill!

Suppose Basil in Bootle buys some machinery from Sidney in Scunthorpe for £10,000. It is agreed that Basil can have six months' credit. On delivery of the machinery Basil will owe Sidney £10,000. If Basil draws a six months' bill in favour of Sidney, there will be an immediate problem as there is no one *on whom* the bill can be drawn. Basil might well, therefore, give Sidney a promissory note for £10,000, there is then only the two parties. This method is often used in such circumstances.

However, it usually happens that when Sidney agrees to give six months' credit, he has already made an arrangement with a financier, Lionel in London, that the bill or note will be immediately discounted with Lionel to finance the transaction. What sort of financial arrangements are made between Basil and Sidney will then depend upon what requirements Lionel in London laid down.

Lionel may well want more than Basil's signature on a promissory note. It will be seen later that, on a note, a drawer must pay it according to its tenor, and is precluded from denying to a holder in due course the existence of the payee and his capacity to indorse.[139] Whereas, if Basil can be made the *acceptor* of a bill, not only must he pay it, but he will be precluded from denying to a holder in due course (Lionel), in addition to the existence of the payee and his then capacity to indorse (as under the note), the existence of the drawer, the genuineness of his signature and his capacity and authority to draw the bill; and if the bill is payable to the drawer's order (which it will be) the then capacity of the drawer to indorse.[140] Obviously, if it can be arranged, Lionel will be in a stronger position if the transaction can be structured with the use of a bill.

The way to do it is this[141]: Sidney the seller from Scunthorpe draws the bill in his own favour on Basil, the buyer from Bootle (on the face of it the roles

138. For Part II see *infra* Chap. 15.
139. Bills of Exchange Act 1882, s. 88. Promissory notes are discussed *infra* in Chap. 9.
140. *Ibid.*, s. 54.
141. See for example the facts in *Lombard Banking* v. *Central Garage & Engineering Co* [1963] 1 QB 220.

are almost reversed). Sidney as payee presents the bill to Basil for acceptance (Basil is now the acceptor); Sidney then indorses the bill over to Lionel.

Lionel, therefore, has a bill accepted by Basil (who owes the money) and indorsed by Sidney. So that not only can Lionel claim against Basil, as acceptor, but if anything goes amiss, he can claim against Sidney as indorser.

Lionel would obviously not agree to be the payee in the bill, as then Sidney (the drawer) could pass it on to Lionel — after Basil's acceptance — as a transferor by delivery, and thus, not be liable himself on the bill. Thus "weakening" the bill to that extent.

Forfaiting[142]

As we have just seen, in what might be termed the *standard* form of transaction involving the giving of credit by a seller to a buyer, all parties require recourse against other parties to the bill of exchange in the event the bill is dishonoured when it is due.

However, in a forfaiting transaction the finance house advancing the money to the seller does so without recourse. What happens is that the finance house (the forfaiter) "forfeits"[143] its rights against the buyer and other parties, and accepts instead a guarantee (the *aval* which we discussed above) from the buyer's bank that the bill will be paid when it falls due.

The way the transaction usually operates is this:

(a) the buyer of the goods or services makes a promissory note for the price drawn in favour of the seller and arranges with its (the buyer's) bank to guarantee the payment of the note;

(b) the note is bought by the forfaiter at a discount. The forfaiter then immediately pays the seller in full;

(c) the forfaiter is paid by the buyer's bank, again in full, upon the maturity of the promissory note.

This is a very simple and straightforward transaction, and saves many of the complications noted earlier when utilising the so-called *standard* form of discounting bills of exchange.

When utilising the forfaiting procedure as outlined above, the following points must be noted:

(1) The guarantee (*aval*) as part of the forfaiting transaction is vital, as also is the ability of the giver of the instrument to negative his liability

---

142. I am indebted for much help and information on this subject to Andy Ripley FCA, a director of London Forfaiting International plc, although Mr Ripley is in no way responsible for the opinions expressed.

143. The word "forfaiting" is derived from the French word "*forfaire*", meaning to forfeit. In German, it is "*forfaitierung*".

on the bill. Much of the attraction to a buyer in a forfaiting transaction would be lost if he were to remain liable *on the bill*. Though whether this negativing of liability will be wholly effective will depend upon which legal system governs the transaction. The system of forfaiting is relatively new, and depends for its efficacy upon the trust which exists among the parties, in particular, on the part of the bank giving the guarantee. The system works well, and is no doubt the reason why so few disputes have needed to have been decided in the courts of the main trading nations.

(2) The instrument used in a forfaiting transaction will usually be a promissory note because in many of these transactions the law governing the use of the commercial paper will be that of a country which has either adopted the Geneva Convention 1930 on Bills of Exchange, or taken the provisions of the Convention into its domestic Code. In particular, the terms of Article 9 of the Geneva Convention (dealing with Bills of Exchange) allows a drawer of a bill to "release himself from the guarantee of acceptance" though it does not allow him to release himself from the liability to pay; however, the provisions of Article 9 do not apply to promissory notes,[144] and so the maker of a note may validly mark the paper *sans recour*, and while the provisions of Articles 43–50, and 52–54 (relating to recourse in case of non-payment), of the 1930 Convention apply to promissory notes, once the note is marked *sans recour* the maker's liability would appear to be at an end, and no action can be brought under the terms of Article 47 which provides, in part:

> All drawers, acceptors, endorsers or guarantors by *aval* of a bill of exchange are jointly and severally liable to the holder.
> The holder has the right of proceeding against all these persons individually or collectively without being required to observe the order in which they have become bound.

(3) The marking of the bill "without recourse" or "*sans recour*" only the liability on a bill of exchange or promissory note (that is, negatives to other persons who are parties to that piece of paper), and does not, of course, affect the basic responsibilities among the parties, in particular, between the buyer and seller. So that under English law, and the laws of many other countries also, the drawer (seller), even if he negatived his liability, if the goods were defective, he would still be liable to the buyer under the main contract. It is only his liability "on the bill" that is negatived.

---

144. See Art. 77 of the Convention.

The cash equivalence principle, whereby the bill of exchange or whatever must be treated as cash, also applies, and so the bill must be paid no matter what dispute there is between the parties as to the goods or services concerned.

(4) Under English law it is not clear whether the maker of a promissory note can immediately negative his liability by marking the note "*sans recour*" or "without recourse" or whatever. The immediate reaction would obviously be that the note marked in this way was valueless, since section 88(1) of the Bills of Exchange Act 1882 provides that the maker of a promissory note "engages that he will pay it according to its tenor", and if he negatives his liability he is doing the very opposite of the terms of s. 88(1). Indeed, it has been argued that the provision of section 16 of the 1882 Act—which allows the "drawer of a bill" to negative his liability—does not apply to the maker of a promissory note at all, because of the difference in definitions in section 2 of the 1882 Act, that a "bill" means a bill of exchange, while a "note" means a promissory note. On the other hand, s. 89(3) clearly states which provisions of the 1882 Act do not apply to "notes" and there is no mention in that subsection of the ability to negative liability, so one must assume the terms of s. 16 *do* apply to promissory notes; particularly so since section 89(1) of the Act states that " . . . except as by this section provided, the provisions of the Act relating to bills of exchange apply, with the necessary modifications, to promissory notes"; therefore the provisions of the Act (s. 16) allowing the negativing of liability would seem to be applicable to promissory notes. Indeed, the negativing of liability by a maker of a promissory note would appear less extraordinary where the note is being guaranteed by his bank (as with an *aval*), since the payee will look to the guaranteeing bank for payment, and the maker of the note (the buyer in the transaction) will remain liable to the payee (the seller in the transaction) under the main contract. While the guaranteeing bank will look to its customer (the buyer) for repayment of the funding in the usual way of banking business, without needing to rely on the promissory note. It is only the maker's liability *on the note*, which is being negatived.

Of course, none of these points have, as yet, come before the English courts for consideration.

(5) The forfaiter will buy the promissory note as has been described, but, as with banks in standard types of discounting bills of exchange, the forfaiter is not involved in the main contract. He will pay the seller no matter what the state of the goods, and is, therefore, not concerned with any disputes which may exist or arise between the buyer and the seller, or the terms of the main contract.

Any attempt to prevent the forfaiter from paying the seller, by, for example, an injunction applied for by the buyer (being the maker of the promissory note), will doubtless fall within the same restrictions relating to documentary credits in general, that is they must be paid unless there is an obvious fraud to the knowledge of the forfaiter.[145]

145. As to which, see Chap. 16 *infra*, "The Contract Between the Buyer and his Bank."

CHAPTER 5

LIABILITY ON THE BILL

We have seen time and again that the giving and taking of a bill of exchange in settlement of an obligation under another contract creates a contract separate from *and additional to* the original contract: the question has also been posed whether, if something goes wrong with the original contract, the contract *on the bill* is likewise put in jeopardy.

It could happen in a number of ways—the most likely being an alleged failure of the payee to carry out fully his part of the original contract. However, the rights under the bill are inviolate and the courts will treat " . . . the execution of a bill of exchange either as analogous to a payment of cash, or as amounting to an independent contract within the wider contract in pursuance of which it was executed, and not dependent as regards its enforcement on the performance of the latter".[1]

THE IMMEDIATE PARTIES

Consequently, as between immediate parties a holder will be entitled to judgment *on the bill* even if the other party has a valid counterclaim under the original contract. For example in

LAMONT v. HYLAND[2]

H employed L to repair a ship, the work to be carried out by an agreed date. Payment was to be made partly by H accepting a bill of exchange. The work was not completed in time and H said a great deal of money was lost in excess of the value of the bill, which

---

1. *Per* Roxburgh J in *Lamont* v. *Hyland* [1950] 1 All ER 929, 931D.
2. [1950] 1 All ER 929. See also *Cebora SNC v. SIP (Industrial Products) Ltd* [1976] 1 Lloyd's Rep. 271; *Jade International Steel Stahl und Eisen GmbH v. Robert Nicholas (Steels) Ltd* [1978] 3 WLR 39. This basic rule of the cash equivalence of bills of exchange has been applied and restated many times. Indeed, the need to make immediate payment on bills of exchange has been upheld by the House of Lords, even where there is pending arbitration proceedings between the parties: *Nova (Jersey) Knit Ltd v. Kammgarn Spinnerei GmbH* [1977] 2 All ER 463. See however the dissenting judgment of Lord Salmon, who, while recognizing the basic rule of cash equivalence if a bill has been negotiated, thought that as between the immediate parties, a stay should be granted to consider any counterclaim.

he refused to pay. L then sued. *Held*—that H had no defence on the bill and judgment was given for L. Any claim under the original contract was a separate matter and judgment could not be stayed pending the trial of that action.

Once a bill has been properly and truly given and delivered, there is really one defence and one defence only to a claim *on the bill* between the immediate parties, that is that there has been a *total* failure of consideration of the original contract.[3] For example,

ELLIOTT v. CRUTCHLEY[4]

E agreed with C to provide refreshments at a naval review. It was agreed that a day or so before the event C would pay an agreed deposit. The agreement provided that in the event of cancellation there was to be no liability on either side. A cheque for the deposit was duly paid by C and the next day the review was cancelled and C stopped the cheque. *Held*—that there was no liability on the cheque.

If there are several bills as part of a transaction, each takes the benefit of the consideration, so that failure of the consideration part way through the contract will not affect bills due before the consideration failed.

FIELDING & PLATT LTD v. NAJJAR[5]

F agreed to supply machinery to a company in the Lebanon of which N was the managing director. There was a lengthy contractual document by which it was agreed the machinery should be installed in stages and paid for by a series of six promissory notes given by N. Work began but when the first note was due it was not paid. F suspended work. The second note fell due and that was not paid. F sued N on both notes. N said the contract for the supply of the machinery had ceased, and so there was no consideration to support the notes. *Held*—that so far as the first note was concerned F had proceeded under the contract and so there was no failure of consideration: however, so far as the second was concerned, before it fell due F had ceased work and, therefore, was not entitled to recover *on the note*, nor of course, any of the others. F was, therefore, left to his remedy in damages under the original contract.

SUBSEQUENT PARTIES

If, as between the immediate parties to the bill, the drawer is to be bound in these circumstances, his position is more hopeless once the bill has been negotiated to a holder in due course or a holder for value. A bill is a negotiable

---

3. See also *Churchill* v. *Goddard* [1937] 1 KB 92, where Scott LJ considered various authorities which established " . . . the well accepted principle that if the consideration for a bill of exchange wholly fails, then as between immediate parties the contract created by the instrument is discharged . . . ", at p. 109.

4. [1906] AC 7.

5. [1969] 1 WLR 357.

instrument and " . . . is to be treated as cash. It is to be honoured unless there is some good reason to the contrary."[6]

The sanctity of negotiability has always been inviolate. As long ago as 1697 it was said:

A drawer of a bill of exchange, though given without consideration shall not be relieved against a third person to whom it was assigned for an honest debt.[7]

Consequently, once a bill has been negotiated the drawer seems always liable to a subsequent holder. For example, in

BROWN SHIPLEY v. ALICIA HOSIERY[8]

X pledged goods with B as security for a loan. X then agreed to sell the goods to A. A enquired of B if the goods were free to be delivered, and was told (it was alleged) the goods were free to be delivered. A then gave X a cheque, which was immediately indorsed to B in repayment of the loan. It then transpired the goods were not free and that there were considerable storage and customs charges to be paid. A refused to honour the cheque and B sued. *Held*—that A had no defence on the cheque, and judgment was given for B, the indorsee.

As Lord Denning MR explained[9]:

. . . judgment should be given upon that bill of exchange as for cash and it is not to be held up by virtue of some counterclaim which the defendant may assert, even as in this case, a counterclaim relating to the specific subject-matter of the contract.

Take another example:

GLASSCOCK v. BALLS[10]

B was indebted to W and gave him a promissory note, together with a mortgage over some freehold property as extra security. Subsequently W transferred the mortgage to H. Later still, W negotiated the promissory note to G who took for value and with no notice of the mortgage or its transfer. G then sued B *on the note*. B contended that he could not be liable both on the note and also under the mortgage. *Held*—that the note was a negotiable instrument, and as G took for value and without notice of any of these circumstances he could recover.

---

6. *Per* Lord Denning MR in *Fielding & Platt Ltd v. Najjar* [1969] 1 WLR 357, 361B. Echoing the words of Pollock CB in *Warwick v. Nairn* (1855) 156 ER 648: "The payment by a bill of exchange is to be taken as the payment of so much cash", at p. 649. Pronouncements in similar vein are legion.

7. Anon (1697) 92 ER 950. If a cheque is indorsed to a holder in due course (the indorsee) he will get a good title to it, even though as between the drawer and the payee (the indorser of the cheque) there had been a partial failure of consideration: *Mackenzie Mills v. Buono, The Times*, 31 July 1986.

8. [1966] 1 Lloyd's Rep. 668.

9. *Ibid.*, p. 669. Harman LJ, while "constrained against my inclination" agreed, though added: "It seems to me there is much to be said for the view that to refuse a stay here is harsh and might indeed work an injustice", at p. 669.

10. (1889) 24 QBD 13.

The position was explained by Lindley LJ in the following words[11]:

It is quite true that, as between the defendant and the payee of the note, after the transfer of the mortgage in equity the right of the payee to sue on the note for his own benefit ceased, because he had parted with all his interest . . . and the payee therefore could be restrained by injunction from suing on the note . . . That would be the equitable right of the defendant as against the payee. But when the note gets in the hands of a bona fide indorsee for value without notice of the facts, there can be no such equity as against him.

Another recent example is

BANCO DI ROMA v. ORRU[12]

Mr Orru carried on business in England under the title "European Food & Wine Co". He agreed to buy a quantity of tins of tomatoes from an Italian company ISPA. Payment was to be by Mr Orru accepting a series of seven, three-month, bills. This he did in respect of six of them (it is not wholly clear why the seventh was not accepted). ISPA indorsed all seven bills to their bank — Banco di Roma — with whom they had an overdraft. When the tins of tomatoes arrived they were blown, and Mr Orru, quite properly, surrendered the consignment to the proper authorities for destruction. Mr Orru refused to pay out on the bills, saying: "To whom do I owe money for goods that I never had?"[13] The bank sued, claiming to be holders in due course. *Held* — that " . . . it is not a question of owing money for goods: it is a question of owing money upon bills of exchange . . . "[14] which Mr Orru had accepted, and which had been negotiated to the bank. The bank, therefore, were able to recover from Mr Orru; he then being left to his remedy under the original contract with ISPA.[15]

Indeed, the sanctity of negotiability is so great that a holder for value can recover, even if he knew at the time he took, that the consideration between the immediate parties had not existed *ab initio* or had failed totally.

We may take as examples the cases of *Fitch* v. *Jones*[16] and *Lilley* v. *Rankin*,[17] the facts of each being very similar:

X became indebted to Y because of a wager which he had lost, and gave a promissory note in settlement. Y indorsed the note to Z. Z claimed payment under the note and when it was refused he sued X.

In both cases the maker of the promissory notes claimed Z (the holder) knew, *at the time he took*, the notes had been given in respect of a gambling transaction and consequently the transaction was void (but not illegal) and so the "consideration" was, in fact, no consideration at all. The courts took the view that the holder was entitled to recover provided (i) he gave value, and (ii) the original "consideration" was simply void and not illegal.[18]

11. *Ibid.*, p. 16.
12. [1973] 2 Lloyd's Rep. 505.
13. [1973] 2 Lloyd's Rep. 505, at p. 507.
14. *Per* Cairns LJ, *ibid.*, p. 507.
15. There was held to be no liability on the bill which had not been accepted.
16. (1855) 24 LJQB (Trin. T.) 293.
17. (1886) 56 LJQB 248.
18. See *per* Lord Campbell, 24 LJQB (Trin. T.) at p. 295; and *per* Smith J, 56 LJQB at p. 251.

It would not be flying in the face of reason to question whether it is proper that a third party, *with knowledge that the original contract on the bill is defective and unenforceable* between the immediate parties, should be able to recover in this way. On the one hand, it can be argued the holder has given value for a bill clearly evidencing a debt by the drawer to the payee (which presumably the drawer intended to pay) and the fact that *the payee* could not sue for the money is by the way: on the other hand, the bill is unenforceable in its original state, and if an indorsee takes with full knowledge of this he has only himself to blame.[19] Yet there is this lingering doubt, and there might well be circumstances, where the above rules would not apply; perhaps, where the indorsee knew that the bill of exchange had been given *for a particular purpose.*

For example, in

LLOYD v. DAVIS[20]

V was being pressed by her creditors and she prevailed upon L to help her. She owned some land and L, on her behalf, agreed it should be sold to D to raise funds. D drew a six months' bill so that it could be given immediately to the creditors. The bill was duly offered to the creditors, who refused it. V was then in danger of being arrested and L stood her bail, in consideration of the bill being indorsed to him. The bill was not presented for payment at the proper time and V died about 12 months later. It was discovered (although the report does not say when) that V had no power to sell the land to D, as she had previously conveyed it to trustees to pay off incumbrances. L sued D on the bill. *Held* — that at the time he stood bail L knew the creditors would not accept the bill and therefore the consideration for it had failed and so he could not recover.

In the course of giving judgment, the court said[21]:

The plaintiffs knew that the consideration for the bill of exchange had failed, and yet they afterwards took upon themselves the responsibility of the original debt . . . If the bill had been presented for payment when it became due, the defendant might have obtained from Miss Vaughan a conveyance of the equity of redemption in the estates. On the grounds, therefore, that the plaintiffs must have known that the consideration had failed, and that they have prejudiced the rights of the defendant, we think this action is not maintainable.

This case was before the 1882 Act, is rather sketchily reported and is not referred to in either *Fitch* v. *Jones* or *Lilley* v. *Rankin* — but the doubt is clearly there, and the doubt increases when one recalls that an injunction can be

---

19. If one carries this argument to its logical conclusion, one can foresee a state of affairs where the payee — being unable to recover — indorses a bill, under an agreement with the indorsee that *he* will sue the drawer!

20. (1824) 3 LJ (o.s.) KB (Mich. T.) 3. There is a suggestion running through the report that perhaps the decision turned partly on the drawer having in some measure been prejudiced by the holder's conduct.

21. *Per* the court, *ibid.*, 39.

obtained to *prevent* negotiation, where consideration has wholly failed by the non-delivery of goods under the original contract.[22]

PARTIAL FAILURE OF CONSIDERATION

The problems arising where there is a *partial* failure of consideration must be considered separately.

If there is only a *partial* failure of the consideration, then, as between the immediate parties, there appears to be no defence *on the bill* under the general rules discussed above, although the part failure can be claimed as a reduction of this liability *pro tanto* in a separate cross-action.[23]

One would think, *prima facie*, it would be more convenient to dispose of the whole matter in one action under RSC Order 18, rule 17 which provides:

Where a claim by a defendant to a sum of money (whether of an ascertained amount or not) is relied on as a defence to the whole or part of a claim made by the plaintiff, it may be included in the defence and set off against the plaintiff's claim, whether or not it is also added as a counterclaim.

However, this rule has been held not to apply to actions on bills of exchange.[24] Even equity is no assistance: "A court of law would say you must pay the bill first and then bring an action . . . ; and apparently where a bill of exchange was concerned equity in this matter followed the law."[25] The reason being that: "The account which a court of equity adjusts must be one of debtor and creditor, and not an account of debts one way and of damages the other way."[26]

It follows, therefore, if something goes wrong with the original contract, say, by the goods to be delivered not being up to quality, "the defendant ought to satisfy the bill and proceed upon the remedy for the breach of warranty."[27]

---

22. *Patrick* v. *Harrison* (1792) 29 ER 653; *Lloyd* v. *Gurdon* (1818) 36 ER 584.

23. *Per* Lord Gorell in *Bow McLachlan* v. *The Ship "Camosun"* [1909] AC 597, 612 (PC), citing *Warwick* v. *Nairn* (1855) 156 ER 648. The need to bring a separate action was, to some extent, ameliorated in the case of *Thoni GmbH & Co KG* v. *RTP Equipment Ltd* [1979] 2 Lloyd's Rep. 282, where the defendants were allowed to bring into court the sum in dispute on the bills. This was, of course, a case between the immediate parties. However, leave was refused in *Montebianco Industrie Tessili SpA* v. *Carlyle Mills (London) Ltd* [1981] 1 Lloyd's Rep. 509.

24. *Lamont* v. *Hyland* [1950] 1 KB 585, 590 *et seq.*

25. *Per* Roxburgh J, *ibid.*, p. 591. *Court* v. *Sheen* (1891) 7 TLR 556 was dismissed by Roxburgh J as being "shortly reported" and must now be of doubtful authority. The same must also be said of *Oscar Harris, Son & Co* v. *Vallarman* [1940] 1 All ER 185, where the Court of Appeal allowed the defendants to argue a possible set off on a claim on a dishonoured bill of exchange, though Slessor LJ (page 187H) thought " . . . the matter is one which may require considerable argument". This was a claim between the immediate parties.

26. *Glennie* v. *Imri* (1839) 160 ER 773.

27. *Per* Pollock CB in *Warwick* v. *Nairn* (1855) 156 ER 648, 649. See also *Morgan* v. *Richardson* (1806) 103 ER 187, and *Trickey* v. *Larne* (1840) 9 LJ Ex 141.

The only ray of hope lies in the possibility however remote that perhaps the court has power to withhold judgment on the bill in a special case if the two transactions (that is, the original contract and the contract on the bill) are sufficiently closely connected. This seems a remote possibility, however, in view of the authorities and the words of Jessel MR[28]:

> I must say, speaking for myself, that I should hesitate long before I allowed a defendant in an action on a bill of exchange to set up a case for damages by reason of the breach by the plaintiff of some other contract or the commission of some tort. I do not say there cannot be a case where the two transactions may not be connected, but at present I cannot even imagine the existence of such a special case.

The rule of liability on the bill seems, therefore, inviolate, at least if the only defence is a possible counterclaim for unliquidated damages. However, it would probably still be open to the courts to allow a defence *on the bill* if the defendant had a fixed, clearly liquidated sum which he could lay before the court. As Channell B explained[29]:

> I do not wish, in thinking this plea good, to throw the least doubt on the decisions which established the rule that a defendant cannot discharge himself with respect to bills of exchange on the ground of partial failure of consideration, where his right to relief is to the extent of unliquidated damages. I do not apprehend that to be the case here. The sum in respect of which the set-off is claimed is made sufficiently definite by the plea to take the case out of the operation of that rule.

The courts have shown no great haste to adopt this concept however, but rather to maintain intact the cash equivalence principle of bills of exchange, with only occasional twinges that, on the special facts of individual cases, they would like to ameliorate some of the effects of the rule.

Yet the fact is that businessmen do not like paying for goods which are defective or, in some cases, they have never had; and while the courts recognize hardship can be caused to buyers who have to pay out in these circumstances, the vast preponderance of decisions, as we have seen, uphold the cash equivalence rule where there has been a *partial* failure of consideration. In the words of Sir Eric Sachs[30]:

> " . . . the courts should be really careful not to whittle away the rule of practice by introducing unnecessary exceptions to it under the influence of sympathy-evoking stories . . . "

---

28. *Anglo-Italian Bank v. Wells and Davies* (1878) 38 LT 197, 199. Thesiger LJ would probably have been prepared to hold that " . . . the counterclaim would have been sufficiently connected . . . " (p. 201), but the facts did not establish a good counterclaim anyway. The dictum of Jessel MR was approved by Lord Denning in the *Brown Shipley* case, at p. 669.

29. *Agra Bank Ltd v. Leighton* (1886) 36 LJ Ex (Mich. T.) 33, 37, which was not cited in *Lamont v. Hyland*. See also *Forman v. Wright* (1851) 20 LJCP (East.) 145, a case incidentally where Serjeant Byles, the learned author of *Bills of Exchange*, was involved as counsel.

30. *Cebora SNC v. SIP (Industrial Products) Ltd* [1976] 1 Lloyd's Rep. 271, at p. 278.

Indeed, analysing the cases, it seems that any discretion the court has, to stay an order for immediate payment, where there has been a partial failure of consideration, will probably be on the following basis, if it is going to be exercised at all:

(1) the action must be between the immediate parties; and
(2) the sum in dispute must be liquidated and clearly ascertainable; and
(3) the court may put the parties on terms.

1. *Between the immediate parties*

The notion clearly is that so long as the bill has not been negotiated, so that no innocent third parties have become involved, it *may* be in order to consider allowing a stay on immediate payment of a bill if the beneficiary of the bill is, or may be, in default under the terms of the main contract, by delivering faulty goods or whatever. This is the main area of "sympathy-evoking stories" referred to by Sir Eric Sachs.

The fact is that in very few transactions are the dealings with bills limited to the immediate parties. Almost always, the bills are discounted with banks, and the question then is: can a bill be *returned* to the original beneficiary (the immediate party) by some far removed bank for the purpose of an action? This is what happened in

JADE INTERNATIONAL STEEL v. ROBERT NICHOLAS (STEELS) LTD[31]

Jade sold steel to Nicholas in two instalments and payment was to be by bill of exchange. When the first consignment arrived it was alleged by Nicholas to be sub-standard. Nicholas refused to accept the second instalment and to pay the bill in respect of the first. The bill in the meanwhile had been discounted by Jade with its bank (the Sparkasse Bank), who in turn had discounted it with the Deutsche Bundesbank, who had then discounted it with Midland Bank. Upon dishonour of the bill it was passed back to the Sparkasse Bank who debited Jade's account and returned the bill to Jade. Jade sued Nicholas, and, since they were the immediate parties, Nicholas claimed they should not be compelled to pay on the bill, until the dispute over the quality of the steel was settled. It was recognized that if any of the banks had sued they would not be immediate parties, but since the bill had been returned to Jade, were Jade and Nicholas still immediate parties notwithstanding the series of discountings? *Held*—that "It is unreal . . . to regard them as having a dual capacity. Indeed, it is something of a logical difficulty to see how they could. I repeat, when they discounted the bill they lost the benefit of their original capacity. . . "[32] The parties were, therefore, no longer the

---

31. [1978] 2 Lloyd's Rep. 13.
32. [1978] 2 Lloyd's Rep. 13, at p. 16.

immediate parties and so no discretion could be exercised and the bill had to be paid.[33]

There appears to be an exception to the "immediate parties rule" based on the old case of *Thornton* v. *Maynard*.[34] To the effect that if the holder of a bill of exchange holds it in part *as trustee* for someone else, then, if the holder/trustee sues on the bill, the defendant (i.e. the party who owes the money) can set up as a defence against the holder/trustee any defence or set-off which could be available as a defence or set-off against the party who was really behind the transaction. This was decided in

BARCLAYS BANK LTD v. ASCHAFFENBURGER ZELLSTOFFWERKE AG[35]

Aschaffenburger agreed to buy machinery from a British company, Black Clawson International Ltd. Payment was to be by a series of bills of exchange accepted by Aschaffenburger. Black Clawson, it was subsequently alleged, were late in delivery, which gave rise to a claim for liquidated damages; and the machinery was defective when installed, which gave rise to another claim for general damages. These disputes went to arbitration. Black Clawson had indorsed the bills to Barclays who sued Aschaffenburger when that company refused to honour the bills because of the alleged defaults of Black Clawson in the way the machinery had been supplied. In indorsing the bills to Barclays, Black Clawson made an agreement with the bank that 73% of the bills would pass to Barclays (and was covered by ECGD to that amount) and the balance would be paid immediately to the account of Black Clawson; so that until payment, Barclays were trustees for Black Clawson for this balance. Aschaffenburger claimed that they should not have to pay immediately to Barclays the balance sum which would, in turn, be passed over at once to Black Clawson. *Held*—that " . . . any defence or set-off which the German company have as against Black Clawson International Ltd is available against Barclays Bank Ltd in so far as the proportion 26.839% is concerned; because to that extent they are trustees for Black Clawson International Ltd . . . Therefore, although there should be judgment for the whole amount with the appropriate interest, there should be a stay as to 26.839% of this claim".[36]

33. In so far as the sanctity of the cash equivalence principle is concerned, the decision is doubtless correct. However, the reasons why any discretion could not be exercised simply because the court seemed to think the parties were no longer "immediate", is of doubtful accuracy. Parties to bills of exchange forever find themselves in two (or possibly more) capacities. The drawer, the payee, the acceptor remain such, and do not lose that capacity, nor the rights and obligations attached to it, because, for example, they also become indorsers. The drawer of a bill does not cease to be liable, as such, just because some third party becomes an acceptor. So, for whatever reasons, if the bill comes back into the possession of the original beneficiary he is just as much an immediate party as he was in the beginning. It is usually the holder at the time of dishonour who sues: in the instant case, the fact that the bill was passed back down the line was exceptional.

There are a number of statements by the learned LJJ which may require comment should the circumstances ever come for consideration again. One, at least, is that Nicholas had the rights of a holder in due course: this certainly could not be the case. It appears from the report that they were payees (and so could not be holders in due course) and when they got possession of the bill again, they took with knowledge of its dishonour and so could not be holders in due course, and s. 29(3) of the Bills of Exchange Act 1882 would not save them. Nor can it be said that, when a dishonoured bill is handed back to a prior party to sue on it, the "handing back" is a "negotiation" to give any *derivative* title.

34. (1875) LR 10 CP 695.

35. [1967] 1 Lloyd's Rep. 387.

36. [1967] 1 Lloyd's Rep. 387. *Per* Lord Denning MR, at p. 389.

Two things seem clear from this case:

(a) A stay can be granted, even if the bill has been negotiated, providing the defendant can show the holder is not beneficially entitled, and is, in reality, a trustee for the supplier under the main contract. This line of argument has not been used or developed in any subsequent case; which is strange, because, if correct, there seems no reason why many transactions should not be structured in this way, since the circumstances are common enough.

(b) Where judgment is given for the full value of the bill, the terms of any stay are vital.[37] Because, as counsel pointed out, if there were to be a stay pending the outcome of an arbitration, immediately those proceedings were over the bank could collect in full, since it already had a judgment for the full amount.

What the court appeared to be overlooking was that the stay pending the foreign arbitration proceedings was not the same as a stay pending proceedings in England, which may result in a cross-judgment wherein the second judgment may reduce the first. In this case, there never could be a set-off because any award of the arbitration in favour of the German company would stand separately, still allowing the bank to collect its judgment in full.

How to overcome the impasse was far from clear[38]:

"Lord Denning MR: Perhaps the better way would be leave to defend as to that proportion — stay that pending determination.

Mr Caplan: That again, if I may say so, shows what a tangle one is getting into because there is in fact nothing to defend.

Lord Justice Harman: Surely the right order is to stay until further order.

Mr Caplan: That may be. I am not saying that there may not be some means of achieving the sort of result which one gathers your Lordships think is just. I was merely pointing out what your Lordship has suggested would be the result, that in two or three years from now the stay would be removed and the judgment would be enforced in its entirety.

Lord Denning MR: I see your point.

Mr Caplan: That does not seem to me to meet what your Lordships have in mind as the justice of the case.

Lord Denning MR: What we had in mind was that they should not be compelled to pay the £26,000 until the other matter is determined.

Mr Caplan: When the other matter is determined presumably they have still got to pay.

Lord Denning MR: It will be taken into account in the other judgment.

Mr Caplan: I do not know how that can be done. . . .

Lord Denning MR: What about what Lord Justice Harman suggested — stay until further order?

Mr Caplan: Assume you have a stay until further order. That means that in perhaps three or four years' time when we come back to a court, almost certainly differently

---

37. This only emerged after judgment had been given, and the point was raised by counsel (Mr Leonard Caplan QC), reported at p. 391 *et seq*.

38. *Ibid.*, p. 392.

composed, we have to ask for a further order in a situation in which all that can be said is: We, Barclays, have a judgment for £110,000, or whatever it is, and we now tell you that Black Clawson have got an arbitration award against them for £1½ million."

The discussion continued at length, and eventually the court adjourned to allow the parties to agree the wording of the stay, and then return to the court. The stay, in fact, was ordered for one year or the determination of the arbitration whichever be the shorter period; and since everyone knew the arbitration would take years to reach a determination, the practical result was, therefore, that the stay in respect of the balance of the judgment was for one year.

Whether this was what the court had in mind originally, one will never know. However, having adhered to the cash equivalence principle by giving judgment for the full amount of the bills, some limitation to the stay was, and, one assumes, always will be, inevitable. The only other possibility seems to be to give judgment for only that part which is to be paid at once.[39]

2. A liquidated sum

Nothing is clearer in this subject than that if the court is prepared to consider a stay as to part, the defendant *must* be able to show he has an exact or calculable sum he is refusing to pay. As we have seen above, a claim for unliquidated damages for defective delivery, or consequential loss, is all too vague, however justifiable it may be in the minds of businessmen who feel it is wrong that they should be asked to pay out on a bill, when, as all the world can see, they have lost vast sums due to the default of the party claiming under the bill. This principle has now been established by the House of Lords in

NOVA (JERSEY) KNIT LTD v. KAMMGARN SPINNEREI GMBH[40]

Nova, an English company, made an agreement with Kammgarn, a German company, to manufacture jersey material in Germany. For this purpose a partnership was set up, and in the agreement, which was subject to German law, there was a widely drawn arbitration clause. Subsequently, and as a separate transaction, Nova sold Kammgarn machines for the manufacture of the material, and Kammgarn leased them to the partnership. The payment was by 24 bills of exchange drawn by Nova and accepted by Kammgarn payable in London. There was no arbitration clause in the sale agreement. Six bills were paid before a dispute arose over the machines and the alleged mismanagement of the partnership, and Kammgarn refused further payment of bills, and immediately began arbitration proceedings in Germany under the terms of the partnership agreement. Nova, in turn, began proceedings in England on the dishonoured bills; and by way of defence, Kammgarn said that the whole matter should stand over for settlement in the German arbitration proceedings. *Held*—that " . . . unliquidated cross-

---

39. This was suggested in discussion by Harman LJ, but only after judgment for the whole amount had been given: *ibid*, p. 392; this is what the court decided to do in *Thoni GmbH & Co KG v. RTP Equipment Ltd* [1979] 2 Lloyd's Rep. 282.
    40. [1977] 2 All ER 463.

claims cannot be relied on by way of extinguishing set-off against a claim on a bill of exchange. As between the immediate parties, a partial failure of consideration may be relied on as a *pro tanto* defence, but only when the amount involved is ascertained and liquidated. The amount claimed here in respect of the machines is certainly neither ascertained nor liquidated, and the claim in respect of mismanagement is one for a wholly unrelated tort".[41]

Moreover, where an unliquidated claim has been rejected by the court, and the defendant has paid the beneficiary on the bill the defendant cannot have a second bite at the cherry, as it were, by claiming rights over that money as security for any subsequent separate action he may bring to obtain damages for the beneficiary's alleged default under the main contract. So that, for example, a *Mareva* injunction will not be granted to prevent a successful plaintiff in an action on a bill of exchange from taking his money out of the jurisdiction; even though the defendant alleges he has a good counterclaim. Bridge LJ in *Montecchi* v. *Shimco (UK) Ltd*,[42] stated the position clearly when he said:

Now of course it is elementary that as between the immediate parties to a bill of exchange, which is treated in international commerce as the equivalent of cash, the fact that the defendant may have a counterclaim for unliquidated damages arising out of the same transaction forms no sort of defence to an action on a bill of exchange and no ground on which he should be granted a stay of execution of the judgment in the action for the proceeds of the bill of exchange . . . It is said that with the enforcement of the judgment by the cash being paid into court or into a joint account, there should be an injunction to restrain the plaintiff from dealing with it. If that were right, presumably the same argument would be available in every case in which a foreign holder of a bill of exchange, being an immediate party to the bill and suing on it, was met with a counterclaim for unliquidated damages by a party liable on the bill. If that were the situation, it seems to me it would have the widest and most undesirable repercussions by way of undermining the well-known principle of international commerce, which the courts have repeatedly upheld, that a bill of exchange is to be treated as having the same value as the equivalent cash.

3. *The parties on terms*

If the court is prepared to allow a stay, or is prepared to give leave to defend, it seems it will not necessarily be unconditional; in that the defendant may well be asked to bring the disputed sum into court. This is what happened in

---

41. [1977] 2 All ER 463, *Per* Lord Wilberforce at p. 469a and b. Lord Salmon dissented, being in favour of a stay, as he was " . . . satisfied that this dispute comes within the arbitration agreement": at p. 477d. The House of Lords' decision reversed that of the Court of Appeal, who had allowed a stay in respect of the immediate payment of the bills, pending the arbitration. The House also held, by way of a preliminary point, that the bills were " . . . governed, as to all matters affecting their substantial effect, by English law": *ibid.*, p. 467f.
42. [1979] 1 WLR 1180, at p. 1183a.

THONI GMBH & CO KG v. RTP EQUIPMENT LTD[43]

RTP was an English company, and they bought fire hoses from Thoni, who carried on business in Austria. The companies had traded with one another over a period of time, and the state of the account between them became confused, due partly to the fact that some hoses were defective and had to be replaced free of charge; and partly, because of payments which had been withheld and invoices resubmitted. Eventually, the parties agreed that RTP would pay off the then balance by monthly instalments, and accept a bill of exchange for one million Austrian schillings. Only two monthly instalments were made before more problems arose over defective deliveries. Thoni then presented the bill for payment, which was dishonoured, RTP claiming that the bill was not to be presented for payment at all, and would be returned once the accounts were cleared. Thoni sued on the bill, and RTP argued that there had been a partial failure of consideration, in that once a further investigation into the accounts had been made, it showed that RTP, at the time they accepted the bill, in fact, owed only 400,897 Austrian schillings, not one million, their stated liability on the bill. *Held*—that " . . . there is a possibility at least that it will be discovered that the indebtedness of the defendants to the plaintiffs was no more than 400,897 Austrian schillings at the date when the bill was accepted . . . there is an arguable case here that there was no consideration for the bill except to the extent of 400,897 Austrian schillings . . . in these circumstances I would . . . give leave to defend in relation to the balance of the amount due on the bill that is to say, 599,103 Austrian schillings upon condition that the defendants bring the latter sum, or the equivalent sum in sterling at today's rate of exchange, into court".[44]

However, this concept has not always met with unqualified approbation. In the words of Sir Eric Sachs: "Pleas to leave in court large sums to deteriorate in value while . . . proceedings are fought out may well . . . seem rather divorced from business realities and should perhaps be examined with considerable caution."[45]

An offer by a defendant to bring such a sum into court is, one supposes, an indication that the proceedings are not merely a delaying tactic on the part of a litigant who cannot really meet its commitments on the bill, but by a party with a genuine claim to pursue. Of course, even if offered in this way the court may still refuse to accept such a condition as a prerequisite to giving leave.[46]

---

43. [1979] 2 Lloyd's Rep. 282.

44. *Per* Buckley LJ, at p. 285. It is not clear from the report whether RTP ever argued that the delivery of the bill was conditional within s. 21(2)(*b*) of the 1882 Act, and, therefore, no delivery at all; nor whether they claimed money was "paid" under a mistake of fact, and, therefore, recoverable. Certainly the authority cited by the court deals not with "failure" of consideration, but with a "want" of consideration at the time the bill was given: see *per* Jervis CJ in *Forman* v. *Wright* (1851) 11 CB 481, at p. 492. This also presupposes that the consideration can be divided or "split" in this way, as will usually be the case with monetary claims.

45. *Cebora SNC* v. *SIP (Industrial Products) Ltd* [1976] 1 Lloyd's Rep. 271, at p. 278.

46. See *Jade International Steel Stahl und Eisen GmbH* v. *Robert Nicholas (Steels) Ltd* [1978] 2 Lloyd's Rep. 13, at p. 14. In *Saga Ltd* v. *Avalon Promotions Ltd* [1972] 2 All ER 545, leave to defend was given on condition that the defendants brought most of the disputed sum into court. This is an odd case, not referred to often in subsequent cases, where the C.A. allowed judgment in default of appearance to be set aside. Salmon LJ, at p. 547f thought the court had discretion, and were not " . . . bound in every case where a claim rests on a dishonoured bill of exchange to give judgment for the plaintiff unconditionally".

DEFENCES TO LIABILITY ON THE BILL

As was said before, once a bill of exchange has been signed (whether by the drawer or an indorser) and delivered, there are few defences open to excuse liability. Although they have been referred to elsewhere it may be helpful to review these defences by collecting them together.

1. Total failure of consideration

Usually, this will be the only defence open, once a bill has been given and delivered. This defence, and the problems of a *partial* failure of consideration, have already been discussed[47] and nothing more need be added here.

2. Lack of capacity

As we have seen[48] if the drawer or an indorser has no capacity in law he will not be liable on the bill.

3. Lack of authority

Once again,[49] if the drawer or an indorser or an acceptor can show that he did not sign himself, and that the person who purported to sign on his behalf did not have authority, he may be able to avoid liability.

In such a case, it may be, that the person who actually signed the bill (that is the purported agent) will be liable personally of course.

4. Not in proper form

Any bill which does not comply with the definition laid down by s. 3(1) of the Bills of Exchange Act 1882 is not a bill of exchange at all,[50] and no liability can attach to the person signing it. It may, however, be evidence of an account stated between the parties. If a bill is defective in form, as we have seen, it may be possible for the holder to complete it, if the person who signed it delivered it "in order that it may be converted into a bill" within s. 20(1) of the 1882 Act.

---

47. The topic of "partial failure of consideration" is discussed in more detail *supra* in Chap. 5.

48. The topic of "capacity" is discussed in more detail *supra* in Chap. 2.

49. The topic of "authority" is discussed in more detail *supra* in Chap. 2.

50. Bills of Exchange Act 1882, s. 3(2). Section 83(1) defines promissory notes in similar terms.

5. Non-delivery

A bill is not deemed to be issued to the payee until it is delivered by the transfer of possession; nor by indorsement unless it is "completed by delivery".[51] Consequently, if it is not delivered there will be no liability. So that if a bill is, for example, stolen, as in *Arnold* v. *Cheque Bank*,[52] the person from whom it was taken will not be liable to a subsequent holder. Unless that holder is a holder in due course, in which case, by virtue of s. 21(2) of the 1882 Act, delivery of the bill is conclusively presumed.

Such cases where want of delivery is being set up as a defence will, as is often the case, be where the instrument is in the hands of an innocent holder and it is a question of whether he or the unfortunate person from whom it was stolen must suffer the loss. The burden of proof is, under s. 21(3) of the 1882 Act on the person attempting to disclaim of course.

The rule is clear, however. There is no liability if a bill is stolen unless: (i) the holder can show he is a holder in due course, in which case, by virtue of s. 21(2) of the 1882 Act, delivery is conclusively presumed; or (ii) the bill was, at the time it was stolen, payable to bearer.

Naturally, the thief can have no title to the instrument.

6. The bill is discharged

If the holder of a bill is attempting to obtain payment, it will be a good defence that the bill is discharged and that all the rights and liabilities under it are extinguished.[53]

The type of case which sometimes arises is where the person against whom the claim is being made states that the bill has been altered in some way, without the consent of all the parties pursuant to s. 64(1) of the 1882 Act.

Once again, in this case, if the holder is a holder in due course, he will be able to claim for the amount of the bill as originally drawn[54] and for which the signer was presumably prepared to be liable.

7. No notice of dishonour

If a bill has been dishonoured, the holder will often attempt to obtain payment from other parties. If a claim is to be made, due notice of dishonour must be given,[55] and, if it is not, any party without notice is not liable on the bill, and as *Yeoman Credit Ltd* v. *Gregory*[56] showed, even slight delay in giving notice can be fatal, as the requirement of notice is strictly enforced, and the defendant

---

51. Bills of Exchange Act 1882, s. 2.
52. (1876) 45 LJCL 562.
53. As to which see *infra* Chap. 7.
54. Bills of Exchange Act 1882, s. 64(1) *proviso*.
55. *Infra* Chap. 8.
56. [1963] 1 All ER 245.

will not be liable even though he "may have sustained no prejudice whatever by the delay".[57]

8. Mistake

If the drawer or an indorser or acceptor has signed a bill in the mistaken belief that he is signing a document of a totally different kind, provided he has not been careless, he will not be liable on it,[58] by virtue of s. 24 of the 1882 Act. However, if he knew the bill *was* a bill, but because of some mistake in the transaction as a whole, he would not have issued it had he known the true facts, he will still be liable *on the bill*.

We are considering here, of course, the discovery of a mistake *before payment*. Once payment has been made under a bill, the problem then is the *recovery* of money paid by mistake, which is an entirely different matter.[59]

The problem resolves itself into this: if a man issues a cheque and then discovers some mistake and immediately "stops" it, is he liable on it? Equally, if a time bill is issued, and before payment some mistake is discovered, can the drawer, acceptor or an indorser disclaim liability? The answer to both questions is that the parties will be liable, and must pursue any counterclaim based on the mistake for the recovery of the money as a separate action.[60] In short, the mistake in this context is no defence *on the bill*.

9. Forgery, fraud, blackmail, duress and undue influence

All these topics are considered later,[61] but their effect is to vitiate the element of consent to the giving of a bill of exchange.

All forgeries are nullities and there is no liability on the part of any person whose signature has been forged: unless, perhaps, if he is estopped from denying the genuineness of his signature by his conduct.[62] As we shall see,[63] there may still be a liability on the bill by persons who sign after a forgery.

In considering fraud as a possible defence to an action on a bill, it must be remembered that the action will often be between two innocent parties who have become involved by the fraud of some third person, who has either disappeared or is not worth suing. As is noted later,[64] in cases of what may be called "general" fraud, that is, where the fraudulent conduct affects the original contract it will be a good defence for the drawer (that is, the person who has been defrauded into parting with his money) to show he was induced by

57. *Per* Megaw J, *ibid.*, p. 256F.
58. See *infra* under the heading "Bills mistakenly signed" in Chap. 6.
59. See for example *infra* "Recovery of money paid by mistake" in Chap. 13.
60. See *supra*.
61. *Infra* in Chap. 6—"The lack of Real Consent".
62. *Greenwood v. Martins Bank Ltd* [1933] AC 51 (CA).
63. *Infra* see Chap. 6, under the heading "Forgery".
64. *Infra* see Chap. 6, under the heading "Fraud".

fraud to sign the cheque or bill,[65] unless the innocent third party (that is, the holder) can prove he is a holder in due course.

If the fraud takes the form of tampering with the instrument itself, other considerations apply. Much will depend upon whether the alteration is apparent or not, and whether the instrument is a time bill,[66] or a cheque.[67]

Clearly, if a man trustingly signs a blank piece of paper, as did the guarantor of a promissory note in *Lloyds Bank* v. *Cooke*,[68] he will be estopped from denying his liability to a bank who honours his apparent instructions. Moreover, since a customer owes a duty to his bank not to draw cheques in a negligent manner, if a cheque is raised because of the customer's carelessness, on the authority of the House of Lords in *London Joint Stock Bank Ltd* v. *Macmillan & Arthur*,[69] the bank will be able to debit his account for the full amount of the cheque as raised. Yet an acceptor, it will be remembered, was held in the case of *Scholfield* v. *Londesborough*,[70] also by the House of Lords, not to be liable for the full amount where his *acceptance* was raised. In the case of a bank, the customer has only himself to blame. If he wants to protect himself from potential fraud he should take more care in the drawing of the cheque, or, as did the prudent customer in *Wilson & Meeson* v. *Pickering*,[71] mark the cheque "not negotiable".

The drawer of a cheque may be able to refute his liability on the instrument if the fraudulent person has so tampered with the document that it becomes "materially altered" within s. 64(1) of the 1882 Act. The drawers in *Slingsby* v. *District Bank*[72] were able to disclaim liability where "the payee" had been fraudulently altered.

Finally, if a bill or cheque has been obtained as the result of "blackmail" (now a statutory offence), duress, or undue influence, then it has not been freely given and the drawer can disclaim liability; although difficult questions of fact will have to be tackled if these circumstances are to be proved.

10. *Lapse of time*

It will be a good defence to a claim by a holder of a bill of exchange that he has allowed time to go by without claiming payment.

If a bill of exchange is not presented for payment on the day it falls due, generally the drawer and indorsers will not thereafter be liable on it.[73] If the bill is payable on demand (as a cheque) presentment must be made within a

---

65. *R E Jones* v. *Waring & Gillow* [1926] AC 670.
66. As to which see the topic of "alterations" in Chap. 6.
67. As to which see "Alteration of cheques" in Chap. 13.
68. [1907] 1 KB 794.
69. [1918] AC 777.
70. [1896] AC 514.
71. [1946] KB 422.
72. [1932] 1 KB 544.
73. Bills of Exchange Act 1882, s. 45(1). There are two exceptions, as to which see *supra* p.51.

reasonable time after issue,[74] otherwise the drawer will be discharged. If the cheque has been indorsed, the indorser will be able to avoid liability if it is not presented for payment within a reasonable time of the indorsement.[75] What is a "reasonable time" in these circumstances is a question of fact of course, and all the facts of the particular case must be looked at, including the nature of the bill and the usage of trade with regard to similar bills.[76]

In considering the limitation of liability in this way it should be remembered that the drawer or an indorser (including a payee) will remain liable *to his immediate indorsee* on the contract between them for the full six-year period, while being discharged from his liability *on the bill* under s. 40 of the 1882 Act, after the elapse of a period which is deemed to go beyond what is reasonable to effect negotiation of the instrument.

Banks will not normally pay cheques which appear to have been in circulation for upwards of six months, treating them as being stale.

With regard to promissory notes, somewhat different rules apply. Ordinarily, presentment for payment is not necessary to render the maker of a note liable,[77] although it is to make an indorser liable.[78] It sometimes happens with a promissory note which is payable on demand that it remains in the hands of the holder a considerable time (as it is intended to do, often by way of security for a loan). In such a case, if payment is not claimed within six years of the date of the note, the holder will have no rights against the maker.[79] If the note has been indorsed, the indorser will not be liable if it is not presented within a reasonable time,[80] which as we saw above, is a question of fact.[81]

No action can be brought on a bill of exchange, unless a writ is issued within six years[82] of the accrual of the claim, under s. 5 of the Limitation Act 1980.

---

74. Bills of Exchange Act 1882, s. 45(2).
75. *Ibid.*, s. 45(2).
76. *Ibid.*, s. 45(2).
77. *Ibid.*, s. 87(1).
78. *Ibid.*, s. 87(2).
79. *Re British Trade Corp* [1932] 2 Ch 1.
80. Bills of Exchange Act 1882, s. 86(1).
81. *Ibid.*, s. 86(2).
82. *Ibid.* s. 86(2). The period of six years runs from the day *following* the accrual of the cause of action: *Radcliffe* v. *Bartholomew* [1892] 1 QB 161. In *Gelmini* v. *Moriggia* [1913] 2 KB 549, Channel J held that the period should run from the day the action accrued, but this was not followed by Havers J in *Marren* v. *Dawson Bentley & Co* [1961] 2 QB 135. See also, *Re Figgis* [1969] 1 Ch 123, *per* Megarry J (as he then was), quoting *Lester* v. *Garland* (1808) 15 Ves. 248, at p. 134G; and *Pritam Kaur* v. *Russel & Sorro Ltd* [1973] QB 336. It is not always easy to say exactly when a cause of action accrues. In tort it is when the actual damage (loss) is sustained; prospective loss is not enough: *First National Commercial Bank plc* v. *Humberts* [1995] 2 All ER 673, *per* Neill LJ, at p. 680e, a case involving loss to a bank because of an alleged negligent property valuation. The bank's claim in contract was statute barred as the action in that form accrued when the valuation was given: p. 679j. Again, for example, if a loan is repayable "on demand" there must be *a demand* as a condition precedent to recovery of the loan, and time only begins to run from the date of the demand being made: *Lloyds Bank Limited* v. *Margolis* [1954] 1 All ER 734; *Boot* v. *Boot, The Times*, 9 May 1996. Most actions relating to bills of exchange will, of course, be based in contract.

Unless the existence of the claim has been acknowledged by the proposed defendant in circumstances which would make the limitation period run afresh.[83] The action will accrue, in the case of a time bill or a bill payable after sight, from the date the bill falls due for payment; in the case of a bill payable on demand or at sight, time runs from the date of the instrument (or the date of its delivery if they are different) and *not* from the date when payment is demanded. If the action is against the drawee for non-acceptance or non-payment, time runs from the refusal.[84] However, if the action is by the drawer suing the drawee, time runs from the drawer suffering actual damage.[85]

Moreover, quite apart from the Limitation Act, if a claim on a bill becomes stale by the lapse of a considerable number of years, no action will lie.[86]

11. Estoppel

As we have seen, estoppel can operate to preclude a person from asserting rights which, by his conduct, he has led someone to believe will not be enforced. So that if a holder of a bill of exchange either expressly, or by implication, leads the drawer, or any other party to the bill, to believe the bill will not be enforced, he will be estopped thereafter from making any claim on the bill.

Obviously, if there is an express waiver of his rights by a holder, this will be a good defence to any subsequent claim.[87] If the waiver is to be implied by conduct, then obviously, difficult questions of evidence to prove the estoppel will arise.

The common law rule is that to operate, the representation must relate to existing facts: there could be no estoppel affecting representations as to *future* intentions.[88] So that, at common law, if a man promised not to take "any proceedings whatsoever" in respect of a judgment debt, if agreed instalments were met, he could still sue for interest on the debt, even if all the instalments had been paid.[89] This seemed a very harsh rule which could cause substantial injustice, and so equity came to the rescue, if at all possible, where it was inequitable to allow the right to be enforced. It is in this context that the doctrine of *equitable* estoppel is sometimes claimed to apply. It was explained by Lord Cairns in the following words[90]:

It is the first principle upon which all courts of equity proceed, that if parties who have entered into definite and distinct terms involving certain legal results, afterwards by their own act or with their own consent enter upon a course of negotiation which has

83. Limitation Act 1980, s. 29(7). See also *Spenser* v. *Hemmerde* [1922] 2 AC 507.
84. *Whitehead* v. *Walker* (1842) 11 LJ Ex 168.
85. *Huntley* v. *Sanderson* (1833) 2 LJ Ex 204.
86. *Per* Jessel MR in *Re Rutherford* (1880) 14 Ch D 687, at p. 692.
87. See Bills of Exchange Act 1882, s. 62.
88. *Jorden* v. *Money* (1854) 5 HLC 185.
89. *Foakes* v. *Beer* (1884) 9 App Cas 605.
90. *Hughes* v. *Metropolitan Rly* Co (1877) 2 App Cas 439, 448.

the effect of leading one of the parties to suppose that the strict rights arising under the contract will not be enforced, or will be kept in suspense, or held in abeyance, the person who otherwise might have enforced those rights will not be allowed to enforce them when it would be inequitable having regard to the dealings which have taken place between the parties.

The principle would apply, for example, if a landlord informed his tenant that the rent under the existing lease would be reduced. If the lower rent was then paid and accepted over the years the landlord could not, thereafter, claim the difference between the lower rent as paid and the rent referred to in the lease.[91] But not where a debtor says he can only pay a lesser sum or nothing. This is not equitable and if the creditor takes the lesser sum he can still sue for the balance, as there is no new *agreement* to accept less, but rather intimidation — accept less or nothing at all.[92] Consequently, particularly in commercial transactions where there has been no more than mere acts of indulgence, the courts have been slow to apply the principle.[93] It is, therefore, sometimes a fine dividing line between cases where the doctrine will be applicable, and where it will not. An example of a case where the rule was applied is

DURHAM FANCY GOODS LTD v. MICHAEL JACKSON (FANCY GOODS) LTD.[94]

D drew a 90-day bill on the defendant company, and sent it to them for acceptance. In doing so D mistakenly wrote on the bill "Accepted payable: Westminster Bank Ltd, 110 Regent Road Salford 5. For and on behalf of M Jackson (Fancy Goods) Ltd Manchester". When it was received, one of the directors, Mr Michael Jackson, signed his name below those words and returned the bill. The bill was dishonoured on presentation and the company went into liquidation. D sued both the company and Michael Jackson, claiming that he was personally liable in signing the bill on behalf of the company without the proper use of the company name. *Held*—that "M" is not an acceptable abbreviation of "Michael". D had placed the wrong name on the bill, and, therefore, was estopped from asserting its error in order to make Michael Jackson personally liable. D could not, therefore, recover.

THE TWO-CONTRACT LIABILITY

Two examples may be given to show the position where there may be conflicts between the liability under the original contract and on the bill of exchange involved with it.

The first example is where payment under a letter of credit is to be made by a bill of exchange. As we shall see below,[95] where a buyer of goods has agreed

---

91. *Central London Property Trust Ltd* v. *High Trees House Ltd* [1947] KB 130.

92. *D & C Builders Ltd* v. *Rees* [1966] 2 QB 617. See also *Ferguson v. Davies* [1997] 1 All ER 315 (CA), where acceptance of a cheque for a lesser sum held not to constitute an accord and satisfaction.

93. See Lord Simonds, *Tool Metal Manuf. Co. Ltd* v. *Tungsten Electric Co Ltd* [1955] 1 WLR 761, 764.

94. [1968] 2 QB 839.

95. *Infra* Chap. 15, "The Credit in Operation".

with the seller that the buyer's bank will irrevocably commit to accepting the seller's bill of exchange by way of payment for the goods, all parties to the bill remain liable on it even though there is a subsequent dispute between the buyer and the seller in respect of the goods or the terms of the main contract. In these circumstances, the buyer cannot prevent his bank from paying under the acceptance to the seller,[96] nor can he escape liability on the bill by attempting to show there is something wrong with the goods or the main supply contract.[97]

It will be noticed, therefore, that where, under the terms of a letter of credit, payment is to be effected by a bill of exchange in the way described above, then *three* contracts will be established: (a) the main supply contract between buyer and seller; and (b) the letter of credit issued by the buyer's bank to the seller; and (c) the contract on the bill of exchange.

In such a case, the parties to the credit can sue and be sued quite independently from any liability on the bill, and *vice versa*.[98]

Moreover, since it is usual in these cases for the seller to discount the bill once it is accepted by the buyer's bank, it will pass into the hands of a holder in due course, or holder for value, and will be enforceable by him, even though there is an ongoing dispute among the parties to the main supply contract, or the letter of credit.

A second example of this dual liability is under a hire-purchase or credit sale contract. It was quite common before the Consumer Credit Act 1974 for a person acquiring goods under a hire-purchase transaction to be asked to give promissory notes as security for the debt to the full amount of the goods, less the deposit. It was also common, for those notes to be discounted with finance houses. This meant that, if something went wrong with the goods or the terms of the hire-purchase agreement, the unfortunate "buyer" remained liable on the notes, even though he was able to return the goods under the terms of the agreement.[99]

With the passing of the Consumer Credit Act, new regulations were enacted in an attempt to protect people in such cases where they might otherwise have been liable on bills of exchange, where they enter into either hire-purchase agreements (when the relationship is that of debtor and creditor), or those of

96. *Hamzeh Malas & Sons* v. *British Imex Industries Ltd* [1958] 2 QB 127; *Power Curber International Ltd* v. *National Bank of Kuwait SAK* [1981] 1 WLR 1233. With the possible exception where there has been fraud on the part of the seller: *Discount Records Ltd* v. *Barclays Bank Ltd* [1975] 1 WLR 315; *Edward Owen Engineering Ltd* v. *Barclays Bank International Ltd* [1978] QB 159. However, see *Hong Kong and Shanghai Banking Corporation* v. *Kloeckner & Co AG* [1989] 3 All ER 513, where the bank claimed successfully to set off debts due to it from the defendant, against monies due *to* the defendant under a standby letter of credit. What seemed significant to Hirst J was that the sum being set off was a liquidated claim, and arose out of the "selfsame transactions"; at p. 522e.

97. *Banco di Roma* v. *Orru* [1973] 2 Lloyd's Rep. 505.

98. See for example, *Re Agra and Masterman's Bank* (1867) LR 2 Ch 391; and *Sassoon & Sons* v. *International Banking Corp* [1927] AC 730.

99. *Acceptance Co Ltd* v. *Cutner* (1964) SJ 298.

simple hire (when the relationship is that of owner and hirer). These new regulations apply if the transaction is covered by a "regulated agreement".[100] Yet, in spite of this new legislation, it is still possible for a dual liability to arise.

The new rules state that the only way the creditor/owner (depending on the type of transaction) can lawfully receive payment is by cash or cheque. He cannot lawfully receive payment by any other kind of negotiable instrument, for example, a promissory note;[101] and if payment is by cheque he must pay it straight into his bank, and not negotiate it.[102] Nor must he take a negotiable instrument by way of security in such circumstances.[103]

The Act recognizes, however, that bills of exchange may still be demanded notwithstanding the new regulations, because it is provided that, "Nothing in the Act affects the rights of the holder in due course of any negotiable instrument",[104] but anyone who takes a negotiable instrument in contravention of these rules cannot be a holder in due course, nor can he "enforce the instrument".[105] This presumably means "with knowledge of the contravention", because the statute goes on to provide[106] that if a "protected person" should become liable to a holder in due course (that is, someone who takes without knowledge of the contravention) the creditor/owner " . . . shall indemnify the protected person in respect of that liability".[107]

There is clearly intended to be a liability on the bill, however, and the unfortunate hirer/buyer will presumably have to pay out before seeking his indemnity. The indemnity may be questionable also, depending entirely on the status of the creditor/owner.

Both the above circumstances are examples showing how the liability on the bill is independent of the terms agreed between the parties in their main

---

100. That is, one made by a private individual, where the amount of the credit does not exceed £15,000: see ss. 8 and 9 of the Consumer Credit Act 1974 and the Consumer Credit (Increase of Monetary Limits) Order 1983, SI 1983/1878. After any contravention of these regulations, the agreement cannot be enforced except by order of the court: s. 124(1) and (2).

101. Consumer Credit Act 1974, s. 123(1). Except consumer hire agreements made in connection with trade goods hired in the course of the hirer's business between the UK and a country outside the UK, or between countries outside the UK: Consumer Credit (Negotiable Instruments) (Exemption) Order 1984, SI 1984/435.

102. Ibid., s. 123(2). An attempted negotiation of a cheque in these circumstances would constitute a defect in his title within the meaning of the Bills of Exchange Act 1882: Consumer Credit Act 1974, s. 125(2).

103. Consumer Credit Act 1974, s. 123(3). It will be deemed to have been taken by way of security if the sum due under the agreement is to be paid in some other way than by the negotiable instrument, and it is to be presented for payment only if the agreed sum is not paid in that other way: Consumer Credit Act 1974, s. 123(4).

104. Ibid., s. 125(4).

105. Ibid., s. 125(1).

106. Ibid., s. 125(3).

107. The subsection speaks of the holder in due course taking from the protected person. It would be essential for the negotiable instrument to be *negotiated* to the holder in due course; taking direct from the protected person as payee, would not render the holder a holder in due course, whether he knew of the contravention of the Act or not.

agreement, but before leaving the topic some other anomalies which can arise with this possible dual liability must be noted.

It will be apparent from all that has been said, that the requirements needed to form the original contract (that is, capacity, consideration, and so forth) are, in fact, needed twice: once to form the original contract, and secondly to support the contract on the bill. In the vast majority of cases, if there is a valid agreement under the *original* contract, there will equally be a valid and enforceable contract on the bill: but not always. The situation must not be taken for granted. The enforceability of the one contract must not be confused with the validity of the other.

Take for example the case of

CHURCHILL v. GODDARD[108]

Churchills were timber brokers and *del credere* agents for a Finnish exporter—Raahes. They negotiated a contract for the supply of timber from Raahes to Goddards, and a formal agreement was entered into between Raahes and Goddards. Churchills paid Raahes the full contract price in accordance with the *del credere* agency—that is, before Churchills received payment from Goddards. The shipping documents were sent by Raahes to Churchills, and Churchills, in turn, drew two bills with themselves (Churchills) as payees, and then sent the bills to Goddards for acceptance. Goddards duly complied. When the timber arrived Goddards rejected it as not being up to standard, and thereupon refused to honour its acceptances. Churchills sued Goddards on the bills. Goddards contended that there was no contract on the bills between them and Churchills who were merely agents for Raahes and could not themselves bring an action on the bills (Raahes not being able to sue, as they had been paid). *Held*—that Churchills " . . . were in no sense trustees or agents for Raahes when they sought to recover on the bills",[109] and consequently, Churchills were entitled to recover, leaving Goddards to sort out the position wih Raahes as to the unacceptability of the timber under the original contract.[110]

Take as another example the case of an infant. We have already seen he has limited liability on a bill of exchange; yet if the original contract related, say, to the purchase of goods necessary for his upkeep, he is liable to pay for them. In short, he has no capacity under the contract on the bill, but *has* as regards the original contract.[111]

Again the original contract may not be enforceable between the parties, yet a bill of exchange given to a third party as agent for one of the original

108. [1937] 1 KB 92.

109. *Per* Lord Roche, *ibid.*, p. 104.

110. It had also been argued that there had been a total failure of consideration. The error here was that—if there had been—it related not to the contract on the bills, but to the contract to supply the timber (of which Churchills were not party). In the words of Scott LJ (p. 111), "I see no ground whatever for the contention that there was any failure of the consideration contained in or given for the bill of exchange contract—which is the only consideration that is material to the action on the bill".

111. Conversely, if an infant "contracted" a debt for which he had no capacity he is deemed still to have no capacity for a bill drawn to satisfy the debt even after he attains his majority: *Smith v. King* [1892] 2 QB 543.

contracting parties is, and it appears not to matter that the agent will then presumably hand the money over to his principal.[112]

Take another example[113]:

R agrees with C to act as its distributor and to purchase C's goods. Their agreement is reduced to writing and includes a clause which provides: "this arrangement is not entered into, nor is this memorandum written as a formal or legal agreement and shall not be subject to legal jurisdiction in the law courts . . . " if a dispute arises. The contract will be unenforceable because of the express clause referred to.

The contract is, of course, not enforceable. However, what would be the position of a bill of exchange given in pursuance of this non-enforceable contract? As we have seen, there are *two* contracts; there is no liability under the original contract, but might not the bill of exchange be enforceable?

The only reason the original contract was not enforceable was the lack of intent to create legal relations—all other requirements including consideration being present. Consequently, no such defect should surely affect the contract on the bill, as by giving a bill a drawer must be taken to intend "legal relations", unless there is overwhelming evidence to the contrary; as by drawing a bill the drawer engages that it will, among other things, be paid and if it is not, that he will compensate the holder or any indorser who has to pay it.[114] The drawer would certainly be liable to a holder in due course.

A similar difficulty must arise where a company enters into a contract *ultra vires* the power given it by its constitution. For example, if a company has powers to carry on the business of "entertainments services" and it undertakes the running of a pig farm, clearly a contract in pursuance of this end is unenforceable.[115] But what of bills of exchange signed on behalf of the company to further this void contract?

Certainly, money borrowed by the company and securities signed are not enforceable, being tainted by the *ultra vires* nature of the company's activities, for " . . . the borrowing is not an end in itself and must be for some purpose of the company".[116] The suggestion is manifest, therefore, that as between the immediate parties a bill given by the company could not be enforced, and perhaps even between remote parties.

Because of this two-tier liability, it does not matter that a cheque given had been cleared, paid (that is the funds are passed from the payee bank to the collecting bank) and discharged in accordance with s. 59(1) of the Bill of Exchange Act 1882, as if the payee or indorsee (that is, the customer of the collecting bank) had no title to the cheque, the drawer may be able to recover the money from the collecting bank.

112. *Pollway v. Abdullah* [1974] 1 WLR 493.
113. The facts are based on those in *Rose & Frank v. Crompton Bros* [1923] 2 KB 261.
114. Bills of Exchange Act 1882, s. 55(1).
115. *Introductions Ltd v. National Provincial Bank* [1969] 2 WLR 791.
116. *Ibid.*, p. 795G.

The reasoning behind this rule was explained by Lord Greene MR in the celebrated case of *Re Diplock*,[117] which involved gifts by will to various charities, which were subsequently discovered to be invalid and the deceased's next of kin claimed to recover the money:

This "money" when "paid" was in the form of a cheque on the executorship account, i.e. a negotiable instrument. This negotiable instrument at the moment preceding its delivery to the charity belonged to the residuary estate of the testator and any of the next of kin, if he had known of the situation, could have secured an injunction restraining the executors from delivering it to the charity . . . The charity accepted the cheque . . . as a volunteer. The first stage, therefore, was that the charity had in its possession a negotiable instrument which in origin belonged to the residuary estate and in which the next-of-kin were, in the eyes of equity, interested. If the next-of-kin had been in a position to interfere at that stage they could . . . clearly . . . have recovered the cheque . . . But the cheque was in fact paid into a banking account in the name of the charity. The next-of-kin claim to follow their "money".[118]

Money can be followed or traced in this way provided: (i) the recipient of the money is a volunteer. If he gave consideration for the cheque, the drawer will not be able to recover; (ii) the money has not become so confused and mixed up with the recipient's own money as to be totally unidentifiable.[119]

This is, of course, a question of degree, and difficult questions of fact must often be resolved in attempting to establish whether the mixing with the recipient's own money is such as to make recovery impossible. It does not matter, for example, that the two moneys have been paid into the same bank account, or have passed through more than one bank account.

BANQUE BELGE v. HAMBROUCK[120]

H was employed by P, who banked with the Banque Belge. H fraudulently drew cheques on this account in his own favour and paid them into his account with another bank, which obtained collection in the usual way. H lived with S and from time to time gave her money (in the form of cheques) which she paid into her account with yet a third bank. The fraud was discovered and the Banque Belge claimed to recover such part of the moneys as at that time stood to the credit of S at her bankers. *Held*—that the bank was entitled to recover from S as she gave no consideration for the money from H, other than the illicit cohabiting which was, of course, no consideration.

Tracing money in this way is not possible, however, if the money has been spent, for example, by use as living expenses, payment of debts and so forth.

---

117. [1948] 1 Ch 465.
118. [1948] 1 Ch 465, at p. 521. " . . . tracing claims depend not on equitable ownership as such but on the concept of an equitable charge": *per* Robert Walker J, *El Ajou* v. *Dollar Land Holdings plc* [1995] 2 All ER 213, 223b citing Millett J ([1993] 3 All ER 717, 736), "Equity's power to charge a mixed fund with the repayment of trust moneys . . . enables the claimants to follow the money, not because it is theirs, but because it is derived from a fund which is treated as if it were subject to a charge in their favour."
119. *Bank Tejarat* v. *Hong Kong and Shanghai Banking Corporation (CI) Ltd* [1995] 1 Lloyd's Rep. 239 at p. 245.
120. [1921] 1 KB 321.

However, where money is in a bank account in this way, it is presumed, under the rule in *Re Hallett's Estate*,[121] that the customer (that is, the recipient of the money) draws on his own money in the account first. This means the money in the account may still be in existence or at least part of it, and capable of being traced.

Once money has been used to purchase property, the problems of tracing it are exceedingly difficult, and a consideration of these problems is outside the scope of this work.

It may, of course, be possible to obtain the return of moneys wrongly paid even if, strictly speaking, tracing is not possible. This is by virtue of the common law doctrine of money had and received, or pursuant to the equitable doctrine of restitution if the money has been paid away without the owner's consent, and it is in the hands of someone who knows or should have known of the want of consent.

For example, in

INTERNATIONAL SALES AND AGENCIES v. MARCUS[122]

A Mr Fancy and a Mr Munsey were business colleagues and close friends. Mr Fancy needed a loan and Mr Munsey recommended he approach a Mr Marcus who was a moneylender. A loan of £30,000 was made by Mr Marcus's company. Subsequently, Mr Fancy became seriously ill, and he told Mr Marcus that if anything happened to him, Mr Munsey would see that the loan was repaid. Mr Fancy died, and it was discovered that his estate was insolvent. Mr Munsey then repaid the debt by drawing in total five cheques on the bank accounts of companies of which he was a director, and which were previously owned by Mr Fancy, and now formed part of his estate. No doubt Mr Munsey repaid the debt in this way as being the only method by which he could satisfy the obligation of his now deceased colleague. When the facts became known, the companies sued Mr Marcus and his company for return of the money. *Held*—the repayments by Mr Munsey were in breach of his fiduciary duties to the companies whose money it was[123] and Mr Marcus knew this, ". . . at the very least Mr Marcus was turning a blind eye to the obvious".[124]

Restitution may also be claimed where money has been paid by one party to another under a contract which is subsequently found to be void *ab initio* as being *ultra vires* one of the parties. The most outstanding recent examples are

---

121. (1880) 13 Ch D 696. The old common law rule as stated in *Clayton's Case* (1816) 1 Mer. 572 was that money in a bank account was deemed to be withdrawn on a first in, first out basis. If no question of invoking the principles of equity arises, the rule in *Clayton's Case* still applies of course. See *Re Yeovil Glove Co* [1964] 2 All ER 849, and *Re James Rutherford Ltd* [1964] 3 All ER 137, both cases involving the liquidation of companies and the claims on moneys in their bank accounts. See also *Barlow Clowes International Ltd (in Liquidation)* v. *Vaughan* [1992] 4 All ER 22, where *Clayton's Case* principles were not applied. The method of distribution being on a *pari passu* basis: at p. 33g to j.
122. [1982] 3 All ER 551.
123. *Ibid.*, p. 557f.
124. *Ibid.*, p. 558h.

the line of cases involving so-called swaps, which are transactions involving the parties, in effect gambling[125] that interest rates would fall, in which case one party would make a profit, but they would incur losses if interest rates rose. A number of local authorities entered the market in the belief that these transactions would be beneficial to their funding, and made swap agreements with numerous banks. However, the district auditor of the Hammersmith and Fulham Council challenged the legality of these transactions, and in *Hazell v. Hammersmith and Fulham London Borough Council*[126] the Court of Appeal held that these transactions were tainted with the improper purposes of speculative trading and were *ultra vires* the council's powers.

There then followed claims by banks and councils for return of moneys paid by one to the other under these " . . . purported contracts . . . " which were " . . . from the start wholly void".[127]

In *Westdeutsche Landesbank Girozentrale v. Islington London Borough Council*[128] the bank was entitled to have returned to it the money they had paid the council, and in *South Tyneside Metropolitan Borough Council v. Svenska International plc*,[129] the council recovered money it had paid to the bank, but the council had to pay another bank on another swap transaction in *Kleinwort Benson Ltd v. South Tyneside Metropolitan Borough Council*.[130]

In these cases, it is not always clear what are the legal grounds for the return of the money. On the one hand, it has been stated that one party or the other had been "unjustly enriched",[131] while on the other[132] it has been stated to be the old common law remedy of money had and received.[133]

Finally, it must be remembered that the giving of a bill of exchange can be evidence of an obligation between the parties, and even though the payee could not sue on the bill, he may still be able to recover under the terms of the original transaction.

For example,

125. However, they are not contracts by way of gaming or wagering: *Morgan Grenfell & Co Ltd v. Welwyn Hatfield District Council* [1995] 1 All ER 1.

126. [1995] 3 All ER 33.

127. *Westdeutsche Landesbank Girozentrale v. Islington London Borough Council* [1994] 4 All ER 890, *per* Hobhouse J, at p. 915b. See now [1996] 2 All ER 961 (HL).

128. [1994] 4 All ER 890.

129. [1995] 1 All ER 545.

130. [1994] 4 All ER 972.

131. *Per* Leggatt LJ, in *Westdeutsche Landesbank Girozentrale v. Islington London Borough Council* [1994] 4 All ER 890, 967c.

132. *Sinclair v. Brougham* [1914] AC 398.

133. Lord Ellenborough stated in *Hudson v. Robinson* (1816) 104 ER 910 at p. 911: " . . . an action for money had and received is maintainable whenever the money of one man has, without consideration, got into the pocket of another." For an "historical perspective" of the subject see *per* Hobhouse J, *Westdeutsche Landesbank Girozentrale v. Islington London Borough Council* [1994] 4 All ER 890, 912d *et seq.*

SHAMIA v. JOORY[134]

J carried on a business as a merchant in Manchester. His representative in Iraq was Y. Y's brother S also lived in England. Various transactions took place between J and Y and when moneys were owing from J, Y asked that £500 should be given by J to S instead of it being remitted to Iraq. J thereupon sent a cheque for this amount to S. There was some irregularity in the drawing of the cheque, and the cheque was returned to J when it was agreed that J would either alter the original or issue a new cheque. Because of the business dealings between J and Y, J ceased to be indebted to Y before the new cheque was issued and—not unnaturally—J did not issue a new cheque or correct the original, as his debt to Y had been cleared. S then sued J for £500 as money had and received. *Held*—that J was liable to S, as at the time the cheque was given J had funds over which he had a right of disposal, however temporary. He was not bound to comply with Y's request, still less, to make any promise of payment (the cheque) to S, and as he did he had only himself to blame.[135] It did not matter that S gave no consideration,[136] and could not, therefore, have sued on the bill.

Cases such as these do not arise very often; however, they do occur from time to time, and are a reminder that when a bill of exchange is introduced to a transaction a new and distinct legal relationship is created, sometimes with surprising results.

SUMMARY

In conclusion, it may be helpful to attempt a summary of the present state of the law.

1. The giver of a bill of exchange is always liable on a bill as cash to his immediate transferee

Except:

  (a) if there has been a *total* failure of consideration; or
  (b) the consideration proved to be illegal; or
  (c) the original contract is subject to statutory control affecting bills of exchange given in respect of it.

or possibly:

  (d) if there is a "special case" where the original contract and the contract on the bill are "sufficiently connected"; or
  (e) the counterclaim is a liquidated sum.

---

134. [1958] 1 QB 448. For some interesting conclusions see J D Davies (1959) 75 LQR 220.
135. Barry J, *ibid.*, p. 459.
136. *Ibid.*, p. 458.

Note: It is unlikely an action on the bill will be stayed while a counterclaim is pursued, but see *supra* the discussion under the heading "Partial failure of consideration".

2. The giver of a bill of exchange is always liable on the bill as cash to a remote party

Except:

- (a) if the consideration proved to be illegal, and no *new* consideration has been given; or
- (b) (possibly) if there is some statutory control affecting bills given in respect of the original contract.

CHAPTER 6

THE LACK OF REAL CONSENT

All agreements involve the parties consenting to be bound by the terms of their bargain. It must follow, therefore, that if there is no consent, there can be no agreement. Life is not quite so straightforward, however, and particularly where bills of exchange are concerned. It may be that a cheque has been given in circumstances where the recipient has defrauded the drawer. In such cases, the drawer consents to giving the cheque, but the consent would not have been forthcoming if he had known all the facts. Then again, cheques may have been obtained under threats of blackmail, and that clearly is not consent. These more subtle methods may well be too slow for some and they resort to direct action by committing forgery.

In all these cases, the recipient has obtained the benefit of the bill by some act, which, if illegal, might well also be a crime, and he cannot get a good title to the bill, of course. But the position with innocent third parties is not always so clear, however.

Each of these cases must now be considered under the following headings:

(1) Forgery.
(2) Fraud.
(3) Blackmail, Duress and Undue Influence.

1. FORGERY

Forgery is the crime of the making of a false document in order that it may be used as genuine.[1]

Section 24 of the Bills of Exchange Act 1882 provides that:

where a signature on a bill is forged . . . the forged signature is wholly inoperative, and no right to retain the bill or to give a discharge therefor or to enforce payment thereof against any party thereto can be acquired through or under that signature, unless the

---

1. Forgery and Counterfeiting Act 1981, s. 1.

party against whom it is sought to retain or enforce payment of the bill is precluded from setting up the forgery . . .

There are three signatures which can be forged.

(a) The drawer's

If the drawer's signature has been forged the document cannot be a bill at all, as s. 3 of the 1882 Act says that a bill is "an unconditional order in writing *signed by the person giving it* . . . " which would obviously not be the case if the drawer's signature were forged.

(b) An indorser's

While the forgery of an indorser's signature is itself a nullity it will not affect the validity of the bill. Take an example. Suppose a bill is drawn "Pay S. Smith or Order.   B. Brown". Smith now has the bill and suppose someone takes the bill and forges Smith's indorsement "Pay J. Jones or Order.   S. Smith". Jones now has the bill (presumably in good faith) and suppose he indorses it "Pay B. Black or Order.   J. Jones". Black now has the bill to which he has, in fact, no title, due to Smith's signature being forged. The bill remains payable to Smith to whom it must be returned, leaving all the parties to recover down the line until the loss should rest with whoever forged Smith's indorsement—if he can be found and is worth suing!

(c) The acceptor's

Where an acceptor's signature is forged this is of no great moment so far as *validity of the bill* is concerned. It means only that the bill has not been accepted and proper presentment must be made.

It is also important to consider whether the forgery is discovered before or after payment of the bill.

(A) Before payment

If the forgery is discovered in time the bill will no doubt be dishonoured.

It is then always possible for the holder to recover from his *immediate indorser* who will then recover from his indorser and so on. More usually, in practice, the holder will try to recover from the drawer (by-passing the intervening indorsers) if he can.[2]

However, as we saw in the example above, if one of the indorsements is forged the chain of liability will be broken and there will be no connection

2. Bills of Exchange Act 1882, s. 55(2)(a).

between the drawer and the holder. In such a case, the holder, if a holder in due course, may recover from all persons who became parties *after* the forgery, as an indorser by indorsing a bill is precluded (that is estopped) from denying to a holder in due course the genuineness and regularity in all respects of the drawer's signature and *all* previous indorsements.[3] It will be remembered that by indorsing a bill one guarantees that all signatures on the bill prior to one's own are valid and genuine.

If the bill has been accepted, the acceptor is not liable to a holder *after* the forgery of an indorsement;[4] but is always liable to pay out if it is the drawer's signature which has been forged.[5]

(B) After payment

If payment has already been made before the forgery is discovered, the problem resolves itself as to whether the acceptor can recover money paid in good faith to an innocent holder.

This depends on whether it is the drawer's or indorser's signature which has been forged:

(i) If the drawer's signature has been forged, the acceptor cannot recover, as by accepting the bill he is precluded from denying to a holder in due course,[6] the genuineness of the drawer's signature.[7]

(ii) If it is an indorser's signature which has been forged, the acceptor will be able to recover, leaving the holder to recover from his indorser and so on down the line, until the unfortunate victim of the fraud bears the loss, unless he can find the forger and sue him, for money received *male fide* can always be recovered if the culprit can be found.[8]

Banks

Where banks pay *cheques* where there have been forged signatures, different considerations apply, and these are dealt with below in Chapter 13.

If the document is a *time bill*, the acceptor, upon acceptance, can, as we have seen, have it presented for payment at his place of business, or his home, or at his bankers. If it is to be at his bank, as it usually will, the holder must then present the bill at that bank.[9] Bills accepted this way are, as we have also seen, called "domicils".

---

3. *Ibid.*, s. 55(2)(*b*).
4. *Ibid.*, s. 54(2)(*c*).
5. *Ibid.*, s. 54(2)(*a*).
6. He could, however, recover from a holder for value.
7. Bills of Exchange Act 1882, s. 54(2)(*a*).
8. *Kendal v. Wood* (1870) LR 6 Ex 243.
9. *Gibb v. Mather* (1832) 1 LJ Ex 87.

Domicils are paid in the usual way; however, if the bank pays anyone but the true owner, they will be liable to their customer, as the protection afforded by the 1882 Act[10] applies only to cheques; so that if the bank paid out to someone who had a defective title, they could not debit their customer's account, and could be compelled to pay again to the true owner.

For example, in

ROBARTS v. TUCKER[11]

X accepted a bill and domiciled it for payment at his bank. There were a number of indorsements on the bill, one of which proved to be a forgery. The bank did not know this and paid out in good faith. *Held*—they were liable and could not debit X's account.

It follows from this that bankers will insist upon an indemnity from their customers before paying domicils.

Bearer bills

If an indorsement is forged on a bearer bill this has no effect, as any indorsement on a bearer bill is not essential and the title of the holder is unaffected.

Dishonour

If a bill is dishonoured, as we have seen, it is possible for the holder to recover from his immediate indorser and so on down the line, or recover from the drawer, *provided* the chain of liability is complete. If there is a forged indorsement there will be no link between the holder and the drawer, consequently, the holder will be able to recover from the indorsers *after* the forgery, with the exception of the acceptor. If, of course, the acceptor has paid the bill before the forged indorsement is discovered, the rightful owner can enforce payment again.

If the drawer's signature is forged and the bill passes through various hands and is then accepted, although there is no valid bill, the acceptor remains tied to the holder and is liable for payment as though there had been no forgery.

Estoppel

It will be remembered that s. 24 of the Bills of Exchange Act 1882 provides that a forged signature is "wholly inoperative" for all purposes, "unless the party against whom it is sought to retain or enforce payment of the bill is precluded from setting up the forgery . . . "

10. Bills of Exchange Act 1882, s. 60.
11. (1851) 16 QB 560.

If a man knows that his signature has been forged and by his actions or his silence willingly leads others to believe that the forgery is his genuine signature he cannot later plead his signature was forged. In short, he will be *estopped* from denying the signature to be his. For example,

GREENWOOD v. MARTINS BANK[12]

Mrs G forged her husband's signature and drew money from his account on various occasions. He knew of this but Mrs G persuaded him not to tell the bank or do anything about it. Finally Mrs G committed suicide and then Mr G sued the bank for recovery of the money paid to the wife. *Held*—that as he had, by his silence, led the bank to believe the forgeries were his genuine signatures he was estopped from denying them to be genuine and he could not recover.

Contrast:

LEWES LAUNDRY CO v. BARCLAY & CO[13]

The company had three directors. The son of one was the company secretary. Some years before, the father knew his son had forged his (the father's) signature, but otherwise had led a blameless life. The son, as company secretary, had charge of all the books, cheque books and so forth. The son then embarked on a series of frauds by forging one of the other director's signatures to cheques which were duly paid by the bank. The forgeries were finally discovered and the company sued the bank for return of the money paid out under the forged signatures. The bank claimed that the company was estopped by virtue of the father's knowledge that his son had been guilty of forgery before. *Held*—that the knowledge of one director was not knowledge of all. There was no estoppel and the company could recover.

2. FRAUD[14]

So far as bills of exchange are concerned, fraud may operate in two ways. First, it may affect the original contract, that is, where the drawer is persuaded to give, say, a cheque in circumstances which but for the fraud (likely some persuasive story), he would not have done. In such cases of what we may call "general" fraud, an innocent recipient of the money will get no title to it, and will have to return any money received, unless he can show he was a holder in due course of the instrument. If he cannot prove this status, he gets no title to the bill. It will be remembered that the unfortunate payee of the cheque in

12. [1933] AC 51. See also *Brown v. Westminster Bank* [1964] 2 Lloyd's Rep.187. It may be, however, that the paying bank can recover the money from the recipient, if the money is still in his possession, as money paid under a mistake of fact, see *National Westminster Bank Ltd v. Barclays Bank International Ltd* [1975] QB 654.

13. (1906) 95 LT 444.

14. When we speak of "Fraud" in this context we mean common law fraud: *Osterreichische Lunderbank v. S Elite Ltd* [1980] 3 WLR 356.

R E Jones v. *Waring & Gillow*,[15] had to refund the money; and the equally unfortunate indorsee in *Wilson & Meeson* v. *Pickering*,[16] had to do likewise.

The second way in which fraud can affect a transaction involving bills of exchange is where the fraud affects the instrument itself. This, in turn, usually can be subdivided into two types of case: (1) where the fraudulent person tells a fairy story and persuades the person signing that the document is not a bill of exchange at all—in other words, where the instrument is mistakenly signed; and (2) where the fraudulent person alters or tampers with the bill *after* it is signed.

(1) Bills mistakenly signed

No person is liable as drawer, indorser or acceptor of a bill who has not signed it *as such*.[17] It is a well-established principle that where someone signs a document of a *totally different kind* to that which he thinks he is signing, there is, in principle, no liability, and the signature is valueless. The signature is *non est factum* (not of his making).

Consequently to avoid liability on a bill of exchange (or any other document for that matter) the person signing must:

(a) be mistaken fundamentally as to the nature of the document he signed; and
(b) not have been careless.[18]

Both points turn on questions of fact, and the burden of proof is, of course, on the person disclaiming. This is so even if the signature is induced by fraud.[19] For example, take the cases of:

FOSTER v. MACKINNON[20]

X presented a paper to Y and said it was a form of guarantee, and asked Y to sign it. It was, in fact a bill of exchange and Y's signature appeared as an indorsement. The bill was negotiated to Z who took in good faith and for value. Z sued Y. *Held*—that Y was

15. [1926] AC 670. An acceptance on a bill obtained by fraudulent representations can be avoided by the acceptor if he repudiates his acceptance as soon as the fraud is discovered: *Ayres* v. *Moore* [1939] 4 All ER 351.
16. [1946] KB 422.
17. Bills of Exchange Act 1882, s. 23.
18. It is sometimes said that he must not have been guilty of "negligence": but this is not a proper term to express the situation. With "negligence" there must be a duty owed not to be negligent, whereas "careless" only indicates that standard of indifference of which a man has been guilty in signing the document.
19. *Saunders* v. *Anglia Building Society (Gallie* v. *Lee)* [1971] AC 1004, where the law is exhaustively reviewed and *Carlisle & Cumberland Bank* v. *Bragg* [1911] 1 KB 489 overruled. See also *R.* v. *Davies* [1982] 1 All ER 513, where the manager of a home in which two old ladies resided, persuaded them to indorse cheques in blank and give them to him, without their knowing the pieces of paper were cheques.
20. (1869) LR 4 CP 704.

not liable. He had not been careless and had signed a document of a totally different nature.

LEWIS v. CLAY[21]

X produced to C a document entirely covered with blotting paper except for some spaces cut in it. X said the document contained a private family matter, and all C was required to do was to sign his name as a witness, in the spaces cut in the blotting paper. In fact the hidden document was a promissory note for a large sum of money in favour of L. In due time C refused payment to L who sued. *Held*—that C was not liable as he believed he was signing a paper of an entirely different kind to that which it turned out to be.

It follows from all this that if a man signs a bill of exchange *knowing it is a bill* the signature will be sufficient to validate the document, and it does not matter that the signature was induced by fraud, or the amount is wrong, or he did not intend the transferor to obtain title.

(2) Alterations

Where a bill is *materially*[22] altered, in almost every case there will be an element of fraud whereby the person making the alteration attempts to gain from his dishonesty. It will, of course, also be a crime.

If *all* the parties to the bill do not consent to an alteration (and they rarely will) they are excused from all liability, and the holder will be left to his remedies, which will depend upon whether the alteration was apparent or not. For example:

A draws a bill for £1,000 payable to B which is accepted by Z. The bill is then negotiated to C who alters the amount to £10,000 and negotiates it to D who in turn passes it on to E and then to F, the holder.

F's rights will depend on whether the alteration was *apparent* (that is, a poor alteration) or *not apparent* (that is, a clever alteration).

If apparent

He can recover from C (the person who made the alteration), D and E (the subsequent indorsers) the full £10,000.[23] F has no right against A, B or Z as, in the words of the Act, they had not "made, authorized, or assented to the alteration".[24]

---

21. (1897) 67 LJ QB 224.
22. As to what is material see *infra* under the heading "Alteration" in Chap. 7.
23. Bills of Exchange Act 1882, s. 64(1). The liability of D and E is based on the fact that they would see the bill for £10,000 at the time they signed and were, presumably, prepared to make themselves liable for this sum. They would also see the apparent alteration and again, presumably, were nevertheless prepared to put their names to the bill.
24. Bills of Exchange Act 1882, s. 64(1).

If not apparent

F can recover from C, D and E the full £10,000 as before. But if he is a holder in due course, he can recover the original £1,000 from A, B or Z.

In practice F would recover £10,000 from E who would then recover from D who would be left to seek out C. If D could not recover from C, D's only course would be to recover on the original tenor of £1,000 from A, B or Z. D would thereby lose £9,000.

Alteration of cheques

Where cheques have been altered different considerations apply, and these are dealt with later in Chapter 13.

3. BLACKMAIL, DURESS AND UNDUE INFLUENCE

Blackmail and duress, although similar, are not the same thing; and duress and undue influence are also similar, but again, not entirely the same thing.

(a) Blackmail

Blackmail is a statutory offence[25] where a person " . . . with a view to gain for himself or another or with intent to cause loss to another makes an unwarranted demand *with menaces* . . . "[26] What consists of "menaces" is not defined, but the *Concise Oxford Dictionary* says the word "menace" means "threat", and the word "threat" is stated to be "such menace of bodily hurt or injury to reputation or property as may restrain a person's freedom of action". The notion of "blackmail" is clear enough, and all such threats are "unwarranted" unless there are reasonable grounds for making the demand, and the use of "menaces" is considered by the court to be a proper means of reinforcing the demand. One can easily conceive of "menaces" that could in no way be deemed "reasonable". However, the exception is to cover legitimate demands for payments and so forth.[27]

(b) Duress

On the other hand, duress is a common law concept that is wide enough[28] to cover threats of violence to the person (but not property), as might the crime

25. Theft Act 1968, s. 21(1).
26. Author's italics.
27. See also s. 40 of the Administration of Justice Act 1970 which makes it an offence to harass a debtor.
28. A number of the older cases of duress could now fall under the crime of "blackmail". For example, extorting money: *Treacy v. DPP* [1971] 1 All ER 110—a prosecution under s. 21 of the Theft Act 1968; threatening to withhold or change testimony unless payment is received: *R v. Clear* [1968] 1 All ER 74; threats of violence: *Talbot v. Von Boris* [1911] 1 KB 854.

of "blackmail", but with the difference that it can *never* be "reasonable", if it is present in any transaction.[29]

For example, in *Société Des Hotels* v. *Hawker*,[30] where an unfortunate tourist was threatened with arrest in Paris unless he gave a cheque (in English form), the hoteliers could not recover on it. This is a good example of duress, but it would almost certainly not be blackmail, if for no other reason than the circumstances happened abroad.

In the case of both blackmail and duress it would negative consent, and hence there could be no agreement, and the payee of any cheque or other bill given in consequence of such menaces, threats or whatever, would get no title to it; and, if a bill is obtained in this way and is then purportedly negotiated, even a subsequent innocent holder will get no title to it, unless he can prove that someone, after the wrongful act, gave value in good faith for the bill.[31]

The burden of proof that duress has influenced the transaction is still on the defendant, however, in spite of the terms of s. 30(2) of the Bills of Exchange Act 1882. So that if a wife signs a bill of exchange under threats of violence from her husband, she will nevertheless, be liable on the bill if she does not prove the payee knew of the duress at the time the bill was issued.[32]

(c) Undue influence

Undue influence was evolved by equity to cover cases where, unlike duress, there had been no violence or threats, but simply a possible interference with the free judgment of one of the parties. The concept would apply, for example, where, as the term implies, the drawer of a bill is not able to exercise the necessary degree of freedom of action, because he is subjected to pressure or inhibiting factors by some other party.

If there is an existing relationship between the parties, then the influence will be presumed: this is the case between parent and child,[33] religious adviser and follower,[34] doctor and patient,[35] trustee and *cestui que trust*;[36] but not, it seems, husband and wife.[37] Where such relationships exist, any cheques or bills of exchange delivered, or property transferred or securities given, can be set aside and the transactions rescinded, the burden of proof being on the beneficiary of the cheque or bill to show there was *no* undue influence.

---

29. For a review of the circumstances of duress, see *Lynch* v. *DPP for Northern Ireland* [1975] 1 All ER 913.
30. (1913) 29 TLR 578.
31. Bills of Exchange Act 1882, ss. 29(2) and 30(2).
32. *Talbot* v. *Von Boris* [1911] 1 KB 854.
33. *Lancashire Loans Ltd* v. *Black* [1934] 1 KB 380.
34. *Allcard* v. *Skinner* (1887) 36 ChD 145.
35. *Re CMG* [1970] Ch 574.
36. *Ellis* v. *Barker* (1871) 7 Ch App 104.
37. *Bank of Montreal* v. *Stuart* [1911] AC 120.

If there is no relationship in this way, then the burden of proof is on the party who wishes to set the transaction aside, to show he has been coerced into the course of action of which he complains. The leading case is *Williams* v. *Bayley*,[38] where a father mortgaged property to a bank to secure the return of promissory notes given by his son, who was in imminent danger of being prosecuted. The mortgage was subsequently set aside on the grounds that the bank had been guilty of undue influence by saying of the son's position: "This is a serious matter. A case of transportation for life." In *Lloyds Bank Ltd* v. *Bundy*,[39] in similar circumstances, the bank lost its guarantee where they had not pointed out that the father should have independent advice before signing a guarantee relating to his son's business account with the bank.

It should be noted that in neither case was there any suggestion that the beneficiary had done anything illegal, being " . . . moved solely by his own self-interest, unconscious of the distress he is bringing to the other".[40] It must also be clear that much turns on the facts of these cases, since: "The influence of one mind over another is very subtle."[41]

38. (1886) LR 1 HL 200.

39. [1975] QB 326. Cf *Cornish* v. *Midland Bank plc* [1985] 3 All ER 513. It is sufficient that the solicitors acting for the bank send the documents for execution to the defendant's solicitors, who, it may be assumed will give proper advice to the defendant: *Bank of Baroda* v. *Shah* [1988] 3 All ER 24. If the wife and her husband are being advised by the same solicitor, "the bank is entitled to assume that the solicitor has given her appropriate advice", including that "she was entitled to take independent advice": per Hoffman LJ (as he then was) in *Bank of Baroda* v. *Rayarel* [1995] 2 FLR 376, 386D. See also *Banco Exterior Internacional* v. *Mann* [1995] 1 All ER 936, a case where the mortgage deed pre-dated *O'Brien*, where the solicitors were not the wife's solicitors at all, and they had acted for the husband and his company. It was nevertheless held (Morritt LJ, and Sir Thomas Bingham MR) that, in spite of her husband's undue influence, Mrs Mann had received independent legal advice, and the bank could rely on the solicitor's certificate to the effect that the contents of the document had been explained. Hobhouse LJ dissented: "The bank did not take any steps to advise the wife. It should have been entirely within their contemplation that the wife might well in fact sign the document under the undue influence of her husband which was in fact what occurred", at p. 948e. Banks and solicitors must act with care. Having given advice to the wife, a solicitor is usually asked to report to the bank as to the advice he gave the wife. This may cause the solicitor difficulty, because circumstances may put his duties to the wife and the bank into conflict: see *BCCI* v. *Aboody* [1992] 4 All ER 955, at p. 982e to h. The wife's claim failed in *Halifax Building Society* v. *Stepsky* [1995] 4 All ER 656, because the solicitors acting for her and her husband in connection with the mortgage were also acting for the building society, and they found themselves with a conflict of interest problem. Mr Stepsky told his wife the loan was for home improvements and carpets, whereas it was to repay business debts. The solicitors knew this, but could not tell the building society without Mr and Mr Stepsky's consent. It was held that the knowledge of the solicitors was not imputed to the building society, who believed the loan was for the joint benefit of husband and wife, and as they had no constructive notice of the husband's misrepresentations and undue influence they were entitled to enforce the mortgage.

40. Per Lord Denning MR, *ibid*., at p. 339.

41. Per Lindley LJ in *Allcard* v. *Skinner* (1887) 36 Ch D 145, at p. 183. Where a beneficiary under a bank guarantee has not made a demand for payment he may be restrained from making the demand if the guarantor can show a *prima facie* case of fraud by the beneficiary, and an interlocutory injunction may then be granted to restrain the encashment of the guarantee pending the trial: *Themehelp Ltd* v. *West* [1995] 4 All ER 215, per Balcombe and Waite LJJ; Evans LJ dissented, in particular at page 231a, where he thought that "Granting an injunction . . . in these circumstances is also harmful . . . to the integrity of the banking system and to standards of commercial morality which the Courts should uphold."

In *Cleese* v. *Thomas*[42] Mr Cleese gave all his savings to his great-nephew (Mr Thomas) to help buy a house in which Mr Cleese was to live for the rest of his days, the balance of the purchase money being provided by a mortgage taken out by Mr Thomas, in whose sole name the property was bought. When Mr Thomas defaulted on the mortgage repayments, Mr Cleese was held entitled to set the transaction aside.[43]

The commonest type of transaction found today where a guarantor might be subjected to some form of undue influence is between husband and wife, where the wife is asked to agree that the matrimonial home is mortgaged to cover bank borrowings by the husband for his business. These circumstances were considered recently by the House of Lords in *Barclays Bank plc* v. *O'Brien*.[44]

Mr and Mrs O'Brien owned their home jointly, and it was subject to a building society mortgage. Mr O'Brien had an interest in a company, and that company needed increased borrowing facilities. The bank agreed to raise the borrowing level provided Mr O'Brien gave additional security. A second charge over the matrimonial home was suggested. Mr O'Brien was left to arrange this with his wife, who was not a customer of the bank. The second charge was duly executed at the bank by Mr and Mrs O'Brien (although neither read the documents), and the facility granted. The company account ran into difficulties, and the bank claimed the right to sell the matrimonial home. Mrs O'Brien raised two defences. First, that she had been put under undue pressure by her husband; secondly, that her husband had not told her the truth, and had misrepresented the terms of the second mortgage which she had signed, saying it was limited to £60,000, and was for a period of three weeks only. *Held*: "A wife who has been induced to stand as a surety for her husband's debts by his undue influence, misrepresentation or some other legal wrong has an equity as against him to set aside that transaction",[45] and, as the bank had not satisfied itself that Mrs O'Brien's agreement to the mortgage had been "properly obtained", the bank was fixed with constructive notice of the husband's wrongful misrepresentation,[46] and, therefore, Mrs O'Brien was entitled to have the charge set aside.

In these transactions the following points must be borne in mind:

(1) Although reference is made to husbands and wives, the position is the same " . . . where there is an emotional relationship between cohabitees".[47] Also, it seems between elderly parent and adult child.[48]

(2) If the bank has notice—actual or constructive—of any undue influence by the husband, the wife will have an equitable right to set the transaction aside.[49]

42. [1994] 1 All ER 35.
43. Unfortunately, when the house was sold the property market had declined, and there were not the funds to repay Mr Cleese in full.
44. [1993] 4 All ER 417.
45. *Per* Lord Browne-Wilkinson, p. 428j.
46. *Ibid.*, p. 429g, and p. 432f.
47. *Ibid.*, p. 431c.
48. *Barclays Bank plc* v. *O'Brien* [1992] 4 All ER 983 (CA), *per* Scott LJ, p. 986d.
49. *Barclays Bank plc* v. *O'Brien* [1993] 4 All ER 417, 425b.

(3) The bank " . . . is put on inquiry when a wife offers to stand surety for her husband's debts",[50] and so will have constructive notice, if it fails to take reasonable steps to verify whether the wife has a right to set aside or not.[51]

(4) A bank " . . . will have satisfied these requirements if it insists that the wife attend a private meeting (in the absence of the husband) with a representative of the [bank] at which she is told of the extent of her liability, warned of the risk she is running and urged to take independent legal advice".[52]

(5) The "extent of her liability" may be different at the time when the bank claims under the security than at the time when the security was given; and so there would appear to be an obligation on the bank to advise the wife from time to time, if the facility to the husband or his business increases significantly.

A wife may be prepared to put herself at risk for £10,000, but not for £100,000. For example, if a wife is a surety of her husband's company's bank account she might prefer to see that company go into liquidation rather than accept an increased personal liability.[53]

(6) The law is now reasonably clear on what the bank must do in future transactions, but "as to past transactions, it will depend on the facts of each case whether the steps taken by the creditor satisfy the test".[54] In reviewing what steps were taken by the bank at the time when the security was given, it may be those steps will be found deficient, and a re-execution of the documents may be advisable. This could lead to problems, of course, as the wife—on being independently advised —might refuse to re-execute, which could leave the bank with a greater problem.

(7) The risk of losing the matrimonial home is, of course, an emotive issue, engendering a strong sense of sympathy; however, as a matter of principle, the protection to be afforded to a wife should equally apply to a charge over any other of her property which she may have given for the benefit of her husband and his creditors.

50. *Ibid.*, p. 429f.
51. *Ibid.*, p. 429b.
52. *Ibid.*, p. 430a, and see footnote 39, p. 122 *supra*. In *Massey* v. *Midland Bank plc* [1995] 1 All ER 929, a case where the mortgage deed pre-dated *O'Brien*, the debtor was present when the solicitor gave this lady advice. "That was not good practice, but fortunately she did receive independent legal advice": *per* Steyn LJ, at p. 934g. The husband was also present in *TSB Bank plc* v. *Camfield* [1995] 1 All ER 951, another case where the mortgage deed pre-dated *O'Brien*, where it was held, in any event, the true motive of the transaction had not been explained, and the mortgage was set aside. Moreover, a bank is under a duty to disclose to a surety " . . . what in general terms can be described as unusual features, unknown to the surety": *Levett* v. *Barclays Bank plc* [1995] 2 All ER 615, 628d. If it does not, it can be ordered to repay moneys recovered from the surety on the account of the customer.
53. See *TSB Bank plc* v. *Camfield* [1995] 1 All ER 951, 954e.
54. *Barclays Bank plc* v. *O'Brien* [1993] 4 All ER 417, 429j.

(8) As the result of the undue influence, the wife need not have suffered loss to have the transaction set aside. A wife "who proves actual undue influence is not under the further burden of proving that the transaction induced by the undue influence was manifestly disadvantageous.[55] "A man guilty of fraud is no more entitled to argue that the transaction was beneficial to the person defrauded, than is the man who has procured a transaction by misrepresentation."[56]

(9) If the mortgage is set aside, it is so in its entirety. Within the rule, there is no scope for allowing a partial enforcement. If this claim is upheld, the court seeks to put that party into the position in which she would have been if the representation had not been made. This involves ascertaining what the position would have been if the transaction had not taken place. It does not involve reforming the transaction to accord with the representation.[57]

(10) If a lady (in these transactions it usually is a wife or a lady partner) obtains independent legal advice, and there is no evidence to suggest she lacked free will, the bank need not enquire as to her motive for giving the security.[58]

---

55. *CIBC Mortgages plc* v. *Pitt* [1993] 4 All ER 433, 439j.

56. *Ibid.*, p. 439g. Lord Scarman in *National Westminster Bank plc* v. *Morgan* [1985] All ER 821, 827h, stated that when considering cases of undue influence, to succeed, the wife must show that the transaction of which she complains " . . . must constitute a disadvantage sufficiently serious . . . " to her. If the transaction conferred a benefit to her, the undue influence, even if it existed, would not enable her to claim relief. The same point was made in *BCCI* v. *Aboody* [1992] 4 All ER 955 where Slade LJ, p. 973h, said that " . . . even . . . a party who affirmatively proves that a transaction was influenced by the exercise of undue influence is not entitled to have it set aside in reliance on the doctrine of undue influence without proving that the transaction was manifestly disadvantageous to him or her". *BCCI* v. *Aboody* is now overruled: *CIBC Mortgages plc* v. *Pitt* [1993] 4 All ER 433, 439c.

There remains the issue of whether, even if there is no undue influence, it is necessary for the wife to obtain benefit from the giving by her of security. Does she need to receive some consideration? If the bank is a mere volunteer may the enforcement of the security fail? In a number of these cases the wife gets no benefit at all, she simply signs away whatever is her interest in the matrimonial home for the benefit of her husband and his creditors. She enters into an agreement in favour of the bank but receives no consideration *from* the bank. Certainly, a mortgage given for an illegal consideration (and hence, no consideration) is unenforceable: *William Hill (Park Lane) Ltd* v. *Hofman* [1950] 1 All ER 1013. One wonders why a wife should be in any worse position, undue influence or not.

57. *Per* Ferris J, in *Allied Irish Bank* v. *Byrne* (1 February 1994) unreported but referred to in *TSB Bank plc* v. *Camfield* [1995] 1 All ER 951, at p. 957c.

58. "It was not the bank's business to ask itself why she was willing to do this": *Banco Exterior Internacional SA* v. *Thomas* [1997] 1 All ER 46, *per* Sir Richard Scott VC, p. 55d.

CHAPTER 7

DISCHARGE OF A BILL

A bill of exchange is discharged, that is, all the rights and liabilities under it are extinguished,[1] in the following ways: (i) payment in due course; (ii) acceptor is the holder at maturity; (iii) express waiver; (iv) cancellation; (v) alteration.

I. PAYMENT IN DUE COURSE

This means payment of the bill by the drawee or acceptor made in good faith at or after maturity to the holder, and without notice that his title to the bill is defective.[2]

Payment in due course can be made only at or after the date of maturity,[3] however, an acceptor can pay a bill *before* the due date, and if he does so, as the bill is still alive and valid, he can put it back into circulation by re-issuing it.

It follows that so long as anyone remains liable on a bill it is not discharged. Thus, if payment is not made by or on behalf of the drawee or acceptor, the bill is not discharged as rights and liabilities still subsist under the bill. For example, if the acceptor refuses to pay and the drawer is compelled to pay it, he can recover from the acceptor. In such a case, although the bill is still alive, the drawer cannot re-issue it.[4]

However, where a bill is paid by an indorser; or payable to the *drawer's* order and is paid by the drawer; either the indorser or the drawer can strike out his own and the subsequent indorsement and negotiate the bill further.[5]

Thus, as we have seen, where the drawer of a bill pays it he can recover from the acceptor. An exception to this is accommodation bills for they are discharged when paid in due course by the party accommodated.[6] The reason

---

1. To prove a bill is discharged and of no further value as a bill the payer can cancel the drawer's signature—as a bank does on payment of a customer's cheque.
2. Bills of Exchange Act 1882, s. 59 (1).
3. *Ibid.*, s. 59(2)(*a*).
4. *Ibid.*, s. 59(2)(*b*).
5. *Ibid.*, s. 59(2)(*b*).
6. *Ibid.*, s. 59(3).

being that the party accommodated cannot have recourse to any other party to the bill.

Payment in due course must be made to the *holder* and if payment is made to any other person (for example, if there has been a forgery of an essential signature), the bill will not be discharged. If the acceptor pays such a bill, as he is not paying the *holder* he can be compelled to pay the true owner. However, so long as he pays *the holder*, even if such person is not the true owner the bill will be discharged.

II. ACCEPTOR IS THE HOLDER AT MATURITY

When the acceptor of a bill becomes the holder of it in his own right (that is, beneficially) at or after maturity, the bill is discharged.[7] This does not happen very often.

III. EXPRESS WAIVER

If the holder of a bill at or after its maturity renounces his rights against the acceptor the bill is discharged. Unless the bill is delivered up to the acceptor, to be a valid waiver, the discharge must be in writing.[8] However, in any event, the acceptor should make a point of getting the bill as well, as the holder could put the bill back into circulation again, and if it comes into the hands of a holder in due course the acceptor will have to pay.[9]

IV. CANCELLATION

Where a bill is *intentionally* cancelled by the holder or his agent, and the cancellation is apparent on the bill, the bill is dischaged.[10]

In the same way any party liable on a bill may be discharged by the *intentional* cancellation of his signature by the holder or his agent. In such a case, any indorser who would have had a right of recourse against the party whose signature is cancelled is also discharged.[11] For example:

A draws a bill payable to B who indorses it to C. The bill is then indorsed to D, then on to E and on to F, the holder. F then strikes out D's signature. D will not be liable on the bill again. As F can so freely discharge D and so destroy the rights of recourse of E

---

7. *Ibid.,* s. 61.
8. *Ibid.,* s. 62(1). No consideration for the giving up of the holder's rights is necessary.
9. *Ibid.,* s. 62(2).
10. *Ibid.,* s. 63(1).
11. *Ibid.,* s. 63(2).

against D it is only fair that E should be relieved of his liability to F. F still, of course, retains the liability of B and C.

Naturally, a cancellation made unintentionally, or by mistake, or without the authority of the holder is inoperative. However, where a bill or any signature appears to have been cancelled, the burden of proof lies on the party who alleges the cancellation was made unintentionally, or by mistake or without authority as the case may be.[12]

V. ALTERATION[13]

Where a bill or an acceptance is *materially* altered without the consent of *all* the parties, the bill is avoidable by all the parties, except those who have made, authorized or assented to the alteration or have become indorsers subsequent to the alteration.[14]

The following alterations are material:[15] (a) the date; (b) the sum payable; (c) the time of payment; (d) the place of payment; (e) the addition of a place of acceptance upon a bill accepted generally; (f) a change in the payee.[16]

12. *Ibid.*, s. 63(3).
13. This is sometimes called the "raising" of bills.
14. Bills of Exchange Act 1882, s. 64(1).
15. *Ibid.*, s. 64(2).
16. *Slingsby* v. *District Bank Ltd* [1932] 1 KB 544.

CHAPTER 8

DISHONOUR

A bill of exchange can be dishonoured in one of two ways. Failure to effect complete acceptance or failure to obtain payment in full.

1. DISHONOUR BY NON-ACCEPTANCE

A bill of exchange is dishonoured by non-acceptance when[1]: (a) it is duly presented for acceptance and the acceptance is expressly refused; or (b) it is duly presented for acceptance and acceptance cannot be obtained; or (c) presentment for acceptance is excused.[2]

As soon as a bill is dishonoured for non-acceptance, the rights of the holder to recourse against the drawer and indorsers arise immediately without any need for presentment for payment.[3]

When a bill is duly presented for acceptance and it is not accepted within the customary time (usually 24 hours)[4] the holder must treat the bill as dishonoured, and notify all prior parties. If he does not, he loses his right of recourse against them.[5]

2. DISHONOUR BY NON-PAYMENT

A bill of exchange is dishonoured by non-payment when[6]: (a) payment is refused; or (b) payment cannot be obtained; or (c) payment is excused, and the bill is overdue and unpaid.

---

1. Bills of Exchange Act 1882, s. 43(1).
2. *Ibid.*, s. 41(2).
3. *Ibid.*, s. 43(2).
4. Nowhere is a time period for acceptance specified. What is "customary" or "reasonable" are a matter of usage or fact in the circumstances. There are some old cases which do no more than illustrate this general rule: for example, see *Fry v. Hill* (1817) 7 Taunt. 398.
5. Bills of Exchange Act 1882, s. 42.
6. *Ibid.*, s. 47(1).

As in the case of non-acceptance, so here, if the bill has been accepted but is dishonoured for non-payment, the rights of the holder against the acceptor, the drawer and indorsers accrue.[7]

If the acceptor or drawee offers to pay part only, the holder can take it or refuse it as he pleases. Usually, he will accept (as part is better than nothing at all) and treat the bill as dishonoured as to the remainder.

If the acceptor or drawee offers to pay by cheque, the bill should not be surrendered until the cheque is cleared; as by accepting the cheque in full settlement the holder is deemed to have waived the bill and it is discharged, and the liability of the parties extinguished. The only right the holder would then have would be on the cheque if *that* was dishonoured.

Notice of dishonour

As we saw above, giving notice of the dishonour whether for non-acceptance or non-payment, is vital. The notice must be given to the drawer and each indorser, and any party to whom notice is not given is discharged from liability on the bill.[8] For example, in

YEOMAN CREDIT LTD v. GREGORY[9]

A series of bills was drawn by Y to cover loans it was to make to E Ltd. These bills were then accepted by E payable at their bank and indorsed by G, E Ltd's managing director. On presentation on 28 January the bills were dishonoured. E Ltd then asked Y to present at another bank, which Y did immediately but the bills were dishonoured here also. Y was informed of this on the morning of 30 January. Notice of dishonour was given at once to G by telephone. Y then sued G, as indorser, to recover the money due under the bills. G claimed he had not received due notice of dishonour. *Held*—that dishonour occurred on the 28th when the first bank refused payment. The telephone communication was irrelevant as this related to the second refusal on the 30th. Therefore Y could not recover from G.

If, after a bill has been dishonoured by non-acceptance, the holder does *not* give due notice, and then negotiates the bill to a holder in due course, the latter will get a good title, and the liability of the prior parties revives in his favour; although to the holder who should have, but did not give notice, they are discharged,[10] so that if the holder in due course recovers from him, he will not be able to claim from anyone else.

Moreover, where a bill is dishonoured by non-acceptance and notice of this is given, and then it is dishonoured for non-payment, it is not necessary to give notice again (that is, of the non-payment) unless the bill in the meanwhile has been accepted.[11]

7. *Ibid.*, s. 47(2).
8. *Ibid.*, ss. 42 and 48 (note, by the way, that in s. 42, in some prints of the Act, reference is given as s. 42(1) but, in fact, there is only one paragraph in the section!).
9. [1963] 1 All ER 245.
10. Bills of Exchange Act 1882, ss. 48(1) and 36(5).
11. *Ibid.*, s. 48(2).

Notice must be given to each transferor, but the holder need not make the communication himself. It is sufficient if he gives notice to his *immediate indorser*, who in turn gives notice to *his* immediate indorser and so on. If any party does not pass on the information he remains liable to the holders, but has no right of recourse against the drawer and the indorsers prior to him. Unless, of course, the delay is caused by circumstances beyond the control of the party giving notice, and the notice is finally given with reasonable diligence after the cause of the delay no longer operates.[12]

An example of how the system works may help.

Drawer	Payee	Indorsers	Holder
A	B	C, D, E, F, G	H

Suppose X is the acceptor who dishonours the bill. H will normally give notice to G, and G to F and so on down the line.

If H gives notice to B, B's liability is retained not only for H himself, but for all the intervening parties C to G, as notice given by *the holder* enures for the benefit of all prior indorsers (as well as any subsequent holders).[13]

Further, if any *indorser* gives notice it enures for the benefit of the holder and all indorsers after the person to whom the notice was given.[14] So that if E gives notice to B, B will be liable not only to C and D but also to F, G and H.

Form of notice

Notice of dishonour must be given in accordance with the following rules:

(i) It must be given by or on behalf of the holder or any indorser who is liable on the bill at the time of giving notice[15]

If notice is given by an agent he can give it either in his own name or in the name of the person on whose behalf he gives the notice.[16]

(ii) No particular form of words is required, so long as the bill is sufficiently identified

Notice can be in writing or by more personal communication,[17] and it is sufficient notice if the bill is returned to the drawer or an indorser.[18] If notice

12. *Ibid.*, s. 50(1).
13. *Ibid.*, s. 49(3).
14. *Ibid.*, s. 49(4).
15. *Ibid.*, s. 49(1).
16. *Ibid.*, s. 49(2).
17. *Ibid.*, s. 49(5). Under the *draft* Deregulation (Bills of Exchange) Order there was suggested an amendment to s. 49(5) of the 1882 Act to allow notice of dishonour to be given by "facsimile transmission or other electronic means", but this was not carried into the Order, nor was the proposal to shift the burden of proof to the recipient of the notice of dishonour to show he did not receive it.
18. Bills of Exchange Act 1882, s. 49(6).

is given in writing, it need not be signed; and if the written notice is not itself sufficient (for example, if the bill is not sufficiently identified) oral communication can supplement it. Even if the bill is misdescribed, the notice is still valid unless the party to whom the notice was given is misled.[19] It is usual to give notice in proper form along the following lines:

To: (the drawer)

Dear Sirs,
   Take notice the undernoted bill of exchange has been dishonoured by non-acceptance/payment and we require immediate settlement from you.
   On settlement we shall return the bill of exchange to you.

Drawer   Acceptor   Amount   Due Date

Yours faithfully,

(iii) The notice may be given either to a party liable on the bill or to his agent[20]

If the party to whom the notice is to be given is dead, the notice should be given to his personal representatives[21] and if bankrupt to his trustee in bankruptcy.[22]
   Where there are two or more parties to whom notice is to be given it must be given to each, unless one has authority to receive notice for the other or they are partners.[23]

(iv) Notice must be given within a "reasonable time"[24] of dishonour

What then is a reasonable time? If both the sender and the recipient live in the same town[25] notice must *reach* the recipient on the *day after* the dishonour.[26]

19. *Ibid.*, s. 49(7).
20. Bills of Exchange Act 1882, s. 49(8).
21. *Ibid.*, s. 49(9).
22. *Ibid.*, s. 49(10).
23. *Ibid.*, s. 49(11).
24. *Ibid.*, s. 49(12).
25. Section 49(12)(*a*) says "the same place". What is meant by "place" has never been defined satisfactorily: see *Hamilton Finance* v. *Coverley* [1969] 1 Lloyd's Rep. 53, where Mocatta J reviews the position and on the facts held two addresses in London, one in W1, the other in EC3, to be "in the same place".
26. Bills of Exchange Act 1882, s. 49(12)(*a*) see *Yeoman Credit Ltd* v. *Gregory* [1963] 1 All ER 245 *per* Megaw J, at p. 256F. "The notice was not given until the second day after there was knowledge on the part of the plaintiffs of that dishonour. Unless special circumstances can be brought in here to justify an extension of that time, the notice of dishonour was out of time, and the inevitable consequence is that the claim on the bill is bad, even though the defendant may have sustained no prejudice whatever by the delay."

If they live in different towns notice must be *sent off* on the *day after* the dishonour, or if there is no convenient post, by the next post on the day after.[27]

Where notice of dishonour is duly addressed and posted, the sender is deemed to have given due notice of dishonour even if there is some miscarriage by the postal authorities.[28]

Notice cannot, of course, be given *before* dishonour, even if all parties know the bill will be dishonoured on presentation. But it does not matter that it is *posted* before dishonour. For example, in

EAGLEHILL LTD v. NEEDHAM LTD[29]

N drew a bill on F payable in four months, the due date being 31 December. F duly accepted the bill, whereupon N discounted the bill with E. F then went into liquidation, which fact was known to all the parties. The bill was duly presented for payment at F's bank on 31 December and, of course, dishonoured. E had already prepared the appropriate notice of dishonour and dated it 30 December. By an oversight, the notice was posted that day and arrived at F's bank on the 31st—the same day that the bill was dishonoured. E sued N who pleaded that they had no liability as the notice was bad. *Held*—that the notice was not invalidated by being posted before the moment of dishonour, and, as there was no evidence to the contrary, the dishonour on the 31st was deemed to be *before* the receipt of the notice. Therefore E could recover from N.

Where a party to a bill *receives* notice of dishonour he has the same time for passing on the information to parties in the chain of liability before him.[30]

Dishonoured bill in the hands of agents

Where a bill when dishonoured is in the hands of an agent, for example, a bank, the agent can give notice himself to the prior parties, or to his principal so that *he* can do so.

If the agent gives notice to his principal he must give the notice within a reasonable time within the rules;[31] thereafter, the principal must give notice to the prior parties within the same rules as to "reasonable time".[32] So if a bank failed to advise a customer of the dishonour in time, and the liability of prior parties was, in consequence, lost, the bank would be liable.

---

27. Bills of Exchange Act 1882, s. 49(12)(*b*).
28. *Ibid.*, s. 49(15). On the face of it, this provision appears to mean that proper notice is deemed to have been "given" when it is *posted* irrespective of when it is received. However, Lord Dilhorne considers that "Rule (15) does not, in my view, provide that posting of a properly addressed letter is deemed to constitute due notice of dishonour but only secures that a notice which would be valid if delivered in the ordinary course of post is not to be regarded as invalid if delayed or lost in the post": *Eaglehill Ltd* v. *Needham Ltd* [1973] AC 992, 1004B. The point was not considered by the other members of the House.
29. [1973] AC 992.
30. Bills of Exchange Act 1882, s. 49(14).
31. *Ibid.*, s. 49(12).
32. *Ibid.*, s. 49(13).

Notice of dishonour dispensed with [33]

The giving of notice of the dishonour of a bill is dispensed with in the following circumstances:

1. When after the exercise of reasonable diligence notice cannot be given.

2. When notice is expressly or impliedly waived—which can be done either before or after dishonour.

For example, under s. 16(2) of the Bills of Exchange Act 1882 a party can waive, as regards himself, some or all of the holder's duties. So that if he places upon a bill words such as "notice of dishonour waived" no holder need advise that party of any subsequent dishonour.

3. There is no need to give *the drawer* notice where: (a) the drawer is also the drawee and the drawee refuses payment: obviously the drawer will already know! (b) the drawee is fictitious or has no capacity. A bill drawn on a fictitious person must always be dishonoured, and the drawer must know this when he draws the bill. Again, the position is the same where a person with no contractual capacity accepts a bill;[34] (c) the bill is presented to the drawer for payment. Obviously in such a case the drawer will know of the dishonour; (d) the drawee or acceptor is under no obligation to the drawer to pay. For example, if the acceptor has not sufficient funds in hand to pay the drawer should know this, and hence there is no need to tell him of the dishonour; (e) the drawer has countermanded payment. Once again, there is no point in telling the drawer what he already knows.

4. There is no need to give *an indorser* notice where: (a) he knew at the time he indorsed the bill that the drawee was fictitious or had no capacity;[35] (b) the bill is presented to the indorser for payment. Obviously, here again he will know of the dishonour; (c) the indorser was accommodated. In such a case, the indorser will know he has no funds to meet the bill, and the holder must look to the accommodation party. It would, therefore, be pointless to have to inform him of facts he well knew.

5. It is never necessary to give the acceptor notice of dishonour.[36]

Liability on dishonour

The liability of the parties to a bill upon dishonour are these:

(a) Before acceptance

(1) The drawer, (2) the payee, (3) the indorsers.

33. *Ibid.*, s. 50(2).
34. Note that s. 22(2) of the 1882 Act (which deals with capacity) does not mention *acceptances* but only the incapacity of drawers and indorsers.
35. Compare the position, *supra*, as to the drawer.
36. Bills of Exchange Act 1882, s. 52(3). Nor to protest the bill to render him liable—as to which see *infra* p. 119.

(b) After acceptance

(1) The acceptor, (2) the drawer, (3) the payee, (4) the indorsers.

If the drawee or acceptor refuses payment, the holder can recover from *any* prior party the *whole* amount of the bill (not pro rata from all the parties). The party who pays the bill will recover from the person next liable down the line, who will then claim from his immediate party and so on down the line, until the drawer ultimately has to pay the bill, the drawer being left to recover from his acceptor if he is able.[37]

Measure of damages[38]

If a claim is made against any party to a bill, the following items can be recovered as damages for dishonour: (i) the amount of the bill; (ii) interest from the date of maturity, unless the bill is payable on demand when interest runs from the date of presentment for payment; (iii) expenses of noting and protesting.

Where interest on a bill is claimed as part of a claim for damages it is within the court's discretion to award it or not, and may be withheld wholly or in part if justice requires it. This applies even if a bill is expressed to be payable with interest at a given rate. So that even in that case, the interest (given as damages) may or may not be awarded by the court at the stated rate of interest.[39]

In foreign transactions, where the bill was in a currency other than sterling, it was possible to claim the amount of re-exchange,[40] since the courts had no jurisdiction to make an award except in the currency of the Realm. This was changed by a decision of the House of Lords in *Miliangos* v. *George Frank (Textiles) Ltd*,[41] and English courts can now give judgment in the currency of any foreign country.[42]

Noting and Protesting

Where a foreign bill[43] is dishonoured either for non-acceptance or non-payment it must be *protested*, and if it is not, the drawer and the indorsers are discharged.[44] A bill which has been protested for non-acceptance may subsequently be protested for non-payment.[45] The method of protesting is this: the

---

37. Bills of Exchange Act 1882, s. 57(1).
38. *Ibid.*, s. 57. See also p. 178 *infra*.
39. *Ibid.*, s. 57(3).
40. *Ibid.*, s. 57(2), now repealed by the Administration of Justice Act 1977, s. 4(2).
41. [1976] AC 443.
42. For a more detailed consideration of the subject, see *infra* Chap. 10.
43. As to which see s. 4 of the Bills of Exchange Act 1882.
44. *Ibid.*, s. 51(2) which says that an inland bill *may* be noted, but this is not necessary to preserve rights against the drawer and indorsers: s. 51(1).
45. *Ibid.*, s. 51(3)

holder takes the bill (or if lost, a copy)[46] to a Notary Public[47] who again presents the bill so as to obtain legal proof of dishonour. If acceptance or payment is still not obtained, the notary must then draw up a protest.

Form of protest[48]

The document embodying the protest must contain and specify the following: (a) the name of the person at whose request the bill is presented; (b) the reason why the protest is made; (c) the demand made to the drawee or acceptor and his answers, if any; (d) a copy of the bill; (e) the signature of the notary.

Time for protesting

A protest must be made by the *day after* the dishonour.[49] This does not allow much time, and the holder frequently takes the opportunity to have the bill *noted*.

"Noting" involves going to a Notary Public as before; he will then represent the bill, and if the acceptance or payment is still refused, he attaches a slip of paper to the bill showing: (a) the fact of the dishonour; (b) the date; (c) his charges for the noting; (d) his initials.

After a bill has been noted in this way the time for protesting is extended indefinitely.[50]

Delay is excused when it is caused by circumstances beyond the control of the holder, provided he notes or protests the bill as soon as the cause for the delay ceases. A protest is dispensed with altogether in any circumstances which would justify dispensing with notice of dishonour as required by s. 50(2) of the 1882 Act.[51]

Where a bill payable at a fixed period after sight is dishonoured by non-acceptance, the time for payment is calculated from the date it is noted or protested.[52]

Place of protesting

A bill must be protested at the place where it is dishonoured.[53] However, where a bill is presented and returned dishonoured by post, it can be protested at the place where it is returned, that is, usually the holder's address.

46. *Ibid.*, s. 51(8).
47. In the unlikely event of a notary not being available, *any householder* will suffice provided he gives a certificate in the form set out in Sched 1 of the 1882 Act, in the presence of two witnesses, each of whom must attest the certificate: s. 94.
48. Bills of Exchange Act 1882, s. 51(7).
49. *Ibid.*, s. 51(4) and the Bills of Exchange (Time of Noting) Act 1917.
50. Bills of Exchange Act 1882, s. 93.
51. *Ibid.*, s. 51(9).
52. *Ibid.*, s. 14(3).
53. *Ibid.*, s. 51(6).

Moreover, if a bill is *drawn* payable by some person other than the drawee, it must be protested at the place where it is expressed to be payable. No further presentment for payment to the drawee is necessary.

Inland bills

Even inland bills can be protested by the holder in the following circumstances: (i) before *any* bill can be accepted or paid "for honour" (which will be considered below) it must be protested;[54] (ii) for "better security" against the drawer or indorsers, a holder can do this where the acceptor becomes bankrupt, insolvent, or suspends payment of a bill before the time of payment is due.[55]

The "better security" means that the bill can be accepted for honour as though actual dishonour by non-acceptance had taken place.

Acceptance and payment for honour

Obviously, great inconvenience arises when the drawee refuses to accept a bill. The whole series of transactions upon dishonour are set in motion and the whole business is very troublesome. In order to avoid all this, the drawer sometimes inserts the name of a *referee in case of need*,[56] and if *he* accepts his acceptance is known as an acceptance "*supra protest*" or "for honour". Perhaps it is because the procedure to recover is too cumbersome, or perhaps it is that people cannot be found who will step into the breach, but for whatever reason this method of proceeding is not much in use today and seems almost extinct.

If it is used the drawer supplies the acceptor *supra protest* with the necessary funds and the acceptor *supra protest* states on the bill that he has accepted *supra protest* for the honour of the drawer. If the bill does not state for whose honour it is accepted it is deemed to be for the honour of the drawer.[57]

Anyone can accept for honour so long as[58]: (a) they are not already liable on the bill; (b) the bill has been protested; and (c) the bill is not overdue.

A bill can always be accepted for honour for part only of the sum for which it is drawn.[59]

The acceptor for honour is liable to a holder and all parties after the party for whose honour he has accepted,[60] for the amount of the bill or the tenor of

---

54. *Ibid.*, ss. 65 and 67.
55. *Ibid.*, s. 51(5).
56. See s. 15. The drawer or any indorser may insert the name of any person to whom the holder may resort in case of need. The holder is not obliged to pursue the referee.
57. Bills of Exchange Act 1882, s. 65(4).
58. *Ibid.*, ss. 65(1) and 67(1).
59. *Ibid.*, s. 65(2).
60. *Ibid.*, s. 66(2).

his acceptance, provided the bill has been presented both for payment and protested for non-payment, and he has received notice to that effect.[61]

Where a time bill is accepted for honour its maturity is calculated from the date of noting for non-acceptance, and not from the date of acceptance for honour.[62]

Requirements

Acceptance for honour *supra protest* in order to be valid must be[63]: 1. written on the bill indicating it is an acceptance for honour; and 2. signed by the acceptor for honour.

Time of presenting for acceptance for honour

As with all notices relating to dishonour, the time allowed for presenting for acceptance for honour is short.

Where the acceptor's address is in the same town[64] where the bill is protested, presentment for honour must be made not later than the day after maturity. If it is not in the same town, the bill must be *sent off* not later than the day following its maturity.[65]

Delay in presentment is excused by any circumstances which would excuse delay in presentment for payment under s. 46 of the 1882 Act.[66]

If the acceptor for honour dishonours the bill it must be protested for non-payment[67] which is done in the usual way and with the same results, that is, anyone can thereafter accept *supra-supra protest*!

Payment for honour

Where the drawee or acceptor of a bill fails to pay it on the due day, *anyone*, even if he is already liable on the bill, can pay it for the honour of any party, so long as it has been noted or protested.[68]

Where a bill has been paid for honour, all parties *after* the party for whose honour the bill is paid are discharged. However, the payer obtains all the rights and duties against the party for whose honour he pays and all parties prior to him.[69] Once more, an example may help:

61. *Ibid.*, s. 66(1).
62. *Ibid.*, s. 65(5).
63. *Ibid.*, s. 65(3).
64. Once again the 1882 Act says "place".
65. Bills of Exchange Act 1882, s. 67(2).
66. *Ibid.*, s. 67(3).
67. *Ibid.*, s. 67(4).
68. *Ibid.*, s. 68(1).
69. *Ibid.*, s. 68(5).

Drawer	Payee	Indorsers	Holder
A	B	C, D, E, F	G

X can pay for the honour of C and if G accepts, D, E, and F will be discharged from liability.

X will acquire rights against C, B, A and the acceptor.

Where two or more people offer to pay the bill for the honour of different parties, the person whose payment will discharge the most parties will have preference.[70]

So, using again the example above, if a person Y offers to pay for the honour of A (the drawer) he would be given preference over X, as Y's payment would discharge B, C, D, E and F.

If the holder refuses to receive payment *supra protest* he will lose his rights of recourse against any party who would have been discharged by the acceptance of the payment.[71]

When the payer for honour pays the holder the full amount of the bill, together with the notarial expenses, he is entitled to the bill and the protest, which the holder must deliver up to the payer. If the holder does not hand over the documents in this way he may be liable in damages.[72]

Evidence of payment

In order to operate as an effective payment *supra protest*, and not merely a voluntary payment, the payment must be evidenced by a "notarial act of honour" that is, a certificate prepared by a notary upon a declaration of the payer or someone on his behalf specifying the name of the payer and for whose honour payment was made.[73] This certificate is then appended to the protest as complete evidence of the whole transaction.[74]

---

70. *Ibid.*, s. 68(2).
71. *Ibid.*, s. 68(7).
72. *Ibid.*, s. 68(6).
73. *Ibid.*, s. 68(4).
74. *Ibid.*, s. 68(3).

CHAPTER 9

PROMISSORY NOTES

Promissory notes are bills of exchange and the Bills of Exchange Act 1882 applies, except where otherwise indicated, with, of course, any necessary modifications.[1]

The basic difference between a promissory note and any other bill is that a note is a *promise* by the maker to pay, whereas an ordinary bill is an *order* to someone else (that is the drawee) to pay.

USE OF PROMISSORY NOTES

Promissory notes are used mainly in transactions involving money-lending, or similar business dealings where money is loaned to the maker. The advantages are:

(a) The note is not only clear evidence of the debt and a promise to pay (or usually more properly repay) it, but being negotiable can be passed on, as for example, on discounting as we saw in Chapter 5.

(b) Terms can be attached to a note. Indeed, s. 83(3) expressly provides that "a note is not invalid by reason only that it contains also a pledge of collateral security with authority to sell or dispose thereof". Frequently, the payment of interest or the giving of additional security for the loan is incorporated in the body of the note.

Ordinary bills would not suffice as, apart from having to be accepted and thus introducing another party, the incorporating of terms giving security and the like would almost certainly render an "ordinary" bill invalid, as requiring something to be done other than the payment of money, within s. 3(1) of the 1882 Act.

The giving of a cheque in similar circumstances would create even greater problems, and would be totally unacceptable to the banking system.

---

1. Bills of Exchange Act 1882, s. 89(1). Promissory notes were in their original conception no more than evidence of a debt rather like an IOU. They could not be transferred or negotiated at common law. By statute—Bills of Exchange Act 1704 (3 & 4 Anne c. 8)—promissory notes were made assignable and indorsable as other bills of exchange.

DIFFERENCE FROM OTHER BILLS

Promissory notes differ in the following respects from other bills of exchange: 1. They do not require accepting.[2] 2. The rules as to bills in a set do not apply.[3] 3. Terms can be added to a note which could render a bill invalid. 4. Notes are *promises* by the maker to pay, not (as are bills) *orders* to third parties to pay.

DEFINITION OF A NOTE

Section 83(1) of the 1882 Act defines a promissory note as:

. . . an unconditional promise in writing made by one person to another signed by the maker, engaging to pay, on demand or at a fixed or determinable future time, a sum certain in money, to or to the order of, a specified person or to bearer.

It will be seen that this definition corresponds closely with that of an "ordinary" bill given in s. 3(1) of the 1882 Act, and the comments and decisions, where applicable, will, of course, apply to the definition of a promissory note.

The definition must now be considered. There must be:

(i) "an unconditional promise in writing"

While the promise can take any form it must be a *promise to pay* and not just an acknowledgement of a debt,[4] otherwise, at best, it will be an IOU which is merely evidence of an "account stated" between the parties and is not, of course, a bill of exchange.[5] The use of somewhat informal words has been deemed a sufficient "promise" to render the document a note. For example:

"John Mason, 14th February 1836 borrowed of M.A.M. his sister the sum of £14 in cash a loan, in promise of payment of which I am truly thankful for"[6]

While similarly informal words have not:

"Borrowed this day of J.H. the sum of £100 for one or two months"

which words were held to be a simple acknowledgement and *not* a note.[7] The note must not undertake to do anything other than the payment of money. However, an otherwise valid note is not invalidated merely by reason that it

2. Bills of Exchange Act 1882, ss. 87(1) and 89(3). Consequently presentment for acceptance and acceptance *supra protest* have no application, except where the note has been indorsed: s. 87(2).
   3. *Ibid.*, ss. 87(1) and 89(3).
   4. *Gould* v. *Coombs* (1845) 135 ER 653; *Akbar Khan* v. *Attar Singh* [1936] 2 All ER 545.
   5. But IOUs are assignable. See *infra* p. 194.
   6. *Ellis* v. *Mason* (1839) 8 LJQB 196.
   7. *Hyne* v. *Dewdney* (1852) 21 LJQB 278.

contains a pledge of collateral security, even if authority is also given to sell or dispose of such security[8]: and frequently a note will contain terms relating to such security.[9] A promise to pay "on or before" a given date is conditional, as it creates an uncertainty and contingency in the time of payment.[10]

(ii) "made by one person"

The reference here to "one" person is extended, in that a promissory note may be made by two or more makers and they can be liable (a) jointly or (b) jointly and severally according to the way the note is made.[11]

"Joint" liability is where there is *one debt* for which all who sign are liable *together*. There is no single liability on any *one* person. "Several" liability is where *each* maker is liable for the *whole amount*, and the holder can bring actions against *each one* for the *whole amount* until he has obtained satisfaction in full. Of course in no case can a holder recover more than the amount of the note!

A new maker cannot be added to a "joint and several" note after it is issued.[12] Nor can there be a series of makers liable severally for their own slice of the total sum,[13] or liable in the alternative.[14]

Where two or more persons sign a note it is deemed to be their "joint and several" note even if it begins "I promise to pay".[15] Payment by one of several makers of a "joint and several" note will discharge it.[16]

A partner, as such, cannot bind his co-partners *severally*, but if he makes a "joint and several" note he can thereby bind the firm jointly[17] and himself *severally*.[18] Moreover, if X, Y and Z are partners and one of them makes a note "I promise to pay . . . " and signs it "for X Y Z" it is a joint note of the firm.[19]

---

8. Bills of Exchange Act 1882, s. 83(3).

9. It is not entirely clear whether the right to the security passes with the note: see *Storm* v. *Stirling* (1854) ER 1353.

10. *Williamson* v. *Rider* [1963] 2 All E.R. 268, Ormrod LJ dissenting. The learned Lord Justice stated at p. 276G that " . . . 'on or before' means that there is a fixed date for payment . . . , that the promisor binds himself to pay on that date, and if he fails can be sued under his promissory note, but if he chooses to pay—and it is purely a matter for him—at an earlier date . . . , then the holder of the bill is under an obligation to accept that payment". This is certainly the understanding of commercial men who regularly provide that payments shall be made "on or before". However, the decision of the majority was unanimously upheld in *Claydon* v. *Bradley* [1987] 1 All ER 522, also a decision of the Court of Appeal. See also Mr A H Hudson, "Time and Promissory Notes" (1962) 25 MLR 593.

11. Bills of Exchange Act 1882, s. 85(1).

12. *Gardener* v. *Walsh* (1855) 24 LJQB 285.

13. *Ibid.*, now each is liable for the whole: Civil Liability (Contribution) Act 1978, s. 3.

14. *Ferris* v. *Bond* (1821) 106 ER 1085.

15. Bills of Exchange Act 1882, s. 85(2).

16. *Nicholson* v. *Revill* (1850) 111 ER 941.

17. *Maclae* v. *Sutherland* (1854) 23 LJQB 229.

18. *Penkivil* v. *Connell* (1850) 155 ER 166.

19. *Ex parte Buckley* (1845) 14 LJ Ex 341.

(iii) "to another"

In fact a note need not be made for the benefit of "another". A note can be made with the maker and the payee being the same person, in such a case if it is payable to the maker's order, it will not be a valid note until it is indorsed by the maker.[20] The reason being that until this is done the note is merely a promise to pay *himself* the sum stated; once it is indorsed it can then be negotiated. If a note is payable "to bearer" specifically, or can be deemed so payable it is, of course, valid *ab initio*.

Moreover, if an instrument is drawn with the drawer and drawee as the same person, or if it is proved the drawee is fictitious or not having capacity to contract, the holder can treat the instrument as a bill of exchange or promissory note as he pleases.[21]

As we shall see a little later, this could, among other things, save the holder the trouble of presentation.

(iv) "signed by the maker"

Nothing need be added here to the remarks made earlier when the definition of a bill of exchange was under discussion.[22]

(v) payment of a note

A promissory note can be payable "on demand" or "at a fixed or determinable future time".

Once again reference should be made to the observations on this subject in relation to "ordinary" bills of exchange. However, it should be noted in the case of promissory notes, if a note payable "on demand" has been indorsed, it *must* be presented for payment within a reasonable time of the indorsement, if it is not, the indorser will be discharged from his liability.[23] In determining what is a reasonable time, regard must be had to the nature of the instrument, the usage of trade, and the facts of the particular case.[24]

Where a note payable on demand has been negotiated, it is not deemed overdue (for the purpose of affecting the holder with defects of title of which he had no notice) just because it appears that a reasonable time for presenting it for payment has elapsed since its issue.[25]

---

20. Bills of Exchange Act 1882, s. 83(2).
21. *Ibid.*, s. 5(2).
22. *Supra* in Chap. 2, heading (v) "Form of a bill".
23. Bills of Exchange Act 1882, s. 86(1).
24. *Ibid.*, s. 86(2).
25. *Ibid.*, s. 86(3). This overrides s. 36(3) which applies only to "ordinary" bills.

While presentment for payment is not necessary to render a maker liable[26] it is necessary to render an indorser liable.[27]

As with an "ordinary" bill of exchange there is no need in the form of a bill to state the place of payment. However, if a place is given, presentment must be made there to render a maker[28] or an indorser[29] liable. If the place is indicated by way of memorandum only (for example, if the note were written on a piece of letter heading), presentment there would be sufficient to render an indorser liable, though presentment to the maker wherever he might be is adequate if the presentment is sufficient in other respects.[30]

(vi) "a sum certain in money"

Once again reference should be made to the observations on this subject made in relation to "ordinary" bills, and nothing further need be added here.

(vii) ". . . to or to the order of . . ."

As before, the same comments apply.

(viii) ". . . a specified person or to bearer"

Regard must again be had to the comments given under this heading as relating to "ordinary" bills. Special note should, however, be made of s. 5(2) of the 1882 Act which gives the holder a choice of treating an instrument as a bill or a note in the following circumstances: (a) if the drawer and drawee are the same person;[31] or (b) the drawee is fictitious;[32] or (c) the drawee has no capacity to contract.

In the case of an "ordinary" bill, if there is a "defect" in the ability of the drawee to pay, obviously the holder will be in a position to claim against the drawer—as is the position under a note; consequently, the holder can treat the instrument as either a bill or a note. The effect is the same.

Moreover, an instrument which is defective as a bill of exchange may nonetheless be a valid promissory note.[33]

---

26. *Ibid.*, s. 87(1).
27. *Ibid.*, s. 87(2).
28. *Ibid.*, s. 87(1).
29. *Ibid.*, s. 87(3).
30. *Ibid.*, s. 87(3).
31. See *Re British Trade Corp* [1932] 2 Ch 1.
32. Nothing is said about the drawee being "non-existent", *cf.* s. 7(3) of the Bills of Exchange Act 1882.
33. *Mason* v. *Lack* (1929) 45 TLR 363, but if it is totally defective it cannot even be a note. See *Britannia Electric Lamp Works* v. *Mandler* [1939] 2 All ER 469, and *Wirth* v. *Weigel* [1939] 3 All ER 712.

FORM OF PROMISSORY NOTES

A not uncommon form of note is as follows:

£100.00   London 1st January 1997.

Twelve months after date hereof I promise to pay Ajax Finance Co. Ltd. of 186 Godminchester Square, London W.53 the sum of One hundred pounds for value received.

John Doe

As we have seen, however, promissory notes sometimes contain conditions or pledges of collateral security. An example of the latter is as follows:

£100.00   London 1st January 1997.

ON DEMAND I promise to pay Ajax Finance Co. Ltd. of 186 Godminchester Square, London W.53 the sum of One hundred pounds for value received with interest thereon at twenty five per cent per annum AND I have deposited with the said Ajax Finance Co. Ltd. and HEREBY PLEDGE to it as collateral security for the same shares numbered 878486–878499 in United Acorns Ltd. for the sum of £100.00. and in default of payment as aforesaid I HEREBY AUTHORISE the said United Acorns Ltd. forthwith either by auction private treaty transfer or otherwise to sell or dispose of the said shares and out of the proceeds of such sale or disposal to reimburse itself the said sum of £100.00 and interest thereon rendering to me any surplus which may be forthcoming from such sale or disposal.

John Doe

LIABILITY ON THE NOTE

In precisely the same way as an "ordinary" bill, a promissory note is often part of a larger transaction, and, as we have seen before, it is necessary for the contract to be properly formed. There must be agreement between the parties, consideration, capacity and so on. A note to be valid must also be delivered to the payee or bearer, until then it is inchoate.[34]

---

34. Bills of Exchange Act 1882, s. 84.

If security is given in addition to the note, the maker is still liable *on the note* even if there is some defect rendering the additional security unenforceable;[35] and this is so even if the note is indorsed to a holder in due course, and the security transferred for value to some other person altogether.[36]

The position of a note covering a hire-purchase contract, and the attendant complications, has already been mentioned in Chapter 5.

LIABILITIES OF THE PARTIES

The 1882 Act provides[37] that in applying the provisions of the Act: the maker is to correspond with the acceptor of a bill; and the first indorser with the drawer of an accepted bill payable to the drawer's order.

The liabilities of the parties must now be considered.

(i) the maker

The maker is the principal debtor. As we have seen, the 1882 Act provides that the maker shall correspond with the acceptor of an "ordinary" bill. However, as the acceptor does not draw (or create) the bill there are two main differences: (a) a note cannot be *made* conditionally,[38] but a bill can be *accepted* conditionally;[39] (b) an acceptor is not liable until presentment to him and he has accepted.[40] No presentment is necessary to render a maker liable.[41]

By making a note, the maker engages that he will pay it according to its tenor,[42] and is precluded from denying to a holder in due course the existence of the payee and his capacity to indorse.[43] Obviously, a maker of a note *must* know in whose favour he is making the promise, and it is not unreasonable to expect him to know whether or not the payee has capacity to indorse.

(ii) the indorser

A promissory note can be validly indorsed in the same way as an "ordinary" bill or cheque, and frequently is.

However, before an indorser will be liable on his signature the note must be presented to the maker for payment.[44]

---

35. *Monetary Advance Co v. Cater* (1888) 20 QBD 785—where a bill of sale of personal chattels was defective, but the accompanying note was held valid.
36. *Glasscock v. Balls* (1889) 24 QBD 13.
37. Bills of Exchange Act 1882, s. 89(2).
38. *Ibid.*, s. 83(1).
39. *Ibid.*, s. 19(2)(*a*).
40. *Ibid.*, s. 53(1).
41. *Ibid.*, s. 89(3).
42. *Ibid.*, s. 88(1).
43. *Ibid.*, s. 88(2).
44. *Ibid.*, s. 87(2). The subsection does not in fact say to whom it must be presented.

As we saw when discussing the form of a note, if in the body of it, it is made payable at some particular place, presentment at that place is essential to retain the liability of an indorser, unless the address was not inserted for that purpose, and was only by way of memorandum. However, in such a case, presentment at that address is sufficient to make the indorser liable.[45]

FOREIGN NOTES

A note which *is*, or on its face *purports* to be, both (a) made; and (b) payable within the "British Islands" is an *Inland* note: any other note is a foreign note.[46]

Unlike a foreign *bill*, where a foreign *note* is dishonoured, it need not be protested in order to retain the liability of the maker and indorser.[47]

45. *Ibid.*, s. 87(3).
46. *Ibid.*, s. 83(4). As to what are the "British Islands" see s. 4. *Cf.* generally with s. 4 as to an inland *bill*.
47. *Ibid.*, s. 89(4). *Cf.* s. 51(2).

CHAPTER 10

INTERNATIONAL LAW FOR INTERNATIONAL BILLS

In international business it happens every day that a bill is drawn in one country and is negotiated, accepted or payable in another. For example[1]:

George draws a bill in England and indorses it to Thomas, also in England. At length it comes into the hands of Pedro in Spain, who indorses it to Gonzalez. The bill, while still in the hands of Gonzalez, is dishonoured. Gonzalez gives notice of dishonour, in Spanish form, to Thomas in England. The notice proves insufficient according to English law.

If Gonzalez sues Thomas in England, the question will then arise as to which legal system will govern the transaction. It will be readily understood that English law may provide one solution, which might be in direct conflict with the provisions of Spanish law. It is for this reason that this branch of English law is sometimes referred to as "The Conflict of Laws";[2] that is, the rules for sorting out which legal system is to apply where a transaction has a foreign element.

THE INTERNATIONAL LAW

There is, in fact, *no* international law of bills of exchange. The law throughout the world is based on two distinct systems:

A. *The Common Law System*

The Common Law System applies to Britain, the United States of America, almost all the Commonwealth countries, and others which originally founded their legal system on the English common law.

B. *The Geneva Convention System*

The Geneva Convention System is based on conventions held in Geneva; the first, of 7 June 1930, entitled "The Unification of the Law Relating to Bills

---

1. These facts are based on those in *Horne* v. *Rouquette* (1878) 3 QBD 514.
2. Sometimes called "Private International Law".

of Exchange", and of 19 March 1931, entitled "The Unification of the Law Relating to Cheques". This system is adopted by most countries of Continental Europe and the USSR as well as Japan and Brazil. However, while some states ratified the Conventions, they took the text of the Uniform Law into their local enactments with various individual amendments, so it could not be said after the adoption of the Conventions there was a "unified" system of law even among the countries that had adopted those Conventions.[3]

When one considers the daily use internationally of bills of exchange it is surprising that there is not a common system operating throughout the world. With this idea in mind in 1966, the United Nations set up a Commission[4] on International Trade Law (UNCITRAL), to study the problem of harmonization of the laws relating to international trade, including a possible new convention on "International Bills of Exchange and International Promissory Notes".

After more than two decades of study, a Convention on International Bills of Exchange and International Promissory Notes was adopted by the General Assembly of the United Nations on 9 December 1988.[5] The Convention applies only to "international" bills and notes (as defined), and does not apply to cheques.[6]

While the General Assembly called upon all Governments to consider becoming party to the Convention, at the time of writing only two of the world's great trading nations—USA and USSR (as was)—have signed.[7] Which illustrates how difficult it is to reach unanimity when framing an "international" set of rules, even given the element of goodwill needed.

There is, of course, already in existence standard codes which are recognized by almost every country in the world, and which are sponsored by the International Chamber of Commerce (ICC).

One relates to letters of credit, and another deals with collection arrangements in export transactions. The first code is called "The Uniform Customs and Practice for Documentary Credits" (UCP), and has been through many revisions over the years since the first edition was adopted at the Seventh Congress of the ICC in Vienna in 1933.

The second, called "Uniform Rules for Collections", replaces the earlier edition which was called "Uniform Rules for the Collection of Commercial

---

3. Not all countries have signed all the conventions however; for example, Austria, Belgium and the USSR have not signed those relating to cheques. Czechoslovakia and Yugoslavia (as they used to be) and Romania and Turkey, adopted the text of the Uniform Law into their metropolitan systems, but did not ratify the Conventions.

4. The Commission began operations on 1 January 1968; see on the subject an article by Professor Clive M Schmitthoff entitled "The Unification of the Law of International Trade", 1968 JBL 105.

5. Resolution 43/165 at the 43rd session of the General Assembly.

6. Article 2.

7. See p. 388 of Multilateral Treaties Deposited with the Secretary General, status 31 December 1991.

Paper", which was first introduced in 1967. The new title was chosen since, in practice, documents collected by banks in these transactions were as likely to have as much "financial" character about them as "commercial". It could, therefore, be said that, in the transactions to which this Second Code applies, there is already in existence an internationally adopted code for these bills and promissory notes.[8]

Litigation and the EEC

It was part of the harmonization of the legal systems of Member States of the EEC, that formalities be simplified which govern the implementation of judgments obtained in the courts of one member state by enforcement in the courts of another; also, that the rules of jurisdiction be standardized between the courts of Member States, so that actions should not be commenced in more than one jurisdiction. It was also necessary to consider the position of actions brought by nationals of non-EEC jurisdictions in the courts of one or other of the Member States. In pursuance of these objects a Convention was signed in Brussels on 27 September 1968.

The Brussels Convention deals only with civil and commercial disputes and only where the defendant in the action is domiciled in an EEC state. In other words, it does not apply to the status or legal capacity of natural persons, or rights in property arising out of matrimonial disputes, nor to wills and succession of property, nor to any social security rights. Also, specifically excluded are insolvency proceedings, arbitrations, revenue and customs matters.

A further convention was signed in Lugano on 19 September 1988, and this extends these regulations to the European Free Trade Area (EFTA) countries of Austria, Switzerland, Iceland, Norway, Finland and Sweden, and where one defendant is domiciled in one of those states.

Both conventions[9] have been given legal efficacy in the UK by the Civil Jurisdiction and Judgments Act of 1982 (which came into force in the UK on 1 January 1987), and which Act is amended to deal with the Lugano Convention by the Civil Jurisdiction and Judgments Act 1991. The text of the Brussels Convention appears in Schedules to the 1982 Act, and these are substituted by new Schedules as of 1 December 1991, by the Civil Jurisdiction and Judgments Act 1982 (Amendment) Order 1990.

---

8. These ICC Codes are considered in detail in section 4 when dealing with "Banker's Documentary Credits". A new Series 500 of the Uniform Customs and Practice for Documentary Credits came into force on 1 January 1994, and new ICC Uniform Rules for Collections, series 522, came into force on 1 January 1996. We also now have ICC Uniform Rules for Bank-to-Bank Reimbursements under Documentary Credits, ICC No 525, which came into force on 1 July 1996.

9. There has become what is called "The Modified Convention" under the 1982 Act, 4th Schedule, where the defendant is domiciled in the UK or where the proceedings are of a kind where jurisdiction in any UK country would apply regardless of domicile, for example where title to land in a UK country was involved.

The provisions of these Conventions can apply both to actions on bills of exchange and bankers' documentary credits, and some of the provisions are considered later in Chapter 17 under the heading of Litigation.[10]

THE CHOICE OF LAW

Therefore, since there is, as yet, no single legal system to apply to international problems relating to bills of exchange, if an issue falls to be decided in England, the rules of English conflict of laws will have to be considered.

Usually, these problems arise in contracts for the buying and selling of goods, and the courts will examine the terms of the main contract between buyer and seller to see whether some legal system is referred to in the documents. If not, then the courts will examine all the facts and circumstances to try to ascertain the legal system with which the transaction has the closest connection. This is referred to as the "proper law" of the contract. It may be, of course, that the "proper law" as applicable to the main contract is not the same legal system that will also be applicable to the contract on the bill of exchange, and the position could be complicated even further by the fact that different aspects of the transaction may be governed by different legal systems. For example, one legal system may govern the format of the bill, and another system altogether the rights in the event of dishonour.[11]

Because it is not always easy in these complicated transactions with parties in different countries to say with certainty what the "proper law" is, it is common for a court to have to decide, as a preliminary point, what legal system it must apply to the problem before hearing the main point of the case. Frequently, these decisions are difficult to make, and it is by no means certain that the express choice of the parties that English law should apply to any dispute shall prevail.[12] Indeed, the "proper law", strictly speaking, cannot be chosen by the parties at all.[13] It is selected by the court as being the system which *the court* thinks the contract has the closest connection. Obviously, however, the wishes of the parties as embodied in their contract will have

10. For a detailed account of these complicated issues, see *Norton Rose on Civil Jurisdiction and Judgments* (1993).

11. "I would regard it as plain that the rules of conflict of laws must be directed at the particular issue of law which is in dispute, rather than the course of action on which the plaintiff relies", *per* Staughton LJ, in *Macmillan* v. *Bishopsgate Investment Trust plc* [1996] 1 All ER 585.

12. See, for example, *Cie Tunisienne de Navigation SA* v. *Cie D'Armement Maritime SA* [1971] AC 572, where English courts refused to have English law govern a contract, although it was substantially in English form and language. Also, *Coast Lines* v. *Hudig & Veder Chartering* [1972] 1 QB 34.

13. *Boissevain* v. *Weil* [1949] 1 KB 482; *cf Vita Products* v. *Unus Shipping Co* [1939] AC 277. In *Turkiyo Is Banhasi AS* v. *Bank of China* [1993] 1 Lloyd's Rep. 132, a telex stated that the proper law of a guarantee was to be Turkish, and that was taken to be impliedly agreed because the defendants did not question it.

substantial weight, provided the choice is made *bona fide*,[14] but such a choice is not, of itself, absolute.[15]

Of course, in England, the *lex fori* (that is, English law[16]) will be applied unless one of the parties considers some other legal system more appropriate, in which case the provisions of that foreign law must be specially pleaded,[17] because there is a presumption that foreign laws are the same as English, unless the contrary is shown. In a case which involved the possible consideration of German law, Lord Dunedin said[18]:

> . . . I am clear that it is for those who say that German law is different from the English to aver it as fact and to prove it. This they have not done, and that being so the German law must be presumed to be the same as the English.

FOREIGN BILLS

We have already seen that a bill of exchange can be either an "inland bill" or a "foreign bill".

14. For example, the choice must not be an attempt to circumvent inconvenient provisions of some other legal system which might have been a more likely choice: see Uniform Laws on International Sales Act 1967, Sched. 1, Art. 4. Where the parties have chosen an exclusive jurisdiction clause they ". . . should be kept to their bargain unless there is good reason to the contrary": *per* Clarke J, in *A/S D/S Svendborg* v. *Wansa* [1996] 2 Lloyd's Rep. 559, 570, applying *The Angelic Grace* [1995] 1 Lloyd's Rep. 87. See also *Egon Oldendorff* v. *Libera Corporation* [1996] 1 Lloyd's Rep. 380.

15. There are authorities to the contrary: see *Rex* v. *International Trustee* [1937] AC 500, *per* Lord Atkin. Speaking of the wishes of the parties he said (at p. 529), " . . . will be ascertained by the intention expressed in the contract, if any, which will be conclusive". Also, speech of Lord Wright in the *Vita Products* case, *supra* (at p. 290), speaking of the parties' choice of law, " . . . it is difficult to see what qualifications are possible, provided the intention expressed is *bona fide* and legal and provided there is no reason for avoiding the choice on the ground of public policy". In *KH Enterprise (Cargo Owners)* v. *Pioneer Container (Owners)* [1994] 2 All ER 250 (PC) the parties agreed the jurisdiction in the event of a dispute as being Taiwan, although the plaintiff, in fact, preferred Hong Kong. When a dispute arose, the plaintiff did not bother with the Taiwan jurisdiction and allowed time there to run out. It was held that a stay of the subsequent Hong Kong proceedings would be granted, since the plaintiff had unreasonably gambled on being permitted to litigate in its preferred forum of Hong Kong instead of the agreed forum of Taiwan.

16. This is not the place for a detailed study of these somewhat involved principles of choice of law, but for the sake of completeness it should be observed that even if an English court does decide that the proper law of the contract *is* English, there is a further problem: does the court apply English *municipal* law (that is, the law as applied to a contract in England, without international connections); or English private international law, the rules of which, it is sometimes found, refer to some other legal system as being the proper law in the particular circumstances. In such a case, the judge could well be faced with applying the rules of that other country to the problem before him, and not "English law" (as probably envisaged by the parties) at all. It was held by Millett LJ in *Macmillan Inc* v. *Bishopsgate Investment Trust plc (No 3)* [1995] 3 All ER 747, a case involving the consideration of whether English law or that of the State of New York should govern priority between holders of competing interests in shares, not only that the laws of the State of New York applied, but also that it was ". . . the domestic law of that State"; at p. 779g to h.

17. RSC Order 18, rule 8. See *Ascherberg Hopwood & Crew Ltd* v. *Casa Musticale Sonzogno di Piero Ostali* [1971] 3 All ER 38.

18. *Dynamit Aktiengesellschaft* v. *Rio Tinto* [1918] AC 292, at p. 293.

A "foreign bill" is defined by the Bills of Exchange Act 1882 as being any bill of exchange other than an inland bill. It will be remembered that an "inland bill" is defined[19] as one which is, or on the face of it purports to be: (a) both drawn and payable within the British Islands[20]; or (b) drawn within the British Islands upon some person resident therein.

It follows, for example, that if a bill of exchange is drawn *on* a bank in a foreign country (the format would show this), and hence payable there, it would be a "foreign bill", even if it was drawn in Britain. Or again, if a bill was drawn abroad (and presumably signed abroad), it would be a "foreign bill" even if drawn on a British bank or other British resident, and in English form. In the latter case, unless there was some indication where it had been drawn and signed (for example, *"fait a Paris"* or whatever), it would not be clear from the face of the bill that it was a "foreign bill", and it would be for a party who wished to allege that it was, to prove the circumstances; because, unless the contrary appears on the face of a bill, a holder may treat it as an inland bill.[21]

The need to consider the distinction between inland and foreign bills is twofold:

(1) If a foreign bill (or on its face appearing to be one) is dishonoured either by non-acceptance or non-payment, it must be protested,[22] and if it has been accepted as to part, it must be protested as to the balance.[23] If it is not protested, the drawer and the indorsers are discharged.[24] Protesting is not necessary for inland bills.

(2) Different rules can apply to inland and foreign bills, where there is a conflict of laws problem, as we shall see below when we consider the rules of choice of law.

MAKING THE CHOICE

We observed above that it was not always easy to decide which legal system should be selected to govern a problem with a foreign element. In contracts involving bills of exchange, s. 72 of the Bills of Exchange Act 1882 assists, to some degree, by stipulating rules as to which legal system shall govern which aspect of the contract on the bill. Each part of the transaction must now be considered.

19. Bills of Exchange Act 1882, s. 4(1).
20. These are defined as "any part of the United Kingdom of Great Britain and Ireland, the Islands of Man, Guernsey, Jersey, Alderney and Sark, and the islands adjacent to any of them being part of the dominions of Her Majesty": Bills of Exchange Act 1882, s. 4(1).
21. *Ibid.*, s. 4(2).
22. *Ibid.*, s. 51(2). It is not necessary to protest for non-payment if the bill has already been protested for non-acceptance.
23. *Ibid.*, s. 44(2).
24. *Ibid.*, s. 51(2).

Capacity

In fact, the Act makes no reference to which system of law should govern the question of capacity. So that if the drawer of a bill, or an indorser, or acceptor wishes to negate the liability for his signature because, so he alleges, he lacks the necessary capacity to commit himself on the bill, the general principles of English conflict of laws must be looked at.

We have already seen that capacity in relation to bills of exchange is the same as capacity under the ordinary law of contract,[25] and capacity to contract is probably governed by one of the following legal systems: (a) the law of the country where the party is domiciled (the *lex domicilii*); or (b) the law of the country where the transaction takes place (the *lex loci contractus*); or (c) the law of the country deemed by the court to be the proper law of the bill of exchange.

It is strange that in this modern day and age there should be no authority on the point.

Subject to what is said at the end of this topic regarding corporations, the *lex domicilii* is not a very attractive choice, since it is frequently difficult to establish a person's domicile anyway; and even if this is clear, it is unlikely that an English court would willingly entertain a disability peculiar to, say, the drawer's domicile if he was competent in all other respects under English law. However, it must be noted that in some countries only traders have the right (that is, the capacity) to issue bills of exchange.

The *lex loci contractus* is marginally better, but only just, since it may be a location quite by accident. It was decided in the old case of *Male v. Roberts*[26] that capacity to contract was to be determined by the law of the place where the contract was made; and this view was supported by Lord Maugham LC in *Baindail v. Baindail*[27] when he said, " . . . it certainly is the view of high authority here that capacity to enter in England into an ordinary commercial contract is determined not by the law of the domicile but by the *lex loci*".

If this view is correct it would mean that an unscrupulous party to a bill could sign it in a country where he had no capacity to do so, and rely on that defect to avoid his liability if subsequently sued in England.

The solution to be preferred, and which certainly gives the court the greatest degree of discretion, is the view that capacity is to be governed by the proper law of the bill. Applied to a commercial contract, this was the decision reached in *Bodley Head Ltd v. Flegon*,[28] where the Russian author, Alexander Solzhenitsyn, gave a power of attorney to his Swiss lawyer, which stated that Swiss law would govern any disputes. It was subsequently alleged that the

---

25. *Ibid.*, s. 22(1).
26. (1800) 3 Esp. 163. See the speech of Lord Eldon. This was cited with approval by the Saskatchewan Court of Appeal in *Bondholders Securities Corp v. Manville* [1933] 4 DLR 699.
27. [1946] P 122, at p. 128.
28. [1972] 1 WLR 680.

author had no capacity to grant such a power under Russian law as his *lex domicilii*, but this was rejected by the court in favour of Swiss law which was held to be the proper law of the power.

The *lex domicilii* appears, however, to have one area of undisputed application, and that is with the capacity of corporations.

A corporation, being a juristic "person" and, hence, a creature of law, takes all its powers, rights and capacity from the terms of its incorporation in whichever country it is formed. This is its domicile, and once having acquired it, it cannot be changed.[29]

Whether a corporation has the capacity to be a party to a bill of exchange can be checked in the country of incorporation, by examining the terms of its constitution or by taking the opinion of a local lawyer. So that, whatever capacity, or incapacity, a corporation has by its *lex domicilii* will be recognized and upheld by the English courts.[30] This has been established by the House of Lords in *Metliss v. National Bank of Greece and Athens SA*[31] which involved a bank in Greece being amalgamated with another, whereby the new bank took over and became the "universal successor" to the rights and obligations of the old one. This concept is unknown in English law, but since the new bank had capacity under its *lex domicilii* to acquire all these rights and obligations, English law recognized and enforced the existing obligations of the old bank against the new.

Requisites of form

Section 72(1) of the Bills of Exchange Act 1882 provides:

The validity of a bill as regards requisites of form is determined by the law of the place of issue, and . . . of the supervening contracts . . . by the law of the place where the contract was made.

In the ordinary way of things, this is the law of the place where the act takes place—*lex loci contractus*. For example, if a foreign law provides that indorsements must be witnessed, and one is not, no action will lie on the bill in England, although such a provision is unknown to English law.

One general observation is in point with the drafting of s. 72(1), and it is that the wording is declaratory, and admits of no variation by the parties. The proper law, for example, can play no part as to form, so that if two Americans agree the format of a bill shall be in accordance with the laws and practice of New York but they happen to be sitting in London when one hands the bill to the other, it is to English law they must look for the "requisites of form".[32]

29. *Gasque v. IRC* [1940] 2 KB 80. Unlike private individuals.
30. *Von Hellfield v. Rechnitzer and Mayer Freres & Co* [1914] Ch 748.
31. [1958] AC 509. The circumstances of this claim have spawned a great deal of litigation. See also *Adams v. National Bank of Greece and Athens* [1961] AC 255, and *National Bank of Greece SA v. Westminster Bank Executor and Trustee Co (Channel Islands) Ltd* [1971] AC 945.
32. See *Guaranty Trust Co of New York v. Hannay* [1918] 1 KB 43.

Two other points about the provisions of the subsection need to be noted:

(1) The place where a bill is first delivered—"the place of issue"—may not necessarily be the place where it is drawn. It is by no means unheard of for a bill to be drawn in Paris and delivered by hand to the payee in London.

(2) Where the supervening contracts are "made" might well be debatable. For example, under English law, if the postal service is being used by the parties as a means of communication, a contract is concluded when the letter of acceptance is posted.[33] According to the laws of a number of Continental countries, it is when the letter is received. This being the case, it is not an easy question for an English court seized of a claim on a bill to decide whether, if a bill is indorsed in Switzerland and posted there to England, the contract on the bill is "made" in Switzerland or England. The answer will depend upon which legal system (Swiss or English) is deemed to govern the act; because the court will not know where the contract is "made" until that issue is decided; and without such a decision the English court could not know which legal system to apply as the *lex loci contractus* under s. 72(1).

The remaining conundrum is, by which legal system, and on what basis, will the English court decide this preliminary point? The position is, to say the least, not wholly clear, but the "putative" proper law of the transaction seems the most acceptable solution; that is, the legal system which would, most likely, be the proper law of the contract, if the contract was validly created.[34]

It may seem strange that such a preliminary issue could be decided by the putative proper law, when, as we saw above, the proper law (whatever it may be) has no part to play in deciding the main issue between the parties.[35]

There are two exceptions to the rule that the *lex loci contractus* governs requisites of form:

(1) English law does not recognize foreign revenue laws. So if a bill is properly drawn in accordance with the rules of the *lex loci contractus*, except that it is not correctly stamped, it will still be valid in England.[36]

(2) If a bill is issued abroad, but is not valid as to form by the local law, it may still be valid "for the purpose of enforcing payment"[37] if: (a) it conforms to the laws of the United Kingdom as regards form; and

---

33. *Household Fire Insurance Co v. Grant* (1879) 4 Ex D 216; *Benaim v. De Bono* [1924] AC 514.

34. See *per* Salmon J (as he then was) in *Albeko Schuhmaschinen v. The Kamborian Shoe Machine Co Ltd* (1961) 111 LJ 519; and *Mackender v. Feldia AG* [1967] 2 QB 590.

35. See also *infra* Chap. 17, under the heading "The Applicable Law", for the same type of problem with documentary credits.

36. Bills of Exchange Act 1882, s. 72(1)(*a*).

37. A holder, claiming a declaration that he need not repay money already received from the acceptor of the bill, is not an action "for the purpose of enforcing payment": *Guaranty Trust Co of New York v. Hannay* [1918] 1 KB 43; on appeal [1918] 2 KB 43.

(b) both the holder and the person he is seeking to enforce the bill against became parties to the bill in the United Kingdom.[38]

The drawing, indorsement and acceptance

The legal system to govern these transactions is stated in s. 72(2) in the following terms:

Subject to the provisions of this Act, the interpretation[39] of the drawing, indorsement, acceptance, or acceptance supra protest of a bill, is determined by the law of the place where such contract is made.

Once again, subject to establishing where a contract is "made", the provision means that the law by which all these matters shall be judged is the *lex loci contractus*.

Some examples may help:

G & H MONTAGE GmbH v. IRVANI[40]

G & H Montage GmbH (Montage), a German corporation, drew a series of bills of exchange on Industrial Development and Service Co Ltd (IDS), a company incorporated in Iran as drawees. The bills were drawn payable to the order of Montage in London at National Westminster Bank plc. The bills were then sent to IDS for acceptance, which was duly done, and Mr Irvani, who was the main shareholder of IDS, then signed the bills on the back without adding any other words or description of why he was signing. The bills were then sent back to Montage, who signed the bills as drawers, and passed them to their bank. The bank then suggested that words should be added on the back of the bills to indicate that Mr Irvani had signed as guarantor, the suggested wording being: *bon pour aval pour les tires*. Mr Irvani agreed to this and those words were typed on each bill by Montage above Mr Irvani's signature in Germany, without the bills being sent back to Iran. Eventually, each bill was duly presented to National Westminster Bank plc at maturity and each was dishonoured but notice of dishonour was not given to Mr Irvani. Montage then sued Mr Irvani personally on the bills in London as guarantor. Mr Irvani contended that by applying English law, and in particular s. 72(2) of the 1882 Act, the court was categorising him as an indorser and not a guarantor, and if that were so, notice of dishonour should have been given to him, and as it had not, he was discharged from liability pursuant to the provisions of ss. 48 and 51(2) of the 1882 Act. *Held*—"Although an *aval* has no counterpart in English law, the obligations which it creates in German law are both recognisable and enforceable in the English courts under s. 72(2) of the 1882 Act." Furthermore, "The overwhelming association geographically with Germany would not . . . be displaced by the fact that it was to [Mr Irvani] in Iran that recourse has to be made for his permission to adjust the

---

38. Bills of Exchange Act 1882, s. 72(1)(*b*).

39. It is not wholly clear what is meant here by the word "interpretation". The *Concise Oxford Dictionary* says it means to "bring out the meaning of"; however, in this context, it is usually taken to have a rather special and legalistic meaning of "the legal effect" or "the essential validity".

40. [1990] 2 All ER 225. Signature on bill of exchange by way of an *aval* (guarantee), while not having a counterpart in English law, was enforceable in England, as the law of the Republic of Germany applied, and the *aval* was recognised there.

bills . . .".[41] Mr Irvani was, therefore, liable as a guarantor[42] on the bills not as an indorser, and the lack of notice of dishonour did not discharge him.[43]

ALCOCK v. SMITH[44]

A bill was drawn in Norway by an Englishman in favour of X. X indorsed the bill to M, who indorsed it to A. Under a judgment obtained in Norway the bill was seized by the sheriff and subsequently sold to K. A sued in England for the amount of the bill, claiming that K, the holder, had no title as the seizure was bad. This was so by English law, but by Norwegian law the seizure by the sheriff and the subsequent sale by him was valid and K had a good title. Which law applied? *Held*—that as s. 72(2) of the 1882 Act provides that the law of the place where the contract is made shall apply, Norwegian law was applied and under that system K had a good title and so A's action failed.

EMBIRICOS v. ANGLO-AUSTRIAN BANK[45]

X in Romania drew a cheque payable to E on an English bank. E specially indorsed it to Y, who was in London. Before it was posted Z, an employee of E, stole the cheque, forged Y's indorsement and obtained payment from a bank in Austria. The Austrian bank then received payment from the drawee bank. The Austrian bank were then sued for conversion in England. By Austrian law the bank got a good title to the cheque, by English law they did not. Which law applied? *Held*—that applying s. 72(2) as the act was in Austria, their law governed the case, and as by that law the holder of a cheque, even after forgery, gets a good title if he has taken in good faith, the Austrian bank succeeded.

KOECHLIN v. KESTENBAUM[46]

X drew a bill in France in favour of Y. It was accepted, payable in London by Z. X indorsed the bill on behalf of and with the authority of Y, and negotiated it to A. Z refused payment as the indorsment was not according to English law (which requires agents to sign "per pro" within s. 32(1) of the 1882 Act). A sued Z in England, relying on French law which did not have this requirement. Which law applied? *Held*—that once again applying s. 72(2), as the indorsement was executed in France, their law applied and A could recover.

From this it will be seen that the legal consequences of an act are governed by the law of the place where it is carried out. To this rule there is one exception:

The proviso to s. 72(2) states:

Provided that where an inland bill is indorsed in a foreign country the indorsement shall as regards the payer be interpreted according to the law of the United Kingdom.

---

41. *Ibid., per* Purchas LJ at p. 244b.
42. The expression used by the learned LJJ is "*avaliste*".
43. A point was also raised that Mr Irvani, if he was a guarantor, could not be liable as there was no note or memorandum in writing within the Statute of Frauds to make him answerable for the "debt, default or miscarriage of another person". It was held that Mr Irvani's liability was *on the bill*, and the Statute of Frauds had no application to liabilities arising under a bill of exchange: *per* Mustill LJ, at p. 238j, and Purchas LJ, at p. 245b.
44. [1892] 1 Ch 238.
45. [1905] 1 KB 677.
46. [1927] 1 KB 889.

The following points must be noted with regard to this exception to the operation of the *lex loci contractus*: 1. It applies only to inland bills: foreign bills fall within the *lex loci contractus* rule.[47] 2. The payer (acceptor) of an inland bill is only liable to a subsequent holder under an indorsement valid by the laws of the United Kingdom.[48] 3. The proviso operates only "as regards the payer"; consequently, it would not apply to a dispute between competing claims as happened in *Alcock v. Smith*.[49]

The duties of a holder

Section 72(3) of the 1882 Act, on the duties of a holder on presentment and dishonour, provides as follows:

The duties of the holder with respect to presentment for acceptance or payment and the necessity for or sufficiency of a protest or notice of dishonour, or otherwise, are determined by the law of the place where the act is done or the bill is dishonoured.

The drafting of this sub-section could be happier.[50] However, attempting an analysis of the wording, the probable intention is this:

1. Presentment: whether for acceptance or payment, is determined by the law of the place where the act was done, that is, as we have seen before, the *lex loci contractus*.
2. Dishonour: the necessity for, or sufficiency of, a protest (for foreign bills), or notice of dishonour, are determined by the law of the place where the bill is dishonoured; again, the *lex loci contractus*.

The problem, however, is which law governs a situation where no act was "done", but was, in fact, overlooked and not done at all. For example, if a foreign bill was not protested, who is to say what are the results of that

47. The proviso establishes statutory force for the decision in *Lebel v. Tucker* (1867) LR 3 QB 77, which was a case of an inland bill; contrast the position of a foreign bill in *Koechlin v. Kestenbaum* [1927] 1 KB 889.
48. There are various references in s. 72 to "the laws of the United Kingdom": in fact, there is no such thing. So far as an English court is concerned, the laws of Scotland, Northern Ireland and the Channel Islands are all "foreign" within the context of a conflict of laws problem. In *Barclays Bank plc v. Glasgow City Council* and *Kleinwort Benson Ltd v. Glasgow City Council* [1994] 4 All ER 865, the defendant council claimed that it was domiciled in Scotland and an English court had no jurisdiction pursuant to the provisions of the Civil Jurisdiction and Judgments Act 1982. Hirst J held that the city council must be sued ". . . in their court of domicile in Scotland", p. 882e, Kleinwort Benson Ltd appealed and the Court of Appeal held that it was desirable to ask the Court of Justice of the European Communities for a preliminary ruling on which jurisdiction should hear the case. "One may be forgiven for wondering why it matters, since it is common ground that the transactions are all governed by English law, and that the proceedings are very likely to end up in the House of Lords, wherever they are tried at first instance." *Per* Lloyd LJ, p. 884b.
49. [1892] 1 Ch 283.
50. Cheshire & North, *Private International Law*, 12th edn. (1992) at p. 526, believe the wording ". . . verges perilously on the unintelligible". Dicey & Morris, *Conflict of Laws*, 12th edn. (1993) Vol. 2 at pp. 1439 and 1440, think there could be a choice of laws, either the place where the act was done *or* the place of dishonour.

omission?[51] Until the point is resolved either by Parliament or the courts, there must be a doubt; however, as the wording of the sub-section is declaratory in form rather than enabling (as is the whole of s. 72), if there is a gap in the rules it would be logical to fall back on the proper law of the transaction, or the bill as a whole, as the case may be.

The sum payable

The sum payable under a bill of exchange is, of course, the amount and currency as shown on the face of the bill, and if it is paid on the due date there will be no problem. In the event that a bill is drawn in one country and payable in another, the due date is determined according to the laws of the place where it is payable.[52]

Difficulties, of course, arise where the bill is dishonoured. The holder is standing out of his money, and he may have to sue the acceptor or other parties for payment.

At one time, in bringing his action in England, there were two obstacles: first, the English court could only give judgment in sterling; secondly, if a foreign currency was involved, the conversion date was taken to be *the date of dishonour*, so that by the time the trial took place, in these days of fluctuating exchange rates, a holder could find himself severely prejudiced.

All these problems were swept away by the House of Lords in

MILIANGOS v. GEORGE FRANK (TEXTILES) LTD.[53]

M, a Swiss national and resident, supplied G, in England, with polyester yarn. Payment was by two bills of exchange drawn on and accepted by G. Action was brought in England on the bills when they were dishonoured. The claim was for 415,522 Swiss francs. Had G paid when he should the rate was 9.9 Swiss francs to the £, but by judgment the exchange rate had fallen to 6.00 Swiss francs to the £. If judgment had to be given only in sterling, G could satisfy the 415,522 Swiss francs by the sterling equivalent of 6.00 to the £—or about £41,000. M argued, however, that he was entitled *not to the sterling equivalent*, but to 415,522 Swiss francs. Consequently, as the rate had gone down, it would cost G more sterling—approximately £60,000—to satisfy the judgment. *Held*—that M was entitled to judgment in Swiss francs, otherwise it would mean that by not paying their obligations when they should, G would get the advantage of their own wrong.

51. Dicey & Morris, *ibid.*, p. 1439, suggest the sub-section would need to be read "where the act is done or *to be* done . . . ". This certainly would remove the problem.
52. Bills of Exchange Act 1882, s. 72(5).
53. [1976] AC 443. Before this the Court of Appeal had decided a foreign money judgment could be given in arbitration proceedings: *Jugoslovenska Oceanska Plovidba v. Castle Investment Co Inc* [1974] QB 292. In the year following they decided in *Schorsch Meier GmbH v. Hannin* [1975] QB 416 that judgment in a foreign currency could be given by an English court. The House of Lords put the issue beyond doubt.

Therefore, English courts can now give judgment in the currency of any foreign country.[54]

Following on from this change, the Administration of Justice Act 1977 amended[55] the Bills of Exchange Act 1882 to allow foreign currency claims and judgments to be made and given in cases of bills of exchange by repealing s. 57(2) (which allowed for re-exchanging with interest until payment, on bills dishonoured abroad) and s. 72(4) (which stated that on a bill drawn out of, but payable within, the United Kingdom the sum would be calculated according to the rate for sight drafts).[56]

The *Miliangos* rule is procedural of course. It simply allows the plaintiff to claim, and get judgment in, the currency of the contract debt or his loss or whatever. It could well be that a bill of exchange is in a currency which has moved *against* the plaintiff, and in such a situation it could be most unfortunate, for all the rule ensures is that the money of account is claimable, and that, as in the *Miliangos* case,[57] " . . . a Swiss franc for good or ill should remain a Swiss franc . . . ". If, because of the non-payment by the defendant/debtor, the plaintiff/creditor finds his bargain ruined by the currency fluctuations of the time, he must seek his remedy in damages for this loss[58]: the *Miliangos* rule will not help him.

Where the action is for a liquidated sum, as would be the case of a bill of exchange or claiming an outstanding debt, the plaintiff must state in his claim the foreign currency, if that is how he wishes the judgment to be ordered.[59] If, on the other hand, the claim is for an unliquidated sum, for example, general damages—and whether in contract or tort—the currency of the claim will be that which the court decides the debtor/defendant knew, or should have

54. This is now a rule of general application, and can apply to claims for damages for breach of contract: *Jean Kraut AG* v. *Albany Fabrics* [1977] 2 All ER 116; and to claims in tort: *The Despina R* [1979] AC 685, *Hoffman* v. *Sofaer* [1982] 1 WLR 1350. However, it has been held that the rule does not apply to cases of winding up of companies: if there is a claim in a foreign currency it must be converted into sterling, as in days of old, at the rate obtaining on the date—if a compulsory winding up—of the order: *Re Dynamics Corp of America* [1976] 1 WLR 757; or—if a creditors' voluntary winding up—as at the resolution: *Re Lines Bros Ltd* [1982] 3 All ER 187.
55. Administration of Justice Act 1977, s. 4(2).
56. The same statute has also repealed: Art. 3(2) of the European Communities (Enforcement of Community Judgments) Order 1972; s. 2(3) of the Foreign Judgments (Reciprocal Enforcement) Act 1933; s. 1(3) of the Arbitration (Investment Disputes) Act 1966.
57. *Per* Lord Wilberforce, [1976] AC 443, p. 466.
58. *Ozalid Group (Export) Ltd* v. *African Continental Bank Ltd* [1979] 2 Lloyd's Rep. 231. Donaldson J seemed to think the plaintiff has a choice of the foreign currency or sterling. He said he could find no trace " . . . of any intention to make a claim in this form obligatory" at p. 233. However, the foreign currency claim seems to be obligatory: *Federal Commerce & Navigation Co* v. *Tradax Export SA* [1977] 1 QB 324, *per* Lord Denning MR at p. 342a. "Once it is recognized that judgment *can* be given in a foreign currency . . . it *should* be given in every case . . . otherwise one side or the other will suffer unfairly by the fluctuations of exchange."
59. Practice Direction (Judgment: Foreign Currency) [1976] 1 WLR 83: which was amended by Practice Direction (Judgment: Foreign Currency) [1977] 1 WLR 197. See RSC Order 42, rule 1(5).

known, the currency in which the creditor/plaintiff's loss probably would be sustained.[60]

When it comes to payment of a foreign currency claim, whether before judgment or afterwards, the debtor has a choice of three methods: (a) to pay the amount of the foreign currency. This would be the expected way of satisfying the claim; or (b) paying the sterling equivalent of the foreign currency claim, with a conversion rate obtaining on the *actual date of payment*;[61] or (c) if there was agreed a *money of payment*, as opposed to a money of account, by settling the claim in that currency, again, with a conversion rate as at *the actual date of payment*.

If the judgment, once obtained, is not satisfied, and enforcement proves necessary, this must be executed in sterling, and hence a conversion from the foreign currency of the judgment will be necessary, at the rate obtaining on the day the court orders enforcement.

60. See *The Folias* and *The Despina R* [1979] AC 685. Without further direction, the currency in which general damages should be calculated is an issue for the proper law of the contract: *Services Europe Atlantique Sud* v. *Stockholms Rederiaktiebolag Svea* [1977] 1 Lloyd's Rep. 39. As is the *right* to interest if none was specified in the bill or the agreement, although the *amount* of interest has been held to be procedural and, hence, for the *lex fori*: *Miliangos* v. *George Frank (Textiles) Ltd (No.2)* [1977] 2 Lloyd's Rep. 434.

61. Prior to *Miliangos*, the conversion date was at breach: *Re United Railways of Havana and Regla Warehouses Ltd* [1961] AC 1007.

SECTION TWO

CHEQUES

CHAPTER 11

THE RELATIONSHIP OF BANKER AND CUSTOMER

INTRODUCTION

A cheque is a bill of exchange[1] which is drawn on a banker[2] and is payable on demand,[3] and, unless otherwise provided, the Bills of Exchange Act 1882 dealing with bills *payable on demand applies to cheques*.[4]

Cheques, being payable on demand, do not have to be presented for acceptance prior to payment.[5] Presentment for payment is effected by taking the cheque to the bank on whom it is drawn and cashing it "over the counter", or paying it into one's bank account for collection through the banker's clearing system in the usual way.

The use of banks in the clearing of cheques introduces another series of parties and obligations, in addition to the drawer, payee, indorser relationship.

THE BANKERS

Before considering the subject of cheques, something must be said of the banks which handle them.

Section 2 of the Bills of Exchange Act 1882 says that a "banker", "includes a body of persons whether incorporated or not who carry on the business of banking". Other than this, there is no definition of what may be considered a "banker" or a "bank". The Cheques Act 1957 follows the same definition, as it is " . . . construed as one . . . " with the 1882 Act.[6]

There can be no problem with the ordinary clearing banks, but in years gone by difficulties in recognizing whether a company or other institution was, or

---

1. Bills of Exchange Act 1882, s. 3(1).
2. See *ibid.*, s. 2, and the discussion *infra* under the heading "The Bankers".
3. Bills of Exchange Act 1882, s. 10(1).
4. *Ibid.*, s. 73.
5. It was, at one time, thought the initialling of a cheque by the drawee bank indicated the bank had accepted it. This is not so: see *Gaden* v. *Newfoundland Savings Bank* [1899] AC 281, at p. 285.
6. Cheques Act 1957, s. 6(1).

was not, a "bank" did occur with the so-called "fringe" or "secondary" banks, and in doubt the problem had to be resolved by the courts.[7]

Reference must now be made to s. 3 of the Banking Act 1979, under which provisions, banks are "recognized" by the Bank of England. It would, therefore, appear that if an institution were recognized by the Bank of England as a "bank" this would be adequate for the purposes of the Bills of Exchange Act and the Cheques Act.[8] Then again, if an institution is carrying on "the business of banking", but is not a recognized bank within the terms of the 1979 Act, one assumes it would still be possible for the courts to hold that it was a "banker" within the Bills of Exchange Act and the Cheques Act, however.[9]

The 1979 Act also created "licensed institutions" (which have become referred to as "licensed deposit takers"), who are not recognized banks, but, as the name implies, they are "licensed" to hold deposits on behalf of customers, and offer other banking services, notwithstanding that they are not "recognized".

New regulations giving the Bank of England greater powers of supervision were introduced by the Banking Act 1987,[10] which largely implemented the proposals contained in the Government's White Paper entitled "Banking Supervision".[11]

The main thrust of the Act is to protect the public from institutions who may receive deposits *from* customers or investors, and then misappropriate them or mismanage them to a point where the business may be forced into liquidation. The main provisions, therefore, are directed to "deposit taking"; the control of advertising for such deposits and the use of names of institutions suggesting they are "banks"; the proper maintenance of accounts and auditing; and the supervision of the management and control of those institutions.

It must be noted, however, that the Bank of England owes no duty of care to individual banks and financial institutions as to how they conduct *their* businesses. Following the Johnson Matthey affair, it was suggested that the Bank of England might be liable in negligence in not discovering the losses in

---

7. See *United Dominions Trust v. Kirkwood* [1966] 2 QB 431, where the subject is exhaustively reviewed, in particular, *per* Lord Denning MR, at pp. 442F to 448C. See also an article by Mr Maurice Megrah QC (1967) 30 MLR 86.

8. Yet this statutory recognition is for no purposes " . . . other than those of this Act . . . ": Banking Act 1979, s. 36(2).

9. For example, in *Lumsden v. London Trustee Savings Bank* [1971] 1 Lloyd's Rep. 114, the court was prepared to say the defendants were "Bankers" even though the Trustee Savings Bank was not recognized within the terms of the 1979 Act. The Trustee Savings Banks are, of course, governed by considerable statutory provisions, notably the Trustee Savings Banks Acts 1981 and 1985. The 1987 Banking Act still does not define a bank as such, but there are variously defined "authorized institutions", ss. 3 and 69, and Sched. 2. See also the Banking Coordination (Second Council Directive) Regulation 1992, SI 1992/3218.

10. 1987, c. 22.

11. Cmnd 9695.

Johnson Matthey's commercial loan portfolio, but this argument failed.[12] A commercial concern cannot look to the Bank of England to make good losses " . . . arising from its own imprudence or carelessness on the basis that the Bank of England should have discovered and dealt with those shortcomings".[13]

S. 1 of the Banking Act 1987 sets out the powers and duties of the Bank of England in relation to "deposit taking".[14] The Bank is given general supervisory duties, including the establishment of the Board of Banking Supervision. The members of the Board advise the Bank of England on the exercise of its functions in this supervisory capacity.

In exercising this control the Bank of England has wide powers, for example, any notice served by the Bank on a financial institution demanding the disclosure of information takes precedence over a High Court injunction ordering that institution not to disclose information to any third party.[15]

Under s. 32 of the Act the Treasury is empowered to make regulations regarding advertisements for deposits and also to regulate the making of unsolicited calls seeking deposits. The Act also controls[16] the use of names which indicate that the institution is a "bank", unless it is so authorized and with a paid-up capital of not less than £5m sterling; under these provisions the Bank of England can object to the use of any name it considers misleading or undesirable.

Under s. 3 of the Act only institutions so authorized by the Bank of England may accept deposits from members of the public in the course of carrying on the business of banking, and such exceptions as there are, are set out in s. 4 of the Act and the Second Schedule to the Act. The Bank has power under the Act to grant or to refuse an application from an institution for leave to be given status of accepting deposits. There are various criteria which the Bank must take into account, one of which is that the institution must have net assets of not less than £1m sterling. It is, of course, an offence under the Act[17] for an institution falsely to describe itself as being authorized to accept deposits or being exempt from the provisions of the Banking Act 1987.

Such institutions must, of course, maintain proper accounts and s. 45 requires the audited accounts of any such institution to be open for inspection, and notice must be given to the Bank of any decision to remove or not

---

12. *Minories Finance Ltd* v. *Arthur Young* and *Johnson Matthey plc* v. *Arthur Young* [1989] 2 All ER 105. The auditors (Arthur Young) were also sued for alleged negligence in not discovering the state of the loan portfolio.

13. *Ibid.*, p. 110f, *per* Saville J.

14. Futures brokers do not carry on a "deposit-taking business . . . " merely by asking their clients to deposit with them money to cover future transactions: *SCF Finance Co Ltd* v. *Masri* [1987] 1 All ER 175, a case under the 1979 Act.

15. *A* v. *B Bank* [1992] 1 All ER 778, at p. 790g, where the Bank of England's powers under the Act are reviewed.

16. Ss. 67 to 73.

17. S. 18.

reappoint an auditor. Indeed, under s. 47 auditors may pass information about the institution to the Bank of England notwithstanding the usual duty which the auditors owe to the shareholders of the institution.

Control is also exercised[18] over changes of directors or managers of a controlled institution, and significant shareholders must also give notice of their interests to the Bank of England. If an authorized institution involves itself in transactions which may put its available capital resources at risk, this must also be reported to the Bank.[19]

Part Two of the Act creates a Deposit Protection Scheme, first established under the Banking Act 1979. Under this Scheme, a fund is established to which authorized institutions must contribute. Under the terms of this Scheme, where an institution becomes insolvent or subject to an administration order, its depositors may receive up to three-quarters of their deposit, provided that deposit does not exceed £20,000; in other words, the maximum refund in such cases would be £15,000.[20]

Further controls are exercised[21] over various "overseas institutions" and "representative offices". Once more the Bank of England has power to object to the use of any name or proposed name of such an institution, and the Treasury may require the representative office of overseas banks to provide information and be subject to the reasonable requirements of the Treasury. In spite of all these regulations we have recently experienced the scandal following the collapse of the Bank of Credit and Commerce International and a call has gone out for still further powers to be given to the Bank of England in the control of businesses holding themselves out as "banks".

So far as branches of a bank are concerned, they are, together with the head office, deemed to be one bank in the eyes of the law.[22] Although, there are a number of exceptions, and one hazards the view that the list of exceptions is far from closed. For example: (a) Payment of cheques can only be claimed at the branch at which the account is situated.[23] (b) A countermand on a cheque is only valid at the branch upon which the cheque is drawn.[24] (c) Notice of proceedings served on the head office is not notice to the branches.[25]

---

18. S. 36.

19. S. 38.

20. The claimant must be entitled to the deposit at the time of presentation of the winding-up petition: Banking Act 1987 (Meaning of Deposit) Order 1991. Before this Order depositors could maximize the amount of their claims by assigning sums of £20,000 to friends, who could then *each* claim £15,000 from the fund: *Deposit Protection Board* v. *Dalia* [1993] 1 All ER 599. On appeal [1994] 1 All ER 539 *per* Russell LJ and Sir Michael Fox, see now [1994] 2 All ER 577 (HL), previous decisions reversed. A depositor means the person who *originally* made the deposit.

21. Under ss. 78 to 81.

22. However, if banks are separate companies, and so independent of one another, they are not branches: *Bank of Tokyo Ltd* v. *Magid Karoon* [1986] 3 WLR 414.

23. *Barclays Bank plc* v. *Bank of England* [1985] 1 All ER 385, at p. 391d.

24. *London Provincial & South Western Bank Ltd* v. *Buszard* (1918) 35 TLR 142; and see *Burnett* v. *Westminster Bank* [1965] 3 All ER 81.

25. See *Z Ltd* v. *A and others* [1982] 1 All ER 556.

If the branch in England is of a foreign bank, then it is subject to the laws of England, *not* to the laws of the country where its head office is situated.[26] Equally, a branch of an English bank in a foreign country is not subject to English law, but to the local law.[27]

It follows from these general principles that payment on a cheque drawn on a foreign bank abroad cannot be claimed on an English branch of the bank,[28] nor the delivery of documents from an English branch of a foreign bank held by that bank in its home country.[29]

1. THE RELATIONSHIP DEFINED

The relationship of a banker and his customer is that of debtor and creditor,[30] but unlike the usual case of debtor and creditor the banker does not have to seek out his customer to pay him.[31]

The general workings of a bank's services are well known.[32] They hold money belonging to a customer, and pay out that money as the customer's agent, on instructions from the customer, usually in the form of printed cheque forms issued by the bank, or by some form of transfer between banks.

A customer may, by agreement, be paid interest on his money held by the bank, usually in what is called a "deposit account" or may borrow money from a bank in any one of a variety of ways and upon varying terms and conditions.

It is rare for the relationship to be reduced to writing, with the exception of the bank "mandate" form which a customer signs when an account is opened, and which sets out the authority of the bank to honour the customer's cheques and other instructions.

---

26. *Power Curber International Ltd* v. *National Bank of Kuwait* [1981] 1 WLR 1233, *per* Lord Denning MR at p. 1241H.

27. *R* v. *Grossman* (1981) 73 Cr App R 302. The Isle of Man is "foreign" for this purpose. An order for discovery of documents held abroad should not be made " . . . save in very exceptional circumstances . . . ": *Per* Hoffman J in *MacKinnon* v. *Donaldson, Lufkin and Jenrette Securities Corporation* [1986] 2 WLR 453, at p. 462G. "As a general rule the contract between a bank and its customer is governed by the law of the place where the account is kept, in the absence of agreement to the contrary": *per* Staughton J in *Libyan Arab Foreign Bank* v. *Bankers Trust Co* [1989] 3 All ER 252, 266e; see also *X AG* v. *A bank* [1983] 2 All ER 464; *MacKinnon* v. *Donaldson, Lufkin and Jenrette Securities Corporation, supra.*

28. *Clare & Co* v. *Dresdner Bank* [1915] 2 KB 576.

29. *Zivnostenska Banka* v. *Frankman* [1950] AC 57.

30. *Foley* v. *Hill* (1848) 9 ER 1002.

31. Indeed, a demand by a customer is a precondition to the liability of the bank to repay the funds it is holding: *National Bank of Commerce* v. *National Westminster Bank* [1990] 2 Lloyd's Rep. 514.

32. Explained by Atkin LJ in *Joachimson* v. *Swiss Bank Corp* [1921] 3 KB 110, 127.

A bank is not a trustee for its customers and it may not necessarily be a trustee of the money it holds. Lord Templeman has stated the position as follows[33]:

A customer who deposits money with a bank authorises the bank to use that money for the benefit of the bank in any manner the bank pleases. The customer does not acquire any interest in or charge over any asset of the bank or over all the assets of the bank. The deposit account is an acknowledgement and record by the bank of the amount from time to time deposited and withdrawn and of the interest earned. The customer acquires a chose in action, namely the right on request to payment by the bank of the whole or any part of the aggregate amount of principal and interest which has been credited or ought to be credited to the account. If the bank becomes insolvent the customer can only prove in the liquidation of the bank as unsecured creditor for the amount which was, or ought to have been, credited to the account at the date when the bank went into liquidation.

However, if the account in which the money is held by the bank is a "trust account" either expressly so designated,[34] or by circumstances which render the bank a constructive trustee,[35] a higher standard of care may well be exacted in respect of the funds it holds.[36] Moreover, money paid to a bank by a customer for a specific purpose is impressed with a trust for that purpose, and cannot be claimed by the bank as a set-off of a customer's general indebtedness to the bank. The money does not need to be in a special account,[37] and the bank cannot claim the money, even if the purpose for which the money was designated does not occur or fails altogether.[38]

Furthermore, if the customer has two or more accounts with the same bank, in the absence of express agreement, the bank cannot set off the credit balance on one against the debit balance on another.[39] However, there has been some conflicting dicta. Lord Cross of Chelsea has observed[40] that there is an implied term in the relationship between banker and customer, so long as the relationship exists " . . . that the bank will not . . . consolidate the two accounts", for " . . . unless such a term is implied no customer could feel any security in

33. *Space Investments Ltd v. Canadian Imperial Bank of Commerce Trust Co (Bahamas) Ltd* [1986] 3 All ER 75, 76e. See also the views of Atkin LJ in the *Joachimson* case, *supra*.

34. *Rowlandson v. National Westminster Bank Ltd* [1978] 3 All ER 370.

35. *Karak Rubber Co Ltd v. Burden* [1972] 1 All ER 1210.

36. In the *Space Investments* case, Lord Templeman stated (p. 76g), "A bank trustee, like any other trustee, may only apply that money in the manner authorised by the trust instrument, or by law."

37. See per Megarry J (as he then was) in *Re Kayford* [1975] 1 All ER 604, 607D and *Carreras Rothmans Ltd v. Freeman Mathews Treasure Ltd* (in liquidation) [1985] 1 All ER 155.

38. *Barclays Bank Ltd v. Quistclose Investments* [1970] AC 567. Note also that when a customer charges by way of security deposits held by his bank, this does not give the bank a proprietary interest in the debt which it owes to the customer, and so is not a "charge", properly so called. *Re: Bank of Credit and Commerce International SA (No 8)* [1996] 2 All ER 121.

39. Per Scrutton LJ in *Bradford Old Bank v. Sutcliff* [1918] 2 KB 833, at p. 847. See also *National Westminster Bank v. Halesowen Presswork Ltd* [1972] AC 785 and *W P Greenhalgh & Sons v. Union Bank of Manchester Ltd* [1924] 2 KB 153.

40. *National Westminster Bank plc v. Halesowen Presswork and Assemblies Ltd* [1972] 1 All ER 641, 653b.

drawing a cheque on his current account if he had a loan account greater than the credit balance on his current account". Lord Kilbrandon,[41] on the other hand, thought a bank had a right of set-off if the customer's accounts are both *current*, but not if one is a loan account, unless there is an agreement expressing or implying the contrary. Lord Denning's view was " . . . that a banker is entitled to combine two accounts unless there is an agreement to keep them separate,[42] without stating whether it mattered that both accounts were current or not, and shifted the emphasis in favour of the bank by stating that ". . . the banker has a right to combine the two accounts whenever he pleases, and set off one against the other, unless he has made some agreement, express or implied, to keep them separate.[43] Confusing though these statements are, the current position would appear to be that a bank has a right of set-off at any time provided:

(a) the two accounts are of the same type, eg both current accounts;[44] and

(b) there is no agreement—express or implied—to keep the accounts separate;[45]

(c) the accounts are under the control of the same customer.[46]

It has long been the practice of banks to obtain a written agreement from their customers to allow a set-off, so as to obviate these problems.

Accounts in the name of several signatories, such as partners or husband and wife, are common enough and care must be taken in the preparation of the mandate to ensure that clear instructions are given and received as to who has authority to sign cheques and other instructions: sometimes it is "any one" signatory, sometimes "all" signatories, or it may be "any two" or "any three".[47]

---

41. *Ibid.*, p. 661h.

42. *Halesowen Presswork & Assemblies Ltd* v. *Westminster Bank Ltd* [1970] 3 All ER 473, 478d, criticising the well-known dictum of Swift J to the contrary in *W P Greenhalgh* v. *Union Bank of Manchester Ltd* [1924] 2 KB 153.

43. *Ibid.*, p. 477f. The right of set-off can also operate in favour of the customer, where he has a credit balance on his own account and there is a larger debit balance on a company account which he has guaranteed as a "principal debtor"; he need pay only the balance: *MS Fashions Ltd* v. *BCCI* [1993] 3 All ER 769: " . . . the set-off is mandatory and cannot be excluded by any contract between the parties", *per* Dillon LJ, at p. 783h.

44. *Re E J Morel (1934) Ltd* [1961] 1 All ER 796, 803c.

45. *Hong Kong and Shanghai Banking Corp* v. *Kloeckner & Co AG* [1989] 3 All ER 513, 519c.

46. *Bhogal* v. *Punjab National Bank* [1988] 2 All ER 296; but not where the control of the account may be in dispute: see *Uttamchandani* v. *Central Bank of India*, *The Times*, 8 February 1989.

47. Needless to say, if instructions to a bank require the signature of *two* people, the bank cannot debit its customer's account on the signature of only one: *National Bank of Commerce* v. *National Westminster Bank* [1990] 2 Lloyd's Rep. 514.

The basis of the relationship

The basis of the relationship is contractual, and, therefore, depends on the contract the bank and the customer make at the time the account is opened, as amended as the relationship goes along, either specifically or by the conduct of the parties in their dealings with one another.

In fact what happens in practice is that both the bank and the customer proceed on what might be termed a general understanding of what the relationship is to be. It is rare that the terms of doing business are discussed in any detail, and, as we saw above, almost never reduced to writing, with the exception of the bank mandate showing who will sign on the account, and what the specimen signatures look like.

Not infrequently, these days, banks will outline the wide range of services they offer, how various types of account operate, and what charges they might make, but laying down terms of conduct for the customer, or the bank for that matter, seem almost never to be mentioned, unless a specific query is raised.

It is, however, common to find some brief terms or advice printed on the inside covers of cheque books, in spite of the fact that it has been said[48] that this is not a good place to give notice to a customer of such terms and conditions applicable to the use of cheques or the account, because, unless the customer has read them, he is not bound by them.

The consideration of other terms and conditions usually only arises if there is a problem, when the courts are invited to indicate what *implied* terms there may be in the relationship.[49] The courts have been slow to place burdens on the customer, however. For example, it was held in *London Joint Stock Bank Ltd* v. *Macmillan & Arthur*[50] that a customer " . . . is bound to exercise reasonable care in drawing the cheque to prevent the banker being misled. If he draws the cheque in a manner which facilitates fraud, he is guilty of a breach of duty as between himself and the banker. . . ". Yet it was said in *Slingsby* v. *District Bank Ltd*[51] that there is no obligation to draw lines after the payee's name up to the printed words "or order". The only other obligation of the customer was laid down in *Greenwood* v. *Martins Bank Ltd*,[52] where it was established that a customer owes a duty " . . . if he became aware that forged cheques are being presented to his banker to inform his banker in order that the banker might avoid loss in the future".

However, this is as far as the customer's obligations go, unless something specific is agreed with the bank. For example, it has long been the case that a

---

48. *Burnett* v. *Westminster Bank* [1965] 3 All ER 81, at p. 87i.
49. When a bank issues traveller's cheques and states they will be replaced if lost or stolen, the agreement is not subject to an implied term that the loss must not be as the result of the customer's own negligence or recklessness: *Elawadi* v. *Bank of Credit and Commerce International SA* [1989] 1 All ER 242, *cf. Braithwaite* v. *Thomas Cook Travellers Cheques Ltd* [1989] 1 All ER 235.
50. [1918] AC 777, at p. 789, *per* Lord Finlay LC.
51. [1932] 1 KB 544, at p. 560, *per* Scrutton LJ.
52. [1932] 1 KB 371, at p. 381, *per* Scrutton LJ; on appeal [1933] AC 51.

customer owes no duty to his bank to examine his pass book or check his accounts with these entries.[53] Indeed, " . . . the true nature of the obligations of the customer to his bank where there is no express agreement is limited to the *Macmillan* and *Greenwood* duties. Clear and unambiguous provision is needed if the banks are to introduce into the contract a binding obligation on the customer who does not query his bank statements to accept the statement as accurately setting out the debit items in the accounts."[54]

A customer can demand his funds held by his bank in cash, no matter how impractical that may be.[55]

The duties of banker and customer

There are, therefore, a number of obligations which are implied on each side, and which form the basis of the relationship. To summarize, the bank has the following duties:

(1) To pay its customers' cheques if it has funds, and the instructions are clearly given.
(2) To preserve its customers' secrets.
(3) To take care of its customers' money and documents left with the bank.
(4) To exercise reasonable skill and judgment in the handling of its customers' business and in giving advice.

(1) Payment of cheques

It is the duty of a bank, if it has funds available, or if it has agreed an overdraft facility, to pay its customers' cheques. In making payment, the bank must, of course, exercise reasonable care and skill and might well be guilty of negligence if, in fact, payment is made by a misapplication of funds.

Contention between banker and customer often arises when a cheque is not paid by the bank. The reason for non-payment usually falls into one of two categories:

Where there is some defect in form

For example, if a cheque is not signed, or not dated, or post-dated, or if it is stale.

53. *Chatterton* v. *London & County Banking Co Ltd* (1891), *The Times*, 21 January 1891. It is a pity this case is not reported in any of the major law reports, although the principle has been upheld often: see *Kepitigalla Rubber Estates Ltd* v. *National Bank of India Ltd* [1909] 2 KB 1010; *Tai Hing Cotton Mill Ltd* v. *Liu Chong Hing Bank Ltd* [1985] 2 All ER 947.
54. *Per* Lord Scarman in *Tai Hing Cotton Mill Ltd* v. *Liu Chong Hing Bank Ltd* [1985] 2 All ER 947, at p. 959d to f.
55. *Libyan Arab Foreign Bank* v. *Bankers Trust Company* [1988] 1 Lloyd's Rep. 259.

Where there are insufficient funds

There must be sufficient funds in the customer's account to cover the whole amount of the cheque. There is no obligation on the bank to pay part, up to the amount in the account: and, of course, a cheque does not operate as an assignment to the payee of the amount standing in the account.[56]

If a bank *wrongfully* dishonours a cheque it will, of course, be liable to the customer in damages. It is not entirely clear whether the marking of a cheque by the drawee bank "Refer to Drawer" or "R/D" is, of itself, libellous. In both *Flack* v. *London and SW Bank*[57] and *Plunkett* v. *Barclays Bank*[58] it was held not to be libellous; but, more recently, in *Jayson* v. *Midland Bank*[59] "this question was put to the jury and the jury answered the question by saying it was defamatory".[60] There is no doubt the words "Refer to Drawer" or "Refer to Drawer, Please Represent" have become translatable, almost exclusively, to mean the drawer is—even temporarily—impecunious![61]

The other problem which arises in these matters is the quantum of damages which will be awarded if the customer is successful. The long established view is "that a person who is not a trader is not entitled to recover substantial damages for the wrongful dishonour of his cheque, unless the damage which he has suffered is alleged and proved as special damage".[62] Consequently, in *Allen* v. *London County & Westminster Bank*,[63] Coleridge J awarded, "as damages such an amount as would relieve the plaintiff of all expenses in connection with the action",[64] but that was all. It is, of course, not only "traders" who can have their reputations prejudiced, and it may well be that the rule could be widened to incorporate others, for as Hilbery J has observed, " . . . nothing about a man travels so fast as that which is to his discredit".[65]

Indeed, this wider view was taken by Evans LJ in *Kpohraror* v. *Woolwich Building Society*[65a] who noted that " . . . history has changed the social factor

56. Bills of Exchange Act 1882, s. 53(1). However, if there is a document of assignment executed, and notice given to the bank the balance in an account can be validly assigned: *Walker* v. *Bradford Old Bank* (1884) 12 QBD 509.
57. (1915) 31 TLR 334.
58. [1936] 2 KB 107.
59. [1968] 1 Lloyd's Rep. 409.
60. *Ibid.*, *per* Danckwerts LJ, at p. 410.
61. And, " . . . it is most important that a cheque should not be an embarrassing document": *per* Lindley LJ in *National Bank* v. *Silke* [1891] 1 QB 435, at p. 438.
62. *Per* Lawrence J in *Gibbons* v. *Westminster Bank* [1939] 2 KB 882, at p. 888, following *Wilson* v. *United Counties Bank Ltd* [1920] AC 102.
63. (1915) 31 TLR 210.
64. *Ibid.*, p. 211.
65. *Davidson* v. *Barclays Bank* [1940] 1 All ER 316, at p. 325b. CA in *Rae* v. *Yorkshire Bank plc* [1988] BTLC 35, dismissed a claim for substantial damages based on "inconvenience and humiliation".
65a. [1996] 4 All ER 119 (CA). The Plaintiff claimed he was a "trader", and so should not have to prove *actual* damage. The Building Society admitted the cheque had been wrongly refused payment, but did not know that the account was to be used for the Plaintiff's business, see at page 127c.

which moulded the rule in the nineteenth century", and went on, "The credit ratings of individuals are as important for their personal transactions, including mortgages and hire-purchase as well as banking facilities, as it is for those who are engaged in trade".[65b]

(2) Customers' secrets

With few exceptions[66] a bank must keep its customers' secrets, and no disclosure can be made without the customer's consent. If, for any reason, accounts or papers in the possession of the bank are needed in legal proceedings, and the customer cannot or will not give the necessary authority to his bank, the applicant's only course is to apply to the court under the terms of the Bankers' Books Evidence Act 1879.[67] In the operation of the Act the following points must be noted:

(1) Disclosure by a bank of its books must be on the order of a judge,[68] who will grant to the party making such an application the right to inspect and take copies of any entries in the books of the banker. The judge has a discretion, of course, and such an order is not demandable as of right. The bank has *three clear days*[69] from the day when an order is served upon it to comply.[70]

(2) "Bankers' books" now include records " . . . on microfilm, magnetic tape or any other form of mechanical or electronic data retrieval mechanism"[71] but not bundles of paid cheques and paying-in slips.[72]

(3) The order can be made, and often is, without the bank being a party to the proceedings, and without the bank attending court or being represented.[73] The bank *can* be represented, of course, and, in any

65b. *Ibid.* page 124b. Though on the facts the damages were held to be too remote, at page 127b: applying *Hadley* v. *Baxendale* (1854) 9 Exch 341.
66. See *per* Banks LJ, in *Tournier* v. *National Provincial and Union Bank of England Ltd* [1924] 1 KB 461, 473, for the suggested exceptions. See also *Robertson* v. *Canadian Imperial Bank of Commerce* [1995] 1 All ER 824 (PC).
67. See for example *Williams* v. *Summerfield* [1972] 2 QB 513. The scope of the 1879 Act does not extend to branches of UK banks abroad: *R* v. *Grossman* (1981) 73 Cr App R 302; see also *McKinnon* v. *Donaldson, Lufkin and Jenrette Securities Corporation* [1986] 2 WLR 453.
68. Bankers' Books Evidence Act 1879, s. 6.
69. Not including Sunday, Christmas Day, Good Friday and any bank holiday: *ibid.*, s. 11.
70. *Ibid.*, s. 7.
71. *Ibid.*, s. 9(2) as amended by the Banking Acts 1979 and 1987. In fact, prior to this amendment it had been held most microfilm records were within the term "bankers' books": *Barker* v. *Wilson* [1980] 2 All ER 81.
72. *Williams* v. *Williams* [1987] 3 All ER 257. To get access to these cheques and paying-in slips it is necessary to apply for a *subpoena duces tecum* requiring a bank officer to attend court with all the necessary documents: see *per* Sir John Donaldson MR (as he then was), p. 258c. There would appear to be no absolute duty to inform the customer of the subpoena: *Robertson* v. *Canadian Imperial Bank of Commerce* [1995] 1 All ER 824 (PC), at p. 830e.
73. *Ibid.*, s. 7.

event, is entitled to its costs in complying with the order, and an indemnity in damages if it is subsequently shown the order should not have been made, and the customer sues.[74]

(4) There is no implied contractual obligation between bank and customer that the bank shall contest the making of such an order.[75]

(5) These orders can be made against accounts of third parties not involved in the court proceedings, but only if such account is in reality the account of the defendant to the action.[76]

There is a new and important exception to a bank's duty of maintaining its customers' secrets contained in the Drug Trafficking Offences Act 1986,[77] s. 24(1) of which provides that if anyone assists a drug trafficker, he can be guilty of an offence under the Act. This can place banks in an invidious position, where moneys are paid into a customer's account which may be the proceeds of drug trafficking. The bank probably has no proof, although the circumstances may be suspicious.[78] Unfortunately, the burden of proof would be on the bank[79] to show it did not know or suspect the arrangements related to drug trafficking.

Therefore, the only course open if the bank has suspicions that something may be wrong, is to avail itself of the provisions of s. 24(3) of the Act, and make a disclosure to the police of the suspicion or belief that funds or investments with which they are dealing may be derived from, or used in connection with, drug trafficking.

If any act has been carried out by the bank, such as transferring money, it is not an offence if disclosure is made on the bank's " . . . initiative and as soon as it is reasonable . . . to make it".[80] Of course, once the disclosure is made, the customer may well be offended, particularly so if it is proved that there is no connection with drugs. The Act covers this point[81] by providing that such a disclosure " . . . shall not be treated as a breach of any restrictions upon the disclosure of information imposed by contract". That, of course, would be a contract between a bank and its customer.

---

74. *Bankers Trust Company* v. *Shapira* [1980] 3 All ER 353.

75. *Barclays Bank plc* v. *Taylor* [1989] 3 All ER 563, which involved an application under the Police and Criminal Evidence Act 1984.

76. *DB Deniz Nakliyati TAS* v. *Yugopetrol* [1992] 1 All ER 205, a case where the application was made *after* judgment had been obtained, and where it was said that the standard of proof as to the likelihood of discovering relevant items was the same whether before or after judgment.

77. In fact, there are a number of statutory provisions which permit banks to disclose details of their customers' affairs. For example, in relation to possible revenue offences, the Taxes Management Act 1970, the Income and Corporation Taxes Act 1988 and the Finance Act 1985. For enquiries into possible irregularities of companies, the Companies Act 1985 (as amended), the Financial Services Act 1986 and the Insolvency Act 1986.

78. See *Agip (Africa) Ltd* v. *Jackson* [1992] 4 All ER 451.

79. Drug Trafficking Offences Act 1986, s. 24(4).

80. S. 24(3)(*b*)(ii).

81. S. 24(3)(*a*).

Under the provisions of s. 8 of the Act, the High Court can make a "restraint order" prohibiting a bank (or anyone else) from dealing with any "realizable property" with such conditions as are specified in the order.[82]

Within the limits of secrecy, banks are entitled to answer enquiries concerning a customer's general financial standing, but great care must be taken. However, where a banker is asked for a reference of this kind it is no " . . . part of his duty to make enquiries outside as to the solvency or otherwise of the person asked about, or to do anything more than answer the question put to him honestly from what he knew from the books and accounts before him".[83] In other words " . . . if a banker gives a reference in the form of a brief expression of opinion in regard to creditworthiness he does not accept, and there is not expected from him, any higher duty than that of giving an honest answer".[84] Over the years, fairly stereotyped answers have been developed by banks in answer to the usual enquiries, which, while being truthful, are not particularly informative!

Sometimes disclosure can occur in an indirect way. For example, in

TOURNIER v. NATIONAL PROVINCIAL ETC. BANK[85]

T was a customer of the bank and received a cheque from X who was a customer of the same branch. T did not pay the cheque into his account but indorsed it to L who was a bookmaker, for a gambling debt. In the course of clearing, the cheque came to the bank, the manager saw it and telephoned the presenting bank to enquire who their customer was and was told it was L whose business was that of a bookmaker. The manager then rang T's employers to enquire T's whereabouts and informed them that several letters had gone unanswered and that he had an overdraft with the bank and a cheque had gone to the credit of a bookmaker's account. T's employers did not renew his employment and T sued his bank for slander and breach of its secrecy obligation. *Held*—that the bank were liable.

This duty of secrecy, of course, continues even *after* an account is closed and the person is no longer a customer of the bank.

(3) Safe custody

Customers frequently deposit valuables or securities with their bank for safe keeping. This has, of course, nothing whatever to do with deposits for the purpose of security for loans or facilities granted by the bank.

---

82. See for example *Re Peters* [1988] 3 All ER 46. There is nothing in the 1986 Act, however, which prevents a bank combining several accounts of a customer pending a confiscation order, if the bank is merely carrying out an accounting operation to establish, between debit and credit items, the indebtedness of the customer, and not making any claim over the funds in the customer's accounts: *Re K, The Times*, 15 July 1989.

83. *Per* Cozens-Hardy MR in *Parsons* v. *Barclay & Co* (1910) 26 TLR 628, 629.

84. *Per* Lord Morris in *Hedley Byrne & Co* v. *Heller* [1963] 2 All ER 575, 594I.

85. [1924] 1 KB 461.

Where a customer leaves valuables or securities in this way, no specific charge is usually made by the bank for this service, and accordingly the bank holds the property as a gratuitous bailee, which means that it must take the same reasonable care as a prudent banker takes of its own property.[86]

In the absence of any agreement to the contrary, the customer can demand the property at any time, thus terminating the bailment.[87]

(4) Skill and judgment

The bank, for its part, must act at all times in a proper and diligent manner, and exercise all reasonable care and skill as might be expected of prudent bankers in the paying and collecting of funds and in transacting business generally.[88]

Customers are also entitled to rely on the ostensible authority of the bank officials with whom they deal for decisions relating to transactions being handled by the bank. If, therefore, a senior manager states that his head office has approved loan facilities for a customer, the bank cannot thereafter decline to proceed on the basis that they no longer wish to handle the customer's business.[89]

While conducting transactions on behalf of customers, information frequently comes into the hands of a bank. If the customer has not specially requested the information, the only obligation on the bank is not to be misleading (which is a question of fact); and even if a customer specifically requests the bank to obtain information, " . . . a bank is not employed as a private enquiry agent. Its field of enquiry is normally limited to what it gets from other banks."[90]

Banks must be careful also when dealing with customers whose interests may conflict with the bank's interests and those of other customers of the bank. For example, if a customer is asked to guarantee or give security to the bank for another customer (say, a company with its account with the bank), the bank owes a duty to see the customer is independently advised. If it does not, any security given may be unenforceable on the grounds of undue influence.[91]

86. If it could be construed as a bailment *for value* a higher standard of care would be implied, and greater safeguards might be demanded than one would take with one's own property.

87. *USA v. Dolfuss Mieg* [1952] AC 582.

88. *Woods v. Martins Bank Ltd* [1959] 1 QB 55, a case concerning negligent advice with a customer's investments; both the bank and the manager personally were held liable. Again, if a manager offers a prediction on the outcome of an application for credit, the bank and the manager personally are liable if such advice proves to have been given negligently: *Box v. Midland Bank Ltd* [1979] 2 Lloyd's Rep. 391. See also *Selangor United Rubber Estates Ltd v. Cradock* [1968] 2 All ER 1073, where it was held that it is no defence for a paying bank to say it did not enquire as it thought the answer would not be truthful.

89. *First Energy (UK) Ltd v. Hungarian International Bank Ltd* [1993] 2 Lloyd's Rep. 194.

90. *Per* Devlin J (as he then was) in *Midland Bank Ltd v. Seymour* [1955] 2 Lloyd's Rep. 147, at p. 158.

91. See *Barclays Bank plc v. O'Brien* [1993] 4 All ER 417; *Lloyds Bank Ltd v. Bundy* [1947] 3 WLR 501. But *cf. Cornish v. Midland Bank plc* [1985] 3 All ER 513.

In fact, it is the modern practice of banks to insist that guarantees and similar documents be executed in the presence of the customer's solicitor, who is asked to confirm to the bank that an explanation of the effect of the document was made to the customer before the formal signing.[92]

The duties a customer owes to its bank are these:

(1) To give his bank clear and unambiguous instructions.
(2) To take care when drawing cheques not to do so in a way that will facilitate fraud.
(3) Not to mislead the bank.

(1) To give clear instructions

A customer must give his bank clear instructions of what he requires of them. For example, cheques are always paid in the order in which they are received through the clearing, and if two or more cheques are received at the same time (for example, in the same postal delivery) and there are funds to pay, say, one only, the bank would be entitled to return *all* the cheques unpaid as its customer had not given clear instructions.

It has been discussed often whether or not a bank should, in an endeavour to be helpful, pay as many small cheques as it can, or the largest up to the standing balance. Practices differ: however, there is little doubt the strictly proper course is to return *all*, as it cannot be any part of a bank's duty to decide which of a customer's creditors should or should not be paid. After all, the customer must know of the dilemma in which he has placed his bank; however, it seems most banks will pay as many cheques as possible with the available funds.

(2) Care with cheques

The customer must take care when drawing cheques that he does not leave "blanks" all over the form, which might make it more easy for the cheques to be raised. If a customer *is* careless, and some fraud is perpetrated by a third party, the customer will not be able to claim against the bank for any loss.[93]

(3) Not to mislead

It need hardly be said that a customer must never mislead his bank. If a customer does, then not only is the bank not liable to the customer for any loss,[94] but the bank can recover any loss from the customer which it suffers.

92. It is assumed the customer's solicitor will give proper advice: *Bank of Baroda* v. *Shah* [1988] 3 All ER 24.

93. *London Joint Stock Bank Ltd* v. *Macmillan & Arthur* [1918] AC 777. The duty is owed only to the bank, however, and not to a third party: *Kepitagalla Rubber Estates* v. *National Bank of India* [1909] 2 KB 1010.

94. *Greenwood* v. *Martins Bank Ltd* [1933] AC 51.

The fact of misleading the bank may also be a crime. For example, it was held in *R* v. *Hassard*,[95] that while a customer can sign a cheque in an assumed name under s. 23 of the Bills of Exchange Act 1882, it is perpetrating a deception and a fraud on the bank to open an account in a fictitious name, unless that name is being used at large, and not merely for the purpose of misleading the bank.[96] It is also a crime for a customer, knowingly, to give incorrect details to his bank in order to gain a pecuniary advantage; and if, for example, a loan is agreed based on this false information, the crime is committed when the facility is granted, even if it is not drawn upon.[97]

2. THE BANKING OMBUDSMAN SCHEME

During the last decade we have become more conscious of the rights of the customer in its widest sense. Including a need for "someone" to do "something" to put things right where there has been an alleged injustice, which, perhaps, is not possible to take to law, or may be too costly to do so. A need for someone the ordinary citizen can contact for a sympathetic hearing.

So we now have the role of the "ombudsman", which is a Swedish word meaning "legal representative". In fact, in its use in English, the word means some official appointed, usually by an organization, to investigate complaints against that organization. In addition to the Banking Ombudsman, we also have the Building Societies Ombudsman and the Insurance Ombudsman.

The Banking Ombudsman Scheme was set up in January 1986 by a group of banks so that complaints from customers could be dealt with, and if possible resolved, when discussions with the particular branch or head office had failed to satisfy the customer.

The Scheme is formally incorporated with the title "The Office of the Banking Ombudsman", and has a Council[98] who appoint the ombudsman, who works within the limits of his terms of reference. The member banks appoint the Board whose main functions are to decide whether to accept recommendations from the Council for changes in the Ombudsman's terms of reference, and to raise subscriptions from the member banks to finance the Scheme's operations.

The service rendered to the public by the Banking Ombudsman is free of charge.[99]

The Banking Ombudsman must, of course, act within his terms of reference which provide for his powers and duties (and the limits on them), and the procedure for dealing with complaints and their possible settlement.

95. [1970] 1 WLR 1109.
96. *Ibid.*, p. 1112C.
97. *R* v. *Watkins* [1976] 1 All ER 578.
98. At the moment it consists of eight members, five of whom are independent, and three of whom are appointed by the member banks.
99. The office of the Banking Ombudsman is at 70 Gray's Inn Road, London WC1X 8NB.

In general terms the Banking Ombudsman can deal with all types of complaint relating to banking business, including problems with cash machines and plastic cards. However, complaints relating to a bank's interest rate policies, or commercial judgement in their wider sense, are outside the scope of the Scheme, unless there has been some specific maladministration or inequitable treatment of a customer.

A complaint to be dealt with must, therefore, fall within the terms of reference, and the main provisions relating to the types of complaint are these:

(1) It must be against a member bank.[100]

(2) The amount being claimed must be less than £100,000.[101]

(3) It must concern a service provided in England, Wales, Scotland or Northern Ireland, as the Scheme does not cover services provided abroad.[102]

Any customer can make a complaint, though if the customer is a company it must be a "small company", as defined in the terms of reference, which broadly means it must have a turnover of less than £1m, and not a member of a group of companies.

The Banking Ombudsman will attempt to mediate between the customer and the bank to see if a settlement can be reached, though if this is not possible the Banking Ombudsman has the power to make an award in favour of the customer, which will be in full and final settlement of the issue. Although these awards are binding on the bank, they are not on the individual, who may reject the award and pursue the problems in the courts.

In reaching a recommendation or award the Banking Ombudsman is not bound by any previous decision made by him (or any predecessor), and he may consult with whom he chooses. In rare cases the Banking Ombudsman may decide the complaint is more appropriate being dealt with by the courts, and may so advise, although he has no power to compel such a course of action.[103]

3. CAPACITY TO OPERATE A BANK ACCOUNT

With very few exceptions, anyone can be a customer of a bank and operate a banking account. However, the following points should be noted:

100. At the present time there are 55 member banks.

101. £50,000 in respect of events occurring before 25 January 1988.

102. Which includes the Channel Islands and the Isle of Man.

103. Complaints against banks rose to a high of 10,200 in 1993, but has fallen to 8,000 as at 30 September 1996. The Voluntary Code of Banking Practice which originally came into force on 16 March 1992 has no doubt helped. The second edition is now in force (March 1994), with the third edition soon to be published.

1. Infants

An infant can operate a bank account, and may be given an overdraft for "necessities" in maintaining himself, as, for example, with a student loan, while living away from home at university. Further, since the Minors Contracts Act 1987[104] he can be sued on a cheque given for the payment of "necessities", including the repayment of any loan granted to him by a bank while he was an infant.[105] Also, any guarantee of the infant's bank account (given by, for example, a parent) may be enforceable against the guarantor.[106]

2. Companies

A company has full powers to operate a bank account in the same way as an ordinary person. The bank will require sight of its certificate of incorporation, and will wish to retain a copy of the company's memorandum and articles of association.

If the company wishes to borrow, then care must be taken to see not only that it has power to do so under its constitution, but the borrowing is for the purpose for which the company was formed. A bank will be unable to recover on security given by a company if the borrowing was for an *ultra vires* purpose.[107]

3. Insolvency

There is, in fact, no rule of law which provides that an undischarged bankrupt cannot operate a bank account. However, since all a bankrupt's assets vest in his trustee-in-bankruptcy, and money he wished to pay into a bank account would vest in the trustee, unless the trustee had consented to those funds being at the disposal of the bankrupt; an example would be a bankrupt's salary, which, as a matter of convenience, may need to be paid into a bank account.

Under the provisions of s. 360 of the Insolvency Act 1986[108] it is unlawful for an undischarged bankrupt to obtain credit to an amount beyond £250[109] without disclosing his status, and a bank could be guilty of an offence if it knowingly allowed an undischarged bankrupt credit, for example, by granting or acquiescing in overdraft facilities.

As a matter of practice, a bank which is approached by an undischarged bankrupt to open an account, should contact the Official Receiver's Office which is dealing with the particular case, and enquire whether, if an account

---

104. See *supra* Chapter 2, III. Capacity and Authority.
105. The Minors Contracts Act 1987 also repeals the Betting and Loans (Infants) Act 1892.
106. *Coutts v. Browne-Lecky* [1947] KB 104 would now appear no longer to be good law.
107. *Introductions Ltd v. National Provincial Bank* [1969] 2 WLR 791.
108. Insolvency Proceedings (Monetary Limits) Order 1986, SI 1986/1996, art. 3.
109. This figure can be reached by aggregating a number of smaller debts.

were to be opened for the bankrupt, any conditions would be placed upon it at the request of the Official Receiver's office; for example, that copies of bank statements be sent regularly to the trustee-in-bankruptcy to allow a monitoring of the account. In each case, it is for the bank to take a commercial decision whether or not to allow the opening of such an account.

In the case of a company it can continue to operate a bank account between the date when the winding up commences and the date when the winding-up order is made. The winding up "commences", in the case of a voluntary winding up, when the company passes a resolution to that effect;[110] and in the case of a winding up by the court, when the petition for winding up is presented.[111]

Difficulties sometimes arise where a bank does not know of its customer's bankruptcy, or, in the case of corporations, a winding up. This is particularly so between the date of the presentation of a bankruptcy petition and the date of the order vesting the bankrupt's assets (including money in his bank account) in his trustee-in-bankruptcy. The rule is[112] that once an individual is adjudged bankrupt any dispositions he attempts to make of his property are void. However, in the case of banks,[113] any such payments by the bankrupt are deemed to have been made *before* the bankruptcy order, providing:

   (i) the bank had no "notice" of the bankruptcy prior to making the payment, or

   (ii) it is not "reasonably practical"—however that may be interpreted—to recover the money paid by the bank from the person who received it, for example, the payee of a cheque.

What this amounts to in practice is that banks caught in these circumstances will be able to debit their bankrupt customer's account with such payments provided they had no notice of the bankruptcy.[114] Presumably, if a bank is subsequently found to have had "notice", they must attempt to recover the payment, unless it is not "reasonably practical", which again will be a term to be interpreted according to the facts. It may, for example, not be "reasonably practical" to attempt to recover a relatively modest sum.

In the case of companies, however, banks are not in such a good position, as the saving provisions of s. 284(5) of the Insolvency Act 1986 do not apply, and a bank will not be allowed to debit the account of a company in respect of funds advanced to it between the date of the petition to wind it up and the

---

110. Ss. 86 and 129(1), Insolvency Act 1986.
111. *Ibid.*, s. 129(2).
112. *Ibid.*, s. 284(1).
113. "Or other person", *ibid.*, s. 284(5).
114. What will constitute "notice" will obviously depend on the circumstances of the individual case.

actual date of the winding-up order,[115] which might of course, be some months. The bank should refer questions of how such accounts are to be operated (if it all) to the court.[116]

4. Persons of unsound mind

If a person (he is now called "a patient") is detained under the provisions of the Mental Health Act 1983, the court has power under s. 95 of that Act to order "the doing of all such things as appear necessary or expedient" for, among other things, "administering the patient's affairs". In carrying out this function regard is to be had, not only to the interests of the patient, but to those of his creditors, notwithstanding the obligations may not be legally enforceable.[117]

It is quite clear that such a person could not *open* a new account, nor operate an existing account. If a person detained under the Act has an existing account, the control will pass to whomsoever the court appoints under s. 95.

If a customer is not "detainable", but is nevertheless of unsound mind (doubtless with periods of lucidity), a bank can be in a very difficult position, which is discussed below when considering the termination of the relationship of banker and customer.

5. Aliens

As we have seen,[118] there is no reason why a foreign national (whether a private person or a corporation) should not open and operate a bank account in Britain. It not infrequently happens that they wish to remit part of their earnings to their home country, or to purchase securities with savings acquired in Britain; or again, to bring into Britain moneys from their home country or, indeed, from some third country.

It must be remembered that while there are now no Exchange Control Regulations in Britain, there may well be in the country of the foreign national, and, depending on the circumstances, the British bank could find itself in

---

115. *Re Gray's Inn Construction Co Ltd* [1980] 1 All ER 814. This was a case before the 1986 legislation, and the proceedings were under the provisions of the 1948 Companies Act. The bank had allowed the company to continue with its banking overdraft facilities between the date of the winding-up petition being advertised (10 August) and the date of the winding-up order (9 October), and the bank did not during this time seek any direction from the court, as it certainly would have been advisable to do. In any winding up by the court, the Insolvency Act 1986, s. 127, makes void any disposition of the company's property, unless the court orders to the contrary. However, there is no "disposition" of the company's property in favour of a bank where the company's account is in credit, and the bank collects on a cheque paid into that account. "The amount standing to the credit of a customer's account is increased in return for the surrender of the cheque which becomes a voucher for payment. It is the drawer of the cheque whose property is disposed of." *Per* Judge Rich QC, *Re Barn Crown Ltd* [1994] 4 All ER 42, 52a.

116. See Insolvency Act 1986, s. 112, under the terms of which a liquidator, any contributor or creditor can apply to the court to have determined any question relating to the winding up.

117. Mental Health Act 1983, s. 95(2).

118. *Supra*, Chap. 2, under the heading of "Capacity".

difficulties in handling a transaction which infringed the regulations of that other country, since under the terms of the Bretton Woods Agreement Act 1945, "exchange contracts"[119] which are contrary to the exchange control regulations of a member country are unenforceable in the territories of any other member.[120]

This creates a problem with bills of exchange if, in the particular circumstances, they are, or could be deemed to be, "exchange contracts", because if a holder takes with knowledge of the possible breach of the foreign exchange control regulations, the instrument in his hand will, almost certainly, be unenforceable. So that with any foreign bill it could be argued that the bank handling it is put on enquiry to see either that: (a) the bill is not, and cannot be deemed to be an "exchange contract"; or (b) it in no way contravenes the foreign regulations.

Both create onerous obligations on the bank, but, clearly, if what they were being asked to do was illegal they must refuse to perform; and, even if the transaction might prove unenforceable, they have a duty to point this out to their customer.

6. Local authorities[121]

At one time, the position of local authorities was somewhat anomalous,[122] in that it seemed never very clear what their powers were to operate a bank account. It was frequently done through a "treasurer", who held the account in his own name as a quasi-trustee for the authority.[123]

Now, in pursuance of s. 151 of the Local Government Act 1972, " . . . every local authority shall make arrangements for the proper administration of their financial affairs and shall secure that one of their officers has responsibility for the administration of those affairs".

The local authority will, in committee, appoint "one of their officers" to administer its financial affairs. They will authorize the opening (or continuation) and operation of their bank accounts, and nominate the signatures within

---

119. What exactly constitutes an "exchange contract" is not wholly clear. For a review of the position, see Mann, *The Legal Aspect of Money*, 5th edn. (1992) pp. 378 *et seq*. See also, *Sharif v. Azad* [1967] 1 QB 605, and *Wilson Smithett & Cope Ltd* v. *Terruzzi* [1976] 1 QB 683. Any commercial contract is capable of being an "exchange contract", but Lord Diplock has stated that it does not include a contract of sale even if there is an obligation to convert from one currency into another for the purpose of payment, except if the contract was "disguised as an exchange contract": see *United City Merchants (Investments) Ltd* v. *Royal Bank of Canada* [1983] 1 AC 168.

120. Bretton Woods Agreement Act 1945, Art. viii, s. 2(*b*).

121. "Local authority" means a County Council, a District Council, a London Borough Council or a Parish Council or Community Council": Local Government Act 1972, s. 270(1).

122. For background see, Paget, *Law of Banking*, 11th edn. (1996), p. 156.

123. As to the position of these "treasurers", see *per* Charles J in *The Guardians of Colchester Union* v. *Moy* (1893) 68 LT 564, at p. 566. Also, *The Guardians of Halifax Union* v. *Wheelwright* (1875) 32 LT 802. For a contrary view, see *The Guardians of Cosford Union* v. *Grimwade* (1892) 8 TLR 775, where the *Halifax Case* was distinguished.

the terms of the mandate they give to their bankers. Under the terms of the 1972 Act, they have power to raise money and issue bills of exchange.[124]

4. OPERATING THE ACCOUNT

The method of operating a bank account is well known. A prospective customer should be asked by the bank for adequate proof of identity, circumstances and respectability. If adequate enquiry is not made, and something goes wrong with the account, the bank may well be guilty of negligence and lose the protection of the 1882 Act. This is particularly so with prospective customers who "walk in off the street". For example, in *Ladbroke* v. *Todd*[125] a fraud opened an account with a stolen cheque, representing himself to be the payee, who was an undergraduate at Oxford. The bank should have, but did not, enquire of the University, nor did it take up any references, and consequently lost whatever protection it might have had under the 1882 Act. In *Hampstead Guardians* v. *Barclays Bank*[126] the same result followed when the bank failed to check the address given by the intended customer, and that of the referee which was given. The bank " . . . took it for granted that the person calling himself Donald Stewart really was Donald Stewart" for "the reference, even if genuine, would only have been good for the genuine Donald Stewart".[127] Again, in *Lumsden* v. *London TSB*,[128] with disastrous results, the bank failed " . . . to check whether either customer or referee appeared in the telephone directory under their home address . . . "[129] and to enquire whether the customer had an account in Australia from where he had travelled. Perhaps, said Donaldson J (as he then was), the bank thought " . . . Australian bank accounts did not count or that Australians could hardly be expected to have bank accounts until they had been exposed for a period to the sophistication of the mother country";[130] "but a bank cannot reasonably be expected to subject *all* prospective customers to a cross-examination".[131] It is, as usual, a difficult question of fact as to what enquiries should be made when an account is opened, but clearly a bank should follow any reference or name given, and if they cannot trace the intended customer or his reference, the bank will proceed at its peril.

124. Local Government Act 1972, Sched. 13(2)(*e*).
125. (1914) 111 LT 43.
126. (1923) 39 TLR 229.
127. *Per* Acton J, *ibid.*, at p. 231.
128. [1971] 1 Lloyd's Rep. 114.
129. *Per* Donaldson J (as he then was) at p. 119.
130. *Ibid.*, p. 119.
131. *Per* Diplock J (as he then was) *Marfani* v. *Midland Bank* [1968] 2 All ER 573, 581.

Once these formalities have been satisfied, the account will be opened. The customer then pays in money or is granted an overdraft, and the bank provides the customer with a cheque book. The customer then makes out cheques to whomsoever he owes money. As we have already noted he must take care in drawing cheques not to leave blanks all over the place which might facilitate some fraudulent person;[132] but there is no obligation to draw lines after the payee's name up to the printed words "Or Order".[133] The customer should remember when drawing cash for himself over the counter he can simply write the word "cash" in the space provided after the printed word "Pay"; he can do the same in payment to anyone else (and his bank will pay it).[134] The instrument can be passed on by delivery, but none of the intervening holders have any rights on it[135]—which one assumes is no concern of the drawer! The customer should remember the bank's only duty is to pay cheques if there are funds available, and it does not say, because the bank allowed "unauthorized borrowing" by paying cheques if there were no funds to meet them on one occasion, that it will be bound to do the same on another occasion.[136]

If overdraft facilities are requested and refused and notwithstanding this the customer draws and issues cheques he can hardly complain as to their dishonour.

A bank is " . . . under no obligation to honour cheques which exceed the amount of the balance or, in other words, to allow the customer to overdraw",[137] so that, without seeking specific permission, "if a customer draws a cheque for a sum in excess of the amount standing to the credit of his account, it is really a request for a loan, and if the cheque is honoured the customer has borrowed money".[138] The bank can then either pay the cheque—thus allowing the borrowing—or return it.

Trouble sometimes arises where overdraft facilities have been acquiesced in by the bank, without a specific agreement as to the borrowing level, and then, for whatever the reason, without notice, cheques are returned. Such conduct by a bank can rarely be justified, unless perhaps where the customer has been guilty of fraud on the bank, for if there is a "course of dealing" it would

---

132. *London Joint Stock Bank Ltd* v. *Macmillan & Arthur* [1918] AC 777.

133. *Per* Scrutton LJ in *Slingsby* v. *District Bank Ltd* [1932] 1 KB 544, 560. An impecunious debtor may sometimes give an *undated* cheque and whether the holder (usually the payee) has authority to complete it is a question of fact: *Re Bethell* (1887) 34 Ch D 561. If the cheque is accepted as conditional payment, it suspends the creditor's rights until paid or dishonoured: *per* Danckwerts LJ in *Bolt & Nut Co* v. *Rowlands, Nicholls & Co* [1964] 2 QB 10, 21. A creditor is deemed "paid" when the cheque is honoured, not when it is received: *Re Hone* [1950] 2 All ER 716—trite perhaps, but see (1951) 14 MLR 65.

134. *N & S Insurance Corp* v. *National Provincial Bank* [1936] 1 KB 328.

135. *Cole* v. *Milsome* [1951] 1 All ER 311.

136. See *per* Pollock CB in *Cumming* v. *Shand* (1860) 29 LJ Ex 129, at p. 132.

137. *Per* Lord Blackburn in *Brooks* v. *Blackburn Benefit Society* (1884) 9 App Cas 857, 864.

138. *Per* Cozens-Hardy MR in *Cuthbert* v. *Robarts, Lubbock & Co* [1909] 2 Ch 226, 233.

"amount to evidence of an agreement between the parties . . . which could not be put an end to without distinct notice".[139]

The moral is obvious. The bank, having allowed a customer to overdraw, should give reasonable and specific notice that it proposes to terminate those facilities. It saves much acrimony and unpleasantness, as there is bound to be ill-feeling, even if it is finally proved that the "course of dealing" did not allow the customer to draw, as in *Parkinson* v. *Wakefield & Co*,[140] where the customer transferred the security for his borrowing, and the bank thereupon "ruled off" the account. Some months later, while the bank were still pressing for repayment, the customer paid in, on separate occasions, cheques for £70 and £30, and then drew one himself for £70 which was returned by the bank. The bank claimed to be entitled to the credits, and to return the customer's cheque. The evidence was confusing as to what exactly was said by the bank, but the court held the customer knew the state of affairs and that the bank were not liable for dishonouring the cheque. Such cases are an unedifying spectacle, and with clear notice need never arise.

The customer should also bear in mind that cheques are intended for use in transferring money on an "immediate payment" basis,[141] and that banks do not much like post-dating, or any other arrangement that involves the customer giving a cheque in the pious hope that funds will be available when the cheque arrives at his bank for payment.[142]

The customer will pay into his account any moneys, cheques or other instruments and his bank will collect payment on his behalf from the other banks on whom the cheques are drawn. It is no part of the bank's business to question the title of its customers to the cheques being paid in, so that if he has stolen them, or obtained them by fraud, it is no concern of the bank; unless the circumstances are suspicious—which of course is a question of fact. For example, in the case of

139. *Per* Pollock CB in *Cumming* v. *Shand* (1860) 29 LJ Ex 129, 132.
140. (1889) 5 TLR 562.
141. *Bank of Baroda* v. *Punjab National Bank* [1944] AC 176, 184.
142. Indeed, if a man draws a cheque knowing perfectly well there are no funds, and there will not be funds to meet it on presentation, he may be guilty of deception under s. 15 of the Theft Act 1968 even though he intends to repay the money at some future time: *Halstead* v. *Petal* [1972] 2 All ER 147. This must not be confused with the case of " . . . the man who, overdrawn on Saturday, draws a cheque in favour of a third party in the honest and well founded belief that funds will be put into his bank on a Monday, [this] is a man who many juries would undoubtedly acquit of dishonesty because there he has a genuine and honest belief that the cheque will be met in the ordinary course of events", *per* Lord Widgery CJ, *ibid.*, p. 151h. The criminal aspects of the law cannot really be discussed here. Suffice to say that where a customer has been advised by his bank that no more cheques will be met, the further issue of cheques may amount to deception under s. 16 of the Theft Act 1968: *R* v. *Fizackerley* [1973] 2 All ER 819; *DPP* v. *Turner* [1973] 3 All ER 124 (HL). Indeed, an offence is committed if a customer is reckless in issuing a cheque not knowing whether it will be met or not: *R* v. *Goldstein* [1976] 1 All ER 1. Where a person, without authority, presents a cheque or sends a telex instruction to a bank to draw on an account in credit or within an agreed overdraft limit, the act of presenting the cheque or sending the telex instruction is the act of theft itself, and not a mere attempt: *R* v. *Governor of Pentonville Prison ex parte Osman* [1989] 3 All ER 701, at pp. 702b and 717b.

MIDLAND BANK LTD v. RECKITT[143]

A solicitor acted for a client under a power of attorney which, among other things, empowered him to sign cheques. He made out and signed several cheques in his own favour and paid them into his own bank account with the Midland Bank. The client died and his personal representatives sued the bank for return of the money. *Held*—that the bank had been negligent in not enquiring of its customer (the solicitor) his authority to receive personally funds of this sort, and so they lost the protection they might have had under the 1882 Act.

Sometimes it may happen that a customer has written a cheque, and having given it to the payee, finds some error or circumstances which he considers disentitle the payee to the money. In such a case the customer (the drawer) can countermand payment, whereupon the authority of the bank to pay the cheque is terminated.[144] This is popularly known as "stopping" a cheque.

A cheque can be "stopped" by written or oral authority from the customer (that is, the drawer of the cheque). However, whether the instructions to the bank are written or oral they *must* reach the attention of the bank, there is no such thing as a constructive countermand.

CURTICE v. LONDON & MIDLAND BANK LTD[145]

C drew a cheque on his bank, and after business hours on the same day countermanded by telegram. The telegram was put into the post box of the bank, but owing to the negligence of the bank staff, the notice did not reach the manager until two days later. In the meanwhile the cheque was paid. *Held*—that the cheque was not countermanded as the notice did not reach the attention of the bank, "although it may well be that it was due to the negligence of the bank that they did not receive notice of the customer's desire to stop the cheque".[146]

A case not easily reconcilable with this is *Burnett v. Westminster Bank Ltd.*[147] This was the case where a customer with an account at two branches used a "Borough" cheque—with suitable amendments—for a transaction on his "Bromley" account. The cheque was printed with magnetic ink in respect of the "Borough" branch for use in the newly installed bank computer. Unfortunately, he changed his mind and gave notice of countermand to the "Bromley" branch (the facts of the case are set out fully *infra* at p. 187, when considering computerized accounting). To have been absolutely sure of his instructions receiving attention, the customer should, perhaps, have given notice to *both* branches, and was perhaps negligent in not doing so. Equally, the bank were negligent in not appreciating fully what was taking place, in that the "Borough" branch received the cheque with the alterations but took no steps to query the position with the "Bromley" branch or the computer; meanwhile, the

143. [1933] AC 1.
144. Bills of Exchange Act 1882, s. 75(1).
145. [1908] 1 KB 293.
146. In any event, a bank is not obliged to recognize an unauthenticated telegram (which is not signed) as sufficient countermand: *per* Cozens-Hardy MR, *ibid.*, p. 298.
147. [1965] 3 All ER 81.

"Bromley" branch, who had not seen the cheque but who had notice of it in its changed form and the countermand, took no steps to query the position with the "Borough" branch or the computer.

Curtice v. *London & Midland Bank Ltd* shows clearly the heavy responsibility on the customer to bring a countermand to the attention of his bank—even if the bank has been negligent. Moreover, for a "stop" to be effective, it must be directed to the appropriate branch upon whom the cheque is drawn.[148] This argument seems not to have been advanced by the bank in the *Burnett Case* (nor the *Curtice* case cited), but to have proceeded solely on the basis of whether or not the bank had fixed the customer with notice of its new methods of operating with the computer. One is left wondering whether adequate notice of the countermand had been given by the customer within the dictum of the *Curtice* case.[149]

In any written countermand the cheque must be described fully, that is, the date, number, payee's name, amount and so on. Considerable care must be taken, as if the customer gives the wrong details or confusing details and the bank "stop" the wrong cheque, the bank will not be liable.[150] If a customer wishes to "stop" a cheque at short notice he may telephone his bank, but the bank will, in such a case, *postpone payment pending confirmation* only, until the written countermand is received.

It must be noted, of course, that although the drawer of the cheque may stop his banker from paying the cheque, he still remains liable to the holder of the cheque so long as that holder has a good title, all it means is that the drawer will have to pay the holder himself in another form.[151]

A bank obtains a general lien over any securities or papers belonging to a customer which come into the bank's hands, if that customer is at that time indebted to the bank. The lien will attach until the indebtedness is discharged or the bank release the lien, or the relationship of banker and customer ends.[152] An example of the operation of a banker's lien is the case of

RE KEEVER[153]

K was a customer of the M bank. He was overdrawn and paid in a cheque which cleared this and placed him substantially in credit. On the day the bank actually

148. *London Provincial & South Western Bank* v. *Buszard* (1918) 35 TLR 142.
149. There are three articles on the topic of stopped cheques which will repay reading: "The bank's right to recover money paid on a stopped cheque"—Professor R M Goode (1981) 97 LQR 254; "Stopped cheques and restitution: another view"—P Matthews [1982] JBL 281; "Stopped cheques and restitution— a reply"—Professor R M Goode [1982] JBL 288.
150. *Westminster Bank* v. *Hilton* (1926) 43 TLR 124, where the customer gave the details of one cheque, but the number of another.
151. If a cheque is received for payment through the bankers clearing or by post from another bank for the credit of a customer, the drawer can "stop" the cheque at any time up to the close of business on that day.
152. For example, on the liquidation of a company: *National Westminster Bank* v. *Halesowen Presswork Ltd* [1972] AC 785.
153. [1967] 1 Ch 182.

received the proceeds, a receiving order was made against K. The trustee in bankruptcy claimed the funds from the bank. The bank contended it had a lien over the cheque on the day it was paid in, and it did not matter that the proceeds were not received until a few days later. *Held*—that " . . . when the cheque was handed to the bank, the bank obtained a lien on the cheque for the amount of the overdraft".[154] Consequently, the bank were a secured creditor in the bankruptcy, and did not need to pass the proceeds of the cheque to the trustee.

Where a customer pays in a cheque, payable "to order" over which the bank thereupon immediately obtains a lien (or gives value by allowing the customer to draw against it uncleared) it does not matter that the cheque is not indorsed.[155] Indeed, since the passing of the Cheques Act 1957 (which relieved banks from the necessity of examining indorsements) indorsement of cheques being paid into the payee's (that is, the customer's) own account is no longer required. Although it is still " . . . the practice of the banks . . . to require the indorsement of a cheque by the payee when it is to be credited to some account other than that of the payee".[156]

Prior to the 1957 Act, a customer (that is, the drawer of a cheque) had the payee's indorsement on a cheque as evidence that he (the payee) had received the money. With the doing away of indorsements in this way, the drawer has been robbed of some of his evidence, although s. 3 of the 1957 Act provides that an unindorsed cheque, which appears to have been paid by the bank, is evidence of the receipt by the payee of the money payable by the cheque.[157]

Cheques must be presented for payment within a "reasonable time" of issue, otherwise the drawer is discharged to the extent of any damage he has suffered because of the delay in presentment.[158] As usual, in determining what is a "reasonable time" regard is to be taken of the nature of the instrument, the usage of the trade and of bankers, and the facts of the particular case.[159] The

154. *Per* Ungoed-Thomas J, *ibid.*, p. 191b.
155. Cheques Act 1957, s. 2. A bank advancing money to a customer on uncleared effects can be a "holder" even though the cheque is not indorsed: *Midland Bank Ltd* v. *R V Harris Ltd* [1963] 2 All ER 685. But see now Cheques Act 1992 if cheque is marked "A/c payee". See also *Westminster Bank Ltd* v. *Zang* [1966] AC 182, where it was held that collection need not necessarily be for the customer's own account. The banker's lien was lost when they passed the cheque to the payee's solicitors so the payee could sue the drawer: *per* Lord Denning, at p. 202g.
156. *Per* Lord Dilhorne, *ibid.*, p. 218g. See the reasoning of Lord Denning, *ibid.*, pp. 201b *et seq*, in the Court of Appeal which was not adopted by the House of Lords.
157. A copy of such a cheque is evidence, if it is made by the bank in whose possession the original cheque is *after* presentation, and is certified by the bank to be a true copy of the original: Deregulation (Bills of Exchange) Order 1996, s. 5.
158. Bills of Exchange Act 1882, s. 74(1). See also s. 45(1) and (2). Sections 74(1) and (3) are curiously drafted, and appear to cover the case of a bank failing (and the drawer's funds being lost) and subsequently a claim being made against the drawer by the holder of a cheque which has not been presented within a reasonable time; that is, while the bank was still functioning.
159. Bills of Exchange Act 1882, s. 74(2). However, see now new s. 74B(2) as inserted by Deregulation (Bills of Exchange) Order 1996, s. 4(1).

drawer can, if he wishes, state what shall be a "reasonable time" within which the instrument must be presented.[160]

In the day-to-day operation of a customer's accounts, banks are in a vulnerable position. If they are not very careful they may be liable for paying a cheque when they should not, or of collecting money for a customer when they should not: in each case they may be liable although they acted in good faith. If things go wrong, it frequently happens that the bank is committed by advantage being taken of the bank's services. For example, in *Lumsden* v. *London Trustee Saving Bank*,[161] an Australian visitor opened an account with a false name and references. He paid in cheques drawn by his employers in favour of business clients, and left the bank liable to repay the employers. In *Baker* v. *Barclays Bank Ltd*,[162] a customer misappropriated cheques into a private account with his bank, which cheques belonged, in fact, to a business in which he was involved. Once again, the bank was left to refund to the business. The customer in *Motor Traders Guarantee Corp* v. *Midland Bank Ltd*,[163] fraudulently indorsed a cheque which belonged to someone else, and paid it into his account and took the proceeds, leaving the bank to repay the rightful owner. One could go on and on. In all these cases there is an echo that more enquiries by the banks ought to have been made, indicating the element of trust which the banks were prepared to extend in accepting whatever explanations were given, only to find their actions (and their trust) being questioned in the subsequent analytical atmosphere of the courts. MacKinnon LJ recognized the dilemma bank staff are often in when he said: "It is true that, in the light of after events, the explanations given . . . may sound improbable to anyone in a suspicious frame of mind; but in my opinion the officials of the banks . . . have not to be abnormally suspicious"[164] and "It is not expected that officials of banks should also be amateur detectives."[165] Yet there are numerous examples of not unreasonable conduct on the part of bank officials which has, nevertheless, been called into question.

Banks, like other businesses, have staff problems. "I recognize that the same degree of intelligence and care cannot be looked for in a cashier as in an official higher in authority, such as a manager . . . I must, however, attribute to the cashiers and clerks . . . the degree of intelligence and care ordinarily required of persons in their position to fit them for the discharge of their duties",[166] so " . . . that if bankers have not got a proper staff to handle the cheques and look

160. *Per* Lord Coleridge J in *Thairlwell* v. *GN Railway* [1910] 2 KB 509, 520.
161. [1971] 1 Lloyd's Rep. 114.
162. [1955] 2 All ER 571.
163. (1937) 157 LT 498.
164. *Penmount Estates Ltd* v. *National Provincial Bank* (1945) 173 LT 344, 346.
165. *Per* Sankey LJ in *Lloyds Bank* v. *Chartered Bank of India* [1929] 1 KB 40, at p. 73.
166. *Per* Bailhache J in *Ross* v. *London County Bank* [1919] 1 KB 678, 685.

after them they must get them".[167] Sometimes a desire more easily expressed than achieved.

5. BANK'S RESPONSIBILITY TO THIRD PARTIES

As a principle, a bank owes no duty to third parties, other than not deliberately to mislead them or to be negligent. It follows that if an account is to be guaranteed a bank is under no duty to *volunteer* information as to the state of the customer's account to the proposed guarantor;[168] and even once the guarantee is signed, the guarantor is entitled to know only the amount of his liability and nothing more.

A bank is not in any way responsible to third parties for the debts or defaults of its customers, although, as we saw with *Midland Bank Ltd* v. *Reckitt*[169] and *Lloyds Bank Ltd* v. *Savory*,[170] it not infrequently happens that some third party succeeds in making a bank liable for its customer's dishonesty, if the bank has been negligent. In the absence of negligence, however, there is no liability.

Garnishee and Mareva orders

It is always possible, of course, for third parties to attempt to claim funds in the hands of banks by obtaining from the courts an order to that effect.

There are two types of order in such cases:

(A) A garnishee order

The effect of this is to order the bank to hand over the whole or such part of the customer's credit balance as will satisfy the debt. No claim can be made on the bank other than in respect of that particular customer's account, however, as " . . . the debt owing by a garnishee to a judgment debtor which can be attached to answer the judgment debt must be a debt due to the judgment debtor alone and that where it is only due to him jointly with another it cannot be attached".[171] Consequently, a debt of a husband cannot be claimed from a joint account of him and his wife.[172]

---

167. *Per* Pickford J in *Crumplin* v. *London Joint Stock Bank* (1913) 109 LT 856, at p. 857.
168. *Cooper* v. *National Provincial Bank Ltd* [1946] KB 1.
169. [1933] AC 1.
170. [1933] AC 201.
171. *Per* Pollock CB, in *Beasley* v. *Roney* [1891] 1 QB 509, at p. 512.
172. *Hirschorn* v. *Evans* [1938] 2 KB 801.

(B) A "Mareva" injunction

This takes its name from the case where it was applied,[173] and is an order of the court which, in effect, "freezes" a bank account pending the hearing of a dispute, where it is feared the defendant (the bank's customer) will attempt to remove from the country, or possibly spend, the money in his bank account.[174] Indeed, a Mareva order can be made on an overdrawn account.[175]

This type of order is a developing concept, and the Court of Appeal in *Z Ltd* v. *A and others*[176] took the opportunity to review the terms of its application, and to give some guidelines to those innocent third parties, such as banks, on how they are affected by these orders. The following are a few of the more important guidelines:

(1) A bank is bound by the terms of the order from the moment of service on the bank, and would be in contempt if the order were to be ignored thereafter.[177] However, there probably would be no contempt if a payment out of a "frozen" account is made by a bank employee in genuine ignorance of the order.

(2) A new account should be opened by the bank in the name of the customer to handle new debits and credits.

(3) Unless the order expressly stipulates, it will not extend to items held by the bank, such as securities, nor will it prevent the bank from carrying out other types of business on behalf of that customer.

(4) If in doubt, the bank can always apply to the court for directions.[178]

The difference between a garnishee order and a *Mareva* injunction is that the former is given to a creditor who has obtained judgment in an action, whereas

---

173. *Mareva Compania Naviera SA* v. *International Bulk Carriers SA* [1975] 2 Lloyd's Rep. 509. In fact, the case where it was first applied was *Nippon Yusen Kaisha* v. *Karageorgis* [1975] 1 WLR 1093, also in the Court of Appeal, but the second case has given it the name. See also *infra* its application to documentary credits.

174. The order is not limited to commercial disputes, and has been granted in police enquiries: *West Mercia Constabulary* v. *Wegener* [1982] 1 WLR 127; *Chief Constable of Kent* v. *V and Another* [1982] 3 WLR 462. But see *Chief Constable of Leicestershire* v. *M* [1989] 1 WLR 20, where the application was refused.

175. *Third Chandris Shipping Corporation* v. *Unimarine SA* [1979] 3 WLR 122.

176. [1982] 1 All ER 556. The court also has power, by the writ *ne exeat regno*, to support a Mareva injunction preventing a defendant leaving the jurisdiction: *Al Nahkel for Contracting and Trading Ltd* v. *Lowe* [1986] 1 All ER 729, where it was alleged the defendant had stolen money in Saudi Arabia, and was passing through London on his way to Manila. In furtherance of such an order, the court has power to order the defendant to deliver up his passport: *Bayer AG* v. *Winter* [1986] 1 WLR 497.

177. See *Z Bank* v. *D1* [1994] 1 Lloyd's Rep. 656.

178. For a recent example involving an application by a bank which was not a party to the action, see *Baltic Shipping Co* v. *Translink Shipping Ltd* [1995] 1 Lloyd's Rep. 673.

the latter is given to hold the *status quo* until the issues can be heard by the courts, and a final judgment made.

6. THE CLEARING SYSTEM

The system of "clearing" cheques is employed by the banks to pass cheques they have received on behalf of their customers to the "paying" banks so that payment can be made.

Reduced to its simplest form, it works like this:

Brown buys goods from Jones, and pays the account of £50 by cheque. Jones will then pay the cheque (together with any others he receives) into his bank. In the course of the day-to-day business among banks Jones' bank will send the cheque to Brown's bank, who will make the necessary entries in their books and debit Brown's account. Jones' bank will have credited his account at the time when Jones paid in the cheque.

The system is not quite so straightforward, however, due mainly to the millions of cheques which are cleared among the banks each day, and while the following account is something of an over-simplification, it will give a general idea of how the system works.[179]

Indeed, because of the continued development of electronic technology, the clearing system is changing to meet the needs of customers for a more efficient processing of cheques, and the Bills of Exchange Act 1882 has recently been amended to accommodate the new technology.

The Deregulation (Bills of Exchange) Order 1996

It was a requirement of the Bills of Exchange Act 1882 s. 45(4), that bills be presented for payment at "the proper place", which, in the case of cheques, meant the address of the drawee bank printed on the cheques. For years, this involved the transporting of millions of cheques around the country each day; however, because of the increasing use of electronic technology the physical presentation of cheques in this way has proved no longer necessary. Therefore, the Cheque and Credit Clearing Company Limited (CCCC), under the auspices of the Association for Payment Clearing Services (APACS), has implemented a new system for the exchange of codeline data between banks—called Inter Bank Data Exchange (IBDE)—and by this procedure the steps in the clearing system can be reduced ("truncated"), and a number of changes have been made to the Bills of Exchange Act.

---

179. For a description of the clearing system which operated in the early 1980s, see the award of Bingham J in *Barclays Bank plc v. Bank of England* [1985] 1 All ER 385, and in the judgment of Brightman J in *Karak Rubber Co Ltd v. Burden* [1972] 1 All ER 1210, at p. 1230d.

So that, so far as cheques are concerned,[179a] the collecting bank may present a cheque for payment to the drawee bank by notifying it of the cheque's "essential features by electronic means or otherwise" instead of by presenting the cheque itself.[179b]

The "essential features" of a cheque for this purpose are (a) the serial number, (b) the drawee bank's sort code, (c) the account number of the customer of the drawee bank, (d) the amount of the cheque.[179c]

If presentation for payment is made in this way both the collecting and drawee banks remain subject to the same duties in relation to collection and payment as if the cheque itself had been presented for payment.[179d]

What this means is that it is no longer necessary to present a cheque for payment at the "proper place", nor at a reasonable hour on a business day.[179e] Having said that, if for any reason the drawee bank wants to see the cheque itself, it can request the collecting bank to present it, and the electronic presentation is then disregarded, provided the request is made before the close of business on the next business day following the electronic presentation.[179f]

The clearing system is co-ordinated by the Association for Payment Clearing Services (APACS), which has substantial responsibilities for all matters relating to money transmission and payment clearing activities in the UK, and membership of APACS includes all financial institutions which play a significant part in the provision of these services. APACS was set up in 1985 to take overall management responsibility for these services.

Under APACS there are three basic areas of activity, which are handled through the medium of separate limited companies:[180]

(1) The Cheque and Credit Clearing Company Ltd, which deals with the bulk cheque clearing and paper credits.
(2) The CHAPS,[181] which deals with the clearing of high value items, including same-day electronic payments and a small number of very high value cheques.

179a. Subject to the various amendments contained in the Deregulation (Bills of Exchange) Order 1996.

179b. See new s. 74B(1) amended by s. 4(1) Deregulation (Bills of Exchange) Order 1996.

179c. See new s. 74B(b) amended by s. 4(1) Deregulation (Bills of Exchange) Order 1996.

179d. See new s. 74B(5) as amended by s. 4(1) Deregulation (Bills of Exchange) Order 1996.

179e. Ibid., new s. 74B(2).

179f. Ibid., new s. 74B(3). Such a request will not constitute a dishonour of the cheque by non-payment: ibid., new s. 74B(4). Also, to operate this new system drawee banks must publish a notice in the London, Edinburgh and Belfast Gazettes giving an address at which cheques drawn on it may be presented: ibid., new s. 74A.

180. In addition, there are two operational groupings which deal with (i) currency clearing, and (ii) cheque card and Eurocheque schemes. APACS covers other aspects of interbank activity including cash, plastic cards and the various City markets, for all of which there are common interest groups which meet under its auspices.

181. The Clearing House Automated Payment System.

(3) BACS[182] Limited, which deals substantially with clearing through the electronic banking systems, including direct debits, standing orders and so forth.

All these activities are under the authority of the Chief Inspector who now has an overview for the general conduct of the business at the Exchange and Settlement Centres, and is responsible for triggering the settlement process over accounts held on behalf of the Members of the Bank of England, while the day-to-day responsibility now rests with the Company Manager.

Cheque and Credit Clearing Company Ltd

This company operates the two major sterling cheque and other commercial paper clearings, being Cheque Clearing (previously known as "General Clearing") and Credit Clearing. Most cheques are cleared through the Cheque Clearing System, and the Credit Clearing operates in much the same way but handles paper credit items. Also, Credit Clearing differs from Cheque Clearing in that the former is not at the moment processed via the Inter Bank Data Exchange (IBDE), so that the whole process is paper based.

There are separate sets of rules for the conduct of both cheque clearing and credit clearing. The procedures are regulated by the APACS Standards Manuals, and cover matters extending from the times when business must be transacted to how settlement is to be effected.

Cheque clearing

The system, very briefly, operates in this way.

(a) When a cheque is paid into a branch of a bank for collection it is stamped by that branch, and, with electronic devices operating now the details of the transaction are captured electronically, and it is encoded by adding the sum payable in magnetic ink (as we all know, the cheque already shows the cheque number, branch reference number of the drawee bank and the customer's account number). This encoding of the sum payable may no longer apply after September 1997, under the new rules. At the close of business that day, the branch sorts the cheques it has received and it makes up bundles of cheques, if necessary, for each drawee bank.

(b) These bundles are collected from the branch that evening, or possibly early in the morning and taken to the clearing department of the collecting bank.

(c) These items are now entered in a "file" which gives details of the transaction referred to above, the file being created between midnight and 11.00am the next morning. This file may contain about

182. Bankers Automated Clearing Services.

1500 items, and is transmitted electronically; that is, without any print out.

(d) At this stage the cheques are not subjected to any examination or inspection relating to their payment; though the Collecting Bank takes steps to ensure the details of the payee, crossing and so forth, are in order.

(e) All cheques have routinely been transported from all over the country to the Exchange Centre in London (which obviously has to deal with many millions of cheques per day), where they have been handed over to the representatives of each drawee bank.[183] It is this procedure which the new rules are intended to dispense with. For the time being however, it is likely that cheques will continue to be delivered to the Paying Bank's Clearing Centre.

(f) The next step is now being centralized by many banks where the cheques are fed into "reader-sorter" machines and compared with the file process referred to above. This electronic device, among other things, sorts the cheques into the appropriate branches on whom they are drawn. This machine also records details of the cheques for onward transmission to the drawee bank's computer where the branch accounts are kept. Of course for the time being, individual banks may decide to accept data presented by the Collecting Banks, and not reprocess the cheques they receive at all.

(g) As all posting to customer's accounts is done from the data on the file, it is at this stage that the various drawers' accounts will be debited as though the cheques have been paid, and a "computer projection" made to that effect.

(h) Once the new system is fully operational (and each bank may have slightly different procedures) the cheques (possibly in bundles for each branch of the drawee banks) will not be sent to the appropriate branch on whom they are drawn.[184] However, this is the moment when the detail of each cheque drawn on that branch will be examined and a decision made whether it can be paid or not; this inspection will take into account whether the drawer (the customer) is in funds or has an agreed overdraft. If there is any doubt about any item, the branch may call for sight of the cheque, as was noted earlier.

---

183. The basic rules for presentment for payment as provided in the Bills of Exchange Act 1882 apply to presentation between banks. See ss. 45, 46 and 47, and *supra*, Chap. 3.

184. The responsibility of the collecting bank to its customer was not discharged until the cheque was physically delivered to the branch of the drawee bank so it could decide whether to pay it or not. It was not enough that it was delivered to the drawee bank's representatives as part of the clearing system: *Barclays Bank plc* v. *Bank of England* [1985] 1 All ER 385. This must now be in question, following the amendment to s. 45(4) of the 1982 Act by the Deregulation (Bills of Exchange) Order 1996.

It should be noted that there are several banks who have stopped putting cheques into bundles as mentioned above, because they have introduced Central Cheque Payment Processes, when demands may be made to the Collecting Bank to provide items as and when the Collecting Bank truncation is fully established. Where central payment has been set up in this way then, until the Collecting Bank truncation is completed, the paper may well be kept in presentation order and extracted where necessary for inspection, for onward transmission to the customer or return, by using the item sequence numbers generated during the clearing process.

(i) If the cheque is paid, the customer's account is debited finally—that is, the "computer projection" effected earlier will take effect.[185] If the cheque is not paid, the original "computer projection" will be reversed. This decision, to pay or not, must be made on the day the details are received by the drawee branch, or the receipt of the cheque itself if that is called for.

(j) The balances are struck by the collecting and paying banks and submitted to the Chief Inspector for checking. They are then settled by inter-bank transfers, through settlement accounts which all the banks maintain at the Bank of England.

Credit clearing

A credit transfer is effected by the payer giving instructions to his bank to make payment to the account of the beneficiary at *his* bank. These instructions signed by the payer do not create a negotiable document, since they never pass into the hands of the beneficiary/payee. Though there will, of course, be an agreement between the payer and the beneficiary (the main agreement) which creates the need to effect the transfer of funds. Consequently, if the transfer is not effected (for example if the paying bank has insufficient funds), the beneficiary could sue the payer under the main contract.

Settlement takes place two days after the transfer is made, or cheque paid in to the collecting bank; in other words on the third day of the transaction, although the time of payment during the third day is not defined. Payment may, therefore, be considered as effected when the paying bank has transferred

185. Except where there has been a manifest error (the Inadvertence Rule) a bank, once having passed debit and credit entries, cannot reverse them next day on the grounds that the final balances were not available from the computer until the following morning: *Momm v. Barclays Bank International Ltd* [1976] 3 All ER 588, but, on specific facts, see *Rekstin v. Severo Sibirsko Gosudarstvennoe Akcionernoe Obschestvo Komseverputj* [1933] 1 KB 47. It is, of course, for the collecting bank to say when value will be given to its customer in respect of any clearing of effects.

the funds to the collecting bank and they are beyond recall;[186] presumably the payer can "stop" the transfer by instructions to his bank at any time up till the close of business on the third day of the transaction.

The collecting bank could well be liable if they receive funds in this way to which their customer was not entitled, though whether the bank could be protected by s. 4 of the Cheques Act 1957 which refers to "any document issued by a customer of a bank which . . . is intended to enable a person to obtain payment . . . " is a question yet to be decided.

Indeed, these are all new concepts, and the legal relationships have not yet fallen for consideration. For example, there are many potential legal issues to be resolved involving the transfer of funds to shopkeepers at point of sale, and the instant access to money provided by cash machines.

CHAPS[187]

The Clearing House Automated Payments System (CHAPS) provides a same-day guaranteed sterling electronic credit transfer service within the UK. It was launched on 9 February 1984, and the system allows for payment of any amount to be transmitted by a branch of a bank to another, using a computer link system through a British Telecom network.

Once again, there are detailed rules governing the conduct of CHAPS business, but the concept is that payment will be made and received between member banks on "an irrevocable guaranteed unconditional sterling payment for same-day settlement" basis.

186. Though always subject to recourse. There have been a number of cases dealing with the question of the timing of clearances. See *Momm* v. *Barclays Bank International Ltd* [1976] 3 All ER 588: " . . . payment in the present case was complete when [the bank] decided to accept . . . instructions to credit the plaintiff's account and the computer processes for doing so were set in motion", *per* Kerr J (as he then was) at p. 598e. See also *The Brimnes* [1974] 3 All ER 88; and *Libyan Arab Foreign Bank* v. *Manufacturers Hanover Trust Co (No 2)* [1989] 1 Lloyd's Rep. 608. In the case of CHAPS, the subject of Risk and Real Time Settlement is only now approaching a solution, with technology which will pinpoint exactly the moment of payment. When funds are transferred between banks in different countries and different time zones, there may be a question of when the payment is effected and the money received. In *The Brimnes* [1974] 3 All ER 88 the Court of Appeal held that payment was not effected when the advice was received by the collecting bank, but two hours later when the advice had been "processed" by the bank's personnel. See also *The Chikuma* [1981] 1 All ER 652; and *Mardorf Peach & Co* v. *Attica Sea Carriers Corporation of Liberia* [1977] 1 All ER 545, where the House of Lords reversed the decision of the Court of Appeal which had stated that payment was effected when the advice was received. The same decision was reached in *Afovos Shipping Co S.A.* v. *Pagnam* [1983] 1 All ER 449. No doubt, with the new procedures being introduced, these decisions, based as they are on systems then obtaining, will have to be reviewed in the future when similar questions call to be decided.

187. Until 1995 there was a system of cheque clearing which applied only in the City of London. This was the so-called "Town Clearing"; it was largely a manual system involving the same day clearing facilities for cheques and other items of a value of half a million pounds sterling or more, which were drawn on and also paid into branches of banks within the City of London. Because of the limited number of transactions each day and, more especially, the limited distance cheques had to travel from one end to the other of the clearing route, the procedures tended to be less detailed. Historically, Town Clearing had its roots going back to the eighteenth century.

BACS Ltd[188]

This company provides an automated clearing house service in the UK which covers the handling of direct debits, standing orders and automated credits, such as the payment of payroll and other purchase ledger payments to company suppliers.

There is a distinction between standing orders and direct debits. For while both involve payments from the payer's bank to the beneficiary's bank, in the case of a standing order, it is the payer who instructs his bank to make payment in accordance with his instructions; whereas in the case of a direct debit, the payer instructs his bank to accept debits originated by the beneficiary on the payer's account, provided these conform to the terms of the instruction.

Payments can be "stopped", even though the payer may still be liable to the beneficiary under the main underlying contract.

Computerized accounting[189]

We saw above that when the cheques are delivered to the clearing departments of the drawee banks, and put through the "reader-sorter" machines, the details of each cheque are entered in the bank's computer, not as a final entry (indeed, the cheques have not been examined for payment at this stage), but as a "computer projection" based on what will probably happen to the cheque —that is, that it will be paid. Therefore, between the time of the computer entry and the actual inspection of the cheque by the drawee branch, there is, obviously, a period when the cheque is in suspense so far as the computer is concerned, and if the "projection" is not reversed, the cheque will be paid and the "computer projection" will become final.

The use of computers in this way is, of course, of great assistance to banks in dealing with the flood of cheques with which they deal, running, as it does, into many millions each day. Problems can arise, however, as usual in the most unexpected ways. In

BURNETT v. WESTMINSTER BANK LTD[190]

B had accounts at both the "Borough" branch of the bank and at the "Bromley" branch. The bank went over to computerized accounting and B was sent a cheque book from the "Borough" branch suitably printed with magnetized ink and a notice on the cover

---

188. This was first established in 1968 as Bankers Automated Clearing Services Ltd. The name was changed in 1986.

189. The following observations are based on the judgment of Mocatta J in *Burnett v. Westminster Bank* [1965] 3 All ER 81, at 84g, in respect of the systems then obtaining.

190. [1965] 3 All ER 81. One must question whether in the future, with the new automated procedures, such circumstances could obtain.

of the cheque book that "cheques . . . in this book will be applied to the account for which they have been prepared". Some months later B made out a cheque from this book but crossed out the word "Borough" and inserted "Bromley" and initialled the alteration. Almost immediately he wanted to "stop" the cheque and telephoned the "Bromley" branch telling them also the cheque was in the changed form. Meanwhile, the cheque reached the computer at the London Clearing House, the details were taken and the cheque itself was sent to the "Borough" branch—the computer having failed to "read" the alteration! The "Borough" branch, of course, knew nothing of the "stop" instructions and they took no steps to "tell" the computer not to pay the cheque. B sued his bank. *Held*—that the bank were liable as they should not have paid the cheque.

Not infrequently money coming into the account is needed for some purpose urgently, and knowing this the bank must exercise reasonable care to collect in the proper way.[191]

In accordance with the APACS procedures, if the Rules are not observed by a bank, whether deliberately or by inadvertence, it will be liable for any loss.[192]

7. THE BANK AS A HOLDER OF CHEQUES

It is the practice of bankers to credit a customer's account with the value of cheques paid in without waiting for those cheques to be "cleared" and the actual funds to be in their hands.

If, therefore, a customer has not sufficient funds and the bank allows its customer to draw against those "uncleared" effects it has, in effect, given the customer some of its money, on the strength of those cheques being met. If they are not, the bank can pursue the drawer of the cheques, the bank being a holder for value or a holder in due course. A recent example is

BARCLAYS BANK LTD v. ASTLEY INDUSTRIAL TRUST[193]

M Ltd were customers of the bank and had a considerable overdraft. Five cheques were paid into the account drawn on A, a finance company, in respect of what appeared to be normal hire-purchase transactions. The bank, on the strength of these cheques, honoured two cheques which M Ltd drew. It transpired that these transactions were fraudulent and A "stopped" their cheques. The bank then sued A, the finance company. *Held*—that the bank were holders for value, and were entitled to recover as they had no notice of any defect of M Ltd's title when they gave value by allowing cheques to be drawn against those uncleared effects.

---

191. *Forman* v. *Bank of England* (1902) 18 TLR 339. The circumstances of this case could, almost certainly, not happen today, but the principle is still good law.
192. *Parrs Bank* v. *Thomas Ashby & Co* (1898) 14 TLR 563.
193. [1970] 2 QB 527. See also *Midland Bank Ltd* v. *RV Harris Ltd* [1963] 2 All ER 685.

Notice must then be given by the bank to the drawer in the ordinary way, as with a bill of exchange that is not a cheque. However, to succeed, it is essential that the bank:

(1) Either allowed its customer to draw against the uncleared effects, or, at least, *agreed* that he could;[194] and

(2) Is a "holder" of the cheque, so as to be in a position to sue in its own right.

These requirements were fully discussed in the case of

WESTMINSTER BANK LTD v. ZANG[195]

Z lost heavily to G in a card game. Z said to a friend T: "I'm in trouble now. Have you any money on you?" T was the "one man" of a one-man company called "Tilley Autos Ltd". T had in his pocket the weekend takings belonging to the company, amounting to over £1,000. Z gave T a cheque for £1,000 made out to T personally, and received, in exchange, the cash. T paid the cheque into his company's bank account—which was overdrawn—at the Westminster Bank, but did not, nor was he asked to, indorse the cheque. The cheque was dishonoured, and the bank claimed from Z, saying they had taken it in reduction of the company overdraft, and had, therefore, given value. *Held*—that (i) the cheque was payable to T "or order", but not indorsed by T, either specially or in blank, so the bank was not a "holder", and so could not sue on it themselves; (ii) in any event, the bank had not shown that there was an express or implied agreement to allow Tilley Autos Ltd to draw against the uncleared cheque. In fact, "the bank put a note on the paying-in slip expressly to prevent any such agreement being implied . . . they cannot have it both ways".[196] The bank could not, therefore, recover from Z.

There is now a further complication. By virtue of the Cheques Act 1992, s. 1, any cheque which is crossed and marked "account payee", or "a/c payee" (whether the word "only" appears or not) is "not transferable", and is only valid "as between the parties thereto". This means that a transferee or indorsee cannot have any title at all; and so if a bank allows its customer to draw against uncleared effects, it would seem the bank can have no title to the cheque representing those uncleared effects; and if the cheque is dishonoured the bank will not be able to sue the drawer in its own right. Of course, the point has yet to be decided, but it is difficult to see any other interpretation which can be put upon the new legislation.

---

194. *Westminster Bank Ltd v. Zang* [1966] AC 182.

195. [1966] AC 182.

196. *Per* Lord Denning, *ibid.*, p. 203b. The bank might have had a lien (as for example in *Re Keever* [1967] 1 Ch 182, see *supra* p. 194 but by handing the dishonoured cheque to T's solicitors so he could take action against Z, the lien was lost: see *per* Danckwerts LJ, *ibid.*, p. 205f. This was altogether an unhappy action for the bank, as T's personal action against Z on the cheque had not been pursued either, and was eventually dismissed for want of prosecution—presumably because T did not wish to incur the costs, even if he recovered from Z, the money would go straight to the bank. If the bank had got the cheque indorsed by T, they would, at least, have been "holders"—but would still have failed as they did not give value.

8. CHEQUE CARDS[197]

With the increase in banking business, and, hence, the vastly increased number of people with cheque books in Britain, the USA and elsewhere, coupled with the mobility of people generally, it was inevitable that there would be a corresponding increase in the numbers of cheques issued that could not be met. The cheque ceased to be an acceptable form of payment unless the payee knew the drawer, or unless there was some on-going relationship. For the vast majority of cases of paying for goods in shops, for example, the cheque no longer carried the approbation it once did.[198]

It so happened that the increase in banking business coincided with the development of the use of computers; indeed, it was, doubtless, the availability of new computer technology that made the banks realize they could handle many more millions of customers, and so triggered the increase in business. It was to this background that the banks devised a system for reliable customers to be issued a piece of plastic which could be used in conjunction with a cheque, to guarantee to the payee that the cheque would be met by the bank in all circumstances. The cheque—backed by the plastic "cheque card"—was as good as cash. Each cheque card is impressed with a number which identifies that that piece of plastic relates to that particular customer's account, and the cheque is cleared in the usual way, and debited to the customer's account; the only difference being that if the cheque is "backed" in this way, the bank is obliged to meet it *vis-à-vis* the payee, even if the customer is without funds or the authority to overdraw.[199]

Of course, there are limitations. The terms of cover in this way are as follows.

The bank guarantees in any single transaction the payment of one cheque taken from one of its own cheque books for up to £100 provided the cheque is not drawn on the account of a limited company, and

> (1) The cheque bears the same name and code number as this card.
> (2) The cheque is dated with the actual date of issue.

---

197. Cheque cards must not be confused with *credit* cards. A *credit* card is a piece of plastic issued by credit card companies, which allows the holder to charge purchases by simply signing a form "backed" by his charge (credit) card. The credit card company then sends a statement, usually monthly, to the customer, which he must then pay direct to the credit card company, who will, already, have paid the shopkeeper or whomsoever supplied the goods or services. At least one credit card in the UK can be used as a cheque card also, but this is not usual.

198. At one time the very fact of a bank issuing a customer a cheque book was taken to be a sign that the bank thought the customer sufficiently trustworthy. These were the days when, within a community, banks knew their customers more so than today.

199. In France, cheque cards do not exist. Every cheque carries the address of the customer, in addition to his name and other usual bank account details. When presenting a cheque for payment, the drawer is asked by the payee for his National Identity Card, which carries his address and a photograph. The payee writes these details on the back of the cheque, so in the event of a problem with the cheque the drawer can be traced quickly—usually by the police, and the penalties for dishonour are heavy. In no sense, however, is the cheque guaranteed by the bank.

(3) It is signed before the expiry of the card in the United Kingdom of Great Britain and Gibraltar in the presence of the payee by the person whose signature appears on this card.

(4) The card number is written on the back by the payee.

(5) The card has not been altered or defaced.

The following points must be noted relating to the operation of cheque cards in this way:

(a) The cheque must be a personal one, bearing the same details as the card.

(b) The limit is £50, £100 or £250 per cheque, "in any one transaction". It would not, at least in theory, be acceptable to give, say, three guaranteed cheques for £100 each to pay for one item costing £300.[200]

(c) The payee has to write the card number on the back of the cheque, usually at the time of payment.

(d) The card (with cheque) can be used not only to buy goods up to a value of £100, but also to obtain cash from any branch of any bank, following the same procedure as a purchase of goods. Only £100 cash per day can be drawn in this way.

(e) The card can only be used in the British Isles; a different card must be obtained from the bank for use abroad.

It will be apparent that cheque cards, operating the way they do, create three separate contracts, between:

(1) The bank and its customer, when the terms of the card are stipulated by the bank and agreed to by the customer when he accepts the card.

(2) The bank and the payee, being a shopkeeper, another bank or whomsoever, that it will honour a cheque to the value of £50 or whatever, on the terms stated.

(3) The customer (drawer) and the payee.

It is only when there are irregularities, of course, that these contractual considerations become important. Because, convenient though the system is, it can have its abuses, which, from the bank's point of view, are, in the main, twofold:

A. The customer may not prove as reliable as the bank originally thought, and he may issue cheques "backed" with the card, when he did not have the funds in his account to meet the cheque, nor the authority to overdraw. In such a case, the bank must still honour the payment to the payee of the cheque, and, while it can sue its customer for the return of the money paid out in this way,

---

200. With Eurocheques, writing more than one cheque to cover a bill for an amount in excess of the maximum guaranteed limit on any one cheque is permitted.

that right may not be worth much. Such acts by a customer could also amount to a criminal offence of course.[201]

The abuse can take a number of forms. If the customer wants cash, he is limited to £100 per day, and must, in accordance with the conditions in the contract between him and his bank, " . . . hand your cheque book as well as the cheque card to the cashier" of the bank, so the cashier can verify that not more than £100 has been withdrawn that day. Yet, in making purchases, the same obligation to check how much the customer has spent that day does not obtain to the shopkeeper it seems. In the case of *Metropolitan Police Commissioner v. Charles*,[202] where the customer, in breach of his agreement with his bank, cashed all 25 cheques in his book at one time, all suitably "backed" by his card, with a gaming establishment for chips, the bank paid out on all the cheques. The customer was charged with "obtaining a pecuniary advantage" by deception;[203] the "deception" being the representation to the payee by the drawer that he is " . . . authorized by the bank . . . and so create a direct contractual relationship between the bank and you that they will honour this cheque".[204]

B. The other problem is that if some thief gets hold of both cheque book and card, and goes about buying goods and services on the strength of the card by forging the customer's signature, the bank cannot debit the customer's account, cheque card or no cheque card, as the signature is a forgery.[205] However, the bank would still be liable to the payee and would have to honour the value of the cheques, and, of course, bear the loss themselves; subject always to its right to sue the forger, for whatever that might be worth.[206]

As we saw above, this type of cheque card is applicable only within the British Isles.[207] To obtain a similar service in other countries the banks have devised the *Eurocheque Encashment Card*, as part of the Uniform Eurocheques system, which the leading commercial banks set up in 1968. The system is made up of "active" members which issue the Eurocheque guarantee cards and cheques; and "passive" members which do not issue cards and

---

201. Under s. 16(1) of the Theft Act 1968. See also *R v. Kovacs* [1974] 1 All ER 1236; *Metropolitan Police Commissioner v. Charles* [1977] AC 177. The Theft Act 1978 replaces s. 16(2)(a) of the 1968 Act, and now covers the crimes of obtaining services by deception, making off without payment, and evasion of an existing liability. Also the offence is committed within the jurisdiction even though the money was obtained from a bank abroad: *R v. Beck* [1985] 1 WLR 22, and *R v. Bevan* (1987) 84 Cr App R 143.

202. [1977] AC 177.

203. Pursuant to s. 16(1) of the Theft Act 1968.

204. *Per* Lord Edmund Davies, *ibid.*, p. 191g.

205. One assumes this to be the case, because of the forged signature: *Sheffield Corp v. Barclay* [1903] 2 KB 580; *Jackson v. White and Midland Bank* [1967] 2 Lloyd's Rep. 68; *Welch v. Bank of England* [1955] 1 Ch 508. However, the point seems not to have been addressed in *First Sport Ltd v. Barclays Bank Plc* [1993] 3 All ER 789 which turned solely on the responsibility of the bank to the payee.

206. *First Sport Ltd v. Barclays Bank Plc* [1993] 3 All ER 789, Kennedy LJ dissenting. Leave to appeal to the House of Lords granted.

207. The ordinary cheque card is not valid outside the UK and Gibraltar.

cheques, but will encash these Eurocheques "backed' with the Eurocard.[208] The system operates upon the following terms and conditions:

(a) A separate plastic "Eurocheque Encashment Card" is issued by the UK bank to its customer; essentially in the format as before.

(b) The UK bank also supplies special Eurocheque forms with the UK bank's name and address printed, but the customer/drawer writes the Eurocheque in the local currency of the country he is in at the time.

(c) Eurocheques can be used to pay for goods and services or to obtain cash while abroad, and they are guaranteed for varying amounts depending on the currency being used.

9. TERMINATION OF THE RELATIONSHIP

It must be made clear that in considering the termination of the relationship of banker and customer, the relationship does not end necessarily at a given moment, as though a guillotine had fallen: a bank cannot throw the ex-customer's money and papers into the street!

For example, if a customer dies the bank have an implied duty to carry on holding any money or securities belonging to the deceased until they receive proper instructions in respect of the effects. What, in effect, has happened is that their *authority* to deal with the account has ceased. Indeed, some aspects of the relationship may continue for ever—for example, the banker's duty to maintain secrecy. With regard to termination the following circumstances need to be considered:

(1) Lapse of time

While, as we saw, the relationship of banker and customer has some of the qualities of debtor and creditor, lapse of time, of itself, does not affect the relationship. If a creditor does not claim for six years he will lose the right to claim his money, but a customer does not lose his rights even if there are no dealings with his account for however long a period. This applies to both current[209] and deposit[210] accounts.

However, if (which seems unlikely) a customer were to make a demand for payment, which for some reason was not executed, time would then run and the customer's rights might then be extinguished after six years under the Limitation Acts.

208. See, for a more detailed explanation, Dassesse and Isaacs, *EEC Banking Law* (1994). Incidentally, the *Eurocheque* can be used in a number of countries outside Europe, for example, Iceland, Sweden, Morocco to mention but a few.
209. *Joachimson v. Swiss Bank Corp* [1921] 3 KB 110.
210. *Atkinson v. Bradford Equitable Building Society* (1890) 25 QBD 379.

(2) *Death*

It is the *notice* of the death, and not the death itself, which terminates the duty to pay cheques.[211] In the absence of strict proof, the notice to the bank must be reliable and not merely a rumour. Moreover, when paying out money to the deceased's personal representatives "Bankers are in a peculiar position, and when asked to hand over large sums of money to persons claiming as executors of a deceased customer, I think they are justified in requiring to be made safe by production of probate."[212]

(3) *Unsoundness of mind*

If a customer is not "detainable" under the Mental Health Acts, but is nevertheless of unsound mind—even with periods of lucidity—the relationship will still continue, but the burden will clearly be on the bank to show the customer's authority existed in any transaction which may be called in question. For, if this authority does not exist (that is, if the customer, because of his unsoundness of mind, has lost capacity altogether) the bank may be liable for any acts carried out on behalf of the customer where it acts as his agent. Moreover, it is the unsoundness of mind, and *not the notice of it*, which terminates the banker's authority to act for his customer.[213] This throws a tremendous responsibility on a bank in these circumstances.

If a customer becomes a "patient" under the Mental Health Acts the position is clearer. The courts will make an order for "the doing of all such things as appear necessary or expedient". This will usually mean the closing of the patient's account and transferring the funds to a new account in the name of the trustee or receiver appointed by the court. Once again, it is the making of the order—not the notice of it—which terminates the bank's authority.

(4) *Insolvency*

If a customer is adjudicated bankrupt, notice will be given to his bank and this will terminate the relationship. Instructions are issued as to the disposal of any credit balance in the customer's accounts, which will be taken over by the trustee in bankruptcy. As a matter of practice, therefore, once a customer is adjudicated bankrupt, as any dispositions of property he attempts to make are void under the terms of s. 284(1) of the Insolvency Act 1986, banks will deal only with the bankrupt's affairs by the direction of the Official Receiver, and to that end the account will be closed.

In the case of a limited company it can continue to operate a bank account between the date when the winding up commences and the date when the

---

211. Bills of Exchange Act 1882, s. 75(2).
212. *Per* Stephen J in *Tarn v. Commercial Bank of Sydney* (1884) 12 QBD 294, 296.
213. *Yonge v. Toynbee* [1910] 1 KB 215.

winding-up order is made. The winding up "commences", in the case of a voluntary winding up, when the company passes a resolution to that effect;[214] and in the case of a winding up by the court, when the petition for winding up is presented.[215]

(5) Express notice

Either the customer or the bank can terminate the relationship. However, while it appears a customer with a credit balance in his account can terminate the relationship almost immediately, the bank, in similar circumstances, must be given reasonable notice.[216]

If the account is to be transferred elsewhere, the relationship still subsists until the transferee (the new bank) is notified of the proposed transfer.[217]

By making a demand for repayment of a loan and closing a customer's account, the relationship between banker and customer does not come to an end.[218]

214. Ss. 86 and 129(1), Insolvency Act 1986.
215. *Ibid.*, s. 129(2). The position of insolvency is also considered *supra*, under the heading of Capacity to operate a bank account. Where a company is being wound up by the court, its property does not automatically vest in the liquidator: s. 145(1), Insolvency Act 1986. In a voluntary liquidation, the company's property remains vested in the company. And see *Re George Gross Ltd* (see *Financial Times*, 23 May 1969) and *Re Operator Control Cabs Ltd* [1970] 3 All ER 657.
216. *Prosperity Ltd* v. *Lloyds Bank* (1923) 39 TLR 372. However, where facilities granted by the bank are "on demand", they can be recalled at any time, and while a period of notice would be the ordinary commercial expectation, it is not a legal obligation: *Sacomex Ltd* v. *Banque Bruxelles Lambert SA* [1996] 1 Lloyd's Rep. 156, 189.
217. See *per* Lord Hanworth in *Rekstin* v. *Severo Sibirsko, etc* [1933] 1 KB 47, at p. 63.
218. *National Bank of Greece SA* v. *Pinios Shipping Co (No. 1), The Maira* [1990] 1 All ER 78.

CHAPTER 12

FORM OF CHEQUES

The form of a cheque and the rules governing it are the same as for ordinary bills of exchange which are payable on demand, and reference should again be made to that section of the book. In practice, banks have printed books of cheques in their own form, and no substantial difference exists among the forms in everyday use.

However, there are several matters relating to form as affecting cheques which need special consideration.

1. UNCONDITIONAL ORDER TO THE DRAWEE BANK

Any order from the drawer to the drawee bank to do any act in addition to the payment of money will render the form of cheque not a cheque or bill of exchange at all! For example, it is the practice of some banks to allow their customers to have designed cheques, which the banks have printed, with a receipt on the back which the payee must sign, as having received the money under the cheque in satisfaction of whatever the sum was for. The obligation is clearly on the paying bank to see this formality is complied with before paying.

Forms of cheques prepared in this way are not, in fact, cheques at all, as such documents are clearly requiring an act to be done "in addition to the payment of money" within s. 3(2) of the Bills of Exchange Act 1882 and are not, therefore, bills of exchange.[1] Such documents are called "conditional orders".

If, however, such a condition can be construed not as being a direction to the drawee bank to get the receipt signed, but only a direction to the *payee* to sign, the document will be a valid cheque and negotiable in the usual way.[2] The same would apply to any term or condition which the drawer of a cheque tried to enforce.

---

1. *Bavins* v. *London and South Western Bank* [1900] 1 QB 270. A cheque drawn, "it will not be honoured after three months from the date of issue" is still a valid cheque and not conditional: *Thairlwall* v. *GN Railway* [1910] 2 KB 509.
2. *Nathan* v. *Ogdens Ltd* (1905) 94 LT 126.

215

ROBERTS v. MARSH[3]

M was indebted to R in the sum of £100 under a contract. He did not have his cheque book with him, and when R insisted on payment, M drew a form of cheque on a blank sheet of paper. He wrote across the face the words "to be retained" and promised he would let R have a cheque on the usual banker's form in substitution for the paper. This M failed to do, and R presented the paper which was dishonoured by M's bank. R sued M who claimed the document was not an "unconditional order". *Held* — that the words "to be retained" were not words which bound the bankers, and were a condition between drawer and payee only.

2. POST-DATING

Where the drawer of a cheque wishes to postpone payment, but nevertheless wishes to give his creditor some proof of his commitment and *bona fides*, he sometimes gives a cheque, but dates it to some time in the future when he hopes or is prepared to have funds available at his bank to meet the liability. For example:

X buys a motor car from Y. The agreed price is £400. X does not have all the purchase price and it is agreed that he will give Y £100 immediately, and three cheques post-dated to the 1st of each month. The presumption is that Y will pay into his bank one cheque on the 1st as and when the cheques fall due.

There is, however, a basic problem in post-dating a cheque in this way. We have seen that a cheque is a bill of exchange which is drawn on a banker and *payable on demand*.[4] If, therefore, the drawer dates a form of "cheque" and the payee accepts it with a date of some time in the future the document is clearly not payable "on demand" and hence is not a cheque! The document is an ordinary bill of exchange (which happens to be drawn on a banker) payable at some future time, and can be indorsed or negotiated in the usual way.[5] For example:

FORSTER v. MACKRETH[6]

X, a solicitor in partnership with Z, wished to borrow £80 for a few days. On 13 July he gave Y a firm's cheque post dated till 20 July for £90 (Y to have £10 for his trouble); whereupon Y made the loan to X. Neither X nor Z had authority to draw, accept or indorse bills of exchange in the name of the firm, but both had authority to draw cheques. The cheque was not paid and Y sued the firm. Z claimed that X had, in fact, given not a cheque but a bill, and as he had no authority the firm was not bound.

3. [1915] 1 KB 42. Before reading this case reference to the Errata at the front of the volume should be made, as there is a vital confusion in the text of the report between "drawee" and "payee"!

4. Bills of Exchange Act 1882, s. 73. As to when a bill is "payable on demand" see s. 10(1).

5. Section 45(2) provides that if a bill is payable on demand (as to which see s. 10(1)) it must be presented for payment " . . . with a reasonable time after its indorsement, in order to render the indorser liable". If a post-dated cheque has been in circulation an unreasonable time after being indorsed an indorser might well be discharged.

6. (1867) 16 LT 23.

Held—that Y's claim failed and Z's view was upheld " . . . we are unable to distinguish this case from giving a bill of exchange at seven days date . . . we are of opinion that this claim upon the cheque fails".[7]

The 1882 Act[8] specifically provides that bills are not invalid by reason of being post-dated, and a post-dated "cheque" is still "regular on the face" for the purpose of creating a holder in due course.

HITCHCOCK v. EDWARDS[9]

On 5 September X gave Y a cheque dated 8 September. On the 6th Y indorsed it to H. On the 7th Y's creditors obtained and had served a garnishee order. H claimed to be a holder in due course and, therefore, entitled to the bill. *Held*—that a post-dated "cheque" is still "regular on the face of it" and H was, therefore, a holder in due course and had a good title.

Bills of exchange of this sort become cheques when the due date arrives,[10] but in the meanwhile they are not cheques and should not be referred to as such.

Banks will not "accept" instruments in this form although there is no *legal* objection to their doing so. They take the view (probably rightly) that their forms of printed cheques are not intended for transactions other than the transfer of money on an "immediate payment"[11] basis, and if delay in payment is desired by the drawer, some other form of document should be used—such as a promissory note.

The problem is in using the bank's printed forms with the bank as drawee. It is, of course, very common for banks to pay its customers' domicils, which have been accepted *by the customer* to be payable at his bank. However, an acceptance in this form does not bind the bank, and they can still refuse payment on presentation for that purpose; whereas, if *they* accepted a bill drawn on their cheque forms they would have to honour it, no matter if the customer had in the meanwhile become insolvent.[12]

Banks will not hold for collection on a post-dated instrument, and if a payee were to attempt to pay it into his bank it would be refused, and returned to him pending maturity of the bill. Likewise, no drawee bank would pay on it, and if by some oversight they did, they would be liable to their customer (the drawer).[13]

7. *Per* Martin B, at p. 25.
8. Bills of Exchange Act 1882, s. 13(2).
9. (1889) 60 LT 636.
10. *Robinson* v. *Benkel* (1913) 29 TLR 475.
11. *Bank of Baroda* v. *Punjab National Bank* [1944] AC 176, 184.
12. Presumably if a bank did accept a post-dated "cheque" they would require specific security as in the case of domicils.
13. At one time banks would accept for collection and payment in the usual way. If the "cheque" were then "stopped" all manner of problems arose. If the collecting bank had allowed its customer to draw against the post-dated "cheque" that bank could, however, recover from the drawer: *Royal Bank of Scotland* v. *Tottenham* [1894] 2 QB 715.

Indeed, banks dislike post-dated "cheques" so much that at one time in the City of London there was a custom (now no longer operating) that the drawee bank would always refuse payment on a post-dated "cheque"—even *after* maturity.[14]

3. IMPERSONAL PAYEES

Cheques are forever being made out to "cash" or "wages" or some such similar terms. As the 1882 Act[15] requires cheques (and other bills) to be payable to " . . . a specified *person* . . . " instruments made out in this way are not cheques at all as the payee is impersonal. These documents cannot be indorsed or transferred from one person to another. For example, in the case of

COLE v. MILSOME[16]

M drew a form of "cheque" made out to "cash" (the words "pay" and "or order" being printed in the usual way). It was given to H. H did not have a bank account and he gave the instrument to C and asked that she should pay it into *her* bank and then draw cheques against it on behalf of H. M discovered some fraud on H's part and "stopped" the "cheque". C sued M. *Held*—that the instrument was not a cheque and consequently could not be passed on from one person to another and, therefore, C could obtain no title to it and her action failed.

In fact, such documents are valueless, except in so far as the *drawee bank* can treat the document as a mandate from its customer to pay the cash to whomsoever is in possession of the document. For example, in

N & S INSURANCE CORP v. NATIONAL PROVINCIAL BANK[17]

X drew a form of "cheque" made out to "cash" (the words "pay" and "or order" being printed in the usual way), and he gave it to Y in payment of work which Y had done. Y paid the "cheque" into his bank and it was cleared in the usual way. X subsequently was adjudicated bankrupt and his liquidator tried to recover the amount of the cheque from X's bank saying that as it was payable "to order" it should have been indorsed and as it had not, the bank should not have paid on it. *Held*—that the document was not a cheque and, therefore, the question of indorsement did not arise. It operated as " . . . a direction to pay cash—by necessary implication, to pay it to the bearer of the document"[18] and the liquidator's action failed.

Moreover, a *collecting bank* can obtain protection in collecting on instruments of this sort although they are not bills of exchange or cheques.[19]

---

14. *Emanuel* v. *Robarts* (1868) 17 LT 646.
15. Bills of Exchange Act 1882, s. 3(1).
16. [1951] 1 All ER 311.
17. [1936] 1 KB 328.
18. *Per* Branson J, p. 336.
19. *Orbit Mining & Trading Co Ltd* v. *Westminster Bank Ltd* [1963] 1 QB 794.

4. CROSSING OF CHEQUES

Crossing is the drawing on a cheque of two parallel lines with or without any further words. A cheque which is not crossed is said to be "open". If a crossing does appear it is a material part of the cheque.[20] No other type of bill but a cheque can be crossed.[21]

The reason for crossing a cheque is to make it more difficult (though not impossible) for a fraudulent person to obtain payment, as the 1882 Act[22] provides that the drawee (paying) bank does not get a good discharge on payment of a crossed cheque unless they pay to a bank or to the true owner. Since banks can never be sure whether or not they are paying the true owner if presentment is made in person over the counter, they obviously and wisely take advantage of the Act and pay crossed cheques only to another bank.

Banks provide cheque books with crossings already printed on the face of the cheques.

Types of crossing

Cheques can be crossed generally or specially[23] either by the drawer or any subsequent holder;[24] and if a cheque is crossed generally the crossing can subsequently be converted into a special crossing.[25]

(i) General crossings: A cheque is crossed *generally* when the words "and company" or any abbreviation ("& Co" is the usual form) is placed between two parallel lines on the face of the cheque; either with or without the words "not negotiable", or merely two parallel lines.[26] For example:

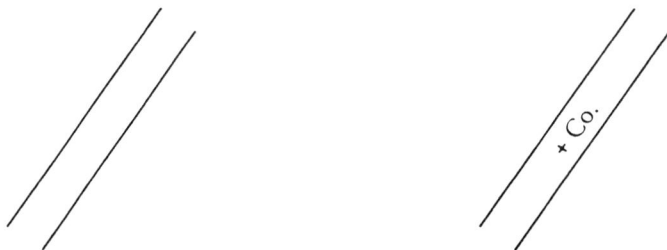

---

20. Bills of Exchange Act 1882, s. 78.
21. However, by s. 95 of the 1882 Act, "the provisions of this Act as to crossed cheques shall apply to a warrant for payment of dividend"; see *infra* Chap. 14, heading 3 (i) "Dividend Warrants" and (ii) "Postal Orders".
22. Bills of Exchange Act 1882, s. 79(2).
23. *Ibid.*, s. 77(1).
24. *Ibid.*, s. 77(2).
25. *Ibid.*, s. 77(3).
26. *Ibid.*, s. 76(1)(*a*) and (*b*).

(ii) Special crossings: A cheque is crossed *specially* when, in addition to the markings which constitute a general crossing, the name of a bank is added.[27] For example:

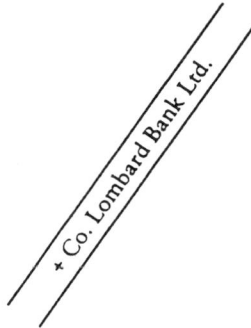

A special crossing must specify one bank only, and if a cheque is crossed specially to more than one bank, for example, "Lombard Bank per Manleys Bank" the bank on which it is drawn should refuse payment, unless, of course, one bank is collecting as agent for another.[28] Where a drawee bank pays, notwithstanding this form of crossing, or ignoring a crossing, general or special, it will be liable to the *true owner* for any loss he may sustain.[29]

Cheques can be crossed at any time. However, if a bank is to obtain protection the cheque must be crossed *before it comes into their hands*.[30]

Of course, if a bank uses the services of another bank for the purpose of collection, there is nothing to stop that bank (that is the second bank) from crossing the cheque.[31] Again, if a cheque is crossed specially, and the bank to which it is crossed uses the services of another bank for the purposes of collection, it can cross specially to the second bank.[32]

Once a crossing is placed on a cheque it cannot legally be removed, as this is a material alteration and would discharge all parties who had not agreed to the alteration, or indorsers who signed after the tampering with the crossing.[33] However, there would appear to be nothing to prevent a *drawer* "opening" a crossing before the cheque is issued by writing "Please pay cash" or some such words and striking out the crossing, provided both are initialled.[34] This then would operate as an instruction to his bank (the drawee) to pay, if needs be

27. *Ibid.*, s. 76(2).
28. *Ibid.*, s. 79(1).
29. *Ibid.*, s. 79(2).
30. See *Capital & Counties Bank v. Gordon* [1903] AC 240.
31. Bills of Exchange Act 1882, s. 77(5).
32. *Ibid.*, s. 77(6).
33. *Ibid.*, s. 64(1).
34. Strictly speaking a bank should insist upon the "opening" of cheques (and any other alterations for that matter) being signed in full although in practice they do accept initialling.

over the counter. It is a definite rule of the clearing banks that they will pay cash against an "opened" cheque only to the drawer's (that is their customer's) *known* agent.

Types of marking

As we have just seen, it is proper to speak of a cheque as "crossed" when there are two parallel lines drawn across its face; however, in addition to the *crossing*, a cheque is often *marked*, for example "not negotiable" or "not transferable".[35] There are three types of "marking" as affecting cheques which must now be examined.

1. "Not Negotiable"

We have seen that the essence of negotiability is that an instrument having this quality is freely transferable *free from equities*. For example, if a thief steals a cheque, which is indorsed in blank (and thus payable to bearer), he can give a good title to anyone to whom he gives the cheque; likewise bankers who accept or pay the cheque. However, if the cheque is marked "not negotiable" the prior rights of the true owner (the person from whom it was stolen) will still subsist, as the person who takes a cheque marked in this way does not get, and cannot give, a better title than that which the person from whom he took had.[36]

Thus, the effect of making a cheque (or any other bill for that matter) "not negotiable" is to ensure that no one can obtain a good title unless he is, in fact, the true owner.

WILSON & MEESON v. PICKERING[37]

W drew a cheque in blank, crossed it and marked it "not negotiable". W handed it to his clerk P to fill in the amount for £2 and "The Commissioners of Inland Revenue" as payees. P, in fact, inserted a sum in excess of her authority and gave the cheque to X in

---

35. Bills of Exchange Act 1882, s. 77(4).
36. *Ibid.*, s. 81. In fact s. 81 says: "Where a person takes a crossed cheque which bears on it the words 'not negotiable . . . '. The effect of a "not negotiable" marking must, however, be the same whether a cheque is crossed or not. See generally *Hibernian Bank* v. *Gysin* [1939] 1 KB 483. However, Paget *The Law of Banking* 11th edn. (1996) p. 251(e), thinks "The words 'not negotiable' have no statutory effect . . . ", unless combined with one of the regular crossings. Paget also considers, p. 251(e), that if the words "not negotiable" appear on a cheque *without a crossing* the words must be construed as having " . . . no effect on its negotiability . . . ". The learned editors argue this is the combined effect of ss. 8 and 81 of the 1882 Act; s. 81, in effect, being an exception to s. 8. On the other hand, the learned author of *Chalmers and Guest on Bills of Exchange, Cheques and Promissory Notes*, 14 edn (1991) p. 655, observes that, "the appearance of the words 'not negotiable' on a cheque which is *not crossed* [author's italics] give rise to some difficulty . . . the drawer presumably intended them to mean something". The supposition is then made that the cheque should be "not transferable" within s. 8(1). But, of course, to confuse matters further, s. 8(1) speaks of the bill then being "not negotiable"—perhaps, the draftsman's slip for "not transferable".
37. [1946] KB 422.

payment of a personal debt. The fraud was discovered and W sued X for return of the money. *Held*—P had no title to the cheque and X had no better title than the clerk had as the cheque was marked "not negotiable". Thus W by marking the cheque "not negotiable" had ensured his liability was only to the true owner, and he could, therefore, recover from X.

It follows that "Everyone who takes a cheque marked 'not negotiable' takes it at his own risk, and his title to the money got by its means is as defective as his title to the cheque itself."[38]

2. "Not Transferable"

A cheque marked "not transferable", whether accompanied by crossings or not, is valid as between the drawer and payee, but cannot be conveyed by the payee to anyone else. The same object could be obtained by drawing a cheque, "Pay John Smith *only*".

This is certainly the safest way to draw a cheque if it is desired to make payment to the payee only; however, it is not often used as it prevents the payee from handing it on to anyone else, even subject to equities.

Banks must take particular care in handling documents of this nature. The drawee bank will require proof that the person seeking payment is the payee, if presentment is made in person (assuming the cheque is open); while the collecting bank, when dealing with such a cheque, must be sure it is collecting for the payee. Therefore, if no enquiries are made they will, *prima facie*, be guilty of negligence and may lose the protection of the Act.

3. "A/c Payee": the common law position

This form of marking has become quite popular over the years. No reference is made to it in the 1882 Act, though we now have a new Cheques Act, as to which see below, which makes specific reference to the words "account payee". The effect of this is a direction to the *collecting bank* to collect only for the payee as named, which means, of course, the cheque is, from a practical point of view, not transferable. However, such a marking does not at common law prevent transferability. "The words merely operate as a warning to the collecting bank that if it pays the proceeds of the cheque to some other account it is put on enquiry and it may be in difficulty in relying on any defence under . . . the Act in an action against it for conversion of the cheque."[39]

For example, in

---

38. *Per* Lord Lindley in *GW Railway Co v. London & County Banking Co* [1901] AC 418, 424.

39. (PC) *Universal Guarantee v. National Bank of Australasia* [1965] 1 WLR 691, 697F, *per* Lord Upjohn. It seems that a bank owes its customer no duty to advise on the propriety or otherwise of handling cheques marked "Not Negotiable—account payee only", where the cheques have been indorsed to the customer: *Redmond v. Allied Irish Bank Plc*, *Financial Times*, 15 July 1987 and [1987] 2 FTLR 264.

NATIONAL BANK v. SILKE[40]

S drew a cheque in favour of M "Pay to the order of M". S crossed the cheque and marked it "Account of M, National Bank, Dublin". M indorsed the cheque and paid it into his bank in Dublin. They, in turn, allowed M to draw on those uncleared effects. S "stopped" the cheque. The bank sued S as holder for value. S said the bank could not sue, as the cheque was incapable of passing to them as holders because of the marking which limited its transferability. *Held*—that the words of marking amounted to nothing more than a direction to the bank to carry the amount of the cheque to M's account. The bank were, therefore, holders and could recover on the cheque.

A grave warning must be sounded, however, for in practice such a marking would certainly have the effect of limiting transferability, for if a bank were to collect for anyone other than the person named as payee, without satisfactory explanation they would, *prima facie*, be deemed guilty of negligence. This is what happened in

HOUSE PROPERTY CO v. LONDON CO & WESTMINSTER BANK[41]

A cheque was drawn in favour of "X or bearer", crossed and marked "A/c payee". The cheque was passed to N who paid the cheque into his own bank account and the bank collected payment for him without making any enquiry as to how he had the cheque when he was not the named payee. The plaintiffs sued the collecting bank for return of the money. *Held*—that the bank was negligent and had to refund the value of the cheque.

Thus, if a cheque is marked "A/c payee" or "A/c payee only", a collecting bank must always collect for the payee, unless they *know* their customer has a good title to the cheque. It should be observed, however, that this marking is no concern whatever of the drawee (paying) bank. In the words of Bigham J:[42]

A crossing is a direction to the paying bank to pay the money generally to a bank or to a particular bank, as the case may be, and when this has been done the whole purpose of the crossing has been served. The paying bank has nothing to do with the application of the money after it has once been paid to the proper receiving banker. The words "Account A.B." are a mere direction to the receiving bank as to how the money is to be dealt with after receipt.

The Cheques Act 1992

The ingenuity of crooks must never be underestimated. In spite of all possible precautions which drawers of cheques and their banks could take (drawers either do not bother—for example where cheques are carelessly drawn—or

40. [1891] 1 QB 435.
41. (1915) 84 LJKB 1846.
42. *Akrokerri (Atlantic) Mines Ltd* v. *Economic Bank* [1904] 2 KB 465, 472. However, it is usually *the drawer* of a cheque who marks it so, which appears to indicate a direction to his (that is, the paying) bank! He hardly has authority to direct the collecting bank! *Quaere* the position of an *indorser* so marking a cheque.

they do not avail themselves of the protection already given by the law), over recent years there has been a growing wave of thefts of cheques while in course of transit in Her Majesty's Mail. Thieves have stolen cheques, forged indorsements and somehow persuaded indorsees and their banks to cash them.

With the problem becoming of epidemic proportions, the banks, having failed to persuade their customers to draw cheques more carefully, prevailed upon the Government to do something. In fact, a remedy was already available, and did not need the further intervention of Parliament.

All that was required was for the banks to print on their cheques the words "not transferable" and part of the problem, at least, could have been solved.[43] However, Parliament *did* intervene by passing the Cheques Act 1992,[44] which came into operation on 16 June 1992.[45]

The new Act provides[46] that where a cheque is crossed, and is marked either "account payee" or "a/c payee" (whether the word "only" appears or not), the cheque "shall not be transferable" and shall only be valid "as between the parties thereto". This is precisely what the Bills of Exchange Act 1882, s. 8(1), provides. It will be remembered that the sub-section states: "When a bill contains words prohibiting transfer, or indicating an intention that it should not be transferable, it is valid as between the parties thereto, but is not negotiable."

One assumes that when the 1882 Act, s. 8(1), and the new Cheques Act, s. 1, speak of "the parties thereto", they both mean the *immediate* parties thereto.

S. 1 of the new Act is a remarkable provision, since it follows that the words "account payee" can now mean "not transferable"!

The banks were quick to respond by printing on their cheques the words "account payee" between the well-known two parallel lines. As we have just seen, under the 1882 Act, s. 8(1), the same result could have been had by printing the words "not transferable", as indeed some banks have done at the request of their customers for many years.

The following points must be noted:

(1) The words "account payee" have the effect intended by Parliament only if the document is a cheque and not any other type of bill of exchange.

(2) Also, that the cheque must be crossed. The appearance of the words "account payee" on an uncrossed cheque will not have this newly created statutory effect, but the words will, presumably, have the effect attributable by the courts (as noted above) as being a direction to the collecting bank to collect only for the payee as named.

43. See Bills of Exchange Act 1882, s. 8(1), and see *Hibernian Bank* v. *Gysin* [1939] 1 KB 483; see also *supra*, p. 60, under heading Restrictive indorsements.
44. 1992 c. 32.
45. S. 4(2), *ibid*.
46. S. 1. This section adds a section 81A to the Bills of Exchange Act 1882.

(3) There is nothing to prevent a drawer, or his bank, marking a cheque —whether crossed or not— with the words "not transferable".

(4) What is not clear is whether the use of the words "account payee" in their new meaning (that is on a crossed cheque) prevents the words from being, *at the same time*, a direction to the collecting bank. In other words, if a collecting bank credits some other account but that of the payee may it lose protection of the 1882 Act if it is sued for conversion of the cheque? It is submitted that a bank would not lose protection, as the words "account payee" on a *crossed* cheque are no longer an instruction to the collecting bank from the drawer.

It is perhaps too early to say what interpretation will be placed upon these words in such circumstances, but since the new Act does not purport to change the law, except as stated, we must presume that the words "account payee" can still be capable of being a direction to the collecting bank as before. Certainly, the protection offered to collecting banks by the Cheques Act 1957 is extended to cheques which fall within the provisions of the new Act.[47] However, while s. 4(3) of the 1957 Act absolves banks from a charge of negligence for failing to concern themselves with, *inter alia*, an irregularity of an indorsement, if a cheque marked "account payee" is received for collection and is indorsed, there must have been an irregularity, since the cheque is not transferable and should, therefore, not be credited to the account of the indorsee—the bank's customer.

(5) The words "account payee" were never any concern of the paying (drawer's) banks, of course; and it would appear that they are not concerned with the terms of the new meaning of the words either, since the new Act[48] states that in considering the protection afforded to the paying bank under s. 80 of the Bills of Exchange Act 1882, a banker is not to be treated as having been negligent by reason only of his failure to concern himself with a purported indorsement of a cheque. This is another strange provision. A cheque marked "account payee" and crossed is not transferable nor are the funds represented by the cheque; therefore, any question of its being indorsed cannot arise. So, if a bank pays a cheque with an indorsement (by the named payee, one supposes) to someone other than the payee's bank, the paying bank must surely recognize an irregularity.

(6) The practical result of this new legislation is probably this:
(a) The drawer of a cheque marked "account payee" and crossed will intend the named payee to receive the money, with no possibility of the cheque being passed to anyone else.

47. S. 3.
48. SS. 1 and 2.

(b) The payee named in the cheque will pay it directly into his bank account and not try to negotiate it.

(c) If the payee *does* try to negotiate it and the indorsee pays it into his bank, the bank should refuse to accept it. The cheque, and the funds the cheque represents, are "not transferable".

(d) It follows, a prospective indorsee should not accept a cheque marked in this way.

(e) Presumably, under the general law, a drawer of a cheque can always delete the marking and initial it to cancel the effect of the new Act. Since the new Act does not imply the words "account payee", they must be expressly written or printed on the cheque for the new provisions to apply.

(f) The Bills of Exchange Act 1882, s. 8(1), continues in force, and transferability can be restricted under its terms in spite of the new Act to cheques (crossed or not) and ordinary commercial bills of exchange.

(g) One of the probably unintended results of the new Act is that cheques crossed and marked "account payee" will no longer be capable of passing into the hands of a bank as holders in their own right. So that, if a bank allows its customer to overdraw against uncleared effects and the cheque which comprises those "uncleared effects" is dishonoured, the bank will have no right to pursue the drawer of the cheque in its own right, since the cheque is, in the terms of the Act, "not transferable".

CHAPTER 13

PROTECTION OF BANKERS

Handling millions of cheques as banks do, it is a sheer impossibility to verify each signature or transaction. If the drawee bank paused to consider with each cheque whether there was an inherent but latent defect in the transaction, or if the collecting bank hesitated each time before crediting its customer's account the whole system would come to a grinding halt.[1] Much has to be taken on trust. It is a pity the trust is sometimes abused—oddly, not always to do down the bank itself, but simply to make use, unlawfully, of the banking system.

The unfortunate victim of a fraud is usually left to recover from the wrong-doer; equally, usually, the culprit has either disappeared altogether, or is not worth suing, and not infrequently has been declared bankrupt! Consequently, the victim will cast about for someone else on whom the responsibility can be fixed—his own bank, if they have paid out when he claims they should not; or perhaps, the collecting bank, which held the money which, he claims, they should never have had in the first place.

Proceedings against a drawee (paying) bank are actions for negligence[2] or for breach of contract. The claim is that money was paid out in circumstances where the bank did not use its proper skill and judgment, or in fact were careless in the way it handled the transaction.

A claim against a collecting bank is for conversion and money had and received.[3] It is against these actions that Parliament has come to the assistance of banks, by giving them statutory protection from the possibility of myriad claims, provided that strict compliance is observed by the banks in meeting the statutory requirements.

---

1. "... to require a thorough enquiry into the history of each cheque would render banking business impracticable": *per* Scrutton LJ in *Lloyds Bank* v. *Chartered Bank of India* [1929] 1 KB 40, 59.

2. Liability for negligence is considered *infra*.

3. "Conversion" is the deliberate interference, without justification, with property belonging to someone else. The act must be *deliberate* though not necessarily with any knowing intention of the prior rights of the claimants to the property; see *per* Sankey LJ in *Lloyds Bank* v. *Chartered Bank of India* [1929] 1 KB 40, at p. 69. While an action for money "had and received" is, as the name implies, an action to recover money wrongfully in the hands of the defendant; that is, money wrongly collected by the bank.

Before considering the statutory protection given to both the drawee and the collecting bank three points of general application must be made:

(1) The person paying or collecting must be a banker. There should usually be no difficulty, as s. 2 of the Bills of Exchange Act 1882 defines a "banker" widely as including a "body of persons whether incorporated or not who carry on the business of banking"; but problems have arisen with what are termed "fringe" banks.[4]

(2) The bank must act in good faith. The reputation of British banks is virtually unimpeachable, and good faith is always presumed and could only be challenged on the clearest and strongest of evidence.

(3) Frequently the bank is required to have acted "without negligence" and a few general words on the subject of negligence may be appropriate.

"Negligence" is the breach of a legal duty to take care which results in damage to one person, which was unintended by the other. Negligence as well as being an independent cause of action (as when for example a man negligently drives his motor car) may also form part of other causes of action. For example, where a banker is accused of acting negligently, the gist of the action is usually the recovery of money paid or received because of the banker's negligence.

In actions of negligence a distinction must be drawn between (i) the duty owed not to be negligent, and (ii) the standard of care required, if the duty exists. There usually is no problem about the first point, since every bank owes a duty to its customers not to be negligent. However, this duty is based on the contract which exists between banker and customer, and no *general* duty to others exists. For example, in

AUCHTERONI v. MIDLAND BANK[5]

A sold goods to X and drew a three months bill on X for the amount, namely £876. X accepted the bill payable at the Midland Bank. At due date W (a servant of A) took the bill to a senior partner of A and got him to indorse it in blank. W then, instead of paying it into A's bank for collection in the usual way, took it in person to the Midland Bank and obtained payment over the counter. A sued the bank for recovery of the money. *Held*—that A was not a customer of the bank and it owed A no duty not to be negligent. However, the bill was an uncrossed negotiable instrument payable to bearer, which had been paid in good faith, and in any event it was not neligence to have paid it over the counter without further enquiries.

Consequently what really is under discussion in all these cases is whether the actions of the bank reached the necessary standard of care. In the words of Lord Warrington:

---

4. See *supra* Chap. 11, under the heading "The Bankers".
5. [1928] 2 KB 294.

The standard by which the absence, or otherwise of negligence is to be determined must, in my opinion, be ascertained by reference to the practice of reasonable men carrying on the business of bankers, and in endeavouring to do so in such a manner as may be calculated to protect themselves and others against fraud.[6]

It is, thus, a question of fact in each case whether the bank has been guilty of the absence of reasonable care; this is, the care which is normally taken by bankers in carrying on their daily business. This does not mean, of course, that because a thing has been done or not done over a long period of time that that is the necessary standard, but it obviously is a useful yardstick. For in all cases where negligence is alleged against a bank, evidence of what other banks would have done in similar circumstances will be considered.

In an attempt to guide the actions of their staff, banks lay down rules which are for the help of managers and other employees. "Such instructions are not of statutory effect but they are clearly a useful guide"[7] to the conduct banks expect from their staff in dealing with these day-to-day problems; " . . . whether they owe their customers the duty of carrying out all the rules which they may lay down as counsels of perfection"[8] is a matter of doubt. The better view is that they do not; these rules being only for internal *guidance*, rather than a mandatory system of regulations, the non-observance of which automatically indicates that the banks *must* have been negligent.

Moreover, the standard of care does not vary with the amount of the transaction, and customers can expect just as diligent service with a cheque for £5 as £50,000.

THE DRAWEE BANK

While it is the duty of the drawee bank, if it has funds available or has agreed an overdraft facility, to pay its customers' cheques, and all manner of thunderbolts will fall if it does not, nevertheless " . . . it seems utterly irrational to suppose that a bank has an absolute unqualified duty to pay and no duty to enquire despite a deep suspicion, approaching but falling short of a certainty, that the funds are being misapplied".[9]

The inevitable question then arises as to what circumstances would give rise to a "deep suspicion". The subject of a "Paying bank's liability to its customer in negligence" has been discussed in some detail by Ungoed-Thomas J in

6. *Lloyds Bank Ltd* v. *Savory* [1933] AC 201, at p. 221.
7. *Per* Sellers LJ in *Orbit Mining & Training Co Ltd* v. *Westminster Bank Ltd* [1963] 1 QB 794, at p. 818.
8. *Per* Goddard J (as he then was) in *Motor Traders Corp* v. *Midland Bank* [1937] 4 All ER 90, at p. 96g.
9. *Per* Brightman J in *Karak Rubber Co Ltd* v. *Burden* [1972] 1 All ER 1210, 1231d. Indeed if the account is a "trust account", there may be a higher standard required in handling dealings in respect of those monies: *Rowlandson* v. *National Westminster Bank* [1978] 3 All ER 370, where the bank was held liable to the beneficiaries.

Selangor United Rubber Estates Ltd v. *Craddock*,[10] but, in the end, it comes down to a question of fact in each case, and the bank using "reasonable care and skill" in carrying out the particular transaction. Ungoed-Thomas J acknowledged that whether or not that standard of care and skill has been attained in any particular case "has to be decided in the light of all the relevant facts, which can vary almost infinitely".[11]

The same point was made by Parker LJ in *Lipkin Gorman* v. *Karpnale*.[12] In speaking of the well-known cases which had been cited, he said that " . . . in my view such cases must be approached with caution, for essentially they are no more than decisions of fact".

The question of what "knowledge" a bank needs to have before it is justified in refusing to carry out the instructions of its customers—or run the risk of a charge of negligence—was exhaustively discussed in *Baden* v. *Société Générale*,[13] where Peter Gibson J stated that " . . . the relevant knowledge must be of facts and not mere claims or allegations". The learned judge went on to consider[14] various types of "knowledge", which may be summarized as follows:

(a) actual knowledge;
(b) wilfully shutting one's eyes to the obvious;
(c) wilfully and recklessly failing to make such inquiries as an honest and reasonable man would make;
(d) knowledge of any circumstances which would indicate the facts to an honest and reasonable man;
(e) knowledge of circumstances which would put an honest and reasonable man on inquiry.[15]

In judging where the line should be drawn between executing a customer's instructions to transfer money, and delaying the execution of those instructions pending further inquiry because the bank has some "knowledge" that a fraud might be perpetrated, Steyn J observed in *Barclays Bank Plc* v. *Quincecare Ltd*[16] that " . . . the sensible compromise, which strikes a fair balance between competing considerations, is simply to say that a banker must refrain from executing an order if and for as long as the banker is "put on inquiry" in the sense that he has reasonable grounds (although not necessarily proof) for

10. [1968] 2 All ER 1073, at pp. 1105d *et seq.*
11. *Ibid.*, p. 1118g.
12. [1992] 4 All ER 409, at p. 439g. The case went to the House of Lords, [1992] 4 All ER 512, but the bank took no part, as the claim against it was not pursued.
13. *Baden and others* v. *Société Generale pour Favoriser le Developpement du Commerce et de l'Industrie en France SA* [1992] 4 All ER 161, p. 235c.
14. *Ibid.*, p. 235g.
15. See *Agip (Africa) Ltd* v. *Jackson* [1991] 4 All ER 451, 467c.
16. [1992] 4 All ER 363, 376g. ". . . the more usual the circumstances and the clearer a representation appears to be, the less the duty to inquire should be", *per* Waller J, *Standard Bank London Ltd* v. *The Bank of Tokyo Ltd* [1995] 2 Lloyd's Rep. 169, 174.

believing that the order is an attempt to misappropriate the funds . . . and, the external standard of the likely perception of an ordinary prudent banker is the governing one."

It is, of course, for the plaintiff to prove the state of knowledge possessed by the bank at the time it effected the transfer of funds, and whether it was sufficient, based on an *ex post facto* rationalization, that the bank should have made further inquiries. This is a high standard of proof to achieve, and it is significant that in none of the cases *Baden* v. *Société Générale*,[17] *Lipkin Gorman* v. *Karpnale*,[18] and *Barclays Bank Plc* v. *Quincecare*[19] were the banks held to have been negligent. Of course, each case turned on its own facts, and, one supposes, with such claims alleging negligence, they always will.

Payment of cheques is effected either to another bank—always if the cheque is crossed—or "over the counter" to the holder, who may, of course, be the drawer when he wishes to draw cash. Presentment in this way could be made by post, in that it would be quite legal within s. 45(8) of the Bills of Exchange Act 1882, but this method is very dangerous and should be employed only in extreme cases, and then only with the clearest and express instructions of the customer. Whichever method of presentment is used it will be apparent from what has been said above that it is not proper that cheques should be paid heedlessly, yet delay may give rise to an action in damages or, at least, lose the bank an otherwise valued customer.

Another problem arises over the verifying of signatures. A bank can never pay out on its customer's (that is, the drawer's) forged or unauthorized signature,[20] and if by chance they do, they will not be allowed to debit their customer's account. For example, in the case of

JACKSON v. WHITE AND MIDLAND BANK[21]

J and W operated a club. They banked with the M bank. W forged J's signature to some cheques and when this was discovered J claimed to recover from both W and the bank. *Held*—that the bank were liable for paying out on the forged signature. The bank could, of course, claim an indemnity from W—for whatever that might be worth.

17. [1991] 4 All ER 161.
18. [1991] 4 All ER 409.
19. [1991] 4 All ER 363.
20. *Sheffield Corp* v. *Barclay* [1903] 2 KB 580.
21. [1967] 2 Lloyd's Rep. 68; *Welch* v. *Bank of England* [1955] 1 Ch 508. There is the awkward case of *Brewer* v. *Westminster Bank* [1952] 2 TLR 568 where, on similar facts, it was held the bank were *not* liable, as with joint accounts the obligation of the bank is *joint* and, therefore, it was said the bank could not be liable to one signatory for the forgery of the other. This seems wrongly decided. It was "not followed" in *Jackson* v. *White* nor in *Welch* v. *Bank of England*, where Harman J (as he then was) said: "I confess I do not follow that decision. None of the cases in equity were cited to the judge", *ibid.*, p. 531. Devlin J (as he then was) in *Baker* v. *Barclays Bank Ltd* [1955] 2 All ER 571 was thankfully able to "distinguish" it. *Brewer* was not followed in *Catlin* v. *Cyprus Finance Corp (London) Ltd* [1983] 1 All ER 809, where Bingham J held that the bank had " . . . a negative duty not to honour instructions not signed by both account holders". At p. 816j.

If it is an indorser's signature which has been forged, or unauthorized, s. 60 of the 1882 Act provides that the bank is not liable for paying out in the ordinary course of business on the cheque so long as the indorsement *appears* genuine.[22]

If the cheque is *crossed* it will be a good defence to a claim made against it if the bank can show it paid the cheque:[23] (i) to another bank; and (ii) without negligence.

It was considered "negligence" if the bank did not examine in detail the indorsers' signatures, and no matter how much time was spent banks could not be very sure that they were genuine. The Cheques Act 1957, s. 1, came to the banks' rescue by providing that if a bank pays a cheque, it incurs no liability if the cheque is not indorsed at all or if it *is* irregularly indorsed. It can, therefore, now not be considered "negligence" for a bank in the paying of cheques[24] to ignore indorsements entirely.

Moreover, s. 19 of the Stamp Act 1853 is still in force and provides:

> . . . any draft or order drawn upon a banker for a sum of money payable to order on demand, which shall, when presented for payment, purport to be indorsed by the person to whom the same shall be drawn payable, shall be a sufficient authority to such banker to pay the amount of such draft or order to the bearer thereof; and it shall not be incumbent on such banker to prove that such indorsement, or any subsequent indorsement, was made by or under the direction or authority of the person to whom the said draft or order was or is made payable either by the drawer or any indorser thereof.

It is curious this section should still be left on foot. It is, in terms, similar to s. 60 of the 1882 Act,[25] but not *identical*. It covers the case of defective indorsements on " . . . any draft or order drawn upon a banker . . . " and covers the same documents as the new s. 1(2)(*b*) of the Cheques Act 1957. Except that the 1957 Act requires a bank to pay "in good faith and in the ordinary course of business", in order to obtain protection, which is not required of s. 19. Consequently, a drawee bank can pay *the bearer* of a document if it is: (i) a draft or order on the bank; and (ii) payable on demand to order; and (iii) indorsed by the payee, without concerning itself that the

---

22. Bills of Exchange Act 1882, s. 60. The section also requires good faith on the part of the bank in its dealings, but this, one hopes, can be taken for granted! The section makes no demand that the bank must act without negligence. In the extremely rare occurrence that a cheque is presented which was originally crossed but the crossing has been erased making it have the appearance of an "open" cheque, so long as the cheque *appears* not to be crossed the drawee bank is not liable for paying it as an "open" cheque, provided payment is made in good faith (as usual) *and* without negligence: s. 79(2).

23. Bills of Exchange Act 1882, s. 80. Once more, good faith is required in all transactions.

24. Or other documents issued by a customer which are not strictly bills of exchange or bankers' drafts: see Cheques Act 1957, s. 1(2).

25. "That section, I think, is impliedly repealed by s. 60 of the Bills of Exchange Act 1882 in the case of bills of exchange and cheques", *per* Slesser LJ in *Carpenter* v. *British Mutual Banking Co* [1938] 1 KB 511, 534, citing Lord Lindley in *Capital & Counties Bank* v. *Gordon* [1903] AC 240, 251.

indorsement of the payee or any subsequent indorsement was made by the authority of the person whose signature it purports to be.

Alteration of cheques

It is not only indorsers' signatures that may be forged of course. The drawee bank may well be faced with a cheque where, for example, the amount or the date has been fraudulently altered.

If a cheque has been altered without the drawer's authority the consequences depend upon whether the alteration is *apparent* (that is, a poor alteration easily discoverable), or *non-apparent* (that is, a clever alteration).

If Apparent—The drawee (paying) bank is fully liable and cannot debit the customer's account.

If Non-apparent—The bank can debit the customer's account for the *original tenor* of the cheque—that is, the amount before alteration. The difference in the amount will be borne by the person who presents for payment, that is, the holder.

Thus, if X draws a cheque for £10 in favour of Y who negotiates it to Z, who alters the amount to £100 and negotiates it to W, who then presents it to X's bank, W will have to bear the loss of the £90, and pursue his remedy against Z for whatever that is worth.

As we have seen, the liability of a bank may always be affected by the negligence of the customer. Every drawer of a cheque owes a duty to his bank (but none other, such as a subsequent indorser) not to be negligent. If the customer does draw a cheque in a careless manner, and "raising" of it follows, the loss will be his, and the bank will be able to debit the account with the *full* amount of the cheque as altered.

LONDON JOINT STOCK BANK LTD v. MACMILLAN & ARTHUR[26]

Messrs Macmillan & Arthur were a firm of general merchants carrying on business in the City of London. They had employed for some years a clerk by the name of Klantschi, who kept the books, made out cheques and was generally in the confidence of the partners. One day, just as Mr Arthur was rushing out to lunch—he had his hat on and was leaving the office—Klantschi came up to him and said he wanted £2 for petty cash and produced a cheque for signature. It was drawn "Pay ourselves or

---

26. [1918] AC 777. In *Lumsden v. London Trustee Savings Bank* [1971] 1 Lloyd's Rep. 114, the plaintiff was held to have been guilty of contributory negligence, and his damages were reduced by 10% under the Law Reform (Contributory Negligence) Act 1945. See also s. 47 of the Banking Act 1979 which provides that in any case under s. 4 of the Cheques Act 1957, where a banker relies on the fact that he has not been negligent, the banker can also set up the defence of contributory negligence by a customer, or any other third party if a duty is owed to them, notwithstanding s. 11(1) of the Torts (Interference with Goods) Act 1977.

Bearer": there were no words at all in the space provided, and the figure "2" appeared in the space provided for the figures. After a few words Mr Arthur signed the cheque and left for lunch. The following day Klantschi did not appear for business. It transpired that Klantschi had "raised" the cheque to £120, cashed the cheque with the London Joint Stock Bank (where the firm had its account) and decamped with the proceeds. The firm sued the bank, asking for a declaration that the bank were not entitled to debit their account with the £120. The bank contended the preparation and drawing of the cheque was so negligent that Messrs Macmillan & Arthur facilitated the fraud. *Held*—that the loss must fall on the firm. "For all practical purposes the cheque was in blank, as the figure '2' in its isolated position afforded no security whatever against a fraudulent increase. The clerk had the authority of the customer to fill up the words denoting the amount in the body of the cheque, and to put other figures before and after the '2' was quite easy owing to its position."[27]

However, if the alteration vitiates the cheque altogether it will be a nullity, and no bank can charge its customer in respect of a nullity.

SLINGSBY v. DISTRICT BANK LTD[28]

Mrs Slingsby was one of four executors of the estate of Henry Turner deceased. The executors' account was kept at the District Bank, Macclesfield. The executors employed a firm of solicitors by the name of Cumberbirch & Potts—James Cumberbirch being the active partner. The executors and their solicitors met one day and decided to invest £5,000 in War Loan. Mr Cumberbirch then drew a cheque for this amount in favour of "John Prust & Co", the appointed stockbrokers. All four executors signed the cheque. Instead of posting the cheque, Mr Cumberbirch altered the cheque by writing in the blank space between the "& Co" of the named payees and the printed "or Order", the words "per Cumberbirch & Potts". Mr Cumberbirch indorsed the cheque, and paid it into the account of a company—the Palatine Industrial Finance Co Ltd of which he was chairman, which account was at the Westminster Bank in Manchester. Mr Cumberbirch was seen no more, and the executors were left to sue the paying bank (District) which they did.[29] *Held*—that the cheque had been "materially altered" within s. 64 of the 1882 Act and the drawers were not, therefore, liable. Moreover, the executors had not been negligent in signing the cheque made out with a space after the payee's name. While a "customer is bound to take all usual and reasonable precautions to prevent forgery",[30] "I am satisfied that it is not at present a 'usual precaution' to draw lines before or after the name of the payee. If this sort of case becomes frequent it may become a 'usual precaution' . . ."[31] The District bank had, therefore, to bear the loss.

27. *Per* Lord Finlay LC, at p. 812.
28. [1932] 1 KB 544.
29. The executors also sued the Westminster Bank but lost: [1931] 2 KB 583, but this was wrongly decided and overruled. The collecting bank *must* have been negligent in making no enquiries as to why a cheque for such a large amount, apparently destined for Prust & Co through the medium of Cumberbirch & Potts, found its way into the account of a company of which Cumberbirch was chairman: Scrutton LJ certainly thought the Westminster Bank was negligent, at p. 556.
30. *Per* Lord Finlay in *Macmillans'* case, at p. 789.
31. *Per* Scrutton LJ in *Slingsby's* case, at p. 560.

Recovery of money paid by mistake

The basic rules are that money paid under a mistake of *fact* is recoverable, whereas if it is paid under a mistake of *law* it is not. This is much too much of a generalization however. The rules governing these cases are by no means settled, but the following principles, from such decided cases as there are, appear to emerge:

(1) Money paid by a drawee bank to a collecting bank under a mistake of *fact* can be recovered, provided the collecting bank still holds the funds.[32] There is no time limit, although a demand for the money's return must be made as soon as the mistake is discovered. Where a mistake was not discovered for two weeks, the paying bank was still held entitled to recover.[33]

(2) The drawee bank is not liable to the payee, and owes the payee no duty of care, and can recover even if the payee has spent the money.[34] Nor does it matter that the bank had the means at its staff's hand to discover the mistake before making the payment.[35]

(3) If the mistake relates to the forgery of a cheque, the drawee bank will still be able to recover, as by paying it, the bank is not taken to represent the drawer's signature, or the cheque as being valid.

(4) If the document under which payment is made is not a cheque, but an ordinary bill of exchange (that is a domicil), the bank will not be able to recover, unless notice of the mistake is given at once, under the rule in *Cocks* v. *Masterman*,[36] which is that the holder of a bill is entitled to know, *on the day when it becomes due*, whether it is to be honoured or dishonoured; and that if he receives payment and retains it during the whole of that day, the parties who paid it cannot recover it back.[37]

32. This is under the general rule that if an agent (who is known to be an agent—as the bank would) receives money for his principal he is not liable once he has parted with it: *per* Cozens-Hardy MR in *Baylis* v. *Bishop of London* [1913] 1 Ch 127, at p. 134.

33. *National Westminster Bank* v. *Barclays Bank International Ltd* [1974] 3 All ER 834, where Kerr J (as he then was) reviews the authorities. Also, *Barclays Bank Ltd* v. *WJ Simms Son & Cooke (Southern) Ltd* [1979] All ER 522, where the law is reviewed in some detail. The important fact seems to be that " . . . there is no evidence of any actual change of position . . . " of the parties: *per* Robert Goff J (as he then was) p. 542f. The fact that the bank obtaining the recovery had made the mistake was irrelevent.

34. *Standish* v. *Ross* (1849) 3 Ex 527; *Larner* v. *LCC* [1949] 2 KB 683. Unless, perhaps, there is some particular duty on the drawee bank to the payee in very exceptional cases: *Skyring* v. *Greenwood* (1825) 107 ER 1064; or if some form of estoppel existed.

35. *Kelly* v. *Solari* (1841) 9 M & W 54; *Imperial Bank of Canada* v. *Bank of Hamilton* [1903] AC 49.

36. (1829) 8 LJ (o.s.) KB (Mich. T.) 77.

37. *Per* Bayley J, *ibid.*, p. 79. See also *London & River Plate Bank* v. *Bank of Liverpool* [1896] 1 QB 7. It will be remembered that notice of dishonour must be given within a "reasonable time": Bills of Exchange Act 1882, s. 49(12). If this is not done all parties are discharged. Delay in giving notice until the second day after dishonour has been held too long, even if the defendant is not prejudiced by the delay: *Yeoman Credit Ltd* v. *Gregory* [1963] 1 All ER 245.

This rule is rigorous in its effect, but is equally strict in its application, so that where there *are* no indorsers to whom notice of dishonour can be given, the law as to the necessity of giving notice of dishonour has no application and the drawee bank can recover from the collecting bank.[38]

(5) If a cheque is paid under a mistake of fact "over the counter", the money is *not* recoverable, unless the party receiving the money was guilty of some illegal act, such as fraud on the bank. The money passes as soon as the cashier places the money on the counter and pushes it across to the person cashing the cheque. It does not matter that the person cashing the cheque stands counting the money before leaving the bank.[39]

(6) Money paid under a mistake of law *cannot* be recovered, unless perhaps there is something in the defendant's conduct which shows he is the person primarily responsible for the mistake.[40]

(7) A particular problem is where a bank has, by a mistake, over-credited an account of its customer. In these circumstances the bank cannot usually recover the money once the customer has acted on the mistake to his detriment:[41] though carelessness on the part of the bank appears to be irrelevant.[42]

In *United Overseas Bank* v. *Jiwani*,[43] Mackenna J gave three conditions which the customer must fulfil if he is to retain the money: (1) The bank must have misstated the balance in the account: and (2) The customer must have been misled by this misrepresentation; and (3) The customer must have changed his position in a way which would make it inequitable to require that he repay the money.[44]

The position between a bank and its customer must not be confused with the position between the customer and some third party who mistakenly transfers money to the customer's bank account. In such a case, there is an obligation on

38. *Imperial Bank of Canada* v. *Bank of Hamilton* [1903] AC 49, at p. 58.
39. *Chambers* v. *Miller* (1862) 7 LT 856. In these days where there is a clear line of the grille separating the bank staff from the customers there should be no doubt that the money passes as soon as it crosses that line.
40. Privy Council in *Kiriri Cotton* v. *Dewari* [1960] AC 192, 204. In *Avon County Council* v. *Howlett* [1983] 1 All ER 1073, an overpayment by mistake of fact was held not to be recoverable because the plaintiffs were estopped, having fed the wrong information into their computer. The law on this exception is far from clear, however. The position is further complicated by the fine distinction which sometimes exists between what is a mistake of law and what is a mistake of fact. A topic outside the scope of this book.
41. *Holland* v. *Manchester & Liverpool District Banking Co* (1909) 25 TLR 386; *Lloyds Bank Ltd* v. *Brooks* (1950). I cannot find this case reported anywhere except in the Journal of the Institute of Bankers, Vol. LXXII, p. 114.
42. *Kelly* v. *Solari* (1841) 9 M & W 54.
43. [1976] 1 WLR 964.
44. See *British & North European Bank* v. *Zalstein* [1927] 2 KB 92.

the recipient to repay the money,[45] and recovery can be claimed by the transferor if a voluntary restoration is not made.[46]

Cheques under advice

A bank can make arrangements with its customers to have cheques paid at other *branches* of the bank to suit a customer's convenience, or arrangements can be made to have cheques paid by other *banks* altogether.

Where a cheque is paid by another *branch* of the bank on which it is drawn, the branch paying will get a good discharge under s. 60 of the Bills of Exchange Act 1882, provided that previous arrangements for the transaction have been made.

Where a cheque is paid by *another bank altogether,* the cheque is not deemed to be *paid* within s. 60, as that section provides protection only if the cheque is paid by "the banker on whom it is drawn". The paying bank in such cases is really buying the cheque, and so if there is a forged indorsement they will be compelled to refund the amount to the true owner. Consequently, it is common practice in these cases for the bank making the arrangements to indemnify the bank which is to cash the cheque in the event of any loss ensuing.

With the proliferation of branches of banks all over the country the need for arrangements of this sort is less today than it used to be, but it may still be encountered in more remote places.

THE COLLECTING BANK

As we have already seen[47] it is no part of a banker's duty to question a customer's title to the cheques he pays into his account. However, if the customer has a defective title—where for example he has obtained the cheque he pays in by fraud—the collecting bank could be sued for conversion.

---

45. It could be a criminal offence under the Theft Act 1968 if the money were not returned: *Attorney-General's Reference (No. 1 of 1983)* [1984] 3 WLR 686—overpayment of salary by direct debit. If a bank makes a payment to another bank twice, that is to say the payment is mistakenly duplicated, recovery can be effected, even if the customer of the collecting bank has gone into liquidation: *Chase Manhattan Bank NA v. Israel-British Bank (London) Ltd* [1979] 3 All ER 1025.

46. *Admiralty Commissioners v. National Provincial & Union Bank of England Ltd* (1922) 127 LT 452; *Larner v. LCC* [1949] 2 KB 683. There is no need to refund if the mistake is one of *law* of course: *Holt v. Markham* [1923] 1 KB 504. The mistaken transfer or payment must have been made under an obligation, however; it seems that a voluntary payment cannot be recovered: *Morgan v. Ashcroft* [1938] 1 KB 49, but see the possibility of "tracing" voluntary payments *supra*, Chap. 5, under the heading "The Two-Contract Liability".

47. For a review of "Problems of the collecting bank" see Mr Gordon Borrie (as he then was) (1960) 23 MLR 16, and for an earlier view Dr AG Davis (1938) 2 MLR 222.

Protection is afforded, however, by s. 4(1) of the Cheques Act 1957[48] and a bank will not be accountable for the proceeds of any cheque it collects provided:

(1) The bank acts without negligence; and

(2) The bank receives payment for a customer; and

(3) The document in question is an instrument to which the section relates.

Each must be considered.

1. The bank must act without negligence

What conduct can be deemed negligent? As we have seen, everything depends upon the facts obtaining in each case.

Negligence, I think, is equivalent to carelessness. It is the price which the bank pays for the protection afforded by the Act in cases where the common law doctrine of conversion would leave the bank without defence.[49]

Two questions must, therefore, be asked: (i) *when* ought enquiries to be made, and (ii) *what* enquiries ought to be made.

(i) When?

"The duty of care owed by the banker to the true owner of the cheque does not arise until the cheque is delivered to him by his customer. It is then, and then only, that any duty to make enquiries can arise."[50] Or put another way: "A bank's decision as to whether it can properly accept a cheque for collection has to be made at the time when the cheque is handed in at the counter or when it is received by post or soon after that before the cheque and paying-in slip are separated and the cheque is sent forward to the clearing house."[51]

It is, of course, a regular practice to pay in cheques to branches, or even banks, other than where a customer has his account. It is a great convenience for customers, but can be a headache for the collecting bank. The clearing system, as we have seen, is such that while the branch which actually receives the cheque over the counter sees the instrument, they will know nothing about the customer or the circumstances relating to the cheque, while the branch at which the customer's account is kept, while knowing the customer, never sees the cheque at all and only credits the amount to his account. This "loophole" was exploited by two dishonest broker's clerks, who misappropriated their

---

48. Replacing s. 82 of the 1882 Act which is repealed: Cheques Act 1957, s. 6(3).

49. *Per* Harman LJ in *Orbit Mining & Trading Ltd* v. *Westminster Bank Ltd* [1963] 1 QB 794, 824.

50. *Per* Diplock LJ (as he then was) in *Marfani* v. *Midland Bank Ltd* [1968] 2 All ER 573, 579.

51. *Per* Sellers LJ in the *Orbit Case*, at pp. 813 *et seq.*

employer's funds, and paid them into City branches for the credit of their accounts in the country. The case went to the House of Lords as *Lloyds Bank Ltd* v. *Savory*,[52] where it was held the bank had been negligent in the method of passing information, in this way, from one branch to another, and they had to refund to the stockbrokers. The practice now is for credits of this kind to be sent for collection to the customer's own branch.

(ii) What?

"What facts ought to be known to the banker? That is, what enquiries should be made and what facts are sufficient to cause him reasonably to suspect that the customer is not the true owner, must depend on current banking practice and change as that practice changes."[53]

It is, therefore, a question of fact in each case whether the enquiries, if any, have been adequate. The burden of proof is on the bank to show it has *not* been negligent. Yet " . . . a bank cannot be held to be liable for negligence merely because they have not subjected an account to a microscopic examination."[54]

As a guide only, it may be helpful to give a few examples either side of the line. It cannot be stressed too strongly, however, that these are *examples* only and much depends on the facts obtaining in each case.

Conduct of collecting bank which has been held negligent

> To receive payment of a cheque drawn, not in favour of the customer, but to his employers without making enquiries.[55]
>
> To receive payment of a cheque drawn, not in favour of the customer but to his business, and not checking with other partners.[56]
>
> To receive payment of a cheque drawn by the customer's employer in favour of some third party without enquiry.[57]
>
> To receive payment of a cheque signed under a power of attorney by a solicitor, in his own favour, without enquiring as to his authority to receive personally funds of this sort.[58]

---

52. [1933] AC 201.
53. *Per* Diplock LJ (as he then was) in *Marfani* v. *Midland Bank Ltd* [1968] 2 All ER 573, 579.
54. *Per* Sankey LJ (as he then was) in *Lloyds Bank* v. *Chartered Bank of India* [1929] 1 KB 40, 73.
55. *AL Underwood Ltd* v. *Bank of Liverpool & Martins Bank* [1924] 1 KB 775. See also, *Bute* v. *Barclays Bank Ltd* [1954] 3 All ER 365.
56. *Baker* v. *Barclays Bank Ltd* [1955] 2 All ER 571.
57. *Lloyds Bank Ltd* v. *Savory* [1933] AC 201.
58. *Midland Bank Ltd* v. *Reckitt* [1933] AC 1

Conduct of a collecting bank held not negligent

Not enquiring into the drawer's authority for signing *per pro* cheques made payable to himself.[59]

Not checking the drawer's signature where two signatures appear on behalf of a company, the cheque being paid into the private account of one of the signatories, made out to him and no indorsement being necessary.[60]

Not keeping itself up to date as to the identity of a customer's employer.[61]

Not asking for a customer's passport to verify identity and relying on one reference only.[62]

Not checking or concerning itself with the absence or irregularities of indorsements.[63]

2. Payment must be received for a customer

There are two considerations which must be made: (a) the person for whom payment is received must be a customer of the receiving bank; and (b) the bank must receive for the customer as his agent, and *not for themselves*.

(a) The person must be a customer

In the usual way there will be little doubt as to whether the person concerned is or is not a customer. The customary rule is that a person becomes a customer as soon as an account is opened upon which he can draw.[64] For example, in

GW RAILWAY CO v. LONDON & COUNTY BANK CO[65]

The L Bank had for 20 years cashed cheques for H although he did not have an account with them. On one occasion H obtained a cheque from the GWR by false pretences. It was crossed and marked "not negotiable". The L Bank cashed the cheque, and paid part into an account of a customer and handed the balance to H. The GWR then discovered H's fraud and sued the L Bank for recovery of the money. The L Bank pleaded protection of the 1882 Act, in that they were not liable to the true owner provided they received payment for a customer in good faith and without negligence. *Held*—that H

59. *Morison v. London County Bank* [1914] 3 KB 356.
60. *Orbit Mining & Trading Co Ltd v. Westminster Bank Ltd* [1963] 1 QB 794.
61. *Per* Harman LJ, *ibid.*, p. 825.
62. *Marfani v. Midland Bank Ltd* [1968] 2 All ER 573. The standard to prove a bank negligent is high. See *Baden v. Société General* [1991] 4 All ER 161 *Lipkin Gorman v. Karpnale* [1991] 4 All ER 409, and *Barclays Bank Plc v. Quincecare* [1991] 4 All ER 363 where none of the banks were held negligent. See *supra*, page 212.
63. Cheques Act 1957, s. 4(3). But see *Thackwell v. Barclays Bank plc* [1986] 1 All ER 676, where the bank, though negligent, escaped liability because the customer had received the cheque as part of an illegal transaction.
64. *Taxation Commission v. English Scottish and Australian Bank* [1920] AC 683.
65. [1901] AC 418.

was not a customer, and hence the bank had no protection and had to repay the money to the GWR.

If there is dispute as to whether a person is or is not a customer, regard should be had to the words of Collins J[66] " . . . the Act means what it says, and that protection is only given for obvious reasons to a bank which does collect for a customer in the real sense . . . ". One bank may, of course, be the customer of another bank.[67]

(b) The bank must receive as agent

Section 4(1)(b) of the Cheques Act 1957 provides that a bank incurs no liability "having credited" a customer's account with the amount of a remittance. In other words, a bank does not have to wait until the cheque is cleared before crediting the amount. At one time it was thought that if a bank credited before clearance they were making themselves liable to their customer and were, therefore, collecting for themselves. The section makes the position clear.[68]

3. The document must be an instrument within the Act

The 1882 Act protected bankers only when collecting cheques[69] and other documents were provided for on a piecemeal basis.[70] Now s. 4(2) of the Cheques Act 1957 sets out the instruments to which the protection afforded will extend. They are:

(1) Cheques, whether open or crossed.

66. *Lacave & Co* v. *Credit Lyonnais* [1897] 1 QB 148, at p. 155.
67. *Importers Co* v. *Westminster Bank* [1927] 2 KB 297.
68. This provision has had a chequered history. For years banks credited the amounts of cheques to customer's accounts immediately on receipt and before they were "cleared". This was long established banking practice and was in accordance with the protection offered under s. 82 of the 1882 Act. However, in 1903 the House of Lords decided (*Capital & Counties Bank* v. *Gordon* [1903] AC 240) that a bank was *not* acting for a customer in these circumstances, but only when the amount of the cheque was credited *after* clearance. This placed banks in a very difficult position, and to avoid the consequences of the decision, it would have meant major alterations in the system of accounting. Parliament came to the rescue by enacting the Bills of Exchange (Crossed Cheques) Act 1906 which provided that banks were still receiving "payment for a customer" within the meaning of s. 82 notwithstanding that it credits its customer's account with the amount of the cheque *before* actually receiving payment. The 1906 Act is now repealed by the Cheques Act 1957, s. 6(3). In fact Cave J in *Clarke* v. *London & County Bank* [1897] 1 QB 552, at p. 554, appears to have sorted the position out quite clearly. The House of Lords (who appear not to have had the benefit of considering the views of Cave J) took a contrary view in the *Gordon Case* and it took Parliament to revert to the position established by Cave J and which is now the law.
69. *Arnold* v. *Cheque Bank* (1876) 45 LJCL 562.
70. For example, *banker's drafts* by s. 1 of the Bills of Exchange (1882) Amendment Act 1932; *"conditional orders"* by s. 17 of the Revenue Act 1893: both provisions now repealed by the Cheques Act 1957, s. 6(3). The protection afforded by s. 4 of the Cheques Act 1957 is available to the collecting bank whether the document is crossed or uncrossed.

    (2) *Any document* issued by a customer which, though not a bill of exchange, is intended to enable a person to obtain payment of the sum mentioned from that bank. This covers "conditional orders" and documents hitherto within s. 17 of the Revenue Act 1893.

For example, in

ORBIT MINING & TRADING CO LTD v. WESTMINSTER BANK LTD[71]

The Orbit company had an account with the Midland Bank and any two directors could sign on the account. Director W was going abroad and director E asked him to sign a few blank cheques before leaving, which W did. E then wrote in the word "Cash" and made up the cheques for amounts which he required and paid them into his own account with the Westminster Bank. In due course the fraud was discovered and Orbit sued the defendant bank for return of the money. *Held*—that the documents were not bills of exchange or cheques but the collecting bank could obtain protection under s. 4(2)(*b*) of the Cheques Act 1957.

    (3) Any document, not being a bill of exchange, issued by a public officer which is intended to enable a person to obtain payment of the sum mentioned from the Paymaster General or the Queen's and Lords Treasurer's Remembrancer.

    (4) Any draft payable on demand drawn by a bank upon itself, whether payable at the head or some other office of his bank. This replaces the Bills of Exchange (1882) Amendment Act 1932.

This is a comprehensive list of instruments, but any which fall outside its terms will place a bank in the position of ascertaining before collecting that its customer has a good title to the document. The most salient omission from the list is the ordinary bill of exchange, which formerly fell within s. 17 of the Revenue Act 1893; s 4(2)(*b*) of the Cheques Act (which replaces s. 17) covers any document issued by a customer "though not a bill of exchange". Henceforward, when collecting payment on an ordinary bill, the customer's title must be verified.

THE DUAL ROLE

It not infrequently happens that a bank receives a cheque for a customer which is drawn on itself by another customer. In such a case, the bank, in order to obtain the full protection of the 1882 Act, must act first as a *collecting* bank and then as a *paying* bank.

It follows that if the statutory protection is sought by the bank it must satisfy the requirements in each capacity, so that it may well not be liable in one capacity, but caught by the self same actions in the other. Put another way, the

---

71. [1963] 1 QB 794.

bank to obtain *full* protection must satisfy the requirements of both s. 60 as regards its capacity as the paying (drawee) bank, and also s. 4 of the Cheques Act (replacing s. 82 of the 1882 Act) as regards its capacity as collecting bank.[72]

These points fell for discussion in the case of

CARPENTER v. BRITISH MUTUAL BANKING CO[73]

The Carpenters' company maintained an account with the defendant banking company. One of their employees, a man by the name of Blackborrow, also banked with the same branch. It was part of Blackborrow's duties to handle the company accounts. He began a series of frauds by getting cheques (all of which were crossed) made payable to tradespeople, and having been properly signed by the officers of the company, forging the indorsements and paying them into his private account. The fraud was, of course, discovered and the company sued the bank for return of the money. *Held*—that "In so far as they received the plaintiff's cheques at Blackborrow's request and credited their customer, Blackborrow, with the proceeds . . . they appear to me to have acted . . . as a receiving bank as well as in the capacity of a paying bank. As a paying banker they may well be protected by s. 60 of the Bills of Exchange Act 1882, in so far as they acted in good faith, which is not disputed, and in the ordinary course of business."[74] However, in its capacity as a collecting bank (s. 82—now s. 4 of the Cheques Act—demands that a bank must act without negligence) the court held, as a question of fact, " . . . that there was negligence, and the protection of s. 82 cannot be invoked by the bank at all".[75] Consequently, the bank was liable in conversion and had to refund the money to the company.[76]

72. S. 4 of the Cheques Act is now amended by the Cheques Act 1992.
73. [1938] 1 KB 511.
74. *Per* Slesser LJ, at p. 533.
75. *Per* Slesser LJ, at p. 536.
76. MacKinnon LJ dissenting.

SECTION THREE

MISCELLANEOUS
DOCUMENTS

CHAPTER 14

MISCELLANEOUS DOCUMENTS

It frequently happens that banks are asked to advance funds in respect of a transaction, the security for which is a document or series of documents giving, or purporting to give, title to goods or money. A good example is a bill of lading relating to goods being shipped to the order of the customer. If the customer needs finance in such a transaction there should be no difficulty, bills of lading and their method of handling being well established in financial circles. However, it may be—and often is—that the transaction, and the relating documents, are not so clearly established; it is then necessary to look closely at the documents being offered, and the surrounding circumstances of the whole transaction.

In the following pages an attempt is made to outline the various types of document usually encountered, and to indicate the principles upon which a decision might be reached whether or not to accept such documents as may be offered.

THINGS IN ACTION

Section 53(1) of the Bills of Exchange Act 1882 provides that a bill, of itself, does not operate as an assignment of funds in the hands of the drawee.

To assign money, or any other kind of property which one cannot claim by physical possession, one needs to execute a document (usually called "an assignment"), and give notice to the holder of the money or the property that the assignment has been made, so that he must now hold the property to the order of someone else—that is the assignee. For example, in

WALKER v. BRADFORD OLD BANK[1]

R banked with the B Bank. R assigned to W, *inter alia*, "the cash at his bankers, and all moneys which might thereafter come to his hands". No notice was given to the bank of the assignment. R died and W gave the bank notice of the assignment. The bank refused to pay, as among other things, no letter of administration to the deceased's estate had

1. (1884) 12 QBD 509.

been granted. *Held*—that the assignment was valid and W was entitled to the balance at the bank.

We normally speak of property of this type as being a "thing in action" or sometimes a "chose (French = thing) in action". It covers a wide variety of property. In the words of Channell J:

"Chose in action" is a known legal expression used to describe all personal rights of property which can only be claimed or enforced by action, and not by taking physical possession.[2]

Debts, money, dividends, bills of lading, bills of exchange, shares in a company, policies of insurance: the list seems endless.

Almost any kind of property[3] can be assigned in this way, with a few exceptions,[4] where statute lays down that a special method must be used; for example, shares in a company can only be transferred as provided by the Companies Act, and policies of assurance under the provisions of the Policies of Assurance Act 1867. These are exceptional cases, however, and most things can be assigned without too much formality, under the provisions of s. 136(1) of the Law of Property Act 1925.

The requirements of a valid assignment are:

    (a) it must be in writing and signed by the assignor. Usually, it will be a formal document prepared by a solicitor, but it need not be.[5]

    (b) the assignment must be "absolute", and not merely by way of mortgage or charge. An assignment is not "absolute" if it relates to part only of the property. For example, one could not assign part of a debt.

    (c) the property being assigned can be "any debt or other legal thing in action" recognized by law.

    (d) express notice of the assignment must be given in writing to the holder of the property, and the effective date is when he *actually receives* it.[6]

The assignment need not necessarily be supported by consideration.[7]

---

2. *Torkington v. Magee* [1902] 2 KB 427, 430.

3. We are not discussing here the question of dispositions of land where different considerations apply altogether.

4. If the parties to a contract involving a chose in action agree that it cannot be assigned, any attempted assignment is invalid: *Helstan Securities Ltd v. Hertfordshire County Council* [1978] 3 All ER 262.

5. It must be stamped at *ad valorem* rates.

6. *Holt v. Heatherfield Trust* [1942] 2 KB 1; however, there are no formal requirements for notice of an assignment: *Van Lynn Developments v. Pelias Construction Ltd* [1969] 1 QB 607. But if the date of assignment is wrongly stated the notice will be ineffective: *WF Harrison & Co Ltd v. Burke* [1956] 2 All ER 169.

7. *Re Westerton* [1919] 2 Ch104. See particularly *per* Sargant J, at p. 111.

If these requirements are fulfilled, the assignment will be effective to pass the legal right to the property from the date of the notice, and, if needs be, the assignee can sue in respect of it in his own name as the new owner.[8] However, the transfer is *not negotiable* and it is, therefore, subject to any equities and prior claims.[9] It might well happen that an attempted assignment is defective in some way, because these requirements have not been wholly satisfied. Such a happening may not be totally without effect, however, as the rules of Equity might well save the purported assignment from being inoperative, as Equity always looked to the intent rather than the form, so that a defective assignment at law may nevertheless be a good assignment in Equity. In these circumstances everything depends upon the particular facts and the intention of the parties. For example, if a bank is advancing money to a customer, and gives notice to debtors of the customer that money should be remitted direct to the bank, that will be a valid equitable assignment of those debts;[10] or, if someone acknowledges that they are holding funds to another's account, this is valid equitable assignment.[11]

Even in Equity, the subject of the assignment must be one which is capable of being assigned, however. For example, contracts for personal services or bear rights to litigation cannot be assigned even in Equity.

It is still not entirely clear whether, unlike a legal assignment, to claim the benefit of an equitable assignment one has to give consideration. The courts have differed in their views,[12] but the better opinion seems to be that consideration is *not* required[13] though the point is still open.

Notice in Equity is not a vital matter; and a defective assignment may well be deemed valid, *as between the assignor and the assignee*, even if no notice is given to the holder of the property. However, the assignee should see that notice of the transaction is given and received for two reasons:

8. If the debtor has a claim against the assignor, it may be set off against the assignee, if the claim had accrued due before the notice of assignment was given, or if it arose out of the same contract as the debt being assigned: *Business Computers Ltd* v. *Anglo-African Leasing Ltd* [1977] 2 All ER 741, 748b.

9. *Roxburghe* v. *Cox* (1881) 17 Ch D 520.

10. *Brandts* v. *Dunlop Rubber Co* [1905] AC 454. See also *Re Kent & Sussex Sawmills* [1947] 1 Ch 177, where the informal assignment of debts to a bank should have been registered under the Companies Act and were void against the customer's liquidator. See also *Re Miller Gibb & Co Ltd* [1957] 2 All ER 266, where undertakings were given under an Export Credits Guarantee Scheme, which amounted to an equitable assignment of funds received by the collecting bank under a bill of exchange. Where there has been an equitable assignment, and the assignor still wishes to bring proceedings in respect of the chose in action, the equitable assignee must be joined in the action, or the assignor must sue as trustee for the assignee on the face of the pleadings: *Three Rivers District Council* v. *Bank of England* [1995] 4 All ER 312.

11. *Gorringe* v. *Irwell India Rubber Works* (1886) 34 Ch D 128.

12. *Per* Atkinson J in *Holt* v. *Heatherfield Trust* [1942] 2 KB 15, at p. 15; *per* Evershed MR in *Re McArdle* [1951] Ch 669, 674.

13. Cheshire Fifoot and Furmston's, *Law of Contract*, 13th edn. (1996) p. 524, citing *Spellman* v. *Spellman* [1961] 2 All ER 498, page 501A.

(1) if no notice is received and the property is transferred to the assignor, the assignee will not be able to demand payment again from whoever was holding the property; and

(2) if the assignor attempted several assignments, the rights of the assignees would depend upon the order in which the holder of the property received the notices.[14]

These matters are of particular importance where businesses discount their invoices under a factoring arrangement, the Finance House taking over the collection of the debts due under the invoices discounted. Clear notice of the assignment must be given to the debtors, and a notice "To facilitate our accountancy and banking arrangements . . . " has been held[15] not adequate notice of the assignment of the debts under the invoices.

The debtor or trustee of funds must always act in accordance with the notice given, and if he does not and ignores it, either deliberately or accidentally, he will be compelled to pay again.[16] To this there is one exception, and that is where he has given a negotiable instrument in respect of the money or the debt.

BENCE v. SHEARMAN[17]

S was the owner of a public house. He asked A if he could find a purchaser for it, in consideration of a commission of £200. A introduced B and the sale was agreed between S and B. A was already indebted to B (to an amount of £200), and he gave B a piece of paper purporting to assign his commission of £200 due from S. S knew nothing of the piece of paper until the day fixed for the completion of the purchase when all three met to finalize matters. The full purchase money was paid by B to S and S gave A a cheque for his commission. It was not clear at what stage B produced the paper, but at all events S gave A the cheque which he went away with, not passing it over to B, who "did not wish to interfere with the regular course of business". B and S were left discussing the purchase, and the purported assignment of the commission was further discussed, after which B persuaded S to "stop" the cheque. B subsequently sued S, claiming the amount of the commission. *Held*—that " . . . having given a cheque on which he is legally liable, his obligation to deal with the holder of the cheque is not altered by notice, after he has given the cheque, that the debt was assigned"[18] S was not,

---

14. This is under what is known as the rule in *Dearle* v. *Hall* (1823) 38 ER 475. Notice otherwise than in writing is of no effect even as regards equitable interests: Law of Property Act 1925, s. 137(3).

15. *James Talcott Ltd* v. *John Lewis Ltd* [1940] 3 All ER 592. Also, under a factoring agreement, if cheques are received by the factoring company, they are subject to a trust, and must be given directly to the factors; to do otherwise, for example, paying them into the company's bank account, would be conversion: *International Factors Ltd* v. *Rodriguez* [1979] 1 All ER 17.

16. "After receipt of that notice the debtor pays the assignor at his peril": *per* Parker LJ (as he then was) in *Walter & Sullivan Ltd* v. *J Murphy and Sons Ltd* [1955] 1 All ER 843, 845d.

17. [1898] 2 Ch 582.

18. Collins LJ, in *Walter & Sullivan Ltd* v. *J Murphy and Sons Ltd* [1958] 1 All ER 843.

therefore, liable to B. S would, of course, still be liable on the cheque unless he had some valid defence.

DOCUMENTS OF TITLE

We saw in the beginning that a bill of exchange was a piece of paper used to transfer money from one person to another. The form developed over the years and is now enshrined in the Bills of Exchange Act 1882. Some instruments used to transfer money are not, as we have seen, bills of exchange at all, although they serve adequately the purpose of transferring title to money. Some bills are negotiable, others are not.

There are a number of documents which are similar in some respects to bills of exchange, some of which are, in fact, negotiable instruments. The difficulty is, in dealing with this amorphous body, to determine which can operate as effective transfers of the property they represent, and whether any can be negotiated.

The problem can be reduced to two questions:

(1) Is *every* piece of paper (other than bills of exchange) capable of representing the ownership and title of the money or goods it represents, and if not, how does one tell?

and having established which instruments are valid documents of title

(2) Are they negotiable, and if so, is it by mere delivery or by indorsement and delivery?

1. The documents

Not every piece of paper is a document of title to the goods or chattels it represents. If X buys a television set, it will be delivered without formality. X will get an invoice and, perhaps, a delivery note, but that is all. There will be no piece of paper to show X owns the set, and hence no piece of paper X can indorse and transfer to someone to whom X subsequently sells the set.

Contrast the case of a motor car.[19] Here, if X buys a car he must see his name is registered with the local authorities and obtain the "registration book" with his name appropriately entered.

19. Problems abound with the transfer of motor vehicles, especially where an element of dishonesty creeps in. In days gone by the owner of the motor vehicle had a "log book" which gave the vehicle details and those of the owner. This was changed to a "registration book" some years ago, and as of March 1997 there is a "Form V 5" which in terms states that it is not a document of title, so it is possible that further complications may arise involving the question of proof of ownership, a subject beyond the scope of this book. The reference to a "registration book" is maintained here, since that is the format of the documentation in the cases cited. A registration book is not, in fact, strictly a document of title: *Joblin* v. *Watkins* [1949] 1 All ER 47, " . . . but it is the best evidence of title. Everyone who buys or sells a second-hand car knows that you cannot give or obtain a clean title unless you have the registration book": *per* Denning LJ (as he then was)

In all these cases, it is a matter of custom. Custom has played a considerable part in the forming of our commercial law, and if it is customary to transfer the ownership of goods in a particular way, that method will, almost certainly, become the method recognized by the law.

These pieces of paper assume considerable importance when, of themselves, they can be used to transfer the ownership of goods and chattels without the actual goods themselves being moved at all; indeed, the goods may well be in the hands of some third party altogether. For example,

ANT. JURGENS v. LOUIS DREYFUS[20]

D had a consignment of seed in his warehouse in Hamburg. He agreed to sell part of this to F who was a broker in London, payment to be made in cash in exchange for the shipping documents and/or a delivery order. F then agreed to resell the goods to M. D accepted F's cheque and gave him a delivery order addressed to the warehouse at Hamburg for release of the goods. F thereupon indorsed the delivery order to M who paid F. F's cheque to D was dishonoured and D refused to release the goods either to F (understandably) or to M. M then sued D for the goods, relying on the indorsed delivery order. *Held*—that the delivery order issued by D was a valid document of title, and had been negotiated by F to M who took in good faith and for valuable consideration, and was, therefore, entitled to the goods.

It is still extremely difficult to say which pieces of paper are or are not documents of title, and banks dealing with funds "against" these documents must exercise great care to establish title before payment is released. As a guide, reference can be made to s. 1(4) of the Factors Act 1889[21] which states that the expression "document of title" shall *include*:

... any bill of lading, dock warrant, warehouse keeper's certificate and warrant or order for the delivery of goods, and any other document used in the ordinary course of business as proof of possession or control of goods, or authorizing or purporting to authorize either by endorsement or by delivery, the possessor of the document to transfer or receive goods thereby represented.

A number of these documents, such as bills of lading, are clearly documents of title and their use has been made clear by long practice and by the courts,

in *Pearson v. Rose & Young Ltd* [1951] 1 KB 275, 289. Consequently anyone who buys without the registration book does so at his peril: *Stadium Finance Ltd v. Robbins* [1962] 2 QB 664, and if the registration book is not handed over the contract of sale or hire-purchase is not complete and cannot be enforced: *Bentworth Finance Ltd v. Lubert* [1968] 1 QB 680, for the handing over of the registration book "... is a practical necessity ... he has to produce it in order to get the car licensed ...", *per* Lord Denning, *ibid.*, p. 684G. A registration book is not a negotiable document, consequently, if the transferor had no right to have the registration book or transfer the car he will (with few exceptions) be able to pass no title to the vehicle: *Pearson v. Rose & Young Ltd, supra*; *Stadium Finance Ltd v. Robbins* [1962] 2 QB 664; *Heap v. Motorists Advisory Agency Ltd* [1923] 1 KB 577. One of the exceptions is where a rogue buys a car, gets the registration book and then his cheque is dishonoured, after he has re-sold to an honest buyer who takes the registration book in good faith: see *Lewis v. Averay* [1972] 1 QB 198. The new computer registration system makes the problem rather worse.
20. [1914] 3 KB 40.
21. 52 & 53 Vict c 45.

but there are others about which confusion still exists. Take, for example, the case of a "delivery order": this was held by Pickford J in *Ant. Jurgens* v. *Louis Dreyfus*[22] to be a document of title, the indorsement of which passed a good title to goods in a warehouse. Whereas Sankey J in *Laurie* v. *Dudin*[23] thought the delivery order *he* was considering to be different from that in the *Jurgens* case, and said that: "A bank, apparently would require the production of a delivery warrant, as distinguished from a delivery order, as security for money advanced";[24] whereas Lord Porter in *Comptoir d'Achat* v. *Luis de Ridder*[25] thought the delivery order before the House was "a preliminary step only" and that: "A complicated procedure had to be followed before the goods would be released." Singleton LJ in *Dumenil* v. *Ruddin*[26] took the view that a delivery order was "a mere promise to deliver", and it was not complete until whoever had control of the goods, such as a wharfinger or ship's master acknowledged to the buyer that the goods were now held on his behalf. The Court of Appeal in *Colin & Shields* v. *Weddel*[27] took the same view.

It is, perhaps, regrettable to have to say so, but there is no rule which can be laid down to indicate in many cases whether the instrument at hand is a document of title or not. So much depends upon the facts of the case, in the absence of a firm decision of the courts having considered that particular document and having pronounced upon it; even then, as we have seen, instruments have been recognized as documents of title in some cases but not in others.

As a general guide, one is thrown back on the wording of the Factors Act " . . . any other document used in the ordinary course of business as proof of possession or control of the goods or authorizing . . . the possessor of the document to transfer or receive goods thereby represented". One has to consider the law merchant and the custom which created it, however, before one can give any real meaning to this very wide definition, which *enables* almost *any* instrument to be a document of title, rather than *specifying* which instruments *are* documents of title.

This is regrettably a confusing answer to give to the first question which was posed. We must now consider the second.

2. Negotiability of documents

Most of the documents which have been discussed, whether valid documents of title or not, can be transferred—usually by delivery, sometimes by indorsement and delivery. The transfer may well be a useless act if the paper is not a

22. [1914] 3 KB 40.
23. [1925] 2 KB 383.
24. *Ibid.*, p. 390.
25. [1949] AC 293, 311.
26. [1953] 1 WLR 815, 817.
27. [1952] 2 All ER 337. See particularly, *per* Denning LJ (as he then was) at p. 343b.

document of title, but it is still transferable. However, by no means is every document a negotiable instrument.

Documents are "negotiable" either by virtue of Act of Parliament (which is extremely rare)[28] or by custom (which is extremely vague). If the custom has been recognized for a long time and has, perhaps, been pronounced upon by the courts, the position is not too difficult; however, so often when problems arise, it is because the document in question is claimed by one party as negotiable, and by another as not having this quality. For example, it took lengthy litigation to prove share certificates are *not* negotiable,[29] but that debentures issued "to bearer" *are*.[30] As a further *guide* as to what is or is not recognized by custom it will be helpful to bear in mind the words of Bigham J[31]:

It is no doubt true that negotiability can only be attached to a contract by the law merchant or by a statute; and it is also true that, in determining whether a usage has become so well established as to be binding on the Courts of Law, the length of time during which the usage has existed is an important circumstance to take into consideration; but it is to be remembered that in these days usage is established much more quickly than it was in days gone by; more depends on the number of the transactions which help to create it than on the time over which the transactions are spread; and it is probably no exaggeration to say that nowadays there are more business transactions in an hour than there were in a week a century ago. Therefore, the comparatively recent origin of this class of securities in my view creates no difficulty in the way of holding that they are negotiable by virtue of the law merchant . . . It is also to be remembered that the law merchant is not fixed and stereotyped.

In cases of doubt, it may not be very satisfactory to say so, but the rule must be, if possible, to treat the document as *not* negotiable, rather than run the risk of treating the document as having this quality only to find that it has not.

It will be convenient here to consider the method by which these documents can be transferred, whether or not they are negotiable instruments.

If Parliament has already legislated that a document is to be transferred in a particular way, that method must be used otherwise no title can pass. For example, shares in a company can only be transferred by virtue of the provisions of the Companies Act, and patents under the provisions of the Patents Act. If the requirements of the appropriate legislation are not satisfied the transfer will be ineffective. So that where shares were being transferred between two foreign nationals, and the necessary statutory approval for the transfer had not been obtained from the Government authorities in London,

28. See, for example, Bills of Exchange (1704) 3 & 4 Anne c 8, which made promissory notes negotiable; see also Companies Act 1985, s. 188(2) which gives negotiability to share warrants.
29. *London & County Bank* v. *River Plate Bank* (1887) 20 QBD 232.
30. *Bechuanaland Exploration Co* v. *London Trade Bank* [1898] 2 QB 658.
31. *Edelstein* v. *Schular* [1902] 2 KB 144, at p. 154.

the transfer had no effect, even though the transferor had signed the form of transfer and sent it to the company.[32] The same applies to the purported transfer of a policy of insurance by a mere indorsement across it, which did not comply with the Policies of Assurance Act 1867.[33]

If there are no statutory rules, the question of what conduct is adequate to create a good transfer is not so easy to answer. The general rule is that a thing in action (with the exception of bills of exchange) cannot be transferred by simply handing over the document.[34] An exception is the pawn-receipt.[35] On surrender of the pawn-receipt (and payment of the amount owing), the pawn-broker[36] must deliver the pawn "to the bearer of the pawn-receipt".[37] The pawnbroker is not liable "to any person" in tort or delict for delivering the pawn to the bearer of the pawn-receipt in this way.[38] To this limited degree it might be said that pawn-receipts are negotiable by delivery.[39]

The position with ordinary cloak-room and other such tickets is not entirely clear, although, probably, and in the absence of negligence, the person to whom goods are entrusted will not be liable for delivering them to whomsoever is in possession of the ticket.[40] Consequently, such tickets would appear capable of passing title by mere delivery.

Once more, it is difficult to be precise in specifying the requirements of a valid transfer of these miscellaneous documents. The rule must be that if the transferor has done all that he can to divest himself of the title to the property—even if that transfer is defective—yet it *may* still be possible for the transfer to be valid in Equity. For example, by indorsement and delivery of a bank deposit receipt[41] even though: "The deposit receipt is clearly not a negotiable

32. *Re Fry* [1946] Ch 312. Complicated questions sometimes arise where the transferor can be deemed a settlor, in such a case, if the settlor has done everything in his power to divest himself of the shares the court may be prepared to perfect the imperfect gift: *Re Rose* [1949] Ch 78. See generally Hanbury and Martin, *Modern Equity*, 14th edn (1993) pp. 117–118 and 138.

33. *Re Williams* [1917] 1 Ch 1.

34. Even the giving of a cheque may not always be adequate: *Jones v. Lock* (1865) 35 LJ Ch (Mich. T.) 117, where a father gave a cheque made payable to him—to his nine-month old son. The case is not very satisfactory as " . . . it did not appear in evidence whether it was payable to bearer or order" (p. 118) and the learned LC thought this point "immaterial" (p. 119).

35. Consumer Credit Act 1974, s. 114. This is the successor to the old pawn-ticket under the Pawn Brokers Acts 1872 to 1960. For the regulations relating to the form of pawn-receipts, see SI 1983/1553, the Consumer Credit (Agreements) Regulations 1983, para. 4.

36. Called in the Act "the pawnee", reminiscent of the tribe of North American Indians.

37. Consumer Credit Act 1974, s. 117(1).

38. *Ibid.*, s. 117(3).

39. Where a person claims to be the owner of the pawn, but does not have the pawn-receipt, he can still redeem by tendering to the pawnee (in place of the pawn-receipt) a Statutory Declaration: Consumer Credit Act 1974, s. 118 and the Consumer Credit (Loss of Pawn-Receipt) Regulations 1983, SI 1983/1567.

40. See *per* Devlin J (as he then was) in *Alexander v. Railway Excutive* [1951] 2 KB 882, 892.

41. *Re Griffin* [1899] 1 Ch 408.

instrument . . . ".[42] Indorsement in such a case is not essential, however; nor is consideration.[43]

MISCELLANEOUS DOCUMENTS CONSIDERED

It will be convenient if we now consider some of the various classes of documents commonly found in daily use. As a matter of convenience only they can be grouped into three divisions: 1. Documents relating to goods or chattels. 2. Documents relating to legal rights. 3. Documents used for payment of money (other than bills of exchange).

1. Documents relating to goods or chattels

What may be termed "goods and chattels" are usually transferred by delivery, and this may not be accompanied by any documentary evidence of title at all; as, for example, the instance of the television set given before.

If an instrument is a document of title it will be freely transferable, usually by indorsement—*but not negotiable*. This is of vital importance where title to goods is purportedly passed on, not by *actual* delivery, but by the transfer of the documents of title.

Among the best known of this type of document is the bill of lading. It has long been established that these bills represent the goods and are, therefore, deemed valid documents of title. It follows that the ownership of the goods can pass by transfer of the bills of lading without any physical movement of the goods at all. In the words of Bowen LJ:[44]

A cargo at sea while in the hands of the carrier is necessarily incapable of physical delivery. During this period of transit and voyage, the bill of lading, by the law merchant, is universally recognized as its symbol, and the indorsement and delivery of the bill of lading operates as a symbolic delivery of the cargo. Property in the goods is passed by such indorsement and delivery of the bill of lading, whenever it is the intention of the parties that the property should pass, just as under similar circumstances the property would pass by an actual delivery of the goods.

A bill of lading is not a negotiable instrument, however. Nevertheless, by virtue of s. 25(1) of the Sale of Goods Act 1979 if a buyer obtains " . . . with the consent of the seller. . . " the documents of title to goods, he can pass a valid title, provided the transferee of the documents receives them " . . . in good faith and without notice of any lien or other right of the original seller in respect of the goods . . . ". It, therefore, followed in *Cahn* v. *Pockett's Bristol*

42. *Per* Byrne J, *ibid.*, p. 411.

43. *Re Westerton* [1919] 2 Ch 104. This is an odd case, as the deposit note had printed on it the words "Not transferable" but was accompanied by a letter addressed to the bank to pay the moneys to the holder. It seems, therefore, the transfer was effected by the letter, the deposit note being merely evidence of the funds which were to be paid to the holder of the note.

44. *Sanders* v. *MacLean* (1883) 11 QBD 327, 341.

Channel Steam Packet Co[45] that when the seller (as was the custom) sent to the buyer for acceptance a bill of exchange with a bill of lading attached and the buyer fraudulently transferred the bill of lading to an innocent buyer of the goods (but did not accept the bill of exchange), nevertheless the innocent buyer got a good title to the goods, the subject of the bill of lading.

As the seller, in most cases, cannot be sure of his buyer, it is now the practice to pass the bill of lading, and other documents, to the seller's bank, who, in turn, will deal with the buyer's bank, thus, eliminating most of these problems. This bank-to-bank relationship is the basis of the whole of international trade.

The subject of bankers' documentary credits is considered below in Section 4.

2. Documents relating to legal rights

There are a variety of legal rights which have no being in themselves—they are said to be *incorporeal*. The existence of these rights is evidenced only by some document or other. For example, one cannot touch or get hold of a share in a company—only the share certificate, which acknowledges the existence of the share. The same can be said of a debt. There may be an invoice or an IOU evidencing the debt, but the debt of itself does not exist.

Share certificates,[46] insurance policies,[47] IOUs,[48] banker's receipts[49] and all similar documents are not negotiable instruments, but, of course, they can be freely transferred, subject to any defects of title which may exist, and, of course, subject to notice to the debtor, or whatever legal requirement there may be, as in the case of share certificates which can only be transferred under the terms of the Companies Acts.

In this class of document there can, of course, be no question of any delivery of the article independently of the documents of title.

3. Documents used for payment of money

This class of document (apart from bills of exchange, cheques, etc.) is used to transfer money for a particular purpose or in a particular manner. Many have characteristics of bills of exchange and, in some cases, bills of exchange —particularly cheques—could be used just as well.

45. [1899] 1 QB 643.
46. *London & County Bank* v. *River Plate Bank* (1887) 20 QBD 232, *per* Manisty J, at p. 239.
47. In fact, it took an Act of Parliament to make them even *transferable*: Policies of Assurance Act 1867.
48. *Wilkinson* v. *L'Eaugier* (1836) 160 ER 437. An IOU is simply an acknowledgement of a debt, and is, therefore, only an account stated between the parties. No particular form is strictly necessary, though the debt and the person creating the note must be clear. If the IOU contains a promise to pay it may be construed as a promissory note.
49. *Beauclark* v. *Greaves* (1886) 2 TLR 837.

(i) Dividend warrants

A dividend warrant is a draft issued by a limited company to a shareholder in respect of his share in the profits of the company for the year, half-year or other period. It is payable on demand and is drawn on the company's bankers. To this extent it is like a cheque. The validity of any usage relating to dividend warrants or their indorsement is specially retained by the 1882 Act.[50]

The provisions of the Bills of Exchange Act 1882 regarding crossed cheques also apply to dividend warrants[51] which means that the 1882 Act and the Cheques Act 1957 apply to *crossed* dividend warrants, as though they were cheques. In fact, dividend warrants can be drawn in such a way that they *are* valid cheques, in which case the ordinary provisions as to cheques will apply: though in most cases dividend warrants will not be cheques.

If a warrant is not a "cheque", a *paying* banker will get protection under s. 1(2)(a) of the Cheques Act 1957 or under s. 19 of the Stamp Act 1853. Both provisions cover instruments such as dividend warrants. Similarly, a *collecting* bank will be covered under s. 4(2)(b) of the 1957 Act.

As we have already seen,[52] it was always the case with dividend warrants that where they were made payable to the order of *two or more payees* they could be validly indorsed by *either or any one* of them. This custom is expressly preserved by s. 97(3)(d) of the Act, although this is not possible with bills of exchange.[53]

It will be convenient under this heading to deal with other company documents similiar to dividend warrants, which can be issued "to bearer" and hence are deemed negotiable.

1. Scrip certificates

Sometimes issued at the time when original shares in a limited company are allotted. The certificate gives the bearer (the holder) the right to claim additional shares, provided the instalments stated in the certificate are paid. The holder can then exchange his scrip for shares in the company. They are, of course, negotiable.[54]

2. Debentures

Issued by a company to raise money—against the securitiy of its assets. They are, in some ways, similar to shares but in other respects totally different. They

---

50. Bills of Exchange Act 1882, s. 97(3)(d).
51. *Ibid.*, s. 95.
52. *Supra*, Chap. 4 under the heading "Requirements of Indorsements".
53. Bills of Exchange Act 1882, s. 32(3).
54. *Per* Mellor J in *Rumball* v. *The Metropolitan Bank* (1877) 2 QBD 194, 197.

are redeemable with interest at the agreed and stated times. If they are issued "to bearer" they are negotiable.[55]

3. Share warrants

Can be issued by a company, if authorized by its articles in respect of shares which are fully paid. The warrant specifies that the holder is entitled to the shares mentioned in the warrant. The shares then become negotiable by delivery of the warrant to the transferee.[56] Where share warrants are issued in this way the company will have no record of the owners of the shares and, consequently, attached to the warrant are usually found coupons which entitle the holder to the receipt of dividends. The company will pay the appropriate dividend to whomsoever presents these coupons for payment.

(ii) Postal orders

A postal order is an instrument issued by the Post Office in exchange for the cash value stated on the face of the order; a small charge (formerly called "poundage") is made by the Post Office at the time of issuing the instrument. It is intended that postal orders are encashed at another (or even the same) Post Office, but they can be paid into a bank account like a cheque for collection from the Post Office. As one can imagine, postal orders are used mainly in the settlement of small debts, frequently by those who do not usually operate bank accounts.

On the printed form the payee's name is blank, as is the Post Office for encashment; these can be filled in by the purchaser of the order, or not, as he wishes. Also, postal orders can be crossed in the same way as cheques, in which case, they will be paid by the Post Office to the collecting bank in accordance with the terms of the crossing.

It must be noted that while a purchaser of an order may leave the form blank at the time he gives, or sends, it to the person he intends should benefit, if it comes into the hands of some unauthorized person the Post Office will pay the blank order to whomsoever is in possession of it; however, postal orders are not inherently negotiable instruments. This was decided in

FINE ART SOCIETY v. UNION BANK OF LONDON[57]

The society banked with the U Bank. The secretary of the society also banked with the U Bank. The secretary paid postal orders belonging to his employers into his own account, and the bank collected in the ordinary course of business. The fraud was

---

55. Per Kennedy J in *Bechuanaland Exploration Co v. London Trading Bank* [1898] 2 QB 658, 666; *Edelstein v. Schular* [1902] 2 KB 144.
56. Companies Act 1985, s. 188(2). See *Webb Hale & Co v. Alexandria Water Co* (1905) 93 LT 339.
57. (1886) 17 QBD 705.

discovered and the society sued the U Bank for return of the money due under the postal orders. The bank contended the orders were negotiable and so they obtained a good title and could not, therefore, be guilty of conversion. *Held*—that the postal orders were not negotiable instruments. "It seems clear that they have not been treated as negotiable instruments by the general practice in England. I do not think it is shown that banker or merchants or the Post Office, for all purposes and with regard to all persons, so treated them. They have none of the attributes of negotiable instruments."[58] The bank were, therefore, guilty of conversion and had to refund the money.

As though to emphasize the point, postal orders are now printed with the words "not negotiable" across the face.

If a bank collects payment of a postal order for a customer, the payment by the Post Office to the bank discharges the order.[59] Moreover, a bank collecting payment on a postal order in this way " . . . shall not incur liability to anyone . . . " except its customer, by reason of the collection. The customer (that is the holder of the order) could, of course, be liable if *his* title were defective.[60] The protection is given only if the bank acts for its customer, however, not where the bank claims as holders in their own right.

An uncrossed order paid by the Post Office "over the counter" is discharged by payment to the person presenting it; and the Post Office is not responsible for checking the signature of the person who purported to sign it.[61]

(iii) Treasury bills

These replaced the old Exchequer bills[62] which were used during the reign of William III (1694–1702) to supply the financial needs of the Realm at the time of the great re-coinage. They are issued by the Government to cover short-term loans, and the holder receives interest at the agreed rate, and on such other terms as have been stated. They have long been recognized as negotiable.[63]

58. *Per* Lord Esher, *ibid.*, p. 710.
59. Post Office Act 1969, s. 70(1).
60. Post Office Act 1953, s. 21(3) as slightly amended by ss. 76, 88 and 139 of and Sch. 4, paragraph 2(8) to the Post Office Act 1969. This is a very wide protection offered to bankers, as there is no requirement that they need act without negligence nor with good faith; nor is there any need that the order be crossed.
61. Post Office Act 1969, s. 70(2). Until a few years ago, the Post Office issued, in addition to "postal" orders, documents of a similar nature, called "money" orders. "Money" orders were issued for amounts larger than "postal" orders, and the formalities of obtaining them were slightly different. As there was no definition of "postal" or "money" orders it is not clear why a distinction was made, and indeed it is the opinion of at least one eminent authority that "postal orders are money orders in a special form": Byles, *Bills of Exchange*, 26th edn. (1988), p. 349. Although both the 1953 and 1969 Acts speak of "money" orders as though they were different documents from "postal" orders.
62. Treasury Bills Act 1877 and see the Treasury Bills Regulations 1968, SI 1968/414 and SI 1991/1667.
63. *Wookey v. Pole* (1820) 106 ER 839.

(iv) Bankers' drafts

These are drafts drawn usually by a branch of a bank upon its head office. They are recognized and treated as cash, and are used extensively by solicitors and businessmen for the payment of purchase money at the completion of property transactions.

They are not strictly bills of exchange, and they are certainly not cheques.[64] However, a banker's draft being drawn by a branch on its head office brings it within s. 5(2) of the Bills of Exchange Act 1882. "That section means in my opinion that where there is a document in the form of a bill of exchange, but which is not a bill of exchange . . . because the drawer and the intended drawee are the same person . . . the holder may, at his option, treat it as though it were a bill of exchange . . . or he may treat it as being what it is not—namely a promissory note."[65]

However, they are freely negotiable (unless restricted) and can be indorsed in the usual way. It is sometimes thought they cannot be "stopped", but this is not so; therefore, the loss of a draft is not catastrophic, *providing* notice is given to the bank before an attempted encashment takes place.

BANKNOTES

In conclusion, something must be said of banknotes, which are, of course, currency of the Realm. In fact they are promissory notes issued by the Bank of England which alone has the right to issue to bearer bills of exchange or promissory notes payable on demand.[66]

They pass freely by delivery and without indorsement,[67] and consequently each transferor is a "transferor by delivery" within the meaning of s. 58 of

64. But see *per* Bailhache J in *Ross v. London & County Bank* [1919] 1 KB 678, at p. 687; and *per* Bigham J in *Brown, Brough & Co v. National Bank of India* (1902) 18 TLR 669, 670.

65. *Per* Romer LJ in *Re British Trade Corp* [1932] 2 Ch 1, at p. 14.

66. Bank Charter Act 1844, ss. 10 and 28, and see s. 97(3)(*c*) of the Bills of Exchange Act 1882. The Bank of England, which was founded in 1694, has occupied an omnipotent position in our banking system for a great many years, yet it was not until the Bank of England Act 1946 (when it was nationalized) that it attained the power to *direct* monetary policy to the commercial banks, which formerly followed the directions of the Bank, but without being obliged to do so.

67. Before 1957 £5 notes were printed on white paper and were much larger in size than those in use today. These ceased to be issued on 20 February 1957 and ceased to be legal tender on 14 March 1961. There grew up a curious custom of asking the transferor to sign his name or put his initials on the back of the note, as a token, presumably, of its *bona fides* and that it was not a forgery. In the days before inflation took over, a £5 note was rarely handled by the ordinary man-in-the-street, and even for shopkeepers they were not a daily occurrence. Presumably, if something did go wrong, the person whose signature was on the note would have been liable as an indorser (see *supra* p. 70). It was not usual to include one's address which may have caused problems in tracing the transferor and it was not uncommon to find more than one set of initials on a £5 note. The practice was dying out long before the notes were changed to their present form. For an interesting case involving the initialling of £5 notes, see Sir Patrick Hastings, *Cases in Court* (Heinemann) at pp. 166 *et seq.*

the Bills of Exchange Act 1882, and is liable only to the person to whom he gave the note. So that if X gives his garage a £5 note for petrol, who in turn gives it as change to another customer Y, if it transpires to be a forgery, X is liable only to his garage, and the garage is liable only to Y. This is of considerable significance since usually it will be impossible for the garage to remember from where the "dud" note came. Any tampering with a banknote makes it void against the Bank of England,[68] and of course they are not liable to pay out on a forgery at all.

Banknotes can, of course, be reissued freely after payment, unlike "ordinary" promissory notes.

Technically, if a banknote is lost it can be "stopped", but this is of little or no practical signifance, as rarely will the unfortunate loser know the number of the note or notes; and, in any event, he will be required to give an indemnity which would put him back exactly where he started.

68. *Suffell v. Bank of England* (1882) 9 QBD 555.

SECTION FOUR

BANKERS' DOCUMENTARY CREDITS

CHAPTER 15

THE CREDIT IN OPERATION

No book on the subject of bills of exchange would be complete without some mention of bankers' documentary credits—or letters of credit, as they are frequently called. This is for two reasons. First, payments under credits are, as often as not, made by the use of bills of exchange as an integral part of the transaction; and, secondly, many of the rules applicable to bills of exchange apply equally to letters of credit, the "cash equivalence" principle being one important example. In the words of Lord Denning MR[1]:

A letter of credit is like a bill of exchange given for the price of goods. It ranks as cash and must be honoured. No set-off or counterclaim is allowed to detract from it. All the more so with a letter of credit. Whereas a bill of exchange is given by buyer to seller, a letter of credit is given by a bank to the seller with the very intention of avoiding anything in the nature of a set-off or counterclaim.

We noted earlier,[2] that almost every country in the world has recognized a standard code, sponsored by the International Chamber of Commerce (ICC) for dealing with letters of credit. This code is called "The Uniform Customs and Practice for Documentary Credits" (UCP), and the most recent revision numbered 500, came into force on 1 January 1994. The Series 400 which is being superseded will, of course, remain effective in respect of bankers' documentary credits in existence prior to that date and which make reference to the Series 400 publication.[3]

METHOD OF OPERATION

As we have seen earlier, sellers of goods are, understandably, wary of shipping to buyers they do not know, in some far off country; payment might never be made. Equally, buyers are wary, as they do not want to pay for goods which might never arrive. Lengthy litigation, which could well be abortive, might then ensue in the case of either party. So, businessmen have introduced a

1. *Power Curber International Ltd* v. *National Bank of Kuwait SAK* [1981] 1 WLR 1233, at p. 1241B.
2. See *supra*, Chap. 10.
3. ICC Publishing SA, 38 Cours Albert 1ᵉʳ, 75008 Paris.

method of payment between the buyer's and the seller's banks which, in most cases, removes the risks and complications.[4]

Over the years the system has become quite sophisticated but, stripped of its trappings, it works like this:[5]

(1) The buyer (who has to pay for the goods) makes an application (the application is on a standard printed form) to his bank (called "the issuing bank") to issue a letter of credit in favour of the seller.

(2) The seller (who is called "the beneficiary" under the credit) instructs his bank[6] to receive the funds in payment of the goods.

(3) The issuing bank then arranges with a bank (called "the advising bank"[7]) in the seller's country to "advise" the seller that the credit is open and on what terms.

(4) The advising bank may do no more than "advise" the existence of the credit, and if so, it has no further reponsibility in the transaction than to take reasonable care to check the apparent authenticity of the credit.[8] If, however, the advising bank cannot establish the apparent authenticity, it must so inform the issuing bank without delay.[9]

(5) It may be, however, that the advising bank has been asked ("nominated" is the word used) by the issuing bank, not only to advise the existence of the credit, but also to effect payment to the seller's bank. In which case the advising bank will also become "the nominated bank",[10] and if it accepts the responsibility to pay,[11] the advising/nominated bank will also become "the paying bank".

(6) What frequently happens in practice is that the seller asks the issuing bank to arrange with a bank in the seller's country to "confirm" the letter of credit, thus enabling the seller to have confirmation from a bank in his own country that payment will be forthcoming, rather than relying on the standing of the issuing bank in the buyer's country.

4. But see *Mannesman Handel AG v. Kaunlaran Shipping Corp* [1993] 1 Lloyd's Rep. 89, where the documents proved to be false, and the bank in Switzerland failed to perform its obligations, and withheld payment contrary to good faith.
5. For the definition of the transaction in UCP, see Art. 2.
6. Throughout, when reference is made to money being received by "the seller", it will, in practice, be received by his bank.
7. Very frequently referred to as "the correspondent bank", but not in the UCP, which always uses "the advising bank", which term is adopted here throughout.
8. UCP, Art. 7a.
9. UCP 7b. If in spite of not being able to establish the apparent authenticity, the advising bank elects to advise the credit, the advising bank must inform the beneficiary that the authenticity has not been established.
10. Since every credit must "nominate" a bank for the purpose of payment: UPC, Art. 10(*b*)(i).
11. Without accepting the obligation to pay, the mere fact of being "nominated" does not constitute any undertaking to pay under the credit: UPC, Art. 10(*c*).

(7) It often happens that the advising/nominated bank will also be invited to "confirm" the credit, and if it accepts, it will also become "the confirming bank".[12]

(8) Sometimes another bank in the seller's country is invited to confirm, and, in such a case, it will become "the confirming bank". If a credit is "confirmed", the confirming bank will be the bank which effects payment, and, hence, "the paying bank" also.

(9) All payments under letters of credit are effected either by a straight-forward transfer of funds between the banks, once the goods are shipped; or by the drawing of a bill of exchange either to be accepted by the paying bank (thereby becoming "the accepting bank" as well); or by that bank negotiating the bill (it would then be "the negotiating bank") on behalf of the seller. In either case, the seller—using a bill of exchange—will get his money without waiting for the goods to arrive.

(10) The paying bank will not, of course, pay until it is satisfied that it has in its possession the various documents of title to the goods (bill of lading, insurance policy and so forth), as agreed between the buyer and the seller as being the trigger mechanism for payment,[13] since these will, ultimately, be sent to the issuing bank as its security while the goods are in transit.

(11) When the documents are received by the issuing bank, it will re-imburse the paying bank for the money paid out to the seller. The documents give title to the goods so that the buyer can receive delivery of them; and, at the same time, the documents also give the issuing bank security for any money or finance it has extended to its customer, the buyer.

Continuity of performance

It is vital, of course, that this credit facility opened by the issuing bank (the buyer's bank) cannot be stopped halfway through the transaction (for exam-ple, once the goods have been shipped), otherwise the seller would be left in an exposed position, having parted with the goods, but having no security for payment.[14] To cover this point, the banking community has developed the "irrevocable" letter of credit, the intention of which, as the name implies,

12. It is quite possible, therefore, for the advising bank also to be the nominated bank, the confirming bank and the paying bank.

13. It is possible for the seller to obtain payment in advance of shipping with the consent of the buyer by having a provision to that effect in the credit. Understandably, this is not very common, and, in days gone by, it used to be written in red ink—it is still called a "Red Clause" credit. A "Green Clause" credit, in addition to advances, also covers storage charges for the account of the bank.

14. For an example of the disasters which can befall a seller under a revocable credit, see *Cape Asbestos Co v. Lloyds Bank* [1921] WN 274.

means it cannot be recalled once given. It is, of course, possible to have a "revocable" letter of credit,[15] but the value of such a document is, to say the least, limited as it can be stopped at will,[16] leaving the seller with his right to sue, which, of course, was what he was trying to avoid in the first place!

Variations on the theme

There are a number of variations in the terms of letters of credit to meet the needs of businessmen, depending upon the requirements of any given transaction.

We saw above that the more usual form is the credit that is both "irrevocable" and "confirmed"; but there can be irrevocable letters of credit that are not "confirmed". Equally, there can be letters of credit that are revocable (that is not "irrevocable") and unconfirmed, or—although unlikely in practice—"confirmed", depending on the needs of the particular transaction.[17]

In addition to these variations, a form of credit that is used often is the "revolving" letter of credit. This is opened with the buyer's bank where the buyer needs an on-going facility, up to an agreed maximum, which will, without any further formality, be renewed over and over again in favour of a named seller to the total agreed value of the facility. This is similar to an instalment credit, which is, however, less flexible, and where the schedule of shipping and payments is agreed upon from the beginning of the transaction.[18]

Of course, the need to provide documentation for each shipment is exactly the same as any other form of such a facility.

Then again, where goods are to be sold and re-sold through several middlemen (sometimes referred to as "string contracts"), it is common to find that each party opens a credit dependent on the others on a back-to-back basis.[19] The whole arrangement is, of course, based on the credit opened by the ultimate purchaser. This final, or "overriding", credit is the one to which all parties will look for the strength of the transaction; but, of course, each and every contract in the chain is separate, and results in independent legal obligations.

15. UCP Art. 6(b). All credits should state clearly whether they are revocable or irrevocable, otherwise they will be irrevocable: sub-para. (c).

16. "A revocable credit may be amended or cancelled by the issuing bank at any moment and without prior notice to the beneficiary": UCP, Art. 8(a); but issuing bank must reimburse paying bank if they paid before notice of cancellation: Art. 8(b).

17. It is possible to confirm a credit issued by an organization which is not a bank: *Barclays Bank Ltd* v. *Mercantile National Bank* [1973] 2 Lloyd's Rep. 541.

18. It must be observed that depending on how the terms are written, the difference between a revolving credit and an instalment credit is sometimes hardly discernable to the naked eye.

19. Sometimes called "countervailing" credits. For an example of how the system works, see *Ian Stack Ltd* v. *Baker Bosley Ltd* [1958] 2 QB 130.

Letters of credit can, of course, be made "transferable",[20] that is, they can be drawn stating clearly that the seller (being the ultimate beneficiary under the credit) has the right to transfer the benefit of the credit to some third party, who will receive the money instead of the seller. This could be used, for example, where the seller owed money to *his* supplier. This type to credit must, of course, have the consent of the buyer in the first place, and he is in no way obliged to provide a transferable credit unless he has specifically agreed to do so[21]; nor is a bank obliged to effect a transfer unless it also expressly consents.[22] It must be noted that under Uniform Customs, Art. 48(g) a transferable credit can be transferred once only, unless partial shipments are not prohibited; in which case, fractions of a credit (not exceeding the total value of course) can be transferred separately.[23]

No summary of the types and terms of letters of credit would be complete unless reference were made to the "standby" letter of credit: it is, in fact, not a letter of credit at all! It is a performance guarantee, and is sometimes demanded of a seller by a buyer who feels the seller may not perform on time, or, perhaps at all.[24] Alternatively, it may be demanded by a seller who has to manufacture specialist goods, and is worried that by the time the documentary credit is due to be opened—perhaps months after the main supply contract was signed—the buyer will either be unable to comply, or has changed his mind about the goods altogether.

METHOD OF PAYMENT

Article 10(a) of the Uniform Customs provides that:

All credits must clearly indicate whether they are available by sight payment, by deferred payment, by acceptance or by negotiation.

This means that a credit has to make clear how the paying bank is to effect payment to the correspondent bank. As will be seen from the wording of this

20. See UPC, Art. 48(*a*).
21. A letter of credit may still be assigned, under the provisions of s. 136 of the Law of Property Act 1925 (as to which see *supra*, p. 230), even though it is not drawn as being transferable. The reason being that a letter of credit is a chose in action, and, hence, is freely assignable as such. UCP, Art. 49 provides that even if a credit is not stated to be transferable, it does not affect the beneficiary's right to assign the proceeds.
22. UCP, Art. 48(*c*). See *Bank Negra Indonesia 1946* v. *Lariza (Singapore) Pty Ltd* [1988] 1 WLR 374 (PC).
23. *Ibid.*, Art. 48(*b*) states, "A credit can be transferred only if it is expressly designated as 'transferable' by the issuing bank. Terms such as 'divisable', 'fractionable', 'assignable' and 'transmissible' do not render the credit transferable. If such terms are used they shall be disregarded." But see *European Asian Bank AG* v. *Punjab and Sind Bank* [1983] 1 Lloyd's Rep. 611, where the court were prepared to accept that a credit marked "divisable" (in fact the word used was "divisionable") meant "transferable".
24. See UCP Arts. 1 and 2. Art. 1 states that the UCP rules apply to Standby Letters of Credit, "to the extent to which they may be applicable".

paragraph, there are three possible methods to effect payment under a letter of credit.

(a) By payment credit

Under a payment credit, the nominated bank is required to pay to the beneficiary (seller) on one of two bases either by:

(1) *Sight payment*, which is essentially "cash against documents". The seller takes the shipping documents to the bank, and, if all is well, payment will be effected immediately. Other than "cash with order", this must be the best terms possible for the seller unless there was to be a Red Clause credit—effectively, "cash before order". In such a case, the buyer has to fund the purchase immediately, and carry whatever risks are involved in paying in this way.

(2) *Deferred payment*, on the other hand, is the equivalent of "cash on delivery", whereby the seller has to ship in advance of payment, or at any rate full payment, the terms being "deferred". Here the risk is on the seller, and he has no security that he will be paid in full at the end of the transaction.

Unless both buyer and seller know one another, and are confident of their dealings, payment credits will probably not be used, and this is where the bill of exchange, coupled with the documentary credit, comes into play.

(b) By acceptance credit

This form of payment is usually accomplished by the buyer arranging for the seller to receive an irrevocable documentary acceptance credit. Put technically, the issuing bank (or some other bank under arrangements with the issuing bank) undertakes irrevocably to accept bills drawn on it by the seller at, say, 90 days or, perhaps, 120 days after sight (acceptance) provided that the bill is accompanied by satisfactory documents.

Based on the strength of the issuing bank's acceptance, the seller will then be able to discount the bill in the market and receive payment at shipment, rather than waiting until the goods are received by the buyer.

What happens is that the seller sends the bill he has drawn, together with the shipping documents, to the bank nominated in the credit as the acceptor, whether this is the issuing bank or some other. If all is, or seems to be, in order, the accepting bank will accept the bill and pass it back to the seller, to enable him to discount it in the market, thus obtaining immediate payment of the value of the bill, less interest and charges.

The accepting bank retains the documents, and passes them to the issuing bank (the bill is then in circulation without the documents), for onward transmission to the buyer to enable him to obtain the goods when they arrive.

In due time, the accepting bank will pay the bill at maturity and be reimbursed by the issuing bank.

(c) By negotiation credit

Again, a bill of exchange is used, only here there is no acceptance, and the seller gets his money by the bank negotiating the bill on behalf of the seller, subject, as before, to the usual charges and commissions.

The negotiating bank takes its authority from the terms of the credit, and, as such, is the agent of the issuing bank.

As with the acceptance credit, the seller will draw a bill and present it, together with the shipping documents, to the nominated bank where the credit is stated to be available, and, after verifying that the documents and the bill are in order, the bank will negotiate the bill on behalf of the seller, and pass the funds to him under the terms of the credit.

ENCASHING THE BILL

As we have observed, bills of exchange can be encashed prior to maturity under the terms of a letter of credit either by discounting or negotiating. If a bill of exchange is not part of a documentary credit, it can still be discounted or negotiated, but if the collecting bank (that is, the holder's bank) has any doubts on the standing of the bill it will simply pass it through for collection in the same way as it would a cheque, taking no responsibility for it other than in that capacity.

The ICC Uniform Rules for Collections

Where the seller of goods wishes to encash his bill before maturity, whether it is part of a documentary credit or not, the basic procedure is the same, and is, in general, governed by the ICC "Uniform Rules for Collections" (URC), the current edition of which came into force on 1 January 1996.[25]

It must be noted that some of the rules apply only to "documentary collections", in other words, to discounting or negotiating under the terms of a letter of credit, while some other of the rules apply whether the bill of exchange is part of a credit or not.

As might be expected, there are a number of definitions stated in the rules which govern their application, and which must be noted before proceeding to consider the rules proper.

A "collection"[26] means the handling by banks, of documents as defined in accordance with instructions received, in order to:

25. See *supra*, Chap. 10, where the subject is first mentioned.
26. URC Art. 2a.

(a) obtain payment and/or acceptance; or

(b) deliver documents against payment and/or against acceptance; or

(c) deliver documents on other terms and conditions.

"Documents" means financial documents and/or commercial documents:

(a) "Financial documents" means bills of exchange, promissory notes, cheques, or other similar instruments used for obtaining the payment of money;

(b) "Commercial documents" means invoices, transport documents, documents of title or other similar documents, or any other documents whatsoever, not being financial documents.

This definition is new, and is intended to show that these collections are those handled *by banks*; and while the Rules may apply to transactions not routed through banks, it may well be the Rules in such cases may not strictly apply. This would be exceptional, of course, but, because of the new definition it is not inconceivable.

As all practitioners know, with the advent of Electronic Data Interchange (EDI Collections), many problems are yet to be resolved, and the ICC Working Party on these new rules felt it was not feasible to make rules at the present time to cover these matters. No doubt in time, these rules will be forthcoming.

The rules speak of a "clean" collection when only financial documents are being handled, and a "documentary" collection when commercial documents are being dealt with, whether or not accompanied by financial documents.[27]

The parties to a collection as referred to in the rules[28] are these:

"The Principal", who is the customer entrusting the operation of collection to his ("the remitting") bank. He will be the seller of goods, and the party who wants to be paid.

"The Drawee" is the party to whom presentation is to be made under the terms of the collection.[29]

"The Collecting Bank" is any bank (other than the "remitting bank") involved in the processing of the collection instructions, and is referred to as the "presenting bank" when making presentation to the drawee.

"The Remitting Bank" is the bank to which the principal has entrusted the collection. It is this bank who wish to receive the remittance on behalf of their customer—the principal.

---

27. *Ibid.*, Art. 2c and d.

28. *Ibid.*, Art. 3.

29. *Ibid.*, Art. 3b. There is no definition of the term "drawee" in the Bills of Exchange Act 1882.

The position of the banks

The principal, being the seller of the goods and the person who wants payment, will instruct his ("the remitting') bank to arrange with a bank in the buyer's country (it could be the issuing bank under a documentary credit) to obtain acceptance or payment. This is the "collecting bank".

The documents and instructions (technically called the "Collection Instruction") can be sent from the remitting bank to the collecting bank directly, or through another bank or branch as an intermediary.

Whenever one bank uses the services of another bank in these transactions it does so for the account, and at the risk, of the principal, who must indemnify the bank against all obligations and responsibilities imposed by the laws and usages of the country in which they operate.[30]

Form of presentation

The Uniform Rules provides in Article 5 new procedures for the presentation of documents. As ever, these rules are detailed, but may be summarised briefly as follows:

(1) The remitting bank will use the nominated collecting bank, but if none is mentioned, it can use any bank of its choice in the country of payment or acceptance, or in any country where terms and conditions have to be complied with.

(2) If the remitting bank does not nominate a presenting bank, the collecting bank can use any bank of its choice.

(3) Documents should be presented in the form in which they are received, except of course, that banks can make endorsements or stamps or identifying marks as customary or required for the collection operation.

(4) The Collection Instruction should state the exact period of time within which any action is to be taken.

Liability of the banks

The banks must, of course, exercise reasonable care,[31] but otherwise under the provisions of Art. 14b of the Uniform Rules, they disclaim liability and responsibility for

---

30. URC, Art. 11a and c. If the collecting bank or drawee bank has to "create" documents, whether Bills of Exchange, Promissory Notes, Trust Receipts, Letters of Undertaking or whatever, because they were not included in the Collection Instruction they are not responsible for the form of wording they provide, because that is the responsibility of the remitting bank: URC Art. 8. Presumably however, the party drafting such documents must use reasonable care and skill.

31. Art. 9. They must also act in good faith, which is usually taken for granted.

... the consequences arising out of delay and/or loss in transit of any messages, letters or documents, or for delay mutilation or other errors arising in the transmission of any telecommunication[32] or for errors in translation or interpretation of technical terms.

Article 14b of the Rules is new, and attempts to extend the banks' disclaimer for "any delays resulting from the need to obtain clarification of any instructions received". In other words, what is being said is that if a bank in its judgement needs to clarify a point, this will almost certainly involve *some* delay, and the bank making these further enquiries ought not to be responsible for the consequences, whatever they may be, of such delay in dealing with the transaction.

Article 13 (which seems to be based largely on Article 15 of the Uniform Customs) is also new, and goes further by attempting to negative the banks' liability for "the form, sufficiency, accuracy, genuineness, falsification or legal effect of any document(s), or for the general and/or particular conditions stipulated in the document(s) or superimposed thereon; nor do they assume any liability or responsibility for the description, quantity, weight, quality, condition, packing, delivery, value or existence of the goods represented by any document(s), or for the good faith or acts and/or omissions, solvency, performance or standing of the consignors, the carriers, the forwarders, the consignees or the insurers of the goods, or any other person whomsover".

This attempt by the Uniform Rules to negative banks' liability in this way could be subject to question under English law. The topic is discussed subsequently[33] when considering similar provisions in the Uniform Customs. In essence, the same comments apply here as obtain in the case of the Uniform Customs.

Again, Art. 15 of the Uniform Rules attempts to excuse the banks from liability for what is called "*force majeure*" situations, being Acts of God, riots, civil commotions and so forth. The Uniform Customs contain similar provisions on this topic also,[34] and the comments on these made subsequently[35] also apply with equal force here.

As we have seen above, banks also refuse responsibility for the genuineness of any signature on bills of exchange[36] or promissory notes or other similar documents.[37]

Some of these attempts to excuse liability may be questionable. However, it is quite reasonable that banks should not be liable or in any way responsible for the goods under a documentary collection.[38] Certainly, unless there is a

---

32. See the use of the word "teletransmissions" in Art. 11 of the Uniform Customs.
33. See *infra*, Chap. 16, under the heading "Limitation of Liability".
34. UCP, Art. 17.
35. See *infra*, Chap. 16, under the heading "Limitation of Liability".
36. URC, Art. 22.
37. *Ibid.*, Art. 23. Nor if instructions they transmit are not carried out, even if the bank issuing the instructions has chosen the other bank which is in default: URC Art. 11b. This Article is new, and is based, no doubt, on the similar provisions of UCP Art. 18b.
38. *Ibid.*, Art. 10a.

prior agreement, a bank has no obligation to take delivery of goods, which must, at all times, remain at the risk and responsibility of the party dispatching them.[39] Moreover, if banks do take any action for the protection of goods, whether on instructions or not, they assume no liability or responsibility for them, nor for the acts or omissions of third parties entrusted with their custody, such as warehousekeepers. There is an obligation on the collecting bank to inform the remitting bank or the principal of any action taken, since all charges and expenses in connection with the protection of goods is for the account of the principal.[40]

The collection instruction

All documents sent for collection must be accompanied by a "Collection Instruction". This is a most vital document in the transaction since it is prepared by the principal and must give "complete and precise" instructions to the banks, which are permitted to act upon those instructions only.[41] If a bank finds itself unable to comply with these instructions it must advise its customer or the instructing bank without delay.[42]

Article 4b specifies the details the Collection Instruction should contain, and those details are comprehensive, the purpose being that the Collecting Banks should not need to look elsewhere for instructions, such as by examining the documents which are received. Indeed, Article 4a(ii) states that "Banks will not examine documents in order to obtain instructions".

In addition, the Collection Instruction should:

(a) Bear the complete address of the drawee, or of the domicile at which presentation is to be made. If the address is incomplete or incorrect and the collecting bank endeavours to find the proper address, it does so without any responsibility;[43] and

(b) Give specific instructions regarding protest (or other legal process in lieu) in the event of non-acceptance or non-payment[44]; and

(c) Indicate clearly and fully the powers of any representative nominated by the principal to act as a "case-of-need"[45] in the event of non--

---

39. URC, Art. 10a and b.

40. *Ibid.*, Art. 10c and d. Notwithstanding the fact that goods should not be despatched to a bank, if they are sent to the collecting bank, and the drawee has honoured the collection by payment or whatever, and the collecting bank arranges the release of the goods, the remitting bank shall be deemed to have authorised the release and must idemnify the collecting bank for all damages and expenses: Art. 10d and e.

41. And in accordance with the Uniform Rules, of course: URC Art. 4a(i).

42. URC Art. 1c.

43. *Ibid.*, Art. 4c(i).

44. *Ibid.*, Art. 24. In the absence of such instructions the banks have no obligation to have the documents protested.

45. As to "referees in case of need", see *supra*, Chap. 8, under the heading "Acceptance and payment for honour".

acceptance or non-payment. It goes without saying the banks will not accept instructions from a person not duly empowered.[46]

(d) State (in respect of a "documentary collection") whether the documents are to be released upon the acceptance of the bill of exchange ("D/A" terms), or whether they are to be released only against payment ("D/P" terms). In the absence of such instructions they will be released only against payment.[47]

The collection instruction should also state any special terms agreed between the parties and which the principal wishes to be demanded as a condition precedent to release of the documents, such as payment of interest,[48] or charges.[49]

The presenting bank must ensure that the documents mentioned in the Collection Instruction are as listed, and if not (as is referred to often in the new Rules) they must advise the remitting bank (from whom the instructions were received) without delay of any documents that are missing. The collecting bank has no further obligation,[50] and may present the documents "as received" without further examination.[51] In fact, if the documents do not appear as listed, the remitting bank is precluded from disputing "the type and number of documents received by the collecting bank."[52] Effectively therefore, the remitting bank is being made responsible for any such documents being lost in the mail or whatever.

The only other obligation on the presenting bank is to see that the form of an acceptance[53] of a Bill of Exchange appears to be complete and correct, but it is not responsible for the genuineness of any signature or for the authority of any signatory to sign the acceptance, or a Promissory Note or other similar documents.[54]

Payment of bills under collection

Bills of exchange will obviously be payable either:

(1) In the (local) currency where payment is to be effected, and in which case the presenting bank, unless otherwise instructed in the collection instruction, must only release the documents against payment in that

46. URC, Art. 25.
47. *Ibid.*, Art. 7b.
48. *Ibid.*, Art. 20.
49. *Ibid.*, Art. 21.
50. *Ibid.*, Art. 12a.
51. *Ibid.*, Art. 12c.
52. *Ibid.*, Art. 12b.
53. *Ibid.*, Art. 22.
54. *Ibid.*, Art. 23. Note also that, as is mentioned in various new rules, the presenting bank is not responsible for the consequences arising out of any delay in the delivery of documents.

currency, which is immediately available for disposal in the manner specified in the collection order,[55] or

(2) In some other currency, in which case the documents should only be released against payment in the appropriate currency which can immediately be remitted in accordance with the instructions given in the collection order.[56]

Under a documentary collection, partial payments will only be accepted if authorized in the collection instruction, and a presenting bank will only release documents against full payment, unless specifically instructed.[57]

In the case of clean collections, partial payments may be accepted " . . . if and to the extent to which and on the conditions on which partial payments are authorized by the law in force in the place of payment".[58] However, no matter what the law says, the documents will only be released when full payment has been received.[59] Any amounts collected, less charges and/or disbursements and/or expenses where applicable, must be made available without delay to the bank from which the collection instruction was received in accordance with the instructions contained in the collection instruction.[60]

Presentation for payment at sight must be made "without delay", and otherwise not later than the appropriate maturity date.[61]

Collecting banks are obliged to advise "fate", that is whether payment or otherwise has been effected in accordance with the following rules:

1. Form of advice

All advices must bear appropriate detail, including the remitting bank's reference number as stated in the collection instruction.[62]

2. Method of advice

It is the responsibility of the remitting bank to inform the collecting bank of the method (telecommunications or whatever) by which it wants the advice to be given; and if the remitting bank does not do so, the collecting bank can choose whichever method of communication it likes, and charge the remitting bank accordingly.[63]

55. URC, Art. 17.
56. *Ibid.*, Art. 18.
57. *Ibid.*, Art. 19b.
58. *Ibid.*, Art. 19a.
59. *Ibid.*, Art. 19a. Documents will only be released to the drawee when funds are readily available: URC Art. 19c, and Arts. 17 and 18.
60. *Ibid.*, Art. 16a. Unless otherwise agreed, the collecting bank will effect payment of the amount collected in favour of the remitting bank only: URC Art. 16b.
61. *Ibid.*, Art. 6.
62. *Ibid.*, Art. 26a. Which rules also apply to acceptances: URC Art. 26c(ii).
63. *Ibid.*, Art. 26b.

3. Advice of payment

The collecting bank must send, without delay, advice of payment, detailing: (a) the amount collected; (b) charges and/or disbursements and/or expenses deducted; (c) method of disposal of the funds, where appropriate.[64]

4. Advice of non-payment

The collecting bank must send, without delay, advice of non-payment, with the reasons therefor if possible.[65]

Where interest is being claimed, if the parties have agreed unconditionally in the bill of exchange or other financial document, that interest will be paid, and there is a clear clause to that effect in the collection instruction, then that amount (that is, both principal and interest) is deemed part of the sum to be collected for release of the documents.[66] If the parties have not reached a clear understanding as to the payment of interest and charges, the party looking for payment may try to impose his will by an instruction in the collection instruction that interest should be collected.[67] Indeed, payment of interest, charges and expenses often causes problems.

Disputes usually arise between the bank presenting the "collection instruction" (and requiring payment), and the drawee bank, who are faced with a demand for payment of interest or charges which they have no immediate instructions from their customer (the buyer of the goods) to make.

It is always possible, unless the collection instruction expressly states that interest[68] or charges[69] may not be waived, for the presenting bank to deliver the documents against payment or acceptance without collecting the interest or charges as the case may be.[70]

In the case of both payment of interest and charges, if the collection instruction provides that payment cannot be waived, and the drawee bank refuses to pay, the presenting bank must[71] not deliver the documents; there will then, doubtless, be a further argument involving not only the banks, but the buyer and the seller, however, the presenting bank "will not be responsible for any consequences arising out of any delay in the delivery of the documents". The

---

64. URC, Art. 26c(i).

65. If the instructions from the remitting bank have not been received within 60 days (under URC 322 it was 90 days) from the advice, the documents can be returned: URC, Art. 26c(iii).

66. Strangely, the wording of Arts. 20 and 21 of the new URC is not so specific as the former Art. 21 on this point.

67. In such a case, the collection instruction must state both the rate of interest, the period covered and the basis of calculation: URC, Art. 20b.

68. *Ibid.*, Art. 20c.

69. *Ibid.*, Art. 21b.

70. *Ibid.*, Arts. 20a and 21a.

71. *Ibid.*, Arts. 20 and 21b says the presenting bank "will not" deliver the documents.

presenting bank must without delay inform the bank from whom their instructions came, that payment has been refused; this must be by telecommunication, or if that is not possible "by other expeditious means".[72]

In the case of charges, it may well be that the collecting bank, if they have been requested to assist with arrangements for delivery of goods, has had to make payment to third parties, for example, for carriage or customs duties. In such cases, where the collection instruction provides for the payment of such charges, the presenting bank "can recover promptly" such disbursements from the bank from which their instructions came.[73]

Indeed, banks may demand payment of charges in advance from the bank from which the collection instruction came, and pending receipt of such payment, they can reserve the right not to carry out those instructions.[74]

Structuring the transaction—Part II

We have noted earlier[75] how a transaction involving a bill of exchange can be structured, and the same general comments apply with regard to bills as a means of payment under documentary credits.

How the bill is to be drawn is a matter for agreement between the buyer and the seller of the goods, and the banks concerned in the transaction, but, as examples, the format could take any of the following:

1. If it is an acceptance credit, the seller may draw the bill in one of two ways:

   (a) In favour of the buyer as payee, on the accepting bank, as drawee. Then the seller will send it to the buyer to obtain his (the buyer's) indorsement, which will be "special" in favour of the seller. The bill will then be passed by the buyer to his (the issuing) bank for acceptance, or, depending upon the terms of credit, passed on to the accepting bank. Once this formality is accomplished, the bill will be returned to the seller for discounting, as already described. The discounting house will, of course, require the seller to indorse in blank, before delivering the bill and receiving payment. The advantage of drawing the bill in this way is that the seller not only has the acceptance of the bank, but also the indorsement of the buyer, who is thereby liable on the bill.

   (b) In favour of himself as payee, on the accepting bank as drawee. He will then indorse the bill in blank, and present it to the accepting bank, together with the shipping documents, for acceptance and return to the seller for discounting. This way is quicker, as the buyer

72. URC, Arts. 20c and 21b.
73. *Ibid.*, Art. 21.
74. *Ibid.*, Art. 21d.
75. See *supra*, part I, Chap. 4.

of the goods is eliminated from this part of the transaction, but it could open the door for disputes at the behest of the buyer subsequently if there were problems with the goods, since he would not be liable on the bill. The buyer would, of course, be liable to his (the issuing) bank under the agreement contained in the application for the credit.

2. If the bill is to be negotiated, the seller draws the bill in his own favour as payee, on the buyer as drawee. The seller will then present the bill, together with the shipping documents, to the negotiating bank. The bank will require the seller to indorse the bill in blank, thus enabling the bank to obtain title, before payment to the seller. The negotiating bank will then send the bill (and documents) to the issuing bank, which will obtain the buyer's acceptance to the bill. By this method, the seller is liable on the bill as drawer and indorser, and the buyer as drawee and acceptor.

METHODS OF ENCASHING THE BILL

We have already noted above that a bill of exchange can be encashed before maturity either by: 1. Discounting; or 2. Negotiation.

Each method must now be considered in a little more detail.

1. *Discounting*[76]

By discounting we mean "selling" the bill to a bank or a finance house, after it has been accepted, so that the strength of the bill will depend almost entirely on the strength of the acceptor. We have seen that discounting is almost always restricted to cases where a bank has accepted under an irrevocable documentary acceptance, though it is possible to arrange a discounting outside a credit, if, within the transaction there is, for example, a prime corporation which could be the acceptor.

Within an irrevocable documentary acceptance credit, the seller will obtain his acceptance, as we have described above. In fact, as we have noted several times before, all these steps are carried out by the banking community, so that the seller's (the presenting) bank is responsible for seeing that the form of the acceptance of the bill of exchange appears to be complete and correct, but is not responsible for the genuineness of any signature or for the authority of any signatory signing the acceptance.[77] The presenting bank must, of course, make presentation for acceptance "without delay".[78]

---

76. Banking terminology speaks of a bill being "discounted" if the seller (the drawer) pays the charges, and "purchased" if the drawee pays them, thus allowing the full value of the bill to pass to the seller. Legally, there is no difference between the two references.

77. URC, Art. 22. The same applies to a promissory note or other similar instrument: URC, Art. 23.

78. *Ibid.*, Art. 6.

Once the acceptance is available, the seller will be in a position to discount his bill (technically now called "an acceptance") in the market. He will do this by taking the acceptance to a finance house or a bank, and he will indorse it to them; they become the owners of the bill (they will, in fact, be holders in due course, as we have seen), and they will pay out the seller—he is at this stage both the seller of the goods under the main contract and seller of the bill.

The finance house being the new holders will, probably, retain the bill until maturity and then present it for payment to the accepting bank; however, they may themselves negotiate the bill to another finance house, and it would be this second holder who would ultimately claim payment. In fact, the bill, once it is accepted in this way, could pass through various hands before it is finally presented for payment. This is why finance houses or banks would not accept restrictive indorsements on a bill, as this would render subsequent negotiation impossible.

It must also be remembered that at this stage the bill is divorced from the other documents relating to the goods. The bill will, of course, have to be paid by the acceptor, who, in turn, will recover from the issuing bank (if they are not the same), and that bank will recover from the buyer of the goods, no matter what the fate of the goods may be.

2. Negotiation

This is similar to discounting, but is carried out where the seller sells his bill *before* acceptance.

Outside the terms of a documentary credit, negotiation of a bill of exchange is usually done with the seller's own bank, rather than with a finance house, since—without the existence of an acceptance—the finance house buying the bill will be relying substantially on the creditworthiness of the seller to reimburse if the bill should subsequently be dishonoured. Certainly, if there is any doubt about the bill, the bank will not buy it, and will simply send it through for collection.[79]

The seller will get the full value of the bill (as with discounting) less the customary charges, which will probably be on a "charges after payment" basis, since it is frequently impossible to know at the time of purchasing the bill what the total deductions for interest and so forth are likely to be; they are, of course, recoverable from the customer, or more usually debited to his account.

The negotiation will make the bank a holder in due course, and if the bill is dishonoured, the bank can claim directly against its customer, as well as from prior parties.

---

79. The bank could, of course, advance money by way of overdraft to their customer (the seller) on the strength of the bill and shipping documents. They would not buy the bill, and would be a holder for value to the extent of their advance.

As a method of payment of a documentary credit, the terms of the credit will state that the nominated bank will "negotiate" the seller's draft. The seller will draw his bill and present it to that bank, which will buy it on the strength of the undertaking of the issuing bank contained in the credit, which, almost certainly, will be "irrevocable",[80] and, hence, the negotiating bank's assurance that they will be reimbursed.

Having "bought" the bill by negotiation (under the terms of the credit), the negotiating bank will send that bill and the shipping documents to the issuing bank for reimbursement by the issuing bank. It is usual for the issuing bank to obtain its customer's acceptance on the bill before releasing the documents to him so that he can make collection of the goods when they arrive. In these circumstances—and in the case of an acceptance credit also—it is common for the issuing bank to ask the buyer (its customer) for a "trust receipt" before releasing the documents, to the effect that the buyer holds the documents, the goods and the proceeds of sale in trust for the bank until any funding as may have been arranged between them is repaid or satisfied.

If the buyer of the goods is of good standing, he will get "D/A" terms—that is, "Documents against acceptance". In other words, the bank will release the shipping documents immediately the bill is accepted, thus allowing the buyer of the goods to collect them without delay. If the strength of its customer's acceptance is not to the bank's liking, it will only grant "D/P" terms, which means the bank will retain the shipping documents as security[81] for the credit it has already paid the negotiating bank until the bill is paid by its customer (the buyer).[82] So that if the goods arrive in the meanwhile, the bank will warehouse and insure them (at the cost of the buyer, of course) until the date of maturity of the bill, or if the buyer of the goods (the acceptor of the bill) pays before maturity.

If the goods are perishable, it may be necessary to sell them before maturity of the bill. In such a case, the instructions of the buyer should be sought by the

---

80. Under an irrevocable credit, the issuing bank handling a negotiation credit must negotiate without recourse to the drawers and/or *bona fide* holders the drafts and other documents drawn by the beneficiary: UCP, Art. 9(b)(iv), under the *previous* UCP rules (Art. 10(a)(iv)), the obligation was to *pay* without recourse.

81. "The general course of international commerce involves the practice of raising money on the documents so as to bridge the period between the shipment and the time of obtaining payment against the documents": *per* Lord Wright, in *TD Bailey Son & Co v. Ross T Smyth & Co Ltd* (1940) 56 TLR 825, at p. 828.

82. These terms should be stated in the collection instruction: URC, Art. 7b. If a bill of exchange is drawn payable at a future date, but the collection instruction states that the commercial documents are to be released against payment and if this causes delay (while the maturity date of the bill arrives) the collecting bank is not responsible: URC Art. 7c. In fact, bills of exchange payable at a future date should not be drawn, if it is intended that the commercial documents be delivered against payment, unless thought is given to the fate of the goods prior to the maturity of the bill: *ibid.*, Art. 7a.

bank, and if no instructions are received then neither the bank nor the ware-
housekeeper (in the absence of any agreement to the contrary) are legally
obliged to take any action. However, if they do decide to sell, they have no
responsibility other than to act *bona fide*, and to inform the buyer of the action
taken.[83]

83. URC, Art. 10c.

CHAPTER 16

THE LEGAL RELATIONSHIPS

Under English law, the Uniform Customs do not apply to contractual arrangements for letters of credit unless they are expressly included, but since it is banking practice always to provide that the Uniform Customs will be included as part of these arrangements, it would be a rare case indeed to find them not applicable in a contract subject to English law.[1] In most other countries the rule is round the other way, in that the Uniform Customs are incorporated automatically, even if no specific reference is made to them in the documentation.

In addition to the Uniform Customs, the ICC has available "Standard Forms for Issuing Documentary Credits", so that the format of the documentation can be standardized, as well as the rules governing the transactions.

The legal relationships which are created by the use of letters of credit were summarized by Lord Diplock in *United City Merchants (Investments) Ltd* v. *Royal Bank of Canada*[2] as follows:

(1) The underlying contract for the sale of the goods, to which the only parties are the buyer and the seller;

(2) The contract between the buyer and the issuing bank under which the latter agrees to issue the credit and either itself or through a confirming bank to notify the credit to the seller and to make payments to or to the order of the seller (or to pay, accept or negotiate bills of exchange drawn by the seller) against presentation of stipulated documents; and the buyer agrees to reimburse the issuing bank for payments made under the credit. For such reimbursement the stipulated documents, if they include a document of title such as a bill of lading, constitute a security available to the issuing bank;

---

1. In *Harlow & Jones Ltd* v. *American Express Bank Ltd and Creditanstalt Bankverein* [1990] 2 Lloyd's Rep. 343, the ICC rules were not specifically incorporated, but it did not matter as all banks operating in England subscribed to those rules. In *Minories Finance Ltd* v. *Afribank Nigeria Ltd* [1995] 1 Lloyd's Rep. 134, the Uniform Rules for collection (1979 Revision) were excluded, but evidence was admitted as to what those Rules provided, and as it was the practice of bankers to abide by the Rules they were applied even though excluded, *per* Longmore J, at p. 140.

2. [1983] 1 AC 168. In fact, there are two other relationships not mentioned by Lord Diplock. 1. That between the seller and his bank; and, 2. That between the seller's bank and the paying bank.

(3) If payment is to be made through a confirming bank, the contract between the issuing bank and the confirming bank authorizing and requiring the latter to make such payments and to remit the stipulated documents to the issuing bank when they are received, the issuing bank in turn agreeing to reimburse the confirming bank for payments made under the credit;

(4) The contract between the confirming bank and the seller under which the confirming bank undertakes to pay to the seller (or to accept or negotiate without recourse to drawer bills of exchange drawn by him) up to the amount of the credit against presentation of the stipulated documents.

Each of these relationships creates a separate contract which, if there is a breach, as we shall see, can give rise to an action at law. We must now examine these different relationships, and some of the problems which arise from them.

1. THE CONTRACT OF SALE

This is the basis upon which the whole transaction begins. It is the agreement between the buyer and the seller, and will deal with all manner of topics apart from the terms of payment.[3]

Opening the credit

The credit must be opened on the day agreed between the parties. If no date is expressly agreed, the following basic rules apply in attempting to fix when the credit must be established:

(a) If it is agreed that the credit is to be established "at once" or "immediately", the credit must be opened within a time that a reasonable businessman would take to open the credit.[4]

(b) If the opening is conditional on the seller doing something, such as advising that the goods are ready for shipment, then the credit must be established immediately after that event.[5]

---

3. The credit is separate from the contract of sale, and banks are in no way concerned with it, even if reference is made to it in the credit: UCP, Art. 3.

4. *Garcia* v. *Page & Co* (1936) 55 Ll.L.Rep. 391.

5. *Plasticmoda SpA* v. *Davidson Manchester* [1952] 1 Lloyd's Rep. 527; see also *Knotz* v. *Fairclough Dodd & Jones Ltd* [1952] 1 Lloyd's Rep. 226, which involved the sending of a provisional invoice as a prerequisite to the opening of the credit. These cases must be distinguished from those where the opening of a credit is a condition precedent to the existence of a contract of sale. In such a case, if there is no credit facility there is no contract at all: *Trans Trust SPRL* v. *Danubian Trading Co Ltd* [1952] 2 QB 297.

(c) If the supply contract is silent as to the date of opening of the credit, it must be opened within a reasonable time before the seller is required to begin shipping, which is a question of fact in each case:[6] and always before shipment begins.[7] If the credit is not opened in a timely and satisfactory way, then the seller is not obliged to ship and can sue the buyer for breach of contract.[8]

(d) If the shipment is to be over an extended period, the credit must be open over the whole period.[9]

Expiry of the credit

Just as important as the commencement date from which the credit will operate is its termination; for after that date, whatever it may be, the credit will have no validity unless extended by the agreement of all parties.

All credits must, therefore, stipulate an expiry date for the availability of the credit, and also an expiry date for presentation of documents whether for payment, acceptance or negotiation, and all documents must, of course, be presented on or before the dates specified.[10] These dates are critical, and their calculation should not be left in doubt. For example, if a bank states that the credit is to be available for "one month" or "six months", or the like, but does not specify the date from which time is to run, the date of issuance of the credit by the issuing bank will be deemed to be the first day from which time is to run, and the period calculated accordingly.[11] Also, words such as "to", "until" and "from" are to be understood to *in*clude the date mentioned; while the word "after" will *ex*clude the date mentioned.[12]

If a month is divided into two halves, the first is to be taken from the 1st to the 15th, and the second half from the 16th to the last day of the month, all dates inclusive;[13] and any reference to "the beginning" of a month shall be taken to be from the 1st to the 10th inclusive; "the middle" of a month is

6. *Sinason Teicher Inter-American Grain Corp* v. *Oilcakes and Oilseeds Trading Co Ltd* [1954] 1 WLR 935.
7. *Pavia & Co SpA* v. *Thurmann-Nielsen* [1952] 2 QB 84.
8. See *Nichiman Corporation* v. *Gatoil Overseas Inc* [1987] 2 Lloyd's Rep. 46.
9. *Pavia & Co SpA* v. *Thurmann-Nielsen* [1952] 2 QB 84.
10. UCP, Art. 42(a) and (b). There is an exception under Art. 44, where a bank is closed (other than by virtue of Acts of God, riots, strikes, etc.—as to which see Art. 17), time shall be extended to the next following business day. No extension will be allowed to the latest day for loading on board, dispatch or taking in charge, and banks will reject the transport documents. When banks do extend under this Article they must issue a certificate to that effect: Art. 44(c). To attempt to change dates of documents to keep within the credit date of validity would amount to fraud: see *United City Merchants (Investments) Ltd* v. *Royal Bank of Canada* [1983] 1 AC 168.
11. UCP, Art. 42(c). "Banks should discourage indication of the expiry date of the credit in this manner."
12. *Ibid.*, Art. 47(a) and (b).
13. *Ibid.*, Art. 47(c).

deemed to be from the 11th to the 20th inclusive; and "the end" of a month from the 21st to the last day, whatever date that happens to be.[14]

It should also be remembered that banks are under no obligation to accept presentation of documents outside their banking hours.[15]

As we know, transactions with letters of credit very often involve the handling of what the Uniform Customs call "transport documents", which are bills of lading or other papers evidencing dispatch of goods. These documents prove that the shipper has the goods, and once these are issued by the shipper (or forwarding agent, in the case of a "forwarder's certificate") they have to be presented to the paying bank for payment—together with whatever other documents are necessary—as soon as possible, and, at all costs, within the time stipulated in the credit; because, if the transport documents presented to the bank bear a date later than as stated in the credit, the bank will refuse acceptance even though the expiry date of the credit has not been reached.

So far as dates for shipment[16] are concerned, it is common for the parties to state that presentation has to be effected "immediately" or "as soon as possible" after shipment. Sometimes these expressions are used because the parties are too lazy to be more precise, but as often as not it is because, at the time the main agreement between them is reached, no more specific dates can be fixed. If such wording is employed, the banks will disregard it.[17]

If a date for shipment *is* stipulated by the parties, it is also common for them to try to cover themselves in the case of any last minute mischance, to say "on or about", or some such expression. If an expression like this is used the banks interpret this to mean that shipment can take place from five days before to five days after the date stipulated by the parties, both end days included.[18]

In all these cases the parties should agree, and state in the credit, the period of time (following the issue of the transport documents) during which the presentation of documents for payment, acceptance or negotiation must be made; because if no period is spelled out, the "banks will not accept documents presented to them later than 21 days after the date of shipment", and, of course, in no case later than the expiry date of the credit.[19] This is a terrifyingly short period of time in which to effect presentation, and a more realistic limitation should always be agreed.

A final word on the subject of timing, unless otherwise stipulated in the credit, a bank will accept a document bearing a date prior to the opening of a

---

14. *Ibid.*, Art. 47(d).

15. *Ibid.*, Art. 45.

16. The word "shipment" used in the context of earliest or latest dates of shipment, will be understood to include the expressions "loading on board", "dispatch", "accepted for carriage", "date of post receipt", "date of pick up" and the like and in the case of a multimodal transport document (as to which see UCP, Art. 26), the expression "taking in charge": UCP, Art. 46(a).

17. UCP, Art. 46(b). The Article states that these expressions "should not be used"!

18. *Ibid.*, Art. 46(c).

19. *Ibid.*, Art. 43(a).

credit, providing it is presented *within* the time limits stated in the credit and in the Uniform Customs.[20]

The documents

It is, of course, for the buyer to inform the seller (and obtain his agreement) to the documents which the buyer wishes to see as a condition of his bank making payment. The requirements must be as clear as possible, since, as we shall see below, endless problems with the acceptability of these documents can occur once they are passed into the hands of the banks, if the details are not as clear as they should have been. The usual documents are those relating to the transport of goods, their insurance and, of course, commercial invoices. If other documents are called for, the credit should stipulate by whom such documents are to be issued, and the appropriate wording or data content. If the credit does not stipulate these documents clearly, banks will accept them, provided the contents are not inconsistent with any of the documents which *are* stipulated.[21]

A problem which arises, not infrequently, is where the buyer demands a long list of detailed documents as a condition of the seller obtaining payment, and which the paying bank must check and verify before parting with the money. As this list is agreed between the buyer and the seller, the banks usually find themselves saddled with the onerous task of dealing with all this detail, before being brought into the transaction; and when finally they have the opportunity to comment, it is often found to be too late to introduce any major changes. Indeed, Art. 5 of the Uniform Customs provides, in part, that:

In order to guard against confusion and misunderstanding, banks should discourage any attempt to include excessive detail in the credit or in any amendment thereto.

However, given the circumstances around which the list of requirements is compiled between buyer and seller, it is a little difficult to see what the banks can do. Certainly, once the banks "accept" the terms of such a list of documents—excessive or not—they are bound to honour their terms to the letter.

It will be convenient now if we consider some of the documents commonly demanded by the buyer, and which the seller must produce as a pre-condition to obtaining payment; and consider also how they are dealt with by the banks.

(a) The commercial invoice

This is one of the most important documents which a seller must provide, consisting as it should of the following: (1) a description of the goods, which

20. *Ibid.*, Art. 22.
21. UCP, Art. 21.

must correspond with the description in the credit;[22] and (2) the name of the buyer, again as stipulated in the credit;[23] and (3) the price of the goods, also as stated in the credit.[24]

(b) The insurance document

When goods are being transported, by whatever means, there is always a risk that they will be lost or damaged in whole or in part, and as the buyer has, in most cases, irrevocably committed himself to pay, he will be faced with honouring that commitment and then recovering his loss from the under-writers. Hence the need for adequate evidence that the goods are insured *before* payment is effected.

The "insurance document" which must be handed over is the insurance policy as stipulated in the credit, "issued and signed by insurance companies or underwriters or their agents",[25] and "cover notes" issued by brokers will not be accepted by the banks unless specifically authorized by the credit.[26]

It is, of course, for the buyer and the seller to agree the type of insurance required, and see to it that this is stipulated in the credit, and dealing with any additional risks they consider should be covered. It is regrettably common for the parties simply to agree that the "usual risks" should be covered, which is not very satisfactory of course, as while banks will accept insurance policies drawn in whatever way they are, so long as they are as stipulated in the credit, they will do so without responsibility for risks not covered.[27] This is also the case if the policy stipulates it covers "all risks" even though some risks are expressly excluded.[28]

The insurance should, of course, be for the full value,[29] and expressed in the same currency as the credit.[30]

22. "In all other documents, the goods may be described in general terms not inconsistent with the description of the goods in the credit": UCP, Art. 37(c). If the description does not correspond the bank may be entitled to reject the documents. In a recent case the bank's contention was not upheld on the facts. "The description of the goods in the commercial invoice did . . . correspond with the description in the credit so as to satisfy Article 37(c) of UCP 500" *per* Sir Thomas Bingham in *Glencore International AG v. Bank of China* [1996] 1 Lloyd's Rep. 135, 154.
23. *Ibid.*, Art. 37(a).
24. Banks may refuse commercial invoices issued for amounts in excess unless other arrangements are made: UCP, Art. 37(b).
25. UCP, Art. 34(a).
26. *Ibid.*, Art. 34(c), and see *Scott v. Barclays Bank Ltd* [1923] 2 KB 1.
27. *Ibid.*, Art. 35(a). The Article states that imprecise terms such as "usual risks" or "customary risks" shall not be used. However, failing specific stipulations in the credit, banks will accept insurance documents as presented to them, without, of course, responsibility for any risks *not* covered: Art. 35(b).
28. *Ibid.*, Art. 36. Banks will accept an insurance document subject to a franchise or an excess, unless otherwise stated in the credit: UCP, Art. 35(c).
29. Unless expressed in the credit, the minimum cover is to be the CIF or CIP value of the goods, plus 10%. Otherwise the banks will accept as the minimum amount 110% of the amount for which payment, acceptance or negotiation is requested by the credit; or, 110% of the gross amount of the invoice—whichever is the greater: UCP, Art. 34(f)(ii).
30. UCP, Art. 34(f)(i).

The effective date of the cover must be, at least, the day of "loading on board"; "taking in charge" or "dispatch", and banks will refuse documents showing a later date, unless there are other provisions stipulated in the credit.[31]

(c) The transport documents

These are the documents which evidence that the goods are in the hands of a carrier for transportation to the buyer, and, to that end, that they have left the control of the seller.

The exact requirements, again, must be agreed between the buyer and the seller, including nominating the ship upon which the goods will be placed, or, perhaps, if that is not possible, then the shipping line to be employed. As we know, it is by no means unusual these days for the transportation to be by more than one form of conveyance. For example, by road from the seller's factory in New Jersey to the quayside in New York; ship across the Atlantic to the West Coast of Africa; then by plane to the final destination in Central Africa. All this must be agreed and provided for in the credit.[32]

To deal with this type of situation the new ICC Publication 500 provides for a "multimodal" transport document, which, in effect, replaces the earlier "combined transport" bill of lading,[33] in whatever form it may be, it is a vital document which a bank will need to have in its possession, and in a satisfactory condition before effecting payment.

If the parties stipulate a bill of lading covering a port-to-port shipment, as always, subject to whatever is said in the credit, the banks will accept the document which[34] (i) appears on its face to have been issued by a named carrier or his agent; and (ii) indicates that the goods have been loaded on board or shipped on a named vessel;[35] and (iii) indicates the port of loading and

31. *Ibid.*, Art. 34(e).
32. Sometimes the services of a "forwarding agent" are used to make the arrangements, and sometimes he will collect the goods from the seller's premises and place them on board the ship. In which case the forwarder is, for this part of the transportation, acting as a carrier: see *The Maheno* [1977] 1 Lloyd's Rep. 81. It is not unknown for the parties to agree, and place the terms in the credit, that a forwarder's certificate, issued under the aegis of *Federation internationale des associations de transitaires et assimiles* (FIATA), be used as a "transport document" entitling the seller to payment, on the basis that he had delivered the goods to the buyer's agent (the forwarder).
33. If the credit provides that the goods are to be sent by post, and calls for a "postal receipt" or "certificate of posting", banks will accept these as "transport documents" if they appear to have been stamped or otherwise authenticated and dated, in the place of dispatch as stated in the credit and in all other respects meets the stipulations of the credit: UCP, Art. 29(a). If a courier service is used their receipt for taking delivery of the goods must indicate the date of pick-up, which will be deemed the date of shipment or despatch: UCP, Art. 29(b).
34. UCP, Art. 23(a). Banks will accept transport documents for payment to a final beneficiary who is not the named consignor of the goods, unless the credit forbids it, which is useful when dealing with back-to-back credits.
35. But note details of UCP, Art. 23(a)(ii).

discharge as stipulated in the credit; and (iv) consists of a full set of originals issued to the consignor if issued in more than one original; and (v) appears to contain all the terms and conditions of carriage; (vi) contains no indication that it is subject to a charter party[36] or that the vessel is propelled by sail[37]; and (vii) meets all other stipulations of the credit.

Unless otherwise authorised in the credit, banks will also accept a bill of lading *covering port-to-port shipments* if the goods have been loaded on board or shipped on a named vessel (and evidence by a notation on the bill of lading),[38] or if the bill of lading indicates a place of receipt or taking in charge different from the port of loading,[39] or if the transport document appears to be issued by a forwarder who has signed either as a carrier or multimodal transport operator, or as agent.[40]

If the parties do not stipulate[41] what kind of transport document[42] they want the banks to recognize as a "transport document",[43] the banks will accept anything which satisfies the list applicable to a marine bill of lading or if the credit calls for a transport document covering at least two different modes of transport, now called "multimodal transport", and the list satisfies that document.[44]

In the case of all types of transport document, the banks must be satisfied if such is the case,[45] that (i) the credit allows a bill of lading subject to a charter party[46] (ii) the vessel is propelled by sale,[47] (iii) it is issued by a forwarder who has signed either as a carrier or multimodal transport operator, or as an agent for the carrier or multi-modal operator;[48] (iv) that the goods will not be loaded on deck even though they may be *carried* on deck;[49] (v) that there is no notation of the bill of lading stating the goods or packaging is defective.[50]

36. It is banking practice not to accept "charterparty" bills of lading because clauses in the charterparty can affect the terms of bills of lading, and a transferee of the bill of lading could not take free from them. The same problem does not arise with "steamship" bills of lading. Note also that not all bills of lading applying to goods carried under a charterparty are necessarily "charterparty bills of lading": see *Enrico Furst & Co* v. *WE Fischer Ltd* [1960] 2 Lloyd's Rep. 340.
37. This is a fact that banks must verify before paying, of course.
38. Unless the bill of lading does not indicate actual port of loading, under the terms of UCP, Art. 23(a)(ii).
39. UCP, Art. 23(a)(ii).
40. UCP, Art. 30.
41. UCP, Art. 31(i). But not if they only "may" be: Art. 31(i).
42. *Ibid.*, Art. 32(b). Credits almost always require "clean on board" documents; that is, a bill of lading which bears no superimposed clauses or notations: Art. 32(c). Documents are "clean" if they comply with the terms of Art. 32(a).
43. That is, not a multimodal or a marine bill of lading, ocean bill or other bill covering carriage by sea, or indicating use of the postal service.
44. UCP, Art. 23(a), which is almost the same as Art. 26(a).
45. There will be no rejection in the circumstances provided for in UCP, Art. 26(b), as UCP, Art. 23(b) is almost identical.
46. UCP, Art. 23(a)(vi) and Art. 25(a)(i), but see Art. 24(a)(vi).
47. *Ibid.*, Art. 23(a)(vi), Art. 24(a)(vi), Art. 25(a)(vii), Art. 26(a)(vi).
48. *Ibid.*, Art. 30.
49. *Ibid.*, Art. 31.
50. *Ibid.*, Art. 32(a).

No matter what form the documents take, the buyer should insist that payment should only be made if the goods are *actually on board the ship*, not merely received by the carrier and stowed, possibly, in a warehouse under his control. Therefore, the buyer and the seller should agree (and again, state clearly in the credit) that payment will only be made against an "on board" notation on the bill of lading transport document. If this is not provided for in the credit, banks are entitled to accept (and pay out on) a document showing only that the goods have been "taken in charge" or "received for shipment",[51] which is not the same thing at all as being secure in the knowledge that the goods are really "on board".

Transshipment[52] of goods involving reloading during the course of carriage is common enough, and unless this is prohibited by the terms of the credit, banks will accept transport documents which indicate that the goods will be transshipped, so long as the entire carriage is covered by one and the same transport document,[53] as the buyer is entitled to have "continuous documentary cover" as against the shipowner over the whole transit.[54] It must be noted that even if transshipment is prohibited by the credit, banks will still accept transport documents, incorporating printed clauses giving the carrier the right to transship, or indicating that transshipment will or may take place provided the entire carriage is covered by one transport document.[55]

It should also be borne in mind that whenever the buyer has agreed to pay the freight charges, that is under contracts CIF or C and F, banks will, nevertheless, accept transport documents stating that the freight charges have still to be paid, unless—as always—something to the contrary is stated in the credit or is inconsistent with the documents when presented.[56]

If the buyer and the seller have agreed, and if the credit so states, that the transport documentation has to indicate that freight has been paid or pre-paid,[57] or other additional costs, such as for loading and unloading, have been paid, the banks will accept documents stating this, so long as the documents show clearly "by a stamp or otherwise . . . or by other means", that this is the case.

With large orders it is usual for the parties to agree that they can, or will, be drawn on and shipped by stated instalments; and payment is normally provided for in the credit to correspond with the delivery schedule. It is generally

---

51. *Ibid.*, Articles 23 (a)(ii), 24(a)(ii), 25(a)(iv) and 26(a)(ii).

52. As to what amounts to "transshipment" see Art. 23(b).

53. UCP, Art. 26(b) and 28(d). If not, the documents can be rejected: *Landauer & Co v. Craven and Speeding Bros* [1912] 2 KB 94.

54. *Per* Lord Asquith in *Holland Colombo Trading Society Ltd v. Alawdeen* [1954] 2 Lloyd's Rep. 45, 53; quoting *Hansson v. Hamel and Horley Ltd* [1922] 2 AC 36. See also *Brazilian and Portuguese Bank v. British American Exchange Banking Corp* (1868) 18 LT 823.

55. See for details UCP, Articles 23(c), 24(c), 26(b), 27(c) and 28(d).

56. UCP, Art. 33(a).

57. *Ibid.*, Art. 33(b) and (d). However, expressions such as "freight prepayable" or "freight to be prepaid" or other similar words will not be evidence of the payment of freight: UCP, Art. 33(c).

understood that delays in the availability of goods for delivery are not unknown, but it is essential to make provision for the credit to continue if delays should occur, because Art. 41 of the Uniform Customs states:

If drawings and/or shipments by instalments within given periods are stipulated in the credit and any instalment is not drawn and/or shipped within the period allowed for the instalment, the credit ceases to be available for that and any subsequent instalment, unless otherwise stipulated in the credit.

This seems an unrealistic provision, and one which should always be neg-atived in a credit covering a contract requiring delivery by instalments.

Unless an instalment contract is agreed, the buyer will, usually, want delivery in one consignment, and so it is common for credits to state that "part shipments" are excluded.[58] Notwithstanding such a restriction in the credit, in a shipment involving, at least in part, a transportation by sea, even if the loading bears either different dates of issuance, or different ports of loading, it will not be deemed a "part shipment" so long as it is on board the same ship and on the same voyage, because it is by no means uncommon for a ship to load at port A then take the tide to nearby port B to load cargo there, which might well include cargo not available for shipment at the tide time of port A.

The same basic rule applies to goods mailed by the seller. If there are several packages it is not deemed a "partial shipment" so long as the postal receipts appear to have been stamped on the same day, from the place indicated in the credit as the point of dispatch.[59] Also, if some other method of transport is used, for example, by air or road, it will not be considered a "partial shipment" if the transport documents are issued by the same carrier, with the same date, from the same place of dispatch and the same destination.[60]

(d) The certificate of origin

This document is necessary where the country of origin of the goods, or some part of them, is important, for example, if preferential tariffs apply to the transaction, say, as is the case among the EEC countries; or, perhaps, where trade embargoes exist between countries, and the buyer needs to know there will be no problems when the goods are eventually delivered.[61]

Once more, it is for the buyer and the seller to agree (and state in the credit) exactly what is required, and by whom the certificate is to be issued, and what the wording must be.[62]

---

58. UCP, Art. 40(a). Unless the credit stipulates otherwise, both partial drawings and partial shipments can be made.
59. *Ibid.*, Art. 40(c).
60. *Ibid.*, Art. 40(d).
61. For example, the shipping of Israeli manufactured goods to Arab countries.
62. If this is not stated in the credit, the banks will accept all documents (except transport, insurance documents and commercial invoices), provided the data content makes it possible to relate the goods to the commercial invoice or the credit: UCP, Art. 21.

(e) Certificates of quality and inspection

The buyer will, in most cases, want to know, prior to the goods being shipped, that they are up to the specification laid down in the agreement between him and the seller; this is particularly so with custom-made items. Consequently, an inspection is provided for a short time before shipment at the seller's factory, or wherever the goods are; this is normally carried out by an independent third party[63] who will issue a certificate that, in his opinion, at the date of the inspection, the goods were in a fit condition within the terms of the main contract between the buyer and the seller, if such is the case, of course.

As always, it is for the parties to agree what exactly is to be certified,[64] and by whom,[65] and then see to it that the terms are incorporated in the credit. To guard against subsequent argument, the main contract should provide that these certificates are, when issued, binding on both parties.

As these certificates are usually given to fulfil the terms of the main contract, and for that purpose alone, they are often referred to as "certificates *in personam*", as opposed to certificates which are addressed to the world at large and which are commonly referred to as "certificates *in rem*".

(f) Certificates of weight and quantity

As the name implies, these are certificates given, usually by independent inspectors, to verify the amount of goods shipped.

When the goods being bought are bulk, such as grain, or coal or some similar type of merchandise, or where the goods are bought by reference to a unit or unit price, the parties should always agree a weight or unit tolerance within which the bulk quantity will be acceptable when delivered. It is usual to fix the price for shipment in advance of knowing exactly what the shipped amount will be, so as to arrange the terms of credit, by agreeing a price *pro rata* with a maximum value of the credit. The credit will then be paid once the bulk is established, and providing it is within the tolerance (say, 5 per cent or whatever), as also agreed in the main contract.

If the parties use expressions in the credit such as "about" or "circa" in connection with the amount of the credit or the quantity or the unit price, these terms will be construed as allowing a difference not to exceed 10 per cent more

63. There are companies which specialize in this service, for example, Bureau Veritas or Cargo Superintendents, who have worldwide representation. Some forwarders accept this responsibility.

64. Otherwise the banks will accept the certificate at its face value within the terms of UCP, Art. 21. For a recent example see *Apioil Ltd* v. *Kuwait Petroleum Italia SpA* v. *Sociedade Nacional de Combustiveis de Angola SA* [1995] 1 Lloyd's Rep. 124.

65. For example, they could provide for a certification as to both "quality" and "condition"—the goods could be within the specification, but not in an acceptable condition. Also, depending on the nature of the goods, a particular type of inspection involving technical detail may have to be provided for: *Commercial Banking Co of Sydney* v. *Jalsard Pty Ltd* [1973] AC 279.

or 10 per cent less than the amount or quantity or the unit price to which they refer.[66]

In the event that the parties do not make provision in the credit for such tolerances, then 5 per cent more or less will be permissible, and the banks will pay out accordingly—even if partial shipments are not permitted by the credit—provided that the amount of the drawings does not exceed the value of the credit, of course.[67] Also, if nothing is said in the credit to the contrary, the banks will accept transport documents which indicate "shipper's load and count" or "said by shipper to contain" or other such expressions,[68] and if a discrepancy is subsequently discovered, it will be too late for the buyer to complain.

Where the credit provides for an attestation or certification of weight, the banks will accept a "weight stamp" or "declaration of weight" which appears to have been superimposed on the transport document by the carrier or the carrier's agent. This is not acceptable: (a) If the credit specifically stipulates the attestation or certification must be by a separate document; or (b) In the case of transportation by sea.[69]

These then are the main documents found in transactions involving letters of credit, but whatever documents are to be used to effect payment and give the necessary security to the buyer, as we have seen time and time again, they are at the discretion of the buyer and the seller. It is for them to agree what will trigger payment, and then state it clearly in the credit.

There is one salient point to remember, and which is of paramount importance in considering this topic, and it is that what is being handled are "documents" not goods or facts.[70] For example, if it is required that goods be shipped on board a vessel belonging to a member of an international shipping conference, what should be demanded is a *certificate*, acceptable to the buyer (and his bank), evidencing the fact that the vessel is so owned: this establishes the documentary position. If this certificate is not used, then someone has to establish to the satisfaction of the paying bank a *fact* without being clear as to how such a fact is to be proved, or what is to happen if the vessel is not owned by a conference member.[71] The moral always is to decide first what document will be required to prove or establish a particular fact or set of circumstances, and then see that it is practical that the seller can supply it; there is no point in demanding something which, from the beginning, will result in breach.

---

66. UCP, Art. 39(a).
67. *Ibid.*, Art. 39(b).
68. *Ibid.*, Art. 31(ii).
69. UCP, Art. 38.
70. *Ibid.*, Art. 4. See *Tukan Timber Ltd* v. *Barclays Bank Plc* [1987] 1 Lloyd's Rep. 171, and *Westpac Banking Corporation and Commonwealth Steel Co Ltd* v. *South Carolina National Bank* [1986] 1 Lloyd's Rep. 311 (PC).
71. See *Banque de l'Indochine et de Suez SA* v. *JH Rayner (Mincing Lane) Ltd* [1983] 2 WLR 841, at p. 855.

Finally, so far as the issuer of any document to be presented under a credit is concerned, it is common for the parties to stipulate a "first class" bank, or a "qualified" or "independent" inspector, or that a certificate must be "official", and, descriptive of what is wanted though these expressions are, they are not at all sufficiently precise for the purpose of giving instructions to the paying bank of what is *really* acceptable. So, if the credit provides for documents described in this way, banks will accept them, so long as they appear on their face to be in accordance with the other terms and conditions of the credit,[72] but the banks will not enquire as to the "qualifications" or "independence" or whatever the terms of these adjectives may be.

The "copy" originals

The documents which are placed before a bank for acceptance as a precondition of payment must all be originals. However, Art. 20(b) of the Uniform Customs provides that banks will accept "as originals" documents produced (or appearing to have been produced) by: (i) reprographic, automated or computerized systems; (ii) carbon copy; provided they: (1) are marked as originals; and (2) appear to have been signed.[73]

One cannot help but observe that, at a time when maritime fraud has reached the level it has, it would appear necessary that original documents need to be better prepared for acceptance than a photocopy with a signature — possibly undecipherable — appearing to have "authenticated" it. For while banks are entitled, under the terms of the Uniform Customs, to rely on these provisions, major problems could occur, especially with papers which are documents of title, such as bills of lading.

As we know, the normal practice is for the shipowner, through the master of the ship, to sign and issue to the seller a bill of lading.[74] In a transaction where payment is by letter of credit, the bill of lading is passed by the seller to the paying bank, together with the other documents to enable payment to be made. The paying bank will send them to the issuing bank, which, in turn, passes them to its customer (the buyer) to enable the goods to be collected. Now, if the paying bank receives, not a real original, but a photocopy suitably "authenticated" it can accept it under the terms of Art. 20(b). However, at the end of the voyage, the master will not deliver the goods unless he receives from

---

72. UCP, Art. 20(a). The Article says that such terms "shall not be used"!

73. A document may be signed by handwriting, by facsimile signature, by perforated signature, by stamp, by symbol, or by any other mechanical or electronic method of authentication: *ibid.*, Art. 20(b). Also, unless otherwise stated in the credit, if a document is required to be "authenticated", "validated", "legalized", "visaed", "certified" or indicating a similar requirement, this will be satisfied by "any signature, mark, stamp or label" on the document that on its face appears to satisfy the requirement.

74. Often bills of lading are issued in a set of two or three, which would only aggravate the circumstances of the example.

the buyer an original bill of lading,[75] and since he will know very well that it is not the original he signed, it is almost certain he will not hand over the goods in exchange for a photocopy marked "original", even though the paying bank had accepted it, and sent it on to the issuing bank and, thence, to the buyer.

Documents in a set

In the days before letters passed freely around the world by airmail a consignee could find that the ship carrying the goods he had bought had arrived, but he had not received the bill of lading to enable him to collect the goods from the master.

This problem was dealt with by executing bills of lading (and bills of exchange also) "in a set", of two or three, as agreed between the buyer and the seller. The practice continues today as a precaution against loss or delay. All are originals; they are signed and dated, all are exactly the same. It is customary, depending how many are in the set, to send one or, perhaps, two by separate airmails and another put into the ship's bag[76] for handing over to the buyer or his representative when the ship docks. With documents in a set it does not matter if one or more is lost or delayed on the way, as the goods can be cleared so long as the consignee has one to produce to the master as proof of title to the goods. The master will deliver the goods to the person who first hands him the bill of lading for collection. The bill is then said to be "accomplished", and the others are void.

Bills of exchange in a set

The situation was (and is) much the same with bills of exchange, so that if one part is lost or delayed in transit it is not a matter of great concern. Where a bill of exchange is drawn in a set each part is numbered and contains a reference to the other parts, and the whole of the parts constitute one bill.[77] Bills in a set must not be confused with a *series* of bills, as these are separate bills meant to be presented for payment at different times, for example, if the price of goods is to be paid by instalments. In such a case, it could happen that a series of bills is issued for payment by instalments, with each bill drawn in a set.

Problems may arise, of course, if a holder of a set indorses two or more parts to different people. In such a case he will be liable on each part, while

---

75. *The Sagona* [1984] 1 Lloyd's Rep. 194; or a letter of indemnity guaranteed by a bank.

76. The ship's bag was, and still is, a method of conveying mail and documents. It is in the custody of the master, but is under the authority of the senior naval officer at each port of arrival or departure of the ship in the UK; similar arrangements apply in other ports throughout the world. When the ship docks, the contents of the bag are delivered to the various addresses, and the letter with the bill of lading is handed to the consignee's representative who (if he has not already received the airmailed documents) can arrange collection of the goods from the master with the bill of lading which had been carried in the ship's bag.

77. Bills of Exchange Act 1882, s. 71(1). The reference usually says for example, " . . . this our first of exchange (second and third of same date and tender unpaid) . . . ".

subsequent indorsers of each will be liable only on the parts they indorse.[78] Where two or more parts are negotiated to different parties who qualify as holder in due course, the holder whose title first accrued (as between the holders in due course) is deemed to be the true owner of the whole bill.[79] Great care must be exercised in indorsing a bill in a set if the whereabouts of the others is not known.

Acceptance of a bill in a set can be written on any part, and must be written on one part only. If the acceptor is foolish enough to accept on more than one part he is liable on each part he accepts as though they were separate bills, if each comes into the hands of a different holder.[80] Equally, where the acceptor pays a bill in a set he should get back the part upon which his acceptance appears; otherwise if that part comes into the hands of a holder in due course, the acceptor will have to pay again.[81] Normally, payment of one part will discharge the whole set.[82]

Under the terms of a documentary credit, it is the correspondent bank that will receive the documents from the seller of the goods, and mail them to the issuing bank. This will be done by separate airmails and, not infrequently, a copy will go in the ship's bag.

One must reflect that with the increasing use of telefax and other electronic means of communication the day cannot be too far away when the rules are changed so that letters of credit, bills of lading and of exchange will all be telefaxed under the terms of a test key system, thus obviating the current and time-honoured practice.

As a last word on the contract between the buyer and the seller, it should be observed that once the credit has been established pursuant to the terms of the agreement of sale, it becomes conditional payment for the goods,[83] and the seller cannot go back on his bargain and attempt to obtain payment from the buyer in some other way.[84]

2. THE CONTRACT BETWEEN BUYER AND HIS BANK

This is the contract between the buyer and his—the issuing—bank, whereby the bank agrees to provide the buyer with the facilities. The bank, of course,

78. Bills of Exchange Act 1882, s. 71(2).
79. *Ibid.*, s. 71(3). Nothing in this sub-section shall affect the rights of a person who in due course accepts or pays the part first presented to him.
80. Bills of Exchange Act 1882, s. 71(4).
81. *Ibid.*, s. 71(5).
82. *Ibid.*, s. 71(6).
83. *WJ Alan & Co Ltd v. El Nasr Export and Import Co* [1972] 2 QB 189; *Maran Road v. Austin Taylor & Co Ltd* [1975] 1 Lloyd's Rep. 156.
84. *Soproma SpA v. Marine & Animal By-Products Corp* [1966] 1 Lloyd's Rep. 367. Except in the unlikely and very exceptional circumstances of the bank going into liquidation: *ED & F Man Ltd v. Nigerian Sweets & Confectionary Co Ltd* [1977] 2 Lloyd's Rep. 50; or, if part of the price was to be paid by bills of exchange, and they are dishonoured: *Sale Continuation Ltd v. Austin Taylor & Co Ltd* [1967] 2 Lloyd's Rep. 403.

in addition to issuing the letter of credit, might also be giving the buyer loan or overdraft facilities to finance the transaction, and the agreement with the bank will, doubtless, provide for repayments on whatever terms are agreed.

However, once the issuing bank has opened an *irrevocable* letter of credit it is bound to pay, and the customer (the buyer) cannot give instructions to halt the payment.[85] "The bank is in no way concerned with any dispute that the buyer may have with the seller. The buyer may say that the goods are not up to contract. Nevertheless the bank must honour its obligations. The buyer may say that he has a cross-claim in a large amount, still the bank must honour its obligations."[86]

Several attempts have been made by buyers to obtain an injunction against their bankers to prevent them making payment, but the courts have been most reluctant to interfere with irrevocable letters or credit. A few examples will illustrate the courts' attitude.

HAMZEH MALAS & SONS v. BRITISH IMEX INDUSTRIES LTD[87]

Hamzeh Malas was a Jordanian company and it bought reinforcing rods from British Imex. The goods were to be shipped in two instalments, and each shipment was to be paid for by a separate irrevocable letter of credit, opened by the Midland Bank in London. After the first shipment had been made and paid for, a dispute arose between the parties and the Jordanian company gave instructions to its bank to withhold payment on the second credit. The bank refused to accept those instructions and an application was made for an injunction to restrain the bank. *Held*—that the instructions were irrevocable, and the injunction was refused.

The case went to the Court of Appeal, and in the course of his judgment Jenkins LJ said:[88]

A vendor of goods selling against a confirmed letter of credit is selling under the assurance that nothing will prevent him from receiving the price. That is no mean advantage when goods manufactured in one country are being sold in another. It is, furthermore, to be observed that vendors are often reselling goods bought from third parties. When they are doing that, and when they are being paid by confirmed letter of credit, their practice is—and I think it was followed by the defendants in this case—to

---

85. UCP, Art. 9(a). For details of terms of payment, see sub-paras (i) to (iv) of Art. 9(a).

86. *Per* Lord Denning in *Power Curber International Ltd* v. *National Bank of Kuwait SAK* [1981] 1 WLR 1233, 1241. See also, UCP, Art. 9(d) which provides: "an irrevocable credit can neither be amended nor cancelled without the agreement of the issuing bank, the confirming bank (if any), and the beneficiary", except in some cases involving transferable credits: see *ibid.*, Art. 48.

87. [1958] 2 QB 127: see also *British Imex Industries Ltd* v. *Midland Bank Ltd* [1958] 1 QB 542, which followed. Also, *Korea Industry Co Ltd* v. *Andoll Ltd* [1990] 2 Lloyd's Rep. 183. However, see *Hong Kong and Shanghai Banking Corporation* v. *Kloeckner & Co AG* [1989] 3 All ER 513, where the bank claimed successfully to set off debts due to it from the defendant, against monies due *to* the defendant under a standby letter of credit. What seemed significant to Hirst J was that the sum being set off was a liquidated claim, and arose out of the "selfsame transactions"; at p. 522e. In other words, if a letter of credit is given to the customer (and not to some third party as is usually the case), the issuing bank may be able to claim a set-off as against its own customer.

88. [1958] 2 QB 127, 130.

finance the payments necessary to be made to their suppliers against the letter of credit. That system of financing these operations, as I see it, would break down completely if a dispute as between the vendor and the purchaser was to have the effect of "freezing", if I may use that expression, the sum in respect of which the letter of credit was opened.

Indeed, the only occasion upon which the courts have, at all, been inclined to interfere is where there is a suggestion that the transaction is tainted with fraud; but even here the standard of proof of fraud is very high. An example of a case where there was an allegation of fraud is

DISCOUNT RECORDS LTD v. BARCLAYS BANK LTD[89]

Discount Records agreed to buy records and cassettes from a French company called Promodisc. Payment was to be by irrevocable letter of credit on Barclays in London. When the goods arrived Discount Records alleged they were not what had been ordered, and that they had been defrauded, whereupon they instructed Barclays not to pay. In keeping with the accepted method of operating, Barclays refused the instructions, and Discount Records applied for an injunction to restrain Barclays from making payment. *Held*—(on the facts) that there was no evidence of fraud, and the injunction was refused, allowing Barclays to pay under the irrevocable letter of credit. The judge said that he " . . . would be slow to interfere with bankers' irrevocable credits, and not least in the sphere of international banking, unless a sufficiently grave cause is shown; for interventions by the court that are too ready or too frequent might gravely impair the reliance which, quite properly, is placed on such credits".[90]

A further and recent example of the inviolacy of letters of credit is:

DEUTSCHE RÜCKVERSICHERUNG AG v. WALBROOK INSURANCE CO. LTD[91]

The dispute involved as plaintiffs two companies in the reinsurance market, one German and the other Belgian. The defendant (Walbrook) was an English company which agreed to transfer substantial loss reserves to the plaintiffs, and it was agreed that the plaintiffs would pay for the transfer of the loss reserves by letters of credit opened by the plaintiff companies and payable in London. At some stage, the plaintiff companies decided they wished to escape from these onerous contractual obligations[92] and attempted to stop payment under the letters of credit by alleging that they (the plaintiffs) had violated the English insurance regulations by carrying on business in

89. [1975] 1 WLR 315. Speaking of the rule that letters of credit must always be paid Lord Denning MR said: "To this general principle there is an exception in the case of what is called established or obvious fraud to the knowledge of the bank": *Edward Owen Engineering Ltd v. Barclays Bank International Ltd* [1978] QB 159, at p. 169. In *Tukcan Timber Ltd v. Barclays Bank Plc* [1987] 1 Lloyd's Rep. 171, an injunction to restrain the bank from paying under the letter of credit was refused, even though fraudulent documents had been submitted on two occasions in an attempt to obtain payment but had been rejected, and even though the customer feared it may happen again. See also, *RD Harbottle (Mercantile) Ltd v. National Westminster Bank Ltd* [1977] 2 All ER 862; *Bolivinter Oil SA v. Chase Manhattan Bank* [1984] 1 WLR 392; *United Trading Corp SA v. Allied Arab Bank Ltd* [1985] 2 Lloyd's Rep. 554.
90. *Per* Megarry J (as he then was) at p. 320. The alleged fraud in this case consisted of the shipment of empty boxes, filled with rubbish, boxes partly filled and others containing wrong materials: see pp. 317H and 318A.
91. [1994] 4 All ER 181.
92. *Ibid.*, *per* Phillips J, 186c.

England without the necessary statutory authorization, and that, therefore, the transfers of the loss reserves and the letters of credit were illegal, void and unenforceable. In other words, the plaintiffs sought to rely on their own illegality, and attempted to obtain an order restraining Walbrook from obtaining payment under the letters of credit. Subsequently, the plaintiffs also alleged fraudulent misrepresentation and/or non-disclosure on the part of the directors of H.S. Weavers (Underwriting) Agencies Ltd., the agency which had handled the administration of the reinsurance, because they had taken an overriding commission which should have been paid to Walbrook. This created a "moral hazard" for the plaintiffs in considering whether to accept the reinsurance risk, because, had they known of this conduct, they might not have been prepared to take the risk.[93] On this further ground Walbrook was not entitled to payments under the contract of transfer, and hence was not entitled to receive payment under the letters of credit. *Held*—that the illegality of the main contracts of reinsurance would not taint the letters of credit,[94] nor, on the question of fraud "where the dishonest conduct has no impact on the risks being reinsured", the judge was disinclined to hold that the plaintiffs could avoid contracts on the grounds of non-disclosure.[95] Indeed, to grant relief in these circumstances " . . . would clot what has been described as the lifeblood of international commerce as surely as an injunction restraining drawing on the credit".[96]

The following points should be noted regarding the attempts to prevent payments under letters of credit:

(1) Where the buyer of goods or services wishes to attempt to prevent his bank from paying under a letter of credit he has opened, usually there is considerable urgency to stop the payment and so an application to the court is often made *ex parte*, and in these circumstances an injunction is sometimes granted for a few days to hold the *status quo* and to allow the other party or parties to attend at court and argue their side. It is a fact however, that as Phillips J observed in *Deutsche Rückversicherung* v. *Walbrook Insurances Co. Ltd*,[97] " . . . there is no reported case where the Court, in *inter partes* proceedings, has approved the grant of an injunction on the basis of the fraud exception".

(2) Even where there is a strong *prima facie* case that the beneficiaries are not entitled under the terms of the main contract to draw on the letter of credit, an application for an injunction to restrain the beneficiaries can be refused.[98]

(3) Of course an injunction can be applied for by the buyer against his bank or against the seller under the main contract who is attempting

93. *Ibid.*, p. 198b.
94. *Ibid.*, p. 186d. This was at an earlier hearing before Clarke J.
95. *Ibid.*, p. 198g.
96. *Ibid.*, *per* Phillips J, p. 202h. The plaintiffs also failed in their claim that they had some proprietary interest in the moneys paid out by the banks under the letters of credit: p. 202c.
97. [1994] 4 All ER 181, 196a.
98. *Howe Richardson Scale Co. Ltd* v. *Polimex-Cekop* [1978] 1 Lloyd's Rep. 161, see *per* Donaldson J (as he then was); also *Tuckan Timber Ltd* v. *Barclays Bank Plc* [1987] 1 Lloyd's Rep. 171.

to obtain payment or both, and there is no difference (that is the test of fraud is the same) in what has to be proved.[99]

(4) It is sometimes suggested that to succeed in his application for an injunction, the buyer must show that his bank has some knowledge of the fraud of the seller—the beneficiary under the letter of credit.[100] However, this is probably "academic once the proceedings have reached the *inter partes* stage",[101] because no matter what the knowledge of the bank was in the earlier course of events, once the proceedings become *inter partes* the bank *must* then have knowledge of the alleged fraud, and so the point is illusory.

Limitation of liability

The issuing bank, at the request of its customer, the buyer, assumes a liability to all other parties to make payment under the terms of the credit, and, as we have seen, this is a responsibility which, once given, cannot be retracted.

The issuing bank, therefore, will demand an indemnity from its customer in consideration of issuing the credit. Indeed Art. 14(a) of the Uniform Customs provides that once the bank pays or incurs a liability to pay against documents which appear to be in accordance with the credit, then, " . . . the Issuing Bank and the Confirming Bank, if any, are bound to reimburse the Nominated Bank which has paid . . . ".[102]

However, Art. 15 is more sweeping in its terms. It provides as follows:

Banks assume no liability or responsibility for the form, sufficiency, accuracy, genuineness, falsification or legal effect of any documents, or for the general and/or particular conditions stipulated in the documents or superimposed thereon; nor do they assume any liability or responsibility for the description, quantity, weight, quality, condition, packing, delivery, value or the existence of the goods represented by any documents, or for the good faith or acts and/or omissions, solvency, performance or standing of the consignor, the carriers, the forwarders, the consignees or the insurers of the goods or of any other person whomsoever.

Taken at its face value, therefore, the buyer cannot claim against his bank (or any others in the transaction for that matter),[103] since, by this wording, they do not accept responsibility for anything; even though, at the end of the day, the buyer has only a collection of documents which gives him title to goods which may no longer exist.

---

99. *Dong Jin Metal Co. Ltd* v. *Raymet Ltd* (unreported) [1993] Transcript 945; and *per* Phillips J, *Deutsche Rückversicherung AG* v. *Walbrook Insurance Co Ltd* [1994] 4 All ER 181, 196e.

100. *Per* Ackner LJ, "the evidence of fraud must be clear, both as to the fact of fraud and as the bank's knowledge": *United Trading Corp SA* v. *Allied Arab Bank Ltd* [1985] 2 Lloyd's Rep. 554, 561.

101. *Per* Phillips J, *Deutsche Rückversicherung AG* v. *Walbrook Insurance Co Ltd* [1994] 4 All ER 181, 195j.

102. Even if the obligations are imposed by foreign laws and usages: UCP, Art. 18(d).

103. See UCP, Art. 20(a).

In addition, the Uniform Customs attempt to relieve the banks of liability when dealing with each other. Article 18 provides that banks assume no liability or responsibility if the instructions they transmit are not carried out, even if they have chosen the bank which is in default. Indeed, the Article goes on to provide that it is the customer who applies for the credit (the buyer of the goods in the main transaction) who must indemnify the banks against all obligations and responsibilities imposed by foreign laws and usages.

If the banks will not accept responsibility for losses arising from their direct acts and omissions, it is not surprising to find the Uniform Customs trying to relieve banks from the possible liability for *consequential* loss in these transactions. Article 16 is also worded widely in its attempt to provide adequate protection if things should go wrong in the banking world. It states:

Banks assume no liability or responsibility for the consequences arising out of delay and/or loss in transit of any messages, letters or documents, or for delay, mutilation or other errors arising in the transmission of any telecommunication. Banks assume no liability or responsibility for errors in translation and/or interpretation of technical terms, and reserve the right to transmit credit terms without translating them.

This must be read together with Art. 12, which deals with "teletransmissions"[104] among banks; sub-para (e) provides that: "Banks shall be responsible for any consequences arising from their failure to follow the procedures set out . . . " in the other sub-paras of Art. 12. Comforting as this is in indicating the banks' willingness to be responsible for "any consequences", if a case were brought in England[105] such loss would, of course, be subject to the rules of English law as to measure of damages,[106] which might well not cover "any consequences".

At all events, one presumes that the cover attempted to be given by Art. 18 would be lost, at least as far as "teletransmissions" are concerned, if the terms of Art. 12 were not observed by the banks. In other words, the banks could not ignore the requirements laid down as to "teletransmissions" in Art. 12, and then, if sued, claim that Art. 18 protected them!

Then again, under Art. 17 of the Uniform Customs the

---

104. This was a new word introduced into the 1984 Revision of the UCP to replace the words "cable, telegram or telex" in Art. 4 of the 1974 Revision. This codeword is not defined in the rules but, doubtless, includes telephone and telefax communications, as well as the methods referred to in the old Art. 4.

105. This would depend upon whether the English courts would accept jurisdiction.

106. It depends on whether the negligence action is based in tort or contract. Shorn of various exceptions, the rule in tort is what the court thinks a reasonable man could have "foreseen": *Overseas Tankship (UK) Ltd* v. *Morts Dock & Engineering Co Ltd—(The Wagon Mound)*—[1961] AC 388; *The Heron 11* [1969] 1 AC 350: in contract, what was in the "contemplation" of the parties: *Hadley* v. *Baxendale* (1854) 9 Exch 341. In either case, the damages may not cover the loss from "any consequences". This is a complicated subject, and it gets more so when the negligence arises out of a breach of contract. See Charlesworth and Percy, *Negligence*, 9th edn. (1997) para 4–301.

Banks assume no liability or responsibility for the consequences arising out of the interruption of their business by Acts of God, riots, civil commotions, insurrections, wars or any causes beyond their control, or by any strikes, or lockouts . . ."

This is an attempt to cover the banks' position in *force majeure* situations as outlined in the wording. As with all such clauses they are interpreted strictly, so that if an event occurs the wording must be looked at carefully to see that the circumstances which have arisen are specifically covered in the language used, because if they are not, the general words " . . . or any other causes . . . " will not be deemed a catch-all. They will be limited to the type of calamity mentioned by the specific words " . . . Acts of God, riots, civil commotions, insurrections, wars . . .",[107] so that the closure of a bank due to inclement weather—not being an Act of God[108]—would probably not fall within the clause,[109] and so the bank could not rely on this to excuse non-performance.

It must also be noted with regard to Art. 19 that it provides that once business is resumed after one of the events set out in the paragraph, the banks will not " . . . incur a deferred payment undertaking, or effect payment, acceptance or negotiation under credits which expired during such interruption of their business", unless "specifically authorized". Because of this provision, the buyer and the seller should ensure that the banks are clearly instructed, within the terms of the credit, that if the banks close in circumstances as outlined in Art. 19, the credit date will be extended automatically, and that they will effect payment on the first day they reopen for business.

All these provisions, which, of course, are deemed to be incorporated into each letter of credit, are undoubtedly weighed heavily in the bank's favour and are a clear attempt to negative any responsibility, even for their own negligence; and the burden would be upon a plaintiff seeking to contest the efficacy of these provisions to show they did not, or should not, apply in the particular circumstances.

Under English law there is little doubt the terms are basically binding upon all parties who sign any forms acknowledging the Uniform Customs (certainly the buyer, being the applicant for the credit), and whether they read the wording or not is immaterial.[110] It is only a question, therefore, of whether the plaintiff can be excused from the full effect of those terms. For example, it may be that in the discussions with the bank there was some oral statement made

107. This is under the *ejusdem generis* rule (of the same kind), which is to the effect that where there are specific words as set out in the clause, followed by general words—" . . . or any causes . . . ". The general words must be interpreted as being of the same kind (*ejusdem generis*) as the specific words.

108. An "Act of God" has been defined as "Circumstances which no human foresight can provide against and of which human prudence is not bound to recognize the possibility . . . ": *per* Lord Finlay LC in *Greenock Corp* v. *Caledonian Railway Co* [1917] AC 556, at p. 571.

109. As with the closure of Manhattan banks by the proximity of hurricane "Gloria" in September 1985. See also *Tillmanns* v. *SS Knutsford* [1908] AC 406.

110. *L'Estrange* v. *Graucob* [1934] 2 KB 394.

by one of the bank's officers, which in some way can be taken to have amended the terms of the exemption claimed subsequently by the bank;[111] or, possibly, if the negligence of the banks is so serious that they should not be allowed to negate the whole agreement, and yet still be able to rely on part of it (namely, the exemption clause),[112] the effect of which would be to defeat the main purpose of the transaction entirely.[113] Moreover, the wording of exemption clauses is always construed strictly, and, hence, in this case *against* the banks, being the party who wishes to obviate the results of its own negligence.[114] Also, the terms of these exemption provisions do, of course, apply only to those who are parties to the particular agreement,[115] and so, while the buyer is clearly bound (having signed the credit application), in spite of the sweeping terms of these Articles, it must be extremely doubtful how far, for example, an issuing bank could rely on them against a seller (the beneficiary under the credit).

However, it cannot really be doubted that if the terms of these exemption provisions are sufficiently clear in their application to the particular circumstances of the case, the banks will, in all probability, be able to rely on them no matter how hard might be the results.[116]

3. CONTRACT BETWEEN ISSUING AND CONFIRMING BANKS

As we have seen, it is the issuing bank which begins the inter-bank contractual relationships when it asks another bank, usually in the seller's country, to advise the beneficiary of the credit or to confirm the credit or whatever. The contract is made between the issuing bank and the advising/confirming bank when that bank signifies its acceptance of the terms to the issuing bank. Until that time there is no contractual obligation on the advising[117]/confirming[118] bank at all. Once acceptance has taken place, then, of course, the banks are bound to carry out the terms of their obligations.

---

111. *J Evans & Son (Portsmouth) Ltd* v. *Andrea Merzario Ltd* [1976] 1 WLR 1078.
112. But this is a question of construction of the wording of the agreement, not a rule of law: *Suisse Atlantique Société d'Armement Maritime SA* v. *NV Rotterdamsche Kolen Centrale* [1967] 1 AC 361.
113. *Glyn* v. *Margetson & Co* [1893] AC 351.
114. Under the *contra proferentem* rule.
115. *Scruttons Ltd* v. *Midland Silicones Ltd* [1962] AC 446.
116. *Photo Production Ltd* v. *Securicor Transport Ltd* [1980] 2 WLR 283. If an exemption clause does apply it will, subject to any particular wording, negative liability in both contract and tort. The subject of exemption clauses is still a very complicated area of the law; see, for a further and more detailed discussion. Cheshire Fifoot and Furmston's *Law of Contract*, 13th edn. (1996) pp. 160 *et seq*.
117. UCP, Art. 10(c).
118. *Ibid.*, Art. 9(c)(i). There is an obligation on the bank invited to confirm to inform the issuing bank "without delay" if it is not prepared to do so. There seems no similar obligation upon the advising bank if it is not prepared to act.

Inter-bank relationships

By nominating another bank or by allowing for acceptance or negotiation in the terms of the credit, or by requesting a bank to add its confirmation, the issuing bank thereby authorizes that other bank to pay, accept or negotiate, as the case may be, and to be reimbursed accordingly. The only defence the issuing bank can have to this obligation is if the other bank did not act on documents which on their face appeared to be within the terms and conditions of the credit.[119] Indeed, in the case of a revocable credit, the issuing bank must reimburse for payments made or documents taken up prior to any cancellation.[120]

If the issuing bank intends that the reimbursement is to be obtained through another branch or office of the issuing bank (or through another bank altogether, for that matter), it must provide that "reimbursing" bank with proper instructions or authorization in good time.[121] In such cases, the issuing bank frequently asks the reimbursing bank to certify that in making payment they have complied with the terms of the credit; but this is not a requirement.[122]

Having made these arrangements for reimbursement, it does not, of course, absolve the issuing bank of its obligations under the credit, if, for any reason, the reimbursing bank does not, in fact, repay the paying bank[123]; the paying bank can still look to the issuing bank to effect the reimbursement. Moreover, the issuing bank will be responsible for any loss of interest if reimbursement is not made on first demand or as specified in the credit or as may be agreed between the banks.[124]

So far as communications between the banks are concerned, the Uniform Customs now provide for "teletransmissions",[125] which is a term not defined, but appears to be broad enough to cover "cable, telegram or telex" (which were the words used in the 1974 Revision),[126] as well as telefax and also telephone.

Where the issuing bank instructs an advising bank "by any teletransmission" to advise a credit, and intends the mail confirmation to be the "operative credit instrument", the teletransmission must state "full details to follow" or some similar expression. The "operative credit instrument" must then follow without delay.[127] If this wording is not used then the teletransmission "will be deemed to be the operative credit instrument".[128] The Uniform Customs and

---

119. UCP, Art. 10(d).
120. *Ibid.*, Art. 8(b).
121. *Ibid.*, Art. 19(a).
122. *Ibid.*, Art. 19(b).
123. *Ibid.*, Art. 19(c).
124. *Ibid.*, Art. 19(d).
125. *Ibid.*, Art. 11. Article 16 uses the word "telecommunication".
126. The old Art. 4.
127. UCP, Art. 11(c).
128. *Ibid.*, Art. 11(a)(i). All this presupposes that the "teletransmission" was not a telephone call!

Practice for Documentary Credits, 1993 Revision, ICC Publication No. 500 applies to all documentary credits " . . . where they are incorporated into the text of the credit,"[129] suggesting that if the UCP are not *expressly* incorporated they will not apply; yet Article 1 goes on to state that the UCP are binding on all parties, " . . . unless otherwise expressly stipulated in the Credit," which is something of a contradiction as yet to be resolved.

If an advising bank receives instructions which are not clear, they have a choice, if they wish, of giving the beneficiary a preliminary notification for information only, and, of course, without responsibility; or of not saying anything.[130] Much will depend upon the circumstances, but usually one would expect the advising bank to verify the facts before making any notification.

Where banks give instructions to issue, confirm or advise a credit in terms similar to one previously provided, and the earlier credit was subject to amendments, it must be understood that the new (and similar) credit will *not* include the amendments from the earlier credit, unless the instructions clearly specify.[131] This is an unhappy way of doing business, and banks will usually not act on such instructions from their customer, which should be discouraged.

Needless to say, if an issuing bank uses the services of an advising bank to have the credit advised to the beneficiary, it must use the services of the same bank to advise of any amendments.[132]

Finally, it must be observed with regard to this relationship with the paying bank that the issuing bank is not relieved from any of its obligations by the paying bank giving notice to the issuing bank of any discrepancies in the documents, or advising that it has paid "under reserve" or against an indemnity or whatever.[133]

Bank-to-bank reimbursements

The ICC has published a set of rules which deal expressly with the topic of bank-to-bank reimbursements. This is ICC publication no. 525 entitled "The Uniform Rules for Bank-to-Bank Reimbursements under Documentary Credits". These rules came into force on 1 July 1996, and they apply "where they are incorporated into the text of the Reimbursement Authorization"[134] and are binding on all parties, "unless otherwise expressly stipulated in the Reimbursements Authorization", which is the document sent by the bank issuing the documentary credit to the bank which is requested to effect payment on its

---

129. *Ibid.*, Art. 1.
130. UCP, Art. 12.
131. *Ibid.*, Art. 5(a).
132. *Ibid.*, Art. 11(b).
133. *Ibid.*, Art. 14(f).
134. Art. 1.

behalf. The rules are not intended to override or change the provisions of the ICC Uniform Customs and Practice for Documentary Credits.[135]

It is the issuing bank which is given the responsibility of initiating the reimbursement procedure,[136] and providing the information required, and is responsible for the consequences of non-compliance.[137] The issuing bank is also responsible for indicating in the documentary credit that reimbursement claims are subject to the rules.[138]

Leaving aside the inevitable detail, the procedure may be summarized as follows:

(1) The bank issuing the documentary credit (the issuing bank) creates the transaction and is responsible for arranging payment of the credit and charges, almost certainly to a bank in another country.

(2) The issuing bank may well ask another bank, again perhaps in that other country, to effect payment of the credit, and that bank (claiming bank) will, of course, have a right to be repaid.

(3) Also, the issuing bank may ask yet another bank, once more perhaps in that other country, to reimburse the claiming bank and if this happens the issuing bank must provide a "Reimbursement Authorization" to that reimbursing bank, which will give detailed instructions of the payments to be made.

(4) The claiming bank will then present a "Reimbursement Claim" to the reimbursing bank who will then pay on behalf of the issuing bank in accordance with the reimbursement authorization.

(5) The claiming bank may well ask the reimbursing bank for an undertaking that repayments will be effected (reimbursement undertaking), so as to be sure of repayment—again, probably from that bank in their own country.

(6) The Rules, of course, are detailed, but the purpose of them is to attempt to ensure the smooth running of these payment and repayment obligations.

(a) The claim

The bank that pays the credit or accepts drafts or whatever, on behalf of the issuing bank, is designated the "Claiming Bank"[139] and is, of course, entitled to be reimbursed. The issuing bank may effect reimbursement direct, or it may instruct another bank—called the "Reimbursement Bank" to effect payment

---

135. *Ibid.*
136. Art. 2a.
137. Art. 5. It must also indemnify the reimbursing bank against all obligations and responsibilities imposed by foreign laws and usages: Art. 13.
138. Art. 1.
139. Art. 2e.

on its behalf.[140] In the latter case, the issuing bank sends a "Reimbursement Authorization" to the reimbursing bank instructing that bank to pay the claiming bank;[141] this reimbursement authorization is, of course, quite independent of the documentary credit.[142]

The reimbursement authorization (and any amendments) is a vital document in the procedure, and it must be "complete and precise"[143] and contain the information mentioned in Article 6d, giving credit number, currency and so forth; also who will pay the charges for the reimbursement.[144]

The reimbursement authorizations and any amendments must be issued either by authenticated teletransmissions or by letter, and the teletransmission[145] will be deemed the operative authorization; if a mail confirmation is sent it will have no effect, and the reimbursing bank has no obligation to check it against the instructions sent by teletransmission.[146] One assumes, therefore, that letters of confirmation will not be used!

The reimbursing bank may well be requested by the issuing bank to give an *undertaking* to the claiming bank, which, if given, is irrevocable, and must contain information similar to that contained in the reimbursement authorization.[147]

Once this "Reimbursement Undertaking" has been given, it cannot be amended or cancelled without the agreement of the claiming bank.[148]

---

140. Art. 2b. However all claims for loss of interest, or value due to exchange fluctuations or revaluations or devaluations are to be settled between the claiming bank and the issuing bank, unless the loss is due to the non-performance of the undertaking given by the reimbursing bank: Art. 17.

141. Art. 2c.

142. *Ibid.*, and Art. 3.

143. Art. 6b and Art. 2d. An irrevocable reimbursement authorization cannot be amended or cancelled without the agreement of the reimbursing bank: Art. 9g(i). If it chooses *not* to issue the amendment, it must inform the issuing bank without delay: Art. 9g(ii). The original authorization, of course, remains in force until the acceptance of the amendment is communicated by the reimbursing bank to the issuing bank: Art. 9g(iv).

144. The reimbursing banks' charges for effecting payment will usually be for the account of the issuing bank, but if they are to be for the account of another party, the issuing bank must give instructions, both in the original credit and in the reimbursement authorization: Art. 16a. Of course, the reimbursing bank must then be obliged to follow those instructions: Art. 16b. If the issuing bank fails to provide instructions as to who is to pay these charges, it is implied that they will be for the account of the issuing bank: Art. 16c. If charges are not paid by the nominated third party (or a claim is never presented for payment) the issuing bank will remain liable for these charges: Art. 16c.

145. See UCP Art. 11.

146. Art. 6a.

147. Art. 9b and 9e. If the reimbursing bank is requested to accept and pay time drafts, the reimbursement authorization must also state the tenor of the drafts, the drawer and the party responsible for the charges of acceptance and discounting. Moreover, issuing banks should not require sight drafts to be drawn on the reimbursing bank: Art. 9c.

148. Art. 9h(i) and (iv). Of course, the original reimbursement undertaking remains in force for the benefit of the claiming bank until that bank accepts the amendment: Art. 9h(iii).

(b) Processing the claim

The reimbursing bank must process claims promptly, though Article 14 absolves the reimbursing bank from liability arising out of delays and/or loss of messages, and for errors in translation. Article 11a(i) states that the period must not "exceed three banking days following the receipt of the Reimbursement Claim"; however, if claims are received outside banking hours they are deemed to be received on the next banking day. In the same way, if the last day for presenting a claim falls on a day when the reimbursing bank is closed for any reason (other than for reasons of *force majeure*),[149] the date for presentation is extended to the first day following, on which the reimbursing bank is open.[150] In fact, except as may be expressly agreed by the reimbursing bank, the reimbursing authorization must not have an expiry date, nor a last date for presentation of the claim at all.[151]

As we have already noted, the banks are at pains to stress that communications shall be by teletransmission, and that confirmation by letter should not be used. Indeed, Article 12 provides that if the issuing bank, when it receives the documents in the transaction, gives a new reimbursement authorization (unless by way of amendment or cancellation), and a duplicate reimbursement takes place, it will be the responsibility of the issuing bank to obtain the return of the amount paid by way of duplication.

In the same way, reimbursement claims must be made by teletransmission, and no mail confirmation is to be sent.[152] As might be expected, the claim must clearly indicate the credit number, the issuing bank, and must state separately the principal amount claimed and charges; also it must, in the case of a reimbursement undertaking, comply with the terms of that undertaking.[153] However, the claiming bank must not indicate that a payment, acceptance or negotiation was made under reserve or against an indemnity.[154] It probably goes without saying that the reimbursing bank assumes no liability for any consequences of the claiming bank failing to follow this procedure.[155]

(c) Failure to pay

If the reimbursing bank, for whatever the reason, decides *not* to effect the reimbursement it must give notice both to the issuing bank and the claiming

---

149. Art. 15.
150. Art. 9f. If the issuing bank requires a pre-debit notification the time taken to effect this is added to the processing period mentioned above: Art. 11a(i).
151. Art. 7. If an expiry date is provided in the reimbursement authorization it will be disregarded.
152. Art. 10a(i).
153. Art. 10a(ii), (iii) and (iv). Note also, the communication for reimbursement must not include multiple claims in one teletransmission: *ibid.*, para. v.
154. Art. 10c. Reimbursing banks assume no responsibility if they honour claims that indicate that payment, acceptance or negotiation was made under reserve or against an indemnity: Art. 11e.
155. Art. 10d.

bank, once more, by telecommunication or by other expeditious means, and if a reimbursement undertaking has been given, the reasons for non-payment must be explained.[156]

The notice of non-reimbursement need not be sent by the reimbursement bank until either, the due date, or at the close of business on the third day following receipt of the claim.[157]

The rule of strict compliance

It will be apparent from all that has been written before that when the issuing bank asks another bank to carry out the issuing bank's obligation to pay it places a heavy responsibility on the paying bank. It must pay strictly in accordance with the terms of the credit, and check the documents presented to it for payment, and eventually pass those documents to the issuing bank.

In handling documents in this way the banks must be careful to deal with them to the letter of their instructions,[158] and while the paying bank can use its own discretion on points of difficulty,[159] if they stray outside the terms of their mandate they may well be liable in damages to their principals. This had led to the doctrine of "strict compliance": either the documents are in order or they are not, and if they are not, the bank can do one of three things:[160] (A) Refuse payment; or (B) Pay and take an indemnity from the beneficiary (the seller) in respect of any loss or damage resulting from the deficiency in the documentation; or (C) Pay the beneficiary "under reserve".

Which course is adopted will depend upon the extent and importance of the deficiencies, and the circumstances of the case.[161] We shall consider each of these possibilities in a little more detail.

156. Art. 11a(ii).

157. Art. 11c(iii). With the addition of time for any requested pre-debit notification, as to which see Art. 11a(i). This paragraph is curiously drafted, since its provisions seem not to apply unless the due date ". . . is more than three banking days following the day of receipt of the Reimbursement Claim".

158. UCP, Art 13(a). In part, it says: "Banks must examine all documents with reasonable care to ascertain whether or not they appear on their face to be in compliance with the terms and conditions of the credit."

159. The terms upon which the paying bank pays, whether "under reserve" or whatever, or rejects, is between them and the payee, and not the issuing bank, which, of course, is still liable under the credit: UCP, Art. 14(f).

160. *Per* Sir John Donaldson MR in *Banque de l'Indochine et de Suez SA* v. *JH Rayner (Mincing Lane) Ltd* [1983] 2 WLR 841, 853H.

161. In making up its mind whether to take up the documents or not, UCP, Art. 14(b) demands that the issuing bank decides " . . . on the basis of the documents alone . . . ", which means, presumably, that the views and wishes of the buyer (its customer) must not influence the bank's decision. Banks must, of course, act in accordance with the instructions given to them, and must accept or reject the documents within the terms of those instructions. They cannot of their own volition introduce terms of acceptance: *Harlow & Jones Ltd* v. *American Express Bank Ltd and Creditanstalt Bankverein* [1990] 2 Lloyd's Rep. 343. See also *Floating Dock Ltd* v. *Hong Kong & Shanghai Banking Corp* [1986] 1 Lloyd's Rep. 65; and *Co-operative Centrale Raiffeisen Boerenleenbank BA* v. *The Sumitomo Bank Ltd* [1987] 1 Lloyd's Rep. 345.

(a) Refuse payment

If the confirming bank is in any real doubt they will, almost certainly, refuse payment. Two examples may help illustrate the point:

EQUITABLE TRUST CO v. DAWSON[162]

Dawsons bought vanilla beans, and they opened a credit in favour of the seller with the Equitable Trust. Payment was to be made upon the presentation of a number of documents, which included a certificate of quality to be given "by experts". There was some confusion in the exchange of cables, and Equitable Trust paid out on a certificate signed by one expert only. As it happened, the seller was fraudulent, and had shipped substantially rubbish, which the single expert failed to discover. Dawsons claimed that Equitable Trust should never have paid out on documents (or at least one of them) that did not comply with the terms of the credit. Equitable Trust sued Dawsons when they refused to have their account debited with the charge. *Held*—that Equitable Trust was not entitled to be reimbursed because they had paid out contrary to Dawsons' instructions, which were to pay on the certificate of at least *two* experts—not one. "There is no room for documents which are almost the same, or which will do just as well."[163]

SOPROMA SPA v. MARINE & ANIMAL BY-PRODUCTS[164]

Soproma, an Italian company, bought fishmeal from Marine & Animal, a New York corporation, on terms which required Marine & Animal to have the bill of lading marked "freight pre-paid", and to provide a certificate that the consignment had a minimum of 70 per cent protein. When the documents were tendered they were defective in that the bill of lading was stamped "collect freight" and, also, the protein content was only 67 per cent. The documents were rejected, and, thereafter, the credit expired. A second tender of the correct documents followed some time later, and was again rejected. *Held*—that as the original tender of the documents was defective, no subsequent tender could correct the irregularity, and the bank were quite correct in refusing payment.

Combination of documents

As we have seen, it is common for banks to receive several documents in respect of any one transaction; for example, the bill of lading, invoice, insurance policy (or certificate), certificate of quality, and so on. In such cases, subject to anything stated in the instructions to the banks, it is enough that all the documents taken together give the bank adequate instructions. The banks need not, unless requested to do so, demand that each document, taken on its own,[165] should satisfy the terms of the banks' mandate. For example, in

---

162. (1926) 27 Ll.L.Rep. 49. See also *Gian Singh & Co Ltd* v. *Banque de l'Indochine* [1974] 2 All ER 754 (PC).
163. *Per* Lord Sumner, at p. 52.
164. [1966] 1 Lloyd's Rep. 367.
165. Note, however, UCP, Art. 13(a) which states: "Documents which appear on their face to be inconsistent with one another will be considered as not appearing on their face to be in compliance with the terms and conditions of the credit." And see *Seaconsar Far East Ltd* v. *Bank Markazi Jomhouri Islami Iran* [1993] 1 Lloyd's Rep. 236, where the bank was held entitled to

MIDLAND BANK LTD v. SEYMOUR[166]

An English company bought ducks' feathers from a seller in Hong Kong. The instructions to the banks, among other things, required that the goods be "Hong Kong duck feathers—85 per cent clean; 12 bales each weighing about 190 lbs". In fact, the bill of lading described the goods only as "12 bales, Hong Kong duck feathers", though all the other documents, taken together, gave an adequate description of the goods. In due course the bank paid out. It was then discovered that the goods were not at all as agreed, and the buyer claimed that the bank must repay the money paid out to the seller, as the seller was in breach because the bill of lading did not properly describe the goods. *Held*—that the bank had discharged its mandate, taking all the documents together, which adequately described the goods.

Timing of rejection

The rule of "strict compliance" does, of course, put the banks in a difficult position where they must make a decision quickly to pay (in accordance with the cash equivalence rule), or refuse because the documents might not be strictly in order. As Lord Diplock pointed out in *Commercial Banking Co of Sydney v. Jalsard Pty*[167]:

Both the issuing banker and his correspondent bank have to make quick decisions as to whether a document which has been tendered by the seller complies with the requirements of the credit at the risk of incurring liability to one or other of the parties to the transaction if the decision is wrong.

If banks do not react quickly it may well amount to ratification of the documents, and the banks may then lose their right of rejection.[168] "Quickly" will, of course, depend upon the circumstances of each case, but in banking practice it is taken to be no more than a few days.[169] The courts have, therefore, adopted the view in these cases that when a banker "acts upon ambiguous instructions he is not in default if he can show that he adopted

reject documents which did not contain the letter of credit number, nor the name of the principal.

166. [1955] 2 Lloyd's Rep. 147.

167. [1973] AC 279, 286. See also UCP, Art. 16, paras (b), (c), (d) and (e).

168. *Bank Melli Iran v. Barclays Bank Ltd* [1951] 2 TLR 1057. In *Bankers Trust Co v. State Bank of India* [1991] 2 Lloyd's Rep. 443, rejection of the documents which took five days was held not to be within a "reasonable time".

169. See *Hansson v. Hamel & Horley Ltd* [1922] 2 AC 36; *Commercial Banking Co of Sydney v. Jalsard Pty* [1973] AC 279. Yet in the *Melli Case* six weeks were allowed, but this has been criticized. The wording of Art. 16(c) in the UCP 400 was that "the issuing bank shall have a reasonable time in which to examine the documents and to determine . . . whether to take up or to refuse the documents". Article 14(d)(i) of UCP 500 states that if the bank is to refuse the documents it must do so " . . . without delay but no later than the close of the seventh banking day following the day of receipt of the documents". There is no implied term that "a reasonable time"—whatever that may be—can be extended so the bank can consult its customer. If it wishes to do so, the consultation must be within the same time: *Bankers Trust Co v. State Bank of India, The Times*, 4 September 1990. For a recent example considered by the House of Lords, see *Seaconsar Far East Ltd v. Bank Markazi Jomhouri Islami Iran* [1994] 1 Lloyd's Rep. 1, which involved the sending of a telex which miscarried, but the list of discrepancies was not received till

what was a reasonable meaning".[170] It follows, therefore, that the bank must "examine with reasonable care all documents presented in order to ascertain that they appear *on their face* to be in accordance with the terms and conditions of the credit".[171] If the documents appear in order, the bank must pay[172]; and once having paid, the bank is then estopped from setting up a claim based on rejection.[173] It is, of course, one thing to state the rule, and another to apply it: questions of fact and degrees of interpretation are constantly arising. A few examples may help show the dilemma in which banks sometimes find themselves. In *Scott v. Barclays Bank Ltd*[174] refusal was justified where the terms of the credit required a policy of insurance, and what was tendered was a *certificate* of insurance. Again, refusal was justified in *JH Rayner & Co Ltd* v. *Hambros Bank Ltd*[175] where the terms of credit referred to "coromandel groundnuts" and the bill of lading specified "machine shelled groundnuts". In *Kydon Compania Naviera SA* v. *National Westminster Bank Ltd*[176] refusal of documents was justified where the terms of credit required a sight draft to be drawn on "Euroasia Carriers", but the draft was, in fact, provided by the Somali Bank.

However, the bank's refusal was considered *not* justified in *British Imex Industries Ltd* v. *Midland Bank Ltd*[177] where the bank refused payment because there was no acknowledgement that a particular clause in the bill of lading had been complied with, when the terms did not require that any particular clause had been satisfied.

(b) Take an indemnity

It is always open to the paying bank, if the documents are in some way defective, to pay instead of rejecting, but before parting with the funds to seek an indemnity from the beneficiary. It is usual for the irregularities notified by

two days later; a further telex seeking authority to pay notwithstanding the discrepancies *was never answered*. Applied in *Bank of Baroda* v. *Vysya Bank Ltd* [1994] 2 Lloyd's Rep. 87. The standard of proof in considering whether jurisdiction has been made out under one of the heads of Order 11 RSC is that of a "good arguable case", not that there should be "a serious issue to be tried" at p. 90.

170. *Per* Devlin J (as he then was) in *Midland Bank Ltd* v. *Seymour* [1955] 2 Lloyd's Rep. 147, 153.

171. *Per* Lord Diplock in *United City Merchants (Investments) Ltd* v. *Royal Bank of Canada* [1983] 1 AC 168, 184E.

172. Unless if there is evidence of fraud known to the bank.

173. *Panchaud Freres SA* v. *Etablissements General Grain Co* [1970] 1 Lloyd's Rep. 53. In a CF contract the right to reject the documents is, of course, a separate right from the right to reject the goods. "The right to reject the documents arises when the documents are tendered, and the right to reject the goods arises when they are landed, and when, after examination, they are not found to be in conformity with the contract": *per* Devlin J (as he then was) in *Kwei Tek Chao* v. *British Traders & Shippers Ltd* [1954] 2 QB 459, 481.

174. [1923] 2 KB 1.

175. [1943] 1 KB 37.

176. [1981] 1 Lloyd's Rep. 68.

177. [1958] 1 QB 542.

the paying bank to the beneficiary to be listed in the form of indemnity; however, sometimes this is not done, and the wording of the indemnity demanded is general in its application.[178]

No one wishes a transaction to be held up needlessly, but giving indemnities like this is not without risk.[179] In truth, it should be no wider in its application than is necessary to protect the bank from the dangers it foresees, and sufficiently clear so as not to expose the beneficiary to a limitless degree.

The indemnity to the paying bank will not extend to cover the issuing bank also, unless the indemnity says so—as it not infrequently does.

Before giving an indemnity the beneficiary should satisfy himself that the discrepancies can be explained and corrected immediately, otherwise the indemnity may well prove limitless as to time. If this is the case, perhaps the paying bank had better refuse the documents in any event.

(c) Pay "under reserve"

Notwithstanding all these rules and guidelines, banks still face difficulties sometimes in deciding whether to reject or not. In such cases, the paying bank may pay "under reserve"; in other words, if the issuing bank subsequently rejects the documents, repayment of the money can be claimed from the beneficiary (the seller) since the bank has made its position clear in reserving its rights in this way. However, since there seems to be no exact meaning of the words "under reserve", it is vital that the form of agreement covering the possible repayment is made clear from the beginning. An example of where this method was used is the case of

BANQUE DE L'INDOCHINE ET DE SUEZ SA v. JH RAYNER (MINCING LANE) LTD[180]

Rayners were merchants in London and sold a quantity of sugar to a buyer in Djibouti. The issuing bank in Djibouti opened an irrevocable letter of credit, which Indochine confirmed in favour of Rayners as sellers. In due course, Rayners tendered documents under the credit to Indochine, which Indochine thought defective. However, after telephone discussions among the parties, Indochine paid out "under reserve". It was then that the issuing bank in Djibouti stated that the buyers could not (or would not) lift the conditions which caused the "reserve". Indochine then sued Rayners for return of the money paid to them, as the payment had been made "under reserve"; in other words, in circumstances which, had the bank wished, they could have refused the documents and payment. Rayners' view was that the bank could not reserve their rights in this way unless the beneficiary under the credit (in this case Rayners) agreed also that the documents were defective. *Held*—that there is no precise meaning of the words "under reserve", and so in using that expression the court must look to the intention of

178. Some banks who are prepared to take a risk try to obtain an indemnity for every conceivable eventuality, including defective goods and liability for consequential loss; this gives them greater cover than under the original terms of the credit!

179. See *Moralice (London) Ltd* v. *ED & F Man* [1954] 2 Lloyd's Rep. 526.

180. [1983] 2 WLR 841.

the parties. In this case " . . . payment was to be made under reserve in the sense that the beneficiary would be bound to repay the money on demand if the issuing bank should reject the documents, whether on its own initiative or on the buyer's instructions".[181]

4. CONTRACT BETWEEN CONFIRMING BANK AND SELLER

It is, as we have seen, the confirming bank—if the credit is confirmed, as it often is—which pays the seller's bank, upon the presentation of whatever documents the buyer and the seller originally agreed would be adequate to release payment. It must be observed that this is the only heading of Lord Wilberforce's analysis where the parties have not negotiated on the terms, and, indeed, in most cases the confirming bank and the seller have no contact with one another at all, until the moment of payment or its refusal. It is a well-established principle, however, and clearly stated by Lord Diplock when he said[182]:

If, on their face, the documents presented to the confirming bank by the seller conform with the requirements of the credit . . . that bank is under a contractual obligation to the seller to honour the credit.

It follows, therefore, that taking the transaction as a whole the seller (who is entitled to payment) can—in his own name—sue the confirming bank, although, in fact, there has been no contractual arrangements directly between the two parties in the accepted sense which would normally lead to privity of contract.[183]

The "cash equivalence" principle is also a fundamental part of this relationship, so that if the documents appear *on their face to be in order* the confirming bank must pay, even if they know of a dispute between the buyer and the seller, and if they do not pay the seller can sue. For example, in

181. *Per* Kerr LJ, at p. 860e. It seems that " . . . as many as two thirds of presentations of documents against confirmed credits in London are thought to deviate from the terms of the credits in some respects, but in the majority of cases this is somehow overcome by agreement". *Ibid.*, p. 859h.

182. *United City Merchants' Case* [1983] 1 AC 168, 183.

183. But see *per* Donaldson J (as he then was) in *Elder Dempster Lines Ltd* v. *Ionic Shipping Agency Inc* [1968] 1 Lloyd's Rep. 529, 535. This contractual relationship may well depend on the inclusion of the Uniform Customs: *Forestal Minosa Ltd* v. *Oriental Credit Ltd* [1986] 1 WLR 631, where the incorporation was made by a note in the margin of the credit to the effect that the credit was subject to the Uniform Customs, "except so far as otherwise expressly stated . . . " at p. 637c. The paying bank can be estopped from claiming that there are discrepancies in the credits to justify non-payment, where an agreement had been reached in respect of those discrepancies, and the seller (being entitled to payment) acted on that agreement: *Floating Dock Ltd* v. *Hong Kong and Shanghai Banking Corporation* [1986] 1 Lloyd's Rep. 65.

URQUHART LINSAY & CO LTD v. EASTERN BANK LTD[184]

Urquharts sold machinery to a customer in Calcutta. The machinery was to be shipped by instalments, and payment was to be made by irrevocable letter of credit opened by the Eastern Bank. After two shipments had been made and paid for, a dispute arose because Urquharts increased their prices for the machinery, as they were entitled to do under the terms of the supply contract. The buyer did not like this, and told his bank to withhold payment pending the resolution of the dispute. The following instalment was therefore not paid for by the bank, and Urquharts sued. *Held*—that the Eastern Bank was liable under the terms of the credit and had to pay out under it, notwithstanding they knew of the dispute between the buyer and the seller.

The basic rule was restated in another more recent case as follows:

UNITED CITY MERCHANTS (INVESTMENTS) LTD v. ROYAL BANK OF CANADA[185]

Glass Fibers, an English company, sold equipment to a buyer in Peru. Payment was to be by irrevocable letter of credit issued by Banco Continental SA (the buyer's bank) in Peru, and confirmed by the Royal Bank of Canada. Glass Fibers subsequently assigned the contract to City Merchants, their merchant bankers in London. As it happened, shipment was made one day later than provided for by the terms of the credit, but the carrier's agent (attempting, no doubt, to accommodate the problem) issued the bill of lading showing the date as though it was the last day of the credit. On presentation of the documents the Royal Bank refused to pay, on the grounds that they had received information to the effect that the shipment was made late and not as stated in the bill of lading. *Held*—that since the documents appeared in order on their face, the bank was obliged to make payment " . . . notwithstanding that the bank has knowledge that the seller at the time of presentation of the conforming documents is alleged by the buyer to have, and in fact has already, committed a breach of his contract with the buyer".[186] The cash equivalence principle was applied, and the fraudulent act of the carrier's agent (which was unknown to the seller) would not justify the refusal of payment.[187]

The seller (beneficiary) cannot, of course, sue other banks in the transaction with which he has no contractual relationship, nor can he intervene in the contract between the buyer and the issuing bank.[188]

184. [1922] 1 KB 318.
185. [1983] 1 AC 168.
186. *Per* Lord Diplock, at p. 183.
187. There was another problem in this case, as in an attempt to subvert the effect of the Peruvian Exchange Control Regulations, it was agreed between the buyer and the seller that the invoice would show a value of twice the agreed price for the goods. It was argued by the bank that this was contrary to Order in Council 1946, Art. VIII, s. 2(b) under the Bretton Woods Agreement, which provided that: "Exchange contracts which involve the currency of any member and which are contrary to the Exchange Control Regulations of that member . . . shall be unenforceable in the territories of any member . . . " The House of Lords held the bank liable to pay that portion of the City Merchants' claim which did not offend the Peruvian Exchange Control Regulations, and to that extent they were prepared to apportion the claim between the enforceable and the unenforceable. The courts are not always prepared to do this, however. See *Etablissement Esefka International Anstalt v. Central Bank of Nigeria* [1979] 1 Lloyd's Rep. 445. However, if the whole transaction is tainted with fraud, the courts will not allow letter of credit procedures to be used by a dishonest person to carry out this fraud: *Rafsanjan Pistachio Producers Co-operative v. Bank Leumi (UK) Plc* [1992] 1 Lloyd's Rep. 513.
188. UCP, Art. 3(b).

CHAPTER 17

LITIGATION

If a dispute cannot be resolved and resort to litigation is necessary two fundamental problems arise: 1. That of jurisdiction. That is, in which country should the action be commenced; and 2. Which system of law governs the dispute.

1. JURISDICTION

The problem of jurisdiction arises because, almost without exception in all these transactions, the parties are based in different countries,[1] and the knock-on effect of such disputes frequently involves all those concerned, from buyer to seller, to issuing bank, through to the confirming bank with each party having its own interests to protect.

Of course, what happens in practice is that the party who is, or feels, aggrieved commences an action in his own country (jurisdiction) if that is at all possible, and where, perhaps, the unfortunate defendant might be at a disadvantage. The defendant then, not infrequently, rushes off to the courts in *his* (or maybe some other) country to try to recover his position. This is illustrated by the recent case of

POWER CURBER INTERNATIONAL LTD v. NATIONAL BANK OF KUWAIT SAK[2]

Power Curber, an American corporation with its place of business in North Carolina (in spite of its name ending in "Ltd"), exported machinery to the Middle East through its representatives, Hammoudeh General Trading in Kuwait. Payment was to be made by a letter of credit as to 25% of the price, and by bills of exchange for the balance. The Kuwaiti (issuing) bank opened the letter of credit; it was irrevocable but not confirmed. The goods were shipped and then problems arose between Power Curber and Hammoudeh. An action was started in Kuwait by Hammoudeh claiming commissions in respect of the transaction, and an order preventing the Kuwaiti bank from paying under the irrevocable letter of credit. Power Curber retaliated by starting an action in North

---

1. There are two EEC Conventions signed in Brussels and Lugano and now enshrined in English law by the Civil Jurisdiction and Judgments Acts of 1982 and 1991.
2. [1981] 1 WLR 1233.

Carolina, but then stopped those proceedings and started an action in England against the London branch of the Kuwaiti bank. In the meanwhile, the Kuwaiti court made an order preventing the bank from paying under the credit. The English court were being asked to make a choice between enforcing the bank's obligation to pay under its irrevocable letter of credit or recognizing the order of the Kuwaiti court.

Held—that the letter of credit must be paid, although it was a ... disagreeable obligation to refuse to recognize the order of a court of a friendly state".[3] The English court felt they would otherwise be doing the Bank of Kuwait a grave disservice, " ... for it would undoubtedly seriously damage their credibility as an international bank if it was thought that their paper was not worth holding".[4]

The paramount consideration in England, at least, has however always been the sanctity of the "cash equivalence" principle,[5] and since the Uniform Customs are adopted worldwide: "If the courts of any of the countries should interfere with the obligations of one of its bankers (by ordering it not to pay under a letter of credit) it would strike at the very heart of that country's international trade. No foreign seller would supply goods to that country on letters of credit—because he could no longer be confident of being paid. No trader would accept a letter of credit issued by a bank of that country if it might be ordered by its courts not to pay."[6]

Some of these sentiments may seem a little strange to businessmen, however, for the standing of a country's national banks has long been a matter that traders have taken into consideration when arranging terms of payment, and is why, in fact, "confirmed" letters of credit are so popular, being a confirmation from a bank in one's own country that payment will be forthcoming, and a reliable defendant if it is not!

The English courts

As we have seen, the party which has suffered the alleged damage will, as likely as not, bring his action in his own country if he can; if, however, he wishes to avail himself of the jurisdiction of the English courts he must serve the defendant with the papers in the proceedings (usually a writ), so that the defendant can be made subject to any order the courts may make. In international cases the service of the proceedings is not as straightforward as in an ordinary domestic case, because the defendant might not be in England. To

3. *Per* Griffiths LJ at p. 1243a. The order was, in fact, obtained *ex parte* and this appeared to influence the English court somewhat: *ibid.*, at g.
4. *Ibid.*, at f.
5. Indeed, it was this principle which, in truth, led the courts to prevent a Central Bank from negating its responsibilites in commercial transactions by trying to hide behind the veil of Governmental immunity: *Trendtex Trading Corp Ltd* v. *Central Bank of Nigeria* [1977] 1 Lloyd's Rep. 581. This was before the State Immunity Act 1978; see also *Hispano Americana Mercantil SA* v. *Central Bank of Nigeria* [1979] 2 Lloyd's Rep. 277. A certificate given by the ambassador of the country involved in the litigation pursuant to s. 13(6) of the Act is taken to be conclusive proof that non-commercial transactions are involved: *Alcom Ltd* v. *Republic of Colombia* [1984] 2 All ER 6; *Gur Corporation* v. *Trust Bank of Africa* [1986] 3 WLR 583.
6. [1981] 1 WLR 1233, *per* Lord Denning MR, at p. 1241d.

overcome this problem the plaintiff has three possible methods of effecting service:

(a) Personal service based on physical presence

Obviously, if the defendant is physically in the country then no problem of service should arise,[7] and even a transient presence is enough for this purpose.[8]

In the case of corporations registered in England under the Companies Act they can be served by leaving the papers at, or sending them by post to, the registered office of the company.[9] In the case of a foreign corporation with a place of business in England it is obliged to file with the Registrar of Companies the name and address of someone within the jurisdiction authorized to accept service on its behalf.[10] If it has failed to do so, or if it has no place of business where service can be made,[11] then "presence" may be shown by the foreign corporation having transacted business in England[12] through an agent in England who had authority to make contracts on behalf of the foreign company,[13] not simply to pass on orders,[14] and service can then be made on the agent.

7. Although, in the case of a private individual, finding him to enable service of the writ to be effected is not an unknown problem.

8. *The Maharanee of Baroda* v. *Wildenstein* [1972] 2 QB 283: service effected while defendant visiting England briefly to attend Ascot races. It is also good service where a copy of the writ in a sealed envelope addressed to the defendant is inserted through the letter-box of the defendant's address within the jurisdiction, if at the time he is out of the jurisdiction, provided he obtains knowledge of the service of the copy writ within seven days: RSC Order 10, r. 1 para. (3)(a), and *Barclays Bank of Swaziland Ltd* v. *Hahn* [1989] 2 All ER 398 (HL) *per* Lord Brightman pp. 402j and 403a. In this case, the defendant did not open the envelope "Because he knew perfectly well what it contained": *ibid.*, p. 403b.

9. Companies Act 1985, s. 725(1). A Scottish company may be served in the same way, if it has a place of business in England: s. 725(2).

10. Companies Act 1985, s. 691(1)(*b*). Service is then effected pursuant to the rules of s. 725(1) *supra*: *The Theodhos* [1972] 2 Lloyd's Rep. 428. RSC Order 65, r. 3(1) provides that "Personal Service of a document on a body corporate may . . . be effected by serving it on [*inter alia*] secretary, treasurer or other similar officer thereof." A "similar officer" has been held to be the cargo accounts officer. While being a junior employee, he was actually conducting the business of the defendant company: *Kuwait Airways Corp.* v. *Iraqi Airways Co.* [1995] 3 All ER 694 (HL) p. 702b, c and h, *per* Lord Goff of Chieveley.

11. In which case see Companies Act 1985, s. 695.

12. Not simply *with* England: see *Attorney-General* v. *Bailey (Malta) Ltd* [1963] 1 Lloyd's Rep. 617. As to a bank having a "place of business" in Great Britain, see *South India Shipping Corp Ltd* v. *Export-Import Bank of Korea* [1985] 2 All ER 219, see *per* Ackner LJ: "They have both premises and staff within the jurisdiction . . . and it matters not that they do not conclude within the jurisdiction any banking transactions", page 224e-f. Leave to appeal to the House of Lords was refused, but granted by the Appeal Committee. No steps for the hearing of an appeal seem to have been taken.

13. *Saccharin Corporation Ltd* v. *Chemische Fabrik von Heyden* [1911] 2 KB 516.

14. *Vogel* v. *R and A Kohnstramm Ltd* [1973] QB 133.

With cases involving letters of credit, as we have seen from the *Power Curber Case*,[15] an English court will accept jurisdiction if there is a branch of the issuing bank in England, even though the transaction has no other connection with the country. In the words of Lord Denning:[16]

... London is an important centre of international trade. Merchants from all the world come here to settle their disputes. Banks from all the world over have branches here to receive and make payments. So far as we can be of service to international trade, we will accept the task and fulfil it to the best of our ability.

Moreover, once having accepted jurisdiction, it follows that an English court can compel the English branch to pay under the credit opened by its head office in another jurisdiction,[17] on the reasoning that "Each branch is treated ... as independent of its parent body. The branch is subject to the orders of the courts of the country in which it operates; but not to the orders of the courts where its head office is situate."[18]

(b) Service by leave of the court

If the prospective defendant, whether a private individual or a corporation, such as a bank, is not in England, it may still be possible to bring an action in England with the leave of the court. The Rules of the Supreme Court, Order 11, gives a list of 17 grounds ((*a*) to (*q*)) upon which an application can be made to the court for leave to have the writ (or notice of it) served out of the jurisdiction, thus enabling an action to be brought even though the defendant is abroad.[19] With this procedure, there has to be a preliminary hearing to obtain the court's consent *before* the action can be commenced; and, of course, if leave is refused, then, so far as the English jurisdiction is concerned, no action can be brought and the prospective plaintiff must seek his remedy in another country.

These applications are made *ex parte* (that is, by the prospective plaintiff without the defendant being present), and the applicant must prove to the satisfaction of the court that: (1) He has a reasonable and arguable case;[20] and

15. *Supra*, p. 241. *Power Curber International Ltd* v. *National Bank of Kuwait SAK* [1981] 1 WLR 1233.
16. *Ibid.*, p. 1242c.
17. *Ibid.*, p. 1242b.
18. *Ibid.*, *per* Lord Denning MR, at p. 1241h. If branches are truly independent, might not the branch in England have believed it could not be ordered to perform something which its parent in Kuwait contracted to do?
19. It is possible to have an application fall within more than one paragraph heading of the order. A prospective plaintiff will not be prejudiced, however, since the " . . . rules under Order 11 are to be read disjunctively and each sub-section is complete in itself and independent of the others": *per* Sellers LJ in *Matthews* v. *Kuwait Bechtel Corp* [1959] 2 QB 57, 62.
20. *Diamond* v. *Bank of London and Montreal Ltd* [1979] 2 WLR 228.

(2) England is a *forum conveniens*;[21] and (3) The court can enforce any order it makes;[22] and (4) It is a proper case for service out of the jurisdiction.[23]

Whilst the original application is made *ex parte*, it is common to find that the court will adjourn the application to allow the defendant, if he wishes, to be legally represented for further argument prior to the court making its decision.

It would be wholly out of place, and quite impossible here, to give an account of each and every heading of the terms of Order 11.[24] Therefore, one or two examples which appear to have particular relevence to letters of credit must suffice. For example, para (f) of Order 11 provides that an application can be made to the courts for permission to serve a defendant "out of the jurisdiction":

(i) Where the contract was made within the jurisdiction.

In such a case as this everything turns on the meaning of the word "made". For this purpose, it is usually taken to be sufficient that the contract was substantially negotiated in England,[25] but, once more, delicate shades of meaning need to be considered. Suppose an issuing bank in Germany posts an offer of credit to a seller (its customer) in England, the offer to remain open for seven days. The seller telexes a reply to the bank in time, but the telex is misdirected, and the offer of credit lapses. According to English law there is a binding contract when the telex is sent,[26] but according to German law not until the telex (the acceptance) is received by the bank. Was the contract "made" in England to enable the seller to apply under this paragraph of Order 11 to issue his writ against the German bank? This is a difficult question, the answer to which would depend on whether the offer from the German bank stated the "proper law" of the offer; if it did not, the English court faced with the Order 11 application would have to consider not only *where* the contract

---

21. If it is not, the application will be refused. The courts are always aware that some plaintiffs cast about to find the locality best suited to their claim, not the most convenient forum—"forum shopping" as it is sometimes called. So far as the jurisdiction of the English courts is concerned it is " . . . not confined to Englishmen. It extends to any friendly foreigner. He can seek the aid of courts if he decides to do so. You may call this "forum shopping" if you please, but if the forum is England, it is a good place to shop in, both for the quality of the goods and the speed of service": *per* Lord Denning MR in *The Atlantic Star* [1973] QB 364, 382. Reversed on appeal [1974] AC 436, where Lord Reid felt obliged to observe that Lord Denning's remarks seemed " . . . to recall the good old days . . . when inhabitants of this island felt an innate superiority over those unfortunate enough to belong to other races . . . " (at p. 453). See also *Mauroux* v. *Sociedade Comercial Abel Pereira Da Fonseca SARL* [1972] 1 WLR 962, see at p. 965 *et seq.* and *Trade Indemnity plc* v. *Forsakrings Aktiebolaget Njord (in Liquidation)* [1995] 1 All ER 796; and *Bank of Credit and Commerce Hong Kong Ltd (in liquidation)* v. *Somali Bank* [1995] 1 Lloyd's Rep. 227.

22. See *British South Africa Co* v. *Companhia de Mocambique* [1893] AC 602.

23. RSC Order 11, rule 4(2).

24. For a detailed study, see Cheshire and North, *Private International Law*, 12th edn. (1992), p. 190 *et seq*; also, Dicey and Morris, *Conflict of Laws*, 12th edn. (1993), p. 270 *et seq*.

25. See *BP Exploration Co (Libya) Ltd* v. *Hunt* [1976] 1 WLR 788, 797.

26. *Household Fire Insurance Co* v. *Grant* (1879) 4 Ex D 216; see also *Benaim* v. *De Bono* [1924] AC 514.

was made (that is whether in England or Germany), but by what system of law the making of the contract was to be tested.

In addition to these legal problems, the English court may have to characterize the facts and events of the transaction before being able to apply the legal principles. If a letter of credit is issued by a Spanish bank through an English bank in London, payable in sterling against documents to be presented in London: is the contract "made" in London, or in Spain by the issuing bank accepting the terms its London agents were able to negotiate?[27]

The prospective plaintiff must feel he has an uphill struggle before him in attempting to resolve issues such as these, as a preliminary to the action he wishes to bring, let alone mounting the action itself![28]

Paragaph (d), sub-para (ii), goes on to state:

Where the contract is made by or through an agent trading or residing within the jurisdiction on behalf of a principal trading or residing out of the jurisdiction.

If a contract is made "by" an agent in England on behalf of a foreign principal the position is reasonably clear; the agent is within the jurisdiction, and, if the consent of the court is obtained, service can easily be effected on the agent, thus rendering the principal liable to the jurisdiction of the English courts.[29]

However, contracts made "through" agents cover wider possibilities than those made "by" agents; since almost any activity, however slight, by an agent resulting in a contract for his overseas principal could be said to have been made "through" him. At all events, this part of the paragraph can apply even though the agent has no authority to finalize contracts in England on behalf of his foreign principal.[30]

This provision is particularly important for banks, as every day there are hundreds of contracts effected in London by agent banks on behalf of their foreign principals (who do not have branches in England); whereby the terms are not finally agreed by the agent bank, but by the foreign principal, to whom the terms are transmitted. In such a case it seems clear that these contracts will have been made "through" the agent, which would bring the contract within

---

27. The example is based on the facts in *Offshore International SA v. Banco Central SA* [1977] 1 WLR 399.

28. If the application is successful, and service abroad is effected, the plaintiff cannot subsequently amend his statement of claim to include causes of action in respect of which he does not have the court's consent to serve out of the jurisdiction: *The Siskina* [1977] 3 WLR 818. In *Seaconsar Far East Ltd v. Bank Markazi Jomhouri Islami Iran* [1993] 1 Lloyd's Rep. 236, it was held that the English courts were clearly the correct forum, but as it was also held there was no arguable case, leave to serve out of the jurisdiction was refused.

29. See *Gibbon v. Commerz und Kreditbank Aktiengesellschaft* [1958] 2 Lloyd's Rep. 113.

30. *National Mortgage and Agency Co of New Zealand v. Gosselin* (1922) 38 TLR 832. Unlike the case discussed *supra*, where a plaintiff effects service on the agent claiming the foreign corporation is "present" in England by virtue of the agent's authority to conclude contracts, and avoiding (the plaintiff no doubt hopes) the need for an application under Order 11. In such a case, of course, the service will be effected by the plaintiff, leaving it to the defendant—the foreign corporation— to apply to the court to have the service set aside.

the terms of the paragraph for the purpose of an application for leave to have the foreign bank brought within the jurisdiction of the English courts.

The third paragraph of para (d) provides for an application to be made for service out of the jurisdiction:

Where the contract is by its terms or by implication governed by English law.

The terms of some credits state clearly what the "proper law" is, and if it is English, then it is possible that the court will grant the application for leave to serve a defendant out of the jurisdiction.[31] To remove all doubt, of course, it would be a lot easier if the terms not only provided for English "proper law", but went on to provide that the parties submitted to the jurisdiction of the English courts; because if this were done, no application under Order 11 should be necessary, since the parties would have already submitted to the jurisdiction. It is a fact, however, that many credits, while providing for a "proper law", make no reference whatever to jurisdiction. If the terms of the credit do not state clearly that English law is to be the "proper law" of the contract, then, obviously, there may be a difficulty in attempting to show that English law applies by "implication". Once more, all the facts and surrounding circumstances will have to be looked at.

As discussed above,[32] trying to find what is the "proper law" of a contract is never easy. If the parties have made no real indication, all the court can do is to attempt to come to a reasoned view as to whether or not English law is the system with which the contract has the closest connection. All the facets of the transaction must be examined; for example, the format of the contract documents,[33] the residence of the parties,[34] where the subject-matter of the contract is situated,[35] any pattern of dealing with a previous transaction[36]: the list of possible points for consideration is endless.[37]

It seems clear, however, that if there is a genuine doubt that the "proper law" is English, then the application based on this paragraph will be refused, and the plaintiff will have to seek a forum other than England.

One final example of the provisions of Order 11 must suffice. Paragraph (1)(b) states that:

---

31. While it is true that the courts can grant leave on the sole ground that English law has been chosen by the parties, it must be remembered that these are discretionary matters, and the applicant has a particularly heavy burden of proof to discharge in showing that England is a distinctly more suitable forum than a foreign court.

32. *Supra*, in Chap.10.

33. *NV Handelmaatschappij J Smits Import-Export* v. *English Exporters (London) Ltd* [1955] 2 Lloyd's Rep. 69.

34. *Jacobs* v. *Credit Lyonnais* (1884) 12 QBD 589.

35. *Kahler* v. *Midland Bank Ltd* [1950] AC 24.

36. *The Freight Queen* [1977] 2 Lloyd's Rep. 140.

37. Simply because the supply contract is governed by English law it cannot be implied that a documentary credit, issued pursuant to that contract, will also be governed by English law: *Attock Cement Co Ltd* v. *Romanian Bank for Foreign Trade* [1989] 1 All ER 1189.

Where an injunction is sought ordering the defendant to do or refrain from doing anything within the jurisdiction (whether or not damages are also claimed in respect of a failure to do or the doing of that thing).

To obtain the consent of the court to have the defendant served abroad under this heading, the equitable remedy of injunction must be the main issue in the suit, and not merely a peripheral form of relief sought only to make the claim fall within the paragraph.[38] This is often the case with disputes involving letters of credit, where the remedy most frequently sought is that of injunction to prevent a bank from making payment. The circumstances where this could arise are if a foreign bank is about to make a payment to an English seller who, the buyer claims, has not satisfied the terms of the credit.

Leave under this heading will not be granted solely to make a claim for a Mareva injunction to restrain the taking of cash or other moveables out of the jurisdiction[39]; before the court will grant a Mareva injunction it must already have jurisdiction in the action.[40] Though an English court can grant a "world-wide" Mareva injunction in aid of proceedings begun in a country which is a member of the Convention on Jurisdiction and Enforcement of Judgments in Civil and Commercial Matters 1968, pursuant to section 25 Civil Jurisdiction and Judgments Act 1982. However, this does not confer jurisdiction on the English court to entertain a counterclaim to the action brought in that other convention country.[41]

(c) Personal service based on consent

If a defendant, who is absent from the country, has submitted to the jurisdiction he can be served with the proceedings even though he continues to be abroad. One can submit to the jurisdiction in several ways; for example, by

---

38. See for example *Rosler* v. *Hilbery* [1925] Ch 250.

39. *Perry* v. *Zissis* [1977] 1 Lloyd's Rep. 607. The Mareva order was varied in *Camdex International Ltd* v. *Bank of Zambia (No. 2)* [1997] 1 All ER 728 (CA), to allow new bank notes printed in England to be transferred to Zambia. For guidelines in respect of Mareva applications see *per* Lord Denning in *Third Chandris Shipping Corp* v. *Unimarine SA* [1979] 3 WLR 122, at p. 137. For "worldwide" Mareva orders there are new guidelines, and a new form of order; also, for the restraining of removal of assets out of the jurisdiction, or disposal within the jurisdiction: Practice Direction [1994] 4 All ER 52.

40. Incidentally, an English court has no power to make orders, such as Mareva injunctions, over movables situated in England if the owner is outside the jurisdiction, and has not been served. Scottish courts have such a power over movables in Scotland however; and the courts of the USA and most Continental countries have similar powers over movables in their jurisdiction if the owner is absent, even if he has not been served with proceedings relating to such property. Indeed, all actions in England are *in personam*, that is, the action is against the defendant, not directly against his specific assets. The only action *in rem* known to English law is against a ship, plane or hovercraft, which must be within the jurisdiction to give the courts authority over the *res*.

41. *Balkanbank* v. *Taher* [1994] 4 All ER 239. Also, where a dispute is subject to arbitration the court has, under a provisions of Arbitration Act 1950 s. 12(6)(f), the same powers to help secure the amount in dispute as in an action in the High Court, and a Mareva injunction will be granted, together with disclosure orders which could extend to assets outside the jurisdiction: *Gidrxlsme Shipping Co. Ltd* v. *Tantomar-Transportes Maritimos Lda* [1994] 4 All ER 507.

agreeing to accept service of the papers in the proceedings,[42] or by commencing an action oneself in England.[43] In commercial cases it is often found that the parties have, by their agreement, accepted that any disputes shall be submitted to the jurisdiction of the courts in England[44]; however, the fact that the contract is to be "governed by English law" does not, of itself, amount to a submission to the jurisdiction.[45]

It may be, of course, that the defendant, having been served with the papers at his place abroad, denies that he has, in fact, consented to the jurisdiction of the English courts; in such a case, the plaintiffs must seek a declaration from the English court that it deems the defendant to have submitted to the jurisdiction because of the circumstances of consent upon which they rely. In these proceedings the defendant is not taken to have consented to the jurisdiction by appearing before the court simply to contest the jurisdiction.[46]

2. LITIGATION AND THE EU

As we saw earlier, the Civil Jurisdiction and Judgments Act 1982[47] accepts the terms of the European Economic Community Convention on Jurisdiction and the Enforcement of Judgments in Civil and Commercial Matters[48] and gives the Conventions " . . . the force of law in the United Kingdom and judicial notice shall be taken of them".[49] The purpose is to simplify formalities governing the reciprocal recognition and enforcement of judgments, and to determine the international jurisdiction of the courts of the Union.

The text of the 1968 Convention, as amended, appears in Schedule 1 to the 1982 Act.[50]

42. Either himself or through a solicitor: RSC Order 10/1/5.
43. RSC Order 11/1/3, *Derby & Co Ltd* v. *Larsson* [1976] 1 WLR 202.
44. See RSC Order 11, (1)(*d*). The parties will be bound by their choice of forum unless one or other can show some good reason to be released from his agreement: see *The Chaparral* [1968] 2 Lloyd's Rep. 158. If an action, which is properly within the English jurisdiction, has already been commenced, it may yet be stayed if the defendant can show a prior agreement to submit disputes to a foreign jurisdiction: see *per* Brandon J in *The Eleftheria* [1970] P 94, 100; *The Sindh* [1975] 2 Lloyd's Rep. 372; *The Makefjell* [1976] 2 Lloyd's Rep. 29. A plaintiff suing *both* in England and abroad can be ordered to stop one action or the other: *The Christiansborg* (1885) 10 PD 141.
45. *Dundee Ltd* v. *Gilman & Co (Australia) Pty Ltd* [1968] 2 Lloyd's Rep. 394.
46. *Henry* v. *Geoprosco International Ltd* [1976] QB 726.
47. 1982, c. 27 and the Civil Jurisdiction and Judgments Act 1982 (Amendment) Order 1989, SI 1989/1346, arts. 3–6 and further amendment, SI 1990/2591, arts. 3–6.
48. Brussels, 27 September 1968; Cmnd 7395.
49. S. 2(1), *ibid.*
50. The Civil Jurisdiction and Judgments Act 1982 gave effect to the Brussels Convention of 27 September 1968 on the Jurisdiction and Enforcement of Judgments in Civil and Commercial Disputes; this Act is now further amended by the Civil Jurisdiction and Judgments Act 1991, which gives the force of law to the Lugano Convention, dated 16 September 1988; s. 3A, *ibid.* The texts of these Conventions can be found in the Schedules to the 1991 Act. The 1968 Convention does not apply to proceedings for the enforcement of judgments given in civil and commercial matters in non-contracting states: *Owens Bank Ltd* v. *Bracco* [1994] 1 All ER 336.

It is in connection with a court's jurisdiction that the Convention needs to be examined with some care, and consideration is given here to the aspects of the Convention that would likely involve Bills of Exchange and Documentary Credits.

Title II, Section 1, Art. 2, states:

Subject to the provisions of this Convention, persons domiciled[51] in a Contracting State shall, whatever their nationality, be sued in the Courts of that State.

Persons who are not nationals of the State in which they are domiciled shall be governed by the rules of jurisdiction applicable to nationals of that State.

Art. 5 goes on:

A person domiciled in a Contracting State may, in another Contracting State, be sued:

(1) in matters relating to a contract, in the courts for the place of performance of the obligation in question;

(2) in matters relating to tort, delict or quasi-delict, in the courts for the place where the harmful event occurred;

(3) as regards a civil claim for damages or restitution which is based on an act giving rise to criminal proceedings, in the court seized of those proceedings, to the extent that that court has jurisdiction under its own law to entertain civil proceedings;

(4) as regards a dispute arising out of the operations of a branch, agency or other establishment, in the courts for the place in which the branch, agency or other establishment is situated;

(5) ...

(6) as regards a dispute concerning the payment of remuneration claimed in respect of the salvage of a cargo or freight, in the court under the authority of which the cargo or freight in question:

(a) has been arrested to secure such payment, or

(b) could have been so arrested, but bail or other security has been given; provided that this provision shall apply only if it is claimed that the defendant has an interest in the cargo or freight or had such an interest at the time of salvage.

It will be apparent, therefore, from the provisions of para. (1) of Art. 5 that it will be a question of fact to establish where performance has taken place. In *Union Transport Group Plc v. Continental Lines SA*,[52] it was held that performance of the contract had taken place in the UK, and that this was adequate to give the English courts jurisdiction, and service of the writ out of the jurisdiction on a Belgian company was, therefore, possible.

It was held in *Shevill v. Presse Alliance SA*,[53] with regard to para. (5) of Art. 5, that the "harmful event" could mean either the Member State where the tort was committed, or the Member State where the damage was suffered, and the plaintiff could sue in either.

---

51. To determine whether a party is domiciled in a given state regard must be had to the provisions of Art. 52.

52. [1992] 1 All ER 161.

53. [1992] 1 All ER 409.

As is often the case with commercial contracts, the parties agree expressly, within the terms of their contracts, in which jurisdiction they wish to settle any disputes they might have. Art. 17, in part, provides:

If the parties, one or more of whom is domiciled in a Contracting State, have agreed that a court or the courts of a Contracting State are to have jurisdiction to settle any disputes which have arisen or which may arise in connection with a particular legal relationship, that court or those courts shall have exclusive jurisdiction. Such an agreement conferring jurisdiction shall be either in writing or evidence in writing or, in international trade or commerce, in a form which accords with practices in that trade or commerce of which the parties are or ought to have been aware. Where such an agreement is concluded by parties, none of whom is domiciled in a Contracting State, the courts of other Contracting States shall have no jurisdiction over their disputes unless the court or courts chosen have declined jurisdiction . . . If an agreement conferring jurisdiction was concluded for the benefit of only one of the parties, that party shall retain the right to bring proceedings in any other court which has jurisdiction by virtue of this Convention.

The agreement to choose a jurisdiction may provide an absolute choice, meaning an "exclusive" jurisdiction and no other; or the agreement may be on a "non-exclusive" basis, that is, that the parties submit to the jurisdiction of, say, the English courts, but another jurisdiction may be used if they wish.

Since the word "exclusive" is used in Art. 17, it may have been thought that any choice stated in an agreement would render the chosen jurisdiction "exclusive". However, it was held in *Kutz* v. *Stella Musical Veranstaltungs GmbH*,[54] that the use of the word "exclusive" in Art. 17 meant only that the jurisdiction as chosen was to have effect to the exclusion of any other jurisdiction which might otherwise have been imposed on the parties by any earlier Conventions.

It will also be noted that for the provisions of this Article to have effect, the choice of jurisdiction must be "in writing or evidenced in writing, or in international trade or commerce, in a form which accords with practices in that trade or commerce of which the parties ought to have been aware", and the inference seems to be that a choice of jurisdiction may be inferred—not being in writing—if there is some custom of trade which might indicate that disputes in that trade are habitually dealt with in the courts of a particular jurisdiction.

Any agreement is, of course, binding on the parties to that agreement, and such a choice has no affect on any third parties who are free to choose their forum as they please.[55]

However, Article 16 of the Convention gives *exclusive* jurisdiction in the following circumstances.

The following courts shall have exclusive jurisdiction regardless of domicile:

---

54. [1992] 1 All ER 630.
55. *Dresser UK Ltd* v. *Falcongate Freight Management Ltd (The Duke of Yare)* [1992] 2 All ER 450.

(1) (a) in proceedings which have as their object rights *in rem* in immovable property or tenancies of immovable property, the courts of the Contracting State in which the property is situated[56] ;

  (b) however, in proceedings which have as their object tenancies of immovable property concluded for temporary private use for a maximum period of six consecutive months, the courts of the Contracting State in which the defendant is domiciled shall also have jurisdiction, provided that the landlord and the tenant are natural persons and are domiciled in the same Contracting State;

(2) in proceedings which have as their object the validity of the constitution, the nullity or the dissolution of companies or other legal persons or associations of natural or legal persons, or the decisions of their organs, the courts of the Contracting State in which the company, legal person or association has its seat;

(3) in proceedings which have as their object the validity of entries in public registers, the courts of the Contracting State in which the register is kept;

(4) in proceedings concerned with the registration or validity of patents, trade marks, designs, or other similar rights required to be deposited or registered, the courts of the Contracting State in which the deposit or registration has been applied for, has taken place or is under the terms of an international convention deemed to have taken place;

(5) in proceedings concerned with the enforcement of judgments, the courts of the Contracting State in which the judgment has been or is to be enforced.

If an action comes within the exclusive jurisdiction of several courts, the court first seised of the proceedings shall have jurisdiction, and any other court must decline jurisdiction.[57]

It follows from these provisions that any judgment obtained from a court which did not have exclusive jurisdiction under the terms of Art. 16, will not be recognized and, therefore, will be unenforceable under the terms of the Convention.

Other than under such mandatory provisions, where a defendant enters an appearance before a court of a Contracting State that will give that court jurisdiction, except where the appearance is entered to contest the jurisdiction.[58]

Where proceedings involving the same cause of action *and* between the same parties[59] are brought in the courts of different Contracting States—for example, one party suing in the courts of his home country, and the other party suing in the courts of his (not an unknown state of affairs)—the court first seised shall have jurisdiction, and any other court of a Member State shall, of

---

56. However, an English court could have jurisdiction *in personam* over a trustee of land in France: see *Webb* v. *Webb* [1992] 1 All ER 17.

57. Art. 23.

58. Art. 18, or where another court has exclusive jurisdiction under Art. 16.

59. An action *in rem* against a vessel is not between the same parties who are suing each other *in personam: The Nordglimt* [1988] 2 All ER 531.

its own motion, decline jurisdiction or stay the proceedings, if the jurisdiction of the court first seised is being contested.[60]

These provisions change the laws of England under the doctrine of *lis alibi pendens*, since the established rule was that there was no automatic right of stay where proceedings were *extant* in another jurisdiction. Everything turned on the facts as to whether one party was subjected to oppression,[61] or, perhaps, where justice could be done in the other country more conveniently and at less expense.[62] In such cases the English courts had a discretion, which has now been removed.

Of course, the Convention does not affect an English court if the other court is in a non-Contracting State.[63]

3. THE APPLICABLE LAW

We have already considered[64] the problems of ascertaining the "proper law" of contracts generally, and those involving bills of exchange in particular. The problems of establishing the "proper law" of contracts involving letters of credit are fundamentally the same, since the identical principles apply. In the absence of any indications which the courts can accept as being an indication of choice by the parties, as we have seen, all the surrounding circumstances must be examined in order to find the system of law with which the letter of credit, or the particular facet of the letter of credit, has the closest connection.

As we shall see, there have been but few cases establishing the principles upon which a choice of law will be made in these relationships with letters of credit. There are a number of reasons for this, among them being the skill of the banks in negotiating around the potential difficulties which arise from time to time; also, in England, the *lex fori* tends to be applied unless one of the parties objects; and judges, in England anyway, tend to deal with these choice of law problems very much on the facts of the particular case, and avoid laying down a general rule, which might well not work in a subsequent case.

---

60. Article 21. The court must decline or stay. The court secondly seized of an action cannot examine the jurisdiction of the court first seized: *Overseas Union Insurance Ltd* v. *New Hampshire Insurance Co* [1992] 2 All ER 138; Court of Justice of European Communities (Case C-351/89).

61. See, for example, *St Pierre* v. *South American Stores (Gath and Chares) Ltd* [1936] 1 KB 382, 389.

62. *MacShannon* v. *Rockware Glass Ltd* [1978] 1 All ER 625.

63. See *S & W Berisford Plc* v. *Hampshire Insurance Co* [1990] 2 All ER 321; and *Arkwright Mutual Insurance Co* v. *Bryanston Insurance Co Ltd* [1990] 2 All ER 335.

64. See *supra*, Chap. 10.

Taking these basic rules and applying them to the contracts of a letter of
credit (and using the same format of the contractual relationships outlined by
Lord Diplock), the various "proper law" situations must now be considered.

1. The contract of sale

This, it will be remembered, is the basic supply contract between the buyer and
the seller, and if there is a dispute between them relating to the payment terms,
it will be a dispute like any other type of dispute between these parties, and the
supply (sale) contract must be looked at to see which legal system appears to
have the closest connection with the contract. As we have seen, trying to reach
a decision on the appropriate legal system might not be easy; the buyer might
be in Saudi Arabia, the seller in Germany, with an agreement to open letters of
credit in New York with a confirmation in Frankfurt. This is what might be
termed the "classic" situation whereby a choice of law problem must be
resolved as a preliminary to the trial of the main issue in dispute.

It must also be remembered that whatever law is ultimately applied to any
dispute under the supply contract as between buyer and seller it does not
necessarily follow that the same legal system will apply to a dispute over the
letters of credit between the banks, or between the banks and other parties.

2. The contract of the issuing bank

If there is a problem between the buyer and his (the issuing) bank, it will
almost certainly be found that in the terms of the credit as offered by the bank
to the buyer and accepted by him, a "proper law" will have been stated. If no
such provision has been made probably no great difficulty will arise in practice
as, very frequently, the buyer and the issuing bank will be found to be in the
same country, and, hence, jurisdiction. If they are not then the "proper law"
will probably be that of the country where the issuing bank carries on its
business and from where it has provided the facilities, on the basis that that
country is the one with the "closest connection" to the contractual activities.
The issuing bank is obviously situated there, the credit is issued there, and,
doubtless, in the form and language of that country. The possibility of choosing the law of the country of the buyer would seem heavily outweighed by the
attachment to the law of the country where the issuing bank is located. This,
of course, is only a presumption, and like all presumptions is rebuttable,
depending on the circumstances.

3. The contract between the banks

Where there is a dispute between the issuing bank and the advising/confirming/
paying bank much will depend upon the nature of the points in issue, as to

what the "proper law" might be, as always, in the absence of a clear statement in the terms of the credit.

As we know, there is always a strong temptation for any court to apply the law of its own country or state, once having accepted jurisdiction. Indeed, as we have seen, in England, there is an obligation on the court to do so, unless one of the parties raises an issue on the applicability of English law.[65]

If the law of the forum is *not* applied then, the law to govern issues of transactions under letters of credit will probably be considered on the basis of the relationship between principal (the issuing bank) and agent (the advising/confirmation/paying bank).[66] This being the case, since the agent's duties will fall to be carried out in the country where it has a place of business, and where the actions of advising/confirming/paying will take place,[67] the probability is that the law of that country will apply to the relationship.[68] This would appear to follow from the case of

OFFSHORE INTERNATIONAL SA v. BANCO CENTRAL SA[69]

Offshore were oil-rig operators incorporated in Panama but with their place of business in Texas. They contracted to construct a semi-submersible oil drilling vessel for Hijos de Barreras SA, a Spanish company; payment to be by irrevocable but unconfirmed letter of credit. The issuing bank in Spain (Banco Central SA) asked the advising bank in New York (Chase Manhattan) to advise Offshore that the credit was open for US $3 million available by Offshore's drafts on Chase at sight, subject to producing various agreed documents. There was no express provision as to the system of law which was to be applied. A dispute arose between Offshore and Hijos, and the matter was referred to arbitration, and this application was made by way of a preliminary point, as to whether the proper law of the credit was Spanish or of New York. *Held*—that in the absence of any express provision as to the system of law, " . . . the letter of credit is governed by the system of law with which it has its closest and most real connection".[70]

65. *Power Curber International Ltd* v. *National Bank of Kuwait SAK* [1981] 1 WLR 1233, where English law appears to have been applied even though the proper law of the credit was held to be that of North Carolina: *per* Lord Denning MR at p 1240f, and Griffiths LJ at 1242e.

66. *Chatenay* v. *Brazilian Submarine Telegraph* Co [1891] 1 QB 79; *Sinfra AG* v. *Sinfra Ltd* [1939] 2 All ER 675.

67. *Offshore International SA* v. *Banco Central SA* [1977] 1 WLR 399. However, Ackner J (as he then was) worked on the "closest connection" rule, and found for the law of the advising bank, but not because of the agency theory. He also thought (at p. 404), if a different legal system were chosen: "The advising bank would have constantly to be seeking to apply a whole variety of foreign laws . . . " Such a state of affairs may well be inconvenient, but convenience has not always been a major factor in reaching decisions in these cases: and it is not unheard of to find different parts of the same contract being subject to different legal systems: *Re United Railways of Havana and Regla Warehouses Ltd* [1960] Ch 52; affirmed, *sub-nom. Tomkinson* v. *First Pennsylvania Banking and Trust* Co [1961] AC 1007.

68. *Brazilian and Portuguese Bank* v. *British and American Exchange Banking Corp* (1868) 18 LT 823.

69. [1977] 1 WLR 399.

70. *Per* Ackner J at p. 401d, referring to *Tomkinson* v. *First Pennsylvania Banking and Trust* Co [1961] AC 1007, but this was not a case on letters of credit, and Lord Ratcliffe (p. 1058) was at pains to say the test of what was the proper law could not be "comprehended under a single phrase", "but *in this case* (Author's italics) . . . the law of the place of performance ought to be regarded as of prepondering importance . . . ".

" . . . on the side of New York law are all matters of performance, whereas, in relation to Spanish law, Spain and a Spanish bank was the source of the obligation. In my judgment, it is with New York law that the transaction has its closest and most real connection."[71]

Lord Denning MR, in the *Power Curber Case*, had no doubts when he said " . . . a debt under a letter of credit is situate in the place where it is in fact payable against documents".[72]

In dealing with any problems with the advising/confirming/paying bank and the seller's bank, since both or all parties are usually in the same country,[73] this should be a purely domestic relationship, with the local law being applied to the dispute; but if this were not the case then the basic rule of choosing the legal system with the "closest connection" to the relationship would apply.

Confusing though it may be, it must always be borne in mind when considering issues involving the "proper law" of these transactions that not all aspects of the same transaction may be governed by the same "proper law". This may be because the parties have chosen different systems of law to govern different aspects of their contract,[74] or, having failed to make a choice, the courts find that a different system, of necessity, has to be applied to separate sections of the transaction. Of course, the courts will not capriciously assign different systems, but sometimes it is unavoidable.

4. Contract between confirming bank and seller

If the confirming/paying bank refuses to pay, and the beneficiary has to attempt to recover by legal action he will, very likely, sue in his own country since, in most cases, the beneficiary and the advising/confirming/paying bank are in the same country. If this is not the case, then the beneficiary will sue, either in the country where the paying bank is situated, or perhaps, in some third country altogether.[75] If that third country is England, then, subject to whatever may be stated in the credit as to the choice of "proper law",[76] the courts will doubtless look for the legal system with the "closest connection" to the contract between the paying bank and the beneficiary, based on the general principles discussed above.

71. *Ibid.*, p. 401h.
72. *Power Curber International Ltd* v. *National Bank of Kuwait SAK* [1981] 1 WLR 1233, at p. 1240f.
73. If the country was, say, the USA, the paying bank and the seller's bank could well be in different states, of course.
74. *Kahler* v. *Midland Bank Ltd* [1950] AC 24, see at p. 42. In *Libyan Arab Foreign Bank* v. *Manufacturers Hanover Trust Co (No. 2)* [1989] 1 Lloyd's Rep. 608, the proper law of the London bank account was stated to be English law, and that of the New York bank account, the laws of the State of New York.
75. Which is what happened in the *Power Curber Case*.
76. It has been observed above, Chap. 16—"(4) Contract between confirming bank and seller", that in most cases there has been no negotiation on the terms between the paying bank and the beneficiary, and hence, probably, no agreement on the "proper law" of their relationship.

The Uniform Customs and choice of law

Since the Uniform Customs apply to all transactions relating to documentary credits the rules will be the same the world over and whether the action is fought in London or Bangkok one should expect the result to be the same. However, this is an over-simplification of the position. Different results could be obtained for a number of reasons, of which the following three are the most salient:

(a) The Uniform Customs are published by the International Chamber of Commerce, not only in English, but also in French, German, Spanish and Arabic. Now, as everyone knows, not every word is capable of exact translation, and anyone who has tried to rely legally upon a translation from an original document will not be surprised to find a divergence in shades of meaning. Hence, if the credit was opened in Paris with the French text of the Uniform Customs, and an action is, subsequently, brought, say, in New York (where, no doubt, the English text would be before the court), it is by no means certain the same meaning will be ascribed to the translation as to the original. So, if the action turns on the fine meaning of words, no amount of argument may convince the judge if he does not speak good commercial French.

(b) The procedural rules in each country are not the same. For example, what can and cannot be given in evidence, and how that evidence is to be given (that is, whether by affidavit or orally), and whether cross-examination of witnessess is permitted, can all affect the outcome of an action, no matter what the basic rules are as relating to the credit.

(c) The basis upon which courts make their decisions on the choice of "proper law" to apply to a transaction are not the same in every country; and, therefore, what one jurisdiction will select as being the "proper law" may not be the same as another. So that, even though the rules of the Uniform Customs may be the same, a difference in interpretation could arise depending upon the courts of which country is seised of the action.

APPENDICES

APPENDIX 1

BILLS OF EXCHANGE ACT 1882*

CHAPTER 61

An Act to codify the law relating to Bills of Exchange, Cheques, and Promissory Notes.

PART I. PRELIMINARY

Short title

1.— This Act may be cited as the Bills of Exchange Act, 1882.

Interpretation of terms

2.— In this Act, unless the context otherwise requires,—
"Acceptance" means an acceptance completed by delivery or notification.
"Action" includes counter claim and set off.
"Banker" includes a body of persons whether incorporated or not who carry on the business of banking.
"Bankrupt" includes any person whose estate is vested in a trustee or assignee under the law for the time being in force relating to bankruptcy.
"Bearer" means the person in possession of a bill or note which is payable to bearer.
"Bill" means bill of exchange, and "note" means promissory note.
"Delivery" means transfer of possession, actual or constructive, from one person to another.
"Holder" means the payee or indorsee of a bill or note who is in possession of it, or the bearer thereof.
"Indorsement" means an indorsement completed by delivery.
"Issue" means the first delivery of a bill or note, complete in form to a person who takes it as a holder.
"Person" includes a body of persons whether incorporated or not.
"Value" means valuable consideration.
"Written" includes printed, and "writing" includes print.

PART II. BILLS OF EXCHANGE

Form and Interpretation

Bill of exchange defined

3.—(1) A bill of exchange is an unconditional order in writing, addressed by one person to another, signed by the person giving it, requiring the person to whom it is

* 45 & 46 Vict c. 61. Reproduced by permission of HM Stationery Office.

addressed to pay on demand or at a fixed or determinable future time a sum certain in money to or to the order of a specified person, or to bearer.

(2) An instrument which does not comply with these conditions, or which orders any act to be done in addition to the payment of money, is not a bill of exchange.

(3) An order to pay out of a particular fund is not unconditional within the meaning of this section; but an unqualified order to pay, coupled with (a) an indication of a particular fund out of which the drawee is to re-imburse himself or a particular account to be debited with the amount, or (b) a statement of the transaction which gives rise to the bill, is unconditional.

(4) A bill is not invalid by reason—

(a) That it is not dated;

(b) That it does not specify the value given, or that any value has been given therefor;

(c) That it does not specify the place where it is drawn or the place where it is payable.

Inland and foreign bills

4.—(1) An inland bill is a bill which is or on the face of it purports to be (a) both drawn and payable within the British Islands, or (b) drawn within the British Islands upon some person resident therein. Any other bill is a foreign bill.

For the purposes of this Act "British Islands" mean any part of the United Kingdom of Great Britain and Ireland, the islands of Man, Guernsey, Jersey, Alderney, and Sark, and the islands adjacent to any of them being part of the dominions of Her Majesty.

(2) Unless the contrary appear on the face of the bill the holder may treat it as an inland bill.

Effect where different parties to bill are the same person

5.—(1) A bill may be drawn payable to, or to the order of, the drawer; or it may be drawn payable to, or to the order of, the drawee.

(2) Where in a bill drawer and drawee are the same person, or where the drawee is a fictitious person or a person not having capacity to contract, the holder may treat the instrument, at his option, either as a bill of exchange or as a promissory note.

Address to drawee

6.—(1) The drawee must be named or otherwise indicated in a bill with reasonable certainty.

(2) A bill may be addressed to two or more drawees whether they are partners or not, but an order addressed to two drawees in the alternative or to two or more drawees in succession is not a bill of exchange.

Certainty required as to payee

7.—(1) Where a bill is not payable to bearer, the payee must be named or otherwise indicated therein with reasonable certainty.

(2) A bill may be made payable to two or more payees jointly, or it may be made payable in the alternative to one of two, or one or some of several payees. A bill may also be made payable to the holder of an office for the time being.

(3) Where the payee is a fictitious or non-existing person the bill may be treated as payable to bearer.

What bills are negotiable

8.—(1) When a bill contains words prohibiting transfer, or indicating an intention that it should not be transferable, it is valid as between the parties thereto, but is not negotiable.

(2) A negotiable bill may be payable either to order or to bearer.

(3) A bill is payable to bearer which is expressed to be so payable, or on which the only or last indorsement is an indorsement in blank.

(4) A bill is payable to order which is expressed to be so payable, or which is expressed to be payable to a particular person, and does not contain words prohibiting transfer or indicating an intention that it should not be transferable.

(5) Where a bill, either originally or by indorsement, is expressed to be payable to the order of a specified person, and not to him or his order, it is nevertheless payable to him or his order at his option.

Sum payable

9.—(1) The sum payable by a bill is a sum certain within the meaning of this Act, although it is required to be paid—

(a) With interest.

(b) By stated instalments.

(c) By stated instalments, with a provision that upon default in payment of any instalment the whole shall become due.

(d) According to an indicated rate of exchange or according to a rate of exchange to be ascertained as directed by the bill.

(2) Where the sum payable is expressed in words and also in figures, and there is a discrepancy between the two, the sum denoted by the words is the amount payable.

(3) Where a bill is expressed to be payable with interest, unless the instrument otherwise provides, interest runs from the date of the bill, and if the bill is undated from the issue thereof.

Bill payable on demand

10.—(1) A bill is payable on demand—

(a) Which is expressed to be payable on demand, or at sight, or on presentation; or

(b) In which no time for payment is expressed.

(2) Where a bill is accepted or indorsed when it is overdue, it shall, as regards the acceptor who so accepts, or any indorser who so indorses it, be deemed a bill payable on demand.

Bill payable at a future time

11. A bill is payable at a determinable future time within the meaning of this Act which is expressed to be payable—

(1) At a fixed period after date or sight.

(2) On or at a fixed period after the occurrence of a specified event which is certain to happen, though the time of happening may be uncertain.

An instrument expressed to be payable on a contingency is not a bill, and the happening of the event does not cure the defect.

Omission of date in bill payable after date

12. Where a bill expressed to be payable at a fixed period after date is issued undated, or where the acceptance of a bill payable at a fixed period after sight is undated, any holder may insert therein the true date of issue or acceptance, and the bill shall be payable accordingly.

Provided that (1) where the holder in good faith and by mistake inserts a wrong date, and (2) in every case where a wrong date is inserted, if the bill subsequently comes into the hands of a holder in due course the bill shall not be avoided thereby, but shall operate and be payable as if the date so inserted had been the true date.

Ante-dating and post-dating

13.—(1) Where a bill or an acceptance or any indorsement on a bill is dated, the date shall, unless the contrary be proved, be deemed to be the true date of the drawing, acceptance, or indorsement, as the case may be.

(2) A bill is not invalid by reason only that it is ante-dated or post-dated, or that it bears date on a Sunday.

Computation of time of payment

14. Where a bill is not payable on demand the day on which it falls due is determined as follows:

(1) Three days, called days of grace, are, in every case where the bill itself does not otherwise provide, added to the time of payment as fixed by the bill, and the bill is due and payable on the last day of grace: Provided that—

- (a) When the last day of grace falls on Sunday, Christmas Day, Good Friday, or a day appointed by Royal proclamation as a public fast or thanksgiving day, the bill is, except in the case herein-after provided for, due and payable on the preceeding business day;
- (b) When the last day of grace is a bank holiday (other than Christmas Day or Good Friday) under the Bank Holidays Act, 1871, and Acts amending or extending it, or when the last day of grace is a Sunday and the second day of grace is a Bank Holiday, the bill is due and payable on the succeeding business day.

NOTE

This subsection was repealed by s. 3 of the Banking and Financial Dealings Act 1971, and the following substituted: "(1) The bill is due and payable in all cases on the last day of the time of payment as fixed by the bill or, if that is a non-business day, on the succeeding business day."

(2) Where a bill is payable at a fixed period after date, after sight, or after the happening of a specified event, the time of payment is determined by excluding the day from which the time is to begin to run and by including the day of payment.

(3) Where a bill is payable at a fixed period after sight, the time begins to run from the date of the acceptance if the bill be accepted, and from the date of noting or protest if the bill be noted or protested for non-acceptance, or for non-delivery.

(4) The term "month" in a bill means calendar month.

Case of need

15. The drawer of a bill and any indorser may insert therein the name of a person to whom the holder may resort in case of need, that is to say, in case the bill is dishonoured by non-acceptance or non-payment. Such person is called the referee in case of need. It is in the option of the holder to resort to the referee in case of need or not as he may think fit.

Optional stipulations by drawer or indorser

16. The drawer of a bill, and any indorser, may insert therein an express stipulation—

(1) Negativing or limiting his own liability to the holder:

(2) Waiving as regards himself some or all of the holder's duties.

Definition and requisites of acceptance

17.—(1) The acceptance of a bill is the signification by the drawee of his assent to the order of the drawer.

(2) An acceptance is invalid unless it complies with the following conditions, namely:

(*a*) It must be written on the bill and be signed by the drawee. The mere signature of the drawee without additional words is sufficient.

(*b*) It must not express that the drawee will perform his promise by any other means than the payment of money.

Time for acceptance

18. A bill may be accepted.

(1) before it has been signed by the drawer, or while otherwise incomplete:

(2) When it is overdue, or after it has been dishonoured by a previous refusal to accept, or by non-payment:

(3) When a bill payable after sight is dishonoured by non-acceptance, and the drawee subsequently accepts it, the holder, in the absence of any different agreement, is entitled to have the bill accepted as of the date of first presentment to the drawee for acceptance.

General and qualified acceptances

19.—(1) An acceptance is either (*a*) general or (*b*) qualified.

(2) A general acceptance assents without qualification to the order of the drawer. A qualified acceptance in express terms varies the effect of the bill as drawn.

In particular an acceptance is qualified which is—

(*a*) conditional, that is to say, which makes payment by the acceptor dependent on the fulfilment of a condition therein stated:

(*b*) partial, that is to say, an acceptance to pay part only of the amount for which the bill is drawn:

(*c*) local, that is to say, an acceptance to pay only at a particular specified place:

An acceptance to pay at a particular place is a general acceptance, unless it expressly states that the bill is to be paid there only and not elsewhere:

(*d*) qualified as to time:

(*e*) the acceptance of some one or more of the drawees, but not of all.

Inchoate instruments

20.—(1) Where a simple signature on a blank [stamped] paper is delivered by the signer in order that it may be converted into a bill, it operates as a primâ facie authority to fill it up as a complete bill for any amount [the stamp will cover] using the signature for that of the drawer, or the acceptor, or an indorser; and, in like manner, when a bill is wanting in any material particular, the person in possession of it has a primâ facie authority to fill up the omission in any way he thinks fit.

Section 32 of the Finance Act 1970 abolished stamp duty on cheques, and the wording of this subsection was amended accordingly.

(2) In order that any such instrument when completed may be enforceable against any person who became a party thereto prior to its completion, it must be filled up within a reasonable time, and strictly in accordance with the authority given. Reasonable time for this purpose is a question of fact.

Provided that if any such instrument after completion is negotiated to a holder in due course it shall be valid and effectual for all purposes in his hands, and he may enforce it as if it had been filled up within a reasonable time and strictly in accordance with the authority given.

Delivery

21.—(1) Every contract on a bill, whether it be the drawer's the acceptor's or an indorser's, is incomplete and revocable, until delivery of the instrument in order to give effect thereto.

Provided that where an acceptance is written on a bill, and the drawee gives notice to or according to the directions of the person entitled to the bill that he has accepted it, the acceptance then becomes complete and irrevocable.

(2) As between immediate parties, and as regards a remote party other than a holder in due course, the delivery—

(*a*) in order to be effectual must be made either by or under the authority of the party drawing, accepting, or indorsing, as the case may be:

(*b*) may be shown to have been conditional or for a special purpose only, and not for the purpose of transferring the property in the bill.

But if the bill be in the hands of a holder in due course a valid delivery of the bill by all parties to him so as to make them liable to him is conclusively presumed.

(3) Where a bill is no longer in the possession of a party who has signed it as drawer, acceptor, or indorser, a valid and unconditional delivery by him is presumed until the contrary is proved.

Capacity and Authority of Parties

Capacity of parties

22.—(1) Capacity to incur liability as a party to a bill is co-extensive with capacity to contract.

Provided that nothing in this section shall enable a corporation to make itself liable as drawer, acceptor, or indorser of a bill unless it is competent to it so to do under the law for the time being in force relating to corporations.

(2) Where a bill is drawn or indorsed by an infant, minor, or corporation having no capacity or power to incur liability on a bill, the drawing or indorsement entitles the holder to receive payment of the bill, and to enforce it against any other party thereto.

Signature essential to liability

23. No person is liable as drawer, indorser, or acceptor of a bill who has not signed it as such: Provided that

(1) Where a person signs a bill in a trade or assumed name, he is liable thereon as if he had signed it in his own name:

(2) The signature of the name of a firm is equivalent to the signature by the person so signing of the names of all persons liable as partners in that firm.

Forged or unauthorised signature

24. Subject to the provisions of this Act, where a signature on a bill is forged or placed thereon without the authority of the person whose signature it purports to be, the forged or unauthorised signature is wholly inoperative, and no right to retain the bill or to give a discharge therefor or to enforce payment thereof against any party thereto can be acquired through or under that signature, unless the party against whom it is sought to retain or enforce payment of the bill is precluded from setting up the forgery or want of authority.

Provided that nothing in this section shall affect the ratification of an unauthorised signature not amounting to a forgery.

Procuration signatures

25. A signature by procuration operates as notice that the agent has but a limited authority to sign, and the principal is only bound by such signature if the agent in so signing was acting within the actual limits of his authority.

Person signing as agent or in representative capacity

26.—(1) Where a person signs a bill as drawer, indorser, or acceptor, and adds words to his signature, indicating that he signs for or on behalf of a principal, or in a representative character, he is not personally liable thereon; but the mere addition to his signature of words describing him as an agent, or as filling a representative character, does not exempt him from personal liability.

(2) In determining whether a signature on a bill is that of the principal or that of the agent by whose hand it is written, the construction most favourable to the validity of the instrument shall be adopted.

The Consideration for a Bill

Value and holder for value

27.—(1) Valuable consideration for a bill may be constituted by,—
  (*a*) Any consideration sufficient to support a simple contract;
  (*b*) An antecedent debt or liability. Such a debt or liability is deemed valuable consideration whether the bill is payable on demand or at a future time.
(2) Where value has at any time been given for a bill the holder is deemed to be a holder for value as regards the acceptor and all parties to the bill who became parties prior to such time.
(3) Where the holder of a bill has a lien on it, arising either from contract or by implication of law, he is deemed to be a holder for value to the extent of the sum for which he has a lien.

Accommodation bill or party

28.—(1) An accommodation party to a bill is a person who has signed a bill as drawer, acceptor, or indorser, without receiving value therefor, and for the purpose of lending his name to some other person.

(2) An accommodation party is liable on the bill to a holder for value; and it is immaterial whether, when such holder took the bill, he knew such party to be an accommodation party or not.

Holder in due course

29.—(1) A holder in due course is a holder who has taken a bill, complete and regular on the face of it, under the following conditions; namely,

    (a) That he became the holder of it before it was overdue, and without notice that it had been previously dishonoured, if such was the fact:

    (b) That he took the bill in good faith and for value, and that at the time the bill was negotiated to him he had no notice of any defect in the title of the person who negotiated it.

(2) In particular the title of a person who negotiates a bill is defective within the meaning of this Act when he obtained the bill, or the acceptance thereof, by fraud, duress, or force and fear, or other unlawful means, or for an illegal consideration, or when he negotiates it in breach of faith, or under such circumstances as amount to a fraud.

(3) A holder (whether for value or not), who derives his title to a bill through a holder in due course, and who is not himself a party to any fraud or illegality affecting it, has all the rights of that holder in due course as regards the acceptor and all parties to the bill prior to that holder.

Presumption of value and good faith

30.—(1) Every party whose signature appears on a bill is primâ facie deemed to have become a party thereto for value.

(2) Every holder of a bill is primâ facie deemed to be a holder in due course; but if in an action on a bill it is admitted or proved that the acceptance, issue, or subsequent negotiation of the bill is affected with fraud, duress, or force and fear, or illegality, the burden of proof is shifted, unless and until the holder proves that, subsequent to the alleged fraud or illegality, value has in good faith been given for the bill.

Negotiation of Bills

Negotiation of bill

31.—(1) A bill is negotiated when it is transferred from one person to another in such a manner as to constitute the transferee the holder of the bill.

(2) A bill payable to bearer is negotiated by delivery.

(3) A bill payable to order is negotiated by the indorsement of the holder completed by delivery.

(4) Where the holder of a bill payable to his order transfers it for value without indorsing it, the transfer gives the transferee such title as the transferor had in the bill, and the transferee in addition acquires the right to have the indorsement of the transferor.

(5) Where any person is under obligation to indorse a bill in a representative capacity, he may indorse the bill in such terms as to negative personal liability.

Requisites of a valid indorsement

32. An indorsement in order to operate as a negotiation must comply with the following conditions, namely:—

(1) It must be written on the bill itself and be signed by the indorser. The simple signature of the indorser on the bill, without additional words, is sufficient.

An indorsement written on an allonge, or on a "copy" of a bill issued or negotiated in a country where "copies" are recognised, is deemed to be written on the bill itself.

(2) It must be an indorsement of the entire bill. A partial indorsement, that is to say, an indorsement which purports to transfer to the indorsee a part only of the amount payable, or which purports to transfer the bill to two or more indorsees severally, does not operate as a negotiation of the bill.

(3) Where a bill is payable to the order of two or more payees or indorsees who are not partners all must indorse, unless the one indorsing has authority to indorse for the others.

(4) Where, in a bill payable to order, the payee or indorsee is wrongly designated, or his name is mis-spelt, he may indorse the bill as therein described, adding, if he think fit, his proper signature.

(5) Where there are two or more indorsements on a bill, each indorsement is deemed to have been made in the order in which it appears on the bill, until the contrary is proved.

(6) An indorsement may be made in blank or special. It may also contain terms making it restrictive.

Conditional Indorsement

33. Where a bill purports to be indorsed conditionally the condition may be disregarded by the payer, and payment to the indorsee is valid whether the condition has been fulfilled or not.

Indorsement in blank and special indorsement

34.—(1) An indorsement in blank specifies no indorsee and a bill so endorsed becomes payable to bearer.

(2) A special indorsement specifies the person to whom, or to whose order, the bill is to be payable.

(3) The provisions of this Act relating to a payee apply with the necessary modifications to an indorsee under a special indorsement.

(4) When a bill has been indorsed in blank, any holder may convert the blank indorsement into a special indorsement by writing above the indorser's signature a direction to pay the bill to or to the order of himself or some other person.

Restrictive indorsement

35.—(1) An indorsement is restrictive which prohibits the further negotiation of the bill or which expresses that it is a mere authority to deal with the bill as thereby directed and not a transfer of the ownership thereof, as, for example, if a bill be indorsed "Pay D. only", or "Pay D. for the account of X.", or "Pay D. or order for collection".

(2) A restrictive indorsement gives the indorsee the right to receive payment of the bill and to sue any party thereto that his indorser could have sued, but gives him no power to transfer his rights as indorsee unless it expressly authorises him to do so.

(3) Where a restrictive indorsement authorises further transfer, all subsequent indorsees take the bill with the same rights and subject to the same liabilities as the first indorsee under the restrictive indorsement.

Negotiation of overdue or dishonoured bill

36.—(1) Where a bill is negotiable in its origin it continues to be negotiable until it has been (*a*) restrictively indorsed or (*b*) discharged by payment or otherwise.

(2) Where an overdue bill is negotiated, it can only be negotiated subject to any defect of title affecting it at its maturity, and thenceforward no person who takes it can acquire or give a better title than that which the person from whom he took it had.

(3) A bill payable on demand is deemed to be overdue within the meaning and for the purposes, of this section, when it appears on the face of it to have been in circulation for an unreasonable length of time. What is an unreasonable length of time for this purpose is a question of fact.

(4) Except where an indorsement bears date after the maturity of the bill, every negotiation is prima facie deemed to have been effected before the bill was overdue.

(5) Where a bill which is not overdue has been dishonoured any person who takes it with notice of the dishonour takes it subject to any defect of title attaching thereto at the time of dishonour, but nothing in this sub-section shall affect the rights of a holder in due course.

Negotiation of bill to party already liable thereon

37.—Where a bill is negotiated back to the drawer, or to a prior indorser or to the acceptor, such party may, subject to the provisions of this Act, re-issue and further negotiate the bill, but he is not entitled to enforce payment of the bill against any intervening party to whom he was previously liable.

Rights of the holder

38.—The rights and powers of the holder of a bill are as follows:

(1) He may sue on the bill in his own name:

(2) Where he is a holder in due course, he holds the bill free from any defect of title of prior parties, as well as from mere personal defences available to prior parties among themselves, and may enforce payment against all parties liable on the bill:

(3) Where his title is defective (*a*) if he negotiates the bill to a holder in due course, that holder obtains a good and complete title to the bill, and (*b*) if he obtains payment of the bill the person who pays him in due course gets a valid discharge for the bill.

General duties of the Holder

When presentment for acceptance is necessary

39.—(1) Where a bill is payable after sight, presentment for acceptance is necessary in order to fix the maturity of the instrument.

(2) Where a bill expressly stipulates that it shall be presented for acceptance, or where a bill is drawn payable elsewhere than at the residence or place of business of the drawee it must be presented for acceptance before it can be presented for payment.

(3) In no other case is presentment for acceptance necessary in order to render liable any party to the bill.

(4) Where the holder of a bill, drawn payable elsewhere than at the place of business or residence of the drawee, has not time, with the exercise of reasonable diligence, to present the bill for acceptance before presenting it for payment on the day that it falls due, the delay caused by presenting the bill for acceptance before presenting it for payment is excused, and does not discharge the drawer and indorsers.

Time for presenting bill payable after sight

40.—(1) Subject to the provisions of this Act, when a bill payable after sight is negotiated, the holder must either present it for acceptance or negotiate it within a reasonable time.

(2) If he does not do so, the drawer and all indorsers prior to that holder are discharged.

(3) In determining what is a reasonable time within the meaning of this section, regard shall be had to the nature of the bill, the usage of trade with respect to similar bills, and the facts of the particular case.

Rules as to presentment for acceptance, and excuses for non-presentment

41.—(1) A bill is duly presented for acceptance which is presented in accordance with the following rules:

(a) The presentment must be made by or on behalf of the holder to the drawee or to some person authorised to accept or refuse acceptance on his behalf at a reasonable hour on a business day and before the bill is overdue:

(b) Where a bill is addressed to two or more drawees, who are not partners, presentment must be made to them all, unless one has authority to accept for all, then presentment may be made to him only:

(c) Where the drawee is dead presentment may be made to his personal representative:

(d) Where the drawee is bankrupt, presentment may be made to him or to his trustee:

(e) Where authorised by agreement or usage, a presentment through the post office is sufficient.

(2) Presentment in accordance with these rules is excused, and a bill may be treated as dishonoured by non-acceptance—

(a) Where the drawee is dead or bankrupt, or is a fictitious person or a person not having capacity to contract by bill:

(b) Where, after the exercise of reasonable diligence, such presentment cannot be effected:

(c) Where although the presentment has been irregular, acceptance has been refused on some other ground.

(3) The fact that the holder has reason to believe that the bill, on presentment, will be dishonoured does not excuse presentment.

Non-acceptance

42.—When a bill is duly presented for acceptance and is not accepted within the customary time, the person presenting it must treat it as dishonoured by non-acceptance. If he does not, the holder shall lose his right of recourse against the drawer and indorsers.

Dishonour by non-acceptance and its consequences

43.—(1) A bill is dishonoured by non-acceptance—

(a) when it is duly presented for acceptance, and such an acceptance as is prescribed by this Act is refused or cannot be obtained; or

(b) when presentment for acceptance is excused and the bill is not accepted.

(2) Subject to the provisions of this Act when a bill is dishonoured by non-acceptance, an immediate right of recourse against the drawer and indorsers accrues to the holder, and no presentment for payment is necessary.

Duties as to qualified acceptances

44.—(1) The holder of a bill may refuse to take a qualified acceptance, and if he does not obtain an unqualified acceptance may treat the bill as dishonoured by non-acceptance.

(2) Where a qualified acceptance is taken, and the drawer or an indorser has not expressly or impliedly authorised the holder to take a qualified acceptance, or does not subsequently assent thereto, such drawer or indorser is discharged from his liability on the bill.

The provisions of this sub-section do not apply to a partial acceptance, whereof due notice has been given. Where a foreign bill has been accepted as to part, it must be protested as to the balance.

(3) When the drawer or indorser of a bill receives notice of a qualified acceptance, and does not within a reasonable time express his dissent to the holder he shall be deemed to have assented thereto.

Rules as to presentment for payment

45.—Subject to the provisions of this Act a bill must be duly presented for payment. If it be not so presented the drawer and indorsers shall be discharged.

A bill is duly presented for payment which is presented in accordance with the following rules:—

(1) Where the bill is not payable on demand, presentment must be made on the day it falls due.

(2) Where the bill is payable on demand, then, subject to the provisions of this Act, presentment must be made within a reasonable time after its issue in order to render the drawer liable, and within a reasonable time after its indorsement, in order to render the indorser liable.

In determining what is a reasonable time, regard shall be had to the nature of the bill, the usage of trade with regard to similar bills, and the facts of the particular case.

(3) Presentment must be made by the holder or by some person authorised to receive payment on his behalf at a reasonable hour on a business day, at the proper place as herein-after defined, either to the person designated by the bill as payer, or to some person authorised to pay or refuse payment on his behalf if with the exercise of reasonable diligence such person can there be found.

(4) A bill is presented at the proper place:—

(a) Where a place of payment is specified in the bill and the bill is there presented.

(b) Where no place of payment is specified, but the address of the drawee or acceptor is given in the bill, and the bill is there presented.

(c) Where no place of payment is specified and no address given, and the bill is presented at the drawee's or acceptor's place of business if known, and if not, at his ordinary residence if known.

(d) In any other case if presented to the drawee or acceptor wherever he can be found, or if presented at his last known place of business or residence.

(5) Where a bill is presented at the proper place, and after the exercise of reasonable diligence no person authorised to pay or refuse payment can be found there, no further presentment to the drawee or acceptor is required.

(6) Where a bill is drawn upon, or accepted by two or more persons who are not partners, and no place of payment is specified, presentment must be made to them all.

(7) Where the drawee or acceptor of a bill is dead, and no place of payment is specified, presentment must be made to a personal representative, if such there be, and with the exercise of reasonable diligence he can be found.

(8) Where authorised by agreement or usage a presentment through the post office is sufficient.

Excuses for delay or non-presentment for payment

46.—(1) Delay in making presentment for payment is excused when the delay is caused by circumstances beyond the control of the holder, and not imputable to his default, misconduct, or negligence. When the cause of delay ceases to operate presentment must be made with reasonable diligence.

(2) Presentment for payment is dispensed with,—

(a) Where, after the exercise of reasonable diligence presentment, as required by this Act, cannot be effected.

The fact that the holder has reason to believe that the bill will, on presentment, be dishonoured, does not dispense with the necessity for presentment.

(b) Where the drawee is a fictitious person.

(c) As regards the drawer where the drawee or acceptor is not bound, as between himself and the drawer, to accept or pay the bill, and the drawer has no reason to believe that the bill would be paid if presented.

(d) As regards an indorser, where the bill was accepted or made for the accommodation of that indorser, and he has no reason to expect that the bill would be paid if presented.

(e) By waiver of presentment, express or implied.

Dishonour by non-payment

47.—(1) A bill is dishonoured by non-payment (a) when it is duly presented for payment and payment is refused or cannot be obtained, or (b) when presentment is excused and the bill is overdue and unpaid.

(2) Subject to the provisions of this Act, when a bill is dishonoured by non-payment, an immediate right of recourse against the drawer and indorsers accrues to the holder.

Notice of dishonour and effect of non-notice

48.—Subject to the provisions of this Act, when a bill has been dishonoured by non-acceptance or by non-payment, notice of dishonour must be given to the drawer and each indorser, and any drawer or indorser to whom such notice is not given is discharged; Provided that—

(1) Where a bill is dishonoured by non-acceptance, and notice of dishonour is not given, the rights of a holder in due course subsequent to the omission, shall not be prejudiced by the omission.

(2) Where a bill is dishonoured by non-acceptance and due notice of dishonour is given, it shall not be necessary to give notice of a subsequent dishonour by non-payment unless the bill shall in the meantime have been accepted.

Rules as to notice of dishonour

49.—Notice of dishonour in order to be valid and effectual must be given in accordance with the following rules:—

(1) The notice must be given by or on behalf of the holder, or by or on behalf of an indorser who, at the time of giving it, is himself liable on the bill.

(2) Notice of dishonour may be given by an agent either in his own name, or in the name of any party entitled to give notice whether that party be his principal or not.

(3) Where the notice is given by or on behalf of the holder, it enures for the benefit of all subsequent holders and all prior indorsers who have a right of recourse against the party to whom it is given.

(4) Where notice is given by or on behalf of an indorser entitled to give notice as herein-before provided, it enures for the benefit of the holder and all indorsers subsequent to the party to whom notice is given.

(5) The notice may be given in writing or by personal communication, and may be given in any terms which sufficiently identify the bill, and intimate that the bill has been dishonoured by non-acceptance or non-payment.

(6) The return of a dishonoured bill to the drawer or an indorser is, in point of form, deemed a sufficient notice of dishonour.

(7) A written notice need not be signed, and an insufficient written notice may be supplemented and validated by verbal communication. A misdescription of the bill shall not vitiate the notice unless the party to whom the notice is given is in fact, misled thereby.

(8) Where notice of dishonour is required to be given to any person, it may be given either to the party himself, or to his agent in that behalf.

(9) Where the drawer or indorser is dead, and the party giving notice knows it, the notice must be given to a personal representative if such there be, and with the exercise of reasonable diligence he can be found.

(10) Where the drawer or indorser is bankrupt, notice may be given either to the party himself or to the trustee.

(11) Where there are two or more drawers or indorsers who are not partners, notice must be given to each of them, unless one of them has authority to receive such notice for the others.

(12) The notice may be given as soon as the bill is dishonoured and must be given within a reasonable time thereafter.

In the absence of special circumstances notice is not deemed to have been given within a reasonable time, unless—

(a) where the person giving and the person to receive notice reside in the same place, the notice is given or sent off in time to reach the latter on the day after the dishonour of the bill.

(b) where the person giving and the person to receive notice reside in different places, the notice is sent off on the day after the dishonour of the bill, if there be a post at a convenient hour on that day, and if there be no such post on that day then by the next post thereafter.

(13) Where a bill when dishonoured is in the hands of an agent, he may either himself give notice to the parties liable on the bill, or he may give notice to his principal. If he give notice to his principal, he must do so within the same time as if he were the holder, and the principal upon receipt of such notice has himself the same time for giving notice as if the agent had been an independent holder.

(14) Where a party to a bill receives due notice of dishonour, he has after the receipt of such notice the same period of time for giving notice to antecedent parties that the holder has after the dishonour.

(15) Where a notice of dishonour is duly addressed and posted, the sender is deemed to have given due notice of dishonour, notwithstanding any miscarriage by the post office.

Excuses for non-notice and delay

50.—(1) Delay in giving notice of dishonour is excused where the delay is caused by circumstances beyond the control of the party giving notice, and not imputable to his default, misconduct, or negligence. When the cause of delay ceases to operate the notice must be given with reasonable diligence.

(2) Notice of dishonour is dispensed with—

(a) When, after the exercise of reasonable diligence, notice as required by this Act cannot be given to or does not reach the drawer or indorser sought to be charged:

(b) By waiver express or implied. Notice of dishonour may be waived before the time of giving notice has arrived, or after the omission to give due notice:

(c) As regards the drawer in the following cases, namely, (1) where drawer and drawee are the same person, (2) where the drawee is a fictitious person or a person not having capacity to contract, (3) where the drawer is the person to whom the bill is presented for payment, (4) where the drawee or acceptor is as between himself and the drawer under no obligation to accept or pay the bill, (5) where the drawer has countermanded payment:

(d) As regards the indorser in the following cases, namely, (1) where the drawee is a fictitious person or a person not having capacity to contract and the indorser was aware of the fact at the time he indorsed the bill, (2) where the indorser is the person to whom the bill is presented for payment, (3) where the bill was accepted or made for his accommodation.

Noting or protest of bill

51.—(1) Where an inland bill has been dishonoured it may, if the holder think fit, be noted for non-acceptance or non-payment, as the case may be; but it shall not be necessary to note or protest any such bill in order to preserve the recourse against the drawer or indorser.

(2) Where a foreign bill, appearing on the face of it to be such, has been dishonoured by non-acceptance it must be duly protested for non-acceptance, and where such a bill, which has not been previously dishonoured by non-acceptance, is dishonoured by non-payment it must be duly protested for non-payment. If it be not so protested the drawer and indorsers are discharged. Where a bill does not appear on the face of it to be a foreign bill, protest thereof in case of dishonour is unnecessary.

(3) A bill which has been protested for non-acceptance may be subsequently protested for non-payment.

(4) Subject to the provisions of this Act, when a bill is noted or protested, it must be noted on the day of its dishonour. When a bill has been duly noted, the protest may be subsequently extended as of the date of the noting.

NOTE

This subsection was amended by the Bills of Exchange (Time of Noting) Act 1917, and now reads:

"Subject to the provisions of this Act, when a bill is noted or protested, it may be noted on the day of its dishonour, and must be noted not later than the next succeeding business day. When a bill has been duly noted, the protest may be subsequently extended as of the date of the noting."

(5) Where the acceptor of a bill becomes bankrupt or insolvent or suspends payment before it matures, the holder may cause the bill to be protested for better security against the drawer and indorsers.

(6) A bill must be protested at the place where it is dishonoured: Provided that—

(a) When a bill is presented through the post office, and returned by post dishonoured, it may be protested at the place to which it is returned and on the day of its return if received during business hours, and if not received during business hours then not later than the next business day:

(b) When a bill drawn payable at the place of business or residence of some person other than the drawee, has been dishonoured by non-acceptance, it must be protested for non-payment at the place where it is expressed to be payable, and no further presentment for payment to, or demand on, the drawee is necessary.

(7) A protest must contain a copy of the bill, and must be signed by the notary making it, and must specify—

(a) The person at whose request the bill is protested:

(b) The place and date of protest, the cause or reason for protesting the bill, the demand made, and the answer given, if any, or the fact that the drawee or acceptor could not be found.

(8) Where a bill is lost or destroyed, or is wrongly detained from the person entitled to hold it, protest may be made on a copy or written particulars thereof.

(9) Protest is dispensed with by any circumstance which would dispense with notice of dishonour. Delay in noting or protesting is excused when the delay is caused by circumstances beyond the control of the holder, and not imputable to his default, misconduct, or negligence. When the cause of delay ceases to operate the bill must be noted or protested with reasonable diligence.

Duties of holder as regards drawee or acceptor

52.—(1) When a bill is accepted generally presentment for payment is not necessary in order to render the acceptor liable.

(2) When by the terms of a qualified acceptance presentment for payment is required, the acceptor, in the absence of an express stipulation to that effect, is not discharged by the omission to present the bill for payment on the day that it matures.

(3) In order to render the acceptor of a bill liable it is not necessary to protest it, or that notice of dishonour should be given to him.

(4) Where the holder of a bill presents it for payment, he shall exhibit the bill to the person from whom he demands payment, and when a bill is paid the holder shall forthwith deliver it up to the party paying it.

Liabilities of Parties

Funds in hands of drawee

53.—(1) A bill, of itself, does not operate as an assignment of funds in the hands of the drawee available for the payment thereof, and the drawee of a bill who does not accept as required by this Act is not liable on the instrument. This sub-section shall not extend to Scotland.

(2) In Scotland, where the drawee of a bill has in his hands funds available for the payment thereof, the bill operates as an assignment of the sum for which it is drawn in favour of the holder, from the time when the bill is presented to the drawee.

Liability of acceptor

54. The acceptor of a bill, by accepting it—

(1) Engages that he will pay it according to the tenor of his acceptance:

(2) Is precluded from denying to a holder in due course:

(a) The existence of the drawer, the genuineness of his signature, and his capacity and authority to draw the bill;

(b) In the case of a bill payable to drawer's order, the then capacity of the drawer to indorse, but not the genuineness or validity of his indorsement;

(c) In the case of a bill payable to the order of a third person, the existence of the payee and his then capacity to indorse, but not the genuineness or validity of his indorsement.

Liability of drawer of indorser

55.—(1) The drawer of a bill by drawing it—

(a) Engages that on due presentment it shall be accepted and paid according to its tenor, and that if it be dishonoured he will compensate the holder or any indorser who is compelled to pay it, provided that the requisite proceedings on dishonour be duly taken;

(b) Is precluded from denying to a holder in due course the existence of the payee and his then capacity to indorse.

(2) The indorser of a bill by indorsing it—

(a) Engages that on due presentment it shall be accepted and paid according to its tenor, and that if it be dishonoured he will compensate the holder or a subsequent indorser who is compelled to pay it, provided that the requisite proceedings on dishonour be duly taken;

(b) Is precluded from denying to a holder in due course the genuineness and regularity in all respects of the drawer's signature and all previous indorsements;

(c) Is precluded from denying to his immediate or a subsequent indorsee that the bill was at that time of his indorsement a valid and subsisting bill, and that he had then a good title thereto.

Stranger signing bill liable as indorser

56. Where a person signs a bill otherwise than as drawer or acceptor, he thereby incurs the liabilities of an indorser to a holder in due course.

Measure of damages against parties to dishonoured bill

57. Where a bill is dishonoured, the measure of damages, which shall be deemed to be liquidated damages, shall be as follows:

(1) The holder may recover from any party liable on the bill, and the drawer who has been compelled to pay the bill may recover from the acceptor, and an indorser who has been compelled to pay the bill may recover from the acceptor or from the drawer, or from a prior indorser—

(a) The amount of the bill:

(b) Interest thereon from the time of presentment for payment if the bill is payable on demand, and from the maturity of the bill in any other case:

(c) The expenses of noting, or, when protest is necessary, and the protest has been extended, the expenses of protect.

(2) In the case of a bill which has been dishonoured abroad, in lieu of the above damages, the holder may recover from the drawer or an indorser, and the drawer or an indorser who has been compelled to pay the bill may recover from any party liable to him, the amount of the re-exchange with interest thereon until the time of payment.

NOTE

This sub-section was repealed by the Administration of Justice Act 1977.

(3) Where by this Act interest may be recovered as damages, such interest may, if justice require it, be withheld wholly or in part, and where a bill is expressed to be payable with interest at a given rate, interest as damages may or may not be given at the same rate as interest proper.

Transferor by delivery and transferee

58.—(1) Where the holder of a bill payable to bearer negotiates it by delivery without indorsing it, he is called a "transferor by delivery".

(2) A transferor by delivery is not liable on the instrument.

(3) A transferor by delivery who negotiates a bill thereby warrants to his immediate transferee being a holder for value that the bill is what it purports to be, that he has a right to transfer it, and that at the time of transfer he is not aware of any fact which renders it valueless.

Discharge of Bill

Payment in due course

59.—(1) A bill is discharged by payment in due course by or on behalf of the drawee or acceptor.

"Payment in due course" means payment made at or after the maturity of the bill to the holder thereof in good faith and without notice that his title to the bill is defective.

(2) Subject to the provisions herein-after contained, when a bill is paid by the drawer or an indorser it is not discharged; but

    (a) Where a bill payable to, or to the order of, a third party is paid by the drawer, the drawer may enforce payment thereof against the acceptor, but may not re-issue the bill.

    (b) Where a bill is paid by an indorser, or where a bill payable to drawer's order is paid by the drawer, the party paying it is remitted to his former rights as regards the acceptor or antecedent parties, and he may, if he thinks fit, strike out his own and subsequent indorsements, and again negotiate the bill.

(3) Where an accommodation bill is paid in due course by the party accommodated the bill is discharged.

Banker paying demand draft whereon indorsement is forged

60. When a bill payable to order on demand is drawn on a banker, and the banker on whom it is drawn pays the bill in good faith and in the ordinary course of business, it is not incumbent on the banker to show that the indorsement of the payee or any subsequent indorsement was made by or under the authority of the person whose indorsement it purports to be, and the banker is deemed to have paid the bill in due course, although such indorsement has been forged or made without authority.

Acceptor the holder at maturity

61. When the acceptor of a bill is or becomes the holder of it at or after its maturity, in his own right, the bill is discharged.

Express waiver

62.—(1) When the holder of a bill at or after its maturity absolutely and unconditionally renounces his rights against the acceptor the bill is discharged.

The renunciation must be in writing, unless the bill is delivered up to the acceptor.

(2) The liabilities of any party to a bill may in like manner be renounced by the holder before, at, or after its maturity; but nothing in this section shall affect the rights of a holder in due course without notice of the renunciation.

Cancellation

63.—(1) Where a bill is intentionally cancelled by the holder or his agent, and the cancellation is apparent thereon, the bill is discharged.

(2) In like manner any party liable on a bill may be discharged by the intentional cancellation of his signature by the holder or his agent. In such case any indorser who would have had a right of recourse against the party whose signature is cancelled, is also discharged.

(3) A cancellation made unintentionally, or under a mistake, or without the authority of the holder is inoperative; but where a bill or any signature thereon appears to have been cancelled the burden of proof lies on the party who alleges that the cancellation was made unintentionally, or under a mistake, or without authority.

Alteration of bill

64.—(1) Where a bill or acceptance is materially altered without the assent of all parties liable on the bill, the bill is avoided except as against a party who has himself made, authorized, or assented to the alteration, and subsequent indorsers.

Provided that, where a bill has been materially altered, but the alteration is not apparent, and the bill is in the hands of a holder in due course, such holder may avail himself of the bill as if it had not been altered, and may enforce payment of it according to its original tenor.

(2) In particular the following alterations are material, namely, any alteration of the date, the sum payable, the time of payment, the place of payment, and where a bill has been accepted generally, the addition of a place of payment without the acceptor's assent.

Acceptance and Payment for Honour

Acceptance for honour supra protest

65.—(1) Where a bill of exchange has been protested for dishonour by non-acceptance, or protested for better security, and is not overdue, any person, not being a party already liable thereon, may, with the consent of the holder, intervene and accept the bill supra protest, for the honour of any party liable, thereon, or for the honour of the person for whose account the bill is drawn.

(2) A bill may be accepted for honour for part only of the sum for which it is drawn.

(3) An acceptance for honour supra protest in order to be valid must—

    (*a*) be written on the bill, and indicate that it is an acceptance for honour:

    (*b*) be signed by the acceptor for honour:

(4) Where an acceptance for honour does not expressly state for whose honour it is made, it is deemed to be an acceptance for the honour of the drawer.

(5) Where a bill payable after sight is accepted for honour, its maturity is calculated from the date of the noting for non-acceptance, and not from the date of the acceptance for honour.

Liability of acceptor for honour

66.—(1) The acceptor for honour of a bill by accepting it engages that he will, on due presentment, pay the bill according to the tenor of his acceptance, if it is not paid by the drawee, provided it has been duly presented for payment, and protested for non-payment, and that he receives notice of these facts.

(2) The acceptor for honour is liable to the holder and to all parties to the bill subsequent to the party for whose honour he has accepted.

Presentment to acceptor for honour

67.—(1) Where a dishonoured bill has been accepted for honour supra protest, or contains a reference in case of need, it must be protested for non-payment before it is presented for payment to the acceptor for honour, or referee in case of need.

(2) Where the address of the acceptor for honour is in the same place where the bill is protested for non-payment, the bill must be presented to him not later than the day following its maturity; and where the address of the acceptor for honour is in some place other than the place where it was protested for non-payment, the bill must be forwarded not later than the day following its maturity for presentment to him.

(3) Delay in presentment or non-presentment is excused by any circumstance which would excuse delay in presentement for payment or non-presentment for payment.

(4) When a bill of exchange is dishonoured by the acceptor for honour it must be protested for non-payment by him.

Payment for honour supra protest

68.—(1) Where a bill has been protested for non-payment, any person may intervene and pay it supra protest for the honour of any party liable thereon, or for the honour of the person for whose account the bill is drawn.

(2) Where two or more persons offer to pay a bill for the honour of different parties, the person whose payment will discharge most parties to the bill shall have the preference.

(3) Payment for honour supra protest, in order to operate as such and not as a mere voluntary payment, must be attested by a notarial act of honour which may be appended to the protest or form an extension of it.

(4) The notarial act of honour must be founded on a declaration made by the payer for honour, or his agent in that behalf, declaring his intention to pay the bill for honour, and for whose honour he pays.

(5) Where a bill has been paid for honour, all parties subsequent to the party for whose honour it is paid are discharged but the payer for honour is subrogated for, and succeeds to both the rights and duties of, the holder as regards the party for whose honour he pays, and all parties liable to that party.

(6) The payer for honour on paying to the holder the amount of the bill and the notarial expenses incidental to its dishonour is entitled to receive both the bill itself and the protest. If the holder does not on demand deliver them up he shall be liable to the payer for honour in damages.

(7) Where the holder of a bill refuses to receive payment supra protest he shall lose his right of recourse against any party who would have been discharged by such payment.

Lost Instruments

Holder's right to duplicate of lost bill

69. Where a bill has been lost before it is overdue, the person who was the holder of it may apply to the drawer to give him another bill of the same tenor, giving security to the drawer if required to indemnify him against all persons whatever in case the bill alleged to have been lost shall be found again.

If the drawer on request as aforesaid refuses to give such duplicate bill, he may be compelled to do so.

Action on lost bill

70. In any action or proceeding upon a bill, the court or a judge may order that the loss of the instrument shall not be set up, provided an indemnity be given to the satisfaction of the court or judge against the claims of any other person upon the instrument in question.

Bill in a Set

Rules as to sets

71.—(1) Where a bill is drawn in a set, each part of the set being numbered, and containing a reference to the other parts, the whole of the parts constitute one bill.

(2) Where the holder of a set indorses two or more parts to different persons, he is liable on every such part, and every indorser subsequent to him is liable on the part he has himself indorsed as if the said parts were separate bills.

(3) Where two or more parts of a set are negotiated to different holders in due course, the holder whose title first accrues is as between such holders deemed the true owner of the bill; but nothing in this sub-section shall affect the rights of a person who in due course accepts or pays the part first presented to him.

(4) The acceptance may be written on any part, and it must be written on one part only.

If the drawee accepts more than one part, and such accepted parts get into the hands of different holders in due course, he is liable on every such part as if it were a separate bill.

(5) When the acceptor of a bill drawn in a set pays it without requiring the part bearing his acceptance to be delivered up to him, and that part at maturity is outstanding in the hands of a holder in due course, he is liable to the holder thereof.

(6) Subject to the preceding rules, where any one part of a bill drawn in a set is discharged by payment or otherwise, the whole bill is discharged.

Conflict of Laws

Rules where laws conflict

72. Where a bill drawn in one country is negotiated, accepted, or payable in another, the rights, duties, and liabilities of the parties thereto are determined as follows:

(1) The validity of a bill as regards requisites in form is determined by the law of the place of issue, and the validity as regards requisites in form of the supervening contracts, such as acceptance, or indorsement, or acceptance supra protest, is determined by the law of the place where such contract was made.

Provided that—

(a) Where a bill is issued out of the United Kingdom it is not invalid by reason only that it is not stamped in accordance with the law of the place of issue:

(b) Where a bill, issued out of the United Kingdom, conforms, as regards requisites in form, to the law of the United Kingdom, it may, for the purpose of enforcing payment thereof, be treated as valid as between all persons who negotiate, hold, or become parties to it in the United Kingdom.

(2) Subject to the provisions of this Act, the interpretation of the drawing, indorsement, acceptance, or acceptance supra protest of a bill, is determined by the law of the place where such contract is made.

Provided that where an inland bill is indorsed in a foreign country the indorsement shall as regards the payer be interpreted according to the law of the United Kingdom.

(3) The duties of the holder with respect to presentment for acceptance or payment and the necessity for or sufficiency of a protest or notice of dishonour, or otherwise, are determined by the law of the place where the act is done or the bill is dishonoured.

(4) Where a bill is drawn out of but payable in the United Kingdom and the sum payable is not expressed in the currency of the United Kingdom, the amount shall, in the absence of some express stipulation, be calculated according to the rate of exchange for sight drafts at the place of payment on the day the bill is payable.

NOTE
This subsection was repealed by the Administration of Justice Act 1977.

(5) Where a bill is drawn in one country and is payable in another, the due date thereof is determined according to the law of the place where is it payable.

PART III. CHEQUES ON A BANKER

Cheque defined

73. A cheque is a bill of exchange drawn on a banker payable on demand.

Except as otherwise provided in this Part, the provisions of this Act applicable to a bill of exchange payable on demand apply to a cheque.

Presentment of cheque for payment

74. Subject to the provision of this Act—

(1) Where a cheque is not presented for payment within a reasonable time of its issue, and the drawer or the person on whose account it is drawn had the right at the time of such presentment as between him and the banker to have the cheque paid and suffers actual damage through the delay, he is discharged to the extent of such damage, that is to say, to the extent to which such drawer or person is a creditor of such banker to a larger amount than he would have been had such cheque been paid.

(2) In determining what is a reasonable time regard shall be had to the nature of the instrument, the usage of trade and of bankers, and the facts of the particular case.

(3) The holder of such cheque as to which such drawer or person is discharged shall be a creditor, in lieu of such drawer or person, of such banker to the extent of such discharge, and entitled to recover the amount from him.

"Presentment of cheque for payment: alternative place of presentment
    74A.—Where the banker on whom a cheque is drawn—

(*a*) has by notice published in the London, Edinburgh and Belfast Gazettes specified an address at which cheques on him may be presented, and

(*b*) has not by notice so published cancelled the specification of that address, the cheque is also presented at the proper place if it is presented there.".

"Presentment of cheque for payment: alternative means of presentment by banker

74B.—(1) A banker may present a cheque for payment to the banker on whom it is drawn by notifying him of its essential features by electronic means or otherwise, instead of by presenting the cheque itself.

(2) If a cheque is presented for payment under this section, presentment need not be made at the proper place or at a reasonable hour on a business day.

(3) If, before the close of business on the next business day following presentment of a cheque under this section, the banker on whom the cheque is drawn requests the banker by whom the cheque was presented to present the cheque itself—

(*a*) the presentment under this section shall be disregarded, and

(*b*) this section shall not apply in relation to the subsequent presentment of the cheque.

(4) A request under subsection (3) above for the presentment of a cheque shall not constitute dishonour of the cheque by non-payment.

(5) Where presentment of a cheque is made under this section, the banker who presented the cheque and the banker on whom it is drawn shall be subject to the same duties in relation to the collection and payment of the cheque as if the cheque itself had been presented for payment.

(6) For the purposes of this section, the essential features of a cheque are—

(*a*) the serial number of the cheque,

(*b*) the code which identifies the banker on whom the cheque is drawn,

(*c*) the account number of the drawer of the cheque, and

(*d*) the amount of the cheque is entered by the drawer of the cheque.

Cheques presented for payment under section 74B: disapplication of section 52(4).

74C. Section 52(4) above—

(*a*) so far as relating to presenting a bill for payment, shall not apply to presenting a cheque for payment under section 74B above, and

(*b*) so far as relating to a bill which is paid, shall not apply to a cheque which is paid following presentment under that section."

(2) This Article has effect in relation to cheques drawn on or after the day on which this Order comes into force.

NOTE

The preceding three sections were inserted pursuant to sections 3 and 4 Deregulation (Bills of Exchange) Order 1996.

Revocation of banker's authority

75. The duty and authority of a banker to pay a cheque drawn on him by his customer are determined by—

(1) Countermand of payment:

(2) Notice of the customer's death.

Crossed Cheques

General and special crossings defined

76.—(1) Where a cheque bears across its face an addition of—

    (*a*) The words "and company" or any abbreviation thereof between two parallel transverse lines, either with or without the words "not negotiable"; or

    (*b*) Two parallel transverse lines simply, either with or without the words "not negotiable";

that addition constitutes a crossing, and the cheque is crossed generally.

(2) Where a cheque bears across its face an addition of the name of a banker, either with or without the words "not negotiable", that addition constitutes a crossing, and the cheque is crossed specially and to that banker.

Crossing by drawer or after issue

77.—(1) A cheque may be crossed generally or specially by the drawer.

(2) Where a cheque is uncrossed, the holder may cross it generally or specially.

(3) Where a cheque is crossed generally the holder may cross it specially.

(4) Where a cheque is crossed generally or specially, the holder may add the words "not negotiable".

(5) Where a cheque is crossed specially, the banker to whom it is crossed may again cross it specially to another banker for collection.

(6) Where an uncrossed cheque, or a cheque crossed generally is sent to a banker for collection, he may cross it specially to himself.

Crossing a material part of cheque

78. A crossing authorised by this Act is a material part of the cheque; it shall not be lawful for any person to obliterate or, except as authorised by this Act, to add to or alter the crossing.

Duties of banker as to crossed cheques

79.—(1) Where a cheque is crossed specially to more than one banker except when crossed to an agent for collection being a banker, the banker on whom it is drawn shall refuse payment thereof.

(2) Where the banker on whom a cheque is drawn which is so crossed nevertheless pays the same, or pays a cheque crossed generally otherwise than to a banker, or if crossed specially otherwise than to the banker to whom it is crossed, or his agent for collection being a banker, he is liable to the true owner of the cheque for any loss he may sustain owing to the cheque having been so paid.

Provided that where a cheque is presented for payment which does not at the time of presentment appear to be crossed, or to have had a crossing which has been obliterated, or to have been added to or altered otherwise than as authorised by this Act, the banker paying the cheque in good faith and without negligence shall not be responsible or incur any liability, nor shall the payment be questioned by reason of the cheque having been crossed, or of the crossing having been obliterated or having been added to or altered otherwise than as authorised by this Act, and of payment having been made otherwise than to a banker or to the banker to whom the cheque is or was crossed, or to his agent for collection being a banker, as the case may be.

Protection to banker and drawer where cheque is crossed

80. Where the banker, on whom a crossed cheque is drawn, in good faith and without negligence pays it, if crossed generally, to a banker, and if crossed specially, to the banker to whom it is crossed, or his agent for collection being a banker, the banker paying the cheque, and, if the cheque has come into the hands of the payee, the drawer, shall respectively be entitled to the same rights and be placed in the same position as if payment of the cheque had been made to the true owner thereof.

NOTE

Now amended by section 2, Cheques Act 1992 by the inclusion of the words "including a cheque which under section 81A below or otherwise is not transferable", after the word "cheque" in the first line.

Effect of crossing on holder

81. Where a person takes a crossed cheque which bears on it the words "not negotiable," he shall not have and shall not be capable of giving a better title to the cheque than that which the person from whom he took it had.

By virtue of section 1, Cheques Act 1992, the following new section is added.

Non-transferable cheques

81A.—(1) Where a cheque is crossed and bears across its face the words "account payee" or "a/c payee", either with or without the word "only", the cheque shall not be transferable, but shall only be void as between the parties thereto.

(2) A banker is not to be treated for the purposes of section 80 above as having been negligent by reason only of his failure to concern himself with any purported indorsement of a cheque which under subsection (1) above or otherwise is not transferable.

Protection to collecting banker

82. Where a banker in good faith and without negligence receives payment for a customer of a cheque crossed generally or specially to himself, and the customer has no title or a defective title thereto, the banker shall not incur any liability to the true owner of the cheque by reason only of having received such payment.

NOTE
This section was repealed by the Cheques Act 1957.

PART IV. PROMISSORY NOTES

Promissory note defined

83.—(1) A promissory note is an unconditional promise in writing made by one person to another signed by the maker, engaging to pay, on demand or at a fixed or determinable future time, a sum certain in money, to, or to the order of, a specified person or to bearer.

(2) An instrument in the form of a note payable to maker's order is not a note within the meaning of this section unless and until it is indorsed by the maker.

(3) A note is not invalid by reason only that it contains also a pledge of collateral security with authority to sell or dispose thereof.

(4) A note which is, or on the face of it purports to be, both made and payable within the British Islands is an inland note. Any other note is a foreign note.

Delivery necessary

84. A promissory note is inchoate and incomplete until delivery thereof to the payee or bearer.

Joint and several notes

85.—(1) A promissory note may be made by two or more makers, and they may be liable thereon jointly, or jointly and severally according to its tenor.

(2) Where a note runs "I promise to pay" and is signed by two or more persons it is deemed to be their joint and several note.

Note payable on demand

86.—(1) Where a note payable on demand has been indorsed, it must be presented for payment within a reasonable time of the indorsement. If it be not so presented the indorser is discharged.

(2) In determining what is a reasonable time, regard shall be had to the nature of the instrument, the usage of trade, and the facts of the particular case.

(3) Where a note payable on demand is negotiated, it is not deemed to be overdue, for the purpose of affecting the holder with defects of title of which he had no notice, by reason that it appears that a reasonable time for presenting it for payment has elapsed since its issue.

Presentment of note for payment

87.—(1) Where a promissory note is in the body of it made payable at a particular place, it must be presented for payment at that place in order to render the maker liable. In any other case, presentment for payment is not necessary in order to render the maker liable.

(2) Presentment for payment is necessary in order to render the indorser of a note liable.

(3) Where a note is in the body of it made payable at a particular place, presentment at that place is necessary in order to render an indorser liable; but when a place of payment is indicated by way of memorandum only, presentment at that place is sufficient to render the indorser liable, but a presentment to the maker elsewhere, if sufficient in other respects, shall also suffice.

Liability of maker

88. The maker of a promissory note by making it—

(1) Engages that he will pay it according to its tenor;

(2) Is precluded from denying to a holder in due course the existence of the payee and his then capacity to indorse.

Application of Part II to notes

89.—(1) Subject to the provisions in this part and, except as by this section provided, the provisions of this Act relating to bills of exchange apply, with the necessary modifications, to promissory notes.

(2) In applying those provisions the maker of a note shall be deemed to correspond with the acceptor of a bill, and the first indorser of a note shall be deemed to correspond with the drawer of an accepted bill payable to drawer's order.

(3) The following provisions as to bills do not apply to notes; namely, provisions relating to—

(a) Presentment for acceptance;

(b) Acceptance;

(c) Acceptance supra protest;

(d) Bills in a set.

(4) Where a foreign note is dishonoured, protest thereof is unnecessary.

PART V. SUPPLEMENTARY

Good faith

90. A thing is deemed to be done in good faith, within the meaning of this Act, where it is in fact done honestly, whether it is done negligently or not.

Signature

91.—(1) Where, by this Act, any instrument or writing is required to be signed by any person, it is not necessary that he should sign it with his own hand, but it is sufficient if his signature is written thereon by some other person by or under his authority.

(2) In the case of a corporation, where, by this Act, any instrument or writing is required to be signed, it is sufficient if the instrument or writing be sealed with the corporate seal.

But nothing in this section shall be construed as requiring the bill or note of a corporation to be under seal.

Computation of time

92. Where by this Act, the time limited for doing any act or thing is less than three days, in reckoning time, non-business days are excluded. "Non-business days" for the purposes of this Act mean—

(a) Saturday, Sunday, Good Friday, Christmas Day

(b) A bank holiday under the Bank Holidays Act, 1871, or Acts amending it:

(c) A day appointed by Royal proclamation as a public fast or thanksgiving day.

Any other day is a business day.

NOTE

The word "Saturday" was added in paragraph (a) by s. 3 of the Banking and Financial Dealings Act 1971.

When noting equivalent to protest

93. For the purposes of this Act, where a bill or note is required to be protested within a specified time or before some further proceeding is taken, it is sufficient that the bill has been noted for protest before the expiration of the specified time or the taking of the proceeding; and the formal protest may be extended at any time thereafter as of the date of the noting.

Protest when notary not accessible

94. Where a dishonoured bill or note is authorized or required to be protested, and the services of a notary cannot be obtained at the place where the bill is dishonoured, any householder or substantial resident of the place may, in the presence of two witnesses, give a certificate signed by them, attesting the disonour of the bill, and the certificate shall in all respects operate as if it were a formal protest of the bill.

The form given in Schedule 1 to this Act may be used with necessary modifications, and if used shall be sufficient.

Dividend warrants may be crossed

95. The provisions of this Act as to crossed cheques shall apply to a warrant for payment of dividend.

Repeal

96. The enactments mentioned in the second schedule to this Act are hereby repealed as from the commencement of this Act to the extent in that schedule mentioned.

Provided that such repeal shall not affect anything done or suffered, or any right, title, or interest acquired or accrued before the commencement of this Act, or any legal proceeding or remedy in respect of any such thing, right, title, or interest.

Savings

97.—(1) The rules in bankruptcy relating to bills of exchange promissory notes, and cheques, shall continue to apply thereto notwithstanding anything in this Act contained.

(2) The rules of common law including the law merchant, save in so far as they are inconsistent with the express provisions of this Act, shall continue to apply to bills of exchange, promissory notes, and cheques.

(3) Nothing in this Act or in any repeal effected thereby shall affect—

(a) The provisions of the Stamp Act, 1870, or Acts amending it, or any law or enactment for the time being in force relating to the revenue:

(b) The provisions of the Companies Act, 1862, or Acts amending it, or any Act relating to joint stock banks or companies:

(c) The provisions of any Act relating to or confirming the privileges of the Bank of England or the Bank of Ireland respectively:

(d) The validity of any usage relating to dividend warrants, or the indorsements thereof.

Saving of summary diligence in Scotland

98. Nothing in this Act or in any repeal effected thereby shall extend or restrict, or in any way alter or affect the law and practice in Scotland in regard to summary diligence.

Construction with other Acts, &c.

99. Where any Act or document refers to any enactment repealed by this Act, the Act or document shall be construed, and shall operate, as if it referred to the corresponding provisions of this Act.

Parole evidence allowed in certain judicial proceedings in Scotland

100. In any judicial proceeding in Scotland, any fact relating to a bill of exchange, bank cheque, or promissory note, which is relevant to any question of liability thereon, may be proved by parole evidence: Provided that this enactment shall not in any way affect the existing law and practice whereby the party who is, according to the tenor of any bill of exchange, bank cheque, or promissory note, debtor to the holder in the amount thereof, may be required, as a condition of obtaining a sist of diligence, or suspension of a charge, or threatened charge, to make such consignation, or to find such caution as the court or judge before whom the cause is depending may require.

This section shall not apply to any case where the bill of exchange, bank cheque, or promissory note has undergone the sesennial prescription.

SCHEDULES

First Schedule

Section 94.

Form of protest which may be used when the services of a notary cannot be obtained.

Know all men that I, *A.B.* [householder], of   in the county of   , in the United Kingdom, at the request of *C.D.*, there being no notary public available, did on the   day of   188   at   demand payment [*or* acceptance] of the bill of exchange hereunder written, from *E.F.*, to which demand he made answer [state answer, if any] wherefore I now, in the presence of *G.H.* and *J.K.* do protest the said bill of exchange.

(Signed)   *A.B.*
G.H.
J.K.   Witnesses.

N.B. The bill itself should be annexed, or a copy of the bill and all that is written thereon should be underwritten.

Second Schedule. Enactments Repealed

.   .   .

APPENDIX 2

CHEQUES ACT, 1957*

An Act to amend the law relating to cheques and certain other instruments.

Protection of bankers paying unindorsed or irregularly indorsed cheques, etc.

1.—(1) Where a banker in good faith and in the ordinary course of business pays a cheque drawn on him which is not indorsed or is irregularly indorsed, he does not, in doing so, incur any liability by reason only of the absence of, or irregularity in, indorsement, and he is deemed to have paid it in due course.

(2) Where a banker in good faith and in the ordinary course of business pays any such instrument as the following, namely,—

(*a*) a document issued by a customer of his which, though not a bill of exchange, is intended to enable a person to obtain payment from him of the sum mentioned in the document;

(*b*) a draft payable on demand drawn by him upon himself, whether payable at the head office or some other office of his bank;

he does not, in doing so, incur any liability by reason only of the absence of, or irregularity in, indorsement, and the payment discharges the instrument.

Rights of bankers collecting cheques not indorsed by holders

2. A banker who gives value for, or has a lien on, a cheque payable to order which the holder delivers to him for collection without indorsing it, has such (if any) rights as he would have had if, upon delivery, the holder had indorsed it in blank.

Unindorsed cheques as evidence of payment

3. An unindorsed cheque which appears to have been paid by the banker on whom it is drawn is evidence of the receipt by the payee of the sum payable by the cheque.

NOTE
Inserted pursuant to section 5 Deregulation (Bills of Exchange) Order 1996.

Unindorsed cheques as evidence of payment

In section 3 of the Cheques Act 1957(a) (unindorsed cheques as evidence of payment) the existing provision shall become subsection (1) and after that subsection there shall be inserted the following subsection—

---

* 5 & 6 Eliz 2, c. 36. Reproduced by permission of HM Stationery Office.

"(2) For the purposes of subsection (1) above, a copy of a cheque to which that subsection applies is evidence of the cheque if—

(a) the copy is made by the banker in whose possession the cheque is after presentment and,

(b) it is certified by him to be a true copy of the original.".

Protection of bankers collecting payment of cheques, &c.

4.—(1) Where a banker, in good faith and without negligence,—

(a) receives payment for a customer of an instrument to which this section applies; or

(b) having credited a customer's account with the amount of such an instrument, receives payment thereof for himself;

and the customer has no title, or a defective title, to the instrument, the banker does not incur any liability to the true owner of the instrument by reason only of having received payment thereof.

(2) This section applies to the following instruments, namely,—

(a) cheques;

NOTE

Now amended by Section 3 Cheques Act 1992 by the inclusion of the words "(including cheques which under section 81A(1) of the Bills of Exchange Act 1882 or otherwise are not transferable)", after the word "cheques".

(b) any document issued by a customer of a banker which, though not a bill of exchange, is intended to enable a person to obtain payment from that banker of the sum mentioned in the document;

(c) any document issued by a public officer which is intended to enable a person to obtain payment from the Paymaster General or the Queen's and Lord Treasurer's Remembrancer of the sum mentioned in the document but is not a bill of exchange;

(d) any draft payable on demand drawn by a banker upon himself, whether payable at the head office or some other office of his bank.

(3) A banker is not to be treated for the purposes of this section as having been negligent by reason only of his failure to concern himself with absence of, or irregularity in, indorsement of an instrument.

Application of certain provisions of Bills of Exchange Act, 1882, to instruments not being bills of exchange

5. The provisions of the Bills of Exchange Act, 1882, relating to crossed cheques shall, so far as applicable, have effect in relation to instruments (other than cheques) to which the last foregoing section applies as they have effect in relation to cheques.

Construction, saving and repeal

6.—(1) This Act shall be construed as one with the Bills of Exchange Act, 1882.

(2) The foregoing provisions of this Act do not make negotiable any instrument which, apart from them, is not negotiable.

(3) The enactments mentioned in the first and second columns of the Schedule to this Act are hereby repealed to the extent specified in the third column of that Schedule.

NOTE

This subsection and the Schedule to the Act, were repealed by the Statute Law (Repeals) Act 1974, Part XI—Spent Repealing Enactments.

Provisions as to Northern Ireland

7. This Act extends to Northern Ireland, but, for the purposes of section six of the Government of Ireland Act, 1920, so much of the provisions of this Act as relates to, or affects, instruments other than negotiable instruments shall be deemed to be provisions of an Act passed before the appointed day within the meaning of that section.

Short title and commencement

8.—(1) This Act may be cited as the Cheques Act, 1957.

(2) This Act shall come into operation at the expiration of a period of three months beginning with the day on which it is passed.

Schedule, Enactments Repealed

.   .   .

CHEQUES ACT 1992*

An Act to amend the law relating to cheques.

[16th March 1992]

Amendment of Bills of Exchange Act 1882: non-transferable cheques

1. After section 81 of the Bills of Exchange Act 1882 there shall be inserted the following section—

> **"Non-transferable cheques**
>
> 81A.—(1) Where a cheque is crossed and bears across its face the words "account payee" or "a/c payee", either with or without the word "only", the cheque shall not be transferable, but shall only be valid as between the parties thereto.
>
> (2) A banker is not to be treated for the purposes of section 80 above as having been negligent by reason only of his failure to concern himself with any purported indorsement of a cheque which under subsection (1) above or otherwise is not transferable.".

Amendment of Bills of Exchange Act 1882: protection to banker and drawer where cheque is crossed

2. In section 80 of the Bills of Exchange Act 1882 (protection to banker and drawer where cheque is crossed) after "crossed cheque" there shall be inserted "(including a cheque which under section 81A below or otherwise is not transferable)".

Amendment of Cheques Act 1957

3. In section 4(2)(a) of the Cheques Act 1957 (protection of bankers collecting payment of cheques, etc) there shall be inserted after the word "cheques" the words "(including cheques which under section 81A(1) of the Bills of Exchange Act 1882 or otherwise are not transferable)".

Citation and commencement

4.—(1) This Act may be cited as the Cheques Act 1992.

---

* 1992 Chapter 32.

THE DEREGULATION (BILLS OF EXCHANGE) ORDER 1996

28th November 1996
No. 2993

Whereas—

(a) the Treasury are of the opinion that certain provisions of the Bills of Exchange Act 1882(a) and which are the subject of this Order impose burdens affecting persons in the carrying on of a trade, business, profession or otherwise and that by amending or repealing the provisions concerned and by making certain other provision it is possible to remove or reduce the burdens, without removing any necessary protection;

(b) the Treasury have consulted such organisations as appear to them to be representative of interests substantially affected by their proposals and such other persons as they considered appropriate;

(c) it appears to the Treasury that it is appropriate, following that consultation, to proceed with the making of this Order;

(d) a document setting out the Treasury's proposals has been laid before Parliament as required by section 3 of the Deregulation and Contracting Out Act 1994(b) and the period for Parliamentary consideration under section 4 of that Act has expired;

(e) the Treasury have had regard to the representations made during that period;

(f) a draft of this Order has been laid before Parliament with a statement giving details of such representations and the change to the Treasury's proposals in the light of such representations; and

(g) a draft of this Order has been approved by resolution of each House of Parliament.

Now, therefore, the Treasury, in exercise of the power conferred on them by section 1 of the Deregulation and Contracting Out Act 1994, hereby make the following Order:

Citation and commencement

1.—(1) This Order may be cited as the Deregulation (Bills of Exchange) Order 1996.

(2) This Order shall come into force on the day after the day on which it is made.

Interpretation

2. In this Order "the 1882 Act" means the Bills of Exchange Act 1882.

Presentment of cheque for payment: alternative place of presentment

3. After section 74 of the 1882 Act there shall be inserted the following section—

"**Presentment of cheque for payment: alternative place of presentment.**
74A.—Where the banker on whom a cheque is drawn—
> (a) has by notice published in the London, Edinburgh and Belfast Gazettes specified an address at which cheques drawn on him may be presented, and
> (b) has not by notice so published cancelled the specification of that address,

the cheque is also presented at the proper place if it is presented there.".

Presentment of cheque for payment: alternative means of presentment by banker

4.—(1) After section 74A of the 1882 Act (as inserted by Article 3 of this Order) there shall be inserted the following sections—

"**Presentment of cheque for payment: alternative means of presentment by banker.**
74B.—(1) A banker may present a cheque for payment to the banker on whom it is drawn by notifying him of its essential features by electronic means or otherwise, instead of by presenting the cheque itself.

(2) If a cheque is presented for payment under this section, presentment need not be made at the proper place or at a reasonable hour on a business day.

(3) If, before the close of business on the next business day following presentment of a cheque under this section, the banker on whom the cheque is drawn requests the banker by whom the cheque was presented to present the cheque itself—
> (a) the presentment under this section shall be disregarded, and
> (b) this section shall not apply in relation to the subsequent presentment of the cheque.

(4) A request under subsection (3) above for the presentment of a cheque shall not constitute dishonour of the cheque by non-payment.

(5) Where presentment of a cheque is made under this section, the banker who presented the cheque and the banker on whom it is drawn shall be subject to the same duties in relation to the collection and payment of the cheque as if the cheque itself had been presented for payment.

(6) For the purposes of this section, the essential features of a cheque are—
> (a) the serial number of the cheque,
> (b) the code which identifies the banker on whom the cheque is drawn,
> (c) the account number of the drawer of the cheque, and
> (d) the amount of the cheque is entered by the drawer of the cheque.

Cheques presented for payment under section 74B: disapplication of section 52(4).
74C. Section 52(4) above—
> (a) so far as relating to presenting a bill for payment, shall not apply to presenting a cheque for payment under section 74B above, and
> (b) so far as relating to a bill which is paid, shall not apply to a cheque which is paid following presentment under that section."

(2) This Article has effect in relation to cheques drawn on or after the day on which this Order comes into force.

Unindorsed cheques as evidence of payment

5. In section 3 of the Cheques Act 1957(a) (unindorsed cheques as evidence of payment) the existing provision shall become subsection (1) and after that subsection there shall be inserted the following subsection—

"(2) For the purposes of subsection (1) above, a copy of a cheque to which that subsection applies is evidence of the cheque if—

(a) the copy is made by the banker in whose possession the cheque is after presentment and,

(b) it is certified by him to be a true copy of the original.".

ICC UNIFORM CUSTOMS AND PRACTICE FOR DOCUMENTARY CREDITS*

A. GENERAL PROVISIONS AND DEFINITIONS

Article 1. Application of UCP

The Uniform Customs and Practice for Documentary Credits, 1993 Revision, ICC Publication No 500, shall apply to all Documentary Credits (including to the extent to which they may be applicable, Standby Letter(s) of Credit) where they are incorporated into the text of the Credit. They are binding on all parties thereto, unless otherwise expressly stipulated in the Credit.

Article 2. Meaning of Credit

For the purposes of these Articles, the expressions "Documentary Credit(s)" and "Standby Letter(s) of Credit" (hereinafter referred to as "Credit(s)"), mean any arrangement, however named or described, whereby a bank (the "Issuing Bank") acting at the request and on the instructions of a customer (the "Applicant") or on its own behalf,

   (i) is to make a payment to or to the order of a third party (the "Beneficiary"), or is to accept and pay bills of exchange (Draft(s)) drawn by the Beneficiary, or
  (ii) authorises another bank to effect such payment, or to accept and pay such bills of exchange (Draft(s)), or
 (iii) authorises another bank to negotiate,

against stipulated document(s), provided that the terms and conditions of the Credit are complied with.

   For the purposes of these Articles, branches of a bank in different countries are considered another bank.

Article 3. Credits v. Contracts

   (*a*) Credits, by their nature, are separate transactions from the sales or other contract(s) on which they may be based and banks are in no way concerned with or bound by such contract(s), even if any reference whatsoever to such contract(s) is included in the Credit. Consequently, the undertaking of a bank to pay, accept and pay Draft(s) or

---

* *Uniform Customs and Practice for Documentary Credits*—1993 Revision (I.C.C. Publication No. 500—ISBN 92-842-1155-7), © International Chamber of Commerce (I.C.C.) 1993. Published in its official English version by the International Chamber of Commerce, Paris, and available from I.C.C. Publishing SA, 38 Cours Albert 1er, 75008, Paris, France and from I.C.C. United Kingdom, 14/15 Belgrave Squae, London SW1X 8PS.

negotiate and/or to fulfil any other obligation under the Credit, is not subject to claims or defences by the Applicant resulting from his relationships with the Issuing Bank or the Beneficiary.

(*b*) A Beneficiary can in no case avail himself of the contractual relationships existing between the banks or between the Applicant and the Issuing Bank.

Article 4. Documents v. Goods/Services/Performances

In Credit operations all parties concerned deal with documents, and not with goods, services and/or other performances to which the documents may relate.

Article 5. Instructions to Issue/Amend Credits

(*a*) Instructions for the issuance of a Credit, the Credit itself, instructions for an amendment thereto, and the amendment itself, must be complete and precise.

In order to guard against confusion and misunderstanding, banks should discourage any attempt:
  (i) to include excessive detail in the Credit or in any amendment thereto;
  (ii) to give instructions to issue, advise or confirm a Credit by reference to a Credit previously issued (similar Credit) where such previous Credit has been subject to accepted amendment(s), and/or unaccepted amendment(s).

(*b*) All instructions for the issuance of a Credit and the Credit itself and, where applicable, all instructions for an amendment thereto and the amendment itself, must state precisely the document(s) against which payment, acceptance or negotiation is to be made.

B. FORM AND NOTIFICATION OF CREDITS

Article 6. Revocable v. Irrevocable Credits

(*a*) A Credit may be either
  (i) revocable,
      or
  (ii) irrevocable.

(*b*) The Credit, therefore, should clearly indicate whether it is revocable or irrevocable.

(*c*) In the absence of such indication the Credit shall be deemed to be irrevocable.

Article 7. Advising Bank's Liability

(*a*) A Credit may be advised to a Beneficiary through another bank (the "Advising Bank") without engagement on the part of the Advising Bank, but that bank, if it elects to advise the Credit, shall take reasonable care to check the apparent authenticity of the Credit which it advises. If the bank elects not to advise the Credit, it must so inform the Issuing Bank without delay.

(*b*) If the Advising Bank cannot establish such apparent authenticity it must inform, without delay, the bank from which the instructions appear to have been received that it has been unable to establish the authenticity of the Credit and if it elects nonetheless to advise the Credit it must inform the Beneficiary that it has not been able to establish the authenticity of the Credit.

Article 8. Revocation of a Credit

(*a*) A revocable Credit may be amended or cancelled by the Issuing Bank at any moment and without prior notice to the Beneficiary.

(*b*) However, the Issuing Bank must:

(i) reimburse another bank with which a revocable Credit has been made available for sight payment, acceptance or negotiaton—for any payment, acceptance or negotiation made by such bank—prior to receipt by it of notice of amendment or cancellation, against documents which appear on their face to be in compliance with the terms and conditions of the Credit;

(ii) reimburse another bank with which a revocable Credit has been made available for deferred payment, if such a bank has, prior to receipt by it of notice of amendment or cancellation, taken up documents which appear on their face to be in compliance with the terms and conditions of the Credit.

Article 9. Liability of Issuing and Confirming Banks

(*a*) An irrevocable Credit constitutes a definite undertaking of the Issuing Bank, provided that the stipulated documents are presented to the Nominated Bank or to the Issuing Bank and that the terms and conditions of the Credit are complied with:

(i) if the Credit provides for sight payment—to pay at sight;

(ii) if the Credit provides for deferred payment—to pay on the maturity date(s) determinable in accordance with the stipulations of the Credit;

(iii) if the Credit provides for acceptance:

(*a*) by the Issuing Bank—to accept Draft(s) drawn by the Beneficiary on the Issuing Bank and pay them at maturity,

or

(*b*) by another drawee bank—to accept and pay at maturity Draft(s) drawn by the Beneficiary on the Issuing Bank in the event the drawee bank stipulated in the Credit does not accept Draft(s) drawn on it, or to pay Draft(s) accepted but not paid by such drawee bank at maturity;

(iv) if the Credit provides for negotiation—to pay without recourse to drawers and/or bona fide holders, Draft(s) drawn by the Beneficiary and/or document(s) presented under the Credit. A Credit should not be issued available by Draft(s) on the Applicant. If the Credit nevertheless calls for Draft(s) on the Applicant, banks will consider such Draft(s) as an additional document(s).

(*b*) A confirmation of an irrevocable Credit by another bank (the "Confirming Bank") upon the authorisation or request of the Issuing Bank, constitutes a definite undertaking of the Confirming Bank, in addition to that of the Issuing Bank, provided that the stipulated documents are presented to the Confirming Bank or to any other Nominated Bank and that the terms and conditions of the Credit are complied with:

(i) if the Credit provides for sight payment—to pay at sight;

(ii) if the Credit provides for deferred payment—to pay on the maturity date(s) determinable in accordance with the stipulations of the Credit;

(iii) if the Credit provides for acceptance:

(*a*) by the Confirming Bank—to accept Draft(s) drawn by the Beneficiary on the Confirming Bank and pay them at maturity,

or

(*b*) by another drawee bank—to accept and pay at maturity Draft(s) drawn by the Beneficiary on the Confirming Bank, in the event the drawee bank stipulated in the Credit does not accept Draft(s) drawn on it, or to pay Draft(s) accepted but not paid by such drawee bank at maturity;

(iv) if the Credit provides for negotiation—to negotiate without recourse to drawers and/or bona fide holders, Draft(s) drawn by the Beneficiary and/or document(s) presented under the Credit. A Credit should not be issued available by Draft(s) on the Applicant. If the Credit nevertheless calls for Draft(s) on the Applicant, banks will consider such Draft(s) as an additional document(s).

(c) (i) If another bank is authorised or requested by the Issuing Bank to add its confirmation to a Credit but is not prepared to do so, it must so inform the Issuing Bank without delay.

(ii) Unless the Issuing Bank specifies otherwise in its authorisation or request to add confirmation, the Advising Bank may advise the Credit to the Beneficiary without adding its confirmation.

(d) (i) Except as otherwise provided by Article 48, an irrevocable Credit can neither be amended nor cancelled without the agreement of the Issuing Bank, the Confirming Bank, if any, and the Beneficiary.

(ii) The Issuing Bank shall be irrevocably bound by an amendment(s) issued by it from the time of the issuance of such amendment(s). A Confirming Bank may extend its confirmation to an amendment and shall be irrevocably bound as of the time of its advice of the amendment. A Confirming Bank may, however, choose to advise an amendment to the Beneficiary without extending its confirmation and if so, must inform the Issuing Bank and the Beneficiary without delay.

(iii) The terms of the original Credit (or a Credit incorporating previously accepted amendment(s)) will remain in force for the Beneficiary until the Beneficiary communicates his acceptance of the amendment to the bank that advised such amendment. The Beneficiary should give notification of acceptance or rejection of amendment(s). If the Beneficiary fails to give such notification, the tender of documents to the Nominated Bank or Issuing Bank, that conform to the Credit and to not yet accepted amendment(s), will be deemed to be notification of acceptance by the Beneficiary of such amendment(s) and as of that moment the Credit will be amended.

(iv) Partial acceptance of amendments contained in one and the same advice of amendment is not allowed and consequently will not be given any effect.

Article 10. Types of Credit

(a) All Credits must clearly indicate whether they are available by sight payment, by deferred payment, by acceptance or by negotiation.

(b) (i) Unless the Credit stipulates that it is available only with the Issuing Bank, all Credits must nominate the Bank (the "Nominated Bank") which is authorised to pay, to incur a deferred payment undertaking, to accept Draft(s) or to negotiate. In a freely negotiable Credit, any bank is a Nominated Bank.

Presentation of documents must be made to the Issuing Bank or the Confirming Bank, if any, or any other Nominated Bank.

(ii) Negotiation means the giving of value for Draft(s) and/or document(s) by the bank authorised to negotiate. Mere examination of the documents without giving of value does not constitute a negotiation.

(c) Unless the Nominated Bank is the Confirming Bank, nomination by the Issuing Bank does not constitute any undertaking by the Nominated Bank to pay, to incur a deferred payment undertaking, to accept Draft(s), or to negotiate. Except where expressly agreed to by the Nominated Bank and so communicated to the Beneficiary, the Nominated Bank's receipt of and/or examination and/or forwarding of the documents does not make that bank liable to pay, to incur a deferred payment undertaking, to accept Draft(s), or to negotiate.

(*d*) By nominating another bank, or by allowing for negotiation by any bank, or by authorising or requesting another bank to add its confirmation, the Issuing Bank authorises such bank to pay, accept Draft(s) or negotiate as the case may be, against documents which appear on their face to be in compliance with the terms and conditions of the Credit and undertakes to reimburse such bank in accordance with the provisions of these Articles.

Article 11. Teletransmitted and Pre-Advised Credits

(*a*) (i) When an Issuing Bank instructs an Advising Bank by an authenticated teletransmission to advise a Credit or an amendment to a Credit, the teletransmission will be deemed to be the operative Credit instrument or the operative amendment, and no mail confirmation should be sent. Should a mail confirmation nevertheless be sent, it will have no effect and the Advising Bank will have no obligation to check such mail confirmation against the operative Credit instrument or the operative amendment received by teletransmission.

   (ii) If the teletransmission states "full details to follow" (or words of similar effect) or states that the mail confirmation is to be the operative Credit instrument or the operative amendment, then the teletransmission will not be deemed to be the operative Credit instrument or the operative amendment. The Issuing Bank must forward the operative Credit instrument or the operative amendment to such Advising Bank without delay.

(*b*) If a bank uses the services of an Advising Bank to have the Credit advised to the Beneficiary, it must also use the services of the same bank for advising an amendment(s).

(*c*) A preliminary advice of the issuance or amendment of an irrevocable Credit (pre-advice), shall only be given by an Issuing Bank if such bank is prepared to issue the operative Credit instrument or the operative amendment thereto. Unless otherwise stated in such preliminary advice by the Issuing Bank, an Issuing Bank having given such pre-advice shall be irrevocably committed to issue or amend the Credit, in terms not inconsistent with the pre-advice, without delay.

Article 12. Incomplete or Unclear Instructions

If incomplete or unclear instructions are received to advise, confirm or amend a Credit, the bank requested to act on such instructions may give preliminary notification to the Beneficiary for information only and without responsibility. This preliminary notification should state clearly that the notification is provided for information only and without the responsibility of the Advising Bank. In any event, the Advising Bank must inform the Issuing Bank of the action taken and request it to provide the necessary information.

The Issuing Bank must provide the necessary information without delay. The Credit will be advised, confirmed or amended, only when complete and clear instructions have been received and if the Advising Bank is then prepared to act on the instructions.

C. LIABILITIES AND RESPONSIBILITIES

Article 13. Standard for Examination of Documents

(*a*) Banks must examine all documents stipulated in the Credit with reasonable care, to ascertain whether or not they appear, on their face, to be in compliance with the terms and conditions of the Credit. Compliance of the stipulated documents on their face with the terms and conditions of the Credit, shall be determined by international standard banking practice as reflected in these Articles. Documents which appear on their face to be inconsistent with one another will be considered as not appearing on their face to be in compliance with the terms and conditions of the Credit.

Documents not stipulated in the Credit will not be examined by banks. If they receive such documents, they shall return them to the presenter or pass them on without responsibility.

(b) The Issuing Bank, the Confirming Bank, if any, or a Nominated Bank acting on their behalf, shall each have a reasonable time, not to exceed seven banking days following the day of receipt of the documents, to examine the documents and determine whether to take up or refuse the documents and to inform the party from which it received the documents accordingly.

(c) If a Credit contains conditions without stating the document(s) to be presented in compliance therewith, banks will deem such conditions as not stated and will disregard them.

Article 14. Discrepant Documents and Notice

(a) When the Issuing Bank authorises another bank to pay, incur a deferred payment undertaking, accept Draft(s), or negotiate against documents which appear on their face to be in compliance with the terms and conditions of the Credit, the Issuing Bank and the Confirming Bank, if any, are bound:

    (i) to reimburse the Nominated Bank which has paid, incurred a deferred payment undertaking, accepted Draft(s), or negotiated,

    (ii) to take up the documents.

(b) Upon receipt of the documents the Issuing Bank and/or Confirming Bank, if any, or a Nominated Bank acting on their behalf, must determine on the basis of the documents alone whether or not they appear on their face to be in compliance with the terms and conditions of the Credit. If the documents appear on their face not to be in compliance with the terms and conditions of the Credit, such banks may refuse to take up the documents.

(c) If the Issuing Bank determines that the documents appear on their face not to be in compliance with the terms and conditions of the Credit, it may in its sole judgment approach the Applicant for a waiver of the discrepancy(ies). This does not, however, extend the period mentioned in sub-Article 13(b).

    (d) (i) If the Issuing Bank and/or Confirming Bank, if any, or a Nominated Bank acting on their behalf, decides to refuse the documents, it must give notice to that effect by telecommunication or, if that is not possible, by other expeditious means, without delay but no later than the close of the seventh banking day following the day of receipt of the documents. Such notice shall be given to the bank from which it received the documents, or to the Beneficiary, if it received the documents directly from him.

    (ii) Such notice must state all discrepancies in respect of which the bank refuses the documents and must also state whether it is holding the documents at the disposal of, or is returning them to, the presenter.

    (iii) The Issuing Bank and/or Confirming Bank, if any, shall then be entitled to claim from the remitting bank refund, with interest, of any reimbursement which has been made to that bank.

(e) If the Issuing Bank and/or Confirming Bank, if any, fails to act in accordance with the provisions of this Article and/or fails to hold the documents at the disposal of, or return them to the presenter, the Issuing Bank and/or Confirming Bank, if any, shall be precluded from claiming that the documents are not in compliance with the terms and conditions of the Credit.

(*f*) If the remitting bank draws the attention of the Issuing Bank and/or Confirming Bank, if any, to any discrepancy(ies) in the document(s) or advises such banks that it has paid, incurred a deferred payment undertaking, accepted Draft(s) or negotiated under reserve or against an indemnity in respect of such discrepancy(ies), the Issuing Bank and/or Confirming Bank, if any, shall not be thereby relieved from any of their obligations under any provision of this Article. Such reserve or indemnity concerns only the relations between the remitting bank and the party towards whom the reserve was made, or from whom, or on whose behalf, the indemnity was obtained.

Article 15. Disclaimer on Effectiveness of Documents

Banks assume no liability or responsibility for the form, sufficiency, accuracy, genuineness, falsification or legal effect of any document(s), or for the general and/or particular conditions stipulated in the document(s) or superimposed thereon; nor do they assume any liability or responsibility for the description, quantity, weight, quality, condition, packing, delivery, value or existence of the goods represented by any document(s), or for the good faith or acts and/or omissions, solvency, performance or standing of the consignors, the carriers, the forwarders, the consignees or the insurers of the goods, or any other person whomsoever.

Article 16. Disclaimer on the Transmission of Messages

Banks assume no liability or responsibility for the consequences arising out of delay and/or loss in transit of any message(s), letter(s) or document(s), or for delay, mutilation or other error(s) arising in the transmission of any telecommunication. Banks assume no liability or responsibility for errors in translation and/or interpretation of technical terms, and reserve the right to transmit Credit terms without translating them.

Article 17. Force Majeure

Banks assume no liability or responsibility for the consequences arising out of the interruption of their business by Acts of God, riots, civil commotions, insurrections, wars or any other causes beyond their control, or by any strikes or lockouts. Unless specifically authorised, banks will not, upon resumption of their business, pay, incur a deferred payment undertaking, accept Draft(s) or negotiate under Credits which expired during such interruption of their business.

Article 18. Disclaimer for Acts of an Instructed Party

(*a*) Banks utilizing the services of another bank or other banks for the purpose of giving effect to the instructions of the Applicant do so for the account and at the risk of such Applicant.

(*b*) Banks assume no liability or responsibility should the instructions they transmit not be carried out, even if they have themselves taken the initiative in the choice of such other bank(s).

(*c*) (i) A party instructing another party to perform services is liable for any charges, including commissions, fees, costs or expenses incurred by the instructed party in connection with its instructions.

   (ii) Where a Credit stipulates that such charges are for the account of a party other than the instructing party, and charges cannot be collected, the instructing party remains ultimately liable for the payment thereof.

(*d*) The Applicant shall be bound by and liable to indemnify the banks against all obligations and responsibilities imposed by foreign laws and usages.

Article 19. Bank-to-Bank Reimbursement Arrangements

(a) If an Issuing Bank intends that the reimbursement to which a paying, accepting or negotiating bank is entitled, shall be obtained by such bank (the "Claiming Bank"), claiming on another party (the "Reimbursing Bank"), it shall provide such Reimbursing Bank in good time with the proper instructions or authorisation to honour such reimbursement claims.

(b) Issuing Banks shall not require a Claiming Bank to supply a certificate of compliance with the terms and conditions of the Credit to the Reimbursing Bank.

(c) An Issuing Bank shall not be relieved from any of its obligations to provide reimbursement if and when reimbursement is not received by the Claiming Bank from the Reimbursing Bank.

(d) The Issuing Bank shall be responsible to the Claiming Bank for any loss of interest if reimbursement is not provided by the Reimbursing Bank on first demand, or as otherwise specified in the Credit, or mutually agreed, as the case may be.

(e) The Reimbursing Bank's charges should be for the account of the Issuing Bank. However, in cases where the charges are for the account of another party, it is the responsibility of the Issuing Bank to so indicate in the original Credit and in the reimbursement authorisation. In cases where the Reimbursing Bank's charges are for the account of another party they shall be collected from the Claiming Bank when the Credit is drawn under. In cases where the Credit is not drawn under, the Reimbursing Bank's charges remain the obligation of the Issuing Bank.

D. DOCUMENTS

Article 20. Ambiguity as to the Issuers of Documents

(a) Terms such as "first class", "well known", "qualified", "independent", "official", "competent", "local" and the like, shall not be used to describe the issuers of any document(s) to be presented under a Credit. If such terms are incorporated in the Credit, banks will accept the relative document(s) as presented, provided that it appears on its face to be in compliance with the other terms and conditions of the Credit and not to have been issued by the Beneficiary.

(b) Unless otherwise stipulated in the Credit, banks will also accept as an original documents(s), a document(s) produced or appearing to have been produced:
  (i) by reprographic, automated or computerized systems;
  (ii) as carbon copies;
provided that it is marked as original and, where necessary, appears to be signed.

A document may be signed by handwriting, by facsimile signature, by perforated signature, by stamp, by symbol, or by any other mechanical or electronic method of authentication.

(c) (i) Unless otherwise stipulated in the Credit, banks will accept as a copy(ies), a document(s) either labelled copy or not marked as an original—a copy(ies) need not be signed.
  (ii) Credits that require multiple document(s) such as "duplicate", "two fold", "two copies" and the like, will be satisfied by the presentation of one original and the remaining number in copies except where the document itself indicates otherwise.

(d) Unless otherwise stipulated in the Credit, a condition under a Credit calling for a document to be authenticated, validated, legalised, visaed, certified or indicating a similar requirement, will be satisfied by any signature, mark, stamp or label on such document that on its face appears to satisfy the above condition.

Article 21. Unspecified Issuers or Contents of Documents

When documents other than transport documents, insurance documents and commercial invoices are called for, the Credit should stipulate by whom such documents are to be issued and their wording or data content. If the Credit does not so stipulate, banks will accept such documents as presented, provided that their data content is not inconsistent with any other stipulated document presented.

Article 22. Issuance Date of Documents v. Credit Date

Unless otherwise stipulated in the Credit, banks will accept a document bearing a date of issuance prior to that of the Credit, subject to such document being presented within the time limits set out in the Credit and in these Articles.

Article 23. Marine/Ocean Bill of Lading

(a) If a Credit calls for a bill of lading covering a port-to-port shipment, banks will, unless otherwise stipulated in the Credit, accept a document, however named, which:
  (i) appears on its face to indicate the name of the carrier and to have been signed or otherwise authenticated by:
      —the carrier or a named agent for or on behalf of the carrier, or
      —the master or a named agent for or on behalf of the master.
      Any signature or authentication of the carrier or master must be identified as carrier or master, as the case may be. An agent signing or authenticating for the carrier or master must also indicate the name and the capacity of the party, i.e. carrier or master, on whose behalf that agent is acting, and
  (ii) indicates that the goods have been loaded on board, or shipped on a named vessel.
      Loading on board or shipment on a named vessel may be indicated by preprinted wording on the bill of lading that the goods have been loaded on board a named vessel or shipped on a named vessel, in which case the date of issuance of the bill of lading will be deemed to be the date of loading on board and the date of shipment.
      In all other cases loading on board a named vessel must be evidenced by a notation on the bill of lading which gives the date on which the goods have been loaded on board, in which case the date of the on board notation will be deemed to be the date of shipment.
      If the bill of lading contains the indication "intended vessel", or similar qualification in relation to the vessel, loading on board a named vessel must be evidenced by an on board notation on the bill of lading which, in addition to the date on which the goods have been loaded on board, also includes the name of the vessel on which the goods have been loaded, even if they have been loaded on the vessel named as the "intended vessel".
      If the bill of lading indicates a place of receipt or taking in charge different from the port of loading, the on board notation must also include the port of loading stipulated in the Credit and the name of the vessel on which the goods have been loaded, even if they have been loaded on the vessel named in the bill of lading. This provision also applies whenever loading on board the vessel is indicated by pre-printed wording on the bill of lading, and
  (iii) indicates the port of loading the port of discharge stipulated in the Credit, notwithstanding that it:

     (*a*) indicates a place of taking in charge different from the port of loading, and/or a place of final destination different from the port of discharge, and/or

     (*b*) contains the indication "intended" or similar qualification in relation to the port of loading and/or port of discharge, as long as the document also states the ports of loading and/or discharge stipulated in the Credit, and

  (iv) consists of a sole original bill of lading or, if issued in more than one original, the full set as so issued, and

  (v) appears to contain all of the terms and conditions of carriage, or some of such terms and conditions by reference to a source or document other than the bill of lading (short form/blank back bill of lading); banks will not examine the contents of such terms and conditions, and

  (vi) contains no indication that it is subject to a charter party and/or no indication that the carrying vessel is propelled by sail only, and

  (vii) in all other respects meets the stipulations of the Credit.

(*b*) For the purpose of this Article, transhipment means unloading and reloading from one vessel to another vessel during the course of ocean carriage from the port of loading to the port of discharge stipulated in the Credit.

(*c*) Unless transhipment is prohibited by the terms of the Credit, banks will accept a bill of lading which indicates that the goods will be transhipped, provided that the entire ocean carriage is covered by one and the same bill of lading.

(*d*) Even if the Credit prohibits transhipment, banks will accept a bill of lading which:

  (i) indicates that transhipment will take place as long as the relevant cargo is shipped in Container(s), Trailer(s) and/or "LASH" barge(s) as evidenced by the bill of lading, provided that the entire ocean carriage is covered by one and the same bill of lading, and/or

  (ii) incorporates clauses stating that the carrier reserves the right to tranship.

Article 24. Non-Negotiable Sea Waybill

  (*a*) If a Credit calls for a non-negotiable sea waybill covering a port-to-port shipment, banks will, unless otherwise stipulated in the Credit, accept a document, however named, which:

  (i) appears on its face to indicate the name of the carrier and to have been signed or otherwise authenticated by:

—the carrier or a named agent for or on behalf of the carrier, or

—the master or a named agent for or on behalf of the master.

Any signature or authentication of the carrier or master must be identified as carrier or master, as the case may be. An agent signing or authenticating for the carrier or master must also indicate the name and the capacity of the party, i.e. carrier or master, on whose behalf that agent is acting, and

  (ii) indicates that the goods have been loaded on board, or shipped on a named vessel.

Loading on board or shipment on a named vessel may be indicated by pre-printed wording on the non-negotiable sea waybill that the goods have been loaded on board a named vessel or shipped on a named vessel, in which case the date of issuance of the non-negotiable sea waybill will be deemed to be the date of loading on board and the date of shipment.

In all other cases loading on board a named vessel must be evidenced by a notation on the non-negotiable sea waybill which gives the date on which the goods have been loaded on board, in which case the date of the on board notation will be deemed to be the date of shipment.

If the non-negotiable sea waybill contains the indication "intended vessel", or similar qualification in relation to the vessel, loading on board a named vessel must be evidenced by an on board notation on the non-negotiable sea waybill which, in addition to the date on which the goods have been loaded on board, includes the name of the vessel on which the goods have been loaded, even if they have been loaded on the vessel named as the "intended vessel".

If the non-negotiable sea waybill indicates a place of receipt or taking in charge different from the port of loading, the on board notation must also include the port of loading stipulated in the Credit and the name of the vessel on which the goods have been loaded, even if they have been loaded on a vessel named in the non-negotiable sea waybill. This provision also applies whenever loading on board the vessel is indicated by pre-printed wording on the non-negotiable sea waybill,
and

(iii) indicates the port of loading and the port of discharge stipulated in the Credit, notwithstanding that it:

    (*a*) indicates a place of taking in charge different from the port of loading, and/or a place of final destination different from the port of discharge, and/or

    (*b*) contains the indication "intended" or similar qualification in relation to the port of loading and/or port of discharge, as long as the document also states the ports of loading and/or discharge stipulated in the Credit,
and

(iv) consists of a sole original non-negotiable sea waybill, or if issued in more than one original, the full set as so issued,
and

(v) appears to contain all of the terms and conditions of carriage, or some of such terms and conditions by reference to a source or document other than the non-negotiable sea waybill (short form/blank back non-negotiable sea waybill); banks will not examine the contents of such terms and conditions,
and

(vi) contains no indication that it is subject to a charter party and/or no indication that the carrying vessel is propelled by sail only,
and

(vii) in all other respects meets the stipulations of the Credit.

(*b*) For the purpose of this Article, transhipment means unloading and reloading from one vessel to another vessel during the course of ocean carriage from the port of loading to the port of discharge stipulated in the Credit.

(*c*) Unless transhipment is prohibited by the terms of the Credit, banks will accept a non-negotiable sea waybill which indicates that the goods will be transhipped, provided that the entire ocean carriage is covered by one and the same non-negotiable sea waybill.

(*d*) Even if the Credit prohibits transhipment, banks will accept a non-negotiable sea waybill which:

    (i) indicates that transhipment will take place as long as the relevant cargo is shipped in Container(s), Trailer(s) and/or "LASH" barge(s) as evidenced by the

non-negotiable sea waybill, provided that the entire ocean carriage is covered
by one and the same non-negotiable sea waybill,
and/or

(ii) incorporates clauses stating that the carrier reserves the right to tranship.

Article 25. Charter Party Bill of Lading

(a) If a Credit calls for or permits a charter party bill of lading, banks will, unless
otherwise stipulated in the Credit, accept a document, however named, which:

(i) contains any indication that it is subject to a charter party,
and

(ii) appears on its face to have been signed or otherwise authenticated by:
—the master or a named agent for or on behalf of the master, or
—the owner or a named agent for or on behalf of the owner.
Any signature or authentication of the master or owner must be identified as
master or owner as the case may be. An agent signing or authenticating for the
master or owner must also indicate the name and the capacity of the party, i.e.
master or owner, on whose behalf that agent is acting,
and

(iii) does or does not indicate the name of the carrier,
and

(iv) indicates that the goods have been loaded on board or shipped on a named
vessel.
Loading on board or shipment on a named vessel may be indicated by pre-
printed wording on the bill of lading that the goods have been loaded on board
a named vessel or shipped on a named vessel, in which case the date of
issuance of the bill of lading will be deemed to be the date of loading on board
and the date of shipment.
In all other cases loading on board a named vessel must be evidenced by a
notation on the bill of lading which gives the date on which the goods have
been loaded on board, in which case the date of the on board notation will be
deemed to be the date of shipment,
and

(v) indicates the port of loading and the port of discharge stipulated in the
Credit,
and

(vi) consists of a sole original bill of lading or, if issued in more than one original,
the full set as so issued,
and

(vii) contains no indication that the carrying vessel is propelled by sail only,
and

(viii) in all other respects meets the stipulations of the Credit.

(b) Even if the Credit requires the presentation of a charter party contract in
connection with a charter party bill of lading, banks will not examine such charter
party contract, but will pass it on without responsibility on their part.

Article 26. Multimodal Transport Document

(a) If a Credit calls for a transport document covering at least two different modes
of transport (multimodal transport), banks will, unless otherwise stipulated in the
Credit, accept a document, however named, which:

(i) appears on its face to indicate the name of the carrier or multimodal transport
operator and to have been signed or otherwise authenticated by:

—the carrier or multimodal transport operator or a named agent for or on behalf of the carrier or multimodal transport operator, or

—the master or a named agent for or on behalf of the master.

Any signature or authentication of the carrier, multimodal transport operator or master must be identified as carrier, multimodal transport operator or master, as the case may be. An agent signing or authenticating for the carrier, multimodal transport operator or master must also indicate the name and the capacity of the party, i.e. carrier, multimodal transport operator or master, on whose behalf that agent is acting,

and

(ii) indicates that the goods have been dispatched, taken in charge or loaded on board.

Dispatch, taking in charge or loading on board may be indicated by wording to that effect on the multimodal transport document and the date of issuance will be deemed to be the date of dispatch, taking in charge or loading on board and the date of shipment. However, if the document indicates, by stamp or otherwise, a date of dispatch, taking in charge or loading on board, such date will be deemed to be the date of shipment,

and

(iii) (a) indicates the place of taking in charge stipulated in the Credit which may be different from the port, airport or place of loading, and the place of final destination stipulated in the Credit which may be different from the port, airport or place of discharge,

and/or

(b) contains the indication "intended" or similar qualification in relation to the vessel and/or port of loading and/or port of discharge,

and

(iv) consists of a sole original multimodal transport document or, if issued in more than one original, the full set as so issued,

and

(v) appears to contain all of the terms and conditions of carriage, or some of such terms and conditions by reference to a source or document other than the multimodal transport document (short form/blank back multimodal transport document); banks will not examine the contents of such terms and conditions,

and

(vi) contains no indication that it is subject to a charter party and/or no indication that the carrying vessel is propelled by sail only,

and

(vii) in all other respects meets the stipulations of the Credit.

(b) Even if the Credit prohibits transhipment, banks will accept a multimodal transport document which indicates that transhipment will or may take place, provided that the entire carriage is covered by one and the same multimodal transport document.

Article 27. Air Transport Document

(a) If a Credit calls for an air transport document, banks will, unless otherwise stipulated in the Credit, accept a document, however named, which:

(i) appears on its face to indicate the name of the carrier and to have been signed or otherwise authenticated by:

—the carrier, or

—a named agent for or on behalf of the carrier.

Any signature or authentication of the carrier must be identified as carrier. An agent signing or authenticating for the carrier must also indicate the name and the capacity of the party, i.e. carrier, on whose behalf that agent is acting,
and

(ii) indicates that the goods have been accepted for carriage,
and

(iii) where the Credit calls for an actual date of dispatch, indicates a specific notation of such date, the date of dispatch so indicated on the air transport document will be deemed to be the date of shipment.

For the purpose of this Article, the information appearing in the box on the air transport document (marked "For Carrier Use Only" or similar expression) relative to the flight number and date will not be considered as a specific notation of such date of dispatch.

In all other cases, the date of issuance of the air transport document will be deemed to be the date of shipment,
and

(iv) indicates the airport of departure and the airport of destination stipulated in the Credit,
and

(v) appears to be the original for consignor/shipper even if the Credit stipulates a full set of originals, or similar expressions,
and

(vi) appears to contain all of the terms and conditions of carriage, or some of such terms and conditions, by reference to a source or document other than the air transport document; banks will not examine the contents of such terms and conditions,
and

(vii) in all other respects meets the stipulations of the Credit.

(b) For the purpose of this Article, transhipment means unloading and reloading from one aircraft to another aircraft during the course of carriage from the airport of departure to the airport of destination stipulated in the Credit.

(c) Even if the Credit prohibits transhipment, banks will accept an air transport document which indicates that transhipment will or may take place, provided that the entire carriage is covered by one and the same air transport document.

Article 28. Road, Rail or Inland Waterway Transport Documents

(a) If a Credit calls for a road, rail, or inland waterway transport document, banks will, unless otherwise stipulated in the Credit, accept a document of the type called for, however named, which:

(i) appears on its face to indicate the name of the carrier and to have been signed or otherwise authenticated by the carrier or a named agent for or on behalf of the carrier and/or to bear a reception stamp or other indication of receipt by the carrier or a named agent for or on behalf of the carrier.

Any signature, authentication, reception stamp or other indication of receipt of the carrier, must be identified on its face as that of the carrier. An agent signing or authenticating for the carrier, must also indicate the name and the capacity of the party, i.e. carrier, on whose behalf that agent is acting,
and

(ii) indicates that the goods have been received for shipment, dispatch or carriage or wording to this effect. The date of issuance will be deemed to be the date of shipment unless the transport document contains a reception stamp, in

which case the date of the reception stamp will be deemed to be the date of shipment,
and

(iii) indicates the place of shipment and the place of destination stipulated in the Credit,
and

(iv) in all other respects meets the stipulations of the Credit.

(b) In the absence of any indication on the transport document as to the numbers issued, banks will accept the transport document(s) presented as constituting a full set. Banks will accept as original(s) the transport document(s) whether marked as original(s) or not.

(c) For the purpose of this Article, transhipment means unloading and reloading from one means of conveyance to another means of conveyance, in different modes of transport, during the course of carriage from the place of shipment to the place of destination stipulated in the Credit.

(d) Even if the Credit prohibits transhipment, banks will accept a road, rail, or inland waterway transport document which indicates that transhipment will or may take place, provided that the entire carriage is covered by one and the same transport document and within the same mode of transport.

Article 29. Courier and Post Receipts

(a) If a Credit calls for a post receipt or certificate of posting, banks will, unless otherwise stipulated in the Credit, accept a post receipt or certificate of posting which:

(i) appears on its face to have been stamped or otherwise authenticated and dated in the place from which the Credit stipulates the goods are to be shipped or dispatched and such date will be deemed to be the date of shipment or dispatch,
and

(ii) in all other respects meets the stipulations of the Credit.

(b) If a Credit calls for a document issued by a courier or expedited delivery service evidencing receipt of the goods for delivery, banks will, unless otherwise stipulated in the Credit, accept a document, however named, which:

(i) appears on its face to indicate the name of the courier/service, and to have been stamped, signed or otherwise authenticated by such named courier/service (unless the Credit specifically calls for a document issued by a named Courier/Service, banks will accept a document issued by any Courier/Service),
and

(ii) indicates a date of pick-up or of receipt or wording to this effect, such date being deemed to be the date of shipment or dispatch,
and

(iii) in all other respects meets the stipulations of the Credit.

Article 30. Transport Documents issued by Freight Forwarders

Unless otherwise authorised in the Credit, banks will only accept a transport document issued by a freight forwarder if it appears on its face to indicate:

(i) the name of the freight forwarder as a carrier or multimodal transport operator and to have been signed or otherwise authenticated by the freight forwarder as carrier or multimodal transport operator,
or

(ii) the name of the carrier or multimodal transport operator and to have been signed or otherwise authenticated by the freight forwarder as a named agent for or on behalf of the carrier or multimodal transport operator.

Article 31. "On Deck", "Shipper's Load and Count", Name of Consignor

Unless otherwise stipulated in the Credit, banks will accept a transport document which:

(i) does not indicate, in the case of carriage by sea or by more than one means of conveyance including carriage by sea, that the goods are or will be loaded on deck. Nevertheless, banks will accept a transport document which contains a provision that the goods may be carried on deck, provided that it does not specifically state that they are or will be loaded on deck, and/or

(ii) bears a clause on the face thereof such as "shipper's load and count" or "said by shipper to contain" or words of similar effect, and/or

(iii) indicates as the consignor of the goods a party other than the Beneficiary of the Credit.

Article 32. Clean Transport Documents

(a) A clean transport document is one which bears no clause or notation which expressly declares a defective condition of the goods and/or the packaging.

(b) Banks will not accept transport documents bearing such clauses or notations unless the Credit expressly stipulates the clauses or notations which may be accepted.

(c) Banks will regard a requirement in a Credit for a transport document to bear the clause "clean on board" as complied with if such transport document meets the requirements of this Article and of Articles 23, 24, 25, 26, 27, 28 or 30.

Article 33. Freight Payable/Prepaid Transport Documents

(a) Unless otherwise stipulated in the Credit, or inconsistent with any of the documents presented under the Credit, banks will accept transport documents stating that freight or transportation charges (hereafter referred to as "freight") have still to be paid.

(b) If a Credit stipulates that the transport document has to indicate that freight has been paid or prepaid, banks will accept a transport document on which words clearly indicating payment or prepayment of freight appear by stamp or otherwise, or on which payment or prepayment of freight is indicated by other means. If the Credit requires courier charges to be paid or prepaid banks will also accept a transport document issued by a courier or expedited delivery service evidencing that courier charges are for the account of a party other than the consignee.

(c) The words "freight prepayable" or "freight to be prepaid" or words of similar effect, if appearing on transport documents, will not be accepted as constituting evidence of the payment of freight.

(d) Banks will accept transport documents bearing reference by stamp or otherwise to costs additional to the freight, such as costs of, or disbursements incurred in connection with, loading, unloading or similar operations, unless the conditions of the Credit specifically prohibit such reference.

Article 34. Insurance Documents

(a) Insurance documents must appear on their face to be issued and signed by insurance companies or underwriters or their agents.

(b) If the insurance document indicates that it has been issued in more than one original, all the originals must be presented unless otherwise authorised in the Credit.

(c) Cover notes issued by brokers will not be accepted, unless specifically authorised in the Credit.

(d) Unless otherwise stipulated in the Credit, banks will accept an insurance certificate or a declaration under an open cover pre-signed by insurance companies or underwriters or their agents. If a Credit specifically calls for an insurance certificate or a declaration under an open cover, banks will accept, in lieu thereof, an insurance policy.

(e) Unless otherwise stipulated in the Credit, or unless it appears from the insurance document that the cover is effective at the latest from the date of loading on board or dispatch or taking in charge of the goods, banks will not accept an insurance document which bears a date of issuance later than the date of loading on board or dispatch or taking in charge as indicated in such transport document.

(f) (i) Unless otherwise stipulated in the Credit, the insurance document must be expressed in the same currency as the Credit.

(ii) Unless otherwise stipulated in the Credit, the minimum amount for which the insurance document must indicate the insurance cover to have been effected is the CIF (cost, insurance and freight (. . . "named port of destination")) or CIP (carriage and insurance paid to (. . . "named place of destination")) value of the goods, as the case may be, plus 10%, but only when the CIF or CIP value can be determined from the documents on their face. Otherwise, banks will accept as such minimum amount 110% of the amount for which payment, acceptance or negotiation is requested under the Credit, or 110% of the gross amount of the invoice, whichever is the greater.

Article 35. Type of Insurance Cover

(a) Credits should stipulate the type of insurance required and, if any, the additional risks which are to be covered. Imprecise terms such as "usual risks" or "customary risks" shall not be used; if they are used, banks will accept insurance documents as presented, without responsibility for any risks not being covered.

(b) Failing specific stipulations in the Credit, banks will accept insurance documents as presented, without responsibility for any risks not being covered.

(c) Unless otherwise stipulated in the Credit, banks will accept an insurance document which indicates that the cover is subject to a franchise or an excess (deductible).

Article 36. All Risks Insurance Cover

Where a Credit stipulates "insurance against all risks", banks will accept an insurance document which contains any "all risks" notation or clause, whether or not bearing the heading "all risks", even if the insurance document indicates that certain risks are excluded, without responsibility for any risk(s) not being covered.

Article 37. Commercial Invoices

(*a*) Unless otherwise stipulated in the Credit, commercial invoices;

  (i) must appear on their face to be issued by the Beneficiary named in the Credit (except as provided in Article 48), and

 (ii) must be made out in the name of the Applicant (except as provided in sub-Article 48 (h)), and

(iii) need not be signed.

(*b*) Unless otherwise stipulated in the Credit, banks may refuse commercial invoices issued for amounts in excess of the amount permitted by the Credit. Nevertheless, if a bank authorised to pay, incur a deferred payment undertaking, accept Draft(s), or negotiate under a Credit accepts such invoices, its decision will be binding upon all parties, provided that such bank has not paid, incurred a deferred payment undertaking, accepted Draft(s) or negotiated for an amount in excess of that permitted by the Credit.

(*c*) The description of the goods in the commercial invoice must correspond with the description in the Credit. In all other documents, the goods may be described in general terms not inconsistent with the description of the goods in the Credit.

Article 38. Other Documents

If a Credit calls for an attestation or certification of weight in the case of transport other than by sea, banks will accept a weight stamp or declaration of weight which appears to have been superimposed on the transport document by the carrier or his agent unless the Credit specifically stipulates that the attestation or certification of weight must be by means of a separate document.

E. MISCELLANEOUS PROVISIONS

Article 39. Allowances in Credit Amount, Quantity and Unit Price

(*a*) The words "about", "approximately", "circa" or similar expressions used in connection with the amount of the Credit or the quantity or the unit price stated in the Credit are to be construed as allowing a difference not to exceed 10% more or 10% less than the amount or the quantity or the unit price to which they refer.

(*b*) Unless a Credit stipulates that the quantity of the goods specified must not be exceeded or reduced, a tolerance of 5% more or 5% less will be permissible, always provided that the amount of the drawings does not exceed the amount of the Credit. This tolerance does not apply when the Credit stipulates the quantity in terms of a stated number of packing units or individual items.

(*c*) Unless a Credit which prohibits partial shipments stipulates otherwise, or unless sub-Article (*b*) above is applicable, a tolerance of 5% less in the amount of the drawing will be permissible, provided that if the Credit stipulates the quantity of the goods, such quantity of goods is shipped in full, and if the Credit stipulates a unit price, such price is not reduced. This provision does not apply when expressions referred to in sub-Article (*a*) above are used in the Credit.

Article 40. Partial Shipments/Drawings

(*a*) Partial drawings and/or shipments are allowed, unless the Credit stipulates otherwise.

(b) Transport documents which appear on their face to indicate that shipment has been made on the same means of conveyance and for the same journey, provided they indicate the same destination, will not be regarded as covering partial shipments, even if the transport documents indicate different dates of shipment and/or different ports of loading, places of taking in charge, or despatch.

(c) Shipments made by post or by courier will not be regarded as partial shipments if the post receipts or certificates of posting or courier's receipts or dispatch notes appear to have been stamped, signed or otherwise authenticated in the place from which the Credit stipulates the goods are to be dispatched, and on the same date.

Article 41. Instalment Shipments/Drawings

If drawings and/or shipments by instalments within given periods are stipulated in the Credit and any instalment is not drawn and/or shipped within the period allowed for that instalment, the Credit ceases to be available for that and any subsequent instalments, unless otherwise stipulated in the Credit.

Article 42. Expiry Date and Place for Presentation of Documents

(a) All Credits must stipulate an expiry date and a place for presentation of documents for payment, acceptance, or with the exception of freely negotiable Credits, a place for presentation of documents for negotiation. An expiry date stipulated for payment, acceptance or negotiation will be construed to express an expiry date for presentation of documents.

(b) Except as provided in sub-Article 44(a), documents must be presented on or before such expiry date.

(c) If an Issuing Bank states that the Credit is to be available "for one month", "for six months", or the like, but does not specify the date from which the time is to run, the date of issuance of the Credit by the Issuing Bank will be deemed to be the first day from which such time is to run. Banks should discourage indication of the expiry date of the Credit in this manner.

Article 43. Limitation on the Expiry Date

(a) In addition to stipulating an expiry date for presentation of documents, every Credit which calls for a transport document(s) should also stipulate a specified period of time after the date of shipment during which presentation must be made in compliance with the terms and conditions of the Credit. If no such period of time is stipulated, banks will not accept documents presented to them later than 21 days after the date of shipment. In any event, documents must be presented not later than the expiry date of the Credit.

(b) In cases in which sub-Article 40(b) applies, the date of shipment will be considered to be the latest shipment date on any of the transport documents presented.

Article 44. Extension of Expiry Date

(a) If the expiry date of the Credit and/or the last day of the period of time for presentation of documents stipulated by the Credit or applicable by virtue of Article 43 falls on a day on which the bank to which presentation has to be made is closed for reasons other than those referred to in Article 17, the stipulated expiry date and/or the last day of the period of time after the date of shipment for presentation of documents, as the case may be, shall be extended to the first following day on which such bank is open.

(*b*) The latest date for shipment shall not be extended by reason of the extension of the expiry date and/or the period of time after the date of shipment for presentation of documents in accordance with sub-Article (*a*) above. If no such latest date for shipment is stipulated in the Credit or amendments thereto, banks will not accept transport documents indicating a date of shipment later than the expiry date stipulated in the Credit or amendments thereto.

(*c*) The bank to which presentation is made on such first following business day must provide a statement that the documents were presented within the time limits extended in accordance with sub-Article 44(*a*) of the Uniform Customs and Practice for Documentary Credits, 1993 Revision, ICC Publication No. 500.

Article 45. Hours of Presentation

Banks are under no obligation to accept presentation of documents outside their banking hours.

Article 46 General Expressions as to Dates for Shipment

(*a*) Unless otherwise stipulated in the Credit, the expression "shipment" used in stipulating an earliest and/or a latest date for shipment will be understood to include expressions such as, "loading on board", "dispatch", "accepted for carriage", "date of post receipt", "date of pick-up", and the like, and in the case of a Credit calling for a multimodal transport document the expression "taking in charge".

(*b*) Expressions such as "prompt", "immediately", "as soon as possible", and the like should not be used. If they are used banks will disregard them.

(*c*) If the expression "on or about" or similar expressions are used, banks will interpret them as a stipulation that shipment is to be made during the period from five days before to five days after the specified date, both end days included.

Article 47. Date Terminology for Periods of Shipment

(*a*) The words "to", "until", "till", "from" and words of similar import applying to any date or period in the Credit referring to shipment will be understood to include the date mentioned.

(*b*) The word "after" will be understood to exclude the date mentioned.

(*c*) The terms "first half", "second half" of a month shall be construed respectively as the 1st to the 15th, and the 16th to the last day of such month, all dates inclusive.

(*d*) The terms "beginning", "middle", or "end" of a month shall be construed respectively as the 1st to the 10th, the 11th to the 20th, and the 21st to the last day of such month, all dates inclusive.

F. TRANSFERABLE CREDIT

Article 48. Transferable Credit

(*a*) A transferable Credit is a Credit under which the Beneficiary (First Beneficiary) may request the bank authorised to pay, incur a deferred payment undertaking, accept or negotiate (the "Transferring Bank"), or in the case of a freely negotiable Credit, the bank specifically authorised in the Credit as a Transferring Bank, to make the Credit available in whole or in part to one or more other Beneficiary(ies) (Second Beneficiary(ies)).

(*b*) A Credit can be transferred only if it is expressly designated as "transferable" by the Issuing Bank. Terms such as "divisible", "fractionable", "assignable", and "transmissible" do not render the Credit transferable. If such terms are used they shall be disregarded.

(*c*) The Transferring Bank shall be under no obligation to effect such transfer except to the extent and in the manner expressly consented to by such bank.

(*d*) At the time of making a request for transfer and prior to transfer of the Credit, the First Beneficiary must irrevocably instruct the Transferring Bank whether or not he retains the right to refuse to allow the Transferring Bank to advise amendments to the Second Beneficiary(ies). If the Transferring Bank consents to the transfer under these conditions, it must, at the time of transfer, advise the Second Beneficiary(ies) of the First Beneficiary's instructions regarding amendments.

(*e*) If a Credit is transferred to more than one Second Beneficiary(ies), refusal of an amendment by one or more Second Beneficiary(ies) does not invalidate the acceptance(s) by the other Second Beneficiary(ies) with respect to whom the Credit will be amended accordingly. With respect to the Second Beneficiary(ies) who rejected the amendment, the Credit will remain unamended.

(*f*) Transferring Bank charges in respect of transfers including commissions, fees, costs or expenses are payable by the First Beneficiary, unless otherwise agreed. If the Transferring Bank agrees to transfer the Credit it shall be under no obligation to effect the transfer until such charges are paid.

(*g*) Unless otherwise stated in the Credit, a transferable Credit can be transferred once only. Consequently, the Credit cannot be transferred at the request of the Second Beneficiary to any subsequent Third Beneficiary. For the purpose of this Article, a retransfer to the First Beneficiary does not constitute a prohibited transfer.

Fractions of a transferable Credit (not exceeding in the aggregate the amount of the Credit) can be transferred separately, provided partial shipments/drawings are not prohibited, and the aggregate of such transfers will be considered as constituting only one transfer of the Credit.

(*h*) The Credit can be transferred only on the terms and conditions specified in the original Credit, with the exception of:
  —the amount of the Credit,
  —any unit price stated therein,
  —the expiry date,
  —the last date for presentation of documents in accordance with Article 43,
  —the period for shipment,
any or all of which may be reduced or curtailed.

The percentage for which insurance cover must be effected may be increased in such a way as to provide the amount of cover stipulated in the original Credit, or these Articles.

In addition, the name of the First Beneficiary can be substituted for that of the Applicant, but if the name of the Applicant is specifically required by the original Credit to appear in any document(s) other than the invoice, such requirement must be fulfilled.

(*i*) The First Beneficiary has the right to substitute his own invoice(s) (and Draft(s)) for those of the Second Beneficiary(ies), for amounts not in excess of the original amount stipulated in the Credit and for the original unit prices if stipulated in the Credit, and upon such substitution of invoice(s) (and Draft(s)) the First Beneficiary can draw under the Credit for the difference, if any, between his invoice(s) and the Second Beneficiary's(ies') invoice(s).

When a Credit has been transferred and the First Beneficiary is to supply his own invoice(s) (and Draft(s)) in exchange for the Second Beneficiary's(ies') invoice(s) (and

Draft(s)) but fails to do so on first demand, the Transferring Bank has the right to deliver to the Issuing Bank the documents received under the transferred Credit, including the Second Beneficiary's(ies') invoice(s) (and Draft(s)) without further responsibility to the First Beneficiary.

(j) The First Beneficiary may request that payment or negotiation be effected to the Second Beneficiary(ies) at the place to which the Credit has been transferred up to and including the expiry date of the Credit, unless the original Credit expressly states that it may not be made available for payment or negotiation at a place other than that stipulated in the Credit. This is without prejudice to the First Beneficiary's right to substitute subsequently his own invoice(s) (and Draft(s)) for those of the Second Beneficiary(ies) and to claim any difference due to him.

G. ASSIGNMENT OF PROCEEDS

Article 49. Assignment of Proceeds

The fact that a Credit is not stated to be transferable shall not affect the Beneficiary's right to assign any proceeds to which he may be, or may become, entitled under such Credit, in accordance with the provisions of the applicable law. This Article relates only to the assignment of proceeds and not to the assignment of the right to perform under the Credit itself.

APPENDIX 6

UN CONVENTION ON INTERNATIONAL BILLS OF EXCHANGE AND INTERNATIONAL PROMISSORY NOTES

The General Assembly

Recalling its resolution 2205 (XXI) of 17 December 1966, by which it created the United Nations Commission on International Trade Law with a mandate to further the progressive harmonization and unification of the law of international trade and in that respect to bear in mind the interests of all peoples, in particular those of developing countries, in the extensive development of international trade,

Aware that the free circulation of bills of exchange and promissory notes facilitates international trade and finance,

Convinced that the adoption of a convention on international bills of exchange and international promissory notes will facilitate the use of such instruments,

Taking note with satisfaction of the decision of the United Nations Commission on International Trade Law at its twentieth session[1] to transmit the text of the draft Convention on International Bills of Exchange and International Promissory Notes[2] to the General Assembly for its consideration,

Recalling its resolution 42/153 of 7 December 1987, in which it requested the Secretary-General to draw the attention of all States to the draft Convention, to ask them to submit the observations and proposals they wished to make on the draft Convention and to circulate those observations and proposals to all Member States,

Recalling also that in the same resolution it decided to consider, at its forty-third session, the draft Convention, with a view to its adoption at that session, and to create to that end a working group, in the framework of the Sixth Committee, to consider the observations and proposals made by States,

Satisfied with the modifications in the draft Convention proposed by the open-ended Working Group on the draft Convention on International Bills of Exchange and International Promissory Notes,[3] and expressing its appreciation for the efforts of the Working Group,

1. *Expresses its appreciation* to the United Nations Commission on International Trade Law for preparing the text of the draft Convention on International Bills of Exchange and International Promissory Notes;

---

1. *Ibid., Forty-second Session, Supplement No. 17* (A/12/17), para. 304.
2. *Ibid.*, annex I.
3. See A/C.6/43/L.2.

2. *Adopts* and opens for signature or accession the United Nations Convention on International Bills of Exchange and International Promissory Notes contained in the annex to the present resolution;

3. *Calls upon*all Governments to consider becoming party to the Convention.

76th plenary meeting
9 December 1988

CHAPTER I. SPHERE OF APPLICATION AND FORM OF THE INSTRUMENT

Article 1

1. This Convention applies to an international bill of exchange when it contains the heading "International bill of exchange (UNCITRAL Convention)" and also contains in its text the words "International bill of exchange (UNCITRAL Convention)".

2. This Convention applies to an international promissory note when it contains the heading "International promissory note (UNCITRAL Convention)" and also contains in its text the words "International promissory note (UNCITRAL Convention)".

3. This Convention does not apply to cheques.

Article 2

1. An international bill of exchange is a bill of exchange which specifies at least two of the following places and indicates that any two so specified are situated in different States:

(*a*) The place where the bill is drawn;
(*b*) The place indicated next to the signature of the drawer;
(*c*) The place indicated next to the name of the drawee;
(*d*) The place indicated next to the name of the payee;
(*e*) The place of payment,

provided that either the place where the bill is drawn or the place of payment is specified on the bill and that such place is situated in a Contracting State.

2. An international promissory note is a promissory note which specifies at least two of the following places and indicates that any two so specified are situated in different States:

(*a*) The place where the note is made;
(*b*) The place indicated next to the signature of the maker;
(*c*) The place indicated next to the name of the payee;
(*d*) The place of payment,

provided that the place of payment is specified on the note and that such place is situated in a Contracting State.

3. This Convention does not deal with the question of sanctions that may be imposed under national law in cases where an incorrect or false statement has been made on an instrument in respect of a place referred to in paragraph 1 or 2 of this article. However, any such sanctions shall not affect the validity of this instrument or the application of this Convention.

Article 3

1. A bill of exchange is a written instrument which:

(*a*) Contains an unconditional order whereby the drawer directs the drawee to pay a definite sum of money to the payee or to this order;

    (*b*) Is payable on demand or at a definite time;
    (*c*) Is dated;
    (*d*) Is signed by the drawer.
  2. A promissory note is a written instrument which:
    (*a*) Contains an unconditional promise whereby the maker undertakes to pay a definite sum of money to the payee or to his order;
    (*b*) Is payable on demand or at a definite time;
    (*c*) Is dated;
    (*d*) Is signed by the maker.

CHAPTER II. INTERPRETATION

SECTION I. GENERAL PROVISIONS

Article 4

In the interpretation of this Convention, regard is to be had to its international character and to the need to promote uniformity in its application and the observance of good faith in international transactions.

Article 5

In this Convention:
    (*a*) "Bill" means an international bill of exchange governed by this Convention;
    (*b*) "Note" means an international promissory note governed by this Convention;
    (*c*) "Instrument" means a bill or a note;
    (*d*) "Drawee" means a person on whom a bill is drawn and who has not accepted it;
    (*e*) "Payee" means a person in whose favour the drawer directs payment to be made or to whom the maker promises to pay;
    (*f*) "Holder" means a person in possession of an instrument in accordance with article 15;
    (*g*) "protected holder" means a holder who meets the requirements of article 29;
    (*h*) "Guarantor" means any person who undertakes an obligation of guarantee under article 46, whether governed by paragraph 4(*b*) ("guaranteed") or paragraph 4(*c*) ("*aval*") of article 47;
    (*i*) "Party" means a person who has signed an instrument as drawer, maker, acceptor, endorser or guarantor;
    (*j*) "Maturity" means the time of payment referred to in paragraphs 4, 5, 6 and 7 of article 9;
    (*k*) "Signature" means a handwritten signature, its facsimile or an equivalent authentication effected by any other means; "forged signature" includes a signature by the wrongful use of such means;
    (*l*) "Money" or "currency" includes a monetary unit of account which is established by an intergovernmental institution or by agreement between two or more States, provided that this Convention shall apply without prejudice to the rules of the intergovernmental institution or to the stipulations of the agreement.

Article 6

For the purposes of this Convention, a person is considered to have knowledge of a fact if he has actual knowledge of that fact or could not have been unaware of its existence.

SECTION 2. INTERPRETATION OF FORMAL REQUIREMENTS

Article 7

The sum payable by an instrument is deemed to be a definite sum although the instrument states that it is to be paid:

(a) With interest;

(b) By instalments at successive dates;

(c) By instalments at successive dates with a stipulation in the instrument that upon default in payment of any instalment the unpaid balance becomes due;

(d) According to a rate of exchange indicated in the instrument or to be determined as directed by the instrument; or

(e) In a currency other than the curency in which the sum is expressed in the instrument.

Article 8

1. If there is a discrepancy between the sum expressed in words and the sum expressed in figures, the sum payable by the instrument is the sum expressed in words.

2. If the sum is expressed more than once in words, and there is a discrepancy, the sum payable is the smaller sum. The same rule applies if the sum is expressed more than once in figures only, and there is a discrepancy.

3. If the sum is expressed in a currency having the same description as that of at least one other State than the State where payment is to be made, as indicated in the instrument, and the specified currency is not identified as the currency of any particular State, the currency is to be considered as the currency of the State where payment is to be made.

4. If an instrument states that the sum is to be paid with interest, without specifying the date from which interest is to run, interest runs from the date of the instrument.

5. A stipulation stating that the sum is to be paid with interst is deemed not to have been written on the instrument unless it indicates the rate at which interest is to be paid.

6. A rate at which interest is to be paid may be expressed either as a definite rate or as a variable rate. For a variable rate to qualify for this purpose, it must vary in relation to one or more reference rates of interest in accordance with provisions stipulated in the instrument and each such reference rate must be published or otherwise available to the public and not be subject, directly or indirectly, to unilateral determination by a person who is named in the instrument at the time the bill is drawn or the note is made, unless the person is named only in the reference rate provisions.

7. If the rate at which interest is to be paid is expressed as a variable rate, it may be stipulated expressly in the instrument that such rate shall not be less than or exceed a specified rate of interest, or that the variations are otherwise limited.

8. If a variable rate does not qualify under paragraph 6 of this article or for any reason it is not possible to determine the numerical value of the variable rate for any period, interest shall be payable for the relevant period at the rate calculated in accordance with paragraph 2 of article 70.

Article 9

1. An instrument is deemed to be payable on demand:
   (*a*) If it states that it is payable at sight or on demand or on presentment or if it contains words of similar import; or
   (*b*) If no time of payment is expressed.
2. An instrument payable at a definite time which is accepted or endorsed or guaranteed after maturity is an instrument payable on demand as regards the acceptor, the endorser or the guarantor.
3. An instrument is deemed to be payable at a definite time if it states that it is payable:
   (*a*) On a stated date or at a fixed period after a stated date or at a fixed period after the date of the instrument;
   (*b*) At a fixed period after sight;
   (*c*) By instalments at successive dates; or
   (*d*) By instalments at successive dates with the stipulation in the instrument that upon default in payment of any instalment the unpaid balance becomes due.
4. The time of payment of an instrument payable at a fixed period after date is determined by reference to the date of the instrument.
5. The time of payment of a bill payable at a fixed period after sight is determined by the date of acceptance or, if the bill is dishonoured by non-acceptance, by the date of protest or, if protest is dispensed with, by the date of dishonour.
6. The time of payment of an instrument payable on demand is the date on which the instrument is presented for payment.
7. The time of payment of a note payable at a fixed period after sight is determined by the date of the visa signed by the maker on the note or, if his visa is refused, by the date of presentment.
8. If an instrument is drawn, or made, payable one or more months after a stated date or after the date of the instrument or after sight, the instrument is payable on the corresponding date of the month when payment must be made. If there is no corresponding date, the instrument is payable on the last day of that month.

Article 10

1. A bill may be drawn:
   (*a*) By two or more drawers;
   (*b*) Payable to two or more payees.
2. A note may be made:
   (*a*) By two or more makers;
   (*b*) Payable to two or more payees.
3. If an instrument is payable to two or more payees in the alternative, it is payable to any one of them and any one of them in possession of the instrument may exercise the rights of a holder. In any other case the instrument is payable to all of them and the rights of a holder may be exercised only by all of them.

Article 11

A bill may be drawn by the drawer:
   (*a*) On himself;
   (*b*) Payable to his order.

Article 12

1. An incomplete instrument which satisfies the requirements set out in paragraph 1 of article 1 and bears the signature of the drawer or the acceptance of the drawee, or which satisfies the requirements set out in paragraph 2 of article 1 and paragraph 2(*d*) of article 3, but which lacks other elements pertaining to one or more of the requirements set out in articles 2 and 3, may be completed, and the instrument so completed is effective as a bill or a note.

2. If such an instrument is completed without authority or otherwise than in accordance with the authority given:

    (*a*) A party who signed the instrument before the completion may invoke such lack of authority as a defence against a holder who had knowledge of such lack of authority when he became a holder;

    (*b*) A party who signed the instrument after the completion is liable according to the terms of the instrument so completed.

CHAPTER III. TRANSFER

Article 13

An instrument is transferred:

    (*a*) By endorsement and delivery of the instrument by the endorser to the endorsee; or

    (*b*) By mere delivery of the instrument if the last endorsement is in blank.

Article 14

1. An endorsement must be written on the instrument or on a slip affixed thereto ("*allonge*"). It must be signed.

2. An endorsement may be:

    (*a*) In blank, that is, by a signature alone or by a signature accompanied by a statement to the effect that the instrument is payable to a person in possession of it;

    (*b*) Special, that is, by a signature accompanied by an indication of the person to whom the instrument is payable.

3. A signature alone, other than that of the drawee, is an endorsement only if placed on the back of the instrument.

Article 15

1. A person is a holder if he is:

    (*a*) The payee in possession of the instrument; or

    (*b*) In possession of an instrument which has been endorsed to him, or on which the last endorsement is in blank, and on which there appears an uninterrupted series of endorsements, even if any endorsement was forged or was signed by an agent without authority.

2. If an endorsement in blank is followed by another endorsement, the person who signed this last endorsement is deemed to be an endorsee by the endorsement in blank.

3. A person is not prevented from being a holder by the fact that the instrument was obtained by him or any previous holder under circumstances, including incapacity or

fraud, duress or mistake of any kind, that would give rise to a claim to, or a defence against liability on, the instrument.

Article 16

The holder of an instrument on which the last endorsement is in blank may:
- (*a*) Further endorse it either by an endorsement in blank or by a special endorsement;
- (*b*) Convert the blank endorsement into a special endorsement by indicating in the endorsement that the instrument is payable to himself or to some other specified person; or
- (*c*) Transfer the instrument in accordance with subparagraph (*b*) of article 13.

Article 17

1. If the drawer or the maker has inserted in the instrument such words as "not negotiable", "not transferable", "not to order", "pay (X) only", or words of similar import, the instrument may not be transferred except for purposes of collection, and any endorsement, even if it does not contain words authorizing the endorsee to collect the instrument, is deemed to be an endorsement for collection.

2. If an endorsement contains the words "not negotiable", "not transferable", "not to order", "pay (X) only", or words of similar import, the instrument may not be transferred further except for purposes of collection, and any subsequent endorsement, even if it does not contain words authorizing the endorsee to collect the instrument, is deemed to be an endorsement for collection.

Article 18

1. An endorsement must be unconditional.

2. A conditional endorsement transfers the instrument whether or not the condition is fulfilled. The condition is ineffective as to those parties and transferees who are subsequent to the endorsee.

Article 19

An endorsement in respect of a part of the sum due under the instrument is ineffective as an endorsement.

Article 20

If there are two or more endorsements, it is presumed, unless the contrary is proved, that each endorsement was made in the order in which it appears on the instrument.

Article 21

1. If an endorsement contains the words "for collection", "for deposit", "value in collection", "by procuration", "pay any bank", or words of similar import authorizing the endorsee to collect the instrument, the endorsee is a holder who:
- (*a*) May exercise all rights arising out of the instrument;
- (*b*) May endorse the instrument only for purposes of collection;
- (*c*) Is subject only to the claims and defences which may be set up against the endorser.

2. The endorser for collection is not liable on the instrument to any subsequent holder.

Article 22

1. If an endorsement contains the words "value in security", "value in pledge", or any other words indicating a pledge, the endorsee is a holder who:
   (a) May exercise all rights arising out of the instrument;
   (b) May endorse the instrument only for purposes of collection;
   (c) Is subject only to the claims and defences specified in article 28 or article 30.

2. If such an endorsee endorses for collection, he is not liable on the instrument to any subsequent holder.

Article 23

The holder of an instrument may transfer it to a prior party or to the drawee in accordance with article 13; however, if the transferee has previously been a holder of the instrument, no endorsement is required and any endorsement which would prevent him from qualifying as a holder may be struck out.

Article 24

An instrument may be transferred in accordance with article 13 after maturity, except by the drawee, the acceptor or the maker.

Article 25

1. If an endorsement is forged, the person whose endorsement is forged, or a party who signed the instrument before the forgery, has the right to recover compensation for any damage that he may have suffered because of the forgery against:
   (a) The forger;
   (b) The person to whom the instrument was directly transferred by the forger;
   (c) A party or the drawee who paid the instrument to the forger directly or through one or more endorsees for collection.

2. However, an endorsee for collection is not liable under paragraph 1 of this article if he is without knowledge of the forgery:
   (a) At the time he pays the principal or advises him of the receipt of payment; or
   (b) At the time he receives payment, if this is later,
unless his lack of knowledge is due to his failure to act in good faith or to exercise reasonable care.

3. Furthermore, a party or the drawee who pays an instrument is not liable under paragraph 1 of this article if, at the time he pays the instrument, he is without knowledge of the forgery, unless his lack of knowledge is due to his failure to act in good faith or to exercise reasonable care.

4. Except as against the forger, the damages recoverable under paragraph 1 of this article may not exceed the amount referred to in article 70 or article 71.

Article 26

1. If an endorsement is made by an agent without authority or power to bind his principal in the matter, the principal, or a party who signed the instrument before such endorsement, has the right to recover compensation for any damage that he may have suffered because of such endorsement against:
   (a) The agent;
   (b) The person to whom the instrument was directly transferred by the agent;

(c) A party or the drawee who paid the instrument to the agent directly or through one or more endorsees for collection.

2. However, an endorsee for collection is not liable under paragraph 1 of this article if he is without knowledge that the endorsement does not bind the principal;

(a) At the time he pays the principal or advises him of the receipt of payment; or

(b) At the time he receives payment, if this is later,

unless his lack of knowledge is due to his failure to act in good faith or to exercise reasonable care.

3. Furthermore, a party or the drawee who pays an instrument is not liable under paragraph 1 of this article if, at the time he pays the instrument, he is without knowledge that the endorsement does not bind the principal, unless his lack of knowledge is due his failure to act in good faith or to exercise reasonable care.

4. Except as against the agent, the damages recoverable under paragraph 1 of this article may not exceed the amount referred to in article 70 or article 71.

CHAPTER IV. RIGHTS AND LIABILITIES

SECTION I. THE RIGHTS OF A HOLDER AND OF A PROTECTED HOLDER

Article 27

1. The holder of an instrument has all the rights conferred on him by this Convention against the parties to the instrument.

2. The holder may transfer the instrument in accordance with article 13.

Article 28

1. A party may set up against a holder who is not a protected holder:

(a) Any defence that may be set up against a protected holder in accordance with paragraph 1 of article 30;

(b) Any defence based on the underlying transaction between himself and the drawer or between himself and his transferee, but only if the holder took the instrument with knowledge of such defence or if he obtained the instrument by fraud or theft or participated at any time in a fraud or theft concerning it;

(c) Any defence arising from the circumstances as a result of which he became a party, but only if the holder took the instrument with knowledge of such defence or if he obtained the instrument by fraud or theft or participated at any time in a fraud or theft concerning it;

(d) Any defence which may be raised against an action in contract between himself and the holder;

(e) Any other defence available under this Convention.

2. The rights to an instrument of a holder who is not a protected holder are subject to any valid claim to the instrument on the part of any person, but only if he took the instrument with knowledge of such claim or if he obtained the instrument by fraud or theft or participated at any time in a fraud or theft concerning it.

3. A holder who takes an instrument after the expiration of the time-limit for presentment for payment is subject to any claim to, or defence against liability on, the instrument to which his transferor is subject.

4. A party may not raise as a defence against a holder who is not a protected holder the fact that a third person has a claim to the instrument unless:

(a) The third person asserted a valid claim to the instrument; or (*b*) The holder acquired the instrument by theft or forged the signature of the payee or an endorsee, or participated in the theft or the forgery.

Article 29

"Protected holder" means the holder of an instrument which was complete when he took it or which was incomplete within the meaning of paragraph 1 of article 12 and was completed in accordance with authority given, provided that when he became a holder:

(*a*) He was without knowledge of a defence against liability on the instrument referred to in paragraphs 1 (*a*), (*b*), (*c*) and (*e*) of article 28;

(*b*) He was without knowledge of a valid claim to the instrument of any person;

(*c*) He was without knowledge of the fact that it had been dishonoured by non-acceptance or by non-payment;

(*d*) The time-limit provided by article 55 for presentment of that instrument for payment had not expired;

(*e*) He did not obtain the instrument by fraud or theft or participate in a fraud or theft concerning it.

Article 30

1. A party may not set up against a protected holder any defence except:

(*a*) Defences under paragraph 1 of article 33, article 34, paragraph 1 of article 35, paragraph 3 of article 36, paragraph 1 of article 53, paragraph 1 of article 57, pargraph 1 of article 63 and article 84 of this Convention;

(*b*) Defences based on the underlying transaction between himself and such holder or arising from any fraudulent act on the part of such holder in obtaining the signature on the instrument of that party;

(*c*) Defences based on his incapacity to incur liability on the instrument or on the fact that he signed without knowledge that his signature made him a party to the instrument, provided that his lack of knowledge was not due to his negligence and provided that he was fraudulently induced so to sign.

2. The rights to an instrument of a protected holder are not subject to any claim to the instrument on the part of any person, except a valid claim arising from the underlying transaction between himself and the person by whom the claim is raised.

Article 31

1. The transfer of an instrument by a protected holder vests in any subsequent holder the rights to and on the instrument which the protected holder had.

2. Those rights are not vested in a subsequent holder if:

(*a*) He participated in a transaction which gives rise to a claim to, or a defence against liability on, the instrument;

(*b*) He has previously been a holder, but not a protected holder.

Article 32

Every holder is presumed to be a protected holder unless the contrary is proved.

SECTION 2. LIABILITIES OF THE PARTIES

A. General provisions

Article 33

1. Subject to the provisions of articles 34 and 36, a person is not liable on an instrument unless he signs it.

2. A person who signs an instrument in a name which is not his own is liable as if he had signed it in his own name.

Article 34

A forged signature on an instrument does not impose any liability on the person whose signature was forged. However, if he consents to be bound by the forged signature or represents that it is his own, he is liable as if he had signed the instrument himself.

Article 35

1. If an instrument is materially altered:
   (a) A party who signs it after the material alteration is liable according to the terms of the altered text;
   (b) A party who signs it before the material alteration is liable according to the terms of the original text. However, if a party makes, authorizes or assents to a material alteration, he is liable according to the terms of the altered text.

2. A signature is presumed to have been placed on the instrument after the material alteration unless the contrary is proved.

3. Any alteration is material which modifies the written undertaking on the instrument of any party in any respect.

Article 36

1. An instrument may be signed by an agent.

2. The signature of an agent placed by him on an instrument with the authority of his principal and showing on the instrument that he is signing in a representative capacity for that named principal, or the signature of a principal placed on the instrument by an agent with his authority, imposes liability on the principal and not on the agent.

3. A signature placed on an instrument by a person as agent but who lacks authority to sign or exceeds his authority, or by an agent who has authority to sign but who does not show on the instrument that he is signing in a representative capacity for a named person, or who shows on the instrument that he is signing in a representative capacity but does not name the person whom he represents, imposes liability on the person signing and not on the person whom he purports to represent.

4. The question whether a signature was placed on the instrument in a representative capacity may be determined only by reference to what appears on the instrument.

5. A person who is liable pursuant to paragraph 3 of this article and who pays the instrument has the same rights as the person for whom he purported to act would have had if that person had paid the instrument.

Article 37

The order to pay contained in a bill does not of itself operate as an assignment to the payee of funds made available for payment by the drawer with the drawee.

B. The drawer

Article 38

1. The drawer engages that upon dishonour of the bill by non-acceptance or by non-payment, and upon any necessary protest, he will pay the bill to the holder, or to any endorser or any endorser's guarantor who takes up and pays the bill.

2. The drawer may exclude or limit his own liability for acceptance or for payment by an express stipulation in the bill. Such a stipulation is effective only with respect to the drawer. A stipulation excluding or limiting liability for payment is effective only if another party is or becomes liable on the bill.

C. The maker

Article 39

1. The maker engages that he will pay the note in accordance with its terms to the holder, or to any party who takes up and pays the note.

2. The maker may not exclude or limit his own liability by a stipulation in the note. Any such stipulation is ineffective.

D. The drawee and the acceptor

Article 40

1. The drawee is not liable on a bill until he accepts it.

2. The acceptor engages that he will pay the bill in accordance with the terms of his acceptance to the holder, or to any party who takes up and pays the bill.

Article 41

1. An acceptance must be written on the bill and may be effected:
   (a) By the signature of the drawee accompanied by the word "accepted" or by words of similar import; or
   (b) By the signature alone of the drawee.

2. An acceptance may be written on the front or on the back of the bill.

Article 42

1. An incomplete bill which satisfies the requirements set out in paragraph 1 of article 1 may be accepted by the drawee before it has been signed by the drawer, or while otherwise incomplete.

2. A bill may be accepted before, at or after maturity, or after it has been dishonoured by non-acceptance or by non-payment.

3. If a bill drawn payable at a fixed period after sight, or a bill which must be presented for acceptance before a specified date, is accepted, the acceptor must indicate the date of his acceptance; failing such indication by the acceptor, the drawer or the holder may insert the date of acceptance.

4. If a bill drawn payable at a fixed period after sight is dishonoured by non-acceptance and the drawee subsequently accepts it, the holder is entitled to have the acceptance dated as of the date on which the bill was dishonoured.

Article 43

1. An acceptance must be unqualified. An acceptance is qualified if it is conditional or varies the terms of the bill.

2. If the drawee stipulates in the bill that his acceptance is subject to qualification:

(*a*) He is nevertheless bound according to the terms of his qualified acceptance;

(*b*) The bill is dishonoured by non-acceptance.

3. An acceptance relating to only a part of the sum payable is a qualifed acceptance. If the holder takes such an acceptance, the bill is dishonoured by non-acceptance only as to the remaining part.

4. An acceptance indicating that payment will be made at a particular address or by a particular agent is not a qualified acceptance, provided that:

(*a*) The place in which payment is to be made is not changed;

(*b*) The bill is not drawn payable by another agent.

E. *The endorser*

Article 44

1. The endorser engages that upon dishonour of the instrument by non-acceptance or by non-payment, and upon any necessary protest, he will pay the instrument to the holder, or to any subsequent endorser or any endorser's guarantor who takes up and pays the instrument.

2. An endorser may exclude or limit his own liability by an express stipulation in the instrument. Such a stipulation is effective only with respect to that endorser.

F. *The transferor by endorsement or by mere delivery*

Article 45

1. Unless otherwise agreed, a person who transfers an instrument, by endorsement and delivery or by mere delivery, represents to the holder to whom he transfers the instrument that:

(*a*) The instrument does not bear any forged or unauthorized signature;

(*b*) The instrument has not been materially altered;

(*c*) At the time of transfer, he has no knowledge of any fact which would impair the right of the transferee to payment of the instrument against the acceptor of a bill or, in the case of an unaccepted bill, the drawer, or against the maker of a note.

2. Liability of the transferor under paragraph 1 of this article is incurred only if the transferee took the instrument without knowledge of the matter giving rise to such liability.

3. If the transferor is liable under paragraph 1 of this article, the transferee may recover, even before maturity, the amount paid by him to the transferor, with interest calculated in accordance with article 70, against return of the instrument.

G. *The guarantor*

Article 46

1. Payment of an instrument, whether or not it has been accepted, may be guaranteed, as to the whole or part of its amount, for the account of a party or the drawee. A guarantee may be given by any person, who may or may not already be a party.

2. A guarantee must be written on the instrument or on a slip affixed thereto ("*allonge*").

3. A guarantee is expressed by the words "guaranteed", "*aval*", "good as *aval*" or words of similar import, accompanied by the signature of the guarantor. For the

purposes of this Convention, the words "prior endorsements guaranteed" or words of similar import do not constitute a guarantee.

4. A guarantee may be effected by a signature alone on the front of the instrument. A signature alone on the front of the instrument, other than that of the maker, the drawer or the drawee, is a guarantee.

5. A guarantor may specify the person for whom he has become guarantor. In the absence of such specification, the person for whom he has become guarantor is the acceptor or the drawee in the case of a bill, and the maker in the case of a note.

6. A guarantor may not arise as a defence to his liability the fact that he signed the instrument before it was signed by the person for whom he is a guarantor, or while the instrument was incomplete.

Article 47

1. The liability of a guarantor on the instrument is of the same nature as that of the party for whom he has become guarantor.

2. If the person for whom he has become guarantor is the drawee, the guarantor engages:
- (a) To pay the bill at maturity to the holder, or to any party who takes up and pays the bill;
- (b) If the bill is payable at a definite time, upon dishonour by non-acceptance and upon any necessary protest, to pay it to the holder, or to any party who takes up and pays the bill.

3. In respect of defences that are personal to himself, a guarantor may set up:
- (a) Against a holder who is not a protected holder only those defences which he may set up under paragraphs 1, 3 and 4 of article 28;
- (b) Against a protected holder only those defences which he may set up under paragraph 1 of article 30.

4. In respect of defences that may be raised by the person for whom he has become a guarantor;
- (a) A guarantor may set up against a holder who is not a protected holder only those defences which the person for whom he has become a guarantor may set up against such holder under paragraphs 1, 3 and 4 of article 28;
- (b) A guarantor who expresses his guarantee by the words "guaranteed", "payment guaranteed" or "collection guaranteed", or words of similar import, may set up against a protected holder only those defences which the person for whom he has become a guarantor may set up against a protected holder under paragraph 1 of article 30;
- (c) A guarantor who expresses his guarantee by the words "*aval*" or "good as *aval*" may set up against a protected holder only:
  - (i) The defence, under paragraph 1(b) of article 30, that the protected holder obtained the signature on the instrument of the person for whom he has become a guarantor by a fraudulent act;
  - (ii) The defence, under article 53 or article 57, that the instrument was not presented for acceptance or for payment;
  - (iii) the defence, under article 63, that the instrument was not duly protested for non-acceptance or for non-payment;
  - (iv) The defence, under article 84, that a right of action may no longer be exercised against the person for whom he has become guarantor;
- (d) A guarantor who is not a bank or other financial institution and who expresses his guarantee by a signature alone may set up against a protected holder only the defences referred to in subparagraph (b) of this paragraph;

(*e*) A guarantor which is a bank or other financial institution and which expresses its guarantee by a signature alone may set up against a protected holder only the defences referred to in subparagraph (*c*) of this paragraph.

Article 48

1. Payment of an instrument by the guarantor in accordance with article 72 discharges the party for whom he became guarantor of his liabilities on the instrument to the extent of the amount paid.

2. The guarantor who pays the instrument may recover from the party for whom he has become guarantor and from the parties who are liable on it to that party the amount paid and any interest.

CHAPTER V. PRESENTMENT, DISHONOUR BY NON-ACCEPTANCE OR NON-PAYMENT, AND RECOURSE

SECTION I. PRESENTMENT FOR ACCEPTANCE AND DISHONOUR BY NON-ACCEPTANCE

Article 49

1. A bill may be presented for acceptance.
2. A bill must be presented for acceptance:
   (*a*) If the drawer has stipulated in the bill that it must be presented for acceptance;
   (*b*) If the bill is payable at a fixed period after sight; or
   (*c*) If the bill is payable elsewhere than at the residence or place of business of the drawee, unless it is payable on demand.

Article 50

1. The drawer may stipulate in the bill that it must not be presented for acceptance before a specified date or before the occurrence of a specified event. Except where a bill must be presented for acceptance under paragraph 2(*b*) or (*c*) of article 49, the drawer may stipulate that it must not be presented for acceptance.

2. If a bill is presented for acceptance notwithstanding a stipulation permitted under paragraph 1 of this article and acceptance is refused, the bill is not thereby dishonoured.

3. If the drawee accepts a bill notwithstanding a stipulation that it must not be presented for acceptance, the acceptance is effective.

Article 51

A bill is duly presented for acceptance if it is presented in accordance with the following rules:
   (*a*) The holder must present the bill to the drawee on a business day at a reasonable hour;
   (*b*) Presentment for acceptance may be made to a person or authority other than the drawee if that person or authority is entitled under the applicable law to accept the bill;
   (*c*) If a bill is payable on a fixed date, presentment for acceptance must be made before or on that date;

    (*d*) A bill payable on demand or at a fixed period after sight must be presented for acceptance within one year of its date;

    (*e*) A bill in which the drawer has staed a date or time-limit for presentment for acceptance must be presented on the stated date or within the stated time-limit.

Article 52

1. A necessary or optional presentment for acceptance is dispensed with if:

    (*a*) The drawee is dead, or no longer has the power freely to deal with his assets by reason of his insolvency, or is a fictitious person, or is a person not having capacity to incur liability on the instrument as an acceptor; or

    (*b*) The drawee is a corporation, partnership, association or other legal entity which has ceased to exist.

2. A necessary presentment for acceptance is dispensed with if:

    (*a*) A bill is payable on a fixed date, and presentment for acceptance cannot be effected before or on that date due to circumstances which are beyond the control of the holder and which he could neither avoid nor overcome; or

    (*b*) A bill is payable at a fixed period after sight, and presentment for acceptance cannot be effected within one year of its date due to circumstances which are beyond the control of the holder and which he could neither avoid nor overcome.

3. Subject to paragraphs 1 and 2 of this article, delay in a necessary presentment for acceptance is excused, but presentment for acceptance is not dispensed with, if the bill is drawn with a stipulation that it must be presented for acceptance within a stated time-limit, and the delay in presentment for acceptance is caused by circumstances which are beyond the control of the holder and which he could neither avoid nor overcome. When the cause of the delay ceases to operate, presentment must be made with reasonable diligence.

Article 53

1. If a bill which must be presented for acceptance is not so presented, the drawer, the endorsers and their guarantors are not liable on the bill.

2. Failure to present a bill for acceptance does not discharge the guarantor of the drawee of liability on the bill.

Article 54

1. A bill is considered to be dishonoured by non-acceptance:

    (*a*) If the drawee, upon the presentment, expressly refuses to accept the bill or acceptance cannot be obtained with reasonable diligence or if the holder cannot obtain the acceptance to which he is entitled under this Convention;

    (*b*) If presentment for acceptance is dispensed with pursuant to article 52, unless the bill is in fact accepted.

2. (*a*) If a bill is dishonoured by non-acceptance in accordance with paragraph 1(*a*) of this article, the holder may exercise an immediate right of recourse against the drawer, the endorsers and their guarantors, subject to the provisions of article 59.

(*b*) If a bill is dishonoured by non-acceptance in accordance with paragraph 1(*b*) of this article, the holder may exercise an immediate right of recourse against the drawer, the endorsers and their guarantors.

(*c*) If a bill is dishonoured by non-acceptance in accordance with paragraph 1 of this article, the holder may claim payment from the guarantor of the drawee upon any necessary protest.

3. If a bill payable on demand is presented for acceptance, but acceptance is refused, it is not considered to be dishonoured by non-acceptance.

SECTION 2. PRESENTMENT FOR PAYMENT AND DISHONOUR BY NON-PAYMENT

Article 55

An instrument is duly for payment if it is presented in accordance with the following rules:

(a) The holder must present the instrument to the drawee or to the acceptor or to the maker on a business day at a reasonable hour;

(b) A note signed by two or more makers may be presented to any one of them, unless the note clearly indicates otherwise;

(c) If the drawee or the acceptor or the maker is dead, presentment must be made to the persons who under the applicable law are his heirs or the persons entitled to administer his estate;

(d) Presentment for payment may be made to a person or authority other than the drawee, the acceptor or the maker if that person or authority is entitled under the applicable law to pay the instrument;

(e) An insrument which is not payable on demand must be presented for payment on the date of maturity or on one of the two business days which follow;

(f) An instrument which is payable on demand must be presented for payment within one year of its date;

(g) An instrument must be presented for payment:
   (i) At the place of payment specified on the instrument;
   (ii) If no place of payment is specified, at the address of the drawee or the acceptor or the maker indicated in the instrument; or
   (iii) If no place of payment is specified and the address of the drawee or the acceptor or the maker is not indicated, at the principal place of business or habitual residence of the drawee or the acceptor or the maker;

(h) An instrument which is presented at a clearing-house is duly presented for payment if the law of the place where the clearing-house is located or the rules or customs of that clearing-house so provide.

Article 56

1. Delay in making presentment for payment is excused if the delay is caused by circumstances which are beyond the control of the holder and which he could neither avoid nor overcome. When the cause of the delay ceases to operate, presentment must be made with reasonable diligence.

2. Presentment for payment is dispensed with:

(a) If the drawer, an endorser or a guarantor has expressly waived presentment; such waiver:
   (i) If made on the instrument by the drawer, binds any subsequent party and benefits any holder;
   (ii) If made on the instrument by a party other than the drawer, binds only that party but benefits any holder;
   (iii) If made outside the instrument, binds only the party making it and benefits only a holder in whose favour it was made;

(b) If an instrument is not payable on demand, and the cause of delay in making presentment referred to in paragraph 1 of this article continues to operate beyond thirty days after maturity;

(c) If an instrument is payable on demand, and the cause of delay in making presentment referred to in paragraph 1 of this article continues to operate beyond thirty days after the expiration of the time-limit for presentment for payment;

(d) If the drawee, the maker or the acceptor has no longer the power freely to deal with his assets by reason of his insolvency, or is a fictitious person or a person not having capacity to make payment, or if the drawee, the maker or the acceptor is a corporation, partnership, association or other legal entity which has ceased to exist;

(e) If there is no place at which the instrument must be presented in accordance with subparagraph (g) of article 55.

3. Presentment for payment is also dispensed with as regards a bill, if the bill has been protested for dishonour by non-acceptance.

Article 57

1. If an instrument is not duly presented for payment, the drawer, the endorsers and their guarantors are not liable on it.

2. Failure to present an instrument for payment does not discharge the acceptor, the maker and their guarantors or the guarantor of the drawee of liability on it.

Article 58

1. An instrument is considered to be dishonoured by non-payment:
   (a) If payment is refused upon due presentment or if the holder cannot obtain the payment to which he is entitled under this Convention;
   (b) If presentment for payment is dispensed with pursuant to paragraph 2 of article 56 and the instrument is unpaid at maturity.

2. If a bill is dishonoured by non-payment, the holder may, subject to the provisions of article 59, exercise a right of recourse against the drawer, the endorsers and their guarantors.

3. If a note is dishonoured by non-payment, the holder may, subject to the provisions of article 59, exercise a right of recourse against the endorsers and their guarantors.

SECTION 3. RECOURSE

Article 59

If an instrument is dishonoured by non-acceptance or by non-payment, the holder may exercise a right of recourse only after the instrument has been duly protested for dishonour in accordance with the provisions of articles 60 to 62.

A. Protest

Article 60

1. A protest is a statement of dishonour drawn up at the place where the instrument has been dishonoured and signed and dated by a person authorized in that respect by the law of that place. The statement must specify:
   (a) The person at whose request the instrument is protested;
   (b) The place of protest;
   (c) The demand made and the answer given, if any, or the fact that the drawee or the acceptor or the maker could not be found.

2. A protest may be made:
   (a) On the instrument or on a slip affixed thereto (*"allonge"*); or
   (b) As a separate document, in which case it must clearly identify the instrument that has been dishonoured.

3. Unless the instrument stipulates that protest must be made, a protest may be replaced by a declaration written on the instrument and signed and dated by the drawee or the acceptor or the maker, or, in the case of an instrument domiciled with a named person for payment, by that named person; the declaration must be to the effect that acceptance or payment is refused.

4. A declaration made in accordance with paragraph 3 of this article is a protest for the purpose of this Convention.

Article 61

Protest for dishonour of an instrument by non-acceptance or by non-payment must be made on the day on which the instrument is dishonoured or on one of the four business days which follow.

Article 62

1. Delay in protesting an instrument for dishonour is excused if the delay is caused by circumstances which are beyond the control of the holder and which he could neither avoid nor overcome. When the cause of the delay ceases to operate, protest must be made with reasonable diligence.

2. Protest for dishonour by non-acceptance or by non-payment is dispensed with:
   (a) If the drawer, an endorser or a guarantor has expressly waived protest; such waiver:
       (i) If made on the instrument by the drawer, binds any subsequent party and benefits any holder;
       (ii) If made on the instrument by a party other than the drawer, binds only that party but benefits any holder;
       (iii) If made outside the instrument, binds only the party making it and benefits only a holder in whose favour it was made;
   (b) If the cause of the delay in making protest referred to in paragraph 1 of this article continues to operate beyond thirty days after the date of dishonour;
   (c) As regards the drawer of a bill, if the drawer and the drawee or the acceptor are the same person;
   (d) If presentment for acceptance or for payment is dispensed with in accordance with article 52 or paragraph 2 of article 56.

Article 63

1. If an instrument which must be protested for non-acceptance or for non-payment is not duly protested, the drawer, the endorsers and their guarantors are not liable on it.

2. Failure to protest an instrument does not discharge the acceptor, the maker and their guarantors or the guarantor of the drawee of liability on it.

B. Notice of dishonour

Article 64

1. The holder, upon dishonour of an instrument by non-acceptance or by non-payment, must give notice of such dishonour;

(*a*) To the drawer and the last endorser;

(*b*) To all other endorsers and guarantors whose addresses the holder can ascertain on the basis of information contained in the instrument.

2. An endorser or a guarantor who receives notice must give notice of dishonour to the last party preceding him and liable on the instrument.

3. Notice of dishonour operates for the benefit of any party who has a right of recourse on the instrument against the party notified.

Article 65

1. Notice of dishonour may be given in any form whatever and in any terms which identify the instrument and state that it has been dishonoured. The return of the dishonoured instrument is sufficient notice, provided it is accompanied by a statement indicating that it has been dishonoured.

2. Notice of dishonour is duly given if it is communicated or sent to the party to be notified by means appropriate in the circumstances, whether or not it is received by that party.

3. The burden of proving that notice has been duly given rests upon the person who is required to give such notice.

Article 66

Notice of dishonour must be given within the two business days which follow:

(*a*) The day of protest or, if protest is dispensed with, the day of dishonour; or

(*b*) The day of receipt of notice of dishonour.

Article 67

1. Delay in giving notice of dishonour is excused if the delay is caused by circumstances which are beyond the control of the person required to give notice, and which he could neither avoid nor overcome. When the cause of the delay ceases to operate, notice must be given with reasonable diligence.

2. Notice of dishonour is dispensed with:

(*a*) If, after the exercise of reasonable diligence, notice cannot be given;

(*b*) If the drawer, an endorser or a guarantor has expressly waived notice of dishonour; such waiver:

  (i) If made on the instrument by the drawer, binds any subsequent party and benefit any holder;

  (ii) If made on the instrument by a party other than the drawer, binds only that party but benefits any holder;

  (iii) If made outside the instrument, binds only the party making it and benefits only a holder in whose favour it was made;

(*c*) As regards the drawer of the bill, if the drawer and the drawee or the acceptor are the same person.

Article 68

If a person who is required to give notice of dishonour fails to give it to a party who is entitled to receive it, he is liable for any damages which that party may suffer from such failure, provided that such damages do not exceed the amount referred to in article 70 or article 71.

SECTION 4. AMOUNT PAYABLE

Article 69

1. The holder may exercise his rights on the instrument against any one party, or several or all parties, liable on it and is not obliged to observe the order in which the parties have become bound. Any party who takes up and pays the instrument may exercise his rights in the same manner against parties liable to him.

2. Proceedings against a party do not preclude proceedings against any other party, whether or not subsequent to the party originally proceeded against.

Article 70

1. The holder may recover from any party liable:
   (a) At maturity: the amount of the instrument with interest, if interest has been stipulated for;
   (b) After maturity:
       (i) The amount of the instrument with interest, if interest has been stipulated for, to the date of maturity;
       (ii) If interest has been stipulated to be paid after maturity, interest at the rate stipulated or, in the absence of such stipulation, interest at the rate specified in paragraph 2 of this article, calculated from the date of presentment on the sum specified in subparagraph (b) (i) of this paragraph;
       (iii) Any expenses of protest and of the notices given by him;
   (c) Before maturity:
       (i) The amount of the instrument with interest, if interest has been stipulated for, to the date of payment; or, if no interest has been stipulated for, subject to a discount from the date of payment to the date of maturity, calculated in accordance with paragraph 4 of this article;
       (ii) Any expenses of protest and of the notices given by him.

2. The rate of interest shall be the rate that would be recoverable in legal proceedings taken in the jurisdiction where the instrument is payable.

3. Nothing in paragraph 2 of this article prevents a court from awarding damages or compensation for additional loss caused to the holder by reason of delay in payment.

4. The discount shall be at the official rate (discount rate) or other similar appropriate rate effective on the date when recourse is exercised at the place where the holder has his principal place of business, or, if he does not have a place of business, his habitual residence, or, if there is no such rate, than at such rate as is reasonable in the circumstances.

Article 71

A party who pays an instrument and is thereby discharged in whole or in part of his liability on the instrument may recover from the parties liable to him:
   (a) The entire sum which he has paid;
   (b) Interest on that sum at the rate specified in paragraph 2 of article 70, from the date on which he made payment;
   (c) Any expenses of the notices given by him.

CHAPTER VI. DISCHARGE

Article 72

1. A party is discharged of liability on the instrument when he pays the holder, or a party subsequent to himself who has paid the instrument and is in possession of it, the amount due pursuant to article 70 or article 71:

(a) At or after maturity; or

(b) Before maturity, upon dishonour by non-acceptance.

2. Payment before maturity other than under paragraph 1(b) of this article does not discharge the party making the payment of his liability on the instrument except in respect of the person to whom payment was made.

3. A party is not discharged of liability if he pays a holder who is not a protected holder, or a party who has taken up and paid the instrument, and knows at the time of payment that the holder or that party acquired the instrument by theft or forged the signature of the payee or an endorsee, or participated in the theft or the forgery.

4. (a) A person receiving payment of an instrument must, unless agreed otherwise, deliver:

(i) To the drawee making such payment, the instrument;

(ii) To any other person making such payment, the instrument, a receipted account, and any protest.

(b) In the case of an instrument payable by instalments at successive dates, the drawee or a party making a payment, other than payment of the last instalment, may require that mention of such payment be made on the instrument or on a slip affixed thereto ("allonge") and that a receipt therefor be given to him.

(c) If an instrument payable by instalments at successive dates is dishonoured by non-acceptance or by non-payment as to any of its instalments and a party, upon dishonour, pays the instalment, the holder who receives such payment must give the party a certified copy of the instrument and any necessary authenticated protest in order to enable such party to exercise a right on the instrument.

(d) The person from whom payment is demanded may withhold payment if the person demanding payment does not deliver the instrument to him. Withholding payment in these circumstances does not constitute dishonour by non-payment under article 58.

(e) If payment is made but the person paying, other than the drawee, fails to obtain the instrument, such person is discharged but the discharge cannot be set up as a defence against a protected holder to whom the instrument has been subsequently transferred.

Article 73

1. The holder is not obliged to take partial payment.

2. If the holder who is offered partial payment does not take it, the instrument is dishonoured by non-payment.

3. If the holder takes partial payment from the drawee, the guarantor of the drawee, or the acceptor or the maker:

(a) The guarantor of the drawee, or the acceptor or the maker is discharged of his liability on the instrument to the extent of the amount paid;

(b) The instrument is to be considered as dishonoured by non-payment as to the amount unpaid.

4. If the holder takes partial payment from a party to the instrument other than the acceptor, the maker or the guarantor of the drawee:

(*a*) The party making payment is discharged of his liability on the instrument to the extent of the amount paid;

(*b*) The holder must give such party a certified copy of the instrument and any necessary authenticated protest in order to enable such party to exercise a right on the instrument. .

5. The drawee or a party making partial payment may require that mention of such payment be made on the instrument and that a receipt therefore be given to him.

6. If the balance is paid, the person who receives it and who is in possession of the instrument must deliver to the payor the receipted instrument and any authenticated protest.

Article 74

1. The holder may refuse to take payment at a place other than the place where the instrument was presented for payment in accordance with article 55.

2. In such case if payment is not made at the place where the instrument was presented for payment in accordance with article 55, the instrument is considered to be dishonoured by non-payment.

Article 75

1. An instrument must be paid in the currency in which the sum payable is expressed.

2. If the sum payable is expressed in a monetary unit of account within the meaning of subparagraph (*l*) of article 5 and the monetary unit of account is transferable between the person making payment and the person receiving it, then, unless the instrument specifies a currency of payment, payment shall be made by transfer of monetary units of account. If the monetary unit of account is not transferable between those persons, payment shall be made in the currency specified in the instrument or, if no such currency is specified, in the currency of the place of payment.

3. The drawer or the maker may indicate in the instrument that it must be paid in a specified currency other than the currency in which the sum payable is expressed. In that case:

(*a*) The instrument must be paid in the currency so specified;

(*b*) The amount payable is to be calculated according to the rate of exchange indicated in the instrument. Failing such indication, the amount payable is to be calculated according to the rate of exchange for sight drafts (or, if there is no such rate, according to the appropriate established rate of exchange) on the date of maturity:

    (i) Ruling at the place where the instrument must be presented for payment in accordance with subparagraph (*g*) of article 55, if the specified currency is that of that place (local currency); or

    (ii) If the specified currency is not that of that place, according to the usages of the place where the instrument must be presented for payment in accordance with subparagraph (*g*) of article 55;

(*c*) If such an instrument is dishonoured by non-acceptance, the amount payable is to be calculated:

    (i) If the rate of exchange is indicated in the instrument, according to that rate;

    (ii) If no rate of exchange is indicated in the instrument, at the option of the holder, according to the rate of exchange ruling on the date of dishonour or on the date of actual payment;

(*d*) If such an instrument is dishonoured by non-payment, the amount payable is to be calculated:

    (i) If the rate of exchange is indicated in the instrument, according to that rate;

    (ii) If no rate of exchange is indicated in the instrument, at the option of the holder, according to the rate of exchange ruling on the date of maturity or on the date of actual payment.

4. Nothing in this article prevents a court from awarding damages for loss caused to the holder by reason of fluctuations in rates of exchange if such loss is caused by dishonour for non-acceptance or by non-payment.

5. The rate of exchange ruling at a certain date is the rate of exchange ruling, at the option of the holder, at the place where the instrument must be presented for payment in accordance with subparagraph (*g*) of article 55 or at the place of actual payment.

Article 76

1. Nothing in this Convention prevents a Contracting State from enforcing exchange control regulations applicable in its territory and its provisions relating to the protection of its currency, including regulations which it is bound to apply by virtue of international agreements to which it is a party.

2. (*a*) If, by virtue of the applications of paragraph 1 of this article, an instrument drawn in a currency which is not that of the place of payment must be paid in local currency, the amount payable is to be calculated according to the rate of exchange for sight drafts (or, if there is no such rate, according to the appropriate established rate of exchange) on the date of presentment ruling at the place where the instrument must be presented for payment in accordance with subparagraph (*g*) of article 55.

  (*b*) (i) If such an instrument is dishonoured by non-acceptance, the amount payable is to be calculated, at the option of the holder, at the rate of exchange ruling on the date of dishonour or on the date of actual payment.

    (ii) If such an instrument is dishonoured by non-payment, the amount is to be calculated, at the option of the holder, according to the rate of exchange ruling on the date of presentment or on the date of actual payment.

  (iii) Paragraphs 4 and 5 of article 75 are applicable where appropriate.

SECTION 2. DISCHARGE OF OTHER PARTIES

Article 77

1. If a party is discharged in whole or in part of his liability on the instrument, any party who has a right on the instrument against him is discharged to the same extent.

2. Payment by the drawee of the whole or a part of the amount of a bill to the holder, or to any party who takes up and pays the bill, discharges all parties of their liability to the same extent, except where the drawee pays a holder who is not a protected holder, or a party who has taken up and paid the bill, and knows at the time of payment that the holder or that party acquired the bill by theft or forged the signature of the payee or an endorsee, or participated in the theft or the forgery.

CHAPTER VII. LOST INSTRUMENTS

Article 78

1. If an instrument is lost, whether by destruction, theft or otherwise, the person who lost the instrument has, subject to the provisions of paragraph 2 of this article, the same

right to payment which he would have had if he had been in possession of the instrument. The party from whom payment is claimed cannot set up as a defence against liability on the instrument the fact that the person claiming payment is not in possession of the instrument.

2. (*a*) The person claiming payment of a lost instrument must state in writing to the party from whom he claims payment:

(i) The elements of the lost instrument pertaining to the requirements set forth in paragraph 1 or paragraph 2 of articles 1, 2 and 3; for this purpose the person claiming payment of the lost instrument may present to that party a copy of that instrument;

(ii) The facts showing that, if he had been in possession of the instrument, he would have had a right to payment from the party from whom payment is claimed;

(iii) The facts which prevent production of the instrument.

(*b*) The party from whom payment of a lost instrument is claimed may require the person claiming payment to give security in order to idemnify him for any loss which he may suffer by reason of the subsequent payment of the lost instrument.

(*c*) The nature of the security and its terms are to be determined by agreement between the person claiming payment and the party from whom payment is claimed. Failing such an agreement, the court may determine whether security is called for and, if so, the nature of the security and its terms.

(*d*) If the security cannot be given, the court may order the party from whom payment is claimed to deposit the sum of the lost instrument, and any interest and expenses which may be claimed under article 70 or article 71, with the court or any other competent authority or institution, and may determine the duration of such deposit. Such deposit is to be considered as payment to the person claiming payment.

Article 79

1. A party who has paid a lost instrument and to whom the instrument is subsequently presented for payment by another person must give notice of such presentment to the person whom he paid.

2. Such notice must be given on the day the instrument is presented or on one of the two business days which follow and must state the name of the person presenting the instrument and the date and place of presentment.

3. Failure to give notice renders the party who has paid the lost instrument liable for any damages which the person whom he paid may suffer from such failure, provided that the damages do not exceed the amount referred to in article 70 or article 71.

4. Delay in giving notice is excused when the delay is caused by circumstances which are beyond the control of the person who has paid the lost instrument and which he could neither avoid nor overcome. When the cause of the delay ceases to operate, notice must be given with reasonable diligence.

5. Notice is dispensed with when the cause of delay in giving notice continues to operate beyond thirty days after the last day on which it should have been given.

Article 80

1. A party who had paid a lost instrument in accordance with the provisions of article 78 and who is subsequently required to, and does, pay the instrument, or who, by reason of the loss of the instrument, then loses his right to recover from any party liable to him, has the right:

(*a*) If security was given, to realize the security; or

(*b*) If an amount was deposited with the court or other competent authority or institution, to reclaim the amount so deposited.

2. The person who has given security in accordance with the provisions of paragraph 2(*b*) of article 78 is entitled to obtain release of the security when the party for whose benefit the security was given is no longer at risk to suffer loss because of the fact that the instrument is lost.

Article 81

For the purposes of making protest for dishonour by non-payment, a person claiming payment of a lost instrument may use a written statement that satisfies the requirements of paragraph 2(*a*) of article 78.

Article 82

A person receiving payment of a lost instrument in accordance with article 78 must deliver to the party paying the written statement required under paragraph 2(*a*) of article 78, receipted by him, and any protest and a receipted account.

Article 83

1. A party who pays a lost instrument in accordance with article 78 has the same rights which he would have had if he had been in possession of the instrument.

2. Such party may exercise his rights only if he is in possession of the receipted written statement referred to in article 82.

CHAPTER VIII. LIMITATION (PRESCRIPTION)

Article 84

1. A right of action arising on an instrument may no longer be exercised after four years have elapsed:
(*a*) Against the maker, or his guarantor, of a note payable on demand, from the date of the note;
(*b*) Against the acceptor or the maker or their guarantor of an instrument payable at a definite time, from the date of maturity;
(*c*) Against the guarantor of the drawee of a bill payable at a definite time, from the date of maturity or, if the bill is dishonoured by non-acceptance, from the date of protest for dishonour or, where protest is dispensed with, from the date of dishonour;
(*d*) Against the acceptor of a bill payable on demand or his guarantor, from the date on which it was accepted or, if no such date is shown, from the date of the bill;
(*e*) Against the guarantor of the drawee of a bill payable on demand, from the date on which he signed the bill or, if no such date is shown, from the date of the bill;
(*f*) Against the drawer or an endorser or their guarantor, from the date of protest for dishonour by non-acceptance or by non-payment or, where protest is dispensed with, from the date of dishonour.

2. A party who pays the instrument in accordance with article 70 or article 71 may exercise his right of action against a party liable to him within one year from the date on which he paid the instrument.

CHAPTER IX. FINAL PROVISIONS

Article 85

The Secretary-General of the United Nations is hereby designated as the Depositary for this Convention.

Article 86

1. This Convention is open for signature by all States at the Headquarters of the United Nations, New York, until 30 June 1990.

2. This Convention is subject to ratification, acceptance or approval by the signatory States.

3. This Convention is open for accession by all States which are not signatory States as from the date it is open for signature.

4. Instruments of ratification, acceptance, approval and accession are to be deposited with the Secretary-General of the United Nations.

Article 87

1. If a Contracting State has two or more territorial units in which, according to its constitution, different systems of law are applicable in relation to the matters dealt with in this Convention, it may, at the time of signature, ratification, acceptance, approval or accession, declare that this Convention is to extend to all its territorial units or only to one or more of them, and may amend its declarations by submitting another declaration at any time.

2. These declarations are to be notified to the Depositary and are to state expressly the territorial units to which the Convention extends.

3. If a Contracting State makes no declaration under paragraph 1 of this article, the Convention is to extend to all territorial units of that State.

Article 88

1. Any State may declare at the time of signature, ratification, acceptance, approval or accession that its courts will apply the convention only if both the place indicated in the instrument where the bill is drawn, or the note is made, and the place of payment indicated in the instrument are situated in Contracting States.

2. No other reservations are permitted.

Article 89

1. This Convention enters into force on the first day of the month following the expiration of twelve months after the date of deposit of the tenth instrument of ratification, acceptance, approval or accession.

2. When a State ratifies, accepts, approves or accedes to this Convention after the deposit of the tenth instrument of ratification, acceptance, approval or accession, this Convention enters into force in respect of that State on the first day of the month following the expiration of twelve months after the date of deposit of its instrument of ratification, acceptance, approval or accession.

Article 90

1. A Contracting State may denounce this Convention by a formal notification in writing addressed to the Depositary.

2. The denunciation takes effect on the first day of the month following the expiration of six months after the notification is received by the Depositary. Where a longer period for the denunciation to take effect is specified in the notification, the denunciation takes effect upon the expiration of such longer period after the notification is received by the Depositary. The Convention remains applicable to instruments drawn or made before the date at which the denunciation takes effect.

DONE at . . . , this . . . day of . . . , one thousand nine hundred and . . . and in a single original, of which the Arabic, Chinese, English, French, Russian and Spanish texts are equally authentic.

IN WITNESS WHEREOF the undersigned plenipotentiaries, being duly authorized by their respective Governments, have signed this Convention.

APPENDIX 7

THE GENEVA CONVENTIONS 1930

UNIFORM LAW ON BILLS OF EXCHANGE PROMISSORY NOTES AND CHEQUES

TITLE I. BILLS OF EXCHANGE

CHAPTER I—ISSUE AND FORM OF A BILL OF EXCHANGE

Article 1

A bill of exchange contains:
1. The term "bill of exchange" inserted in the body of the instrument and expressed in the language employed in drawing up the instrument;
2. An unconditional order to pay a determinate sum of money;
3. The name of the person who is to pay (drawee);
4. A statement of the time of payment;
5. A statement of the place where payment is to be made;
6. The name of the person to whom or to whose order payment is to be made;
7. A statement of the date and of the place where the bill is issued;
8. The signature of the person who issues the bill (drawer).

Article 2

An instrument in which any of the requirements mentioned in the preceding article is wanting is invalid as a bill of exchange, except in the cases specified in the following paragraphs:

A bill of exchange in which the time of payment is not specified is deemed to be payable at sight.

In default of special mention, the place specified beside the name of the drawee is deemed to be the place of payment, and at the same time the place of the domicile of the drawee.

A bill of exchange which does not mention the place of its issue is deemed to have been drawn in the place mentioned beside the name of the drawer.

Article 3

A bill of exchange may be drawn payable to drawer's order.

It may be drawn on the drawer himself.

It may be drawn for account of a third person.

Article 4

A bill of exchange may be payable at the domicile of a third person either in the locality where the drawee has his domicile or in another locality.

Article 5

When a bill of exchange is payable at sight, or at a fixed period after sight, the drawer may stipulate that the sum payable shall bear interest. In the case of any other bill of exchange, this stipulation is deemed not to be written (*non écrite*).

The rate of interest must be specified in the bill; in default of such specification, the stipulation shall be deemed not to be written (*non écrite*).

Interest runs from the date of the bill of exchange, unless some other date is specified.

Article 6

When the sum payable by a bill of exchange is expressed in words and also in figures, and there is a discrepancy between the two, the sum denoted by the words is the amount payable.

Where the sum payable by a bill of exchange is expressed more than once in words or more than once in figures, and there is a discrepancy, the smaller sum is the sum payable.

Article 7

If a bill of exchange bears signatures of persons incapable of binding themselves by a bill of exchange, or forged signatures, or signatures of fictitious persons, or signatures which for any other reason cannot bind the persons who signed the bill of exchange or on whose behalf it was signed, the obligations of the other persons who signed it are none the less valid.

Article 8

Whosoever puts his signature on a bill of exchange as representing a person for whom he had no power to act is bound himself as a party to the bill and, if he pays, has the same rights as the person for whom he purported to act. The same rule applies to a representative who has exceeded his powers.

Article 9

The drawer guarantees both acceptance and payment.

He may release himself from guaranteeing acceptance; every stipulation by which he releases himself from the guarantee of payment is deemed not to be written (*non écrite*).

Article 10

If a bill of exchange, which was incomplete when issued, has been completed otherwise than in accordance with the agreements entered into, the non-observance of such agreements may not be set up against the holder unless he has acquired the bill of exchange in bad faith or, in acquiring it, has been guilty of gross negligence.

CHAPTER II—ENDORSEMENT

Article 11

Every bill of exchange, even if not expressly drawn to order, may be transferred by means of endorsement.

When the drawer has inserted in a bill of exchange the words "not to order" or an equivalent expression, the instrument can only be transferred according to the form, and with the effects of an ordinary assignment.

The bill may be endorsed even in favour of the drawee, whether he has accepted or not, or of the drawer, or of any other party to the bill. These persons may re-endorse the bill.

Article 21

An endorsement must be unconditional. Any condition to which it is made subject is deemed not to be written (*non écrite*).

A partial endorsement is null and void.

An endorsement "to bearer" is equivalent to an endorsement in blank.

Article 13

An endorsement must be written on the bill of exchange or on a slip affixed thereto (*allonge*). It must be signed by the endorser.

The endorsement may leave the beneficiary unspecified or may consist simply of the signature of the endorser (endorsement in blank). In the latter case, the endorsement, to be valid, must be written on the back of the bill of exchange or on the slip attached thereto (*allonge*).

Article 14

An endorsement transfers all the rights arising out of a bill of exchange.

If the endorsement is in blank, the holder may:
(1) Fill up the blank either with his own name or with the name of some other person;
(2) Re-endorse the bill in blank, or to some other person;
(3) Transfer the bill to a third person without filling up the blank, and without endorsing it.

Article 15

In the absence of any contrary stipulation, the endorser guarantees acceptance and payment.

He may prohibit any further endorsement; in this case, he gives no guarantee to the persons to whom the bill is subsequently endorsed.

Article 16

The possessor of a bill of exchange is deemed to be the lawful holder if he establishes his title to the bill through an uninterrupted series of endorsements, even if the last endorsement is in blank. In this connection, cancelled endorsements are deemed not to be written (*non écrits*). When an endorsement in blank is followed by another endorsement, the person who signed this last endorsement is deemed to have acquired the bill by the endorsement in blank.

Where a person has been dispossessed of a bill of exchange, in any manner whatsoever, the holder who establishes his right thereto in the manner mentioned in the preceding paragraph is not bound to give up the bill unless he has acquired it in bad faith, or unless in acquiring it he has been guity of gross negligence.

Article 17

Persons sued on a bill of exchange cannot set up against the holder defences founded on their personal relations with the drawer or with previous holders, unless the holder, in acquiring the bill, has knowingly acted to the detriment of the debtor.

Article 18

When an endorsement contains the statements "value in connection" ("*valeur en recouvrement*"), "for collection" ("*pour encaissement*"), "by procuration" ("*par procuration*") or any other phrase implying a simple mandate, the holder may exercise all rights arising out of the bill of exchange, but he can only endorse it in his capacity as agent.

In this case, the parties liable can only set up against the holder defences which could be set up against the endorser.

The mandate contained in an endorsement by procuration does not terminate by reason of the death of the party giving the mandate or by reason of his becoming legally incapable.

Article 19

When an endorsement contains the statements "value in security" ("*valeur en garantie*"), "value in pledge" ("*valeur en gage*"), or any other statement implying a pledge, the holder may exercise all the rights arising out of the bill of exchange, but an endorsement by him has the effects only of an endorsement by an agent.

The parties liable cannot set up against the holder defences founded on their personal relations with the endorser, unless the holder, in receiving the bill, has knowingly acted to the detriment of the debtor.

Article 20

An endorsement after maturity has the same effects as an endorsement before maturity. Nevertheless, an endorsement after protest for non-payment, or after the expiration of the limit of time fixed for drawing up the protest, operates only as an ordinary assignment.

Failing proof to the contrary, an endorsement without date is deemed to have been placed on the bill before the expiration of the limit of time fixed for drawing up the protest.

CHAPTER III — ACCEPTANCE

Article 21

Until maturity, a bill of exchange may be presented to the drawee for acceptance at his domicile, either by the holder or by a person who is merely in possession of the bill.

Article 22

In any bill of exchange, the drawer may stipulate that it shall be presented for acceptance with or without fixing a limit of time for presentment.

Except in the case of a bill payable at the address of a third party or in a locality other than that of the domicile of the drawee, or, except in the case of a bill drawn payable at a fixed period after sight, the drawer may prohibit presentment for acceptance.

He may also stipulate that presentment for acceptance shall not take place before a named date.

Unless the drawer has prohibited acceptance, every endorser may stipulate that the bill shall be presented for acceptance, with or without fixing a limit of time for presentment.

Article 23

Bills of exchange payable at a fixed period after sight must be presented for acceptance within one year of their date.

The drawer may abridge or extend this period.

These periods may be abridged by the endorsers.

Article 24

The drawee may demand that a bill shall be presented to him a second time on the day after the first presentment. Parties interested are not allowed to set up that this demand has not been complied with unless this request is mentioned in the protest.

The holder is not obliged to surrender to the drawee a bill presented for acceptance.

Article 25

An acceptance is written on the bill of exchange. It is expressed by the word "accepted" or any other equivalent term. It is signed by the drawee. The simple signature of the drawee on the face of the bill constitutes an acceptance.

When the bill is payable at a certain time after sight, or when it must be presented for acceptance within a certain limit of time in accordance with a special stipulation, the acceptance must be dated as of the day when the acceptance is given, unless the holder requires that it shall be dated as of the day of presentment. If it is undated, the holder, in order to preserve his right of recourse against the endorsers and the drawer, must authenticate the omission by a protest drawn up within the proper time.

Article 26

An acceptance is unconditional, but the drawee may restrict it to part of the sum payable.

Every other modification introduced by an acceptance into the tenor of the bill of exchange operates as a refusal to accept. Nevertheless, the acceptor is bound according to the terms of his acceptance.

Article 27

When the drawer of a bill has indicated a place of payment other than the domicile of the drawee without specifying a third party at whose address payment must be made, the drawee may name such third party at the time of acceptance. In default of this indication, the acceptor is deemed to have undertaken to pay the bill himself at the place of payment.

If a bill is payable at the domicile of the drawee, the latter may in his acceptance indicate an address in the same place where payment is to be made.

Article 28

By accepting, the drawee undertakes to pay the bill of exchange at its maturity.

In default of payment, the holder, even if he is the drawer, has a direct action on the bill of exchange against the acceptor for all that can be demanded in accordance with Articles 48 and 49.

Article 29

Where the drawee who has put his acceptance on a bill has cancelled it before restoring the bill, acceptance is deemed to be refused. Failing proof to the contrary, the cancellation is deemed to have taken place before the bill was restored.

Nevertheless, if the drawee has notified his acceptance in writing to the holder or to any party who has signed the bill, he is liable to such parties according to the terms of his acceptance.

CHAPTER IV — "AVALS"

Article 30

Payment of a bill of exchange may be guaranteed by an "aval" as to the whole or part of its amount.

This guarantee may be given by a third person or even by a person who has signed as a party to the bill.

Article 31

The "aval" is given either on the bill itself or on an "allonge".

It is expressed by the words "goods as aval" ("*bon pour aval*") or by any other equivalent formula. It is signed by the giver of the "aval".

It is deemed to be constituted by the mere signature of the giver of the "aval" placed on the face of the bill, except in the case of the signature of the drawee or of the drawer.

An "aval" must specify for whose account it is given. In default of this, it is deemed to be given for the drawer.

Article 32

The giver of an "aval" is bound in the same manner as the person for whom he has become guarantor.

His undertaking is valid even when the liability which he has guaranteed is inoperative for any reason other than defect of form.

He has, when he pays a bill of exchange, the rights arising out of the bill of exchange against the person guaranteed and against those who are liable to the latter on the bill of exchange.

CHAPTER V — MATURITY

Article 33

A bill of exchange may be drawn payable:
At sight;
At a fixed period after sight;
At a fixed period after date;

At a fixed date.

Bills of exchange at other maturities or payable by instalments are null and void.

Article 34

A bill of exchange at sight is payable on presentment. It must be presented for payment within a year of its date. The drawer may abridge or extend this period. These periods may be abridged by the endorsers.

The drawer may prescribe that a bill of exchange payable at sight must not be presented for payment before a named date. In this case, the period for presentment begins from the said date.

Article 35

The maturity of a bill of exchange payable at a fixed period after sight is determined either by the date of the acceptance or by the date of the protest.

In the absence of the protest, an undated acceptance is deemed, so far as regards the acceptor, to have been given on the last day of the limit of time for presentment for acceptance.

Article 36

Where a bill of exchange is drawn at one or more months after date or after sight, the bill matures on the corresponding date of the month when payment must be made. If there be no corresponding date, the bill matures on the last day of this month.

When a bill of exchange is drawn at one or more months and a half after date or sight, entire months must first be calculated.

If the maturity is fixed at the commencement, in the middle (mid-January or mid-February, etc.) or at the end of the month, the first, fifteenth or last day of the month is to be understood.

The expressions "eight days" or "fifteen days" indicate not one or two weeks, but a period of eight or fifteen actual days.

The expression "half month" means a period of fifteen days.

Article 37

When a bill of exchange is payable on a fixed day in a place where the calendar is different from the calendar in the place of issue, the day of maturity is deemed to be fixed according to the calendar of the place of payment.

When a bill of exchange drawn between two places having different calendars is payable at a fixed period after date, the day of issue is referred to the corresponding day of the calendar in the place of payment, and the maturity is fixed accordingly.

The time for presenting bills of exchange is calculated in accordance with the rules of the preceding paragraph.

These rules do not apply if a stipulation in the bill or even the simple terms of the instrument indicate an intention to adopt some different rule.

CHAPTER VI—PAYMENT

Article 38

The holder of a bill of exchange payable on a fixed day or at a fixed period after date or after sight must present the bill for payment either on the day on which it is payable or on one of the two business days which follow.

The presentment of a bill of exchange at a clearing-house is equivalent to a presentment for payment.

Article 39

The drawee who pays a bill of exchange may require that it shall be given up to him receipted by the holder.

The holder may not refuse partial payment.

In case of partial payment the drawee may require that mention of this payment shall be made on the bill, and that a receipt therefor shall be given to him.

Article 40

The holder of a bill of exchange cannot be compelled to receive payment thereof before maturity.

The drawee who pays before maturity does so at his own risk and peril.

He who pays at maturity is validly discharged, unless he has been guilty of fraud or gross negligence. He is bound to verify the regularity of the series of endorsements, but not the signature of the endorsers.

Article 41

When a bill of exchange is drawn payable in a currency which is not that of the place of payment, the sum payable may be paid in the currency of the country, according to its value on the date of maturity. If the debtor is in default, the holder may at his option demand that the amount of the bill be paid in the currency of the country according to the rate on the day of maturity or the day of payment.

The usages of the place of payment determine the value of foreign currency. Nevertheless, the drawer may stipulate that the sum payable shall be calculated according to a rate expressed in the bill.

The foregoing rules shall not apply to the case in which the drawer has stipulated that payment must be made in a certain specified currency (stipulation for effective payment in foreign currency).

If the amount of the bill of exchange is specified in a currency having the same denomination, but a different value in the country of issue and the country of payment, reference is deemed to be made to the currency of the place of payment.

Article 42

When a bill of exchange is not presented for payment within the limit of time fixed by Article 38, every debtor is authorised to deposit the amount with the competent authority at the charge, risk and peril of the holder.

CHAPTER VII—RECOURSE FOR NON-ACCEPTANCE OR NON-PAYMENT

Article 43

The holder may exercise his right of recourse against the endorsers, the drawer and the other parties liable:

At maturity:

If payment has not been made;

Even before maturity;

(1) If there has been total or partial refusal to accept;

(2) In the event of the bankruptcy (*faillite*) of the drawee, whether he has accepted or not, or in the event of a stoppage of payment on his part, even when not declared by a judgment, or where execution has been levied against his goods without result;

(3) In the event of the bankruptcy (*faillite*) of the drawer of a non-acceptable bill.

Article 44

Default of acceptance or of payment must be evidenced by an authentic act (protest for non-acceptance or non-payment).

Protest for non-acceptance must be made within the time fixed for presentment for acceptance. If, in the case contemplated by Article 24, paragraph 1, the first presentment takes place on the last day of that time, the protest may nevertheless be drawn up on the next day.

Protest for non-payment of a bill of exchange on a fixed day or at a fixed period after date or sight must be made on one of the two business days following the day on which the bill is payable. In the case of a bill payable at sight, the protest must be drawn up under the conditions specified in the foregoing paragraph for the drawing up of a protest for non-acceptance.

Protest for non-acceptance dispenses with presentment for payment and protest for non-payment.

If there is a stoppage of payment on the part of the drawee, whether he has accepted or not, or if execution has been levied against his goods without result, the holder cannot exercise his right of recourse until after presentment of the bill to the drawee for payment and after the protest has been drawn up.

If the drawee, whether he has accepted or not, is declared bankrupt (*faillite délarée*), or in the event of the declared bankruptcy of the drawer of a non-acceptable bill, the production of the judgment declaring the bankruptcy suffices to enable the holder to exercise his right of recourse.

Article 45

The holder must give notice of non-acceptance or non-payment to his endorser and to the drawer within the four business days which follow the day for protest or, in the case of a stipulation "*retour sans frais*", the day for presentment. Every endorser must, within the two business days following the day on which he receives notice, notify his endorser of the notice he has received, mentioning the names and addresses of those who have given the previous notices, and so on through the series until the drawer is reached. The periods mentioned above run from the receipt of the preceding notice.

When, in conformity with the preceding paragraph, notice is given to a person who has signed a bill of exchange, the same notice must be given within the same limit of time to his *avaliseur*.

Where an endorser either has not specified his address or has specified it in an illegible manner, it is sufficient that notice should be given to the preceding endorser.

A person who must give notice may give it in any form whatever, even by simply returning the bill of exchange.

He must prove that he has given notice within the time allowed. This time-limit shall be regarded as having been observed if a letter giving the notice has been posted within the prescribed time.

A person who does not give notice within the limit of time mentioned above does not forfeit his rights. He is responsible for the injury, if any, caused by his negligence, but the damages shall not exceed the amount of the bill of exchange.

Article 46

The drawer, an endorser, or a person guaranteeing payment by *aval* (*avaliseur*) may, by the stipulation "*retour sans frais*", "*sans protêt*", or any other equivalent expression written on the instrument and signed, release the holder from having a protest of non-acceptance or non-payment drawn up in order to exercise his right of recourse.

This stipulation does not release the holder from presenting the bill within the prescribed time, or from the notices he has to give. The burden of proving the non-observance of the limits of time lies on the person who seeks to set it up against the holder.

If the stipulation is written by the drawer, it is operative in respect of all persons who have signed the bill; if it is written by an endorser or an *avaliseur*, it is operative only in respect of such endorser or *avaliseur*. If, in spite of the stipulation written by the drawer, the holder has the protest drawn up, he must bear the expenses thereof. When the stipulation emanates from an endorser or *avaliseur*, the costs of the protest, if one is drawn up, may be recovered from all the persons who have signed the bill.

Article 47

All drawers, acceptors, endorsers or guarantors by *aval* of a bill of exchange are jointly and severally liable to the holder.

The holder has the right of proceeding against all these persons individually or collectively without being required to observe the order in which they have become bound.

The same right is possessed by any person signing the bill who has taken it up and paid it.

Proceedings against one of the parties liable do not prevent proceedings against the others, even though they may be subsequent to the party first proceeded against.

Article 48

The holder may recover from the person against whom he exercises his right of recourse:

    (1) The amount of the unaccepted or unpaid bill of exchange with interest, if interest has been stipulated for;

    (2) Interest at the rate of 6 per cent. from the date of maturity;

    (3) The expenses of protest and of the notices given as well as other expenses.

If the right of recourse is exercised before maturity, the amount of the bill shall be subject to discount. This discount shall be calculated according to the official rate of discount (bank-rate) ruling on the date when recourse is exercised at the place of domicile of the holder.

Article 49

A party who takes up and pays a bill of exchange can recover from the parties liable to him:

    (1) The entire sum which he has paid;

    (2) Interest on the said sum calculated at the rate of 6 per cent., starting from the day when he made payment;

    (3) Any expenses which he has incurred.

Article 50

Every party liable against whom a right of recourse is or may be exercised, can require against payment that the bill shall be given up to him with the protest and a receipted account.

Every endorser who has taken up and paid a bill of exchange may cancel his own endorsement and those of subsequent endorsers.

Article 51

In the case of the exercise of the right of recourse after a partial acceptance, the party who pays the sum in respect of which the bill has not been accepted can require that this payment shall be specified on the bill and that he shall be given a receipt therefor. The holder must also give him a certified copy of the bill, together with the protest, in order to enable subsequent recourse to be exercised.

Article 52

Every person having the right of recourse may, in the absence of agreement to the contrary, reimburse himself by means of a fresh bill (redraft) to be drawn at sight on one of the parties liable to him and payable at the domicile of that party.

The redraft includes, in addition to the sums mentioned in Articles 48 and 49, brokerage and the cost of stamping the redraft.

If the redraft is drawn by the holder, the sum payable is fixed according to the rate for a sight bill drawn at the place where the original bill was payable upon the party liable at the place of his domicile. If the redraft is drawn by an endorser, the sum payable is fixed according to the rate for a sight bill drawn at the place where the drawer of the redraft is domiciled upon the place of domicile of the party liable.

Article 53

After the expiration of the limits of time fixed:

>   For the presentment of a bill of exchange drawn at sight or at a fixed period after sight;
>   For drawing up the protest for non-acceptance or non-payment;
>   For presentment for payment in the case of a stipulation *retour sans frais*,

the holder loses his rights of recourse against the endorsers, against the drawer and against the other parties liable, with the exception of the acceptor.

In default of presentment for acceptance within the time limit of time stipulated by the drawer, the holder loses his right of recourse for non-payment, as well as for non-acceptance, unless it appears from the terms of the stipulation that the drawer only meant to release himself from the guarantee of acceptance.

If the stipulation for a limit of time for presentment is contained in an endorsement, the endorser alone can avail himself of it.

Article 54

Should the presentment of the bill of exchange or the drawing up of the protest within the prescribed limits of time be prevented by an insurmountable obstacle (legal prohibition (*prescription légale*) by any State or other case of *vis major*), these limits of time shall be extended.

The holder is bound to give notice without delay of the case of *vis major* to his endorser and to specify this notice, which he must date and sign, on the bill or on an *allonge*; in other respects the provisions of Article 45 shall apply.

When *vis major* has terminated, the holder must without delay present the bill of exchange for acceptance or payment and, if need be, draw up the protest.

If *vis major* continues to operate beyond thirty days after maturity, recourse may be exercised, and neither presentment nor the drawing up of a protest shall be necessary.

In the case of bills of exchange drawn at sight or at a fixed period after sight, the time limit of thirty days shall run from the date on which the holder, even before the expiration of the time for presentment, has given notice of *vis major* to his endorser. In the case of bills of exchange drawn at a certain time after sight, the above time-limit of thirty days shall be added to the period after sight specified in the bill of exchange.

Facts which are purely personal to the holder or to the person whom he has entrusted with the presentment of the bill or drawing up of the protest are not deemed to constitute cases of *vis major.*

CHAPTER VIII—INTERVENTION FOR HONOUR

1. *General provisions*

Article 55

The drawer, an endorser, or a person giving an *aval* may specify a person who is to accept or pay in case of need.

A bill of exchange may, subject as hereinafter mentioned, be accepted or paid by a person who intervenes for the honour of any debtor against whom a right of recourse exists.

The person intervening may be a third party, even the drawee, or, save the acceptor, a party already liable on the bill of exchange.

The person intervening is bound to give, within two business days, notice of his intervention to the party for whose honour he has intervened. In default, he is responsible for the injury, if any, due to his negligence, but the damages shall not exceed the amount of the bill of exchange.

2. *Acceptance by intervention (for Honour)*

Article 56

There may be acceptance by intervention in all cases where the holder has a right of recourse before maturity on a bill which is capable of acceptance.

When the bill of exchange indicates a person who is designated to accept or pay it in case of need at the place of payment, the holder may not exercise his rights of recourse before maturity against the person naming such referee in case of need and against subsequent signatories, unless he has presented the bill of exchange to the referee in case of need and until, if acceptance is refused by the latter, this refusal has been authenticated by a protest.

In other cases of intervention the holder may refuse an acceptance by intervention. Nevertheless, if he allows it, he loses his right of recourse before maturity against the person on whose behalf such acceptance was given and against subsequent signatories.

Article 57

Acceptance by intervention is specified on the bill of exchange. It is signed by the person intervening. It mentions the person for whose honour it has been given and, in default of such mention, the acceptance is deemed to have been given for the honour of the drawer.

Article 58

The acceptor by intervention is liable to the holder and to the endorsers subsequent to the party for whose honour he intervened, in the same manner as such party.

Notwithstanding an acceptance by intervention, the party for whose honour it has been given and the parties liable to him may require the holder, in exchange for payment of the sum mentioned in Article 48, to deliver the bill, the protest, and a receipted account, if any.

3. Payment by intervention

Article 59

Payment by intervention may take place in all cases where, either at maturity or before maturity, the holder has a right of recourse on the bill.

Payment must include the whole amount payable by the party for whose honour it is made.

It must be made at the latest on the day following the last day allowed for drawing up the protest for non-payment.

Article 60

If a bill of exchange has been accepted by persons intervening who are domiciled in the place of payment, or if persons domiciled there have been named as referees in case of need, the holder must present the bill to all these persons and, if necessary, have a protest for non-payment drawn up at the latest on the day following the last day allowed for drawing up the protest.

In default of protest within this limit of time, the party who has named the referee in case of need, or for whose account the bill has been accepted, and the subsequent endorsers, are discharged.

Article 61

The holder who refuses payment by intervention loses his right of recourse against any persons who would have been discharged thereby.

Article 62

Payment by intervention must be authenticated by a receipt given on the bill of exchange mentioning the person for whose honour payment has been made. In default of such mention, payment is deemed to have been made for the honour of the drawer.

The bill of exchange and the protest, if any, must be given up to the person paying by intervention.

Article 63

The person paying by intervention acquires the rights arising out of the bill of exchange against the party for whose honour he has paid and against persons who are liable to the latter on the bill of exchange. Nevertheless, he cannot re-endorse the bill of exchange.

Endorsers subsequent to the party for whose honour payment has been made are discharged.

In case of competition for payment by intervention, the payment which effects the greater number of releases has the preference. Any person who, with a knowledge of the facts, intervenes in a manner contrary to this rule, loses his right of recourse against those who would have been discharged.

CHAPTER IX — PARTS OF A SET, AND COPIES

1. *Parts of a set*

Article 64

A bill of exchange can be drawn in a set of two or more identical parts.

These parts must be numbered in the body of the instrument itself; in default, each part is considered as a separate bill of exchange.

Every holder of a bill which does not specify that it has been drawn as a sole bill may, at his own expense, require the delivery of two or more parts. For this purpose he must apply to his immediate endorser, who is bound to assist him in proceeding against his own endorser, and so on in the series until the drawer is reached. The endorsers are bound to reproduce their endorsements on the new parts of the set.

Article 65

Payment made on one part of a set operates as a discharge, even though there is no stipulation that this payment annuls the effect of the other parts. Nevertheless, the drawee is liable on each accepted part which he has not recovered.

An endorser who has transferred parts of a set to different persons, as well as subsequent endorsers, are liable on all the parts bearing their signature which have not been restored.

Article 66

A party who has sent one part for acceptance must indicate on the other parts the name of the person in whose hands this part is to be found. That person is bound to give it up to the lawful holder of another part.

If he refuses, the holder cannot exercise his right of recourse until he has had a protest drawn up specifying:
  (1) That the part sent for acceptance has not been given up to him on his demand;
  (2) That acceptance or payment could not be obtained on another of the parts.

2. *Copies*

Article 67

Every holder of a bill of exchange has the right to make copies of it.

A copy must reproduce the original exactly, with the endorsements and all other statements to be found therein. It must specify where the copy ends.

It may be endorsed and guaranteed by *aval* in the same manner and with the same effects as the original.

Article 68

A copy must specify the person in possession of the original instrument. The latter is bound to hand over the said instrument to the lawful holder of the copy.

If he refuses, the holder may not exercise his right of recourse against the persons who have endorsed the copy or guaranteed it by *aval* until he has had a protest drawn up specify that the original has not been given up to him on his demand.

Where the original instrument, after the last endorsement before the making of the copy contains a clause "commencing from here an endorsement is only valid if made on the copy" or some equivalent formula, a subsequent endorsement on the original is null and void.

CHAPTER X — ALTERATIONS

Article 69

In case of alteration of the text of a bill of exchange, parties who have signed subsequent to the alteration are bound according to the terms of the altered text; parties who have signed before the alteration are bound according to the terms of the original text.

CHAPTER XI — LIMITATION OF ACTIONS

Article 70

All actions arising out of a bill of exchange against the acceptor are barred after three years, reckoned from the date of maturity.

Actions by the holder against the endorsers and against the drawer are barred after one year from the date of a protest drawn up within proper time, or from the date of maturity where there is a stipulation *retour sans frais*.

Actions by endorsers against each other and against the drawer are barred after six months, reckoned from the day when the endorser took up and paid the bill or from the day when he himself was sued.

Article 71

Interruption of the period of limitation is only effective against the person in respect of whom the period has been interrupted.

CHAPTER XII — GENERAL PROVISIONS

Article 72

Payment of a bill of exchange which falls due on a legal holiday (*jour férié légal*) cannot be demanded until the next business day. So, too, all other proceedings relating to a bill of exchange, in particular presentment for acceptance and protest, can only be taken on a business day.

Where any of these proceedings must be taken within a certain limit of time the last day of which is a legal holiday (*jour férié légal*), the limit of time is extended until the first business day which follows the expiration of that time. Intermediate holidays (*jours fériés*) are included in computing limits of time.

Article 73

Legal or contractual limits of time do not include the day on which the period commences.

Article 74

No days of grace, whether legal or judicial, are permitted.

TITLE II. PROMISSORY NOTES

Article 75

A promissory note contains:
  (1) The term "promissory note" inserted in the body of the instrument and expressed in the language employed in drawing up the instrument;
  (2) An unconditional promise to pay a determinate sum of money;
  (3) A statement of the time of payment;
  (4) A statement of the place where payment is to be made;
  (5) The name of the person to whom or to whose order payment is to be made;
  (6) A statement of the date and of the place where the promissory note is issued;
  (7) The signature of the person who issues the instrument (maker).

Article 76

An instrument in which any of the requirements mentioned in the preceding article are wanting is invalid as a promissory note except in the cases specified in the following paragraphs;

A promissory note in which the time of payment is not specified is deemed to be payable at sight.

In default of special mention, the place where the instrument is made is deemed to be the place of payment and at the same time the place of the domicile of the maker.

A promissory note which does not mention the place of its issue is deemed to have been made in the place mentioned beside the name of the maker.

Article 77

The following provisions relating to bills of exchange apply to promissory notes so far as they are not inconsistent with the nature of these instruments, viz.:
  Endorsement (Articles 11 to 20);
  Time of payment (Articles 33 to 37);
  Payment (Articles 38 to 42);
  Recourse in case of non-payment (Articles 43–50, 52 to 54);
  Payment by intervention (Articles 55, 59 to 63);
  Copies (Articles 67 and 68);
  Alterations (Article 69);
  Limitation of actions (Articles 70 and 71);
  Holidays, computation of limits of time and prohibition of days of grace (Articles 72, 73 and 74).

The following provisions are also applicable to a promissory note: The provisions concerning a bill of exchange payable at the address of a third party or in a locality other than that of the domicile of the drawee (Articles 4 and 27); stipulation for interest (Article 5); discrepancies as regards the sum payable (Article 6); the consequences of signature under the conditions mentioned in Article 7, the consequences of signature by a person who acts without authority or who exceeds his authority (Article 8); and provisions concerning a bill of exchange in blank (Article 10).

The following provisions are also applicable to a promissory note: Provisions relating to guarantee by *aval* (Articles 30–32); in the case provided for in Article 31, last paragraph, if the *aval* does not specify on whose behalf it has been given, it is deemed to have been given on behalf of the maker of the promissory note.

Article 78

The maker of a promissory note is bound in the same manner as an acceptor of a bill of exchange.

Promissory notes payable at a certain time after sight must be presented for the visa of the maker within the limits of time fixed by Article 23. The limit of time runs from the date of the visa signed by the maker on the note. The refusal of the maker to give his visa with the date thereon must be authenticated by a protest (Article 25), the date of which marks the commencement of the period of time after sight.

CHAPTER I—THE DRAWING AND FORM OF A CHEQUE

Article 1

A cheque contains:
1. The term "cheque" inserted in the body of the instrument and expressed in the language employed in drawing up the instrument;
2. An unconditional order to pay a determinate sum of money;
3. The name of the person who is to pay (drawee);
4. A statement of the place where payment is to be made;
5. A statement of the date when and the place where the cheque is drawn;
6. The signature of the person who draws the cheque (drawer).

Article 2

An instrument in which any of the requirements mentioned in the preceding article is wanting is invalid as a cheque, except in the cases specified in the following paragraphs:

In the absence of special mention, the place specified beside the name of the drawee is deemed to be the place of payment. If several places are named beside the name of the drawee, the cheque is payable at the first place named.

In the absence of these statements, and of any other indication, the cheque is payable at the place where the drawee has his principal establishment.

A cheque which does not specify the place at which it was drawn is deemed to have been drawn in the place specified beside the name of the drawer.

Article 3

A cheque must be drawn on a banker holding funds at the disposal of the drawer and in conformity with an agreement, express or implied, whereby the drawer is entitled to dispose of those funds by cheque. Nevertheless, if these provisions are not complied with the instrument is still valid as a cheque.

Article 4

A cheque cannot be accepted. A statement of acceptance on a cheque shall be disregarded.

Article 5

A cheque may be made payable:
>   To a specified person with or without the express clause "to order", or
>   To a specified person, with the words "not to order" or equivalent words, or
>   To bearer.

A cheque made payable to a specified person with the words "or to bearer", or any equivalent words, is deemed to be a cheque to bearer.

A cheque which does not specify the payee is deemed to be a cheque to bearer.

Article 6

A cheque may be drawn to the drawer's own order.

A cheque may be drawn for account of a third person.

A cheque may not be drawn on the drawer himself unless it is drawn by one establishment on another establishment belonging to the same drawer.

Article 7

Any stipulation concerning interest which may be embodied in the cheque shall be disregarded.

Article 8

A cheque may be payable at the domicile of a third person either in the locality where the drawee has his domicile or in another locality, provided always that such third person is a banker.

Article 9

Where the sum payable by a cheque is expressed in words and also in figures, and there is any discrepancy, the sum denoted by the words is the amount payable.

Where the sum payable by a cheque is expressed more than once in words or more than once in figures, and there is any discrepancy, the smaller sum is the sum payable.

Article 10

If a cheque bears signatures of persons incapable of binding themselves by a cheque, or forged signatures, or signatures of fictitious persons, or signatures which for any other reason cannot bind the persons who have signed the cheque or on whose behalf it was signed, the obligations of the other persons who have signed it are none the less valid.

Article 11

Whosoever puts his signature on a cheque as representing a person for whom he had no power to act is bound himself as a party to the cheque and, if he pays, has the same rights as the person for whom he purported to act. The same rule applies to a representative who has exceeded his powers.

Article 12

The drawer guarantees payment. Any stipulation by which the drawer releases himself from this guarantee shall be disregarded.

Article 13

If a cheque which was incomplete when issued has been completed otherwise than in accordance with the agreements entered into, the non-observance of such agreements may not be set up against the holder unless he has acquired the cheque in bad faith, or in acquiring it, has been guilty of gross negligence.

CHAPTER II—NEGOTIATIONS

Article 14

A cheque made payable to a specified person, with or without the express clause "to order", may be transferred by means of endorsement.

A cheque made payable to a specified person, in which the words "not to order" or any equivalent expression have been inserted, can only be transferred according to the form and with the effects of an ordinary assignment.

A cheque may be endorsed even to the drawer or to any other party to the cheque. These persons may re-endorse the cheque.

Article 15

An endorsement must be unconditional. Any condition to which it is subject shall be disregarded.

A partial endorsement is null and void.

An endorsement by the drawee is also null and void.

An endorsement "to bearer" is equivalent to an endorsement in blank.

An endorsement to the drawee has the effect only of a receipt, except in the case where the drawee has several establishments and the endorsement is made in favour of an establishment other than that on which the cheque has been drawn.

Article 16

An endorsement must be written on the cheque or on a slip affixed thereto (*allonge*). It must be signed by the endorser.

The endorsement may leave the beneficiary unspecified or may consist simply of the signature of the endorser (endorsement in blank). In the latter case, the endorsement, to be valid, must be written on the back of the cheque or on the slip attached thereto (*allonge*).

Article 17

An endorsement transfers all the rights arising out of a cheque.

If the endorsement is in blank, the holder may:
(1) Fill up the blank either with his own name or with the name of some other person;
(2) Re-endorse the cheque in blank to some other person;
(3) Transfer the cheque to a third person without filling up the blank and without endorsing it.

Article 18

In the absence of any contrary stipulation, the endorser guarantees payment.

He may prohibit any further endorsement; in this case he gives no guarantee to the persons to whom the cheque is subsequently endorsed.

Article 19

The possessor of an endorsable cheque is deemed to be the lawful holder if he establishes his title to the cheque through an uninterrupted series of endorsements, even if the last endorsement is in blank. In this connection, cancelled endorsements shall be disregarded. When an endorsement in blank is followed by another endorsement, the person who signed this last endorsement is deemed to have acquired the cheque by the endorsement in blank.

Article 20

An endorsement on a cheque to bearer renders the endorsement liable in accordance with the provisions governing the right of recourse; but it does not convert the instrument into a cheque to order.

Article 21

Where a person has, in any manner whatsoever, been dispossessed of a cheque (whether it is a cheque to bearer or an endorsable cheque to which the holder establishes his right in the manner mentioned in Article 19), the holder into whose possession the cheque has come is not bound to give up the cheque unless he has acquired it in bad faith or unless in acquiring it he has been guilty of gross negligence.

Article 22

Persons sued on a cheque cannot set up against the holder defences founded on their personal relations with the drawer or with previous holders, unless the holder in acquiring the cheque has knowingly acted to the detriment of the debtor.

Article 23

When an endorsement contains the statement "value in connection" ("*valeur en recouvrement*"), "for collection" ("*pour encaissement*"), "by procuration" ("*par procuration*"), or any other phrase implying a simple mandate, the holder may exercise all rights arising out of the cheque, but he can endorse it only in his capacity as agent.

In this case the parties liable can only set up against the holder defences which could be set up against the endorser.

The mandate contained in an endorsement by procuration does not terminate by reason of the death of the party giving the mandate or by reason of his becoming legally incapable.

Article 24

An endorsement after protest or after an equivalent declaration or after the expiration of the limit of time for presentment operates only as an ordinary assignment.

Failing proof to the contrary, an undated endorsement is deemed to have been placed on the cheque prior to the protest or equivalent declaration or prior to the expiration of the limit of time referred to in the preceding paragraph.

CHAPTER III — "AVALS"

Article 25

Payment of a cheque may be guaranteed by an "aval" as to the whole or part of its amount.

This guarantee may be given by a third person other than the drawee, or even by a person who has signed the cheque.

Article 26

An "aval" is given either on the cheque itself or on an "allonge".

It is expressed by the words "good as aval", or by any other equivalent formula. It is signed by the giver of the "aval".

It is deemed to be constituted by the mere signature of the giver of the "aval", placed on the face of the cheque, except in the case of the signature of the drawer.

An "aval" must specify for whose account it is given. In default of this, it is deemed to be given for the drawer.

Article 27

The giver of an "aval" is bound in the same manner as the person for whom he has become guarantor.

His undertaking is valid even when the liability which he has guaranteed is inoperative for any reason other than defect of form.

He has, when he pays the cheque, the rights arising out of the cheque against the person guaranteed and against those who are liable to the latter on the cheque.

CHAPTER IV — PRESENTMENT AND PAYMENT

Article 28

A cheque is payable at sight. Any contrary stipulation shall be disregarded.

A cheque presented for payment before the date stated as the date of issue is payable on the day of presentment.

Article 29

A cheque payable in the country in which it was issued must be presented for payment within eight days.

A cheque issued in a country other than that in which it is payable must be presented within a period of twenty days or of seventy days, according to as whether the place of issue and the place of payment are situated respectively in the same continent or in different continents.

For the purposes of this article cheques issued in a European country and payable in a country bordering on the Mediterranean or *vice versa* are regarded as issued and payable in the same continent.

The date from which the above-mentioned periods of time shall begin to run shall be the date stated on the cheque as the date of issue.

Article 30

Where a cheque is drawn in one place, and is payable in another, having a different calendar, the day of issue shall be construed as being the corresponding day of the calendar of the place of payment.

Article 31

Presentment of a cheque at a clearing-house is equivalent to presentment for payment.

Article 32

The countermand of a cheque only takes effect after the expiration of the limit of time for presentment.

If a cheque has not been countermanded, the drawee may pay it even after the expiration of the time-limit.

Article 33

Neither the death of the drawer or his incapacity taking place after the issue of the cheque shall have any effect as regards the cheque.

Article 34

The drawee who pays a cheque may require that it shall be given up to him receipted by the holder.

The holder may not refuse partial payment.

In case of partial payment the drawee may require that the partial payment shall be mentioned on the cheque and that a receipt shall be given to him.

Article 35

The drawee who pays an endorsable cheque is bound to verify the regularity of the series of endorsements, but not the signature of the endorsers.

Article 36

When a cheque is drawn payable in a currency which is not that of the place of payment, the sum payable may, within the limit of time for the presentment of the cheque, be paid in the currency of the country according to its value on the date of payment. If payment has not been made on presentment, the holder may at his option demand that payment of the amount of the cheque in the currency of the country shall be made according to the rate on the day of presentment or on the day of payment.

The usages of the place of payment shall be applied in determining the value of foreign currency. Nevertheless, the drawer may stipulate that the sum payable shall be calculated according to a rate expressed in the cheque.

The foregoing rules shall not apply to the case in which the drawer has stipulated that payment must be made in a certain specified currency (stipulation for effective payment in a foreign currency).

If the amount of the cheque is specified in a currency having the same denomination but a different value in the country of issue and the country of payment, reference is deemed to be made to the currency of the place of payment.

CHAPTER V – CROSSED CHEQUES AND CHEQUES PAYABLE IN ACCOUNT

Article 37

The drawer or holder of a cheque may cross it with the effects stated in the next article hereof.

A crossing takes the form of two parallel lines drawn on the face of the cheque. The crossing may be general or special.

The crossing is general if it consists of the two lines only or if between the lines the term "banker" or some equivalent is inserted; it is special if the name of a banker is written between the lines.

A general crossing may be converted into a special crossing, but a special crossing may not be converted into a general crossing.

The obliteration either of a crossing or of the name of the banker shall be regarded as not having taken place.

Article 38

A cheque which is crossed generally can be paid by the drawee only to a banker or to a customer of the drawee.

A cheque which is crossed specially can be paid by the drawee only to the named banker, or if the latter is the drawee, to his customer. Nevertheless, the named banker may procure the cheque to be collected by another banker.

A banker may not acquire a crossed cheque except from one of his customers or from another banker. He may not collect it for the account of other persons than the foregoing.

A cheque bearing several special crossings may not be paid by the drawee except in a case where there are two crossings, one of which is for collection through a clearing-house.

The drawee or banker who fails to observe the above provisions is liable for resulting damage up to the amount of the cheque.

Article 39

The drawer or the holder of a cheque may forbid its payment in cash by writing transversally across the face of the cheque the words "payable in account" ("à porter en compte") or a similar expression.

In such a case the cheque can only be settled by the drawee by means of book-entry (credit in account, transfer from one account to another, set off or clearing-house settlement). Settlement by book-entry is equivalent to payment.

Any obliteration of the words "payable in account" shall be deemed not to have taken place.

The drawee who does not observe the foregoing provisions is liable for resulting damage up to the amount of the cheque.

CHAPTER VI—RECOURSE FOR NON-PAYMENT

Article 40

The holder may exercise his right of recourse against the endorsers, the drawer and the other parties liable if the cheque on presentment in due time is not paid, and if the refusal to pay is evidenced:

    (1) By a formal instrument (protest), or

    (2) By a declaration dated and written by the drawee on the cheque and specifying the day of presentment, or

(3) By a dated declaration made by a clearing-house, stating that the cheque has been delivered in due time and has not been paid.

Article 41

The protest or equivalent declaration must be made before the expiration of the limit of time for presentment.

If the cheque is presented on the last day of the limit of time, the protest may be drawn up or the equivalent declaration made on the first business day following.

Article 42

The holder must give notice of non-payment to his endorser and to the drawer within the four business days which follow the day on which the protest is drawn up or the equivalent declaration is made or, in case of a stipulation (*retour sans frais*), the day of presentment. Every endorser must, within the two business days following the day on which he receives notice, inform his endorser of the notice which he has received, mentioning the names and addresses of those who have given the previous notices and so on through the series until the drawer is reached. The periods mentioned above run from the receipt of the preceding notice.

When, in conformity with the preceding paragraph, notice is given to a person who has signed a cheque, the same notice must be given within the same limit of time to his *avaliseur*.

When an endorser either has not specified his address or has specified it in an illegible manner, it is sufficient if notice is given to the endorser preceding him.

The person who must give notice may give it in any form whatever, even by simply returning the cheque.

He must prove that he has given notice within the limit of time prescribed. This time-limit shall be regarded as having been observed if a letter giving the notice has been posted within the said time.

A person who does not give notice within the limit of time prescribed above does not forfeit his rights. He is liable for the damage, if any, caused by his negligence, but the amount of his liability shall not exceed the amount of the cheque.

Article 43

The drawer, an endorser, or an *avaliseur* may, by the stipulation "*retour sans frais*", "*sans protêt*", or any other equivalent expression written on the instrument and signed, release the holder from having a protest drawn up or an equivalent declaration made in order to exercise his right of recourse.

This stipulation does not release the holder from presenting the cheque within the prescribed limit of time, or from giving the requisite notices. The burden of proving the non-observance of the limit of time lies on the person who seeks to set it up against the holder.

If the stipulation is written by the drawer, it is operative in respect of all persons who have signed the cheque; if it is written by an endorser or an *avaliseur*, it is operative only in respect of such endorser or *avaliseur*. If, in spite of the stipulation written by the drawer, the holder has the protest drawn up or the equivalent declaration made, he must bear the expenses thereof. When the stipulation emanates from an endorser or *avaliseur*, the costs of the protest or equivalent declaration, if drawn up or made, may be recovered from all the persons who have signed the cheque.

Article 44

All the persons liable on a cheque are jointly and severally bound to the holder.

The holder has the right to proceed against all these persons individually or collectively without being compelled to observe the order in which they have become bound.

The same right is possessed by any person signing the cheque who has taken it up and paid it.

Proceedings against one of the parties liable do not prevent proceedings against the others, even though such other parties may be subsequent to the party first proceeded against.

Article 45

The holder may claim from the party against whom he exercises his right of recourse:

(1) The unpaid amount of the cheque;
(2) Interest at the rate of 6% as from the date of presentment;
(3) The expenses of the protest or equivalent declaration, and of the notices given as well as other expenses.

Article 46

A party who takes up and pays a cheque can recover from the parties liable to him:

(1) The entire sum which he has paid;
(2) Interest on the said sum calculated at the rate of 6%, as from the day on which he made payment;
(3) Any expenses which he has incurred.

Article 47

Every party liable against whom a right of recourse is, or may be, exercised, can require against payment, that the cheque shall be given up to him with the protest or equivalent declaration and a receipted account.

Every endorser who has taken up and paid a cheque may cancel his own endorsement and those of subsequent endorsers.

Article 48

Should the presentment of the cheque or the drawing up of the protest or the making of the equivalent declaration within the prescribed limits of time be prevented by an insurmountable obstacle (legal prohibition (*prescription légale*) by any State or other case of *vis major*), these limits of time shall be extended.

The holder is bound to give notice without delay of the case of *vis major* to his endorser and to make a dated and signed declaration of this notice, on the cheque or on an *allonge*; in other respects, the provisions of Article 42 shall apply.

When *vis major* has terminated, the holder must without delay present the cheque for payment and, if need be, a protest to be drawn up or an equivalent declaration made.

If *vis major* continues to operate beyond fifteen days after the date on which the holder, even before the expiration of the time-limit for presentment, has given notice of *vis major* to his endorser, recourse may be exercised and neither presentment nor a protest nor an equivalent declaration shall be necessary.

Facts which are purely personal to the holder or to the person whom he has entrusted with the presentment of the cheque or the drawing up of the protest or the making of the equivalent declaration are not deemed to constitute cases of *vis major*.

CHAPTER VII — PARTS OF A SET

Article 49

With the exception of bearer cheques, any cheque issued in one country and payable in another or payable in a separate part overseas of the same country or *vice versa*, or issued and payable in the same or in different parts overseas of the same country, may be drawn in a set of identical parts. When a cheque is in a set of parts, each part must be numbered in the body of the instrument, failing which each part is deemed to be a separate cheque.

Article 50

Payment made on one part operates as a discharge, even though there is no stipulation that such payment shall render the other parts of no effect.

An endorser who has negotiated parts to different persons and also the endorsers subsequent to him are liable on all parts bearing their signatures, which have not been given up.

CHAPTER VIII — ALTERATIONS

Article 51

In case of alteration of the text of a cheque, parties who have signed subsequent to the alteration are bound according to the terms of the altered text; parties who have signed before the alteration are bound according to the terms of the original text.

CHAPTER IX — LIMITATION OF ACTIONS

Article 52

Actions of recourse by the holder against the endorsers, the drawer and the other parties liable are barred after six months as from the expiration of the limit of time fixed for presentment.

Actions of recourse by the different parties liable for the payment of a cheque against other such parties are barred after six months as from the day on which the party liable has paid the cheque or the day on which he was sued thereon.

Article 53

Interruption of the period of limitation is only effective against the person in respect of whom the period has been interrupted.

CHAPTER X — GENERAL PROVISIONS

Article 54

In the present law the word "banker" includes the persons or institutions assimilated by the law to bankers.

Article 55

The presentment or protest of a cheque may only take place on a business day.

When the last day of the limit of time prescribed by the law for performing any act relating to a cheque, and particularly for presentment or for the drawing up of a protest or the making of an equivalent declaration, is a legal holiday, the limit of time is extended until the first business day which follows the expiration of that time. Intermediate holidays are included in computing limits of time.

Article 56

The limits of time stipulated in the present law shall not include the day on which the period commences.

Article 57

No days of grace, whether legal or judicial, are permitted.

APPENDIX 8

BILLS OF EXCHANGE

1. Standard form of bill in a set

£10,000   London 1st January 1997

One hundred and eighty days after sight[1] of this our First Exchange (Second and Third of the same date and tenor unpaid) pay Anglo-Transilvanian Trading Co Ltd or Order the sum of Ten thousand pounds Sterling,[2] payable at the collecting bank's selling rate for sight drafts on London, with interest at nine per cent. per annum added thereto from date hereof to due date of arrival of remittance in London, value received which charge to the account of the Sydney Trading Syndicate at Marleys Bank plc, Lombard Street, London EC, for shipment of one million tons of coal per SS *Enterprise* reference 97/1000/5/31/004.[3]

                                        Sydney Trading Syndicate

To Basil Industries Ltd
Bootle
Lancs.

NOTES:
1. Or "after the date hereof" or "after presentation".
2. The bill may be in some other currency of course.
3. This reference will identify the bill with the main contract and other documents.

---

2. Short form of bill payable on demand

£10,000   London, 1st January 1997

On demand[1] pay Anglo-Transilvanian Trading Co Ltd or Order the sum of ten thousand pounds Sterling for value received.

To: Basil Industries Ltd[2]
Bootle
Lancs.

NOTES:
1. Or "at sight", or "on presentation".
2. Be sure the drawee and his address is clear and unmistakable so presentation can be effected without difficulty. Remember a bill cannot be drawn on drawees *in alternative* or *in succession*:

s. 6(2), Bills of Exchange Act 1882. If one of several payees is named this does not prevent the document being a bill of exchange (s. 7(2), *ibid*), but in such a case, provision should be made for the discharge of the drawee's obligation under the bill upon payment to either payee or any one of several.

---

3. Short form of bill payable not on demand and with interest

£10,000   London, 1st January 1997

Ninety days after sight[1] pay Anglo-Transilvanian Trading Co Ltd or Order[2] the sum of ten thousand pounds Sterling with interest at Marleys Bank plc's Base Rate[3] obtaining from time to time for value received

                                                              Sydney Trading Syndicate

To: Basil Industries Ltd
Bootle
Lancs.

NOTES:
1. It could be drawn "after the date hereof".
2. The words "*sans recours*", or "without recourse", may be added here to negative the drawer's liability on the bill: s. 16(1), Bills of Exchange Act 1882.
3. It is better practice to state not only the bank whose rate is to be used, but also *which* of the bank's various rates.

---

4. Acceptances

(*a*) *General acceptance*

Accepted payable by Basil Industries Ltd at their offices Bootle, Lancs.
                                                              Bert Basil for
                                                              Basil Industries Ltd
                                                              1st March 1997

(*b*) *Qualified local and as to delivery of documents*

Accepted payable at Marleys Bank plc London EC only[1] and on the delivery to that bank of bills of lading for shipment of one million tons of coal per SS *Enterprise* reference 97/1000/5/31/004.[4]
                                                              Bert Basil for
                                                              Basil Industries Ltd
                                                              1st March 1997

NOTES:
1. This is a "local" acceptance: s. 19(2)(*c*) Bills of Exchange Act 1982.
The use of the additional words "and not elsewhere" seems to have gone out of fashion.
2. This is a "conditional" acceptance, that is, the acceptance does not take effect until the documents *and the bill* are presented to the bank.

PROMISSORY NOTES AND FORMS OF DISHONOUR AND PROTEST

PROMISSORY NOTES

1. SIMPLE FORM

£10,000 London, 1st January 1997

Twelve months after date hereof[1] I promise to pay Ajax Finance Co Ltd of 186 Godminchester Square, London W.53 the sum of One hundred pounds Sterling for value received.

John Doe[2]

NOTES:

1. It could, of course, be payable "on demand" or "on sight"; if payable "after sight", the note would need to be presented to the maker to fix the due date of payment.
2. It is usual to add the full address of the maker.

---

2. JOINT AND SEVERAL NOTE TO ORDER

£100 London, 1st January 1997

We John Doe and Richard Roe jointly and severally[1] promise to pay Ajax Finance Co Ltd or Order[2] on demand the sum of one hundred pounds Sterling for value received.

John Doe
Richard Roe

NOTES:

1. If these words were not used the signing by two makers would render the note a "joint" liability only.
2. The note could, of course, be drawn "or Bearer".

459

3. NOTE ALSO GIVING SECURITY

£100   London, 1st January 1997

ON DEMAND I promise to pay Ajax Finance Co Ltd of 186 Godminchester Square, London W53, the sum of One hundred pounds for value received with interest thereon at twenty five per cent per annum AND I have deposited with the said Ajax Finance Co Ltd and HEREBY PLEDGE to it as collateral security for the same shares numbered 878486–878499 in United Acorns Ltd for the sum of £100.00 and in default of payment as aforesaid I HEREBY AUTHORISE the said United Acorns Ltd forthwith either by auction private treaty transfer or otherwise to sell or dispose of the said shares and out of the proceeds of such sale or disposal to reimburse itself the said sum of £100.00 and interest thereon rendering to me any surplus which may be forthcoming from such sale or disposal.

John Doe

NOTE:
It is not entirely clear whether the right to the security passes with the negotiation of the note: see *Storm* v. *Stirling* (1854) ER 1353. In the author's opinion it does not, because, without more, this document gives the payee of the note only an equitable charge over the security which would not pass by delivery to an indorsee.

---

4. NOTE PAYABLE BY INSTALMENTS WITH INTEREST

£100   London, 1st January 1997

I John Doe of 15 Mansion Towers, London W.22, promise to pay Ajax Finance Co Ltd or Order the sum of One hundred pounds Sterling for value received by four instalments of twenty five pounds each payable on the first day of March, the thirtieth day of June, the thirtieth day of September and the thirty-first day of December 1997 WITH INTEREST on the balance for the time being outstanding payable (together with the repayment of the capital sum) on the above dates at Marleys Bank plc's Base Rate obtaining from time to time AND IN DEFAULT of payment of any instalment to pay to you on demand the whole balance then unpaid with interest as above to the date of repayment.

John Doe

NOTE:
Over recent years there has grown up the practice of lenders, instead of taking a promissory note in these terms, taking a series of post-dated cheques, with a loan agreement. This may be a little more cumbersome, but it is felt the cheque is a more direct method of obtaining payment (albeit without the interest accrued), and whose dishonour would render an action for recovery that much easier.

FORMS OF DISHONOUR AND PROTEST

1. Notice of dishonour   1st February 1997

To:

Sydney Trading Syndicate
High Road Works
Scunthorpe
Lincs.

TAKE NOTICE[1] that a bill of exchange dated 1st day of January 1997 drawn by
you on Basil Industries Ltd of Bootle, Lancs for £10,000 payable to Anglo-
Transilvanian Trading Co Ltd or Order one hundred and eighty days after
sight[2] has been dishonoured by non-acceptance[3] and that you are held responsible therefor.

Rupert Hentzau for
Anglo-Transilvanian Trading Co. Ltd.

NOTES:

1. Notice must be given as a matter of *real urgency*, although the 1882 Act uses the words
within a "reasonable time": see s. 49(12)

2. If the notice is given to an indorser insert here the words "and bearing your indorsement".
The notice to the indorser will be in addition to that sent to the drawer of course.

3. Or "non-payment" as the case may be. The words "and protested" need to be added if the
bill is a foreign bill, and, of course, protested: s. 51(2), Bills of Exchange Act 1882.

---

2. Notice of dishonour — Short form

To:

Sydney Trading Syndicate   1st February 1997
High Road Works
Scunthorpe
Lincs.

TAKE NOTICE the undernoted bill of exchange has been dishonoured by non-
acceptance and we require immediate settlement from you. On settlement we
shall return the bill of exchange to you.

Drawer	Acceptor	Amount	Date
Sydney Trading Syndicate	Basil Industries Ltd	£10,000	1st January 1997

Rupert Hentzau
Anglo-Transilvanian Trading Co. Ltd.

3. Protest

ON the first day of February 1997 at the request of Anglo-Transilvanian
Trading Co Ltd the holder of the original bill of exchange,[1] of which a true
copy is attached hereto, I, John Smith, of 104 Lincolnmans Square, London
EC, a Notary Public by lawful authority and duly sworn did exhibit the
original of the said bill of exchange to Basil Industries Ltd[2] the person on
whom the same is drawn[3] at their offices at Bootle, Lancs, the place of
payment specified in the said bill of exchange and demanded acceptance,[4] of
it to which I received an answer that they would not accept the same,[5]
WHEREFORE I, the said John Smith, at the request of Anglo-Transilvanian
Trading Co Ltd did and do by these presents protect against the drawer of the
said bill of exchange and all other parties to it and all others concerned for all

costs of exchange and re-exchange and all costs, damages and interest present and to come for want of acceptance[4] of the said bill of exchange. Thus protested in the presence of Richard Whittington and Albert Weir witnesses.[6]

Which I attest
John Smith
Notary Public[7]

[COPY OF BILL ATTACHED]

NOTES:

1. A foreign bill, as defined in the 1882 Act, *must* be protested to maintain the liability of the drawer and indorsees: s. 51(2), Bills of Exchange Act 1882. Protest is not necessary in the case of a foreign promissory note: s. 89(4), *ibid*. Protesting must be carried out no later than the day after dishonour: s. 51(4) *ibid*. This does not allow much time, and so the holder can ask a notary to have the bill "noted", after which, time for protesting is extended indefinitely: s. 93, *ibid*. Noting involves the notary presenting a bill as for a protest, so if he can do that one assumes he could carry out the formalities of protest.

2. This is the drawee, but protesting may be made to a bank if that is what the bill requires.

3. If the bill had been accepted, the words "and by whom the same was accepted", should be added here.

4. If the bill had been accepted, the word "payment" must be substituted.

5. Whatever answer the notary received will be included here.

6. Witnesses are not required by the 1882 Act, but it is the practice to have them present.

7. In the unlikely event of a notary not being available, a protest can be carried out by "any householder" or "substantial resident": s. 94 *ibid*. The form to be used in such a case appears in the First Schedule to the 1882 Act.

APPENDIX 10

ICC UNIFORM RULES FOR COLLECTIONS*

A. GENERAL PROVISIONS AND DEFINITIONS

Article 1. Application of URC 522

a. The Uniform Rules for Collections, 1995 Revision, ICC Publication No. 522, shall apply to all collections as defined in Article 2 where such rules are incorporated in the text of the "collection instruction" referred to in Article 4 and are binding on all parties thereto unless otherwise expressly agreed or contrary to the provisions of a national, state or local law and/or regulation which cannot be departed from.

b. Banks shall have no obligation to handle either a collection or any collection instruction or subsequent related instructions.

c. If a bank elects, for any reason, not to handle a collection or any related instructions received by it, it must advise the party from whom it received the collection or the instructions by telecommunication or, if that is not possible, by other expeditious means, without delay.

Article 2. Definition of collection

For the purposes of these Articles:

a. "Collection" means the handling by banks of documents as defined in sub-Article 2(b), in accordance with instructions received, in order to:
  i. obtain payment and/or acceptance,
  or
  ii. deliver documents against payment and/or against acceptance,
  or
  iii. deliver documents on other terms and conditions.

b. "Documents" means financial documents and/or commercial documents:
  i. "Financial documents" means bills of exchange, promissory notes, cheques, or other similar instruments used for obtaining the payment of money;
  ii. "Commercial documents" means invoices, transport documents, documents of title or other similar documents, or any other documents whatsoever, not being financial documents.

c. "Clean collection" means collection of financial documents not accompanied by commercial documents.

d. "Documentary collection" means collection of:
  i. Financial documents accompanied by commercial documents;
  ii. Commercial documents not accompanied by financial documents.

---

* ICC No. 522. Reproduced by permission of ICC Publishing SA. © ICC Publishing SA.

Article 3. Parties to a collection

a.   For the purposes of these Articles the "parties thereto" are:
     i.   the "principal" who is the party entrusting the handling of a collection to a bank;
     ii.   the "remitting bank" which is the bank to which the principal has entrusted the handling of a collection;
     iii.   the "collecting bank" which is any bank, other than the remitting bank, involved in processing the collection;
     iv.   the "presenting bank" which is the collecting bank making presentation to the drawee.
b.   The "drawee" is the one to whom presentation is to be made in accordance with the collection instruction.

B. FORM AND STRUCTURE OF COLLECTIONS

Article 4. Collection instruction

a.   i.   All documents sent for collection must be accompanied by a collection instruction indicating that the collection is subject to URC 522 and giving complete and precise instructions. Banks are only permitted to act upon the instructions given in such collection instruction, and in accordance with these Rules.
     ii.   Banks will not examine documents in order to obtain instructions.
     iii.   Unless otherwise authorised in the collection instruction, banks will disregard any instructions from any party/bank other than the party/bank from whom they received the collection.
b.   A collection instruction should contain the following items of information, as appropriate.
     i.   Details of the bank from which the collection was received including full name, postal and SWIFT addresses, telex, telephone, facsimile numbers and reference.
     ii.   Details of the principal including full name, postal address, and if applicable telex, telephone and facsimile numbers.
     iii.   Details of the drawee including full name, postal address, or the domicile at which presentation is to be made and if applicable telex, telephone and facsimile numbers.
     iv.   Details of the presenting bank, if any, including full name, postal address, and if applicable telex, telephone and facsimile numbers.
     v.   Amount(s) and currency(ies) to be collected.
     vi.   List of documents enclosed and the numerical count of each document.
     vii.   a. Terms and conditions upon which payment and/or acceptance is to be obtained.
         b. Terms of delivery of documents against:
           1) payment and/or acceptance
           2) other terms and conditions.
         It is the responsibility of the party preparing the collection instruction to ensure that the terms for the delivery of documents are clearly and unambiguously stated; otherwise banks will not be responsible for any consequences arising therefrom.

      viii.   Charges to be collected, indicating whether they may be waived or not.

      ix.   Interest to be collected, if applicable, indicating whether it may be waived or not, including:

          a. rate of interest

          b. interest period

          c. basis of calculation (for example 360 or 365 days in a year) as applicable.

      x.   Method of payment and form of payment advice.

      xi.   Instructions in case of non-payment, non-acceptance and/or non-compliance with other instructions.

c.   i.   Collection instructions should bear the complete address of the drawee or of the domicile at which the presentation is to be made. If the address is incomplete or incorrect, the collecting bank may, without any liability and responsibility on its part, endeavour to ascertain the proper address.

      ii.   The collecting bank will not be liable or responsible for any ensuing delay as a result of an incomplete/incorrect address being provided.

C. FORM OF PRESENTATION

Article 5. Presentation

a.   For the purposes of these Articles, presentation is the procedure whereby the presenting bank makes the documents available to the drawee as instructed.

b.   The collection instruction should state the exact period of time within which any action is to be taken by the drawee.

      Expressions such as "first", "prompt", "immediate", and the like should not be used in connection with presentation or with reference to any period of time within which documents have to be taken up or for any other action that is to be taken by the drawee. If such terms are used banks will disregard them.

c.   Documents are to be presented to the drawee in the form in which they are received, except that banks are authorised to affix any necessary stamps, at the expense of the party from whom they received the collection unless otherwise instructed, and to make any necessary endorsements or place any rubber stamps or other identifying marks or symbols customary to or required for the collection operation.

d.   For the purpose of giving effect to the instructions of the principal, the remitting bank will utilise the bank nominated by the principal as the collecting bank. In the absence of such nomination, the remitting bank will utilise any bank of its own, or another bank's choice in the country of payment or acceptance or in the country where other terms and conditions have to be complied with.

e.   The documents and collection instruction may be sent directly by the remitting bank to the collecting bank or through another bank as intermediary.

f.   If the remitting bank does not nominate a specific presenting bank, the collecting bank may utilise a presenting bank of its choice.

Article 6. Sight/acceptance

In the case of documents payable at sight the presenting bank must make presentation for payment without delay. In the case of documents payable at a tenor other than sight the presenting bank must, where acceptance is called for, make presentation for acceptance without delay, and where payment is called for, make presentation for payment not later than the appropriate maturity date.

Article 7. Release of commercial documents

Documents Against Acceptance (D/A) vs Documents Against Payment (D/P)

a. Collections should not contain bills of exchange payable at a future date with instructions that commercial documents are to be delivered against payment.

b. If a collection contains a bill of exchange payable at a future date, the collection instruction should state whether the commercial documents are to be released to the drawee against acceptance (D/A) or against payment (D/P).
    In the absence of such statement commercial documents will be released only against payment and the collecting bank will not be responsible for any consequences arising out of any delay in the delivery of documents.

c. If a collection contains a bill of exchange payable at a future date and the collection instruction indicates that commercial documents are to be released against payment, documents will be released only against such payment and the collecting bank will not be responsible for any consequences arising out of any delay in the delivery of documents.

Article 8. Creation of documents

Where the remitting bank instructs that either the collecting bank or the drawee is to create documents (bills of exchange, promissory notes, trust receipts, letters of undertaking or other documents) that were not included in the collection, the form and wording of such documents shall be provided by the remitting bank; otherwise the collecting bank shall not be liable or responsible for the form and wording of any such document provided by the collecting bank and/or the drawee.

D. LIABILITIES AND RESPONSIBILITIES

Article 9. Good faith and reasonable care

Banks will act in good faith and exercise reasonable care.

Article 10. Documents vs. Goods/services/performances

a. Goods should not be despatched directly to the address of a bank or consigned to or to the order of a bank without prior agreement on the part of that bank.
    Nevertheless, in the event that goods are despatched directly to the address of a bank or consigned to or to the order of a bank for release to a drawee against payment or acceptance or upon other terms and conditions without prior agreement on the part of that bank, such bank shall have no obligation to take delivery of the goods, which remain at the risk and responsibility of the party despatching the goods.

b. Banks have no obligation to take any action in respect of the goods to which a documentary collection relates, including storage and insurance of the goods even when specific instructions are given to do so. Banks will only take such action if, when, and to the extent that they agree to do so in each case. Notwithstanding the provisions of sub-Article 1(c) this rule applies even in the absence of any specific advice to this effect by the collecting bank.

c. Nevertheless, in the case that banks take action for the protection of the goods, whether instructed or not, they assume no liability or responsibility with regard to the fate and/or condition of the goods and/or for any acts and/or omissions on the part of any third parties entrusted with the custody and/or protection of the goods. However, the collecting bank must advise without delay the bank from which the collection instruction was received of any such action taken.

d.   Any charges and/or expenses incurred by banks in connection with any action taken to protect the goods will be for the account of the party from whom they received the collection.

e.   i.   Notwithstanding the provisions of sub-Article 10(a), where the goods are consigned to or to the order of the collecting bank and the drawee has honoured the collection by payment, acceptance or other terms and conditions, and the collecting bank arranges for the release of the goods, the remitting bank shall be deemed to have authorised the collecting bank to do so.

       ii.   Where a collecting bank on the instructions of the remitting bank or in terms of sub-Article 10(e)i, arranges for the release of the goods, the remitting bank shall indemnity such collecting bank for all damages and expenses incurred.

Article 11. Disclaimer for acts of an instructed party

a.   Banks utilising the services of another bank or other banks for the purpose of giving effect to the instructions of the principal, do so for the account and at the risk of such principal.

b.   Banks assume no liability or responsibility should the instructions they transmit not be carried out, even if they have themselves taken the initiative in the choice of such other banks(s).

c.   A party instructing another party to perform services shall be bound by and liable to indemnify the instructed party against all obligations and responsibilities imposed by foreign laws and usages.

Article 12. Disclaimer on documents received

a.   Banks must determine that the documents received appear to be as listed in the collection instruction and must advise by telecommunication or, if that is not possible, by other expeditious means, without delay, the party from whom the collection instruction was received of any documents missing, or found to be other than listed.
       Banks have no further obligation in this respect.

b.   If the documents do not appear to be listed, the remitting bank shall be precluded from disputing the type and number of documents received by the collecting bank.

c.   Subject to sub-Article 5(c) and sub-Articles 12(a) and 12(b) above, banks will present documents as received without further examination.

Article 13. Disclaimer on effectiveness of documents

Banks assume no liability or responsibility for the form, sufficiency, accuracy, genuineness, falsification or legal effect of any document(s), or for the general and/or particular conditions stipulated in the document(s) or superimposed thereon; nor do they assume any liability or responsibility for the description, quantity, weight, quality, condition, packing, delivery, value or existence of the goods represented by any document(s), or for the good faith or acts and/or omissions, solvency, performance or standing of the consignors, the carriers, the forwarders, the consignees or the insurers of the goods, or any other person whomsoever.

Article 14. Disclaimer on delays, loss in transit and translation

a. Banks assume no liability or responsibility for the consequences arising out of delay and/or loss in transit of any message(s), letter(s) or document(s), or for delay, mutilation or other error(s) arising in transmission of any telecommunication or for error(s) in translation and/or interpretation of technical terms.
b. Banks will not be liable or responsible for any delays resulting from the need to obtain clarification of any instructions received.

Article 15. Force majeure

Banks assume no liability or responsibility for consequences arising out of the interruption of their business by Acts of God, riots, civil commotions, insurrections, wars, or any other causes beyond their control or by strikes or lockouts.

E. PAYMENT

Article 16. Payment without delay

a. Amounts collected (less charges and/or disbursements and/or expenses where applicable) must be made available without delay to the party from whom the collection instruction was received in accordance with the terms and conditions of the collection instruction.
b. Notwithstanding the provisions of sub-Article 1(c), and unless otherwise agreed, the collecting bank will effect payment of the amount collected in favour of the remitting bank only.

Article 17. Payment in local currency

In the case of documents payable in the currency of the country of payment (local currency), the presenting bank must, unless otherwise instructed in the collection instruction, release the documents to the drawee against payment in local currency only if such currency is immediately available for disposal in the manner specified in the collection instruction.

Article 18. Payment in foreign currency

In the case of documents payable in a currency other than that of the country of payment (foreign currency), the presenting bank must, unless otherwise instructed in the collection instruction, release the documents to the drawee against payment in the designated foreign currency only if such foreign currency can immediately be remitted in accordance with the instructions given in the collection instruction.

Article 19. Partial payments

a. In respect of clean collections, partial payments may be accepted if and to the extent to which and on the conditions on which partial payments are authorised by the law in force in the place of payment. The financial document(s) will be released to the drawee only when full payment thereof has been received.
b. In respect of documentary collections, partial payments will only be accepted if specifically authorised in the collection instruction. However, unless otherwise instructed, the presenting bank will release the documents to the drawee only after full payment has been received, and the presenting bank will not be responsible for any consequences arising out of any delay in the delivery of documents.

c.   In all cases partial payments will be accepted only subject to compliance with the provisions of either Article 17 or Article 18 as appropriate.

Partial payment, if accepted, will be dealt with in accordance with the provisions of Article 16.

F. INTEREST, CHARGES AND EXPENSES

Article 20. Interest

a.   If the collection instruction specifies that interest is to be collected and the drawee refuses to pay such interest, the presenting bank may deliver the document(s) against payment or acceptance or on other terms and conditions as the case may be, without collecting such interest, unless sub-Article 20(c) applies.

b.   Where such interest is to be collected, the collection instruction must specify the rate of interest, interest period and basis of calculation.

c.   Where the collection instruction expressly states that interest may not be waived and the drawee refuses to pay such interest the presenting bank will not deliver documents and will not be responsible for any consequences arising out of any delay in the delivery of document(s). When payment of interest has been refused, the presenting bank must inform by telecommunication or, if that is not possible, by other expeditious means without delay the bank from which the collection instruction was received.

Article 21. Charges and expenses

a.   If the collection instruction specifies that collection charges and/or expenses are to be for account of the drawee and the drawee refuses to pay them, the presenting bank may deliver the document(s) against payment or acceptance or on other terms and conditions as the case may be, without collecting charges and/or expenses, unless sub-Article 21(b) applies.

Whenever collection charges and/or expenses are so waived they will be for the account of the party from whom the collection was received and may be deducted from the proceeds.

b.   Where the collection instruction expressly states that charges and/or expenses may not be waived and the drawee refuses to pay such charges and/or expenses, the presenting bank will not deliver documents and will not be responsible for any consequences arising out of any delay in the delivery of the document(s). When payment of collection charges and/or expenses has been refused the presenting bank must inform by telecommunication or, if that is not possible, by other expeditious means without delay the bank from which the collection instruction was received.

c.   In all cases where in the express terms of a collection instruction or under these Rules, disbursements and/or expenses and/or collection charges are to be borne by the principal, the collecting bank(s) shall be entitled to recover promptly outlays in respect of disbursements, expenses and charges from the bank from which the collection instruction was received, and the remitting bank shall be entitled to recover promptly from the principal any amount so paid out by it, together with its own disbursements, expenses and charges, regardless of the fate of the collection.

d.   Banks reserve the right to demand payment of charges and/or expenses in advance from the party from whom the collection instruction was received, to cover costs in attempting to carry out any instructions, and pending receipt of such payment, also reserve the right not to carry out such instructions.

G. OTHER PROVISIONS

Article 22. Acceptance

The presenting bank is responsible for seeing that the form of the acceptance of a bill of exchange appears to be complete and correct, but is not responsible for the genuineness of any signature or for the authority of any signatory to sign the acceptance.

Article 23. Promissory notes and other instruments

The presenting bank is not responsible for the genuineness of any signature or for the authority of any signatory to sign a promissory note, receipt, or other instruments.

Article 24. Protest

The collection instruction should give specific instructions regarding protest (or other legal process in lieu thereof), in the event of non-payment or non-acceptance.

In the absence of such specific instructions, the banks concerned with the collection have no obligation to have the document(s) protested (or subjected to other legal process in lieu thereof) for non-payment or non-acceptance.

Any charges and/or expenses incurred by banks in connection with such protest, or other legal process, will be for the account of the party from whom the collection instruction was received.

Article 25. Case-of-need

If the principal nominates a representative to act as case-of-need in the event of non-payment and/or non-acceptance the collection instruction should clearly and fully indicate the powers of such case-of-need. In the absence of such indication banks will not accept any instructions from the case-of-need.

Article 26. Advices

Collecting banks are to advise fate in accordance with the following rules:

a. FORM OF ADVICE
    All advices or information from the collecting bank to the bank from which the collection instruction was received must bear appropriate details including, in all cases, the latter bank's reference as stated in the collection instruction.
b. METHOD OF ADVICE
    It shall be the responsibility of the remitting bank to instruct the collecting bank regarding the method by which the advices detailed in sub-Articles (c)i, (c)ii and (c)iii are to be given. In the absence of such instructions, the collecting bank will send the relative advices by the method of its choice at the expense of the bank from which the collection instruction was received.
c. i. ADVICE OF PAYMENT
        The collecting bank must send without delay advice of payment to the bank from which the collection instruction was received, detailing the amount or amounts collected, charges and/or disbursements and/or expenses deducted, where appropriate, and method of disposal of the funds.
    ii. ADVICE OF ACCEPTANCE
        The collecting bank must send without delay advice of acceptance to the bank from which the collection instruction was received.

iii. ADVICE OF NON-PAYMENT AND/OR NON-ACCEPTANCE

The presenting bank should endeavour to ascertain the reasons for non-payment and/or non-acceptance and advise accordingly, without delay, the bank from which it received the collection instruction.

The presenting bank must send without delay advice of non-payment and/or advice of non-acceptance to the bank from which it received the collection instruction.

On receipt of such advice the remitting bank must give appropriate instructions as to the further handling of the documents. If such instructions are not received by the presenting bank within 60 days after its advice of non-payment and/or non-acceptance, the documents may be returned to the bank from which the collection instruction was received without any further responsibility on the part of the presenting bank.

ICC UNIFORM RULES FOR BANK-TO-BANK REIMBURSEMENTS UNDER DOCUMENTARY CREDITS*

A. GENERAL PROVISIONS AND DEFINITIONS

Article 1. Application of URR

The Uniform Rules for Bank-to-Bank Reimbursements under Documentary Credits ("Rules"), ICC Publication No 525, shall apply to all Bank-to-Bank Reimbursements where they are incorporated into the text of the Reimbursement Authorisation. They are binding on all parties thereto, unless otherwise expressly stipulated in the Reimbursement Authorisation. The Issuing Bank is responsible for indicating in the Documentary Credit ("Credit") that Reimbursement Claims are subject to these Rules.

In a Bank-to-Bank Reimbursement subject to these Rules, the Reimbursing Bank acts on the instructions and/or under the authority of the Issuing Bank.

These Rules are not intended to override or change the provisions of the ICC Uniform Customs and Practice for Documentary Credits.

Article 2. Definitions

As used in these Rules, the following terms shall have the meanings specified in this Article and may be used in the singular or plural as appropriate:

(a) "Issuing Bank" shall mean the bank that has issued a Credit and the Reimbursement Authorisation under that Credit.

(b) "Reimbursing Bank" shall mean the bank instructed and/or authorised to provide reimbursement pursuant to a Reimbursement Authorisation issued by the Issuing Bank.

(c) "Reimbursement Authorisation" shall mean an instruction and/or authorisation, independent of the Credit, issued by an Issuing Bank to a Reimbursing Bank to reimburse a Claiming Bank, or, if so requested by the Issuing Bank, to accept and pay a time draft(s) drawn on the Reimbursing Bank.

(d) "Reimbursement Amendment" shall mean an advice from the Issuing Bank to a Reimbursing Bank stating changes to a Reimbursement Authorisation.

(e) "Claiming Bank" shall mean a bank that pays, incurs a deferred payment undertaking, accepts draft(s), or negotiates under a Credit and presents a Reimbursement Claim to the Reimbursing Bank. "Claiming Bank" shall include a bank authorised to present a Reimbursement Claim to the Reimbursing Bank on behalf of the bank that pays, incurs a deferred payment undertaking, accepts draft(s), or negotiates.

(f) "Reimbursement Claim" shall mean a request for reimbursement from the Claiming Bank to the Reimbursing Bank.

---

* ICC No. 525. Reproduced by permission of ICC Publishing SA. © ICC Publishing SA.

(g) "Reimbursement Undertaking" shall mean a separate irrevocable undertaking of the Reimbursing Bank, issued upon the authorisation or request of the Issuing Bank, to the Claiming Bank named in the Reimbursement Authorisation, to honour that bank's Reimbursement Claim provided the terms and conditions of the Reimbursement Undertaking have been complied with.

(h) "Reimbursement Undertaking Amendment" shall mean an advice from the Reimbursing Bank to the Claiming Bank named in the Reimbursement Authorisation, stating changes to a Reimbursement Undertaking.

(i) For the purposes of these Rules branches of a bank in different countries are considered separate banks.

Article 3. Reimbursement Authorisations Versus Credits

A Reimbursement Authorisation is separate from the Credit to which it refers, and a Reimbursing Bank is not concerned with or bound by the terms and conditions of the Credit, even if any reference whatsoever to the terms and conditions of the Credit is included in the Reimbursement Authorisation.

B. LIABILITIES AND RESPONSIBILITIES

Article 4. Honour of a Reimbursement Claim

Except as provided by the terms of its Reimbursement Undertaking a Reimbursing Bank is not obligated to honour a Reimbursement Claim.

Article 5. Responsibilities of the Issuing Bank

The Issuing Bank is responsible for providing the information required in these Rules in both the Reimbursement Authorisation and Credit and is responsible for any consequences resulting from non-compliance with this provision.

C. FORM AND NOTIFICATION OF AUTHORISATIONS, AMENDMENTS AND CLAIMS

Article 6. Issuance and Receipt of a Reimbursement Authorisation or Reimbursement Amendment

(a) All Reimbursement Authorisations and Reimbursement Amendments must be issued in the form of an authenticated teletransmission or a signed letter. When a Credit, or amendment thereto which has an effect on the Reimbursement Authorisation, is issued by teletransmission, the Issuing Bank should advise its Reimbursement Authorisation or Reimbursement Amendment to the Reimbursing Bank by authenticated teletransmission. The teletransmission will be deemed the operative Reimbursement Authorisation or the operative Reimbursement Amendment and no mail confirmation should be sent. Should a mail confirmation nevertheless be sent, it will have no effect and the Reimbursing Bank will have no obligation to check such mail confirmation against the operative Reimbursement Authorisation or the operative Reimbursement Amendment received by teletransmission.

(b) Reimbursement Authorisations and Reimbursement Amendments must be complete and precise. To guard against confusion and misunderstanding, Issuing Banks must not send to Reimbursing Banks:

    (i) a copy of the Credit or any part thereof or a copy of an amendment to the Credit in place of, or in addition to, the Reimbursement Authorisation or

Reimbursement Amendment. If such copies are received by the Reimbursing Bank they shall be disregarded;

    (ii) multiple Reimbursement Authorisations under one teletransmission or letter, unless expressly agreed to by the Reimbursing Bank.

(c) Issuing Banks shall not require a certificate of compliance with the terms and conditions of the Credit in the Reimbursement Authorisation.

(d) All Reimbursement Authorisations must (in addition to the requirement of Article 1 for incorporation of reference to these Rules) state the following:

    (i) Credit number;

    (ii) currency and amount;

    (iii) additional amounts payable and tolerance, if any;

    (iv) Claiming Bank or, in the case of freely negotiable credits, that claims can be made by any bank. In the absence of any such indication the Reimbursing Bank is authorised to pay any Claiming Bank;

    (v) parties responsible for charges (Claiming Bank's and Reimbursing Bank's charges) in accordance with Article 16 of these Rules.

Reimbursement Amendments must state only the relative changes to the above and the Credit number.

(e) If the Reimbursing Bank is requested to accept and pay a time draft(s), the Reimbursement Authorisation must indicate the following, in addition to the information specified in (d) above:

    (i) tenor of draft(s) to be drawn;

    (ii) drawer;

    (iii) party responsible for acceptance and discount charges, if any.

Reimbursement Amendments must state the relative changes to the above. Issuing Banks should not require a sight draft(s) to be drawn on the Reimbursing Bank.

(f) Any requirement for:

    (i) pre-notification of a Reimbursement Claim to the Issuing Bank must be included in the Credit and not in the Reimbursement Authorisation;

    (ii) pre-debit notification to the Issuing Bank must be indicated in the Credit.

(g) If the Reimbursing Bank is not prepared to act for any reason whatsoever under the Reimbursement Authorisation or Reimbursement Amendment, it must so inform the Issuing Bank without delay.

(h) In addition to the provisions of Articles 3 and 4, Reimbursing Banks are not responsible for the consequences resulting from non-reimbursement or delay in reimbursement of Reimbursement Claims, where any provision contained in this Article is not followed by the Issuing and/or Claiming Bank.

Article 7. Expiry of a Reimbursement Authorisation

Except to the extent expressly agreed to by the Reimbursing Bank, the Reimbursement Authorisation must not have an expiry date or latest date for presentation of a claim except as indicated in Article 9.

Reimbursing Banks will assume no responsibility for the expiry date of Credits and if such date is provided in the Reimbursement Authorisation it will be disregarded.

The Issuing Bank must cancel its Reimbursement Authorisation for any unutilised portion of the Credit to which it refers, informing the Reimbursing Bank without delay.

Article 8. Amendment or Cancellation of Reimbursement Authorisations

Except where the Issuing Bank has authorised or requested the Reimbursing Bank to issue a Reimbursement Undertaking as provided in Article 9 and the Reimbursing Bank has issued a Reimbursement Undertaking:

(a) The Issuing Bank may issue a Reimbursement Amendment or cancel a Reimbursement Authorisation at any time upon sending notice to that effect to the Reimbursing Bank.

(b) The Issuing Bank must send notice of any amendment to a Reimbursement Authorisation that has an effect on the reimbursement instructions contained in the Credit to the nominated bank or, in the case of a freely negotiable Credit, the advising bank. In the case of cancellation of the Reimbursement Authorisation prior to expiry of the Credit, the Issuing bank must provide the nominated bank or the advising bank with new reimbursement instructions.

(c) The Issuing Bank must reimburse the Reimbursing Bank for any Reimbursement Claims honoured or draft(s) accepted by the Reimbursing Bank prior to the receipt by it of notice of cancellation or Reimbursement Amendment.

Article 9. Reimbursement Undertakings

(a) In addition to the requirements of sub-Article 6(a), (b) and (c) of these Rules, all Reimbursement Authorisations authorising or requesting the issuance of a Reimbursement Undertaking must comply with the provisions of this Article.

(b) An authorisation or request by the Issuing Bank to the Reimbursing Bank to issue a Reimbursement Undertaking is irrevocable ("Irrevocable Reimbursement Authorisation") and must (in addition to the requirement of Article 1 for incorporation of reference to these Rules) contain the following:

(i) Credit number;
(ii) currency and amount;
(iii) additional amounts payable and tolerance, if any;
(iv) full name and address of the Claiming Bank to whom the Reimbursement Undertaking should be issued;
(v) latest date for presentation of a claim including any usance period;
(vi) parties responsible for charges (Claiming Bank's and Reimbursing Bank's charges and Reimbursement Undertaking fee) in accordance with Article 16 of these Rules.

(c) If the Reimbursing Bank is requested to accept and pay a time draft(s), the Irrevocable Reimbursement Authorisation must also indicate the following, in addition to the information contained in (b) above:

(i) tenor of draft(s) to be drawn;
(ii) drawer;
(iii) party responsible for acceptance and discount charges, if any.

Issuing Banks should not require a sight draft(s) to be drawn on the Reimbursing Bank.

(d) If the Reimbursing Bank is authorised or requested by the Issuing Bank to issue its Reimbursement Undertaking to the Claiming Bank but is not prepared to do so, it must so inform the Issuing Bank without delay.

(e) A Reimbursement Undertaking must indicate the terms and conditions of the undertaking and:

(i) Credit number and Issuing Bank;
(ii) currency and amount of the Reimbursement Authorisation;
(iii) additional amounts payable and tolerance, if any;
(iv) currency and amount of the Reimbursement Undertaking;

(v) latest date for presentation of a claim including any usance period;

(vi) party to pay the Reimbursement Undertaking fee, if other than the Issuing Bank. The Reimbursing Bank must also include its charges, if any, that will be deducted from the amount claimed.

(*f*) If the latest date for presentation of a claim falls on a day on which the Reimbursing Bank is closed for reasons other than those mentioned in Article 15, the latest date for presentation of a claim shall be extended to the first following day on which the Reimbursing Bank is open.

(*g*) (i) An Irrevocable Reimbursement Authorisation cannot be amended or cancelled without the agreement of the Reimbursing Bank.

(ii) When an Issuing Bank has amended its Irrevocable Reimbursement Authorisation, a Reimbursing Bank which has issued its Reimbursement Undertaking may amend its undertaking to reflect such amendment. If a Reimbursing Bank chooses not to issue its Reimbursement Undertaking Amendment it must so inform the Issuing Bank without delay.

(iii) An Issuing Bank which has issued its Irrevocable Reimbursement Authorisation Amendment, shall be irrevocably bound as of the time of its advice of the Irrevocable Reimbursement Authorisation Amendment.

(iv) The terms of the original irrevocable Reimbursement Authorisation (or an Authorisation incorporating previously accepted Irrevocable Reimbursement Authorisation Amendments) will remain in force for the Reimbursing Bank until it communicates its acceptance of the amendment to the Issuing Bank.

(v) A Reimbursing Bank must communicate its acceptance or rejection of an Irrevocable Reimbursement Authorisation Amendment to the Issuing bank. A Reimbursing Bank is not required to accept or reject an Irrevocable Reimbursement Authorisation Amendment until it has received acceptance or rejection from the Claiming Bank to its Reimbursement Undertaking Amendment.

(*h*) (i) A Reimbursement Undertaking cannot be amended or cancelled without the agreement of the Claiming Bank.

(ii) A Reimbursing Bank which has issued its Reimbursement Undertaking Amendment shall be irrevocably bound as of the time of its advice of the Reimbursement Undertaking Amendment.

(iii) The terms of the original Reimbursement Undertaking (or a Reimbursement Undertaking incorporating previously accepted Reimbursement Amendments) will remain in force for the Claiming Bank until it communicates its acceptance of the Reimbursement Undertaking Amendment to the Reimbursing Bank.

(iv) A Claiming Bank must communicate its acceptance or rejection of a Reimbursement Undertaking Amendment to the Reimbursing Bank.

Article 10. Standards for Reimbursement Claims

(*a*) The Claiming Bank's claim for reimbursement:

(i) must be in the form of a teletransmission, unless specifically prohibited by the Issuing Bank, or an original letter. A Reimbursing Bank has the right to request that a Reimbursement Claim be authenticated and in such case the Reimbursing Bank shall not be liable for any consequences resulting from any delay incurred. If a Reimbursement Claim is made by teletransmission, no mail confirmation is to be sent. In the event such a mail confirmation is sent, the Claiming Bank will be responsible for any consequences that may arise from a duplicate reimbursement;

(ii) must clearly indicate the Credit number and Issuing Bank (and Reimbursing Bank's reference number, if known);

(iii) must separately stipulate the principal amount claimed, any additional amount(s) and charges;

(iv) must not be a copy of the Claiming Bank's advice of payment, deferred payment, acceptance or negotiation to the Issuing Bank;

(v) must not include multiple Reimbursement Claims under one teletransmission or letter;

(vi) must, in the case of a Reimbursement Undertaking, comply with the terms and conditions of the Reimbursement Undertaking.

(b) In cases where a time draft is to be drawn on the Reimbursing Bank, the Claiming Bank must forward the draft with the Reimbursement Claim to the Reimbursing Bank for processing, and include the following in its claim if required by the Credit and/or Reimbursement Undertaking.

(i) general description of the goods and/or services;

(ii) country of origin;

(iii) place of destination/performance;

and if the transaction covers the shipment of merchandise,

(iv) date of shipment;

(v) place of shipment.

(c) Claiming Banks must not indicate in a Reimbursement Claim that a payment, acceptance or negotiation was made under reserve or against an indemnity.

(d) Reimbursing Banks assume no liability or responsibility for any consequences that may arise out of any non-acceptance or delay or processing should the Claiming Bank fail to follow the provisions of this Article.

Article 11. Processing Reimbursement Claims

(a) (i) Reimbursing Banks shall have a reasonable time, not to exceed three banking days following the day of receipt of the Reimbursement Claim, to process claims. Reimbursement Claims received outside banking hours are deemed to be received on the next banking day.

If a pre-debit notification is required by the Issuing Bank, this pre-debit notification period shall be in addition to the processing period mentioned above.

(ii) If the Reimbursing Bank determines not to reimburse, either because of a non-conforming claim under a Reimbursement Undertaking, or for any reason whatsoever under a Reimbursement Authorisation, it shall give notice to that effect by telecommunication or, if that is not possible, by other expeditious means, without delay, but no later than the close of the third banking day following the day of receipt of the claim (plus any additional period mentioned in sub-Article (i) above). Such notice shall be sent to the Claiming Bank and the Issuing Bank and, in the case of a Reimbursement Undertaking, it must state the reasons for non-payment of the claim.

(b) Reimbursing Banks will not process requests for back value (value dating prior to the date of a Reimbursement Claim) from the Claiming Bank.

(c) Where a Reimbursing Bank has not issued a Reimbursement Undertaking and a reimbursement is due on a future date:

(i) The Reimbursement Claim must specify the predetermined reimbursement date.

(ii) The Reimbursement Claim should not be presented to the Reimbursing Bank more than ten (10) of its banking days prior to such predetermined date. If a Reimbursement Claim is presented more than ten (10) banking days prior to the predetermined date, the Reimbursing Bank may disregard the Reimbursement Claim. If the Reimbursing Bank disregards the Reimbursement Claim it must so inform the Claiming Bank by teletransmission or other expeditious means without delay.

(iii) If the predetermined reimbursement date is more than three banking days following the day of receipt of the Reimbursement Claim, the Reimbursing Bank has no obligation to provide notice of non-reimbursement until such predetermined date, or no later than the close of the third banking day following the receipt of the Reimbursement Claim plus any additional period mentioned in (a)(i) above, whichever is later.

(d) Unless otherwise expressly agreed to by the Reimbursing Bank and the Claiming Bank, Reimbursing Banks will effect reimbursement under a Reimbursement Claim only to the Claiming Bank.

(e) Reimbursing Banks assume no liability or responsibility if they honour a Reimbursement Claim that indicates that a payment, acceptance or negotiation was made under reserve or against an indemnity and shall disregard such indication. Such reserve or indemnity concerns only the relations between the Claiming Bank and the party towards whom the reserve was made, or from whom, or on whose behalf, the indemnity was obtained.

Article 12. Duplications of Reimbursement Authorisations

An Issuing Bank must not, upon receipt of documents, give a new Reimbursement Authorisation, or additional instructions, unless they constitute an amendment to, or a cancellation of an existing Reimbursement Authorisation. If the Issuing Bank does not comply with the above and a duplicate reimbursement is made, it is the responsibility of the Issuing Bank to obtain the return of the amount of the duplicate reimbursement. The Reimbursing Bank assumes no liability or responsibility for any consequences that may arise from any such duplication.

D. MISCELLANEOUS PROVISIONS

Article 13. Foreign Laws and Usages

The Issuing Bank shall be bound by and shall indemnify the Reimbursing Bank against all obligations and responsibilities imposed by foreign laws and usages.

Article 14. Disclaimer on the Transmission of Messages

Reimbursing Banks assume no liability or responsibility for the consequences arising out of delay and/or loss in transit of any message(s), letter(s) or document(s), or for delay, mutilation or other errors arising in the transmission of any telecommunication. Reimbursing Banks assume no liability or responsibility for errors in translation.

Article 15. Force Majeure

Reimbursing Banks assume no liability or responsibility for the consequences arising out of the interruption of their business by Acts of God, riots, civil commotions, insurrections, wars or any other causes beyond their control, or by any strikes or lockouts.

Article 16. Charges

(a) The Reimbursing Bank's charges should be for the account of the Issuing Bank. However, in cases where the charges are for the account of another party, it is the responsibility of the Issuing Bank to so indicate in the original Credit and in the Reimbursement Authorisation.

(b) When honouring a Reimbursement Claim, a Reimbursing Bank is obligated to follow the instructions regarding any charges contained in the Reimbursement Authorisation.

(c) In cases where the Reimbursing Bank's charges are for the account of another party they shall be deducted when the Reimbursement Claim is honoured. Where a Reimbursing Bank follows the instructions of the Issuing Bank regarding charges (including commissions, fees, costs or expenses) and these charges are not paid or a Reimbursement Claim is never presented to the Reimbursing Bank under the Reimbursement Authorisation, the Issuing Bank remains liable for such charges.

(d) Unless otherwise stated in the Reimbursement Authorisation, all charges paid by the Reimbursing Bank will be in addition to the amount of the Authorisation provided that the Claiming Bank indicates the amount of such charges.

(e) If the Issuing Bank fails to provide the Reimbursing Bank with instructions regarding charges, all charges shall be for the account of the Issuing Bank.

Article 17. Interest Claims/Loss of Value

All claims for loss of interest, loss of value due to any exchange rate fluctuations, revaluations or devaluations are between the Claiming Bank and the Issuing Bank, unless such losses result from the non-performance of the Reimbursing Bank's obligation under a Reimbursement Undertaking.

INDEX